Lady (*interviewing maid*). "Do you belong to the Church of England?"
Maid. "Well, m'm, Father goes to chapel, but personally I'm wireless."

The Churches an
British Broadcasting C
1922–1956

THE CHURCHES
AND THE
BRITISH BROADCASTING
CORPORATION
1922–1956

The Politics of Broadcast Religion

KENNETH M. WOLFE

SCM PRESS LTD

334 01932 X

First published 1984
by SCM Press Ltd
26–30 Tottenham Road, London N1

Photoset at The Spartan Press Ltd, Lymington, Hants
and printed in Great Britain by
The Camelot Press Ltd
Southampton

TO MY WIFE

CONTENTS

PART THREE

WAR 1939–1945:
NATIONAL CHRISTIANITY AND THE CHURCHES

PART FIVE
MORALS AND MISSIONS:
THE PARTING OF THE WAYS 1951–1955

PART SIX
EXPOSURE AND COMPETITION: TELEVISION
1951–1956

FOREWORD

This detailed study of the evolution of religious broadcasting has a
double interest. For historians of broadcasting it provides a valuable
description and analysis of a particular branch of broadcasting to
which the BBC attached special importance, and, equally important in
this particular case, of its impact on other branches of broadcasting.
For historians of religion in a century of far-reaching and often
confusing social change, it will be perhaps even more interesting and
important. All religious groups were bound to be affected by the new
balance between local and national influences, and in time by the
emergence of new modes of presentation of 'religious programmes'. Yet
different groups with their different traditions – and contemporary
challenges – some large, some small, were affected in different ways as
broadcasting began to appeal to a wider audience than any of them had
been able to reach. Not surprisingly questions of bias and exclusion as
well as of opportunity and initiative often figured on the agenda. Like
every other branch of broadcasting there were crises and turning points
in the story and, as in most previous periods of history, there were
divisions inside and between different religious groups on particularly
critical issues which could introduce a strident note into the history.

There is a forbidding mass of evidence available inside and outside
the BBC Archives, not all of it designed for public attention, and it has
never been subjected before to such close scrutiny. Yet the facts and
ideas on which policy was based were essentially 'British', with
Scotland and Wales as well as England determining a particular
pattern of religious broadcasting which was unique. More work needs
to be done on comparative broadcasting history, and Dr Wolfe's study
will itself provide important evidence. It is only by exploring the detail,
as he does, that it will ever be possible to establish the broad
generalizations.

24 May 1983   ASA BRIGGS

ACKNOWLEDGMENTS

This volume examines the first phase in the relations between the religious and broadcasting institutions in the United Kingdom, from 1922 until the advent of independent television in 1956, and considers the principal aspects and evolution of BBC policy in respect to religious broadcasting. Apart from the relatively brief treatment given by Asa Briggs in his four-volume history, there has been no analysis of the place of religion in the politics of broadcasting, notwithstanding Melville Dinwiddie's small book *Religion by Radio* (1968), which is descriptive and somewhat rose- coloured. I hope that this book will not only contribute to broadcasting history, but will be of interest to social historians and to those concerned with the fortunes of religious faith, ritual and utterance in the seemingly uncongenial climate of the twentieth century. It is the outcome of a substantial research fellowship at the Centre for the Study of Religion and Society at the University of Kent, funded by the Leverhulme Trust. I greatly valued the generous appreciation shown by the Director and Trustees of the importance of the subject and the complexity of the task. I have been particularly glad of the meticulous help I received from Jean Cunningham and the editorial staff of SCM Press.

I am specially grateful to Lord Briggs whose monumental *History of Broadcasting* in part stimulated this investigation and who offered valuable advice and practical assistance particularly at the outset. I must also acknowledge the support and encouragement of Professor David Martin of the London School of Economics and Dr Michael Tracey of the Broadcasting Research Unit at the British Film Institute.

The major raw materials are the prodigious archives of the BBC. The enormous collection at the Written Archive Centre is watched over by a diligent and unfailingly helpful staff under Mrs Jacqueline Kavanagh. Gwynever Jones deserves a special medal for her diligence and patience in the face of many pressures and notably my insistence that what may appear to have been lost could surely be found! I must also acknowledge the generous help given by Miss C. Poyser of the Archives of the Archbishop of Westminster; Miss M. Barber of the Lambeth Palace

Library; Mrs B. Hough of the Church House Archives; Mr P. Barr of the York Minster Library; Mrs G. Councell of the Livesey Museum in South London; Miss F. Williams of the British Council of Churches Archives in the Selly Oak Colleges, Birmingham; the Public Record Office, Kew; and the BBC Reference Library, London. I am obliged also to Dr Gerald Ellison, former Bishop of London, for assistance with the diary of Cyril Garbett of Winchester and York, and Dr Edward Carpenter, Dean of Westminster, with respect to the former Archbishop of Canterbury, Geoffrey Fisher.

I have also been greatly helped by persons close to or directly involved in this story who have given their time, hospitality and judgments: in particular, Bishop Agnellus Andrew, Dr Kathleen Bliss, the Rev. Brian Cooper, Geoffrey Dearmer, the Rev. and Mrs Eric Fenn, Mr Anthony Flemming, the Rev. and Mrs Kenneth Grayston, Sir Hugh Greene, Mr Harman Grisewood, Lord Hailsham, Miss Joy Harington, the Rev. and Mrs Francis House, the late Miss Nancy Hughes, the Rev. Oliver Hunkin, Sir Ian Jacob, the Hon. Kenneth Lamb, the Rev. and Mrs Roy McKay, Professor and Mrs Geoffrey Parrinder, the Rev. Stanley Pritchard, the Rt Rev. George Reindorp, the Rev. Edwin H. Robertson, the Rt Rev. David Say, the Rev. Ronald Selby Wright, Mr Bernard Sendall, Lord Soper, the Rev. and Mrs Vernon Sproxton, the Rt Rev. Mervyn Stockwood, the Rev. and Mrs Cyril Taylor, the Rev. and Mrs Robert Walton, Mrs Mary Welch, the Rev. and Mrs John G. Williams, the Rev. and Mrs Stephen Winward, Mr Dennis Wolferstan and Mr Lawson Wood.

I am grateful to the BBC for permission to reproduce the photographs and to the proprietors of *Punch* for permission to print the cartoons, with the exception of those by Osbert Lancaster on pp 507 and 520; for permission to reproduce these I thank Messrs John Murray.

Finally my thanks to an ever patient Valerie Rivers for typing the manuscript again and again, to Carol Wilson for help with the proofs and Jane Clarke for the index.

LIST OF ILLUSTRATIONS

ABBREVIATIONS

BAFTA	British Association of Film and Television Arts
BBC	British Broadcasting Corporation
BCC	British Council of Churches
CCSB	Central Council for Schools Broadcasting
CRAC	Central Religious Advisory Committee
ITA	Independent Television Authority
LDOS	Lord's Day Observance Society
LR	Listener Research
MRA	Moral Re-armament (= the Oxford Group Movement
OB	Outside Broadcast
PMG	Postmaster-General
RAC	(Regional) Religious Advisory Committee
RBD	Religious Broadcasting Department
RPA	Rationalist Press Association
SBC	Schools Broadcasting Council
SCM	Student Christian Movement

INTRODUCTION

This volume chronicles for the first time the relationship of two major institutions in British culture, the BBC and the churches, from the beginning of broadcasting until 1956. The central matter of this history is how the two bodies co-operated and how they defined their mutual policy and agreed the output. It was not always easy: broadcasters invaded sacred territories and had their own convictions about the nature of religion and did not always charm the clergy into more efficient and co-operative utterance. The churches on their side regarded the BBC as a distinctly establishment institution and expected that it would do as it was told or at least as it was advised. This volume examines their changing relationship and the variations which developed in the commitment of both institutions to the place of Christianity in the culture. In 1922 there was only one broadcasting institution which nevertheless provided anyone listening with several choices not only in the broadcast material but, very soon, by regional, national and foreign contributions. By the end of the First World War, as Professor Briggs illustrates in his first volume of the *History of Broadcasting*, there had already been clear signs that radio was sure to have immense social consequences. Among churchmen, however, it was regarded as a triviality which belonged chiefly to technically-minded enthusiasts; they thought it none of their business – which perhaps is hardly surprising. Such men had been reared on the printed word for which a substitute could hardly be conceived. They mostly showed little interest until it soon became clear quite to the more perceptive that the business of talking – which the clergy did with varying degrees of skill – could be singularly well served by the wireless.

In 1922 the Rector of Whitechapel gave the first religious address for Reith's new Company on Christmas Eve. He would surely be speaking now, he said, to more people than did St Paul in his whole lifetime. There was one distinct difference, he added: he could not see those to whom he now spoke. For the first time for most clergy the concept of a congregation that might only switch off metaphorically gave over to that of an audience which could do so literally. Choosing one station meant inevitably rejecting the remainder unless, of course, there were domestic facilities for recording. During our period there were not. The broadcasters controlled the output which the public either accepted or rejected and herein lies the key motif in the history of broadcasting, which since the beginning was about the choices made by a very few on the basis of what they guessed would be both wanted by and good for the great majority.

Religion was one such provision defined and decided by the churches and the BBC and dominated by Reith's conviction that broadcasting should be an agent of education. The relations between the churches and the increasingly confident broadcasting institution offer a profile of the religious utterance in a demonstrably Christian culture in which the supremacy of the historical churches was in subtle decline. Nevertheless, the early broadcasters were obliged to comply with the dictates of the denominations over questions about the place of broadcasting during the traditionally sensitive and much abused 'Reithian Sunday'. It was the consequence of political interaction between both the church and BBC hierarchies and of the endeavour by the latter to maintain the support of a Christian culture whilst at the same time serving an increasing and diversely conceived audience. The BBC naturally developed its own outlook on the broadcasting of religion. Whilst a very few churchmen approached the subject positively and constructively, weighty and widespread reactions were more often cautious or belligerently negative; broadcasting seemed to threaten clerical and eccesial autonomy. Others, however, began to see that this new invention could achieve far more than any individual evangelist; the ascendancy of Christianity might now begin. But whose version? Christianity could no more be conceived without its institutional substance than politics. There was only one BBC which had to deal with a plurality of religious bodies, each vigorously concerned with its own identity.

During the first thirty-four years until the coming of independent television it was the mainstream churches which asserted their special rights both to a place within the broadcast output and to protection from what they regarded as unwelcome innovations by broadcasters in the realms of education, entertainment and of course, religion. At the same time, the BBC hierarchy was committed to a species of Christian culture which some radical churchmen were anxious to question. This polarity was nowhere more marked or controversial than during the Second World War, when the notion of Christian Britain was under considerable strain and religious utterance became demonstrably yet another species of propaganda. Accomplished broadcasters were suddenly refused access to the microphone and disputes raged between churchmen over the relation between church and state in time of war. The BBC spoke for the increasing numbers of unchurched with growing confidence and challenged the faithful to greater precision, intelligibility and honesty. Broadcasting penetrated the sensitive recesses where clerical and theological authorities seemed much less secure than they had before the First World War. The BBC provided evidence with increasing accuracy that the definitions or pictures of a Christian culture shared by the leaders of the mainstream churches were slowly becoming obsolete. Broadcasting in the first thirty years would reveal aspects of Christian belief running the gauntlet of social and intellectual revolution. It would challenge those images of a Christian culture shared particularly by churchmen which suggested that the vast majority of people were still favourably disposed towards the churches in general and Christian belief in particular. Broadcasting gave new stature to doubts and questions about the nature of religion and the relevance of Christian belief.

The churches insisted that answers and explanations on the air should reflect a proper denominational diversity and thus the Corporation was embroiled in the historical disputes of centuries. Theological, philosophical and biblical issues had to be presented greatly simplified for the widest audience and churchmen were naturally divided over the extent to which broadcasting should restate religious truths about which the churches themselves were divided. Could the sacramental in religion be made 'available' through broadcasting, or was this casting pearls before swine? Even so modest a matter of broadcasting hymns engaged the Corporation in a wrangle which lasted two decades and raised almost every issue in the sociology of religion. Attempts at dramatizing the historical Jesus struck at the most profoundly sensitive roots of Christian creed and provoked squalid rows between those who believed Holy Writ should not be touched and those who were sure the gospels could be the basis for historical assertions. To their cost the churches fought tooth and nail throughout our period to avoid any fundamental questioning of Christian faith on the air for fear it would destroy what they believed were the simple certainties of the great majority. It was a time when all belief seemed subject to emerging intellectual stresses upon the culture of post-war mid-twentieth century Britain. The complex political disputes between the mainstream Christian religious institutions and the BBC from 1922 until 1956 comprise a struggle for supremacy. At the end of this period, it was clear to informed wisdom in the churches that with the establishment of

the ITA, there would henceforth be more than one agency of control
and more than one ideology behind the provision of religious programmes. The churches towards the end of our period had never had it quite
so good; and yet however vigorous and often acrimonious their disputes
with the Corporation, a thread of orthodoxy in broadcasting tradition
had provided a workable basis for co-operation between them.
Orthodoxy however, like many a fragile Grecian vase, was full of hair-
line cracks; broadcasting had become an ominous vibrant instrument
with which Christianity had never had to reckon. The revolution of
printing had betokened a literate response; that of broadcasting,
however, engaged any who had ears to hear. The following pages thus
concentrate upon the special era of radio which was to take the
churches, like every one else, by surprise. In 1922 no one had heard of
John Reith, but they soon would. A distinct new era in British culture
was about to begin: everyone would be affected by this business of
communicating without wires and it was a remarkable coincidence that
its direction was the responsibility of one to whom religion was
curiously and painfully important.

PART ONE

EXPERIMENTS AND PREPARATIONS
1922–1933

1

BEGINNINGS

A. John Reith

In the summer of 1922 a congregation in Peckham in south-east London heard the voice of their minister, Dr J. Boon, from the Burndept Aerial Works in Blackheath. His sermon was heard for a radius of around one hundred miles; the Peckham Christian Union had set up a three-valve receiving set and speaker at the pulpit rails and most of the congregation heard radio for the first time. Boon told the *Daily Telegraph* that he had no doubt that broadcasting had come to stay:

> I am convinced it will prove a valuable means of bringing the gospel into the very homes of the people. But there must be no squabbling in the church over this – it must remain united . . . every church in the land could never have its own transmitting centre, it simply could not be done, but one sermon at least should go out each Sunday by wireless . . . The church should strike out now and at once. If not, a chance may pass never to return.[1]

Had John Reith noticed the widespread press coverage of this remarkable innovation, he might have shared this evangelical sentiment and would doubtless have agreed that any kind of 'free for all' would have been unthinkable; the wireless must speak with one voice. Broadcasting involved a limited natural 'space' in the spectrum of air waves and any replication would be – as Boon recognized – the Tower of Babel all over again! Monopoly was implied by the wavelengths.[2] During October, John Reith became Managing Director of the British Broadcasting Company, and henceforth only this company was permitted to engage in broadcasting.[3]

The new manager was a young man to whom religion mattered a great deal. He had been born into it as a son of the manse; his father was later Moderator of the General Assembly of the United Free Church of Scotland. His diaries (many sections of which remain unpublished) reveal his attitude to religion as more than slightly superstitious and certainly not an accurate reflection of his Presbyterian upbringing. His headstrong character led to clashes with his parents and elder brothers, so that, though he wished to go to university and read philosophy, literature and history, he was instead apprenticed as a mechanical engineer. Though his relationship with his father was restored during the First World War, he felt after the latter's death in 1919 that he had never really known him. In his scrapbook Reith preserved a letter which he had received from him at the age of six: 'Jesus is now in heaven and the happiest boy is the one who loves Jesus.' It was a notion that would penetrate and persist. He wrote years later, in 1920, that the 'best for mankind' could be quickest attained by an 'unqualified deliberate manly aggressive doctrine of the principles expounded by Christ and that the loftiest and surest foundations for political guidance are to be found in some of the volcanic utterances of the Old Testament Jehovah'. At the same time his opinion of the church was less than sanguine: it failed to show the practical application of Christianity to the problems of the day. 'A strong exposition of its wonderful principles would cause a profound impression and turn again the captivity of England and make her path pleasantness and peace.'[4] His Christianity was unrealistic but lyrical; the harsh poetry of his Presbyterian origins embraced personal piety enmeshed in notions of duty which in turn were bound up with his troubled relationship with his father. It was a Christianity impatient with the churches and indignant with the culture south of the border which seemed more and more obviously to be doing without it. Civic duty went hand in hand with Presbyterian orthodoxy; he was desperate to be accepted for some public task. 'I am conscious of abilities which overwhelm me and yet with nothing to do. . . . I am eager to pass on the fire of inspiration from pulpit or pew or printed page which burns within me.' He repeated parts of the creed 'as a talisman to exorcise the demons of doubt, depression and even despair'.[5]

In June 1922, he paid his first visit to St Martin's-in-the-Fields in London and was much impressed: 'Next day I wrote this on a bit of paper: "I believe in God the Father almighty at this time when I am living in great anxiousness . . . as to my future works." ' Reith had a strong sense that he should 'bring Christ's kingdom to men in whatever capacity God calls me to'.[6] The idealism inherited from his father was based on the relation of Scottish Presbyterianism to Scottish society and constituted that manifestation of 'established Christianity' which Reith saw as wholly positive and practical. His 'evangelicalism' was as Scottish as it was Christian: it was about Christian 'nationhood' as well as Christian manhood. Holding these views, he was all the more troubled in the post-war period by an attitude towards organized religion shared by very many for whom the war had shaken religious confidence to the marrow. 1919 had seen the appearance of a devastating report, *The Army and Religion*,[7] which, however incomplete its statistics, concluded that the churches were living in a fool's paradise: 'The rigid ecclesiastical structures are no longer adequate for the necessities of our spiritual life.'[8] The report made it quite clear that the average soldier was confused about and remote from the teaching of Christianity and the language and style of common worship; religious education had failed. One of the 'rigid ecclesiastical structures' was the formal language of liturgy to which Reith was sensitive: he had heard it in the moving conditions of the Front. His admiration for the clerics who had seen the war alongside the rank and file animated his enthusiasm for H. R. L. Sheppard and his like. He regarded them as eminently representative of that style of Christian utterance which would be appreciated by the mass of untutored soldiers who had become vaguely acquainted with the faith through the efforts of padres in uniform. In contrast, the churches were impractical in outlook and parochial in style.[9]

Reith shared his impatience and his sentiments with Sheppard, whom he met in the summer of 1923. Sheppard had also returned unhappy from the war; he was now vicar of St Martin's and Reith found in him a kindred spirit.

B. The Sunday Committee

Reith was anxious to have the Christian religion feature within the broadcast output of his new broadcasting company. His own almost superstitious regard for Sunday meant that religion must have a place. Throughout his diary, Reith attests his high regard for the vital importance of Sunday and worship. In London he was drawn towards almost any church, but there was no real substitute for his father's 'College Church' in Glasgow. He had to admit, however, that there was 'mighty little in many churches to attract'.[10]

Reith was never a really committed 'churchman'; he was committed to the protection and promulgation of 'dynamic' Christianity in national and personal life, and Sunday was the one institution which, he believed, belonged to the maintenance of a Christian presence. He would defend the working man against being exploited and expose him to the best preaching which the churches could provide.

During 1923, since Alexander Fleming (of St Columba's, Pont Street, in Kensington) had started the Sunday evening broadcast addresses,[11] there came a point when Reith needed practical advice on how to choose the speakers; the question of denomination and sect was uppermost and he wanted advice on whom the churches would regard as suitable. Thus began a delicately balanced relationship between the churches and the Company. Within a decade they would have to put a man of their own into the broadcasting administration to bridge the divide which Reith felt existed in 1923 between expectations of the broadcasters and hopes of the few churchmen who were aware in a small way of the potential for religion in radio broadcasting. Reith met with George Bell, the Archbishop's Chaplain, who arranged for him to meet Archbishop Davidson: 'I wanted his co-operation in some sort of control for the religious side.'[12] On 19 March, the now well-known meeting took place: Archbishop and Mrs Davidson visited the Reiths at their home. Reith discreetly switched on his wireless (disguised as a sideboard) and his guests were thunderstruck.[13] On 20 April, Davidson summoned a meeting at the House of Lords of leading ecclesiastics including Cyril Garbett, Bishop of Southwark, whom Davidson then appointed as chairman. The first meeting of the 'Sunday Committee' took place on Friday 18 May 1923. The Church of England was represented by Garbett and by Canon C. S. Woodward and H. R. L. Sheppard, whom Davidson had suggested, the Nonconformists by Mr R. Nightingale of the National Council for Evangelical Free Churches and Dr R. C. Gillie of the English Presbyterian Church, and the Roman Catholics by the only layman, Mr Herbert Ward. The ostensible purpose was to advise and provide the Company with Sunday speakers (Rev. J. A. Mayo, the Rector of Whitechapel, had already given the first BBC talk on Christmas Eve, 1922, as had subsequently others from diverse denominations).

At the first meeting each member was asked to provide a list of names for use by the Company; they all agreed that no fees, only expenses, should be paid to speakers and that they should submit their scripts at least three days prior to the date of the address.[14] Reith had the support of Lord Gainford, the first chairman of the Company, who had also pressed his fellow directors to get religious talks into the Sunday programme. Gainford claimed some measure of the credit for getting the Board to accept an advisory committee at all.[15]

C. Broadcasting church services

During 1923, broadcast religion took the form of the concert interval talk, and for Reith this was appropriate enough to his concept of the Christian Sunday; many speakers had a reputation derived from chaplaincy service during the First World War. They had been tested amid bombs and in the trenches in the most intolerable circumstances of war.[16] The broadcasting success of men such as Studdart-Kennedy and 'Tubby' Clayton had linked broadcasting with the Christian Sunday and with a special style of vibrant and eloquent Christian message which Reith particularly appreciated. They had whetted the appetite of the Christian public and not the least the invalid, hospitalized and bed-ridden community. Before long people began to write and ask for more; they wanted not only the voice of the preacher but the context in which he is normally at work; they wanted church services – they wanted the BBC to provide a corporate liturgical event. Should it come from a BBC studio or from an actual church? But then, whose church? Reith needed yet more advice. He was not an ecclesiastic, and had little grasp of the subtleties of confessional history or ecumenical debate. He turned to the central cathedrals for permission to broadcast their ordinary services. But the Chapter of Westminster had already refused to broadcast the wedding of the Duke of York and Lady Elizabeth Bowes-Lyon,[17] and Reith had also been snubbed by St Paul's: Canon J. G. Simpson had said the year before that 'he was opposed to introducing sensational methods into worship'.[18] The clergy believed that church services were for the faithful and that broadcasting would amount to an invasion by a secular body in theological affairs far beyond its competence.

Reith told his Sunday Committee that since the central, nationally recognized churches would not open their doors to the broadcasters, the BBC would go elsewhere. He thought church services made for good broadcasting – it was for the public good and especially valuable to the housebound. He later reflected that there were problems and delicacies of another order not to be encountered in any other broadcasting field.[19] From the point of view of Christianity itself, he believed the broadcasting of church services could only benefit the churches. But he had already discovered at St Paul's that there were clerical energies opposed to anything that smacked of competition; the churches opposed almost anything which weakened the fragile loyalties of the vast majority who should be at church on a Sunday.[20] Reith sympathized with this attitude.

Cyril Garbett of Southwark, however, was unsure of the wisdom of broadcasting actual ordinary services, partly because he thought people would find cathedral services rather boring. He certainly would not have communion services broadcast. Reith looked for a good broadcaster and the excellent music of a 'national shrine' at Westminster Abbey or at St Paul's. Nonconformists were not so suitable in that they had too many words and not enough music. Reith wanted the best in broadcasting to serve the general public (which he believed had a deep religious faculty) and the churches themselves. Since St Paul's and the Abbey would not co-operate, he thought of perhaps Southwark Cathedral or St Martin's or the Temple. Garbett was uncertain about his Chapter and the Master of the Temple, William H. Draper, was not willing. Reith had to look elsewhere than to the nation's central shrines, and thus began his relation with H. R. L. Sheppard and the supremacy of St Martin's-in-the-Fields as the church soon to be listened to by millions. Sheppard had given his first broadcast in July 1923, only a month after his first meeting with Reith, when the idea of broadcasting a complete service had been discussed. Earlier that month, the Sunday Committee had irked Reith by refusing to alter the time of the Sunday evening religious talk from 9.0 p.m. to 8.30; the later time came in the middle of the main broadcasting period. Sheppard had been absent from this meeting, and thus was not to be blamed for the Committee's high-handed and not altogether co-operative attitude at only its second meeting.

Despite this snub, Reith was anxious not to offend the Anglicans on the Committee, who might well agree that St Martin's was by no means a national shrine and lacked a musical tradition as eminent as St Paul's. Garbett and Woodward, however, agreed that St Martin's was a good choice, as did the Committee. Sheppard was keen to construct a special service for broadcasting, as he agreed with Garbett that an ordinary Prayer Book service with psalms, etc. would not be suitable and might raise hostile reactions. He was as much influenced by Reith on questions of broadcasting and the listening public as Reith was influenced by him on questions of the Christian message and the worshipping public. St Martin's had a reputation which went back to the First World War and Sheppard's ministry stood for a special service to central London and to the troops who waited for trains to take them to the trenches.[21] 'There are many strong "Catholic" and "Protestant" centres in which men and women with those convictions can feel at home,' claimed Sheppard, 'but St Martin's stands for a diffused rather than a sectional Christianity.'[22] St Martin's and its special Christianity could communicate itself to the so-called common man and particularly those serving in the trenches whom Reith the soldier had tried – with some success – to influence in 1915.[23] Sheppard had been in France – in the trenches – and had ministered to the dying. Now, four years after the Armistice, St Martin's was that special haven for the poor and destitute, for people on the move to whom Sheppard tried so hard to speak the message of Christianity in an uncluttered and only imperceptibly ecclesiastical manner. Reith wanted Sheppard to produce a service for broadcasting which would appeal to a vast mass of people who might not now be true worshippers but who might have been once, who would still respond to sincere prayer and who recognized the quality of true religion when they saw it. This they saw in Sheppard – and whilst Cyril Garbett might have thought Westminster Abbey would be ideal, St Martin's could at least be tried as an experiment once a month. Sheppard was delighted, although he feared he would be heavily criticized for staging a 'stunt' – a word of common abuse for projects out of the ordinary.[24] The Sunday Committee agreed that services from St Martin's should begin in 1924 and Sheppard rehearsed the congregation the week before. On 6 January queues formed outside the church for the 8.15 event: 'Tonight we begin the happy, if difficult, task of making contact with a great multitude of unseen people which no man can number. It is our ambition that one day this may ripen into a friendship.'[25] Sheppard's biographers have scanned the response which that first broadcast received: overwhelming support across all kinds of social, ecclesiastical and educational boundaries.[26] There was however a good deal of abusive reaction by those who saw some of the implications of this event; it was an innovation which in the eyes of many might usurp the churches' own task by a cheap, artificial device which, it was thought, could make Christianity acceptable to the vast majority, notwithstanding all the efforts of the churches themselves.

D. The mainstream churches: striking the boundaries

The broadcast of 6 January 1924 was the real beginning of religious broadcasting and of a special relationship between churchmen and broadcasters who together sought to provide a twofold service: to those who could no longer attend church for themselves, and to the 'non-attending churched': those with trenchant memories of youthful engagement in church and Sunday school who might be led into greater maturity and even a living commitment which, it was hoped, would issue in a return to active church life. One way and another, this was to be the fundamental objective of those who were to engage in broadcasting religion; they assumed with Reith that the country was 'instinctively' Christian, that broadcasting expressions of Christian piety might bring innate Christian teaching to surface in practical action, and that the churches would at last stem the ebbing flow of the nation's adulthood from active membership. Reith had no doubt that the protection of fundamental – as against sectional – Christianity was a principal justification of the monopoly granted by the Postmaster-

General.[27] Furthermore, this Christianity was to be defined as 'non-denominational'.

At the first meeting of the Sunday Committee following the commencement of the monthly St Martin's services, the Nonconformists raised the question of their share of the Sunday services and whether certain central Nonconformist churches might be wired up along with St Martin's. Garbett had been quick to get the approval of A. F. Winnington-Ingram, the Bishop of London, for Nonconformists (those approved by the Committee) to preach in the pulpit of St Martin's. For the Free Churches, Nightingale claimed – as Sheppard and others had said a year before – straight 'ordinary' services would not do for broadcasting and moreover, there was as much the likelihood of opposition among Free Churchmen as there had been and still was from the Church of England over St Martin's. Winnington-Ingram's approval was accepted: St Martin's service would accept the Nonconformists suggested by the Committee and no doubt there would be others. Donald Soper would be among many Free Churchmen invited by Sheppard to devise a service for broadcasting around a non-Anglican pivot, i.e. a good quality talk. The Church of England and the Free Churches represented by the Free Church Federal Council, together with the Church of Scotland, had been singled out by Reith and Davidson and subsequently approved by the Committee itself. The Committee had decided its own boundaries: about anyone outside they could only advise that 'they could not advise' or they simply could not approve. The Jews who had requested access were left to the decision of the Company, whereas the Christian Scientists and Rationalists certainly could not be included in a Sunday programme, and it was for the Company to decide whether it would allow them on a weekday.[28] The matter was not to rest so easily: there would soon be those, notably the Rationalist Press Association, who would fiercely contest the Christian monopoly of the Corporation and the manner in which the 'accepted' churches were approved and others rejected. The Sunday Committee's unanimous opinion that 'the introduction of non-Christian talks on Sunday would open the door to possible abuse'[29] was manifestly subjective and in the interests of the Christian establishments which the members represented and with which the Company – notably Reith – wished to deal; so far, their interests were in common. In May 1923, Reith had told the Sykes Committee that the BBC had never yet broadcast anything controversial and was taking every care not to do so.[30] Non-Christian talks were regarded as controversial and thus forbidden. Underneath this first piece of 'sculpturing' of the BBC's Christian format were serious questions about propaganda, sectarianism, and bias in broadcast material and how powerful would be the lobby of any plaintiff group which had been offended or 'excited' by the broadcasting of material on behalf of another group with which they disagreed and by which they might have been offended. In the field of religion, it would depend on who was being offended. Eventually the Corporation was to tread a narrow and perilous path between orthodoxy and various party lines in religion presented by organizations outside the Corporation as well as within it. At the Crawford Committee in 1926, Reith asked for more freedom; he wanted to broadcast controversial material and he wanted news coverage; this latter was furiously controversial – the newspaper publishers were threatened. But there were varieties of controversy: theological or ecclesiastical differences involving material and ideas known only to university dons were not likely to excite any major sector of the listening population to write to their MPs or begin a concerted campaign in the newspapers. But Reith would not allow any preacher or religious speaker to attack the 'position' of another, especially when it involved religious groups or parties. The question which the Company in 1924 could not answer was who and how many and how powerful were those who might take offence and where exactly was the central ground of Christian consensus.

By saying 'No' to non-Christian talks on a Sunday, the Committee had played a significant hand in programming policy; it had delineated a boundary between the broadcasters and the churches and had thus decided what the Company itself could consider for broadcasting (during the week in this case) and preserved its own authority over Sunday talks and over the use of Sunday itself. If there was to be broadcasting at all on a Sunday, it should be appropriately Christian in style as well as content, and that assumed, implicitly, the protection of Christianity 'in a manner that would not offend'. The question was simply 'whose Christianity?' – the answer was by no means solved with the simple answer of the Protestant majority. Cyril Garbett, the chairman, thought the Company had been fair and impartial and the Committee, including the Nonconformists, agreed.[31] In 1927, Garbett was emphatic that the Christian Scientists were 'unorthodox' and 'if the door were open to them, it would be impossible to avoid throwing it open to Theosophists, Buddhists and other similar bodies'.[32] All agreed that Christian Science was controversial but were divided as to whether its precepts raised a controversy over religious issues or, as Woodward thought most likely, over scientific issues. Garbett thought that even if a Christian Scientist could give a non-controversial and helpful talk on a Sunday, it would be construed that the Committee endorsed Christian Science views. So long as this was believed, it would contribute to the widespread notion that whatever was in fact actually broadcast must have the support of the BBC and its advisers. The issue was not quite so clear in the discussion on the Spiritualists, who had also made an overture to the Corporation. Garbett saw no harm in much of the religious teaching of the Spiritualists provided again that any such talk or debate was not broadcast on a Sunday. He thought a debate on psychic research could be undertaken without bringing in the religious aspect; Reith, however, thought otherwise and did not approve it. He had the support of Herbert Ward, who knew that Roman Catholics would certainly be offended. Indeed, anything which attacked the principles of Christian Protestant orthodoxy was to be barred from the air. Yet for Reith, the church institution itself could comprise an offence to the traditional faith and tradition in poor quality preaching. Throughout his time at the BBC, Reith criticized the churches for their lack of imagination and, at the same time, he welcomed their strong support particularly when his 'idealism' and his lofty expectations of broadcasting were so clearly stated, time and time again. He did so in 1924.

That year saw the appearance of Reith's *Broadcast Over Britain*. He complained that people were being 'repelled by the impractical and morbid manifestations which pass for the real thing on the one hand, and by the inconsistencies or the absence of the practice of the elementary principles of religion in the ordinary lives of those who are professing Christians, on the other hand'.[33] Any complaint should be 'against the real thing and not the imperfection of its human interpretation'. The church in broadcasting must therefore see that it does not 'put a stained glass between the observer and the facts'. Reith castigated the abuse of the Christian Sunday in recreations 'found only in the distractions of excitement'. The majority of the clergy would doubtless have agreed, but then few of them as yet were prepared to pay attention to wireless on a Sunday – or any other day! Few of them took it seriously, although the *Church of England Newspaper* urged them to in its review of Reith's book: 'The immense importance and incalculable value of the broadcast message to a "congregation" of possibly two million people does not need emphasizing . . . the church must not be satisfied with anything less than "the best".'[34] The review heartily endorsed Reith's final sentence of the chapter on religion: 'If the churches recognize their new opportunity there will not be room enough to hold their people.'[35] This was a challenge to the clergy, for it was they, after all, who influenced Christianity for good or ill. Reith had been turned down by St Paul's from the beginning and he thought the

Dean and Chapter had been particularly discourteous. George Bell, however, now Dean of Canterbury, readily accepted Reith's offer of regular services on a quarterly basis; he told Reith that they would be 'of rather a special character for broadcasting.'[36] Reith felt the Company was 'honoured' by the co-operation of Canterbury Cathedral; it was the best accolade yet. Broadcasting was in an excellent position to provide what the churches were not providing – 'thoroughgoing, manly and optimistic' religion. Significantly for his broadcasting policy, he believed that 'attendance at church while excellent and desirable, is not necessarily of any religious or spiritual value'.[37] It was an echo of many clergy like Sheppard who had been tested by the war and, like so many of the rank and file, had returned in despair of established leadership and, not the least, the remote men in pulpits who had never seen a spade, let alone had to speak of one. Sheppard himself wrote:

> A lack of interest in churches and church affairs may be perfectly compatible with a genuine and sincere enthusiasm for Christianity. It is here that religious broadcasting had an opportunity which probably none of us even yet recognizes.[38]

Having read *Broadcast Over Britain*, Davidson told Reith how he watched 'with keen interest all that is happening in regard to broadcasting; [I] only wish I were able to be more help in this matter.'

By 1929 the place of religion in broadcast programmes had increased enormously; Sunday services, weekly evensong from Westminster Abbey and a daily service.[39] Opportunities for the clergy in broadcasting were increasing and around the country the rush for the microphone was troubling the BBC station directors. The BBC and its Central Committee were concerned with increasingly complex questions about broadcasting and about the authority exercised by station directors to decide who would and who would not be allowed access to the microphones and whose church would be wired. Some clergy were beginning to feel that they had a right to broadcast. By 1927, the BBC had twenty stations, each with its own committee usually chaired by the local Anglican bishop, and they arranged their own services when not taking St Martin's from London. On the second Sunday of each month, St Martin's was broadcast with no alternative and 'Dick' Sheppard soon became a household word among those very millions who he thought 'had little interest in church affairs'. The Church of England was particularly concerned about the quality of broadcast sermons: Cosmo Gordon Lang, still at York, suggested at the Bishops' Meeting in October 1927 that there should be a school especially for preachers (not to be confused with the theological colleges) set up somewhere 'in the middle of Britain' to improve the ability of the clergy in the communicating arts, particularly oratory. The Bishop of Edinburgh was prepared to resign his See and organize it.[40] Reith wanted men to persevere in broadcasting 'a non-sectarian Christianity, confined in respect of doctrine to those simplest essentials to which all Christians of the West can adhere' and who could on radio 'maintain the devotional character which differentiates a service from a mere intimate talk upon serious things'.[41] The churches had to try.

E. Sermons and talks: preaching and teaching

In 1924, one John C. Stobart, an inspector of schools, was seconded from the Board of Education as the BBC Director of Education. 'He was a quiet scholarly man, with a good sense of fun, inclined to be bored with day to day affairs but full of ideas.'[42] He was a classicist. Reith worked hard on this procurement and noted in April 1924, having fixed up Stobart's appointment: 'He is likely to be as good as we can get'.[43] He was to co-ordinate the work of all stations on such matters as pertain to the transmission of general and particular information.[44] Stobart was therefore to be responsible for the BBC's religious output and particularly for the standards which the BBC would set the clergy not only in broadcast sermons from both church and studio but, as broadcasting hours were extended on Sunday, other material of a religious nature both for adults and children. Stobart had the problem of raising the standards without upsetting the ordinary parish clergy by presenting them with the well-established models in the personalities whom the BBC was now projecting round the country: Sheppard, Donald Soper, George MacLeod, Alexander Fleming and others.

Stobart attended his first Sunday Committee in June 1925; thereafter he would present his progress report to each meeting. At the BBC Control Board in November 1926, Reith expressed the view that 'we should be content with nothing else than the best preachers on every possible occasion and the best men should be encouraged'. However much the provincial stations felt they should pull their weight and provide their share of preachers, Reith wanted the best, whether locally or simultaneously broadcast to the nation. This was Stobart's brief: Christian utterance was to improve. Reith had already had conversations with a Canon of Westminster (whom he would not name) who remarked to him in September 1926 that not only is the 'standard of religion not high enough' but moreover that in his opinion 'there are not fifty men in all the denominations put together who are qualified to speak to such an audience as the BBC provides'. Reith strongly urged the BBC hierarchy[45] in the person of Nicolls, Stobart and Eckersley 'to take more steps to ensure really decent sermons being broadcast'. He thought that 'performance' records ought to be kept, as with artists, but recognized the influence of local committees over denominational allocation and the inevitable urge to broadcast by the clergy in any locality. Within months Stobart was pressing all stations 'to raise the quality of Sunday evening addresses by the exploiting of notable preachers from wherever they may be speaking' – to have a local man 'nationalized' for the benefit of all. He also wanted services from studios to some degree standardized in that they should contain certain common elements of liturgical form which could be extricated from the prayer book or service-book context and 'rebuilt' into a formation which made for good broadcasting: elements of contrast and variety which would not overtax the listener, who could neither see nor 'experience' the material other than through a receiver which was doubtless cheap and thus gave a poor reception; over all such odds the speaker must prevail.

Stobart's appointment linked the BBC to the world of education and by 1928 the Hadow Report on Adult Education was given wide publicity, not the least by an enthusiastic editor of the *Sunday School Chronicle*, Dr Basil Yeaxlee, formerly secretary of the Educational Settlements Association and later to be Principal of West Hill Training College. The Hadow Report stressed the need for 'expert presentation of new knowledge and new perspectives', but that broadcast education 'should be closely related to the normal interests of the general public'.[46] Yeaxlee was one of the very few prepared and eager to co-operate with Charles Siepmann and Stobart on the provision of religious talks for the general public. He was aware of the dangers and told Stobart that Sunday afternoon talks, 'while making fuller provision for real education, must not invoke the criticism of people who are not students and are only too ready to resent the "highbrow" '. He tried hard through his weekly *Sunday School Chronicle* to have the churches take more interest in the general talks: 'The relation of religious education to the BBC programme is much broader than talks on specifically religious subjects.' But the starting points for the public envisaged by Stobart lay in Bible and church. The concerns of the Advisory Committee, however, were the provision of services for both the committed and the 'non-attending' Christian population who were already informed on the fundamentals of Christian belief through Sunday school and day school. As Sunday afternoon broadcasting increased, there arose the 'competition' for space within the Talks

Department; Stobart was anxious not to 'overdo the religious element' but realized it would be a compromise between claims: adult education talks or a short service for children and the bi-monthly talks on missionary themes (travel talks specially designed to enlist support and sympathy for the missionary effort). The Sunday Committee had volunteered Canon Woodward for the monthly children's service from St John's, Smith Square, Westminster.[47] These were very popular as they involved children participating in the service, and in 1930 the Cardiff Station Director, E. R. Appleton, was to begin his series of dramatic programmes under the general title *For the Children*. Both Reith and Stobart were enthusiastic about a monthly series of Bible readings and from 1925 onwards were especially anxious to make the Old Testament more widely known as fine literature (in any question about intelligibility Reith always preferred the Authorized Version). The Sunday Committee advised most strongly that on no account (there were 'ceremonial' exceptions!) should any Sunday broadcast service take place during normal church hours, namely 6.0—7.45 p.m.; this was based on the firm fundamental assumption shared by all the members that broadcasting church services would keep the faithful away from the churches; Sunday afternoon broadcasts for children would keep them from Sunday school. Thus for the BBC planners – each clamouring for a portion of the extra space on Sundays – no time was really safe.

R. S. Lambert (later first editor of *The Listener*) was, in 1928, in charge of Adult Education and knew Yeaxlee to be in full support of the BBC's work. Siepmann also contributed to the *Sunday School Chronicle* and wanted Yeaxlee on the Central Council for Broadcast Adult Education; he would represent Christian educational interests for the Free Churches via their Council of Christian Education which also included the YMCA, the SCM and the Adult School Union. For the Church of England, he would cover the Teaching Church Group[48] (based at St Albans), St Christopher's College and the Church of England Sunday School Institute. Yeaxlee would cover all these interests and avoid the problem of over-representation on BBC Committees. The Sunday Committee since July 1926 the Central Religious Advisory Committee, (henceforth referred to as CRAC) was not asked to nominate, nor did they show a great interest. Siepmann wanted some part of the religious element of Sunday to be directly educational and suggested a course of talks aimed at the teachers of religion in schools. This would mean a shift in the listenership and Stobart did not wish to lose his non-highbrow audience by the introduction of an educational element. Yeaxlee was confident that a transition period would suffice to add the missionary talk/Bible-reading audience to the vast numbers of the committed and the 'non-attending committed' who wished to take a more intelligent look at their own faith with the assistance of very able popular teachers as exemplified by William Temple and Canon Vernon Storr at Westminster. Temple had already excelled with the programme *Points of View*[49] and his sermon to the SCM.[50] In 1930, the first major series of Adult Education talks was started with two talks by Professor Eric S. Waterhouse on Psychology and Religion.[51] In 1932 a series of fifteen talks entitled *What are Saints?* was given by Fr Cyril Martindale, the Jesuit from Farm St. He was already acceptable and indeed had become one of the most widely appreciated speakers in the BBC's galaxy of preachers. Yeaxlee was satisfied but looked forward to the time when his fellow student at theological college, C. H. Dodd, would give courses which would bring the results of biblical scholarship to the mass of the committed – whatever their confessional colour.

The controversy about broadcasting and education in the field of religion ran parallel to the deliberations of CRAC and its concern to educate the listening public through sermons. Most of the clergy invited to preach did not regard their pulpits or the Savoy Hill Studio as in any way akin to a lecture room or classroom. Basil Yeaxlee told Reith that he did not want to 'turn all the preachers at Savoy Hill into lecturers, heaven forbid!' But if, as the anonymous Canon of Westminster and CRAC had advised, the same preachers should be deployed time and again, what possibilities could be achieved when a man might be heard in a series of three or more services? In March 1928, CRAC approved the first connected series of addresses from the St Martin's pulpit by Eric Southam, a close friend both of Reith and of Garbett. (The series dealt with questions of Christian evidence and led eventually to a book by Bishop F. T. Woods of Winchester, *What is God Like?*[52]) Reith, Stobart and Garbett agreed that the resources of broadcasting should be used not merely or only to carry the voice of the local preacher to a wider 'locality' if he was rather ordinary, or to the nation if he was exceptional. The BBC must take an initiative (notwithstanding the difficulties of finding the acceptable and common core of Christian tradition) to enlarge the knowledge of Christianity and Christian insight among the vast mass of the listening public, whatever the degree of commitment.

2

ANGLICAN APPROVAL:
THE ELY COMMITTEE OF 1931

By 1929 the BBC was broadcasting regular services on Sundays, talks for children and the regular Epilogue which Basil Nicolls had aptly named for the short programme to end the Sunday broadcasts.[1]

In 1927, Reith gave one of his characteristic speeches to church bodies – this time in Glasgow – on the subject of broadcasting in general and religion in particular. Whilst he extolled the enormous BBC potential, there was, however, a great deal that the churches could do. Reith asked the impossible of the churches; as Asa Briggs points out, his concept of religion was itself, to say the least, controversial. However much Reith wanted Christian morality to prevail in the doings of men and women, the churches, he said, were doing themselves no good in airing their differences in public, thus exposing their theological flanks to attack, or even in exposing points of theological difference between various denominations or sections. He supported CRAC in its constant refusal to consider the non-central and sectarian branches of the Christian 'fringe'.

In 1930 the Committee strengthened its centralist Protestant position by including more Nonconformists, whose denominations were thus to be regarded *de jure* on the same footing as the Church of England. Nevertheless, the Church of England was the principal church of the land and not surprisingly had the most churches and clergy. In broadcasting terms during this period of around eight years, the Church of England had around 45 per cent of the broadcasts, with the remaining 55 per cent shared among the Free Churches (24 per cent), the Roman Catholics (12 per cent), and the remainder shared between the Church of Scotland and others such as the Quakers and Salvation Army. The BBC had issued *Hints to Speakers* in 1924 on how to have the address prove helpful to *all* listeners and reprinted sections of some broadcast addresses in the *Radio Times* as models to be read by others (Hilda Matheson had enlisted the help of H. W. Fox of the *St*

Martin's Review, an Anglican cleric, to whom Stobart sent sermons for approval as a way of assessing who should or should not broadcast). In 1927, the BBC had drawn up a book of services but it was not published; the proofs were, however, revised by Canon Dwelly of Liverpool Cathedral and it was eventually published in 1930, under the title *Services for Broadcasting*.[2]

Throughout the late twenties, Reith was still conscious of opposition to broadcast religion by the general run of the clergy and criticized them for their conservatism and timidity – 'possibly not uncommon characteristics of clerical organizations'. He believed there was general appreciation by the vast majority who listened to religious services. Nevertheless, the BBC had a moral responsibility; it was 'not doing half enough to counteract the pernicious effect of modern ethics nor with respect to the intellectual standard so lowered by the press'.[3] The churches, he had always felt, were being consistently negative. Reith told Bell in June 1928 that he believed that the most encouraging co-operation came from the nation's cathedrals, prepared as they were to mount special services between 8.0 and 8.45 p.m. on Sundays.

In July 1929 Reith was again invited to address himself, this time to the diocese of Coventry. On the policy of the BBC he told them that analysis of letters and the general reaction in the press, both religious and secular, showed that the religious services etc. were 'the most highly appreciated activities of the wireless in the whole week'. Furthermore, as Reith was fond of saying, no initiative had come from the churches themselves, at the outset, simply because the limited reaction of the clergy was fear; they were more anxious about the possible, in his view hypothetical, diminution in their own congregations than the spread of a religious message over fifteen million people. After all, he asked, was attendance a supreme consideration in church? The disparity between the popularity of religious broadcasts and the demise of the church in the country at large suggested something wrong: 'There was not a proper co-ordination between the somewhat indefinite wireless effort and the specialized concentrated effort of the churches.' A great deal more was needed and this could only be done by the churches; radio aroused people's interest but when they entered their local church they were disappointed.[4] Much press comment presented Reith as the enemy of the clergy: he was not offering any constructive suggestions as to what could be done. He defended himself in the *St Martin's Review* of the following January: 'I do not find theological doctrine or dogma of much practical significance in the world today.'[5] His opponents rejected a non-dogmatic and blandly non-doctrinal interpretation of religion which seemed only incidentally

Christian. Reith had already recognized that perhaps a cleric was needed to take responsibility for religious broadcasting in the BBC itself: 'it needed proper handling'.[6]

The Bishop of Coventry thanked him for 'frank and sympathetic criticism which is not easy to get and is just what a Diocesan Conference needs from a non-ecclesiastical layman!' Reith told Basil Yeaxlee a week later that he had intended no attack on the church or the clergy and thought that much of the press coverage was sensational and out of context. He lunched with Lang at Lambeth in October and there discussed the issues. Lang assured him that he had 'more influence probably than any man before or now'.[7]

The publication of his expansion of the Leamington appraisal in *St Martin's Review* caused a ripple throughout the Church of England. Garbett thought the issues and opinions should be tested in the context of Convocation itself. The Dean of Winchester, E. G. Selwyn, a close friend of Garbett, brought a motion to the Convocation of Canterbury, the centre of the church's foremost arena of policy making. He wanted Lang to appoint a committee of both Houses to 'consider the religious value of broadcasting services and their bearing on public worship; it would be lacking in courtesy if the House did not answer the criticisms of John Reith',[8] said Selwyn. Reith wanted the church to act and the clergy wanted 'clearer guidance as to the ways in which it was possible for the church to deepen and extend the good influences that broadcasting has brought to bear'. The church must have a policy, not only because the BBC's religious policy was 'creating considerable interest in religion' but because the BBC was broadcasting 'lectures on the subject of religion . . . not always sympathetic to Christianity'. It was to be a matter of growing contention when men of letters could lecture – as did H. G. Wells and Shaw – on matters which raised controversial religious beliefs; but also when theologians did the same over questions of theology. Selwyn paraded the limitations of broadcast religion before the House: it would tend to replace attendance at church and induce passive worship; sermons would be without gesture and 'most serious of all, censorship' would be imposed. A great many broadcast sermons were without 'a good deal of the salt they ought to have'. He reminded the House that the sermons which had the greatest attraction were those from Roman Catholics – they were 'more definite and precise in their teaching'. Thus he articulated a desire felt now by CRAC, by Stobart, by the educationalists and by Yeaxlee, that something more was wanted: systematic exposition of the Christian faith to enable the rank and file to develop a more mature understanding of its central beliefs and the basic knowledge of a Christianity appropriate to mature adults. Selwyn thought the Committee might well consider 'a more intellectual and definite kind of religious teaching than was being given. People were tired of being told that they ought to live the Christian life better.' Perhaps sermons could be 'classified' and be arranged in 'courses'.

Reith was anxious to co-operate and provide Convocation with the necessary material. Stobart prepared a long statement written 'in a spirit of optimism' not because of the 'marvellous growth and progress' but because 'problems and difficulties have melted away; . . . the public confidence in the BBC's honesty of purpose seems to have dissipated the old atmosphere of hesitation and cynical or jealous disparagement.' Reith himself knew that this was just not true; the very existence of a Committee appointed by Convocation would be a means to bring widespread opposition into the open and to have responsible church-men consider the issues intelligently. The cautious Bishop of Durham, Hensley Henson, supported Selwyn in his opposition to radio religion poaching the congregations from the churches.[9] Reith knew that Henson 'was not convinced that wireless is doing as much good as harm to religion',[10] whereas Davidson from the beginning – having been given a wireless receiver by Reith – was impressed by 'what broad-casting may now mean for the world for good or ill'. Stobart's report went on to express the churches' concern at the BBC's 'present machinery for attracting the best preachers of all denominations' (which was one way of saying that CRAC was not yet quite willing to pick the best preachers for the BBC at the inevitable sacrifice of the less than best). Reith's opinions are clear in this document: '. . . in a word, broadcast sermons are dull'.[11] Religion, for Reith, was a possession of the people held in safe custody or 'serviced' by the churches. Religion for his critics was the property of the church, and those who in the Church of England criticized the BBC for competing in one way or another were most often those who opposed the close relation of the church with the establishment – the Prayer Book issue was still remembered. It was not censorship (over which much blood had already been spilled) which made sermons dull but rather those characteristics of a pulpit style – high-flown rhetoric, affectation and epigrams with which churchgoers were familiar and which they perhaps actually wanted; the vast millions of 'non-attending churched' who had acquired a species of well-developed Christian superstition had to be attracted to listen, helped to listen and by so doing to resuscitate that religion of Christian Britain which could be of practical value. The churches, by and large, however, wanted their already half-empty churches refilled and whatever good radio was doing for religion, it was not substantially reversing that trend. The Reith/ Stobart defence went on to suggest that more preparation would help if preachers would only be willing to submit to 'the possible indignity of rehearsal'. Many clergy simply were not prepared for this and found the interference of production an impertinence often more than they could bear. Some who really wanted to broadcast successfully were pleased to be 'produced' and they were open or intelligent enough to see the peculiar needs of the microphone audience and could square the co-production of their sacred pulpit utterance with both the Holy Spirit and the Corporation's Duty Officer! Stobart's document outlined the possibilities: broadcast religion – whilst doing good work for the housebound and invalid – might act as a stimulant and even a means of recruitment for the churches. Why not use the rediffusion technique and bring loud-speakers into the churches and have a few good preachers address the widest possible congregation? Experiments had been made.[12] Neither the churches nor society at large were prepared for the implications of this notion; many asked what would become of all the low-grade preachers whilst the Sopers and MacLeods were popularizing the faith during the local evensong?

Stobart was boldly assertive; the BBC had shaped its policy 'so that there shall be as little as possible of rivalry or counter-attraction' and that had meant no broadcasting during church service hours and no secular alternatives when broadcast services were in progress. But rivalry there inevitably was, and, as in other fields, the BBC created a 'standard by which local preachers may be judged and thus render congregations less tolerant of mediocrity than they used to be'. That might have been true in music, but in religion the vast numbers awakened to these insights were mostly not to be found in a church on Sunday; for a great number of clergy, therefore, radio was a rival. Moreover, at the Lambeth Conference in 1930, while consideration was given to the church's approach to the general public 'increasingly afforded through the press', the BBC was conspicuous by its absence from the report.[13]

The Committee under the chairmanship of L. J. White-Thomson, Bishop of Ely, included a number of well-known men: C. L. Carr, Bishop of Coventry, who had invited Reith to speak at Leamington; Canon Guy Rogers, Rector of Birmingham and Chairman of the BBC North Region Religious Advisory Committee (RAC); Dean Selwyn of Winchester, and Sheppard's successor at St Martin's, Pat McCormick. Lang had asked Garbett to be the chairman but he refused: it would be too embarrassing as he was chairman of CRAC.[14] On 21 January 1931, the Committee presented its report to Convocation.[15] The first unanimous finding was of appreciation for the BBC's original determination to find a place for religion in its broadcast programme: 'It has brought religion once again into the market place.' There were all manner of advantages in having religion discussed between men in the mines and in factories, 'under the lee-side of a hedge and in bars'. For those whose work kept them from church, for all those in distant lighthouses and ships, 'for how many settlers has the broadcast from some English country church, the movement of the congregation and even the scraping of a chair revived the sense of fellowship well-nigh forgotten'. There were excellent services provided for the young and for the sick. The first and unanimous finding was one of heartfelt and strongly worded approval.[16]

The report then turned to its suggestions and here its approval was qualified! Broadcast religion was perhaps too emotional, with insufficient instruction: 'We are not suggesting controversial subjects' but the 'body of theology which all who profess and call themselves Christian may be said to hold in common'. The general concepts of God were erroneous and the central words of Christian belief needed more frequent restatement such as were to be found in the syllabus of religious instruction for church and county council schools through which framework 'the religious life of the nation may be built on an abiding foundation'.[17] Religious speakers should encourage the notion of fellowship so that people should see listening and active participation in a local church as one. The report finally suggested talks for schools and agreed with the policy of the Corporation not to broadcast Holy Communion.[18]

It then addressed 'some remarks to our brethren': 'We wish the clergy would realize that broadcasting has come to stay and to be one of the most potent factors in the nation's life.'[19] That meant particularly its educational uses but, more generally, 'we should . . . gradually wean them from the cheap and the mean'. One last point it desired to make more strongly than anything – the BBC had introduced a renewed appreciation of the liturgical heritage, but when people went to their own or local churches 'they have too often been discouraged by indifferent preaching and inferior reading and singing'– exactly Reith's point; he approved of quality even when he didn't appreciate it – and he was never greatly moved by choral evensong; he preferred to sing a metrical psalm (which he could only do in Scotland). 'The truth is', said the report, 'broadcast services have raised the tone of public opinion. A better type of service and better reading are demanded and our brethren should do their utmost to meet this demand. Even a village choir can aid worship at home so that listeners can follow easily.'

Introducing the report in the Upper House of Convocation, the Bishop of Ely said very little by way of amplifying the recommendations. He mentioned the offer of the BBC to provide an alternative Sunday evening evensong for outlying and rural congregations: they could have a loudspeaker in the church. 8.0 p.m. was, however, too late, as they were bound not to broadcast during church hours. The Bishop wanted the BBC to be thanked by Convocation and his seconder, the Bishop of Hereford, echoed this gratitude, 'having regard to what broadcasting might have become had it not been for the splendid ideals of the leaders'. Whether splendid or not, Reith's conviction had welded religion into the output. Carr positively assured his fellow bishops that the gramophone trade, theatres and concert halls, had all done well by virtue of broadcasting; how could they think people were being diverted from the churches? A 'real attempt to improve services . . . would lead to increased congregations'. Garbett, in his remarks, believed broadcasting was a 'wonderful influence' and he scotched the notion that broadcast services kept people from church attendance: 'Those who said they listened to broadcast services instead of going to church were people who would be in any case unlikely to attend church.' This was undoubtedly true.

Bishop Barnes of Birmingham spoke in favour of the series *Science and Religion*[20] in which he had taken part. When men of distinction were asked to speak they should be given complete freedom: 'They should be asked to be courteous' but beyond that there should be no restriction. He wanted freedom of religious discussion over the air: 'the best thought of their epoch led men to Christ'. Bishop Barnes soon provoked opposition. The Bishop of Salisbury warned that the wireless put a greater responsibility on the clergy to 'forewarn their people against the atmosphere of criticism in which they must live'. Temple had agreed with Barnes, but 'when one side is put, the other side must be put fairly soon'.

In the Lower House, the report was introduced by Selwyn, who found that the final version contained but few relics of the originality present in the draft; the message had become quite simple: the church was grateful to the BBC and the clergy should take care about their manners in the liturgy. Pat McCormick thought it should record special appreciation to the BBC for their determination to refrain from broadcasting during church service hours, notwithstanding the enormous pressure to do so. He doubted whether the church as a whole realized what this meant for the 'cause of religion in this country'. Some speakers were aware that what broadcasting meant for the cause of religion was distinct from the inevitable competition that prevailed between the 'local' and the 'broadcast' experience: attendance at one's local service followed by a speedy return home in time to hear yet another on the wireless was common! Whilst all agreed with a Cornish archdeacon who wanted to avoid any suggestion that broadcast services were a substitute for public worship, another speaker wanted these broadcasts to be much more scholarly. Selwyn, however, preferred 'addresses of a more theological character' and was clearly contrasted with McCormick and Guy Rogers of Birmingham who both wanted to have the church see broadcasting in a much wider perspective: 'the whole subject of religious broadcasting in relation to science' must be discussed, they claimed. Rogers reproached those who criticized the BBC for broadcasting anti-Christian propaganda in series such as *Science and Religion,* which involved Huxley, Malinovsky and others. The church could not have it both ways, Rogers argued: if clergy felt they could speak, even though as non-experts, in such fields as economics, then they could not 'resent the expression of views on religion by journalists, novelists and scientists'. He hoped that they would all agree on the general question that people should not be 'prevented from hearing things with which the clergy did not agree'. The BBC were to be congratulated on the balance between one view and another. The report was accepted, and the clergy were warned; the BBC was congratulated and asked for more theology on the style of the listening groups organized by adult education. Here was the chance for the churches to educate their congregations in the foundations of theology around which their liturgy revolved.

Thus the principal beneficiary of the BBC had given a qualified vote of thanks for the services broadcast from both churches and studios. The Ely Report focused on several major aspects of broadcast religion which were to occupy the attention of both parties until the sixties.

1. Broadcasting did well for the cause of Christianity and church; some thought the BBC should entirely protect Christianity; others thought the BBC should reflect the wider debate between, e.g., scientific discourse and theological discourse.

2. Broadcasting did well for the cause of religion, especially among those not normally in church. By religon was meant Christianity and its mission to the non-churched. Standards must be raised in both liturgy and utterance to benefit those on both sides of the divide which separated active and participant Christianity from that indigenous religious consciousness embedded by school and by Christian elements in culture at large. It was this group which naturally formed the largest number and to which the broadcasters should give more of their attention. There would come a time when the Corporation would have considerable aspects of its policy influenced simply by the numbers of people actually listening.[21]

3

RELIGIOUS CONTROVERSY

Since 1922 Reith, Lord Gainford and the Sunday Committee had ensured that Christianity itself should not be open to attack nor abused in the broadcast programmes. Reith had not allowed an alternative secular programme during the broadcast service on Sunday evening, and told George Bell that he had even been prepared to resign over the issue. The question of controversial broadcasting had troubled Reith from the beginning.[1] If, as Briggs says, the Post Office was 'frightened of the BBC dabbling in controversy', Reith constantly pressed for freedom to handle 'a certain amount of controversial matter under adequate safeguards of impartiality'[2] and in another letter only a few weeks later he expressed his frustration more succinctly: 'On practically all subjects of first rate importance, the Service is silent.'[3] The Crawford Committee eventually recommended a 'moderate amount' of controversial matter provided it was 'of high quality . . . and distributed with scrupulous fairness'. Notwithstanding the plea of the BBC (it is notable that the Sunday Committee was not in support: Garbett had merely submitted in its behalf the great success and appreciation of broadcast services which were non-controversial, extremely popular and highly appreciated[4]), the Government would not have the BBC dabbling in arenas which belonged to political discourse backed up by the strength of the newspaper lobby with which politicians would have to contend. The refusal by the Postmaster-General in January 1927 forbade any statement of opinion by the Corporation on issues of public policy and speeches/lectures 'containing statements on topics of political, religious or industrial controversy'. It is interesting to note that Reith thought that the proceedings of the Church Assembly over the revision of the Prayer Book would have been entirely appropriate for broadcasting. In February 1927 he thought it 'the hottest subject of religious controversy' and whilst he was torn between being topical and offending the extremists, it was something actually happening and thus worth reflecting in a broadcast talk. Doubtless such a talk would have to be confined to facts but 'it must not be given in such a way as to minimize the changes or excuse them'. It was important that this debate should be reported, especially since the press was giving the issue such wide coverage.[5] Notwithstanding Reith's importunity, the Postmaster-General replied that '. . . if the subject matter comes within the area of. . . religious controversy, it would be well for the present not to accept it'.[6] In July 1927, Reith and Clarendon met the Postmaster-General about the removal of the ban: 'a hopeless business', wrote Reith. 'I have contempt for the Postmaster-General, and Clarendon is a puppet with him. This is most unfortunate for the BBC.'[7]

Reith and the Board of Governors requested the Postmaster-General again in February 1928 to re-consider the question of controversy. Finally on 5 March the ban was lifted and within two days Reith called a meeting of all his top aides, Cecil Graves, the Controller-General, R. H. Eckersley, Organizer of Programmes, Gladstone Murray, Director of Publicity, J. C. Stobart, Director of Education, and Hilda Matheson, to discuss the implications. Together they decided that the lifting of the ban 'will not involve any vital change in the methods of religious broadcasting'. This was far-reaching and central to the discussion of the BBC's initiative as to how religion should be tackled. This meant that, as Reith had told the Postmaster-General, 'nothing must offend or provoke', especially since the BBC 'has the support of the vast majority'. Nevertheless, it did not preclude lectures or debates on religion, 'provided that these are treated with requisite self-restraint, impartiality and authority'. The Central Religious Advisory Committee, (so-called to distinguish it from the Regional Committees and to remove any suggestion that the Sunday Committee had served only the London Regional Station) reaffirmed this view and agreed a statement in March which drew a clear distinction between questions of content and questions of style; there could be debates and lectures on weekdays but nothing at any time to offend: 'In regard to religion the removal of the ban on controversy creates a new position for the BBC in theory rather than in practice . . . this policy excludes sectarian propaganda and the expression of extreme views or contentious argument.'[8] It was well meant but oppressive: there should be no voice for the Christian and other religious sects clamouring for the microphone. Reith was not prepared to have Christianity wash its linen – of whatever hue – in public. This matter was to come fully into view in CRAC's debate with the Roman Catholics.

However under-represented the principal Free Churches might have been at this time, the Committee could confidently agree to advise the BBC on the choice of speakers and by so doing filter out the sectarian propagandists who wanted their particular and identifiable social grouping to be recognized by the BBC and thus widely publicized. This policy quite clearly favoured the mainstream denominations and particularly the Church of England; the BBC simply called on Protestants at the centre to resist any temptation to identify their sectional interests as against the interests of that Christianity which, as Reith had always said, was above denominational self-interest. In 1930 CRAC added Free Church representatives with the addition of the Regional Advisory Committee chairmen, who were mostly Bishops or Anglicans of high rank.[9]

The BBC was assailed by three sorts of groups interested in the lifting of the ban and diminishing the strength of the mainstream churches on the Advisory Committees. First, the Christian sects with either North American or European origins felt themselves to be part of the wider spectrum of Christian tradition and felt they had a right to a small place in the regular pattern of religious programmes and particularly Sunday services. These included the Christian Scientists, Spiritualists, Christadelphians, the Free Church of England, Unitarians, Swedenborgians, Churches of Christ, Seventh Day Adventists and others such as the Oxford Group Movement.

In the second group came the Freethinkers, the Rationalists, the British Humanist Association, *Psychic News*, the Ethical Society, the Fabians and those smaller groups who between them demanded a right to challenge the BBC on its relation to the mainstream and the Christian monopoly. No one, they claimed, was permitted explicitly to deride or question the central beliefs of the Christian position at the microphone, least of all in the manner in which these bodies were accustomed to question the claims of Christianity (perhaps with a measure of directness and even belligerency which had a clear motive). This lobby was, of course, propagandist and sectarian and the BBC were no more free to encourage such sectionalist interests than promote the explicit interests of the Church of England over the Methodists.

In the third group might be put the smaller fringe bodies allied and animated by a particular objective; foremost here were the Lord's Day Observance Society along with the Imperial Alliance for the Defence of Sunday, the Temperance League, Protestant Truth Society, and the World's Evangelical Alliance, all bodies whose interests were threatened by the dissemination of particular views or information to which they might take objection. Most notable were the bodies concerned with the protection of Sunday and of Protestant institutions.

Throughout its history, the BBC was to be besieged by enthusiasts in these three groups opposed to one or other aspect of its religious policy – not only in the context of religious broadcasting but of any broadcast material which questioned the foundation on which, it was believed, British society rested.

No sooner had the ban on controversy been lifted than Siepmann and Stobart were organizing the notable series of adult talks on *Science and Religion*.[10] It was to embrace Huxley and Haldane, Dick Sheppard and Dean Inge and would focus very clearly on several major issues of policy. The talks were scheduled to run from September to December 1930. Reith had met Temple at York the year before planning began. Reith persuaded the Board of Governors to minute that 'there was to be no attack on the Christian religion and not even reasons for unbelief'.[11] Yeaxlee's Council for Broadcast Adult Education wanted not merely controversy but the systematic statement of the non-Christian position. Whilst Yeaxlee did not want Bertrand Russell for fear he might be 'cynical and flippant and not put in a good reasoned argument', he definitely wanted the Christian position scrutinized.[12] Yeaxlee, like Temple, was confident that Christianity could only benefit from reasoned scrutiny. Reith was unsure and feared the effect of this upon the faithful. He asked Temple for his advice; he wanted a formula which he could pass on to the speakers as to what they were permitted to say.[13] About this extraordinary position Reith had no doubt. He told Temple that the speakers could say anything provided they did not offend those 'whose religion was the deepest and greatest thing in life'. Here was the central problem of the broadcasting authority: the BBC could not easily select listeners who had the stamina to listen to this and not to that; broadcasting was blanket coverage unless it was possible to school people into not listening and into being selective for themselves. Reith was concerned for those whose religion was so fragile as to be 'far more influenced by a few minutes' anti-religious comment by someone of repute than by hours of religious teaching, no matter how well done'. And what of those whose moral position is controlled by some 'form of Christian principle? This may be a Sunday school sort of outlook to start with but it is better than nothing . . . if we shake Christian principle, its authority and validity, what is to be the effect?' Whilst Reith felt flexible over the whole issue, it was a matter of considerable anxiety to him. More than anything else in BBC policy the general religious issue troubled him: 'I could not myself endure the thought that I had been party to anything in the nature of a denial of Christ.'[14]

Temple, not surprisingly, was glad that 'our wireless service is in the hands of someone who cares as you do for sound moral standards and for religion'. But he was troubled at Reith's idea of controlling what was to be said by the speakers in the *Science* series; they would surely not accept an invitation and that was educationally unsatisfactory. The best minds of the day would be lost. More important was the religious question. 'Nothing can be more disastrous in the long run than to let the notion get around that religious people dare not let the case against their convictions be frankly stated.' Temple felt the dilemma. 'On the other hand, listeners must be protected against any insult to their beliefs or feelings.' Exactly how to define Temple's listeners who should be protected was difficult enough, but 'the argument against religion should not be left unanswered'. He suggested a rule for producers, that in every *series* which might bear on religious matters, a preponderance of speakers should be religious men; and for speakers, 'that they shall treat religious matters with reverence and respect for the deep feelings of others; they should avoid any unfair exploitation of their opportunity to say what may give pain.' Temple thought the BBC should, like those who appointed the Gifford Lecturers – and he quoted the fourth requirement of the terms of Lord Gifford's will – 'use diligence to secure that they be able, reverent men, true thinkers, sincere lovers of and enquirers after the truth'.

As preparations continued, Stobart was locked in earnest debate with Father C. C. Martindale, SJ, who took an entirely different view. Martindale believed that the nation's mental machinery was being less and less used due partly to the cinema and 'partly to the debauching nature of inferior education'; on the other hand, the series *Science and Religion* would not enlighten. The only thought-out philosophies affecting people, he thought, were Bolshevism and Catholicism. Martindale believed that any sectarian interest which was so far from the public mind as to need a complete explanation must be regarded as propaganda – an unsavoury word in broadcasting philosophy, at least as regards religion. The criterion seemed to be that while the central Christian fundamentals (which Reith believed broadcasting must protect) were not attacked, support for them and thus for the recognized institutions which promoted and enshrined them could come to the microphone from nearly any quarter. In effect, these were few: CRAC had decided in favour of the Salvation Army and the Society of Friends, even though there were doubts about broadcasting so much silence! By the same token the Jews were supported by CRAC almost as soon as broadcasting began, although it was many years before an actual Jewish service was broadcast. The Chief Rabbi was allowed to give a talk around Passover time.[15]

The lifting of the ban on controversy was to make little real difference to the policy of the BBC in respect to Christianity; it was not to be attacked and this meant, in effect, that it was not to be discussed. Fringe sectarian groups were not permitted and nor were lobbying bodies who were offended by the Reithian-dominated programme on Sundays (no alternative programmes during religious services). Notwithstanding the *Science and Religion* series of September 1930, the policy of refusing minority groups, and especially those such as the National Secular Society, was maintained. The Rationalist Press Association and National Secular Society met the Corporation in 1928 and were told the official policy. Their argument in reply was simple: Britain was no longer a Christian country, given falling church attendance and declining religious observance; therefore the BBC should not be financed to propagate the religious outlook of only one section of the population. This was to be the hub of the campaign by all those minority groups which claimed that the BBC should provide a forum for good-mannered but open expressions of convictions, whatever their relation to the generally accepted Christian view. They wanted to use broadcasting to attack the entrenched supremacy of the mainstream churches just as they did through their publications.

In 1927 the Board had (following CRAC) refused time on the air to Philip Kerr (later Lord Lothian), the Astors and other Christian Scientists. Garbett was vigorously opposed to them, as were all of the Board except Mrs Snowdon, who thought they should not be refused simply because the Board believed that they did not accept Christianity.[16] Whatever he might say to Kerr, Reith was quite clear about what was orthodox and what wasn't; whatever an objective scrutiny of Christian Science might afford, the microphone was not the place for it. This would be sectarian propaganda and, far from wanting to divide Christian groups, including, of course, the major churches, the BBC wanted their differences minimalized. However, there was to be one major exception and complication – relations with Roman Catholicism.

4

THE ROMAN CATHOLICS

A. Relations with the Protestant establishment

In 1928, the first published *BBC Handbook* declared confidently that the 'policy on religion' (especially the Sunday services) had been 'welcomed by the church authorities and the general public alike' and that 'the co-operation of the Christian churches has been secured'.[1] It might have been more accurate had the vital word 'Protestant' been inserted before 'Christian' in that assertion. There had been co-operation with and from the Roman Catholics from the very beginning, but there were grave differences both of principle and theology which caused considerable worry to the BBC and to the Roman Catholic authorities in Westminster, in the north of England and Northern Ireland.

As I have said, the policy from the beginning had been eclectic and perhaps 'pan-Protestant'; it had assumed a measure of Protestant Christian conviction in the population of Britain upon which Reith and his kind could happily build in broadcasting policy. Evangelicals within Protestantism would predictably baulk at such a suggestion, and even quote church attendance statistics in support of their claim that the country was now just as much in need of conversion as ever, if not more so. Whilst the decade from 1922 saw a continuing rise in church attendance,[2] most Roman Catholics would share the Evangelicals' view: judging by attendance at places of worship, the country's Christian foundation was being more and more eroded by changing lifestyles, etc. As we have noticed in the thinking of Reith and Sheppard, the policy on religious broadcasting made one crucial assumption – that attendance at church was not necessarily an index of Christian conviction or moral rectitude. There was an inbuilt Christianity in the population which made it possible to speak of Christian Britain as Reith did to the Crawford Committee in 1925:

It is suitable that there should be a definite association with the Christian religion in particular. Christianity is the official religion of the country and . . . in these critical days a service can be rendered by broadcasting the fundamentals of the Christian religion.[3]

This reflected the sense of urgency and idealism which very largely governed Reith's whole attitude to broadcasting. Reith's impatience with the churches had been fired by Sheppard's; they saw that a new sort of Christianity – unlike the Christianity which was widely believed to have failed – must be promulgated to post-war Britain. Broadcasting gave this urgency space. Here was the churches' great opportunity.

The Roman Catholics were not so easily led by this sense of missionary endeavour. It was not merely a task of resuscitating people's dormant faith, whether they attended church or not; for Roman Catholics there were vital issues of identity at stake. They were not quite alone in this. Some Anglicans and most Nonconformists at the centre of Protestantism were also concerned with their identity; however they were more amenable to recognizing common elements and promoting an intelligible message of common witness; they were more able to concentrate on what 'unites rather than divides'.[4] Whilst the Roman Catholics were a minority church, three important facts had to be remembered:

1. There were nearly three million Roman Catholics in Britain.[5]

2. They had a strong and widely recognized hierarchy related, across barriers of nationality and language, with Rome.

3. They shared a worldwide liturgy in the Latin rite and centrally the Mass.

These factors and the theological and ecclesial principles behind them were not easily negotiable or easily assimilated into any common core of Christian dogma which could be servant to an easily recognizable message coined for the broad British public.

In 1922 Reith invited Cardinal Bourne of Westminster to attend the first meeting of the Sunday Committee and to bring suggestions for suitable broadcasters. Bourne appointed Herbert Ward, the Secretary of the National Catholic Congress, to represent him. He was the only layman on the committee; he was to feel this fact acutely as the difficulties between the Roman Catholic Church and the BBC increased. Very soon, Roman Catholic preachers made their mark in studio services each month, among them Fr Bede Jarrett from St Dominic's Priory in North London and Mgr Ronald Knox.[6] Fr Martindale of Farm Street soon gained a most favourable response from both Roman Catholic and Protestant listeners. As the BBC expanded its stations, however, co-operation was not always forthcoming; Scottish Catholics would have nothing to do with broadcasting at all. In Manchester, Bishop Casartelli joined the North Regional RAC but in Nottingham the Bishop would not. The Station Director of Bournemouth in September 1924 declared to Eckersley that 'the Roman Catholics are distinctly averse to broadcasting'.

Reith seemed little worried by this aversion. His appreciation of the Catholic Church was as much for its ritual as its grandeur and its confidence, but 'if they don't wish for our normal efforts, I don't think we're called on to be abnormal and we aren't altering our policy'.[7] He did want to know the situation around the country: did the Romans generally co-operate on the local station advisory groups? The general response was poor simply because the presence or not of a member involved a decision of the Roman Catholic hierarchy, and its general attitude was rather negative, even though some speakers were nominated or volunteered. Edward Liveing, the Manchester Station Director, thought the greatest support came from the younger intellectuals. Some nominated members never came to meetings and when they did come, as the Cardiff Station Director neatly noted: 'They are against it; in the studio they are one religion among many and in a church they are censored.' The most co-operative support came from Liverpool and Manchester: there were services once a month and the response had been altogether positive.

It soon became clear that the BBC's policy of requesting a manuscript up to ten days in advance of the broadcast would cause problems for Roman Catholics, whose priests were not accustomed to submitting their sermons for any sort of lay assessment; the BBC and its staff were simply not regarded as competent to wield the blue pencil, even though from the beginning most speakers suffered little or no threat of excision on grounds of doctrine or principle; it was merely anything offensive or propagandist which should be avoided. Fr Parker of Liverpool reflected later that in the days of the Company[8] 'things were very crude; one pushed in as much dogma as possible to see how far it would escape the blue pencil'.[9] But it was to be some years before Cardiff and Birmingham would co-operate. Fr Parker on the Manchester Station Committee was one of the most outspoken of the Romans in aiding the discussion; he wanted above all to protect the peculiar and distinct interests of the Catholics and have any censorship entrusted to an intermediary on or off the local advisory committee so as to avoid censorship by a lay person. His position was indeed quite consistent; since the BBC were asking each denominational representative to submit speakers, they should actually make the decision as to who should be invited. However, he was quickly reminded that since the Crawford Committee in 1925, it was established that the BBC was wholly responsible for its broadcast output.

By 1928, when the ban on controversy was lifted, about twelve per cent of the broadcast services were Roman Catholic. Herbert Ward was able to 'express himself quite satisfied with the consideration given to Roman Catholics', notwithstanding the fact that he represented London and was thought to be too amenable and not able to fight hard enough for the Catholic interests in particular localities such as Lancashire. Unlike the widely accepted St Martin's experiment, which the Protestant establishment broadly regarded as a great advance in denominational co-operation, the Roman Catholics had no such liturgical form which was sufficiently malleable to produce an acceptable liturgical hybrid for broadcasting. At one end was the Latin Mass, which, merely because it was in Latin, was likely to cause much provocation. Herbert Ward and Cardinal Bourne were strongly against the Mass being 'desacralized'.[10] At the other end were the services produced in churches and in studios which took a number of basic liturgical components and sandwiched a sermon between them. Some Catholics did this supremely well; Fr Martindale was to excel here. Opposition, however, came from others who regarded the impression given by such services as crude and not at all in the interests of the Catholic Church. They were simply not authentic. Martindale was a vociferous defender of Catholic interests; he regretted that any Catholic should join hands with the rationalists and oppose broadcast religion.[11] Stobart felt this lack of a liturgical home in broadcasting and felt that logically broadcasting the Mass was the only safe conclusion. It would be announced that this was a Roman Catholic Mass for Roman Catholics. Time and again Stobart would be thwarted – it was contrary to policy; religious broadcasting could not be sectional or denominational; this would be to encourage broadcasting by minorities and go in the face of the general public's generous response to the religious policy of the BBC so far. Roman Catholics were thus forced to find forms generally acceptable and could not appeal to their own people alone; this would have undermined the movement of co-operation and unity between all Christian confessions. Apart from occasional broadcasts of the Mass in Northern Ireland, the Roman Catholic Mass would not be generally broadcast until the war. Notwithstanding a suggestion in a leader in *The Universe* that the BBC might well relay the broadcast Mass from Hilversum, technical as well as other considerations made this too difficult. Mass and Holy Communion (taken together by the BBC) were rejected; it was 'casting pearls before swine'.

By the end of 1927, the Cardinal Archbishop had put paid to the suggestion of Reith and Stobart that perhaps in Benediction there was a liturgical form possible for broadcasting which was neither a 'stunt' (as Fr Kerr of the Brompton Oratory had feared) nor a 'hybrid'. At the same time, Filson Young (a Roman Catholic whom Reith had taken on as a general programme adviser) expressed a growing disquiet among Catholics that Roman Catholic issues should be subject to a Protestant Advisory Committee. Stobart thought it was a pity that Benediction was linked so closely with the Mass; only Roman Catholics would be aware of this subtle point. Young was convinced that Benediction could be broadcast distinct from the Mass and an approach was made to Kerr of the Brompton Oratory, who naturally wanted the Cardinal's approval. Stobart had therefore to ask that the Oratory should put on a special afternoon Benediction. In November the Cardinal replied to Stobart that he was 'strongly of the opinion that no service that is in any way connected with the Blessed Sacrament such as Mass or Benediction should be broadcast'. Stobart was sorry that the BBC had 'exposed itself to this rejection'. Bourne was the only one to object; the Bishops of Southwark, Liverpool and Birmingham approved. Bourne would only approve of Catholic music, but even then not broadcast from a church.[12]

B. Controversy and identity

The lifting of the Postmaster-General's ban on controversy in 1928 proved particularly significant for Roman Catholics. Just one year before, the Archbishop of Liverpool, Dr Keatinge, complained through Ward[13] that a 'discourse' of his had been so censored that he was forced to withdraw it. Stobart had no patience with such a complaint; he was convinced that there were 'prelates [who] thought of broadcasting as a kind of Hyde Park rough and tumble in which various denominations score off one another'. He told Reith that censorship was absolutely necessary. However he politely answered Archbishop Keatinge, through Ward, that whilst they reluctantly had to exercise the blue pencil by the terms of the charter, they would rather not. Ward was reminded that at the very first meeting of the Sunday Committee all agreed that manuscripts should be subject to so-called censorship, since they knew that some preachers would regard the microphone as an opportunity for polemics. In Keatinge's instance, remarks about the Reformation and Martin Luther had been sufficient to arouse controversy by the mere statement of the Catholic position. Stobart thought *The Universe* leader was helpful in the matter; the mere fact that famous Catholics such as Knox and Martindale had passed scrutiny 'would prove that we do not desire to prevent Catholics from speaking as Catholics'. The Cardinal Archbishop had impressed the same idea on Ward for his deliberations on the Sunday Committee. 'We are, of course, agreed that controversy must be eliminated, but it is equally necessary that Catholics should speak as Catholics and not be expected to speak in non-Catholic tones.'[14]

The whole discussion was compounded by a lack of definition and by prejudice on the part of many Catholics not involved in broadcasting who had come by the notion that Catholics were being censored. There was no other appropriate word to describe this process whereby the men at the BBC (with rather more sympathy for Catholics than Reith entertained) made sure that the Catholics did not arouse adverse comment by praying for the conversion of England – as did one priest during 1926 – or by being discreetly critical of the origins of the Protestant movement. At the same time, the BBC wanted Catholics to get the best from their broadcasts; Reith believed the general public would benefit by the Roman Catholic contribution.

Once the ban on controversy had been lifted, Ward felt insufficiently qualified as a layman to serve on the Sunday Committee and participate with sufficient competence in the increasingly complex debates on theological issues. Bourne, therefore suggested Martindale, already a very widely popular speaker. Stobart said he could not have wished for a happier choice.[15]

In March 1928 the Committee was disturbed by a memorandum from a Liverpool priest with the backing of his Archbishop, Keatinge. The Rev. W. Sheppard from St Anne's, Edge Hill, sent his long memorandum to Bourne; it was critical of the BBC's Reithian view of a non-controversial Christianity 'unassociated with any particular creed or denomination'.[16] Sheppard's view was not ungenerous: he paid tribute to all the BBC had done but could not help saying that 'it has adopted a theory of Christianity which is itself conspicuously controversial'.[17] Every utterance made from any pulpit was controversial and must be so. Furthermore, no Catholic could subscribe to the Reithian view no matter how much they wanted to join in the broadcasting movement. He admitted that the BBC had to exercise censorship and this had always been done with the utmost courtesy and consideration, but there was a principle at stake: 'The Catholic preacher is an expert in the science of theology and an official exponent.' The censors had excised simple phrases such as 'extreme unction' and 'Holy Viaticum' on the grounds that they would surely arouse 'controversy'. Sheppard's solution was to let all and each denomination 'take its own standpoint and if people didn't wish to hear they could always switch off'. This was perfectly logical provided there was nothing beyond 'the bound of exposition or exhortation in matters of faith and morals'. The necessary censorship should not be ruled by any doctrine peculiar to any particular denomination; each should have its own 'qualified' censor so that all would be consistent and equitable. 'Each denomination will give of its best and the listener will be able to choose for himself the preachers and the doctrines that have . . . the strongest appeal.'

This was dynamite in the Committee, coming just as it was asked to approve the lifting of the ban on controversy, even if this was 'in theory rather than practice'.[18] Martindale wanted distinctly Catholic services allowed and described as such. The Committee only agreed that the 'BBC was to broadcast the ethical and spiritual message that all the Christian churches were trying to deliver'.[19] Pat McCormick from St Martin's equated distinctive ecclesial identity with propaganda. Claiming that 'all church services, even the Church of England, were adapted for broadcasting', and further that the Roman Catholics had so far opposed the broadcasting of their distinctive Mass and Benediction, was a quaint way of saying that anything distinctly Catholic in broadcasting must adapt itself to the pan-Protestantism of the Reithian/CRAC policy. Reith wanted to avoid wrangling between denominations and he wanted the churches – if they were to use the microphone – to speak with one voice: Dick Sheppard and others had done so, and so the rest should try. He told Ward in March that he regretted his words in *Broadcast Over Britain*: 'The Christian religion is or should be non-controversial.'[20] Reith was not a theologian! It was no wonder that Martindale and the Catholic leadership (notably the Bishops of Liverpool and Salford) regarded the BBC as a Protestant institution filtering out those distinctly Roman Catholic utterances thought to be provocative and which would divert the listener's attention from the central and fundamental Christian message which the BBC was sure the broadcast preachers could – and more to the point, should – deliver. This message was to transcend all strictly denominational emphasis and any resort thereto – Protestant or Catholic – was propaganda and would only draw attention to the churches' divisions and faults.

Martindale criticized the Sheppard/Keatinge paper. He had a much more intelligent perception of Christianity in Britain: statistics were meaningless.

The country by and large believes in some sort of providence and would refuse to call itself atheist but has little idea of what it means by 'God'; it has a conscience and distinguishes right from wrong; it respects the memory of our Lord with a sort of respectful halo and reserves its dislikes for the churches, by which it means 'religious conventionalism', though the mass of the working class regards the Anglican church as bound up with privilege and there is still a great deal of prejudice against Catholics.

Hence a Catholic 'looking at the nation and wishing to give it "Catholic" help will . . . give it milk and not meat'.[21] Martindale quoted an incident in Cardiff where a Catholic had given a sermon on the Immaculate Conception and raised a storm of protest. Bad psychology, he thought; people were listening to what they could not understand and were angry. 'Hence it would be bad psychology to say nearly anything that the BBC would object to our saying.' His intention was evangelical. 'And if we succeeded in causing millions to touch as much as the fringe of our Lord's robe, they would begin to experience His healing.' And that meant basic religion rather than 'ultimate deductions' which belonged to the language of the inner community; 'it is idle to try to build the upper storeys such as papal infallibility etc., before the basics of our faith. . . . The Pope means nothing to people who have no idea of the Church.' Martindale knew that articulation of Roman Catholicism as against Anglicanism would do no good at all, and was all for a censor who would be not only fair but useful as indicating what in his experience he knew would irritate.[22] 'If we withdraw because we don't like being "censored" (Martindale recognized that it was this word which caused the irritation!) we hand over the entire BBC to non-Catholic indoctrination of the land and to do so would be mad.' He wanted a priest-consultant somewhere in the machine.

Notwithstanding the objections by the Bishops of Liverpool and Salford to the agreed statement of 3 April 1928, the Roman Catholics through the good offices of Martindale came eventually to accept the broad policy that 'if the BBC censorship implies nothing more than an elimination of provocative, offensive and propaganda matter, it is all to the good'. That was how Martindale argued the case to the northern Bishops and he assured the Cardinal Archbishop that Garbett was in full agreement that any doctrinal utterance was potentially controversial to those 'on the inside' but may not at all be provocative to those on the 'outside' who would not understand. The Advisory Committee agreed that since censorship rarely arose, it was enough to continue the 1928 policy and hold the BBC entirely responsible for Roman Catholic studio services and the diocesan authorities for services from their churches – increasingly required by both the Bishops and the listening public. This had been worked out in the principal Roman Catholic areas, especially Birmingham, and now Manchester, Liverpool and all Yorkshire would comply.

To maintain the BBC's policy, Stobart needed all his patience and wit. Some supremely imaginative Catholics such as Martindale recognized the evangelical possibilities of broadcasting and agreed that it was possible for Christians from all the mainstream churches to say something sensible to the broad general public. Other Catholics in Northern Ireland would simply not co-operate; there had been delegations from the Belfast office of the BBC in 1927 and again in 1929, but with little progress. It was at the Northern Ireland RAC that Stobart came to the view that Roman Catholic services would, after all, have to be clearly and distinctly billed as such, simply because in Northern Ireland the Catholics would certainly not accept the Protestant undenominationalism of the BBC. The Northern Ireland Committee did not agree – it would open the door to all manner of sectarianism. In Newcastle, whilst the Romans had no wish to be offensive, the Station Director in 1929 was under pressure to allow Catholics freedom to air their own opinions on the 'fallacy of Luther's doctrine, the Lourdes miracles and transubstantiation'.[23]

Stobart's policy was to make haste slowly and use Martindale as a filter for the Catholic authorities. Unfortunately, Martindale was always travelling and frequently not available for consultation. On one side of divided Catholic opinion, Stobart encountered those who wanted the Roman Catholic broadcasts identifiable by normal Roman Catholic services, specifically, the Mass in Latin. On the other side, Martindale was certainly against it. The pressure for outside church broadcasts was all the more eager following a significant experiment by the Bishop of Pella at Vauxhall (St Anne's) which was generally well received. Stobart was pleased. The Bishop sent the BBC two large batches of correspondence from listeners all delighted that for the first time they could hear a 'real Catholic service'. Stobart was optimistic that a *modus vivendi* would be reached by experiment. He had spent a good deal of time at the regional committees and was gratefully aware that many Roman Catholics broadly accepted the 'London dominance in broadcasting generally', not because of headquarters tyranny but the 'obvious fact of metropolitan against provincial resources'. Martindale and Cardinal Bourne were good friends.

In 1931, however, Stobart was in dispute with the Roman Catholic programme adviser, Filson Young. The official Roman Catholic figure for broadcast services stood at 8 per cent of the total. Young thought this was quite misleading; he wanted to include all the other services, epilogues, evensongs, etc., which would cast a quite different light on the figures. Instead of Stobart's total of 72 services of which the Roman Catholics got 8 per cent, Young calculated a total of 440 Protestant religious 'events' as against the six Catholic services; it was thus 1.3 per cent. (This figure did not include epilogues.) He told Reith this proportion was too small: if Catholic services continually came from a studio, rank and file Catholics would not recognize them and therefore would not ask for them. With a shortened Compline with Benediction the situation would be different but the Cardinal Archbishop would not agree to this. In spite of all his efforts the situation caused Stobart no end of anxiety and his health began to suffer. In the meantime Roman Catholic relations depended upon the offices of Martindale as intermediary, aided by his widespread popularity as a broadcaster.

5

EXPANSION AND RESISTANCE

As has been noted, Reith's attitude towards Sunday was in one sense a reflection of contemporary middle-class attitudes of churchgoers to the religious significance of the Sabbath. From the beginning he found ready and even enthusiastic support for his feelings in the Sunday Committee. In 1925, Reith told the Crawford Committee that 'consideration must be given to the broadcast observance of Sunday'. Everywhere people are calling for freedom, he noted, but 'broadcasting', at any rate, 'should not assist the secularization of the day; the Sunday programmes should be framed with the day itself in mind without being dull – and they should not encroach on church hours.'[1] Notwithstanding the support of all leading churchmen, including Davidson and later, Lang, for efforts to protect Sunday on social rather than religious grounds, it was the 'church hours' issue which was to dominate the discussions on the churches' side about what should or should not be broadcast on Sunday. Reith wanted to maintain a subtle blend of religious conviction (deriving from the puritan Sunday) with an early twentieth-century desire to protect the working man from being exploited on Sunday.[2] With the growing means of mass mobility this process was already, in the late twenties, in full swing and Reith was appalled by it.

By 1929, Sunday afternoons on the BBC were dominated increasingly by words: lectures, readings and talks following Filson Young's Bach Cantata series at 3.0 p.m. It was also increasingly clear to Stobart, Wellington and Eckersley that Sunday, which had the largest potential audience, in the opinion of many people offered the least attractive programmes, aimed at the religious minority.[3] The Regional Directors had complained in October 1929 that more material in drama or features was needed, but it was hard to find. Yet when pressure came from Val Gielgud for dramatic presentations, Reith rather unexpectedly accepted the idea.[4]

Hilda Matheson wanted religious talks and was to produce a series on the English Mystics by Fr Martindale. Stobart and Wellington agreed that the 4.30–6.30 p.m. period was the peak listening time, although Stobart himself had no time for anything resembling listening figures. He thought there was too much talk but was anxious to do the right thing by both CRAC on the one hand and Yeaxlee's Council for Broadcast Adult Education on the other.

In 1928 'The Wireless League' presented its case to Stobart with evidence that (1) people would not be put off church by broadcasting services during 6.30–8.0 p.m. periods; (2) people wanted actual services broadcast and not those specially prepared for broadcasting; (3) this was a better time for hospital patients (on this point Stobart had evidence from a questionnaire sent to 1,500 hospitals that 8.15 p.m. was the best time). The wireless was silent from 6.30–8.0 p.m. and, on Stobart's suggestion that appropriate material might be broadcast, CRAC and Cyril Garbett were adamantly negative. Garbett warned the BBC staff, notably Eckersley and Stobart, that the clergy would express their grave opposition to any competition by the broadcasting of *anything* whilst the nation was at its devotions; this was a threat which the Corporation had to take seriously. The Committee unanimously agreed that people who went to church wished to be home in time to hear the broadcast service at 8.0 p.m.[5] Garbett urged the Committee to avoid any formally negative advice and agree only that the BBC should not alter the time of the broadcast services.

On the initiative of Yeaxlee's Council for Broadcast Adult Education, talks on Sunday afternoon were becoming less devotional and distinctly less related to the Bible and missionary context, which had been the original policy. Yeaxlee and Siepmann wanted education on much broader lines as did Stobart; it was this trend that would lead away from distinctly religious material on Sunday afternoon to secular talks and eventually other non-religious material which would extend into the church service hours. CRAC viewed this with alarm: they were in favour of the series by Eric Waterhouse on Psychology and Religion and Edward Carpenter in the *Religion and Life* series on Old Testament religion – they both conformed to the BBC's Sunday policy. But they did not wish for 'educational talks of a purely secular nature'.[6] For more than a year Siepmann had been pressing to fill the silence of Sunday on continental lines: strict religious observances for the devout followed by a 'jolly afternoon' were, he argued, 'the only good alternatives to the blessed silence of Sunday: proper religious observances and first-class entertainment can and should happen on the same day.'[7] He wanted drama and music and a permanent feature comprising all the arts based on an appropriate theme having varied appeal. Stobart and Reith were both in favour.

By 1928 CRAC's composition was significantly strengthened: the churches were more comprehensively 'represented' – something Reith had always resisted; he had wanted advice, but the churches – and especially the Free Churches – wanted representation.[8] Stobart wanted the net for catching 'star' Free Church preachers cast wider. In October 1930, Stobart put the case to the Committee that it should denote its 'centrality' much more concretely, particularly as the regions regarded their own committees as on a par with London. Garbett's suggestion was to have the chairmen of the regional committees plus a representative from the mainstream Free Churches: Baptist, Methodist and Congregational. It became a sort of 'leap-frogging' with Sydney Berry (Congregationalist), M. E. Aubrey (Baptist) and J. T. Barkby (Methodist) joining the Committee in 1930. Garbett shared Reith's view that the Church of England was under-represented: the Committee now comprised five Free Churchmen and two Anglicans. By 1931, therefore, the Anglican Chairmen of North Region, Cardiff and Midland, were formally invited and this was predictably followed by Martindale's suggestion of a third Roman Catholic member. The Committee agreed that, since Martindale travelled so much, his place should be taken by Fr. Martin D'Arcy but that at any one meeting only two Catholics should attend. At the sixteenth meeting the Committee comprised thirteen members under the Chairman, newly translated from Southwark to Winchester. The new Free Churchmen were all warmly supportive of the BBC's policy: Barkby wrote to Reith that he 'could not appreciate too highly what you are doing to keep the soul of the people alive'.[9] Reith thought this was a 'good attitude' towards broadcasting in general even if Barkby didn't offer much to elucidate the particular problems and principles involved in broadcasting from day to day!

Broadcasting policy reflected the nation's general interest in Sunday as a day distinct from the rest of the week and associated with leisure in one form or another. In broadcasting terms this implied entertainment. The listening public had a way of showing its intelligent disapproval and Reith was certainly conscious of a dilemma: how to cater for minorities and how to entertain the majority (which latter had certainly not yet learned to switch off if they heard what they regarded as objectionable; on the contrary, it would be listened to and followed by protest of one kind or another). Broadly understood, the majority of listeners were Christian in some sense.

There was also the problem of balance: too much of one style would make for bad broadcasting; too much spoken word, or a paucity of music, would become tedious and would defeat the objectives of serving the general interest of the listener. Broadcasting had to be variegated and recognizable; it had to be popular in the very real sense that whatever the subject matter of any programme, the broadcaster, no matter how 'expert' and accomplished, must begin in his mind with an audience comprising ones and twos sitting at home, probably within earshot of children.

In the religious policy from the beginning, Reith had made his assumptions about the essential 'simplicity' of the Christian religion. Those who advised him shared the same assumptions. Christianity could be made intelligible to the simplest of 'souls' and in practice it must be possible to convey this simple Christianity through the voice of the preacher, the traditional exponent of Christian tradition and teaching. Everyone recognized the good and bad among them but Reith and later Stobart assumed that somehow the churches could be persuaded to see the great advantages of broadcasting for religious utterance. In fact they generally did not.[10] Nevertheless, both Reith and Whitley, the Chairman of the Governors, were not satisfied and informed CRAC that broadcast services were 'not effective'; 'too often preachers missed the opportunity of delivering a real spiritual message which would convince unbelievers and strengthen the cause of religion'.[11] What exactly was the 'real spiritual message'? In what way could unbelievers be convinced? CRAC members were asked to find better speakers. The churches wanted their access to the microphone and the Corporation its access to the congregations; both wanted 'authenticity' in one guise or another. St Martin's was a good example, but St Martin's had become almost an adjunct of the BBC; almost an outside studio where the broadcast services were more or less as Reith had conceived them and to which CRAC had generally agreed. Reith wanted more control over the choice of the broadcast preacher. The Programme Board, in 1926, had asked Stobart to investigate the possibility of the BBC's using the Savoy Chapel immediately behind their offices in Savoy Hill. Long negotiations came to nothing. Such motivations naturally played into the hands of those who accused the Corporation of purveying a type of 'BBC Religion'. By now, the BBC's religious output was mostly from churches; the weight of criticism by both the churches and the listening public was in favour of church as against 'studio' worship which was thought artificial and colourless. Indeed, some clergy simply could not cope with the microphone in the studio. M. E. Aubrey, the new Baptist member of CRAC, felt unnatural and restrained before the microphone: 'I am the sort of preacher who finds it practically impossible to write a sermon out beforehand for it is seeing the eyes of the people and the hungry look in their faces that draws me out.' Only a few had shown an inbuilt aptitude for that directness and simplicity which many thousands appreciated from the start.

The Daily Service had begun in January 1928 and, as Briggs notes,[12] was the product not of a BBC initiative but of private pressure. Miss Kathleen Cordeux was passionately concerned both for the maintenance of a Christian Britain and also for the needs of the sick and housebound which could best be met by radio. With great persistence and energy, she organized widespread public support for her appeal for a daily religious service on the wireless and thus helped to establish the longest running radio programme in broadcasting history. By the end of 1929 the whole country could receive this simple service, conducted by the Rev. Hugh Johnston, one of Dick Sheppard's staff at St-Martin's-in-the-Fields. The unaccompanied singing of the BBC Singers soon became a hallmark; Johnston thought it provided 'the most finished part-singing in the wireless programme'.[13] This service embodied the Corporation's religious broadcasting policy. As Eckersley had ruled,[14] it was first of all to be of high quality; but it was significant that the BBC had absolute control over both style and content. It was not an outside broadcast; it had no parochial or confessional identity. It crystallized. a liturgical blend of music and words – hymns and prayers – going out to a wide spectrum of listeners, but especially the housebound, as Miss Cordeux had hoped. The audience would range from the firmly committed congregational and participant Christian to those who might barely recollect their church involvement from times past or even think that religion had a proper place in the order of broadcasting. Like the services from St Martin's-in-the-Fields, the Daily Service recognized the distinction between religious participation by those bodily present in a local act of worship, and those varied and subtle responses which might be made by all shades of Christian allegiance across a nominally Christian culture. For Miss Cordeux and successive Directors of Religious Broadcasting, the Daily Service was an instrument of private meditation at home and was not designed to evoke any sense of participation in or alongside someone else's active worship; the wireless could properly bring religious piety to the hearer rather than draw him away to some churchy actuality. Some clergy, however much they appreciated the provision of this service, had reservations: the BBC was promoting a species of Christian piety and worship in a context of entertainment; all the arguments about meditation were outweighed by the suspicion that broadcasting religious services from the studio would encourage passivity and put it abroad that such services were an acceptable substitute for one's presence in church. Nevertheless, the public response was very substantial and Hugh Johnston was encouraged to produce two service books which prepared the way for *New Every Morning*.[15]

The Epilogue was designed to bring the broadcast day to a close and on Saturdays perhaps prepare the faithful for Sunday. Not long before the first Daily Service in January 1928, the Cardiff Director, E. R. Appleton, had, in good BBC tradition, taken an unusual initiative and on Sunday evenings begun broadcasting his own Epilogue entitled *The Silent Fellowship*. When in 1927 the Daventry transmitter made it possible for Appleton's *Silent Fellowship* to be heard by the whole country, it became very popular. Whereas this was a sort of brief 'heart-to-heart', the London Epilogue was deliberately impersonal and anonymous. Appleton gave homilies and encouragement and gained an enormous following which Reith found irksome. Once a month, the whole country could hear not only the regular Epilogue but also *The Silent Fellowship*, and the response encouraged Appleton to request that the latter should replace the Epilogue monthly! Reith was quite against it, particularly from a religious point of view. Appleton recognized the inconsistency of following the Benediction of the Epilogue, which had been included to close the day. Under Stobart, the Epilogue had become rather more highbrow and Appleton focused the need for more direct and popular religious programmes such as Reith had always had in mind in the BBC's religious policy. Having got his monthly broadcast, Appleton then asked for every week and was refused: *The Silent Fellowship* was simply not good enough on aesthetic grounds and Reith would not have people confused into thinking that the Cardiff offering was a continuation of the London Epilogue. The issue was all the more muddled by virtue of the former freedom which Appleton had exercised and the resultant conflict with the central and growing influence, by the end of the twenties, of Savoy Hill. Furthermore, Reith had to be so careful of the 'BBC Religion' charge that a ruling had to be put into force in December 1927 forbidding any BBC employee to give religious addresses. By 1930, Stobart was strongly against the influence of *The Silent Fellowship* and of Appleton's methods, which had encouraged people to write their opinions and claimed a response of forty thousand to these literary mosaics on Sunday evenings. Stobart thought it a 'retrograde step and one full of danger for the BBC to have its own gospel and its own "chaplain",[16] especially if the latter were not fully accredited', as he told Reith. Appleton might claim immense support, but the crucial issues were first that he was exercising a traditional role of the formerly relatively isolated Station Director who now, by virtue of 5XX, was now in touch with the whole country; and, secondly that the BBC was appearing to encourage its own popular spokesman on religion. Stobart was responsible for all religious affairs but he did not broadcast himself and in no sense acted as a representative of the churches or even a channel for their opinions; he was a programme administrator. There was a case for a BBC religious expert, particularly as the religious advice to the Corporation was almost wholly vested in a non-BBC body.

6

POPULAR THEOLOGY:
'GOD AND THE WORLD
THROUGH CHRISTIAN EYES'

By 1931, the BBC had developed the studio service for which it took particular responsibility and the services of the various mainstream churches in closer collaboration with CRAC. By this time too the Bishop of Ely's Committee had made its recommendations and had formally congratulated the BBC for its service to the Christian religion and the Church of England in particular. The Committee was keen to have the BBC move on from the popular style of common religious utterance to broadcasts which were designed to educate. Lamentations that the public was hopelessly under-educated in Christianity were widespread and the Ely Committee asked for 'more scholarly broadcasts'. Since 1926 Stobart had produced series on subjects like the Psychology of Religion and the Beginnings of Christian Theology; these had been satisfactory, but did not appeal to the larger numbers who were in church sometime on Sunday and were only interested in the broadcast service at 8.15 p.m. Garbett and Reith were both strongly in favour of the 'scholarly' recommendations of the Ely Committee. Reith wanted to educate not only listeners who both went to church and listened to the service but also the substantial number who were non-churchgoers. The Christian faith must be presented intelligently and systematically. Only by such exposure to Christian dogma could the nation reappraise the Christian faith on the basis of proper evidence. Reith wanted such talks to be within the setting of the evening service and not in the educational context of Sunday afternoon. He cleverly and perhaps deviously planned that there should now be an alternative church service on the regional wavelengths for the popular audience. The majority of listeners would have no real choice; they would either listen to one or other of the church services or switch off! In this way, Reith believed the BBC would be providing both the 'robust, sensible attitude towards religion which will appeal to the man in the street and be broadminded' and also be giving 'more prominence to doctrine and dogma'.[1] Filson Young had persuaded Reith that to most Roman Catholics good sermons were to do with belief and intellect and the theology of church and gospel rather than what he thought was the 'free and easy style' – ('Go home and say a kind word to the wife – I know it's difficult') of Dick Sheppard and Eric Southam. Young, like Ronald Knox, believed that such sermons 'do not get people anywhere'. Ronald Knox was even more scathing:

> Englishmen are fond of an occasional spiritual titillation as long as it makes no particular claim on the intellect; many would not be consciously confused if they heard flat atheism talked all the week, rounded off by a hymn or two, and a straightforward manly religious talk on the Sunday evening.[2]

Martindale wanted the BBC to raise the standard for theology and philosophy; to re-establish the sermon as a vehicle of the church's exposition of the nature of belief – its voice to every new generation. That meant 'experts' were needed. The Reithian 'manly' religion was not sufficient. The St Martin's service was powerfully protected by the Committee[3] and could not be made educational. Stobart, however, had a suspicion of theology; to substitute philosophical and theological talks for religious addresses would 'prove a disappointment to vast numbers of listeners who prefer a straight sermon and like to have an alternative to a studio preacher'. Listeners would regard 'philosophy as being out of place in their Sunday evening service; it would strike them as chilly and abstract'.

> Even if our preachers sometimes miss the mark and talk platitudes, the service with its familiar hymns and Bible reading is a great joy and comfort to the masses, and there are very few preachers who do not give some inspiration to simple folk.

He regarded the bulk of theology 'as being definitely part of the lumber of the past and rather abhorrent to the men of today'. He construed dogma in terms of controversial material unsuitable for broadcasting and regarded the battles over Arianism as 'indications of how evanescent are the warfares of theology'. Stobart believed that modern man's chief desire was to 'live a decent life; to believe in an all-wise and all-merciful Creator; to help his fellow men in the spirit of Christ who helped us. Such teaching is what we get in various tones and accents Sunday by Sunday . . . it may not get us anywhere except possibly to heaven.'[4] It was not that scholarly, theological and biblical talks were unknown. C. H. Dodd widened his reputation as a scholar by a 1930 series on the Bible.[5] The problem was acute even for Dodd, who was reminded by C. A. Siepmann that he could assume no knowledge in his hearers: 'Interest must be evoked by a constant stimulus as you proceed.'[6]

Reith, Stobart and Siepmann had to respond to the call of the Ely Committee for more scholarship. One such response was an idea for a long series of talks which had come mainly from the 'Club' – a group of eminent and radical clergy around Percy Dearmer of Hampstead of which Temple was a member. Reith told Lang about this; he was anxious to reassure Lang that the BBC could handle such a delicate matter efficiently; Lang agreed to mention the series in his Canterbury address on 1 January 1933. Pat McCormick wanted him to do even more – to instruct that a letter be read in all pulpits, but he refused. He did, however, pass the information on to his Bishops' meeting.[7]

In November 1932 Stobart (now very ill) published details of the projected series and assured the press that whilst he wanted to avoid broadcasting 'polite dogfights' the BBC wanted honest theology without offending the feelings of any who might be listening.[8] The series was to be edited by Leonard Hodgson, Canon of Winchester, whom Bell had suggested to Reith in the spring of 1932. Hodgson was much impressed by the idea of a complete course of lectures for adults; such a thing had never been done before. The series *God and the World through Christian Eyes* 'is offered to those who will "gird up the loins of their minds" and seek to understand the faith which has done so much to mould our civilization'.[9] By the end of the year his collaboration and co-operation with Garbett had produced the synopsis, while on the BBC side, Stobart had produced the men who would speak on every other Sunday for a whole year!

Garbett told Convocation he doubted if a course of lectures had ever had such a number of distinguished teachers and theologians taking part. Christianity was under attack, mostly by those who were ignorant and who thus attacked 'some false conception they had formed of it', not least Mr Bernard Shaw, whose recent book on religion, *The Adventures of the Black Girl in Her Search for God*, 'displayed a lamentable ignorance' of the faith. The series would probably appeal, said Garbett, to the large numbers of thoughtful non-churchgoers who might hear Christian teaching for the first time. For the speakers[10] – now broadcasters – he hoped they would not use 'highly technical and highly theological language but bear in mind the thoughtful, educated man who might be asking questions about religion'. He also hoped they would instruct the churches and the faithful – themselves lacking in knowledge – who were at the mercy of the modern critics of religion. Cosmo Lang, however, requested of the prospective speakers an impossible task: the language of philosophy and theology was totally unintelligible to 'masses of educated people; terms that are simple to us are technical and largely unintelligible to them'. The speakers must remember that while their argument may be as deep as possible, 'the presentment of it ought to be in a very simple form and that so far as possible theological or philosophical terms should be avoided.'[11] One might imagine the dilemma: the speaker must speak to the 'educated' but not use their language!.

The response to the series was mixed: generous appreciation and firm rejection; acceptance by the minority of educated churchmen and opposition from the Stobart view which wanted much greater simplicity and who believed that one could not anyway appeal to all groups of Christians at any one time. Lang's chaplain, Alan Don, records that as they listened to Temple giving his talk – the first of the series on *What Does Man Know of God?* – 'C. G. [Lang] was somewhat befogged – William was too philosophical and not simple enough – the average listener would not carry much away.'[12] It was a beautifully argued lecture for a cultivated listener for whom argument, analysis and reflection were activities to which he was accustomed.

The series was generally well received by the churches. The principal criticism was that the lectures were too intellectual and way above the heads of the average listener.[13] Indeed they were! But what the BBC had hardly thought out, and the churches via CRAC not at all, was exactly how broadcasting should define 'average' – was there an average 'layman' or an average, non-churchgoing individual (albeit still familiar with the Bible and with hymns) for whom these talks would be unintelligible? Or did the series fail because the pressures on the BBC via CRAC and Reith were such that broadcasting was conceived by churchmen as in their gift? Certainly great attention was paid by Reith and Stobart and, their colleagues to the opinions and expectations of the leading Anglicans, notably Convocation. The Bishop of Ely's report in 1931 had asked for more consistent exposition and *God and the World* was the prodigious response. But that Committee had assumed that those who listened to Dick Sheppard would be happy to listen to William Temple, Fr D'Arcy and Charles Raven. It further assumed that those who left their churches and rushed to their wireless sets for 8.15 p.m. – the Christian 'apologists' in the pew – were in the greatest degree likely to benefit from the 'course work' which broadcasting could uniquely provide. Unfortunately, the rank and file in the pews were, it seemed, more ignorant than either the BBC or Garbett had bargained for! The response in general was divided between those who wanted a didactic university-style sermon to sound like a talk, and those who wanted a propagandist sermon to sound like a homily; the talk should be non- technical and the sermon non-propagandist.

Whilst the BBC sought to satisfy the widespread thirst for knowledge and perspective which could be met by accomplished minds with a special flair for being profound without being technical, the churches were not able to respond quite so readily – perhaps because such enquiry was, in the minds of so many churchmen, in danger of upsetting the simple faith of the committed, unaccustomed as they were to the rigours of argument and analysis; they might be faithful and even enthusiastic for church and witness; but they were not skilled in the disciplines of believing. They were intelligent but untrained just as Garbett had told his fellow prelates. It was not simply a matter of presentation; complex things could be said simply, as Lang had said. But the *God and the World* series had said them none too clearly, and only for those who had ears to hear. They were fine for the committed and those who were prepared to attend one of 220 groups around the country in church halls, public libraries and private houses for further discussion. As far as the BBC could ascertain in late 1933 and early 1934 through the Talks Department, only 75 of these groups had stayed the course. A group meeting in Leicester Public Library, however, averaged an attendance of about sixty throughout the course. The Borough Librarian, who had organized that group, claimed that religious book borrowing increased by seventy-five per cent and, notwithstanding the lack of microphone technique and the 'too academic and expert tone', the religious life of Leicester, he thought, must have greatly benefited.[14] However the reaction from the churches via the BBC Regional Officers made it clear that the BBC had made an error of judgment; it had engaged in scholastic activity under excellent guidance but against the overriding interests of the general listener. Reith was disappointed with the criticism; 'high-brow' religion militated against his evangelical instincts. *God and the World* was the most obvious symbol of the BBC's religious inventiveness; the series had demonstrated the closest co-operation yet enjoyed between churchmen and the BBC. It was not only a problem of administration but ecclesial and theological judgment; more was needed inside the Corporation to pursue the interests of the BBC in addition to the advice of the churches through CRAC and the press. The BBC needed a professional, as Reith had thought for some time.

PART TWO

CONSOLIDATION:
THE CHURCH IN THE BBC
1933–1939

7

THE SEARCH FOR A DIRECTOR

For all his diligence, Stobart, the rather conservative Anglican layman, could not be responsible for religion, adult education and children's programmes. Reith looked for a cleric. Since the early popularity of Dick Sheppard, Reith had wanted him to take responsibility for the religious output. Through Dick Sheppard, Stobart had been in touch with a freelance cleric-turned-journalist, H. W. Fox, who wrote for the *St Martin's Review* and who advised on the quality of sermons submitted for broadcasting. Fox, according to Stobart, had the 'greatest difficulty in finding a passage of any distinction in them'. Fox was also in touch with W. J. Fuller, Editor of the *Radio Times*, for whom he chose the 'Broadcast Pulpit' articles. Fuller proposed to Stobart a 'new and independent department', of which Fox should be put in charge. Stobart was not in favour and did not care much for Fox's advice on the sermons; his reports had little bearing. He once told Reith they were 'not worth a guinea'. In February 1926 Reith explained to Gladstone Murray that religious matters should be 'handled more definitely' and a specialist was needed.[1] Fox was passed over as 'much too entrenched in Anglicanism' for Stobart's liking. The other obvious choice was Dick Sheppard, but his health was now failing. In 1927, his friend Cosmo Lang already regarded Sheppard's 'ministry and life [as] broken'.[2] Sheppard was a household name and in touch with a variety of BBC servants on all matters of broadcasting, not only religion. A rumour that he was to be given a significant position was scotched by the BBC in 1927. From his convalescence he wrote sadly to Reith in October that if he could be of the 'faintest service to the religious side of the BBC, I could count it the greatest honour possible'. He felt 'sure that Reith's religious initiative in broadcast religion had brought such thousands to know their Lord'. The BBC made it known that they still wanted his 'effective association with their work but no changes are contemplated'.[3] Sheppard knew he was too ill for the job and by June knew that there was no hope of being offered it.[4] In October 1927 the Board of Governors decided firmly against Sheppard on the advice of Reith, who was rather embarrassed by Sheppard's new book, *The Impatience of a Parson*, which Lang himself also regretted.[5] In this book, Dick Sheppard castigated the church in a way that did not endear him to church leaders. 'The church . . . is subsidiary to the adventure of Christian living,'[6] he cried, and with sharp directness he blamed the church for the nation's lack of interest in Christianity. The BBC had been criticized for not having courage to employ him and thus have the Corporation associated with his denunciation of humbug.[7] Reith told the Board of Governors that Sheppard could not carry the job, nor should he be associated solely with the religious work which was now adequately covered by Stobart. Reith's compromise was to suggest a part-time consultancy – 'a roving commission with an honorarium of £500' notwithstanding that the 'difficulty would be to prevent him from trying to do too much'. He did not want the embarrassment of Sheppard; it would clearly have strained the BBC's relationship with Lang.

The search for a Director was resumed after several years. For a time Reith thought a layman would be preferable, but failed to secure a suitable one. Finally Lang suggested F. A. Iremonger for a post combining the BBC work with the Savoy Chapel.

Reith had first met Iremonger in 1923, with George Bell and W. J. B. Odhams, Reith's father-in-law. The following year Iremonger had seen the Radio Wembley Exhibition, and heard the broadcast by George V. He was chaplain to Lang, and a close friend of Sheppard, and also of Temple, whose biographer he later became; he knew the Church of England scene well. He had been president with Garbett of the 'Life and Liberty' movement, and was a member of the Poplar Labour League. After eleven years in East End parishes, he had become editor in 1923 of the Church of England newspaper, *The Guardian*, but had resigned in 1927 after a disagreement with its owner, Hugh Smith, who later told Reith that Iremonger always wanted too much of his own way! Some of his interviews with famous churchmen had appeared in book form as *Men and Movements in the Church*; he had also reviewed books for *The Times Literary Supplement*. He was a teacher and propagandist, and believed strongly in an educated laity.

Since he had left *The Guardian* he had been a parish priest in Garbett's diocese of Winchester, where he had just been offered the Deanery. However in May 1933 Reith, who had given up the idea of a lay Director, offered the job to Iremonger, He was surprised to be asked, but 'assured me that he was prepared to do as he was told here'.[8] Reith was glad that Iremonger belonged to Boodles Club and not the Athenaeum! This was proof of his 'essential humanity and freedom from ecclesiasticism'. After the interview Reith gave him a Bible reading audition and told him he read badly and was typically parsonic.[9] 'I think he will do,' Reith concluded. The two men were to build a close friendship and enormous respect for each other. Iremonger was to praise Reith in days to come as few others on the staff would do. Reith accepted Iremonger's criticism all the more readily because he 'had status in the Church of England without being conventional'.[10] Iremonger later reflected that Reith was one of the only two people 'who seemed to understand me at once and always: if any good has come from me, it is largely you who have drawn it out of me. In this and many other things I can't be grateful enough to you'.[11]

8

FREDERICK A. IREMONGER

F. A. Iremonger began what the BBC has called[1] 'the years of consolidation', which were to establish more firmly the relations between the Corporation and the leaders of the mainstream churches, notably the Church of England. Much had been done by Stobart, who died on 11 May 1933. He had organized the initiative of the Corporation to which the churches had made a somewhat confused and half-hearted response; the problem of acting together and burying their confessional identities in the broadcast message was squarely tackled by some but opposed rather more by others. The churches had the well-established reputation of being the custodians of the BBC Sunday, and many thought they did themselves no good by advising against unsuitable or 'unedifying' broadcasting on Sundays; and by allowing no alternatives to church services whilst they were being broadcast around 8.0 p.m. and no unsuitable material during the period that ordinary liturgical services were going on in the churches up and down the land. The churches wanted broadcasting to serve their interests on the oft-questioned assumption that Christianity and religion were best served by people not being diverted from the possibility of attending their churches and not being offered any substitute for that congregational and participatory aspect which, of course, belonged to church worship. A major underlying motivation was the belief that by radio access to the population, Christianity could be re-established as never before. Unfortunately, no one actually knew how successful these religious services and talks, etc. were. Early on, Reith and Stobart were firmly against any notion of what was later called listener research, and were happy to rely upon the popular response of people prepared to put pen to paper. This they did in great numbers, especially in respect of regular features of popular religious interest, notably the Epilogue on Sunday, the Daily Service and a new hybrid, broadcast midweek service begun in the summer of 1931 from St Michael's, Chester Square, London, by the Rev. W. H. Elliott. He illustrated a BBC dilemma.

Elliott had been Vicar of Holy Trinity, Folkestone, and had first broadcast from there in 1927. He subsequently met Reith at St John's, Smith Square, near to where Reith lived. Reith wrote in his diary that he 'did not care for him'. Reith nevertheless requested the Dean of St Paul's to have W. H. Elliott give a talk following the Thursday evensong from Westminster Abbey during Lent 1928. In 1930, Elliott became Vicar of St Michael's, Chester Square, and by Septembr 1931 had made considerable impression, so that Reith invited him to start a midweek service in the context of the national crisis of the summer of 1931. The suggestion of W. H. Elliott came from Ramsay MacDonald. Reith claimed this invitation was his own and reflects his strong conviction that not only was there an 'increasing revolt against materialism' but that the BBC could meet a crucial need and provide the population at large with some expression of hope and comfort in the crisis. W. H. Elliott had a peculiar gift for simplicity and, like Sheppard and others, managed to tap a source of enthusiasm in the nation's Christian conviction which was considered by many to be the basis of a morality which was being overshadowed by contemporary movements. He began this simple broadcast service every Thursday evening at 10.15 p.m. in the autumn of 1931 and, at the time of a summer break in 1932, Elliott asked listeners to write a postcard to the BBC if they wished the service to continue. In about a month 10,000 cards had been received! This was characteristic. Elliott had so many letters that the BBC even consented to pay for his secretary. It was the first substantial religious programme in the weekday evening schedule.

W. H. Elliott recognized and exploited the peculiar advantages of broadcasting. The broadcaster must talk to the microphone as an old friend, not thinking of the millions but of one person by the fire.[2] He was against the present 'artificiality' and 'performance' or 'recital' of religious music and word in the Epilogue. The authenticity of the church environment was crucial: 'All the service should be congregational but when it comes to the sermon, the congregational part of it ends; the preacher must forget the congregation and speak to the microphone confidentially.'[3] W. H. Elliott rightly thought 70 per cent of church preachers failed in broadcast services because they preached to the gallery. His Thursday evening service was short – fifteen minutes – and consisted of the most basic liturgical components: a hymn, reading from the Bible, a talk and a final prayer. The talks themselves were published, and before long he was writing a regular piece for Kemsley's *Sunday Pictorial*. Elliott was sentimental and yet encouraging. He reflected the common aspiration for security in a puzzling world and made no attempt at analysis beyond saying that religion was necessary for us all, and that the eternal values of fellowship, courage and hope were part and parcel of that religious consciousness that all men needed to help them through the dangers of life. He made no attempt at a Christian apologetic, and rarely spoke of Jesus. He asked people to imagine (within the reach of their education and upbringing) some of the simple and practical distillations of the Christian ethic: such basic Christian behaviour as consideration for others,[4] honesty and kindliness.

Elliott attracted an enormous following, which was sustained throughout almost the whole of Iremonger's time with the BBC. He called for a return to Christian virtue and thus shared considerable affinity with the fast growing Oxford Group Movement which itself attracted considerable numbers concerned with the future of the Christian community and nation. Many of its followers were in high places in the government and law as well as in the churches. It was Elliott's Thursday evening service from 1931 which focused aspects of the BBC religion about which many churchmen complained, notably the Roman Catholics. Like Dick Sheppard, Elliott and the enthusiasts of the Oxford Group were immersed in fringe Christian movements but derived their Christian identity from their respective denominational roots. Their radicalism seemed to many a chimera in that it called for a return to basic Christian teaching in all spheres of life, but did not ask radical questions of theology or ecclesiology or even ethics. On the air for six years, it was a search for comfort which Elliott expressed with supreme success.

In 1933, as we have noted,[5] the experimental series *God and the World* had started from the other end: the dons of the theological faculties provoked no public appeal to Reith that the series should continue through the summer as did Elliott's services. This was a different audience, but nevertheless did not by any means exclude the intelligent people who listened to Elliott and thought, as did even Ramsay MacDonald, that Elliott's was a message to restore the spirits of the people. He was widely recognized for his skill in the pulpit. 'He has a deep clear voice', wrote Alan Don in his diary, 'and great gifts as a popular preacher, but personally I should quickly tire of his style of oratory'.[6] This precisely indicated a dilemma for the BBC and, in 1933, for Iremonger. Elliott was a popular religious broadcaster in the weekday context, in strong contrast with the Sunday evening services, even including St Martin's.

Iremonger inherited the controversial BBC Sunday which was largely in the hands of the churches. He also inherited the BBC weekday religion, the Daily Service and Elliott's Thursday evening service – largely bearing the obvious mark of BBC policy: simplicity and a large audience.

Prior to Iremonger's arrival the BBC Sunday had been under considerable pressure and Reith had a problem. The Newspaper Proprietors' Association was anxious because during the silent period, 6.30–8.0 p.m., listeners were being wooed in large numbers by continental stations and the newspapers were losing advertising.[7] The Regional Advisory Committees were all asked to consider it and decided that come what may the times of broadcast church services should not change. The BBC could, however, broadcast secular material 'in conformity with the well-known Sunday policy of the Corporation'.[8] Garbett told Reith privately that he would be very sorry if the broadcast religious services were moved; he expected very strong opposition to any direct competition with broadcast evening services. Iremonger joined the Corporation in July of that year just as the whole programme policy was coming under quite new scrutiny; his title was Religious Director.

In the review of policy in 1943, the BBC regarded the foundations of religious broadcasting policy as having been laid by the time Iremonger took the job. It might be more accurate to speak of a door being opened. By 1933, the door had opened sufficiently to let the churches into the bureaucracy of the Corporation and in the person of Iremonger they now had a secure position. Iremonger represented the broadest interests both of Anglicanism and of British Christianity as a whole. He had been editor of a Church of England newspaper concerned with the relations of the Anglican church with contemporary society, and he thus knew a great number of people in high places both in Britain and abroad. He was neither an Evangelical nor a high churchman, but recognized the crucial importance of establishment and statecraft in relation to church affairs. As secretary of the 'Life and Liberty' movement, he marked himself as a radical and alongside William Temple sought to influence church opinion towards reform and putting its house in order. Church patronage and the 'inexcusable disparity between clerical incomes which seemed to bear no relation to the work involved . . . these, and other abuses in . . . the church militated against its witness and stultified its message'.[9] The most notable demand was liberty from Parliament. Iremonger, like Sheppard, held that the present generation was resistant to the church, and not to its Founder. He now found himself alongside the Director-General who himself shared this point of view.

In Iremonger the church had a 'mole', a 'wooden horse' who developed his vast connections and relationships and thus laid a foundation for a strategy of broadcasting policy which for a while enabled the Christian churches to maintain not only a firm hold on

religious policy, but the widest relationship between general broadcasting and the religious sensitivities of the broad mass of churchgoers –
and indeed, the many more who did not attend but who might have
done (so Iremonger believed) but for the abuses which the 'Life and
Liberty' radicals sought to alleviate. Thus in Iremonger, the widest
diversity of Christian interests were represented on the Corporation's
executive in one man. He could be contrasted with the influence of the
Advisory Committees which, whilst speaking mostly, as Garbett later
optimistically reflected, with one voice, nevertheless represented
diverse and powerful denominational interests. These were so arranged
that contention would not arise. Issues which they discussed usually
looked towards general objectives in the interests of Christianity rather
than specific programme policy – little understood by most. The
appointment of Iremonger was the beginning of the years of expansion,
diversity and consolidation. By the end of his six years – he would then
be sixty-one – broadcast religion would increase and range more widely
outside Sunday.[10] Iremonger was eager to draw more of the major
departments of the growing Corporation, notably talks and drama, into
relationship with religion. He wanted the BBC to take initiatives in the
business of speaking and communicating the message of Christianity
and the church to the widest possible audience. Not until the end of his
time would the first really useful piece of audience research be available
for the broadcasters of religion.[11] Iremonger also took seriously the
growing place of broadcasting in schools and the specialized work in
relation to young children outside day school and on Sunday. He
wanted specialists in all the fields in which he felt religion should be
represented. Men who were popular in the centres and on the edges of
the denominations were drawn into broadcasting and given wider
scope, publicity and popularity, Donald Soper and Leslie Weatherhead for the Methodists, George MacLeod in Scotland and J. S. Whale
for the congregationalists, William Temple and W. R. Matthews for
the Anglicans. At the two ends of a confessional spectrum that extended
from Roman Catholics to Baptists it was not easy to find personalities.
The Catholic emphasis was upon liturgy rather than the preacher,
while for the Baptists the emphasis was upon pulpit rather than
microphone. Aubrey admitted to Iremonger that some of the ablest
men at the microphone were 'perfect terrors for forgetting themselves
when they preach'. Preaching accounted for the great bulk of religious
broadcasting from both church and studio. Iremonger had inherited a
growing conviction within CRAC that random disconnected sermons
from random churches were not enough; broadcasting demanded a
consecutive and argued utterance. There was a continuum – a

sequential structure implicit in broadcasting which carried over from week to week and day to day. It was argued that people listened to particular things at particular times on particular days. With the aid of the 'service book' in the *Radio Times*, the listening public comprised a diversity of minority passions, with each group regularly finding its own interest. Regional factors added to this pattern, notably in Scotland. Dinwiddie and Iremonger gave each other mutual support, and Iremonger was particularly concerned to give Scotland a good showing, even though the balancing act became increasingly unsteady as the denominational pattern changed north of the border. Moreover, now that religion had its own Department, and its distinct broad-casting identity, Iremonger's workload increased accordingly, and his endeavours grew more diverse. Happily the Corporation provided an accomplished civil servant as 'Religion Executive' in Dennis Wolfer-stan. Iremonger now had an indefatigable co-ordinator of the in-creasing numbers of people involved with religious broadcasting, and the Department had added status within the Corporation, even though the output was – much to Iremonger's irritation – more or less confined to the first day of the week.

Sunday programmes remained a much debated issue for the nation, churches and broadcasters throughout Iremonger's period and until the coming of the Second World War. Furthermore, as the technology of broadcasting became more sophisticated, people could hear more stations and with increasing quality they had greater choice. Moreover, by 1933, greater mobility in transport facilities – of both goods and persons – meant the greater expansion of leisure pursuits on the one day when the vast majority of the population was not working. People increasingly objected to the Reithian Sunday; the churches which had established their authority in broadcasting policy were reluctant to accede to this objection; on the other hand, they wanted yet more broadcasting on Sunday themselves. If broadcasting hours were to be extended to virtually the whole day, the churches wished to retain their hold on policy, at least as strongly as any of the Advisory Committees could. Reith was only too willing to comply with the ecclesial expectation for Sunday. Leisure was foreign to him. He lamented that there was no longer any place for silence and peace; but at any rate the BBC 'would not be guided by the lowest common denominator of public taste'.[12]

9

SUNDAY POLICY

In 1934, the newly appointed Controller of Programmes, Colonel Alan Dawnay, set out to review the timing of Sunday programmes.[1] One important suggestion he made to the Board of Governors was that, since each region broadcast a religious service at 8.0 p.m. every Sunday, for the London Regional programme alone the service should be abolished in favour of a secular item. Eighty-five per cent of the country could still receive a service on the national programme and those services and times would, of course, not be changed. Dawnay appreciated the churches' views but wanted the changes; he was aware of pressure but wanted the principle established at least for London, if at this moment nowhere else. The Newspaper Proprietors' Association the year before had increased public pressure for less strict observance of Sunday. Reith told Iremonger in April 1934 that he was reluctantly changing his mind. Dawnay wanted opinion on changing the service from 8.00 to 6.30 p.m. – the normal church hours. In January 1935 Dawnay asked Iremonger to collate the churches' official opinions. Iremonger wrote to the denominational representatives on CRAC, to William Temple and Cosmo Lang. All opposed such change; competition from broadcast services during church hours would 'almost certainly interfere with church attendance . . . there would always be the temptation to listen to good singing and preaching instead of attending the more familiar and ordinary church services'.[2] Temple was more positive and suggested the value of an experiment, particularly as radio 'is bound to have a very profound effect upon the occasions when people gather for any kind of discourse'.[3] The Vicar of Ramsgate had given Iremonger yet another idea about which he became quite enthusiastic – rediffusion. Let urban churches install loudspeakers (as a few had done in outlying areas) and have the BBC broadcast specific services for specific denominations. A strong plea had come from the Roman Catholics, who by this means could have Catholics broadcasting to Catholics; the same would apply to all the other denominations.[4] Martindale, Iremonger told Lang, could then say what he liked about the Pope, and whatever the reactions, it would be 'better that each separate church should be able to give its own particular message on certain days in the year rather than that their spokesmen should all be fumbling about for the lowest common denominator which satisfies very few'.[5] Aubrey, for the Baptists, wanted it both ways; no competition, either by straight broadcast services or those broadcast via loudspeakers in churches, but rather broadcast services at a time when congregations were just home from their own churches, so that they could have the benefit both of star preachers and – crucially central to Sunday morning services – of participation.[6] This had always been a complaint by churchmen against BBC religious services: they detracted from a religious activity,[7] from physical participation. (In the later 'sacrament' debate, the participation issue was central.[8]) Rediffusing broadcast services by loudspeakers might have resolved the problem in this regard, but would certainly have raised the hackles of the urban clergy whose sermons might have been every bit as good as the next man's broadcast. The Bishop of Ripon, E. A. Burroughs, had made a very successful experiment from his cathedral whereby great numbers of churches installed sets in order to hear a North Region Whitsun broadcast relayed to the USA. It was a perfectly logical scheme, 'a corporate spiritual adventure in which a diocese might unite'.[9] As Briggs has noted, Reith was against any notion of 'open access' for any denominational purposes: this was an unacceptable form of propaganda. It was approved in this and some other instances (a Bristol church had done the same in 1925) simply because it was an Anglican venture.

Dawnay, however, wanted more secular material on Sunday evenings; religion was being 'squeezed' – as Reith saw quite clearly – in favour of entertainment. He lamented that there was not to be one day 'clear of such stuff'. Peter Eckersley, in charge of entertainment, thought Sunday programmes should be broadened even in the interests of religion itself: 'It is hardly fair that religion only should be available at what is perhaps the greatest peak hour of the whole week.' He told Dawnay that CRAC was 'ungenerous' and 'narrow' and 'may be doing their own cause harm'. Garbett, on the other hand, felt that a firm stand should be taken by the churches: 'The witness of no alternatives to the religious service was something at a high cost we should keep up.' Iremonger, however, was looking ahead. Already in 1934 there were moves to propose a Sunday morning service; the daily morning service for invalids and the housebound had become a well-established fixture but they were denied it on Sunday morning.[10] Iremonger made clear to Dawnay that if there was to be a loss of programmes on Sundays then

Old-fashioned Lady. "No, I never listen-in on Sundays. I should hate to think I was causing extra work."

compensation should be made by way of religious programmes during the week.[11] It was a significant piece of bargaining. Nevertheless, Iremonger was most afraid of the 'gradual absorption by secular subjects during Sunday broadcasting'. He expected the changes would start in the autumn of 1934 and that CRAC should be ready to deal with the proposed offers by the Programme Revision Committee of alternatives to 8.0 p.m. on the London region: i.e. 9.30 a.m. or 6.30 p.m. (the latter directly at the time of normal Sunday evening church services). The Governors, however, decided firmly against any alternative to the 8.0–8.40 p.m. period, and thus the question was back to the first square as to how Sundays could be lightened without offence to (and if possible with the co-operation of) the churches represented by CRAC.

By January 1935, Dawnay looked for further lightening of Sunday programmes and again Iremonger amassed opinion in order to make his official reply; this took three months and in March he produced his considered and extensive observations on Sunday programmes.[12] In this whole discussion Reith had always regarded Sunday as a day not only of religion, but of refreshment and rest. He wanted his staff to realize that Sunday policy 'does not mean simply the exclusion of anything which is incompatible with the religious observances of the day – and at this rate, half of what we are doing already would go out – but a rather different intellectual standard'. Iremonger, as Religious Director, was in effect being called upon to issue a sort of *ex cathedra* utterance to the BBC which he did in his long memorandum to Dawnay of 4 March. The consequences were significant.

He told Dawnay that any change must be gradual – he recognized the force of the potential opposition; it would not only be The Lord's Day Observance Society but a 'solid block of English and Scottish conviction that desires Sunday broadcasting to be largely different from weekdays'. He opposed the negative suggestion that Sundays could be just another weekday without the unsavoury material such as jazz! More positively, the programmes should be varied: a broader definition of plays and not only Shakespeare. More music of light opera type, he thought, would be the most drastic alteration. As for the rising popularity of the Wurlitzer organ, it was vulgar in the extreme! Why could they not use the BBC organ in the concert hall? Gerald Cock, the Outside Broadcast Director, wanted Jack Hylton without jazz or vocalizing, but Iremonger wanted to hear more of it before making a judgment (Geraldo's orchestra was not to be barred provided it did not play dance music!).[13] The Regional Directors wanted features: biographical, dramatic and historical; and Iremonger thought there was 'room for development' here. They also quite naturally wanted local alternatives to the style and content of the National Programme as well as more variety. Dawnay eventually agreed with this 'not too bold' programme for lightening Sunday and coping with the competition from the continent. The changes were modest: more varied drama and features and the use of the BBC organ for lighter fare. Most significantly Dawnay now recommended to Reith that the Religious Director be vested with 'special powers as the "keeper of the public conscience" in the whole domain of Sunday programmes'.[14] It was an extraordinary capitulation to the churches.

By the end of 1935 Iremonger was still rather disappointed that nothing much had come of Dawnay's suggestions. This well suited CRAC, which had no urge to change the traditional if rather vague concept of the English Sunday. Aubrey told Reith in 1936 he thought the pressure to lighten Sundays came from 'a faction which has shown small concern for the welfare and authority of the nation'. This was an opinion at the opposite end of the spectrum of criticism which had been levelled at BBC Sunday policy since the emergence of the commercial stations. Even the *Church Times*[15] spoke of giving at least some of the public some more of what it wants. It was a conflict of objectives; those who had no need of wireless as a 'diversion' could more readily regard it as an instrument of education; the remainder of the six million licence holders could use the more expensive available sets and receive lighter entertainment from the continent. Those with simpler sets had to make do with serious music, lecture-styled programmes and religious services all ending with the Epilogue. Not until 1938 would the situation drastically change by the extension of broadcasting hours. In the meantime, Iremonger was effectively the churches' censor for Sunday programmes. The Controller of Programmes and Reith had deferred to Iremonger on the question of the lightening of Sunday and the result, from the point of view of the critics, was timid and almost a policy of denial. The BBC, some said, was in the hands of CRAC and imposed an austere diet on an unwilling public. There was no choice and no real alternative to a doubtless excellent diet of intellectually demanding and heavily rewarding programmes, provided one had a background in the subjects and thus a ready soil to receive the seed. Many people called for a less rigorous diet and certainly more variety. The notorious Bach cantata series introduced in May 1928 had not been dropped until June 1931. The week by week broadcasting of all the Bach Cantatas was perhaps the most utterly typical enterprise of Reith's Sunday policy.[16] He had no love of Bach.

Producers and departments were naturally not happy with the ruling that their scripts had to be censored by the head of another department who had little facility in the whole area of production but who must weigh up all contributions in the light of a broadcasting philosophy which was thoroughly partial. In May 1937 a Sunday short story producer, C. V. Salmon, suggested D. H. Lawrence's *The White Stocking*. It was rejected by Iremonger as 'mud'. Salmon complained that either the Religious Director should produce it himself or the story should have a new title and his own department would take no responsibility for it. On other issues, the Roman Catholic, Martindale, went even further, and managed to have the Committee demand of Siepmann's department – he regarded him contemptuously as 'bitterly red' – that when talks related to civilization and the 'left-wing or sceptical point of view it [the department] represented', the BBC should secure 'adequate representation of the Christian point of view'.[17]

A more compelling challenge came in 1938 when proposals from the new Controller of Programmes, Cecil Graves, were to be canvassed around the regions. Siepmann meanwhile had put a somewhat hypothetical case to Iremonger over the vexed question of BBC competition with the continentals. Since 1933 the formerly silent period between 6.15 and 8.00 p.m. had been filled in. CRAC, whilst not approving, had agreed, provided, of course, that the fill-in programmes complied with Sunday policy. Listening to continental broadcasting was heaviest on Sundays.[18] Briggs says: 'The BBC weekday service remained more popular than that of all foreign commercial stations combined, and British listening to foreign stations reached its peak when none of the Corporation's stations was transmitting'.[19] Worst of all was Sunday without any broadcasting in the morning before 12.30 p.m. It was a matter of deep concern, and by the end of 1937 plans were afoot for clawing back a considerable portion of this audience from abroad. The demand for more popular material on Sundays went hand-in-hand with the common complaint about paying licence fees and being forced over to foreign stations on Sunday morning. The churches had gained yet more control over Sunday morning by the institution of the Sunday morning service at 9.30 a.m., which was followed by silence.[20]

What should be broadcast during yet another notorious silent period between 10.45 and 12.30 on Sundays? In early 1938 Siepmann wanted to know from Iremonger what were the 'limits within which you would still insist that what we term Sunday policy must be observed?' Siepmann was now in charge of Regional Representation and was much concerned with democratic ideology in respect to the identity and interests of the regions. Iremonger was firmly committed to a centralist approach and wanted the CRAC to call the tune and set the patterns for the rest of the nation, with the understandable exception of Scotland. There was no love between Iremonger and Siepmann who, Iremonger thought, was the 'devil of the piece'.[21] Siepmann wondered whether Iremonger would approve of serials and features: *In Town Tonight* ('obviously not in a jazz setting!'), and the dramas of Mabel Constanduros and other light entertainment. At the same time Cecil Graves was concerned to attract the support of CRAC for lighter music in the morning silent period and they were to discuss the matter on 3 March 1938. Iremonger wanted to answer Siepmann after that meeting which he knew would be 'definitely against the proposal'.[22]

At the CRAC meeting, Graves presented a paper which outlined the problem but assured that the proposed 'light' programme 'would be of a type compatible with the Corporation's Sunday policy and of a higher grade than the foreign stations'.[23] Views were aired and they decided to leave the decision 'in the Corporation's hands'.[24] With all respect to Professor Briggs, this response was not a 'sign of trust in the BBC'.[25] It was, in fact, most surely a posture of defiance. CRAC hoped that those responsible for programme planning would win their fight for the protection of Sunday against the pressure to compete as gracefully as possible with the continentals: it was veiled opposition. Only a week later Graves announced to all the regions that the new programmes for 10.45 a.m. would begin on 24 April – and 'continue without alternative until 4.0 p.m'.

The Scottish Advisory Committee for its part requested that the new programmes should not be transmitted into Scotland: 'The reasons that have led the Corporation to this decision do not obtain in Scotland.'[26] Dinwiddie, the Scottish Director,[27] did not agree and was much pressured by all the Protestant denominations. They had been the first in Scotland to protest: Guthrie, for the Lord's Day Observance Society (LDOS), wrote to London with vigour that the proposal for programmes between 10.45 and 4.0 was 'subversive of the Lord's day, unseemly and repugnant and certainly the desire for lighter programmes does not emanate from Scottish listeners'. They then sent a deputation to Dinwiddie on 12 April 1938. They were determined to take the matter to London and Dinwiddie had no choice but to warn John Reith that they were coming. The deputation had been organized by the LDOS of Scotland and was a powerful line-up of Scottish divines representing the Presbytery of Edinburgh, the Baptists, Congregationalists, Methodists and Free Church of Scotland. The deputation thought it a 'moral wrong to broadcast such programmes on Sunday'. They also deprecated the secular plays in the evening. Altogether it was a plea for the protection of the Sabbatarian Sunday: the new proposal was 'contrary to our national spirit'. Notwithstanding Dinwiddie's reply that the BBC had a duty to those who did not wish for religious programmes and that invalids and the hospitalized would also benefit, the Linlithgow Presbytery maintained that this was beside the point and 'when a protest was made by a national church, the BBC as a national body should meet it'. Secular programmes amounted to a 'lowering of the flag and a retrograde step' and the BBC's concern over quality of reception for Scottish listeners was quite beside the question: 'Light programmes did not come within the real joy of the Christian Sunday.' Andrew Stewart for the BBC tried to emphasize that people in Scotland did want non-religious programmes and if the BBC could raise the standards of such lighter programmes, people could be wooed back from the Continent. But the silent period 'reflected our national character abroad', claimed the Rev. E. J. Hagan, the Moderator of the Edinburgh Presbytery. The deputation wanted silence – after the noise of solemn assemblies – at 10.45 p.m. No hardship, they claimed, was being done to any section of the community by these silent hours. Dr Archibald Main, the Chairman of the Scottish RAC, reported the unanimous decision of his Committee against the proposals. But since

1. John Reith

2. H. R. L. Sheppard

3. J. C. Stobart

4. Studio 3E

these programmes must be broadcast, the BBC should give programmes not just as people wanted but 'more than they wanted and better than elsewhere'. The BBC could at least raise the non-religious standards since they were not broadcasting religion during these hours.

The Scottish deputation represented and focused the clear disquiet and opposition (expressed with characteristic bitterness by the LDOS) to the invasion by the BBC of arenas belonging to the established churches and in this case, the use of Sunday. The Scottish leaders recognized that the churches were less than full, but the BBC should not be allowed to encourage secularization no matter how much that agency might do for religion itself. The deputation certainly appreciated the broadcast religious services but to some extent took them for granted: the BBC was a servant of the churches, who provided the broadcast preachers. Iremonger's concern, on the other hand, was that the BBC might find its own preachers as it had done since 1922. Sheppard had been the first of the few and they were devilish difficult to come by, as Iremonger so painfully complained.

Dr Archibald Chisholm, notable as the Chairman of the influential Church of Scotland 'Church and Nation' Committee, and four other Scottish church leaders met with Reith and Dinwiddie a month later. The deputation doubted, as had CRAC, just how strong was the demand for lighter programmes. Lighter programmes were really not required at all in Scotland, they claimed. Reith sharply pointed out that the Church of Scotland had never supported the BBC Sunday programme policy and, if the forthcoming General Assembly discussed it at all, it could be the first time it had considered BBC matters. Reith, however, averred that it was not the desire of the BBC to invade Sunday silence but in view of the licence question, etc., it had a duty to the country at large. He was, after all, under pressure from Government.[28]

Reith, that same afternoon in May, met the 'Imperial Alliance for the Defence of Sunday' – another Protestant body concerned for the protection of Sunday more on secular and social grounds than the strictly Sabbatarian one of the LDOS (albeit they both shared many patrons in common; Iremonger, for example, belonged to the LDOS.) The deputation from the Alliance had a notable leader, the Marquis of Aberdeen. Graves, the Roman Catholic, had little respect for the bland opinions expressed rather incoherently by the Marquis. The same story as before: the BBC was making a mistake; everyone liked the Epilogue and 'Sunday was as old as the Christian era'. Graves thought the deputation was satisfied with the BBC explanation about Luxembourg etc. 'Lord Aberdeen made another stand-up speech which was full of polite nothings and lasted quite a little while.'[29] Graves reported that finance would be found for Dinwiddie to put on his own light programme of a serious kind for the Scottish transmitter.[30] Apart from Scotland, there were no other regional protests. All other Advisory Committees had agreed with the decision of the Central Committee. They had voted against the proposal but sent no deputations.

The process of lightening Sunday programmes continued to the end of Iremonger's term around the close of 1938. In November the Controller in charge of programme output, the Anglican Basil Nicolls, gathered up his ideas for policy change for the Control Board on 22 November. He had Iremonger's approval for a historical appraisal to be put to the Board of Governors later in the month. For Nicolls the Sunday audience could be divided between the churchgoing public and the church-listening public; put together they were, he believed, still a minority. He insisted on good alternative programmes to the religious service and felt that no principle was at stake, since alternatives were broadcast during the weekday Evensong and Elliott's midweek service; so why not on Sunday? Nicolls was sure that 'refusal of alternatives is an act of religious oppression which should not be tolerated in a free country'.[31] He strongly opposed the conviction Iremonger shared with the LDOS that the 'silence was an internationally recognized witness for the nation'. The old objection that Sunday broadcasting involved extra work for the BBC staff no longer obtained – it was simply a matter of degree. Iremonger had pleaded for a restriction of outside broadcasts (OBs), which made for even more work. Nicolls agreed with Iremonger that Sunday should be distinct, but thought that religious services should be part of a balanced Sunday programme distinct from the rest of the week in terms of its consistent high quality but now was not the time to go the whole way. He was also worried that the Religious Director had a dampening effect upon the responsibility of the various output departments who had to get their programmes past Iremonger. He should, in future, act rather as a 'consultant'; the climate was changing. For all this, Iremonger believed firmly in the principle that the BBC Sunday should be essentially different from the rest of the week and that the general audience wanted a different 'quality' Sunday. Those who wanted lighter programmes had a real choice; they could tune to the continent! Here he reflected Garbett's opinion that there was quite enough of light variety during the week and naturally differed from Reith, who knew that the BBC must provide a choice. The Post Office knew this too, and the Ullswater Committee[32] had likewise called for a brighter Sunday; the Corporation had to 'hasten slowly' and gradually introduce choices to those who paid the piper. Iremonger believed that the stable listeners to the BBC were in the country towns and villages. They were the centres of not only churchgoing but of the strongest sense of identity, where people would wish to protect the traditional characteristics of English life. It was not here that the clamour for a lighter Sunday was aired. But Reith knew he was running a Corporation, not a charity.

Iremonger was asked to serve on a sub-committee of the Control Board with Graves and Nicolls. Their conclusions were not startling. The Religious Director was, after all, to retain his censorship over Sunday programmes, but output departments had themselves to make sure that the slightly wider style of programmes should conform to Sunday policy. There should be more OBs on Sunday and most crucial of all, CRAC should be asked to consider a secular alternative to the broadcast religious service at 8.0 p.m. and the placing of the religious service on the *regional* wavelengths, leaving the national programme free for a secular alternative. This was driving the wedge in further and Iremonger knew it. The Control Board's final proposal to the Governors included a recommendation that the St Martin's-in-the-Fields monopoly should cease[33] and that discussions might take place on subjects other than those dealing with political controversy or those that would 'embitter feelings'. By this time, however, Iremonger was considering resignation. Reith had resigned and Iremonger, now almost sixty-one, wanted a change. He knew himself to be too old for the task. He had told Martindale in July 1938 that as he had struck sixty last week he was 'too old for a job in which one wants to be constantly inventive and full of imagination'.[34]

10

INITIATIVES AND INNOVATIONS

A. Sunday morning service

As early as Easter 1931, Reith had asked Stobart for an occasional service on Sunday morning, and since then irregular requests had been made for a regular Sunday morning broadcast. There was a good deal of correspondence from the committed Daily Service listeners who pointed out that they could enjoy a service every weekday, and asked 'Why not on Sunday?' Reith also felt that Sunday broadcasting would be enhanced by a morning service broadcast for the benefit of invalids and the hospitalized, and even those who wanted both a religious service and the advantage of the remainder of Sunday at leisure. Throughout 1934, Iremonger's first complete year, it was discussed by engineers and OB staff, and CRAC quite naturally supported the idea of a service from either studio or church, starting at 9.0 or 9.30 a.m., and lasting about forty minutes. It would not clash with normal services in churches;[1] such services as did take place at that hour were usually Sung Eucharists, and were therefore excluded. The only problem would be to find outside churches which could produce a service (and a congregation) suitable for broadcasting at an abnormal hour. Iremonger asked the regions to suggest central churches with a congregation of two to three hundred and 'a man of some personality'.[2] He wanted a man who could talk well for about ten minutes – 'anything longer would not be tolerable at a morning service'. Either way, the service would have to be a special one for broadcasting, and here again the BBC would attract criticism for encouraging the churches to produce curious liturgical hybrids for the non-church-going public. In Scotland, Dinwiddie considered the chief demand was for services for the sick and housebound and those in far-off places. Otherwise he thought it was sacrilegious; the growing vogue for hiking and Sunday motor travel, and the preparations for them, did not make for 'a mood to listen seriously – just as people were not attracted to church early or late on Sunday'.[3] Dinwiddie was concerned with the concept of participation. He recognized the dilemma that pervaded the whole range of concepts related to broadcast liturgy. The objective of broadcasting would justifiably serve as a creditable alternative to church attendance for the sick and housebound. But if it were to attract the 'out-of-doors listener and the lazy churchgoer, it is doubtful if we shall succeed in getting the former to worship and if the latter do listen, the churches are likely to suffer'. For all listeners the concept and the experience of wireless participation was yet hardly understood. Dinwiddie at least recognized that the greatest value of broadcast services was in the provision of a surrogate congregational experience for the sick. Iremonger knew this too and constantly pressed the engineers as well as the Advisory Committees to 'reproduce' a congregation of a substantial size and above all create the atmosphere of a church. Hence his concern to find central churches which could hold such numbers. Arthur Buxton, the Vicar of All Souls, Langham Place, was keen to help but on Sunday morning, like many Anglicans, he wanted to broadcast his service of Sung Eucharist.[4] West Region declared that the idea was out of the question: they simply could not create a 'scratch' congregation at that hour except for a Sung Eucharist. Surprisingly, the Anglicans did not jump – as did so many churches by this time – at the esteemed privilege of broadcasting a special service and so gaining publicity: again it looked too much like a stunt. In the north, the Methodists were particularly keen and the North Region Director assured Iremonger of Leslie Weatherhead's value as a star preacher. Unfortunately he was not a regular attender on the Northern RAC, and was earning the jealous feelings of other Nonconformists who felt he was succeeding rather too speedily in gaining support for a Northern equivalent of St Martin's.

B. Sacramental events

Mainstream Anglicans and Roman Catholics regarded the Mass/ Eucharist as a central and indispensable part of their liturgical identity.[5] For Nonconformists it was infrequent and rather more marginal. The broadcasting of this supremely intimate rite was to remain one of the most vexed questions discussed between churchmen and theologians during the period and until the late fifties. It arose out of the need to produce a morning service for broadcasting on Sundays at a time when increasing numbers of Church of England congreg- ations attended a Sung Eucharist. The motivation to develop a 'St Martin's' in the morning was born furthermore out of the desire to have a comparable broadcast to the Daily Service on Sunday. Reith wanted it and so did Iremonger. The development of such a service at the increasingly common 'eucharistic' time on Sunday morning touched upon issues of sacrality, religious and theological sensitivities which raised the most profound convictions and most subtle relationships – even tensions – between broadcasting authenticity and ecclesiastical privacy. It also touched firmly on the role of the Roman Catholics and the Mass: the Romans had been urging the broadcasting of the Mass in some quarters as the only authentic broadcast; ever since 1923, however, Reith had reaffirmed the policy of the Corporation that the Eucharist of all acts in the churches' liturgical life, would not be broadcast.[6] He had reassured Davidson and Lang of this. Eventually, Reith considered the matter much more positively under the influence of the St Martin's clergy and specially McCormick who thought with many that it should be broadcast for the sick and housebound – the obvious audience.

Well before the advent of the Sunday morning service in 1935, Garbett had reiterated his support of a policy he had helped to maintain in the face of the demand by Roman Catholics for the Mass, especially in the northern areas. He had told Stobart in 1932, as he told Iremonger in 1935, that he was quite definitely opposed to the suggestion. In 1934 Martindale had broadcast a descriptive talk on the Sacrament of Mass in connection with the Buenos Aires International Eucharistic Congress of the Roman Catholic Church in October. This had raised considerable dust from the more evangelical and right-wing Protestant groups, including the World's Evangelical Alliance, which had been consistently vocal since 1925. The Alliance was loudly anti-Roman Catholic and had the ear of Reith who had 'every sympathy with them in this line'.[7] It also had support in high places, especially from the former Solicitor-General, Sir Thomas Inskip, MP, who complained to Reith that this Roman Catholic broadcast was 'a grave affront to the prevailing religious sentiment of the country'; this was quite polite compared with other reactions from that end of the 'Protestant-evangelical-British Christianity' spectrum. Inskip's name with many others appeared on the letterheads of many such bodies including the Protestant Truth Society and the LDOS; he was also President of the National Church League. Iremonger himself had no love of the Roman Catholics: his 'dislike of the whole Papal system was so intense' that it spilled over against Anglo-Catholics. But as he told H. M. Gooch, Secretary of the Evangelical Alliance ('this man Gooch', who had irritated Reith by his persistent and aggressive tone), he thought the BBC should be the mouthpiece of national Protestantism. Reith approved the ideal but not their bellicose methods. The Roman Catholics should have a place in broadcasting and 'our duty is to hold the scales as evenly as possible.'[8] Men like Gooch could always claim that any Roman Catholic broadcast, let alone the Mass, would be regarded as controversial and therefore against accepted policy. Iremonger would not accept this any more than he could accept Gooch's underhand tactics of writing tendentious letters to Cosmo Lang who would not enter into any such wrangles.[9] Iremonger suggested to Lang that 'Gooch should be told to go and boil his head and play with the gravy'.[10]

The broadcasting of the Mass-Eucharist was explosive not only because of the extensive, albeit dormant, anti-Catholic sentiment in the country. In 1934 CRAC had approved the idea of the Sunday morning service, which they eagerly supported without appreciating that the very protective covering by which they wished to surround the BBC Sunday was being undermined. The BBC would then have to fill yet more hours of Sunday, i.e. between 10.30 and 12.30, with 'suitable' material which many churchmen would soon regard as yet another attack on the Sabbath peace. The Roman Catholics asked for the Mass even though many, including Martindale, were concerned about the extent to which radio would allow random listening by people without any intention to participate. It was reminiscent of the attitude of the Westminster Chapter over the wedding of the Duke of York to Lady Elizabeth Bowes-Lyon in 1923;[11] Dean Ryle had refused to allow it to be broadcast for fear men in public houses would listen with their hats on. Garbett told Iremonger in March 1935 after a meeting of CRAC at which the matter had been raised but deferred for further research, that if they did ask, it would be difficult to refuse. The Committee was not at one on the subject; however Martindale sought advice from Archbishop Hinsley, who ruled that Mass should most definitely *not* be broadcast. Garbett's problem was now solved; the Church of England could not and need not broadcast Sung Eucharist. Meanwhile, CRAC thought Iremonger should investigate the matter fully. Garbett had told the Archbishop that whatever the Roman Catholics did, this 'should not be regarded as a precedent for the Church of England'. He admitted that he had always taken a definite stand against it. 'I intensely dislike the thought of the sacred mysteries being broadcast to all who cared to listen whether they were Christian or not.'[12] Whilst Garbett wanted Lang's view, and not simply his own prejudices, to prevail, he rightly expected Lang's concurrence.[13] They met in July 1935 and Lang confirmed Garbett's view: broadcasting the sacrament was casting pearls before swine – holy words being listened to by outsiders. Lang had been apprised of the prevailing diverse views through Iremonger who, during 1934, had elicited a response from a number of notable people across the ecclesial spectrum. The Anglo-Catholic R. Ellis Roberts shared the fear of irreverence; it could only be offered for invalids and the housebound if 'we could secure that no one else listens; their forgoing of privilege will be of greater benefit to them and the Christian body than the risk of general irreverence'.[14] The Dean of Winchester, E. G. Selwyn, close to both Garbett and Iremonger, took the 'invalid' position and felt that reverence would be safeguarded by the time of 9.30; no one else would be listening (*sic*!). Temple supported Iremonger on the public relations aspect. If the church's broadcast is always in the form of matins, Iremonger had suggested, it will give the impression that this is the only form of Anglican worship. Temple thought this would only affect 'those who know nothing about us and that matters comparatively little'.[15] Iremonger did *not* agree with this; he was concerned with the large number who would listen simply as interested non-attenders, because there was such a programme available. Iremonger realized that once the airtimes were filled, there would be vast numbers listening to whom the church should be addressing itself. Temple, however, agreed with Lang that the question of participation was more important than the fear of irreverence: 'the act of Communion is really one of two foci of the Eucharist, the consecration being the other. You cannot broadcast the reception and therefore I am myself on balance disposed to resist the broadcasting of the Eucharist altogether.'[16] The problem of irreverence in the listener was a real argument, but not decisive. For Temple it was a question of principle.

Notwithstanding the strong opposition by both Archbishops and by Temple Iremonger feared the public would get the wrong idea about Anglican worship without the broadcasting of the sacrament. In the Roman Catholic Mass the words of consecration – the most sacred of all the components – were inaudibly spoken by the priest and the central elevation of the Host was marked by a bell – singularly appropriate for broadcasting. Similarly, for Anglicans these holy words were central, mysterious and sacred. Garbett had rightly directed Iremonger to this sensitive area: these were the pearls before the swine. (When Hinsley pronounced strongly against the Mass, the issue was shelved until after the war.)

Iremonger therefore had to construct yet another service for the listener, 'both devotional and reverent and yet simple and homely', as he told E. K. Talbot, the Superior of the Community of the Resurrection at Mirfield in Yorkshire. 'We are blazing a new trail here and do not want a chapel evening service, but rather to be distinctive and beautiful and full of a real spirit of religion.' The first broadcast

Sunday morning service celebrated Harvest from Croydon Parish Church under Edward S. Woods, later Bishop of Lichfield, where Iremonger became, eventually and unwillingly, Dean. Of the thirteen services between October and December 1935, there were several from Croydon Parish Church, which became a sort of 'morning St Martin's'. The denominational balance was seven Church of England services, two Methodist and for the rest, one each. Leslie Weatherhead, minister of Brunswick Methodist Church in Leeds, was described by Iremonger as 'one of the most appreciated of our morning preachers.' The monthly pattern of services was: first Sunday, Croydon Parish Church; second Sunday, a London studio; third Sunday, another outside broadcast; fourth Sunday, a regional outside broadcast and when there was a fifth Sunday, a regional studio. The wide reception of the Sunday morning service was mostly appreciative but as increasing numbers of churches were celebrating at or around 9.30 there came complaints not so much that it was keeping potential worshippers from church, but that the benefits of the service were being lost to those who were already in church. They wanted both services, largely – as Iremonger was aware –because the quality of radio preaching was much higher than that which people were generally used to. He wanted more 'stars' of Weatherhead's calibre.

C. Improving the preachers

Iremonger thus decided to push the RACs to think more boldly about the quality of preaching. In May 1936 he called together a handful of diverse enthusiasts including L. S. Hunter, Archdeacon of Northumberland, Donald Soper for the Free Churches, Ellis Roberts and Dick Sheppard. The whole message of this small advisory 'wheel-within-a-wheel' was a demand for 'feature rather than preacher', a way of saying, perhaps, that no matter how hard the BBC might try to influence the clergy with such hand-outs as *Hints to Sunday Speakers* and advice-giving in print and in person, broadcasting was disregarded by most clergy. They agreed that broadcasting showed up the average cleric as unable to speak to a non-tutored audience. Iremonger thus began a tradition of inner consultation; of bringing together a handful of people 'younger and brighter than the members of our Central RAC', as he told Graves. He even thought Soper was too old at around thirty-three – he wanted young people of inventive minds who understood the limitations and possibilities of the microphone.

In 1937 Iremonger produced his own major critique of the churches' contribution to broadcasting. He criticized above all the preaching. Whilst he wanted services which were impersonal and full of the 'spirit of religion', as he often put it, two-thirds of the preachers on the wireless were doing more positive harm than good. He presented these insights to CRAC in March 1937.[17] They were significant because they questioned the right of CRAC to protect the broad denominational policy, however much it might be weighted in favour of the established Church of England. Iremonger's report was a radical questioning of CRAC in its representative role; it suggested bringing the best personalities, whatever the denomination, to the microphone and sometimes, as in the case of Weatherhead, Soper, Matthews, Hugh Martin, George MacLeod and F. A. Cockin, keeping them there regularly.

Iremonger was a radical churchman. He wanted to have the faith of the church seen to be relevant and practical by the vast public who, he believed, did not hear 'the true gospel or see the true church with sufficient clarity'. He told Cockin that he wanted the churches to tackle 'social and industrial questions'. However, as he recognized, the rule on controversy threatened to impose silence both from the side of the BBC hierarchy and from the churches themselves. The BBC were happy with Elliott because vast numbers listened. Iremonger was increasingly not happy because what these vast numbers received were a 'few words of fortitude inevitably associated in the British mind with worship and the presentation of religious truth'.[18] He thought that two-thirds of broadcast sermons had a 'strange lack of religion in them'. They lacked 'vital religious experience' or had only moral messages or, worse, were of the Elliott type where challenge is missing: 'The preacher says what he thinks the more comfortable of his listeners want him to say.' Or again, the broadcast sermon is unintelligible: too many technical words from the vocabulary of the doctrinaire clergyman who sounded less like a theologian than he should.

Church services lacked aesthetic stature simply because local parish churches attempted to copy the cathedral service and the result on the air was simply dull. Iremonger made a scathing criticism of the music of most churches; it was lacking in vitality and beauty. He especially deplored the intoning of prayers by minor canons who robbed most of them of their devotional value. Prayers were too long and contained interminable lists of the world's problems with hardly a gesture towards understanding or depth. Iremonger's complaint was against the 'lack of excellence' in almost every aspect of communicable religious utterance in speech or in music. Whilst he recognized the principles of choice in denominational balance and the variety of mainstream religions represented by the wide variety of both religious experience and aspiration amid the listening public, Iremonger's concept of the sermon combined literary and oracular excellence coupled with simple and concise and even entertaining instruction. He likened his hopes to those of the Talks Department, which obtained the services of the best man in a given area. If the BBC could broadcast *fewer* services Iremonger thought they might be better. Thus, until the 'general standard of preaching in the churches is raised' the BBC should only invite the best obtainable. If the Talks Department could successfully distinguish between 'good popular' and 'bad popular' speakers, Iremonger thought the churches should do the same. 'Good popular' ones were men like Soper, Weatherhead and Martindale. It had been BBC policy up until then, when the quarterly allocations were made, to fill in the denomination and then find the preacher; this was wrong. Iremonger believed that the stress on denominational balance 'militates more than any other one thing against our being sure of broadcasting a good service'. He wanted CRAC to agree to two things: relax the denominational rule for six months, use well-known competent and tested churches, and resist the temptation to have a church chosen simply because it had not yet had its turn. To these centres of excellence Iremonger wanted the best preachers sent to preach again and again in order to have the Christian gospel taught in a manner that was intelligent but not abstruse, erudite without being obscure. Iremonger envisaged an ideal preacher, teacher and communicator, this invariably meant a man with considerable experience of the modern and particularly the under-privileged sector of society, as indeed he had experienced it himself in Bethnal Green soon after his ordination. He wanted broadcasting to teach and inspire; he wanted broadcasting to attend to the mind of the listening population as well as to the emotions. Broadcasting could supremely well service the church at worship and the church in its tangle with contemporary ideas.

Two ways were open to him: to improve the standard both of preaching and liturgy. Two men were to become particularly valuable to Iremonger's hopes; J. S. Whale and Sir Walford Davies.

D. Sermons in sequence

In 1931 Convocation had called for more 'regular instruction' in addition to the myriad broadcast sermons. *God and the World Through Christian Eyes* was the first attempt, and for all its erudition and eminence – or even because of it – turned out to be a failure. Iremonger

inherited this disappointment in July 1933. Before the series had ended
Iremonger, only a month into the job, could confidently inform all the
regional directors that 'in spite of their interest to a very limited
number, they have been definitely unpopular'.[19] The Belfast Programme Director noted that the series had been criticized by the public
generally, but his RAC, comprised mainly of the clergy, not surprisingly, agreed on its excellence. He shrewdly noted: 'Perhaps we are
going beyond our legitimate functions in providing what virtually
amounts to a course in theology instead of simple Christian teaching.'[20]
Dinwiddie in Scotland thought most church people found them too
abstract and could not, himself, 'quite see what the difference would be
between a popular simple lecture and ordinary sermons'. Iremonger
thus agreed that the second proposed series on *God and the World* should
be delayed to October 1934 instead of beginning in January. He told
Reith that it would be difficult to win back great numbers of listeners
who, he believed, were lost through the first series. Iremonger's small
sub-committee on *God and the World*, which included Martindale and
McCormick, agreed that a new series must be shorter and simpler.
Iremonger wanted first to avoid the academic overtones of 'lecture' and
use the term 'talk' to describe the next series. Secondly, he wanted,
characteristically, to start with man and to illustrate from the human
condition man's longing for God. Leonard Hodgson, the Editor, was
not moved by this approach. He wanted solid intellectual grounds for
belief analysed more simply perhaps than in the first series (which
began boldly with the Doctrine of God). Hodgson thought Iremonger's
scheme would upset the theologians because it is wrong, he thought, 'to
teach men to think of God as being what they want instead of
proclaiming the prophetic message of God's revelation and leaving
men to make what they can of it'.[21] He accused Iremonger of a
characteristically nineteenth-century outlook, but recognized that he
was concerned with his audience, whose theological outlook was
probably a generation old! Iremonger's point was that the bulk of the
audience had no theological outlook at all (apart from the minority,
including the clergy, who had some degree of theological and
philosophical training but who did not listen). The motivation for the
original series was to inform; to lead the general populace from a
jaundiced view of Christianity towards what most clergy would regard
as a sound understanding from which an intelligent counter-attack
might be launched.[22]

Iremonger conceived his task as a public relations exercise in favour
of what he and his intimates regarded as that interpretation of the faith
which would attract the common man of East London to a faith

somehow elevated beyond the scandals and mundane preoccupations of church bureaucrats. He was committed to such movements as would restore the image of Christians, particularly those organized in what men view publicly as the 'church'. Broadcasting sorted the clerical men from the boys: those who had been through the war, especially the chaplains who had seen the worst of any kind of life, from those who had grown up in privilege and passed through to ordination without ever having been forced to converse with the under-educated and those who had left school at fourteen. Hence the importance which he attached to his years as a curate in Bethnal Green. The church had to find a way of speaking, a mode of discourse which would bring an intelligible understanding of Christian tradition and knowledge within the grasp and scope of the uneducated. Perhaps it was an impossible objective. Certainly *God and the World* had not achieved it.

Iremonger intended to make erudition popular alongside the developing Talks policy.[23] The Corporation realized that not every utterance could be made popular, even though many different talks animated great numbers who were, indeed, not schooled in a particular subject but were interested to learn, provided they were not subjected to technical jargon. *God and the World* was a theological 'course' and people had switched off in great numbers. As the late John Stobart had said, theology was 'unwanted lumber'. How that came about must be laid at the door of the clergy who, in addition to being too few, were themselves neither equipped nor always inclined to provide theological courses; that was not the proper use of the pulpit. Vast numbers did not attend church to be taught, as the Religious Director was constantly reminded. There were a great many listening groups, but compared with the already substantial audience which the Corporation believed it had for religious broadcasting, these groups involved a small fraction of a small minority. People mostly went into church not to be taught but to worship – to engage in activities which strengthened and reinforced beliefs and creeds in such a way that they protected those utterances and poetical, stylized formations from discourses which belonged elsewhere, such as in the university or academy. From Reith's beginnings, the views of the churches on the RACs had been influenced almost entirely by the resistance of the clergy to the competitive nature of broadcasting, particularly on Sunday. Intellectual and aesthetic interests came second to considerations as to how broadcasting would introduce people in general to alternative ways of appreciating Christianity.

It fell to Iremonger in 1934 to conceive and structure another series to follow *God and the World* which would combine two elements: the lecture and the sermon. The sermon was generally held in poor repute and the clergy had no clear idea as to its exact objectives in relation to both the broadcast audience and the broadcast subject matter. Much of the response to the first series had called not for philosophical or speculative discourses, however well-meaningly simple the language, but for something profoundly different: for dramatic, biographical exposition of the teaching and especially the significance of Jesus. For the moment, Iremonger devised the new series with only twelve lectures instead of the previous thirty-six and in two distinct parts: 'What is Man?' and 'Does God Speak?' Hodgson was right: the theologians did not agree on the underlying concepts of the scheme. Charles Raven, the Regius Professor of Divinity at Cambridge, agreed with Iremonger on starting with man: 'To start with God is to begin with a jump that many will not take.'

Conversely, N. P. Williams, Lady Margaret's Professor at Oxford, believed the programme was 'too worldly and sacrificed much of the real charm and fascination of historic Christianity'. C. H. Dodd, for his part, was unhappy with the isolatedness of each contributor and contribution; it was not a real course; it existed only on paper and was insufficiently examined from an educational and audience point of view. No one, including Temple, expected widespread popularity. In his Foreword to the first volume of the published talks, he wrote: 'If the discourses become technical, they will miss their public; . . . if they are only "popular", as the word is commonly understood, they will miss their object' – a neatly-phrased but ambiguous admission that they could only be expected to appeal to a minority embracing an unimaginable mix of broadly intelligent listeners, most of whom had been church attenders at one time or another.[24] Iremonger gave the introductory talk in the *Way to God* series, and appealed to his audience for 'a patient and sympathetic hearing of these lectures by those who sit rather loosely to their convictions, if indeed they have any at all'.[25] And, as if to capture the atmosphere of Dick Sheppard, Iremonger speculated about this lack of conviction: 'Are you quite sure that you have not mistaken this gospel for some poor human interpretation of it and that you merely "don't hold with parsons"?'

Though this series was shorter than its predecessors, many regarded it as still much too long. All the speakers had masses of correspondence; W. R. Matthews, Dean of St Paul's, was glad of it and said so in his 'Answers to Listeners' Questions' (a broadcast 'endpiece' to respond to the correspondence, notwithstanding the difficulties of reducing diverse questions to a manageable reply). Speakers testified to the character of so much of this correspondence as testimony and recital – a desire to express feeling and form some connection with this or that speaker.

Following these two major adventures in broadcast sermons, Iremonger was, by 1936, perfectly well aware of the problem of their academic style; future talks would have to be much more personal. Iremonger turned to J. S. Whale, President of Cheshunt College, Cambridge, this time for an even shorter series of three consecutive Sunday sermons. David Lloyd George had recommended him to Reith in 1933 and since then he had given several studio services and was now asked by Iremonger to participate in his concept of a 'radio mission' – there were to be many more, and by 'mission' Iremonger meant a consistent and consecutive series of sermons designed to evangelize rather than inform.

J. S. Whale had given the 'What is Man?' section of the *Way to God*[26] series and confessed great difficulty in producing a simple style. Iremonger had insisted on it, Whale complaining that if one asked for a talk with profound metaphysical implications 'you cannot really expect utter simplicity throughout'. He had had three hundred letters in response to the first programme. Iremonger, ironically, was convinced that his particular 'Answers to Listeners' Questions' was the best of all his talks. CRAC discussions on shorter series reflected the denominational interests of the Committee and some felt that each should have an opportunity of one of the sermons. Iremonger insisted on one man, and that man Whale; finally the Committee endorsed the scheme. The Corporation, much to Reith's pleasure, was at last taking an initiative, irrespective of any denominational bias. It was a modest victory. Fr Martin D'Arcy, for the Catholics, called it a Protestant scheme but Iremonger insisted 'this was not denominational'. He had got his way! Iremonger's document of March 1935 to CRAC, so heavily critical of two-thirds of broadcast sermons, had been supported by encouragement from Reith to relax the denominational emphasis in favour of excellence; Whale was to give five sermons during 1938. Iremonger wanted evangelistic sermons rather than convincing talks; furthermore, they would be in a studio where he had maximum control. He told Whale he wanted a call to commitment and decision and this time (as contrasted with *God and the World* and *The Way to God*) 'no speculative prolegomena'. Whale wanted some argument based upon a 'great chunk of apologetic' but Iremonger was firm: 'The BBC has made up its mind.' Iremonger had, at any rate! The outcome was Whale's series, *This Christian Faith*.

The BBC organized a great number of interesting talks on the church and aspects of Christianity for a weekday audience. They were not sermons. Iremonger was not much worried about the studio talks: William Paton, Ronald Preston, Howard Marshall could speak well to an intelligent weekday audience. He was more concerned at the input from the churches, over which he sought increasing control. This concept of mission was a 'glorious adventure', he told Whale, who in the meantime struggled with the 'bigger question', intelligibility. Iremonger wanted to awaken the churches, the converted and the committed. The church was doing the faith little good. He wanted Whale's sermons to evangelize this group and have it realize its supreme responsibility for the way Christianity speaks to the social problems of its contemporaries. Whale was increasingly unhappy and began to find 'this broadcasting of religion difficult and distasteful'. He was not so optimistic as Iremonger with his faith in good sermons addressed to the converted, and thought that by 'sticking to these conventional religious forms you put off the very people you want to attract'. The series *The Christian Answer to the Problem of Evil* was broadcast in 1936, published by SCM Press and altogether well received. Iremonger always went on Monday to buy his potted meat from Fortnums and even received a good word about the series from one of the shop walkers who normally gave him a measure of abuse appropriate to the sermon on the previous Sunday! Iremonger believed Whale was the 'pioneer of quite a new method of broadcast addresses'.

The same year the new Dean of St Paul's, W. R. Matthews, undertook a similarly successful series on *The Hope of Immortality*; it is noteworthy that the two subjects, immortality and evil, were chosen because it was these two issues which were raised in greatest numbers by correspondents following the *Way to God* series.[27] Iremonger believed that by these two divines in particular, the 'answers' requested by the public could be so presented as to be a challenge and testimony to the place of the Christian apologetic in an increasingly non-participating Christian society, and similarly a way of apprehending the superstitious element in popular Christianity which sought enlightenment on the fundamental questions of death and suffering, i.e. of immortality and evil.

E. Music courses

From the very outset of his appointment, Iremonger was concerned not only about the standard of the broadcast sermons from churches but also about the standard of their music. English cathedrals were struggling and the general standard of cathedral music was not exceptionally high. Early Sunday policy had taken up a suggestion by the Roman Catholic, Filson Young, for the broadcasting of Bach's Church Cantatas, and had done so each Sunday afternoon from May

1928 to June 1931. This was hotly debated and there was much complaint that this highly specialized music, no doubt of the profoundest beauty in all Christendom, nevertheless was not good for broadcasting policy and doing no good to the cause of religion. By December 1933 Iremonger had encouraged Sir Walford Davies, by now one of the most accomplished broadcasters, on to the RBD staff, to devise a programme of sacred music which not only entailed a straight musical offering but which would serve to improve the music in churches by aiding, on a limited technical basis, the work of choirmasters and organists. Walford Davies wanted to let listeners hear some of the many ways sacred words formulate themselves into musical forms. The series *Melodies of Christendom* was broadcast on the fourth Sunday in each month and soon gained an enormous following. It continued intermittently until 1939.[28] Reith was enthusiastic and Iremonger, after almost a year, realized how well it was 'taking on as a mission'. He had ample evidence that choirmasters and organists were being helped by the mixture of semi-technical and popular music.[29] The programme usually ended with a straight performance by the Wireless Singers, following short studies of four or five sections of anthems, amens, alleluias, etc., which Davies would explain to both choir and organist – all with a view to better performance among their own congregations. Walford Davies was profoundly committed and constantly over-ran his programme time (much to the annoyance of Wellington, the Presentation Director). From both the church press and *The Musical Times* came a request that the programme should give more practical help to the innumerable church choirs struggling against severe difficulties of a lack of training and leadership. Walford Davies also wanted to venture out into new music: ten minutes of choral team practice to precede twenty minutes of enjoyment of choral music itself. In June 1937, Walford Davies made the extraordinary suggestion that local church choirs be brought into the BBC Concert Hall to exemplify the problems they faced in their own congregations. It was tried in October 1937 with considerable success, and again, on Sunday 13 February 1938, 115 members from four choirs joined Walford Davies in the Concert Hall. Graves was concerned, as were many correspondents, at the risk of turning a recital into a lesson and removing the sense of beauty for those who listened without any technical or performing interests.

Not all the regions would take *Melodies of Christendom*. The North had its own hymn programmes during the week and these were very popular indeed. There was also resentment at the imposition of a Southern interest in choral music contrasted with hymn singing which the North Region Programme Director thought a more 'sturdy' programme for the area. It is also interesting that in the development of *Melodies*, Walford Davies took his cue for more practical help to choirs from an initiative of the Midland Region which arranged for the organist and choirmaster of Derby Cathedral to present a programme of more recent church music and help choirs to undertake such performances. They were not, he emphasized, 'musical appreciation lectures'. He also estimated that there were 'at least half a million – largely amateurs – staffing the choirs of places of worship in England alone'. (Scotland by contrast called for metrical psalms of which Reith approved almost instinctively.[30])

Iremonger wanted above all to co-ordinate the whole country and asked for details as to what each region was doing in this area. For the most part he was disappointed: there was much choral music – oratorios, metrical psalms in Scotland, festivals in cathedrals and the singing of the ubiquitous popular hymn – wanted everywhere and supplied by the programme planners in considerable and regular quantities. R. S. Thatcher, the Deputy Director of Music, regretfully told Iremonger in 1938 that among regional music directors there was 'a definite disinclination to fall in with a national scheme; local activities have a large and enthusiastic following'. Iremonger was not surprised that there would be opposition to what he hoped could be co-ordinated work: 'It seems to me lamentable that local prejudice should stand in the way of a carefully thought out scheme for the regions.' The initiative of Walford Davies remains significant as the first attempt by the BBC to have a programme of education and practical assistance organized towards the objective of raising the standards of church music. Iremonger wanted it among the preachers too and this, of course, was resented among the sectional interests of the regions where the balance between the national and local interest fluctuated. The churches saw broadcasting facilities as access to the public to which they each in turn had a right.

F. Denominational co-operation

As has been said, Iremonger was in close touch with movements of all kinds in the churches towards a more radical approach to theological and ecclesial questions affecting the place of Christian witness. Hugh Martin, a Baptist who had been closely involved for many years with the Student Christian Movement, put to Iremonger in late 1934 the idea that the BBC should do something quite specific for the cause of church union and the co-operation now taking place not only in the United Kingdom, but in America and particularly in Europe. Martin, like so many, regarded the BBC as an institution which could be of great service to the Christian cause and particularly to movements of which the great bulk of the deeply and not so deeply committed Christians in the United Kingdom were unaware. William Paton of the International Missionary Council went even further and saw the BBC as perhaps the only way by which to bring to the rank and file those insights and activities within the churches largely confined to the leaders of denominations and those privileged to attend international conferences: 'We are in a time when international Christianity is terribly needed and people know so little about it,' he told Iremonger. Iremonger was in touch with the World Council of Churches (still in process of formation) and with Temple, Hodgson and George Bell; they discussed a series of preparatory programmes in connection with the Oxford and Edinburgh ecumenical conferences on 'Life and Work' and 'Faith and Order' planned for 1937.[31] In December 1935 the Programme Board had approved a weekday setting for a series of five talks eventually to be entitled 'Church, Community and State', designed to reflect the very issues with which these conferences were concerned.[32] The issues were wide: the relations between the church and the state, the duty of the world-wide church to state and community and not only as conceived and discussed in the elevated atmosphere of the enclaves in Lausanne and Stockholm.[33]

Iremonger wanted the BBC to engage the general listener in the concerns of these conferences and see how the churches were considering the reactions to the emerging political movements and social changes in Western society. As a consequence of the *God and the World* series, the Corporation was in touch with a considerable number of people, mostly clergy, from around the country – about four hundred, about a quarter of whom met in February 1936 in Broadcasting House. Reith was present and delighted to have dignitaries in such numbers in his Concert Hall.[34] Temple and J. H. Oldham discussed plans for literature, etc., and the meeting decided that the five talks should have the widest possible listening potential and voted for 9.0 p.m. on Sundays. Graves, the Controller of Programmes, thought, however, that there was a psychological point: if such a programme was on Sunday evening, people would regard it as 'just another religious talk and switch over'. If Sunday was insisted on it would have to be in the context of the 8.15 p.m. religious service time. Graves saw the danger of burying what he regarded as at least a significant series in a Sunday liturgical hole and losing it. He wanted a weekday, as indeed did Iremonger – only then would the clergy be listening. The February meeting disagreed; the clergy would be more likely to listen on Sunday

– they were too busy during the week! Iremonger lamented their lack of understanding.

Who should give the talks was another question. Oldham, who was the real power behind the series, favoured laymen in contrast to Reith, who was very keen on the series but wanted to hear church leaders speaking. Oldham himself was ruled out; he had a severe stutter. He made up in sincerity what he lacked in diction.[35] Oldham had hammered out the scheme of talks based upon and deriving from the concerns of the two conferences: the Christian conception of man and spiritual values against the triumph of materialist and humanist values. Iremonger was delighted with Oldham's precision and was sure that he and the BBC were breaking new ground: 'Such a series would be more concerned with the present problems of the world as distinguished from the private belief of the individual than any religious talks we have yet had.' In the end, the talks were given on Tuesday evenings by laymen such as Lord Lothian, Walter Moberly, Arnold Toynbee and T. S. Eliot. It was an impressive line-up. Later in the year John Maud (later Sir John Maud) broadcast a review of the twelve-day Oxford Conference on 'Church, Community and State'. He was, he told the national audience, impressed by three things; 'a vision of one church; the liturgy of the Russian Orthodox Church; and that all the sections of the Conference spoke of the churches' need to repent: we Christians were shamefully involved in the foulness of the world.' The BBC prepared a pamphlet which sold[36] around 5,000 copies. Iremonger was well pleased that there were about four hundred groups around the country discussing these talks.

Iremonger's innovations in religious talks were designed not only to serve the causes of the radical church movements and personalities who wanted changes but – as Reith had always declared – to set before the listeners a 'balanced view' – the expression of both sides of the argument. Iremonger wanted not only to raise the repute of Christendom but to do so by the exposure of its best men to the non-churchgoing Christian public through the talks series on Sunday afternoons. The views and intentions of Iremonger himself were reflected in the choices of both subjects and speakers. Two eminent conservatives, Sir Thomas Inskip and H. Hensley Henson, the Bishop of Durham, discussed establishment; Evelyn Underhill discussed spirituality, and Canon Grensted, an Oxford philosopher of religion and noted supporter of the Group Movement, examined questions of philosophy. Characteristically, Iremonger wanted the views of the young aired, and a notable series of five talks on *The Church I Look For* brought a number of younger men to conceptualize their 'visions'. The established and reputable leaders were given voice in yet another outlet for new ideas when Howard Marshall interviewed such people as Temple and MacLeod in a series called *What is the Church For?* followed by *What is the Church Doing?* Iremonger also wanted people who, once having heard, would also read; radio was a route towards deeper Christian formation undertaken by and through literature. R. Ellis Roberts, eventually Sheppard's biographer, began in 1934 to review Christian books once every quarter. The reviews were continued by Iremonger himself after his retirement in April 1939, in the series called *From a Deanery Window*.

While it was strongly affirmed by those who opposed the religious policy that the BBC was in the firm hands of the churches, the axis upon which broadcast religion turned had two distinct pivots, CRAC at one end and Iremonger at the other. Considerable numbers of talks were initiated entirely by him without reference to CRAC at all. Over 'Church, Community and State' the Committee entirely endorsed the initiative (although there was some unease about the selection of speakers: D'Arcy thought they should have been chosen by the Committee; Iremonger simply replied that this was an entirely undenominational issue). Iremonger regarded himself as a servant of the BBC and thus took decisions and initiatives as a churchman in the service of an institution which unlike any hitherto, could enable the church, or sections and styles within it, to address the public and have itself exposed to the public gaze. By this means, the religion of church and nation would be both scrutinized, especially in talks and Iremonger's studio sermon series, and demonstrated to the widest conceivable public. As yet there was no scientific machinery for telling exactly how many of the public were actually listening.[37] Services were either routine or ceremonial. The supreme example of the latter was the coronation of 1937 in which Iremonger both excelled and nearly suffocated! It fell to him to give 'the majestic rubrics of the historic service' from a tiny box of a room above the triforium in the Abbey, which had no ventilation whatsoever.[38] This most successful broadcast, for which Iremonger was highly praised, brought the religious significance of the coronation clearly home to the vast numbers who listened. Many churches requested the BBC to allow rediffusion by loudspeaker, and the coronation committee under the Duke of Norfolk gave permission. Reith, however, was sorry Norfolk would not allow television cameras into the Abbey.[39] Never before could the ordinary man have heard a coronation service, a national event of a very special kind in all its grandeur as a religious as well as a ceremonial spectacle. F. A. Cockin thought it a good occasion – in a broadcast sermon – to extrapolate on BBC policy. This prompted R. S. Lambert, the Editor of *The Listener*, to offer a leading article[40] which presented a

BBC religious policy with three aims: national, aesthetic and didactic. Religious broadcasting focuses the relation of church and state in national events of supreme significance to the identity of a people; secondly, it presents the best in worship and raises the standard; and thirdly, it has the aim to instruct, as for instance in *God and the World*, J. S. Whale's addresses, and 'Church, Community and State'. The BBC was not dispensing a new brand of religion and it had, said *The Listener* leader, 'undoubtedly exercised a harmonizing influence upon denominational distinctions within the churches', which was not exactly how Iremonger saw it! He had not been consulted by *The Listener*'s Editor. The article is important for the comment it aroused, especially from the Bishop of Durham, Hensley Henson. Iremonger thought his contribution was essentially sectarian propaganda, and so asked for the correspondence to close. Cockin in his sermon had claimed that radio 'provides a form of worship which can meet a need common to Christians of all types and conditions'. Henson did not think so: the popular broadcast service, he said, 'is the product and shadow of competitive sectarianism and decorates a form of self-indulgence with the name of Christian worship'; it was not worship – it had no participating congregation. He was both right and wrong. There was participation by the listener in broadcast worship, but not of the type which the churches broadly accepted as legitimate and authentic. He thought there was no evidence that broadcasting helped to improve attendance at public worship. 'Wireless may be the "handmaid of the churches" but there is hardly any function of the church which the BBC is not undertaking.' E. N. Porter Goff, the Vicar of Streatham, disagreed with the severely negative Bishop of Durham. He thought the parochial clergy should be grateful; some listeners were helped to renew their practice of worship. Broadcasting was doing what the churches should be doing; instructing, raising standards and increasing intelligence in all matters of faith, order and witness. Cardinal Hinsley complained of the BBC's 'lowest common denominator' and wished that Catholics could have more talks. Not surprisingly, Iremonger thought the leader article had simply given rise to sectarianism in the subsequent letter pages; he knew that Hinsley's letter had been written by Martindale, with whom Iremonger often clashed.[41] He asked Graves to stop this harmful publicity. Graves obliged and the correspondence ceased; it was the very picture that Iremonger wanted to avoid.

G. Service books: first steps towards a hymn book

R. S. Lambert's *Listener* leader did, however, make mention of a significant BBC publication, *New Every Morning*, which appeared in 1936 and by 1937 had sold over 100,000 copies. This was a service book and not the first to be available to the public for use with broadcast orders of service. In 1930, the BBC had published *Services for Broadcasting* from Savoy Hill. Prayers were set under subjects and there were orders for Epilogues rather similar to the broadcast Epilogue to which millions of listeners were enthusiastically committed. It had been compiled (though his name never appeared) by Canon F. W. Dwelly of Liverpool Cathedral who, in 1930, was sharply aware of the reverberations that the term 'BBC Religion' produced on everyone from Reith downwards. He insisted in the preface that this book was 'in no way an attempt to impose any new type of religious worship'; it was, he said, a 'humble adaptation of existing forms'. He might have better said 'distillation', since there were so many forms of worship represented and featured in the BBC's religious output that some refraction would inevitably be reflected in any publication of broadcast religious material for worship. He continued, somewhat defensively, that apart from regular worshippers and the sick, 'there are great numbers who do not habitually form part of any congregation. The scope of this book therefore is exceptionally wide.' Indeed! It was exactly the habitually non-churchgoing worshippers for whom Iremonger had so much sympathy. They might have rubbed shoulders or crossed swords with the churches and gone on their way for reasons good or ill.

Dwelly's *Services for Broadcasting* had not been the first. Hugh Johnston, who had conducted the Daily Service from 1928 to 1932, had produced *This Day* in 1928. He followed it in 1932 with *When Two or Three*, which grouped prayers around themes reflecting the nature of the Daily Service which resembled a species of Family Prayers concentrating on one main idea. He wanted this book to be useful in the life of the church, and not only to the listeners to the Daily Service, but to clergy and congregation alike when shorter or special 'orders' were necessary. A principal difficulty in all broadcast services was the origin and choice of hymns, and there was a constant debate in the Religious Broadcasting Department concerning the extent to which preachers should choose hymns from this book or that.[42]

In 1935, however, Iremonger, McCormick and Hugh Johnston thought that *When Two or Three* had done its work. Iremonger wanted Reith's general approval for a new prayer book for the Daily Service, a more elaborate one. He wanted to eliminate second-rate prayers and especially descriptive prayers which were poetic ways of interpreting religious conviction and seemed to inform the deity of our mundane historical situation to date! He wanted classical collects, prayers from the Book of Common Prayer which have 'worn well' and new material from contemporary anthologies. Iremonger himself expected to be the final editorial authority, albeit he had strong collaborators in Hugh Martin, Editor of SCM Press, A. C. Craig of Glasgow, L. S. Hunter and Edward Shillito the Congregationalist. Basil Nicholls, Controller of Administration, thought it time the BBC had a worthy book for the Daily Service; he thought *Where Two or Three* a rather 'scrubby affair'. Iremonger told Reith that he had given a detailed report to CRAC merely to be civil and tactful and to avoid 'giving them the impression that we had settled everything without asking their advice'. Iremonger was constantly in touch with Reith and submitted for his comment two 'modern' prayers, one on the subject of 'road accidents' and one for 'shop assistants and domestic servants'. Reith would have liked a prayer 're litter and the spoliation of the countryside'. The book was published in October 1936 and Iremonger wrote politely in the *Radio Times* that *New Every Morning* was to aid the 'large number of listeners who, however loosely they may be connected with organized religion, still look for guidance and inspiration in their daily life to Jesus Christ and his Gospel'.[43]

This was typically Iremonger's attitude toward broadcast religion. The churches were in no position to label non-attenders as excommunicate or apostate because of their disaffection with their former 'mother church'. It was also to assert that the BBC had a Christian style which could and indeed most certainly did appeal to vast numbers who gained something from such services as the Epilogue and Daily Service, especially, as Iremonger exphasized in his paper to CRAC in 1937, that in these broadcasts there were no sermons. Reith wanted recognizable grandeur in such a book as befitted the immense labour entailed in it. The Editor of the *Daily Express* was glad of the road accident prayer – 'A grand thing for weekend motorists'! It sold prodigiously, 80,000 within three months and 130,000 by February 1939. *The Times*[44] thought it 'a difficult piece of work excellently done' because while it contained good modern prayers, it did not try to update the 'matchless compositions' of earlier centuries. The *Daily Mirror*'s verdict was that 'nothing could be better' and it particularly appreciated prayers for road users, policemen and 'even for journalists'.[45] The church press received it warmly and commended it for use by ministers. With the *Church Times*, however, Iremonger knew that no amount of traditional religion would send the vast audience for the Daily Service back into the churches. Notwithstanding the modest objections of some publishing houses to the BBC venturing into publication,[46] *New Every Morning* had been smoothly launched with the help of Father H. H. Kelly of The Society of the Sacred Mission, Kelham.

One serious liturgical technicality remained for Iremonger: which hymns? Every denomination had its own hymn book, some included the same hymn with different tunes or indifferent versions, and the constant question was which books should be referred to in the *Radio Times*. *Songs of Praise* was Percy Dearmer's most recent collection and increasingly popular. Iremonger thought it 'compiled by advanced modernists who deliberately excluded many of the best and still truest of the old hymns; and "highbrows" who showed their sympathy with modern thought by such lines as "All the little atoms go dancing on their way" – a rather specialized conception for congregational worship'.[47] Thus, no sooner was *New Every Morning* off the press, but Iremonger wanted a new hymn book in which there would be 'nothing that was not first class; in which the good popular hymns would not be left out and all the best of the new ones included'.[48] He was blithely optimistic that the BBC was the 'only one body without any sectional bias which would meet with the general approval of most of the churches'.

As far back as 1927 Nicolls had suggested that the BBC mount a competition 'to produce our own hymn and prayer book for use on Sunday evening'.[49] It was not proceeded with on account of pressure from the publishers of existing hymn books, and also opposition to the BBC being involved in any publishing other than the *Radio Times*. Again in 1934 a suggestion for a BBC hymn book was put forward but rejected; it was thought that the churches as well as the hymn book publishers would be against it.

In 1937, however, Iremonger's somewhat naïve hopes were high; his optimism and even vision on this aspect as on others would not be matched by the response of the churches, who could so easily be provoked into seeing broadcasting either as a threat to religion or merely an adjunct to the churches' sectional interests. Iremonger wanted broadcasting to serve Christianity and its founder and wanted the churches to move forward into the twentieth century and join with the BBC in new objectives and methods. As for the hymn book, the war would delay it yet another decade, although his connection with it would not cease when he resigned in 1939. However, for the moment, Reith and the Board of Governors approved it, and in July 1937 work began very slowly indeed. It also had to be confidential; Iremonger's optimism was still tempered by fear of criticism from the churches. Soon enough the word got out and Iremonger was pleased to hear from the Chairman of The Hymn Society who provided a selection of about two hundred and twenty of what he called the common denominator of the twenty English-language hymn books.[50]

The first thing was to get an interdenominational committee together and work out a basis for discussion. (This was not the first: a BBC staff committee had considered the idea in 1929.) Leslie Hunter, Archdeacon of Northumberland, Hugh Martin, the Baptist editor of SCM Press, Ellis Roberts, Albert Peel for the Congregationalists and W. A. L. Elmslie for the Presbyterians met in October to pool their collection: each had chosen from the various denominational books and altogether the Committee produced around two hundred and fifty hymns. 'Not enough!' said Iremonger: he had soon enough realized that whilst the selection was required for broadcast services and in particular, the Daily Service, if the BBC were to publish, any new hymnal would have to be attractive to the churches and profitable to whoever actually published it. The Oxford University Press showed sympathy from the beginning.[51]

The committee expanded its choice to around eight hundred pieces and ended up with five hundred and twenty three hymns with 'settled' tunes. By August 1938, this Committee had done its work and the list was then to be sent to the BBC referees. The initiative was firmly with the Corporation and there was no intention of consulting CRAC at this stage – if at all: Iremonger had made it clear to his Committee that whilst he was grateful for all their help, it would now be up to the Corporation's chosen referees to turn this selection into a hymnal with a distinct style of its own. It would be a companion-book to *New Every Morning*. Leslie Hunter however put his finger on a crucial issue: hymns for broadcasting were not always the same as hymns for general congregational use; why not publish two books complementary to each other? This however was unrealistic and would not be financially viable; OUP was certainly sympathetic but feared the consequences of co-operating with the Corporation in ordinary book publishing. There was a further problem: of the proposed BBC book's five hundred and twenty-three hymns, three hundred and thirty-seven were already to be found in OUP's *Songs of Praise*.

Iremonger's Committee had produced the draft and it was now the turn of the referees. They were, for the BBC, Sir Walford Davies, R. S. Thatcher, Deputy Director of Music, his colleague Trevor Hervey and the Director of Music for the Midland Region, W. K. Stanton. Outside the Corporation were Dykes-Bower, the organist of St Paul's, Henry Ley, the organist of Eton College, G. W. Briggs of Worcester Cathedral, W. T. Cairns for the Church of Scotland and people from the Hymn Society and the Society of the Sacred Mission at Kelham. Iremonger hoped that when all their suggestions had been put together, they would be sent to the OUP via the BBC Copyright

Department and the BBC Hymnal would be on its way. By the spring of 1939, Iremonger was about to leave the Corporation but would stay for another two months to settle in his successor; he hoped he could complete the hymn book from his new home, the Deanery at Lichfield.

He had not however reckoned with impending conflicts; the country was moving perilously towards war and the proposed hymn book towards stiff resistance. It had been a relatively simple operation for Iremonger to have the OUP publish *New Every Morning*. It was of course designed for use at home in conjunction with the Daily Service. Clergy and others could use it elsewhere as they pleased and moreover it involved no musical issues. Questions of copyright over texts of prayers were very few and OUP had gone ahead without hindrance.

The proposed hymn book immersed the Corporation in questions of copyright not only of the hymn texts but of the tunes. In the spring of 1939 just as Iremonger was handing over, Ralph Vaughan Williams, Music Adviser to OUP, expressed himself rather strongly on behalf of those who stood to suffer the most from sales of the BBC book, namely the widow of Percy Dearmer, the compiler of the somewhat notorious *Songs of Praise*, and Martin Shaw, Vaughan Williams' musical co-editor, who had written many of the new tunes. The new book would cause 'severe financial loss' and therefore compensation should be paid. William Temple was similarly concerned for Nan Dearmer's interest and wrote in a similar tone both to Iremonger and the Director-General.[52] Vaughan Williams certainly did not wish to exercise the ultimate veto and refuse copyright to the Corporation: it would go ahead anyway and their book would be all the worse for the inferior alternatives that would result. He thought, predictably, that *Songs of Praise* was the finest English hymn book and saw no real need of another – all the more since increasing competition from this 'formidable rival' would result in a serious loss of income.[53] OUP for its part had stipulated that no words over which it had copyright control should be set to any other than the *Songs of Praise* tune without the consent of Vaughan Williams and Shaw; Vaughan Williams, it was widely believed, had become the 'unfettered dictator' of OUP.[54] Whether that was true depended upon one's point of view. If, however, the BBC was to pursue a book involving music, Vaughan Williams was involved and his influence had to be faced in the negotiations with OUP. It was clearly no longer a matter now, of sending a draft to the BBC's 'referees'; a highly respected music committee would have to deliberate and somehow gain the confidence and co-operation of Vaughan Williams.

Iremonger and his BBC advisers met in August and decided that any music edition of their embryo hymn book was going to be a long job. Let the words-only edition founded upon the work of Iremonger's original Church Committee be published by the BBC and available from Broadcasting House only: it might even be bound in with *New Every Morning*. All agreed that a 'Music Committee' be appointed with people acceptable to both Vaughan Williams, effectively for OUP, and Walford Davies similarly for the BBC. Perhaps the revered Sir Hugh Allen, the BBC's adviser on opera, would take the chair. They would fit the necessary tunes to the already published words and the BBC and OUP would together reap the profits; they expected the music edition to appear two to three years after the words.[55] For his part, Iremonger thought Vaughan Williams would be 'better out of the way',[56] as would Briggs of Worcester, who, he believed, wanted only his hymns in the book.

Iremonger believed the BBC book could do what Dearmer's *Songs of Praise* could not: it would supersede *Hymns Ancient and Modern* which he thought would soon be outmoded. He thought the churches and the worshippers that comprise them 'simply will not stand for about five sixths of the words and music still served up to them; good church music will always make its appeal'.[57] He thought Percy Dearmer had 'overawed his *Songs of Praise* Committee and they were glad to have the theological responsibility taken off their shoulders'.[58] It was this theological position to which Iremonger so strongly objected; the new hymn book must reflect the piety of the British more faithfully and particularly the subjectivism of much in evangelical Christianity. *Songs of Praise* suffered from Dearmer's 'blunder' of partiality and Iremonger hoped the Corporation's choice in theology, music and poetry would be nothing less than definitive.[59] Such a production would not only take time to produce; it would need to be tested in and out of the churches. The words edition would benefit from a couple of years as a draft, to be followed by a final edition accompanied by the music. But for one crucial factor, it was a neat if rather non-commercial scheme. War broke in September 1939 and Iremonger's advice was that the project should be delayed; there would be such a small market for it now, not to mention a lack of paper. Iremonger 'retired' to Lichfield with his drafts, intending to go quietly on with it.[60] He thought the Music Committee would find it difficult to meet during hostilities, and so the task to all intents and purposes was dropped for the duration.

11

FOR CHILDREN AND SCHOOLS

Before Iremonger's time, initiatives had been taken to produce acceptable programmes on Sunday afternoons for the young. BBC's Children's Hour, to which a great deal of energy and attention was given by the slender company staff, had started very early in 1923.[1] This however was a weekday entertainment. CRAC's attention was first directed towards Sundays by C. S. Woodward, Canon of Westminster. He wanted one man to organize an acceptable programme on Sunday afternoons, and there was a good deal of interest in plays which would not only make good use of the medium but would convey the message of the Bible in a simple way, provided that 'historic facts were not mutilated and that imaginary words were not put into the mouths of historic persons such as the Virgin Mary'.[2] Plays were preferable to readings, the Committee thought; they should be written by an 'expert dramatist' and subject to 'careful censorship'. They were predictably cautious of any tampering with Holy Writ, but prepared to consider at least the use of the medium of radio and radio drama in the service of religious and ecclesial objectives. Another major caution concerned the time of the broadcast: it should not interfere or clash with the traditional times when church Sunday schools met. Reith wanted Canon Woodward to be responsible for the co-ordination of the broadcasting to children, and the production of a style of service directed to and involving children. These came first from a studio and later from St John's, Smith Square. In 1926, a local minister in Manchester devised broadcast missionary services on Sunday afternoons, and talks on the life of missionaries and their adventures were broadcast bi-monthly with great appeal. These talks were selected and edited for the BBC by the Far and Near East Press Bureau, and were designed to enlist sympathy with missionary effort through travel talks.[3] By 1929, with the gradual expansion of Sunday broadcasting, a church service was broadcast on the first Sunday of each month, St John's taking its turn with other churches. On other Sundays there were short dramatic programmes to illustrate and enforce the lessons of scriptural texts. These came under the general title of *For the Children*. In 1930, E. R. Appleton, the Cardiff Station Director, began his broadcasts of dramatized biblical stories under the title of *Joan and Betty's Bible Story*.[4] Again these were outside the churches' Sunday school times. Indeed, the BBC had assured the Sunday School Union in 1923 that this hour would not be invaded.

In 1929, Basil Yeaxlee had become principal of West Hill College, Birmingham, and had gathered a group of people representing wide interests in religion and education including the 'Teaching Church Group', a Church of England body based in St Albans. Yeaxlee's group kept an interested eye on the BBC's work among the young and before long he headed a committee of ten – half Church of England and half Free Church – to be responsible for *For the Children* on the third and fifth Sundays in the month. Yeaxlee was the churches' representative on the Central Council for Broadcast Adult Education, and there he was pushing hard for adult religious talks also on Sunday afternoons; he thus felt a conflict of interests. By 1932 the BBC was being advised by Yeaxlee's Committee and by CRAC, some of which were by no means happy about what Yeaxlee's committee produced, nor the rather trite *Joan and Betty* series from Cardiff, popular as that was. Graves wanted to 'clean up Sunday', as indeed did Stobart, and this had serious implications for those organizing outside broadcasts from churches. The planners wanted more studio services for the children and somewhat later than mid-afternoon. They preferred early evening, when outside broadcast services could not possibly be organized for children only minutes away from Evensong.

With the arrival of Iremonger, the problem was to find more people who could successfully undertake work among children. There was, it appeared to him, little imagination to hand. He brought Percy Dearmer, Canon of Westminster, into the work; children's Sunday services, taken by Dearmer in a Broadcasting House studio,[5] now alternated with Appleton's Bible stories. Dearmer brought a handful of children with him who asked questions which he answered; in effect he provided a course of consecutive Bible teaching.[6] Hymns were sung with the help of members of the Wireless Singers, and he designed the services so that children at home could not only learn but sing some of the hymns they heard. There were dialogues between older children and the clergy who took the services, but very little headway was made to investigate possibilities of drama for children on which Iremonger pinned enthusiastic hopes. After just over two years, however, he was 'by no means satisfied with our radio broadcasts', and hoped by the end of 1936 to evolve new plans. He expected Yeaxlee's 'features' to come to an end before long, which would leave two Sundays in the month empty.

Dearmer died in May 1936, so changes became necessary. Iremonger wanted to present biblical material in dramatized forms, but taking care that when the voice of Jesus was heard there would be no imaginary material: a narrator would speak his words from the Authorized Version. By October 1936, Dearmer's son, Geoffrey, was

"Do you think I could ask the B.B.C. Announcer to say my prayers for me? He speaks so beautifully."

taken on to organize *For the Children* on a weekly basis with collaboration from Lance Sieveking, the dramatic producer in the Features Department, who had a 'daring and creative mind'.[7] Iremonger had put in train a number of ideas which were to be developed during wartime by his successor who, like Yeaxlee, was an experienced educationalist and a man who, rather more substantially than Iremonger, understood children's needs and the complex issues discussed by philosophers of education.

Iremonger's initiatives among the young included ideas for religion in BBC broadcasting to schools, and yet showed a singular lack of imagination in the light of all that had been achieved by Stobart and Somerville since broadcasting to schools began in 1924.[8] The so-called 'Kent experiment'[9] – an attempt to gauge broadcasts from the receiving end – had recommended closer relations between the Corporation and the school and education authorities. Thus the Central Council for Schools Broadcasting (CCSB) was set up, with Mary Somerville as secretary. The BBC was already well and truly committed to the implications of having a specialized audience under the aegis of the schools, from which there was, not surprisingly, much resistance in the initial stages to broadcasts 'taking over the role of the teacher'. The CCSB was the advisory link between broadcasting and the schools. In 1927, the CRAC had discussed broadcasting religion to schools in some fashion. Stobart had told them that one of the most useful services the BBC could render 'would be to give an undenominational religious lesson at the start of the school day'. He was well aware, as many on the Committee were not, that few enough teachers interested in teaching the subject had any real knowledge apart from their own religious upbringing and whatever they had gained in church and congregation. In 1927 Stobart thought such a broadcast was still a long way off and 'hardly practical politics as yet'.

The first official and weighty approach to the Corporation for schools broadcasts came from the forward-looking Association for Teachers of Religious Knowledge, which had Sir Henry Hadow as its Chairman and such presidents as J. H. Oldham and B. H. Streeter, and included among its leadership Basil Yeaxlee and J. W. D. Smith. Under Yeaxlee and Oldham's guidance, the Association at its annual meeting in January 1934 passed a resolution asking the CCSB to investigate the possibility of broadcasting programmes of Bible study or religious knowledge for the 'benefit of the upper forms of secondary and public schools'. The CCSB referred this request to their executive in March, and a sub-committee was set up which included Iremonger. This sub-committee pondered the issue until the end of the year, and came out strongly in favour of the desirability of providing material for the older age group. Progress was slow and not until May 1935 did the executive of the CCSB meet again. Notwithstanding the strong support for the idea, there was also strong opposition. The sub-committee had recommended that such teaching should only be for the children of fifteen or over who, it was assumed, 'possess some superficial knowledge of and an undoubted interest in the problems of behaviour and belief and are therefore better fitted to appreciate the issues'.[10]

Not everyone thought the idea was a good one, nor that the CCSB should actually sponsor the proposal. Several bodies represented on the Council were in favour of the series – as were most representative members – but were anxious that the initiative should remain with the educationalists. The representatives of the London County Council

5. F. A. Iremonger

6. C. F. Garbett

7. Eric Fenn conducting the Daily Service, 1942

8. Cardinal Hinsley

9. W. H. Elliott

10. F. W. Ogilvie

11. B. E. Nicholls

and the National Union of Teachers, however, were concerned with the question of conscience. The Association of Assistant Masters were in favour of what they called 'simple Bible teaching', but were concerned with the liberty of conscience in the profession as a whole. There would be a problem if teachers were obliged to conduct classes involving broadcast religious material; it could be open to the construction that religious teaching was being authorized and supported by a particular teacher whose religious views, or lack of them, might be offended. The CCSB finally agreed that a divided vote would not be helpful and gave limited support to the idea. They were 'unwilling to abandon the proposals outright' and would be 'glad to see the Corporation itself undertake the experiment'.[11] The initiative was thus given to Iremonger and the Religious Broadcasting Department.

Iremonger was a close friend of the Dean of Windsor, Anthony Deane, who had been giving studio sermons and various talks since before 1933.[12] He had won a reputation for his broadcasts, and Iremonger thought he was the one person 'giving a message in plain English'. Deane was asked to devise a series of sixteen talks for the upper years of schools for the beginning of 1936. *Sixth Form Religion* was the result. They must be neither sermons nor academic essays, nor duplicate the scripture lesson already supplied.[13] He told Iremonger:

> The rising generation must be given a chance of being Christian by being taught the Christian faith, for which no mere benevolence and goodwill and vague aspiration can serve as an equivalent. The BBC's religious work has the greatest value when it teaches the main factors of the Christian faith; it can do much to Christianize England.[14]

Deane was a good friend of Reith, and with him believed that the BBC had an important task in teaching the Bible. Every other aspect of the Department's work rested on the teaching of the Bible, and the BBC should provide this 'intelligent knowledge'. Through broadcasting, the rising generation could so be provided with this intelligent knowledge of Bible and faith that commitment would arise from intelligent responses and not from traditional or family or class precedents alone. He thought no expense should be spared for the training of teachers and making the Church of England colleges efficient. 'Upon their work, the future of religion among the great mass of people in this country depends.' Yeaxlee agreed in part, but was aware that the educational system was being gradually secularized – that it would not entertain the preaching of Christianity in the curriculum. Deane's talks covered a variety of biblical subjects, and there were soon approving replies from a number of schools. He was greatly encouraged.[15] On the CCSB side, the Chairman, W. W. Vaughan, former Headmaster of Wellington and Rugby, and Mary Somerville, the Secretary, were somewhat disturbed that Deane was talking down in these broadcasts and treating the listening teenager as a Sunday school adolescent. Vaughan admitted to Somerville that he was reluctant to write to Deane for fear he would give him ground for thinking that the CCSB was discreetly vetting his scripts. Iremonger had his theological doubts about some of Deane's talks, especially on such controversial and complex subjects as the miracle narratives of the New Testament. Notwithstanding these strictures, he was regarded as one of the few capable expositors and was thus asked to do another series for May and June of the same year.

Within a year, Deane's Bible talks were being listened to, as far as the Schools Broadcasting Department could determine, by approximately two hundred schools of which only twenty-one were public schools, the remainder being secondary and elementary in equal numbers.[16] His first two series were followed in autumn 1936 by a series on the Bible by Dr C. A. Alington. The chief criticism by the schools was more on the grounds of presentation than substance. Charles Baty, the Headmaster of the King's School, Chester, for example, thought Alington was 'rather stating reasons for religious belief instead of giving a background against which the school could study the Old or New Testament'. This went to the heart of the problem which faced Iremonger: how to find people who not only could present their material and themselves in compelling ways appropriate to the classroom, but also were able to discuss the Bible and its religious and theological content in a rather more objective and rather less propagandist fashion than might be expected of the clergy. They indeed were often fearful of the influence of these talks outside schools.[17] Deane had already been severely critized by a vicar in Suffolk who complained to Iremonger that 'by means of radio he (Deane) enters the very homes of my people and by a single sentence strikes a blow at the teaching in this parish for the last fifty years; . . . the BBC should inspire confidence in the Bible rather than doubt; there is no other way to national revival.' This man conceived his relationship to 'his own people' as the clergy at large believed the relationship of the churches should be to the BBC. Broadcasting belonged to those responsible for the maintenance of faith; just as the clergy should protect the rank and file from doubt, so should the BBC in its religious policy. For Iremonger and Deane, the schools presented a difficulty because of the charge which threatened every teacher of religion: 'indoctrination'. In the 1930s it was linked with denominationalism, and indeed the Association of Assistant

Masters and Mistresses formally asked for more denominations to be represented in whatever lists of speakers would be drawn up for future series. Iremonger thought that good education in religion could only do the cause of Christianity a good service, even though he would not talk as the Suffolk vicar did of 'national revival'.

At a meeting of the CCSB in November 1936 there was much discussion on the question of objectivity, and the need to provide a background to the New Testament and church history rather than investigating complex issues of belief which, to many teachers, sounded rather propagandist. This was not a doctrinaire refusal to look at the challenge of religious belief, but a recognition of the strong lobby of the National Union of Teachers and others which were not prepared to do the churches' own work. The new secretary, A. C. Cameron, was sympathetic towards the place of religion in schools broadcasting, and suggested to the CCSB that they should recommend a course on the historical development of Christianity up to the Reformation, which would cover the history of the church from the Acts of the Apostles onwards. Charles Baty, an important member of the Council (he was also Chairman of the CCSB Modern Languages Committee) wanted wider denominational representation among the speakers and uncontroversial religious matter. By that he meant that religious debate should be kept away from the classroom, at least in the broadcasts themselves. He wanted authoritative scholarship. He was supported enthusiastically by the Association of Teachers of Religious Knowledge, and especially by Basil Yeaxlee at West Hill. Most syllabuses in secondary schools, the CCSB believed, reflected a discreetly Protestant approach and were narrowly biblical. They ended with the Acts and would then go abruptly back to Genesis, said Cameron. The BBC could fill this need for history beyond Acts and have Roman Catholics on the list of speakers. Iremonger agreed and hoped C. H. Dodd would undertake the first four centuries!

In the meantime, Deane and H. Wheeler Robinson were preparing another series of Bible talks for January to Easter 1937, and Iremonger planned the history series. Dodd could not do it, so Iremonger turned to A. E. Rawlinson, the Bishop of Derby, to co-organize this two-year series of fifty-six talks. On 13 April 1937 Iremonger called a significant meeting of scholars, including Yeaxlee, D'Arcy, Baty and W. R. Matthews. Yeaxlee's place was significant because he was the only one involved in pioneering the reforms in the teaching of religion in schools which was very largely undertaken by non-specialists. Yeaxlee favoured the Deane/Alington experiment; they were scholars. But to use only these few could be to play into the hands of the opponents among the teachers who believed that broadcasting sought to take the place of the teacher. It was comparable indeed to the fears of the clergy that their own authority would be undermined. Yeaxlee wanted broadcasts from specialist teachers who had specialist qualifications without necessarily being first-class scholars. The whole enterprise would only succeed finally if broadcasters were as much teachers as they might be priests, bishops or other ecclesiastics. C. H. Dodd was by the end of the 1930s well known in both capacities. The BBC could do for school-teaching what Iremonger had always hoped it could do for preaching: show the incompetent how it could be done!

Yeaxlee went to the Easter 1937 meeting with these notions in mind and found himself greatly disturbed by the plans for the proposed church history course. It was too long and occupied the whole post-School Certificate Course for 16–18 year-olds, thus precluding any investigation of modern thought and Christian ethics. Yeaxlee was firmly convinced that the course was of no use to secondary schools and of questionable value to the public schools. He was sorry that 'the BBC with its unique power to revitalize the teaching of religion in multitudes of schools, should adopt a scheme so unlikely to be used by any but a small fraction. The scheme appears to be evolved by clergy and scholars and not by practical teachers with school conditions in their minds.'[18] He was involved at the forefront of change in religious schooling, and told Iremonger that was why he cared so much about what the BBC was doing. He complained that Baty, who had prepared a draft syllabus and was effectively the planner of the course, really did not grasp the situation in the secondary schools, where there was only rarely somebody equipped to take the invariable one period per week of religious knowledge, which always came at the beginning of the school day. The course was too highly specialized: 'For those schools which can take it, it will be magnificent, but in the nature of things they will be few.' The series began on 27 September 1937 and the BBC's official handout declared that the course would fill a gap and supplement school studies.

The general response to the announcement was favourable. Cosmo Lang thought that the programmes would be useful and the National Sunday School Union (NSSU) declared that the BBC was 'rendering a very important service to Christian education'. The producer of the series, Evelyn Gibbs, for the CCSB, was not so confident as the NSSU. Only about one-hundred and fifty secondary schools had signified they would take the programmes; this was a much smaller number than expected by Baty and his committee. Enquiries around the London schools and beyond proved rather depressing; the talks were mostly too advanced for their sixth form pupils. By December 1937, the signs were not encouraging even though there was some optimism. Bryanston School wanted more relevance to today and others complained about the presentation; the broadcasting was poor. Production was difficult because collaboration was not always possible. At root, as Evelyn Gibbs confessed to Mary Somerville, the speakers were either clergy or university professors or both, and even if they had broadcasting experience, as Charles Raven and Nathaniel Micklem had, they hardly collaborated, except on the day of the broadcast, in order to organize their scripts. If they had no broadcasting experience, they were not easily adapted to the microphone; they could not quickly develop a professional technique. Cameron nevertheless thought that the course had got off to a good start and that he had to accept 'as inevitable those which have not been ideal'.

In some cases, either because a contributor's voice was poor or because of distance or his heavy commitments, lectures were read by announcers. Yet the Corporation was not in a position to dragoon a highly dignified scholar into producing a manuscript, and then ask him not to read it simply because he had not been trained at the microphone as the 'schools' people wanted, i.e. in a manner more akin to classroom teaching than either the lecture platform or the pulpit. For all his excellence as a 'star' broadcaster, Deane had the same problem.

But it was not only questions of presentation that were raised by the critics. Head teachers complained that the series was not only too advanced or 'academic', but that it did not help sixth-formers to formulate and deal more maturely with the ethical and religious questions related to the changing life of a sixteen-year-old. This was Iremonger's dilemma in the relationship of his department with the CCSB. He, too, wanted to have broadcasts to schools relating religious issues of the present to the central origins of the Christian faith. He asked Cameron to raise the matter in the CCSB: 'I wish these schools broadcasts could deal with the realities of life and religion as much as with history.' Mary Somerville pointed to the practicalities: these lectures were being given by experts who could not broadcast. Training the speakers to be broadcasters or preparing the material for radio would involve a staff commitment which the Corporation just did not have. Because the CCSB had not actually sponsored the series, Iremonger could make no demands; he was on his own. And the Secretary, Cameron, felt strongly that the job of the BBC was to provide data for people to make up their own minds. He claimed that he had always held, from the first discussion in the Council 'that you could not by broadcasting teach Christianity'; he wanted 'background rather than content'. Iremonger wished for relevance. The course was right to concentrate on the background; anything more relevant was in danger of censure from the CCSB over indoctrination – and also of criticism from those in the Corporation who felt that 'relevance' belonged to the churches and not to the CCSB. Those who first met in April 1937 to launch the series met for the second time, again under Sir Henry Richards (Chairman of the CCSB), and approved the series but noted, first that the talks were too full, and secondly, that the single voice was not a good vehicle for the classroom. The Committee then set out to plan the second series for 1938–9. They resolved this time that more attention must be paid to producers; they also took note of Evelyn Gibbs' constructive criticisms: e.g. 'word pictures are more acceptable than summaries'; 'good broadcasters are more important than experts'; talks about persons are more important that talks about historical facts; it is better to be concrete than abstract – e.g. 'Life in Corinth' rather than 'St Paul's Epistles'. The third series beginning in October 1939–40 would pursue the same policy as that which Iremonger sought among the churches: fewer and better. The listening schools, however, remained few.

12

THE BBC AND CHRISTIAN ORTHODOXY

Throughout Iremonger's period, he and the Corporation were besieged both directly and in the press by those who wanted to widen the scope of broadcasting in respect to religious and moral issues. Pressure was exercised by fringe Christian institutions and small denominations, as well as non-Christian groups which demanded air-time in order to refute the claims of the Christians. The BBC developed gradually both concepts and arguments in support of what it broadly termed 'mainstream' Christianity and more specifically the mainstream churches. There were many facets to this pressure, particularly among the Protestant groups which had sprung up in the nineteenth century and which were concerned to promulgate a view of Christian Britain and protect it from the less worthy aspects of broadcasting such as the bad language associated with drama and the stage.

The mention of birth control, for example, in a series of talks during April 1937 on the world's population raised immediate opposition; it was to be mentioned although not discussed. Both Protestants and Roman Catholics on CRAC thought it would be offensive to listeners. The issue was very sensitive and had been discussed by the Board of Governors and ratified by the General Advisory Committee which had allowed only its mention.[1] D'Arcy respected the care in its handling but preferred that it should not be mentioned at all. Nor was he alone. Garbett told Iremonger that he would thoroughly object to any discussion. Lord Fitzalan, a Catholic member of the Upper House, had complained to Reith, who felt obliged to admit that the BBC regarded the matter as controversial and would say so clearly. D'Arcy had been asked by Cardinal Hinsley to request that the concept should not be mentioned anywhere – not even in non-religious talks.[2] For the Protestants, Mrs Bramwell Booth of the Salvation Army began what amounted to a campaign. She wrote strong letters to the Prime Minister, to the Archbishop of Canterbury and to Reith. She was one of many who protested on grounds which might be described as Victorian. The radio had power to corrupt. 'It cannot be right', she complained, 'to lay bare the intimate relationships of married life before those who are too young to understand. . . . Wireless is available where mixed companies congregate, servant halls and mixed clubs. Artificial birth control is repulsive to a large part of the population and to impose this controversial subject by radio is most undesirable.' Lang agreed with her, but he complied with Reith and the General Advisory Committee who had listened to Garbett's view but had maintained its position. Reith replied to Mrs Booth, who was understanding but implacable. 'The widespread sale of contraceptives is a great evil and the depraved youngster can hear little of truth and honour except via the radio.' Such a letter epitomized the reaction of much Protestant opinion to issues which, when put before an untutored or unprotected public, were thought to threaten national unity or national identity, or indeed the foundation of the monarchy and the very fabric of society itself. Much of the Protestant indignation against the BBC was fired by the participation of Roman Catholics in the programmes and on the staff of the Corporation.[3] The protection of the 'Sabbath' from increasing Sunday leisure and the protection of Protestant Britain from the Roman Catholics was a familiar aim. On the other hand, pressure came from rationalist and humanist groups which claimed the right to offer an alternative view to that supported, and they believed promulgated, by the Corporation.

By the time of Iremonger's arrival in 1933, policies in respect to orthodox Christianity were formulated and firmly written into the programme policy, which in turn derived from the advice of the CRAC. Henceforth this would be distilled through an Anglican Religious Director. There were, in the organizations which approached and badgered the Corporation, men and some women in high places who had given their names or who were stalwart enthusiasts of their cause. Reith and subsequent Directors-General had therefore to take note of the influence such people could wield, especially in either House at Westminster. Lady Astor was a Christian Scientist and several MPs were known to be Unitarians. There were eminent men who were also Spiritualists and thus such movements had access to the leadership and policy-making personnel in broadcasting. They all wanted their turn at the microphone either on the grounds that their following was socially and numerically significant, or that their beliefs were orthodox; or indeed, that in a liberal and democratic culture they had a right to air their views and beliefs, no matter how easily or quickly the BBC would cry 'controversy' and hide behind the screen of good taste and avoidance of offence, and thus behind a concept of the Christian majority. What was at stake was an agreed orthodox Christianity; 'agreed', that is, by those whom the Corporation deemed 'agreeable'! Two particular groups were thorns in its side.

A. Christian Science

Within the first year of broadcasting, the Company had received requests from the Christian Scientists, and Reith was obliged to put the matter to Garbett's 'Sunday Committee' in October 1923. It predictably said 'no' to broadcasting Christian Science in Sunday programmes. The Committee did, however, explicitly say that the BBC could do as it pleased on weekdays and consigned to the Company in principle the freedom to make judgments on certain theological issues and decide whether to broadcast non-orthodox Christian material outside Sundays. The Sunday Committee recognized its limitations and would advise only on matters pertaining to the orthodox and mainstream churches; it was only there to choose Christian preachers. In 1927 this ban on Sunday was endorsed as it was again in 1928 following the Postmaster-General's lifting of the ban on controversy. (The *Christian Science Monitor* in 1928 had offered to provide the Corporation with a free copy of the paper for the BBC's waiting room, but Eckersley had turned it down politely!) In 1927, it had been Garbett's personal view which prevailed: Christian Science was unorthodox and if the door was opened to it 'it would be impossible to avoid throwing it open to theosophists, Buddhists, and other similar bodies'.[4] He told Stobart that there would also be complaints from the medical profession. There was some call for debate in CRAC, but Reith saw controversy looming and recommended that these bodies should not be given broadcasting time on Sundays: it would only give the impression that they were approved and even accepted by the orthodox mainstream churches and the Committee was vociferous in saying that they definitely were not! In 1931, CRAC made the grounds of the ban more specific and theologically explicit: speakers were now barred if they represented 'religious bodies which do not accept the deity of Christ'. Throughout these deliberations, the Board of Governors upheld the decisions of CRAC, although Mrs Snowdon in 1927 had opposed the suggestion of a ban on the grounds of theological unorthodoxy and not some other subversive characteristic.

In August 1933, however, pressure came from the former secretary to Lloyd George, Philip Kerr, now Lord Lothian. He had served in South Africa and was secretary to the Prime Minister from 1916–21. He was an outstanding figure in the League of Nations discussions and held a minor office in the National Government of 1931. He had already broadcast on Africa and on disarmament and was a close friend of Siepmann. He had been reared a Roman Catholic. His letter to Reith claimed orthodox status for Christian Science: it was good for public consumption and it re-stated traditional religion in modern terms. He also examined the grounds of the past bans and the policy of the BBC in respect to CRAC. 'To deny the public, on principle, an opportunity of hearing its message, would convict the BBC of being a censor of what is good for the public.' Christian Scientists should have the chance to be heard and he thought 'this question should be decided by the authorities of the BBC itself and not left to the decision of a committee of religious denominations, however fairminded, who can hardly be expected not to view the question from their own denominational point of view'. Lothian claimed that Christian Scientists were free in other countries to broadcast their service, as well as any talks. Reith replied that Sunday evenings must be confined to those who are 'more or less orthodox (don't ask me what this means)' but there might be a possibility of a Sunday afternoon talk in which Lothian could put the case of Christian Science. Rendall, in charge of Talks, suggested one in a series *What I Believe* which, however, would end with a Christian having the last word. Lothian refused to be assessed by an orthodox Anglican and resented being put among the fringe bodies excluded from the hallowed Sunday evening period, which was the preserve of the 'orthodox'. Reith consulted Iremonger, who claimed that the only question was whether Christian Science could be included in the category of 'orthodox' and thus embraced by CRAC policy. Christian Science makes 'a definite break with Christian theology' and Mrs Eddy's metaphysics are 'fundamentally inconsistent with all the main positions of Christian theology'.[5] H. A. L. Fisher, Warden of New College, Oxford, had recently published *Our New Religion*,[6] which was uncompromisingly critical. Iremonger proposed that the *status quo* should remain.

On the other hand, Christian Science was growing and he thought therefore its proponents should have the chance to 'say their piece', perhaps in some series on the varieties of belief. Christian Science should also be responded to by behavioural scientists with a summing up by W. R. Matthews of St Paul's. Lothian, however, had gone further and asked for a Christian Science seat on CRAC, together with Sunday services and readings from Mrs Eddy's *Science and Health* and a weekday talk! Reith was afraid that it was plainly propagandist. Propaganda was a pejorative label for sectarian and sectional interests outside the mainstream. The Christian Scientists were theologically unorthodox, and no matter how great their numbers they could not compete with the assumption that interpreted Britain as an orthodox Christian country, and therefore with numbers which amounted to millions. Propaganda was always what opponents said. Reith asked Iremonger's view again before the projected meeting with Lothian. Iremonger was firm against this very significant challenge to the supremacy of the mainstream churches on CRAC; they should have no seat on CRAC and no Sunday services: 'How could we ever hold up our heads again as a sane Corporation if we allowed the representatives of any society to broadcast such a sentence as "Obesity is an adipose belief in yourself as a substance; no need to give up bread or potatoes but just think your fat away"!'. About the proposal for a weekday talk, he said: 'We should make ourselves a laughing stock if we were not at pains to see that any statement was followed by a rebuttal given by a doctor, philosopher and a Christian theologian . . . we must ensure that a hearing is given to those who believe Christian Science to be false.'[7] But Reith was sufficiently moved by Lothian's argument to ask Iremonger to modify his position by giving them a Sunday afternoon – not the 'holy' evening – and thus treating them as semi-orthodox. They would submit a script with 'no propaganda – still less anything which would offend the churches'. Reith was in a real dilemma. How was he to please Lothian and avoid a row, and at the same time keep faith with CRAC? How could Christian Scientists be refused 'their say', even though such utterance over the air would raise considerable controversy, not to mention opposition. There would surely be cries of 'Heresy' from CRAC if not elsewhere. To this Iremonger responded with equal conviction: the Christian Science movement were infiltrators and trying to get themselves acknowledged as orthodox. If they had a Sunday afternoon and did not employ propaganda, this would be insidious and suggest that they were after all orthodox and that by their presence on the air on Sunday they were approved by both the Corporation and the churches.

Iremonger was angered by Lothian's statistics compiled from the number of attendances at lectures in 1933. He thought it was tantamount to misrepresentation of the truth to say that three thousand lectures were attended by three million people. Perhaps, he suggested, the same three thousand went time and again. The 1926 USA census stated that Christian Science members were just over two hundred thousand and thus, in spite of their propaganda and big money, the membership was less than one fifth of one per cent. Iremonger had the support of R. C. Norman, Vice-Chairman of the Governors, who was equally concerned about the BBC's dilemma and even more amazed that Lothian, a Liberal and brought up a Roman Catholic, could be so strongly attracted by a body which could 'transform the faith out of all recognition'.[8] Reith finally replied in August 1934 that he couldn't offer the Sunday service without consultation with CRAC. Lothian replied with another appeal accusing CRAC of basing their advice on 'some degree of religious prejudice and not on any real knowledge'. His new appeal was not now based on numbers but directed to broadcasting philosophy; the public were interested and might be comforted by it. Further, 'our propaganda', he observed, 'is just the same as other Christian churches', and therefore there is no reason why we should be placed in a position different from other . . . Christian denominations each of whose doctrinal tenets are highly controversial.'[9] Here he was wrong. To a Protestant nation, orthodox Protestant propaganda or preaching was not controversial. Any who contested the centrality of the Trinity or the veracity of Holy Scripture or the Sabbath might and indeed often did provoke offence and give rise to discussion. Either way, Iremonger and CRAC behind him were not going to allow Reith to 'sell the pass' to the Christian Scientists. When the Director-General had offered Lothian the talk and refused the Sunday service, Lothian inisted that CRAC be consulted. In October it predictably endorsed Iremonger's view: no service and no seat on CRAC. On the weekday talks 'the committee tendered no advice'.[10] Reith felt the dilemma rather acutely; both 'establishments' were in danger of being offended and even alienated. This he could not afford.

Later, in May 1935, a 'memorial' was addressed to the Chairman by eleven members of both Houses of Parliament including Lord Airlie, the Astors and Lord Lothian. The grounds this time were that the BBC's decisions on all points 'contravened the principle of religious freedom'. The Board met and again offered the talks but not the service, just as Iremonger had suggested to the Director-General. Iremonger had yet another weapon: since they have appealed to Caesar, 'let them find a metaphysician of any standing who has ever taken (them) seriously.' This was not quite the point. Christian Science wanted consideration on the grounds of religious freedom, and of this Reith would not approve, however much he might have wanted to make a reasonable concession to Lothian and the Astors. Iremonger played this card with vision. The British Israelites had also been putting on the pressure. This movement had, as Iremonger reminded Reith, support by intelligent people in high places, but as with other sects and societies, it had been refused. This was consistent with BBC and CRAC policy.[11] The Church of England had first claim and the Roman Catholics and Nonconformists on the Committee accepted their less central position. The Christian Scientists were, however, far beyond the boundaries of orthodoxy and so were refused. Iremonger made his experience of Christian Science quite clear: they were 'insidious'. 'It would be possible for Christian Science to say nothing in a talk that would strictly speaking be controversial while all the time they would suggest by their "cures" the contention that they alone held the secret of the pure Gospel of Jesus Christ.'[12] The Board told Lothian that CRAC did not 'impose' a decision on the BBC as he had suggested. CRAC had a difficult task and could not see how Christian Science could be orthodox, but its advice was accepted by the Corporation. Lothian could be forgiven for regarding this as a discreet imposition. The letter finally claimed that no Christian body, not even the 'national church' is permitted to broadcast its own particular tenets no matter how important they are held to be. Not surprisingly, the critics in the church like Hensley Henson, and E. W. Barnes, the Bishop of Birmingham, and Sidney Mozely of the *Daily Herald* claimed that the BBC was broadcasting a religion of its own. It was 'essential' Christianity such as Reith had conceived from the beginning, or so he believed.

It is, of course, a matter of speculation as to whether the Governors would have been prepared to make any concession had Iremonger not been the spokesman of the churches in CRAC. Throughout BBC history, CRAC had defended an entrenched position from which it offered advice; the extent to which it 'imposed' it, as Lord Lothian claimed, is more than a semantic question. With Reith as Director-General and Iremonger in charge of religion, BBC religion was protected by a formidable armoury. It in turn was to protect mainstream orthodoxy from the minorities who clamoured at the door for a place on the airwaves; and there were as many as thirty which made applications of one kind or another and with a greater or lesser degree of influence. It is quite clear from the decisions made by CRAC that there were categories of approval. At one end of the scale the Strict Baptists were regarded as the most fundamentalist and strenuously sectarian branch of the Baptists in England. In response to their application the BBC was advised to accept a service on Sunday on the basis of merit and recommendation provided that they did not propagate, emphasize or elucidate their own identity or uphold Baptist 'strictness' on the air and during the service. Aubrey, himself an 'ordinary' Baptist, was not keen to recommend them: 'they regard ordinary Baptists pretty much as the Jews regard the Samaritans', albeit they did have some men of a recommendably high standard. The same applied to the Churches of Christ and the Brotherhood movement. At the other end were quite naturally the Freethinkers, the Ethical Society and the Rationalists, whose motivation was the refutation of the Christian message and whose complaint to the BBC was on grounds of freedom of speech. CRAC was unmoved; there was no question of such debates being organized either on Sunday or during the week. On Sunday it was not Christian and during the week it was controversial! The Moslems came into this category; they were anti-Christian and were therefore refused a broadcast of their services from a central London mosque.

Somewhere in the middle were those groups which emphasized a certain distance from the mainstream, e.g. the Christadelphians, who were refused because they did not belong to the Free Church Federal Council. On theological and controversial grounds, Spiritualism was refused, as was the Swedenborgian New Church since it did not recognize the deity of Christ as a central theological basis of its creed. Other groups such as Pacifists and Temperance enthusiasts were considered worthy but not actually allowed to speak, only to be spoken about. CRAC recommended that talks be given on the Oxford Group movement or psychic research rather than granting access to the representatives of such bodies to talk about themselves or defend their special tenets or promote their special identity. In the case of the Christian Scientists, as we have seen, the support of people in high positions naturally meant that the BBC's hierarchy would be accessible to such as the Marquis of Lothian and Lady Astor. The Greek Orthodox Church was also considered, but since its members in Britain were so few in number it was considered not appropriate to broadcast their services. However, a recital of Orthodox Church music might be considered. Like so many of these applicant groups, they commanded very little authority. There were, however, groups that did command sturdy support, for example the World's Evangelical Alliance, which in the early days made a successful overture and was granted a talk at the New Year by one of its supporters, among whom were many bishops and almost all the leaders of the Free Churches. It was a pan-Protestant rather than an ecumenical movement and had the support not only of churchmen but also of Members of Parliament.

B. The Unitarians

Two years before Iremonger arrived, CRAC had finally decided that the test for those wishing to broadcast officially should be no longer institutional but theological. Herbert Ward, the Roman Catholic on CRAC in the very early days, quite naturally felt that for all non-

Anglicans and non-Roman Catholics, attachment or affiliation to the Free Church Federal Council was no real test and he cited the Society of Friends, whose members did very occasionally broadcast. In 1931, CRAC decided that the test should be based rather on attitude to the deity of Christ than on institutional affiliations. This question had arisen in connection with the Christian Scientists but became particularly acute over the Unitarians, a body so nearly orthodox as to be almost acceptable.

Cyril Garbett was strongly against their having any time on the air, and was supported by the Committee. He did not approve of the presence of a Unitarian on the Belfast RAC and was irritated by Stobart's liberal attitude which considered them 'hardly distinguishable from other Free Churchmen'. Stobart did ask Garbett if he should unseat the Belfast Unitarian. Garbett told the BBC that it must do as it pleased and recognized that Unitarians 'come very near to orthodox Christianity . . . but there is a quite clear difference in the formularies of the churches'; the committee should 'not depart from the deity of Christ principle' . . . (which of course the Unitarians could not hold) . . . 'whatever the attitude of the BBC towards all such groups as Jews and Christian Scientists, etc'. 'If the BBC invites a Unitarian,' Garbett icily told Stobart, 'then CRAC will have nothing to do with it.'[13] Stobart saw nothing objectionable provided a Unitarian could avoid either a denunciation of the deity of Christ or expression of any anti-orthodox views, and would in any sermon emphasize those theological aspects which Unitarians held in common with the mainstream denominations. Garbett wanted to maintain the 'purity' and orthodoxy of CRAC and, because of this concern, forced Stobart and Reith (and later Iremonger) to make their own decisions. The BBC was confronted by a shade of Christianity which in many respects hardly differed from the orthodox or 'mainstream' churches but by which Garbett wished CRAC not to be sullied. The BBC had to decide on other grounds whether it should respond and take up an opinion on the Unitarian issue. Ironically, in view of the earlier discussion on whether the name of the advisory body should include the word Christian or religious, CRAC's concern was most firmly with Christian orthodoxy. Garbett could only force the BBC to advise itself – as it eventually did.

The Unitarian General Assembly (of Unitarians and Free Christian Churches) was told by Stobart in 1932 that he could not invite them to nominate preachers officially 'but we are always ready to consider suggestions for good broadcast preachers'. Recognizable broadcasting styles were more important than subtle theological issues which few could discern. Reith had always agreed that he saw no good reason why the Unitarians shouldn't do a studio service. Stobart found Garbett's attitude rather embarrassing. Iremonger later asked Reith, as Director-General; Reith thought Garbett would not object 'so long as he [the chosen Unitarian] doesn't unitarianize!'[14] He knew that Garbett's opposition forced the Corporation into a discourteous action against CRAC. In the event, the Committee was asked to renounce its interest in the BBC's (namely Iremonger's) invitation to a Unitarian. Garbett, however, accepted the difficulty of the theological test and felt there was a case for the simpler institutional test: membership of the Church of England, the Roman Catholic church or the Free Church Federal Council, especially as he thought that some Unitarians as individuals were hardly different 'from some of our own modernists – especially Congregationalists. The Unitarians definitely repudiate what Anglicans, Roman Catholics and Free Churches regard as essential.' He counselled that the BBC invite individuals and not representative Unitarians. Iremonger was thus able to invite Henry Gow of Manchester College, Oxford, to take a studio service. It was billed as a religious service and Dr Gow was obliged to hide his Unitarianism behind the microphone! Between 1934 and the beginning of the war there were about a dozen invitations to Unitarians, but the matter was not left to rest. There was a consistent lobbying by a Liberal MP among others and by a deputation from the Unitarian General Assembly which complained that the BBC's attitude was 'grudging admission at long intervals'. They were allowed an occasional broadcast which eventually became an annual service, but only from one of the regions.

Iremonger and his successors thought the Unitarians were hard pressed to find good preachers, and notwithstanding the overtures and pressures from such as Tom Driberg, MP, the standard BBC reply was simply that services were occasionally granted and that there was insufficient space for every group. Iremonger, meanwhile, had created a precedent in pushing for a Unitarian broadcast against the wishes of CRAC in the cause of high standards of Christian utterance; Gow was an excellent preacher (as was L. P. Jacks,[15] another well-known Unitarian and the hero of Dick Sheppard).

Iremonger and Reith, by going against CRAC and Garbett, did set an interesting new course. The BBC now had a religious policy quite outside and independent of the 'Christian' Advisory Committee; it was a policy on religion, whereas CRAC's policy was strictly Christian without being sectarian. However strongly Garbett wanted to have the BBC promulgate in services, talks and even general programme output a definite Christianity tied none too closely to any kind of denominationalism, his grasp of orthodoxy was equally strong; sectarianism and the various heresies propagated by diverse groups should not be acceptable to CRAC, which was in business to maintain Christianity, no matter how eclectic the variant 'orthodoxies' of the Church of England, the Roman Catholics and the Free Church Federal Council. The BBC was a Christian Corporation.

C. St Martin's-in-the-Fields

Perhaps nowhere was this 'eclectic orthodoxy' better experienced nationally than through the broadcasts from St Martin's-in-the-Fields each month. Since 1924 St Martin's had broadcast a regular service twice a month, and eventually once a month, with no efforts spared to ensure that it was taken without alternatives by the regions. Dick Sheppard had been the inspiration in these broadcasts. In Scotland, from 1929, there had developed a similar 'St Martin's' in the preaching of George MacLeod from St Cuthbert's Church, Edinburgh. Otherwise the regions were obliged to take the St Martin's service simultaneously, once a month. St Martin's was the spearhead of the BBC religious broadcasting policy which was, among other things, as Stobart explained to the North Region RAC 'to achieve a national unity of religious feeling and to secure the best preachers without regard to their denomination but their excellence and worthiness; it was to widen the sympathies of the public and to spread a broad general religious teaching.'[16] Garbett would by no means have cared for Stobart's definition, moving as it did from Christianity in particular to religion in general. However, Stobart made this emphasis clear to the North Region RAC which wanted more and more opportunity to respond to the pressure from local churches to broadcast from representative denominations instead of, as Stobart asked, from the main centres of the population. St Martin's was at the centre of this discussion. The RACs wanted an alternative on their own wavelength, and resented the compulsion to listen only to St Martin's.

Most strongly articulate of all were the Roman Catholics who, especially in the North and Midlands, were deeply resentful of the imposition of St Martin's uniformity. The BBC, by way of reply, complained that there were too few applications to broadcast by competent people. So many Roman Catholics, they were told, held the Corporation in such low regard that they would not treat broadcasting seriously. The North Region made a formal proposition for consideration by CRAC in March 1931, but a decision was constantly delayed. The Midland Region similarly resented this compulsion; some on the Committee regarded McCormick as by no means as universal in his appeal as Sheppard had been. Northern Ireland's Director, Beadle, was beset by the Presbyterians on the Committee who laboured the point that they comprised a third of the population; why should they remain obliged to take St Martin's? Beadle's constant observation and warning to Stobart had been that denominational balance could not be disregarded in any major area of the United Kingdom in the manner that it could be done in London. In 1934, the issue was brought before the Governors and they decided quite clearly against any alternative programme during the St Martin's service at 8.0 p.m. They would not yield to pressure for a 'brighter Sunday'.[17]

The services continued for almost two years more until late 1935, when Iremonger conducted a serious investigation through discussions and correspondence and considerable consultations in the regions. The matter had been postponed for three sessions of CRAC and could be no longer. Iremonger, in a note to Siepmann before the CRAC meeting in March 1936, clarified the reactions under four heads: (1) a general dislike of preferential treatment of one church; (2) Anglicans who objected to deviations from the Book of Common Prayer; (3) Noncon-formists who found the preaching insufficiently evangelical; and (4) a larger and mixed group who objected to the emphasis on the social and industrial implications of Christianity as against their more individual-istic approach, which Iremonger rather mistakenly regarded as gradually passing away. The only criticism he was prepared to accept was that in the opinion of some, St Martin's was not what it was and that since Sheppard and McCormick had enjoyed a good innings at St Martin's there was now a call for greater variety. Iremonger had no sympathy with ambitious Anglicans and jealous Nonconformists who resented the centrality and apparent privilege of the preference for St Martin's. 'It strikes me as one of the less refined forms of selfishness for church- and chapel-goers, after receiving spiritual sustenance in their own places of worship, to expect to get something exactly like it from us with hardly a thought of the enormous majority who are unattached and to whom the St Martin's services do stand, to put it at its lowest, for some kind of uplift in their lives.'[18]

Finding another regional St Martin's, one for each area, was not a good idea. Iremonger thought this suggestion by the regional Directors not helpful:

The churches-and-preachers whom we could trust completely with an SB [simultaneous broadcast] service can be numbered on the fingers of two hands ... I do not think there are half a dozen churches or chapels where one finds the atmosphere of simple and sincere devotion with good congregational singing which is the chief characteristic of St Martin's.

Iremonger was convinced of the importance of St Martin's and was not going to lose it.[19] Regional identity might have been to some extent at stake, but what irked him so strongly was that notwithstanding the opportunities which the regions enjoyed on their own wavelength three Sundays out of four, they should want even more, even to the extent of dismantling the witness of St Martin's and the singularly representative and special character of its service which had become familiar to so many. Iremonger, however, agreed that instead of Sheppard and McCormick having nine out of twelve sermons, this proportion could be changed somewhat; they could have five and invite visitors for the remaining seven. 'In this way we would secure a service of the "good popular" kind which to many, is no less important and profitable than the sermon,' he told CRAC.

The Committee accepted Iremonger's analysis. Fr Parker of Liverpool proposed an alternative but it gained no support. The centre had won a crucial contest over regional interests, the St Martin's service was and would continue to be the focus of the most successful regular Sunday BBC religious broadcast. The regions wanted to develop their own 'centres of excellence', and it was clear to Iremonger that St Anne's, Manchester, under Canon F. Paton-Williams and Carrs Lane Congregational Church in Birmingham under Leyton Richards, for example, would have made excellent alternatives; but it was a risk he would not take. Central control over religious policy was at stake and Iremonger was not prepared to let St Martin's be denied to the many thousands outside organized religion who listened to this one monthly service and very probably, to no other. St Martin's was only threatened in 1939 when the pressure to wean the Luxembourg public back to BBC programmes would propose a secular alternative during the Sunday evening service.

D. The Oxford Group Movement

Iremonger's first months at the BBC coincided with the growing influence of the Oxford Group Movement, established by Dr Frank Buchman and becoming significantly influential among leading churchmen. Iremonger received several requests from members of the Group to explain their beliefs on the radio. He was not at all impressed by this imported religious sect; however he recognized that the Movement had scored a number of hits among the leaders of the established churches, not to mention the leaders of the nation. Buchman, an American Lutheran minister, was known worldwide and had support from European and American churchmen. Among the former was Nathaniel Söderblom, who told Buchman in 1931 that 'the work that God has chosen you for doing cannot be too highly appreciated'.[20] Among those who shared an interest was L. W. Grensted, the Nolloth Professor of Philosophy of the Christian Religion at Oxford, who had become a good friend of Buchman and done a great deal of travelling for the Movement. In the foreword to *What is the Oxford Group?*[21] he was glad to recommend this anonymously written apologia for Group thinking; he wanted to help the image and increase the popular understanding of the Movement 'to bring home to them that challenge for which alone the fellowship stands'. In his introduction to *The Person of Christ*[22] Grensted acknowledged his debt to the Oxford Group; his recent experience, he felt, 'affected my presentation of a living Christianity . . . Bible and church alike have come to mean more and not less.' W. R. Matthews thought Grensted had been 'captivated' by the Movement and his theological precision impaired.[23] In October 1932, Buchman had been invited to Lambeth Palace with a hundred or so companions for high tea, followed by a service in the chapel. Lang thought it would convince them that the Church of England 'has no wish to cold-shoulder them'.[24] J. W. C. Wand, Dean of Oriel and future Bishop of London, had also given guarded support,[25] as did Fr D'Arcy, SJ, of Campion Hall, a member of CRAC. Requests had been made by the Movement to broadcast, although there is no record at this time of Buchman ever approaching Reith personally.

The issue came before CRAC in 1933, and in view of the ambiguity of the Movement's reputation and L. W. Grensted's public and bold association with it (and his reputation as a highly distinguished scholar), the Committee decided to invite him to take a studio service.[26] Iremonger wanted to avoid hearing an American speaker on the issues and had confidence in Grensted – he had broadcast before, in Manchester during 1922, and was accomplished at the microphone. In his talk in February 1934 he spoke of the attraction of the 'new honesty' and the challenge to sacrifice and find a new life arising out of the old. It was a kind of second conversion, calling Christians to present a united front to the severe problems of the world. Iremonger had offered him a free hand, as he was sure Grensted would 'not exceed the controversial limits we feel bound to impose'.

There were frequent attempts to have the BBC broadcast Group Movement propaganda and, in October 1934, CRAC decided that permission should not be granted to the Movement to have special services broadcast. There were, of course, very many dignitaries of the stature of Grensted who did support the Movement and who were at the microphone from time to time. This was permitted, provided there was no overt Group propaganda. Charles Raven and Evelyn Underhill gave qualified approval to the Movement in *The Meaning of the Groups*, published in 1934, which the Bishop of London, Winnington-Ingram, in a brief preface, thought the fairest account yet. Raven, another regular broadcaster for the Department, could admit of the leader, Buchman, that 'his power as an instrument for conversion remains his supreme endowment'. 'I am sure that Dr Buchman and his groups can infect men with the love of God.'[27] Raven was invited to the microphone again and again and regarded himself as a friendly critic of this Movement.

Reith had been much pressured during the Movement's London campaign in 1933. He told Lady Harrowby, who had written on its behalf asking for microphone publicity, that no such publicity could be given without a reply from its opponents. This very idea would be deemed controversial and thus against the BBC policy, because it would raise opposition in certain quarters and begin to open the door to sectarian access, which as yet the BBC was not prepared to give. He assured Lady Harrowby that supporters of the Movement among churchmen were often already at the microphone. The BBC avoided giving status or recognition to the Movement *qua* Movement; Movement it might be but denomination or sect it was not.

In 1935 the British Industries Fair was held at Castle Bromwich, and the Movement asked for a broadcast as Buchman was to make a speech. Dunkerly, Midland Regional Director, told Iremonger that he felt he should leave it firmly alone. Remarkably enough, the BBC were prepared to offer technical facilities to the Dutch Radio Corporation to re-transmit to the USA.[28]

In July 1937, *The Times* carried a number of letters, most notably one by Lord Salisbury, which encouraged people to write to the BBC and request publicity for the Movement's aims and methods. More pressure brought an item in a news bulletin under *Points from Today's Speeches*. The actress, Margaret Rawlings, was guest speaker at Catherine Foyle's literary lunch. Miss Rawlings sat next to Tom Driberg and in her speech attacked Buchman, who during lunch had spoken of personal confession and its value, a principal tenet of the Group's ideology. She remarked that this was 'psychic exhibitionism as indecent . . . as if someone took off all their clothes in Piccadilly Circus'.[29] Sir Cooper Rawson, MP, who had contributed to *The Times* correspondence in July, said the BBC was to blame for this attack on the Movement. He wrote to the Chairman, R. C. Norman, quoting Lang, who had been reported as saying that the Movement was doing what the church exists to do – change lives.[30] Norman made it quite clear to Rawson that the Movement would get news coverage if it was of general interest; otherwise specific requests for coverage would be referred to CRAC. This brought forth another storm and the matter, with all these local pressure points, came before CRAC in October. On a vote only half the members were in favour of a series of talks on evangelistic movements, of which the Movement could be one.[31] By 1938, the pressure was at last successful and in October a series of three objective talks on Moral Re-Armament was given by Sir Walter Moberly, Sir William Bragg and Lord Kennet, and gave rise to a lively correspondence in *The Listener* through to December. Finally, the BBC was persuaded to broadcast Buchman himself. The talk, *Chaos against God*,[32] went out on 27 November. Lord Salisbury was instrumental in persuading Ogilvie to grant the Earl of Athlone a broadcast on 1 December 1939. With the onset of World War II, the pressure would get even stronger to have Buchman's call broadcast more frequently. This resistance by both the RBD and the BBC hierarchy was to continue into the fifties and beyond.[33]

13

BROADCASTING STATISTICS:
DEFINING THE AUDIENCE

In 1936 Robert Silvey had been appointed to co-ordinate and strengthen the Corporation's methods of obtaining accurate information as to who exactly was listening to the programmes. There had been much discussion and dissension over the value of such research, particularly as methods were not easy to devise and the results were often a dubious foundation for programme making.[1] Not until the end of Iremonger's time did the issue have any significance. In July 1939 Silvey passed to the Department the first major report on the audience for religious broadcasts.[2] It was the first attempt at a reliable and scientifically calculated estimate of listening, contrasted with the guesswork of previous years among those who kept an eye on the press and an ear to the ground. Iremonger had essentially catered for the committed and recognized that, if his hopes for increased broadcasting of religious programmes during the week were to be fulfilled, his programmes would have to stand up to competition with others. Without the strong backing of Reith, the Department would, before the new decade was out, have to fight for space not on grounds so much of good religion but of good broadcasting, not always the same thing. As the methods and results of listener research became more accurate, the more subtle the task for all departments and certainly religion in particular. This first report was to show why. The 4,000 people who were log-keepers were, as Silvey admitted, 'keen listeners' who kept records of their listening during the four months from December 1938 to April 1939. Had these 4,000 been a more random sample of listeners, the general levels of response would have been lower.[3] The results of this exercise broadly confirmed that of all religious broadcasts, the Sunday evening services (in particular St Martin's) were the most popular, being listened to by a third of the sample. More listened to church services 'proper' than to services from studios, which were appreciated more by the middle classes than the working class who, in turn, listened rather more to Sunday morning services than did the middle classes, who might well have been in church anyway. W. H. Elliott's midweek service was again listened to by more working-class than middle-class log-keepers, and not surprisingly the numbers slumped when the alternative programme provided a boxing commentary! Rather surprisingly, the report discovered that most religious listening was done in the Western Region embracing Gloucestershire and from Portsmouth down to the Cornish coast. The report also showed that there were about thirteen per cent occasional and regular listeners to the Daily Service and again most of the occasional listeners were working-class. Moving from services to talks, the figures were discouragingly low but predictable: there were twice as many middle-class as working-class listeners, and the overall figure was around ten per cent of the total sample.

Church services and in particular those from St Martin's were widely listened to, as were Elliott's from Chester Square. 'Studio Religion', including talks and involving specially arranged music for 'recital', was not liked as much as congregational singing relayed from churches during their own service times. It is interesting that the report did not examine the response to the mid-week Evensong – especially suitable for radio, as the music was of a high quality and demanded no concentration upon a sermon. The report also indicated quite clearly that religious programmes, doubtless like other serious programmes, suffered badly from the competition of alternative programmes when these existed. The Sunday services, as we have seen, were still protected, and on the second Sunday of each month the St Martin's evening service itself was protected even from the competition provided by the alternative regional church services. In many parts of the country away from London, there was a higher concentration of listening to religious services than in the south, and not surprisingly the RACs had to be persuaded to forgo a regional church in favour of the London-imposed St Martin's or some other special service. Iremonger had fought to maintain the central influence of Broadcasting House and CRAC over urges in the regions to have their own local 'pulpit talent' brought to the microphone, and sometimes to the whole country. That is certainly how men such as Leslie Weatherhead became even more popular in the nation as a whole than they were in their own regions.

The report gave clear indications that the major group of listeners to the religious output after seventeen years of religious broadcasting were among the vast sector of the population not to be found in the churches. They were attracted by the unpretentious approach: familiar hymns and the popular and low-brow styles of religious utterance exemplified by nationally recognized broadcasters like W. H. Elliott and George MacLeod, among others. The report made clear that such utterance could overcome and counteract the tendency to switch off by those for whom religion normally provoked negative responses; it could, in a word, be 'entertaining'. It was not, however, a word the churches were easily able to acknowledge.

14

THE CENTRAL RELIGIOUS ADVISORY COMMITTEE: THE CONSTITUTION

Since the expansion of the Committee in 1931 there had been no change either of the members or of the constituencies. In 1938 Iremonger contemplated a revision of the constitution, and in February brought a proposal before CRAC that the 'central' members (as against the ex-officio members from the regions) should retire three at a time each year in order of seniority. The Chairman should retire every five years. (Garbett had often told Iremonger of his wish to retire – he had been Chairman since 1922.) The Committee was well aware that this was an innovation which threatened their influence over the policy discussions. Now that the notion of permanence was giving over to a rather more cyclical engagement of personnel, the Committee rather feared that relations with the churches would be 'less easy'.[1] Above all, Iremonger and Reith had always stressed the fact that since they were advisory, the members might be suggested by the churches in an unofficial way. The BBC 'appointed' the members and thus held the real power: they were not representatives. Reith's earlier policy was to have the top people in order to have the most authoritative access to the best preachers of any one denomination. With the coming of Iremonger and his connections with the churches, this function of CRAC as a 'preacher agency' became less important. At a meeting in March fifteen members 'approved' the changes by a dubious figure of five to three with the rest abstaining. The Governors approved it, and after some consultation around the regions, Iremonger sent around a draft Constitution which made the relationships clear: the Religious Director was to be indisputably in control and the regional committees would work 'in co-operation' with the Central Committee. Decisions by the latter were binding on the former 'save where local customs or interests suggest that divergence is desirable'.[2]

Before the March vote, Iremonger had complained to Nicolls, the Controller of Programmes, as often before, that many of the permanent members never turned up at all! Some were handicapped by age; others were simply not interested in broadcasting and were there, as in the early days, merely to act as a 'buffer between the Corporation and the churches'. This would not do. The new constitution included the provision that failure to turn up for more than two meetings 'without good reason' meant the sack! Iremonger was clear that he wanted his successor in a stronger position than hitherto with regard to the formation of broad policy outlines. It was not enough to have the support of Garbett.[3] Iremonger wanted younger men who were in touch with other younger men whose religious outlook would be of greater service to the Committee and Corporation than those who had been there for so long simply to secure their share of broadcasts. (This motivation was never to be absent from the Committee.) Iremonger wanted CRAC to assist not essentially in the formation of policy but in the working out of a policy already framed. It was not a matter of wresting power from CRAC so much as a new expectation of how it would enable the churches to respond to initiatives by the Corporation. The Corporation was developing a clear identity in its religious 'convictions' which would increasingly give CRAC a role as a link between the Corporation's Board of Governors and the churches. This was the church in a new arena – in a quite new 'missionary' situation, not so much amid the heathen but alongside an established and powerful body which organized and administered a mass communication machine the implications of which few could imagine, least of all those in the churches and sometimes not even within the Corporation itself.

For the 'representing' churchmen on CRAC, the meeting of March 1939 brought a threat to almost the last formal vestige of protection, the time of the Sunday evening broadcast service hour. The two evening services, one national and the other regional, offered no alternative except of denomination. Only very rarely would an Anglican national broadcast be accompanied by similar services on the regional programmes near or within range. Nicolls wanted an alternative to religious services just at the times when significant numbers were listening to Normandie and Luxembourg and the press was campaigning for 'brighter Sundays'.[4] Would CRAC accept the regional service at 5.30 so that an alternative programme could at last be provided – appropriate, of course, to the BBC Sunday policy? Predictably the Chairman was against it and so were most of the Committee. Iremonger, too, thought that now in the circumstances of national crisis the BBC religious service was an act of 'national witness and recognition which no other country undertook'; furthermore there would be great resentment by the clergy at such a change. An ironical impasse. The Committee did not think that the people listening to Radio Normandie would be attracted by the BBC 'Sunday policy secular alternative' so the case was not proven. The Committee was not ready to look at the evidence of figures, and contended that 'there was no evidence of a desire for a change among listeners'.[5] Guy Rogers of Birmingham and Dr Scott Lidgett moved that it was in the best interests of religion 'that the present arrangement should continue'. The churches were being asked to accept an innovation which went directly against their Sunday interests and attitudes, and to recognize that broadcasting now had religious objectives of its own. The charges of 'BBC religion' would inexorably take shape as the Corporation judged for itself the potential audience for religious programmes. The difference was simply that what the Corporation thought might be good for the listener, CRAC believed was not so good for the nation.

15

THE END OF AN ERA:
REITH AND IREMONGER RETIRE

Much to the astonishment of the outside world and the churches, Reith retired from the BBC in June 1938.[1] He was to go somewhat unwillingly to Imperial Airways and thence to the Ministry of Information. Within less than a year, Iremonger was to retire – his asthma was increasingly troublesome and, as he later put it, his 'boss had gone'. Just before Reith departed, Iremonger confessed to him that he had never been trusted by anyone so much as by Reith, and that whatever good had come from the religious work was largely what Reith had drawn out of him. Iremonger could not work under Reith's successor and through Garbett's influence went to the Deanery at Lichfield, notwithstanding his aversion to the liberal Bishop Edward Woods. He told Reith how thankful he was that six years earlier he had chosen the BBC instead of going with Garbett to the Deanery at Winchester: 'You and my first rector are the only two people I can think of who seemed to understand me at once and always.'

For several years Reith had been uncertain about his life as Director-General; it is interesting that at different times over the years he had sought advice from Lang, Bell and Temple.[2] Lang, on hearing of Reith 'being restless at the BBC', told him that he had a Christian duty to stay there for a time – the talk 'reconciled me to staying with the BBC for a bit'.[3] From his scrapbook it is easy to see how Reith cherished the warm responses the announcement of his retirement evoked.[4] Garbett wrote, 'I don't think we overestimate the influence the BBC has had on religion. I believe it has been the most effective antidote to secularism . . . and without your conviction and courage, the wireless might have become mere entertainment.' And not only the religious programmes were appreciated; Sidney Berry of the Congregational Union was grateful not only because Reith gave the churches their chance to 'get their message across' but for the 'tone of the programmes for which we owe you so much'. Lang was sorry that he would be no longer there to uphold his high ideals and the Baptist Aubrey speculated that 'if Britain ever had to turn to a dictator, John Reith would be the man for the job'. He was, as everybody knew, an outstanding Protestant of the twentieth century.

What had worried Aubrey, and many more staunch Protestants, was exacly who would take his place. As Briggs explains, the main contenders were Graves, now Deputy Director-General, and Sir Stephen Tallents, Controller of Public Relations. Graves was a Roman Catholic, as everyone knew, and had come in for 'considerable abuse' from the Protestants when Reith had made him Controller of Programmes in 1935. The 'Protestant Alliance' had appealed to the Governors for Graves to behave like a Protestant and not 'insinuate his bias towards Roman Catholicism in censorship and supervision'. They even wanted him to reply to a questionnaire; if he refused it would be a tacit admission he was not fit for the job. Even Aubrey, hardly a Protestant extremist, had expressed his concern to Reith on behalf of Free Churchmen that 'Roman Catholics are securing . . . appointments to all sorts of key appointments; but I am not afraid of them running away with the BBC so long as you are there.' Reith, for all his avowed Presbyterianism, was never so imbued with the Protestant neurosis about what Iremonger often called 'Romanism'. He once told Jerrold, the Editor of Eyre and Spottiswoode, a Roman Catholic, that he admired the Catholic Church for its authoritarian approach to doctrine provided it was not disposed to write off a man who endeavours to live by Christ's teaching and yet is bewildered by the church's theology.[5] Poor Graves was even abused by the Rationalist Press Association, usually rampant against the abuses of extremists. On this occasion they, ironically, joined their ranks, warning their readers that 'Roman Catholics are notorious for their intolerance' and that anxiety about the new Controller was justified! Now that Reith was leaving and the press was putting Graves forward as his successor, the Protestant lobby became even more vocal. The Women's Protestant Union complained that there would only be more prominence given to the Roman Catholics. Sir Thomas Inskip, a leading supporter of the Protestant Truth Society and other Sabbatarian causes, wrote to the Postmaster General hoping there would be 'no chance of Graves, a Roman Catholic, being put in charge of one of the biggest education systems in the country'. Inskip was President of the National Church League, another right-wing Protestant body, and, encouraged by its President, it wrote to Lang with the same complaint. Graves was described by J. A. Kensit of the Protestant Truth Society as 'a pervert to the Church of Rome'. Iremonger had got on well with Graves, finding him an ally in his concern for the place of religion and particularly of Christianity in broadcasting policy.[6] (In the event the choice fell upon neither Graves nor Tallents, but upon F. W. Ogilvie.)

On Iremonger's retirement Charles Raven hoped that the church would find 'some means of making use of his unique and very valuable experience'. But this hope was largely unfulfilled. However at the end of his six years he bequeathed to his successor a wide range of programmes, some with mass appeal, others aimed at small minorities, some distinctively denominational, others non-confessional in style; the services from St Martin's contrasted sharply with the distinct identities of the Salvation Army and the weekly Cathedral Evensong at either end of the range. He had established teaching courses on popular Christianity through the Sunday afternoon talks and through the series of sermons to deliver which an increasingly select and recognizable group of clergy were invited. The radio brought to clergy already popular within their denomination an even wider fame. Above all, Iremonger had put the growing Corporation in touch with an increasing number of radical but not revolutionary churchmen from all the 'mainstream' churches.

Iremonger and Garbett were an excellent team with a single objective, which was to strengthen the faith of the churches and the Christian knowledge of the committed.[7] They were determined to give a true picture of the relevance and stature of the Christian religion to the widest possible public which after 1933 (apart from Roman Catholics[8]) attended places of worship in smaller and smaller numbers, whatever other forms their allegiance to Christianity in Britain might take. As broadcasting wavelengths increased, so did the scope for recognizing regional aspects, even though by and large Reith and CRAC, more firmly Protestant since 1931, wanted a greater sense of unity displayed at the cost of both regional and confessional variations. Iremonger wanted every skill and aspect of broadcasting brought into play for the Christian faith and its mission. Hence the development of a teaching programme on Sunday afternoons which brought some of the best exponents of the complex issues in biblical and systematic theology to the microphone. Iremonger appointed Ellis Roberts, the biographer of H. R. L. Sheppard, to review books regularly. The scope was exceedingly wide and reflected every aspect of religious study, both Christian and occasionally outside. Iremonger wanted young speakers, and in the notable series *The Church I Look For* encouraged criticism and intelligent reflection from the rising generation. He also saw the public relations aspect of broadcasting and the necessity to present the Christian witness in its best light, from the integrity of sacrificial commitment to projects like the Iona Community under George MacLeod. He wanted the intelligent listener to construe a balanced picture of church and faith and not be left only with the impression of historic piety and liturgy to which a relatively small section of the community were committed. Like Sheppard, he wanted the post-war failure of the churches to be met by the clear advances in the thinking of churchmen of all kinds, men who were able to articulate the questions which many outside the ranks of committed Christians were still asking, about spirituality and about society, about new political movements and the deep changes taking place in society. Against the wishes of CRAC he resisted the temptation to protect Christian institutions from the increase in social and intellectual mobility – of which broadcasting was the most significant development beside the motor vehicle.

The development of broadcasting and of leisure-time pursuits went hand-in-hand as people were increasingly free to travel. They were no longer imprisoned in their own localities on Sundays. Churchgoing thus became increasingly one option among others; a Sabbatarian outlook prevailed less and less. Iremonger clearly recognized this trend and tried gently to shift the centre of gravity in religious broadcasting from Sunday to weekdays, and thus reflect the changing interests of radical clergy like Temple in making religion intelligible and attractive in a non-liturgical presentation. In this connection, the institution of a weekday Evensong was regarded very highly and accorded with Iremonger's concept of 'impersonality', which he believed was appropriate to the medium. Evensong embodied the sounds of the Christian cultus and was made all the more appealing by virtue of its aesthetic aspect. In contrast with this impersonality was the endless array of invited clergy from up and down the land. Iremonger tried to reduce the numbers but also to improve the quality, both theological and stylistic. By searching out and encouraging a few well-known apologists, he brought the BBC into special relation with the churches. Garbett gave his support, since he recognized the problems for the rising generation of clergy in the wake of the post-war decade, and also that the clergy were generally poorly trained in pulpit utterance.

In fact, most had no training at all nor wished for it. Iremonger's task was to find preachers who had that special facility, style and insight, which made for an accomplished confidence at the microphone. Men who displayed such skills in their respective localities were likely to be brought from their pulpit to a BBC studio and used again and again. The problem was to find such men; Iremonger was effectively but not entirely on his own. He was not only concerned to find men who were, by the standards of oracular excellence, good preachers. He had to consider theology, denomination and the subtleties of utterance in the language of popular faith and churchmanship. He could not be everywhere at once and thus had to rely upon the programme directors and staff of the regional offices and in some cases the Regional Director himself. Their task was to find the best churches, choirs and preachers and, not surprisingly, some that were thought to be swans in the regions, Iremonger regarded as geese. He needed an assistant and after much exertion the Controllers approved – without spelling out with any precision what his duties would be.[9] The office in London, however, was not the only BBC religious broadcasting operation: there were the regions, each with its particular identity. Religion in many cases tended to be the poor relation.

As Professor Briggs has explained, the regions in the thirties had few specialist executive staff, and people were expected to be adaptable. This is not the place to examine the developing regional policy of the Corporation up to the outbreak of war,[10] except to note that during Iremonger's period, in 1936, Siepmann's *Report on Regions* on the Corporation's regional policy had clear implications for the Corporation's religious policy. It wanted the regions to contribute to the nation as a whole as well as to reflect themselves to themselves. Siepmann believed that the regions were the 'seed ground of talent and the ultimate source of supply for our London programmes'.[11] Such talent, however, was by no means sufficiently adapted to the wider audience. This was precisely Iremonger's problem. From the beginning of broadcast church services (as contrasted with those in a studio) the concept of 'production' had been emerging. BBC staff wanted to see that the clergy gave their best; but this was only possible if they would submit to the peculiar disciplines of microphone speaking. Iremonger wanted more than 'hints' to Sunday speakers – he knew there were rules. It was not merely a matter of finding the reputedly good clergy; they also had to be 'trained', prepared and 'produced' for broadcasting. He could not be everywhere at once.

There was another hindrance: if religion was the half-hearted responsibility of a regional director or someone less prestigious, the local clergy would not regard their commitment to their local Advisory Committee quite so seriously. The Corporation would be open to the further criticism that it was not concerned with regional religious initiatives and by implication, that the metropolitan output was all that mattered. Iremonger, for his part, claimed that regional broadcasters were more anxious to reflect and articulate local characteristics than to contribute to a single Christian utterance marked neither by denominationalism nor regionalism.

The most notorious were the Scots! Siepmann thought their 'self-consciousness' was best left alone.[12] They were in a very strong position, however, because Reith had appointed Melville Dinwiddie as the Scottish Regional Director. He was a Church of Scotland minister; he had been a chaplain in the First World War, where he had served with Reith and been decorated for his bravery. Religion in Scottish broadcasting affairs was all the more perceptively organized. The Church of Scotland in the main supported the BBC religious policy but wanted it, in Scotland at any rate, more subject to the decisions of the General Assembly. Reith consistently maintained that finally it was the BBC that appointed members of its advisory committees.[13] When other denominations complained, as they frequently did, that the Church of Scotland was overrepresented on the Scottish RAC, Dinwiddie argued, much to Iremonger's irritation, that 'We have to make a distinction between those denominations that are essentially Scottish and others that are branches in Scotland.'[14] Dinwiddie believed the Daily Service was too Anglican by half and campaigned to have Scotland represented in the broadcast, and for mention of hymn numbers from the Scottish *Church Hymnary*. 'It will require all our artillery to make him [Iremonger] capitulate,' said Dinwiddie.[15] Some Scottish Presbyteries thought the Scottish output too restricted and one went to the trouble of complaining to the General Assembly. Dinwiddie questioned whether it was the function of broadcasting to teach theology; it should 'enable listeners to share in the worship of the church'.[16] People like George MacLeod of St Cuthbert's succeeded supremely in his services designed to appeal to the indigenous Christianity in the non-churchgoing public. But Dinwiddie was disappointed that so many of his colleague ministers resented the dominance of men like MacLeod. He commanded considerable public interest in connection with his work at Iona,[17] and his services from St Cuthbert's, in Edinburgh had been the Scottish equivalent of St Martin's in London.

It was clear to Iremonger towards the end of his term that Scotland at any rate put distinct limits on the amount of control that would be accepted from London in the religious output. The Church of Scotland's General Assembly stood as firmly behind the Scottish Advisory Committee as did Lambeth Palace (perhaps more discreetly) behind CRAC. Elsewhere, however, the situation was not at all satisfactory. In the Midlands the Secretary of the RAC was an outsider not on the BBC staff, Canon Stuart Morris; in 1937 he followed Dick

Sheppard into the Peace Pledge Union and all but abandoned his interest in broadcasting. A staff member was urgently needed.[18] At an earlier meeting of the Committee, in February 1937, there was the suggestion of a 'religion scout', perhaps borrowed from Geoffrey Dearmer's early 'scouting' for Iremonger before he took up the children's work. They had a local barrister in mind. In the Western Region, religion was the 'Cinderella of the programme department' simply because of staff shortage. Iremonger thought the quality of the output well below standard. He wanted people to give their whole time. In Wales and Northern Ireland E. R. Appleton and G. Beadle, the Regional Directors, had both organized the religious programmes as best they could. Appleton was particularly committed, but his positon had become difficult when his *Silent Fellowship* programmes were dropped. A seventy-year-old retired Major, Edgar Jones, took over the organization of the religious programmes on a part-time basis.[19] There was a full-time man in the North Region, Holgate Morris. Iremonger believed that this should be the case throughout the country; ideally there should be a specialist, in other words a cleric: 'We are barely scratching the surface of the religious work in the regions' – it was time that the religious output kept pace with the gradual expansion of the regional developments. Iremonger wanted above all a man of imagination: 'There must be a good groundwork of religion in him . . . and not a "crusted" worshipper.' He had prepared the ground for an assistant in London and his successor would no doubt take advantage of it. The Controllers' meeting had approved the idea in July 1938. With the coming of war, however, the notion of regional emphasis would be quickly superseded by the single wavelengths.[20]

Iremonger had succeeded in convincing the Executive and Reith above all that the reputation of the Corporation was at stake; if the Corporation was to be accused of purveying its own style of religious utterance that image could only substantially be negative so long as poor quality sermons continued to arrive on the national wavelengths from regions which were anxious to have their place in the national output. Possible improvement might have come about if the churches had recognized the technological and engineering potential in rediffusion: relaying a church to the churches. He thought it a lost opportunity that the clergy and churches were not open to the visiting, unseen preacher. The Bishop of Ripon had proposed a scheme in the mid-thirties, but CRAC was not interested; it wanted no part in such artificiality. It believed strongly in the value of broadcast services for invalids and the housebound; in these cases the impossibility of physical participation was obvious; but for the churches themselves to substitute the loudspeaker for the living voice was, predictably, too much to expect.

Iremonger remained as Director until April 1939, much longer than he had expected. It was by no means easy to find a competent and suitable replacement. Both he and Reith had begun to look for one as early as October 1937. (In view of the confidence Reith had in Iremonger, it is fair to assume that Iremonger knew of Reith's intentions and wished to leave at about the same time.) In January Reith consulted Lang, who suggested Leslie Hunter (later Bishop of Sheffield). Reith was certain now that he wanted a priest of the Church of England; before Iremonger's appointment he had not been quite so sure. Lang had earlier suggested Sir Walter Moberly, John Maud, a Fellow of University College, Oxford, and Hugh Johnston, Rector of Cranleigh, who had effectively brought the Daily Service into operation back in 1928. Temple was also consulted; it was clearly to be a Church of England appointment. Many names were put forward, but not one candidate of all the Anglican clergy, high or low, was both suitable and willing. Nicolls in some desperation wrote to both Oxford and Cambridge University Appointments Committees for suggestions. Parsons, he lamented, were reluctant to abandon familiar work and preachers their reputations. There had to be balance; only theoretically could the man be a layman – better for him to be in orders and an Anglican.[21]

In August 1938 Hunter finally refused the position, regarding the job as 'too limiting'. He did, however, recommend an acquaintance, one James Welch, the thirty-eight-year-old principal of St John's Training College in York, who was an education specialist. (He had done post-graduate work as an anthropologist in Nigeria, and had broadcast in the series *Life among Native Tribes* in 1932.[22]) Welch had met Iremonger, for some minor programme discussion, late in August. Iremonger was soon sure they had the right man and asked Lang to persuade him. He did:

> I regard the post of Religious Director as one of the very greatest importance in the religious life of our country. It is difficult to exaggerate the influence which broadcasting has had and may still have in that religious life . . . what a misfortune it would be if the appointment could not be kept in the hands of the Church of England.[23]

Lang wanted an Anglican to maintain that 'tone and ideal' which he naturally assumed to be the Christian outlook established and sustained in the nation by the Church of England. They were fortunate to have found not so much a typical parish priest as an exceptional one, one who was also an educationalist. Iremonger told Lang that he was 'an ideal man', and to Lang's relief, Welch accepted the post in September 1938.[24]

PART THREE

WAR 1939–45
NATIONAL CHRISTIANITY
AND THE CHURCHES

16

NEW APPROACHES: JAMES WELCH

As Welch took up his responsibilities in April 1939, with the title of Director of Religious Broadcasting, the war clouds were already gathering. He wanted religious broadcasting to take initiatives in two quite major directions. On numerous occasions he was to examine his role both as a priest of the Church of England and as a servant of the Corporation which had, he believed, given him this particular environment in which to exercise both types of ministry. That he was paid by the BBC was almost immaterial. He felt called to exercise this bi-polar ministry and therefore committed, as had Iremonger been before him, both to reflect and to influence the churches; to use broadcasting to discipline them to see the implications of the medium more clearly. In June, almost as soon as he was installed, he called together a notable group of associates including Oliver S. Tomkins, General Secretary of the SCM, Professor T. S. Boase, Principal of the Courtauld School of Art, Donald Soper of Kingsway, Eric Fenn and Geoffrey Dearmer. They were to discuss how Sunday in wartime could be used 'for the kingdom of God and the British nation'. It was 'all to the good', the group decided, that the strict puritan Sunday should no longer be enforced. Notwith-standing Donald Soper's suggestion that the breakdown of Sunday had meant that 'serious reading' had disappeared, Sunday in broadcasting should be significantly different and 'restore depth to life in all its range including the cultural and recreational'. This was perfectly in accord with the traditional concept of the BBC Sunday, but without that strenuous protective cover that CRAC had for so long maintained. With a single programme for the whole country, that would no longer be possible. Indeed, in early June the Control Board had decided to 'disregard the advice of the Religious Advisory Committee on the question of secular alternatives to Sunday services'.

Welch was also determined to carry on Iremonger's tradition of not allowing the broadcast sermon to be a random affair over which the BBC had no control. He wanted to avoid a succession of Sunday services with sermons again and again on the war issue. What was good for this or that local congregation on a single Sunday was not good for the general audience week after week. The local congregation got something out of it; the general audience did not. So, again in June 1939, Welch had called together a further group to discuss the whole notion of the broadcast sermon as a course of instruction over a period; this group included J. S. Whale, W. R. Matthews, Leslie Hunter, and the Baptist, F. Townley Lord. The clergy invited to take part would have to submit to a BBC 'lectionary discipline'; a smaller number of preachers and courses planned in advance would avoid the fault often complained of, that most sermons were roughly the same – extolling courage and faith and offering mostly consolation but little challenge. This was Welch's overall consideration: Christianity must challenge both church and nation alike, especially the latter, through testimony to the relevance and value of Christian tradition. Broadcasting was a means for the church to renovate its public image on a hitherto unimagined scale. Welch's group agreed that the BBC's image simply did not offer challenge, and Whale thought that only the Roman Catholics gave expression to the 'deep evangelical truths of the faith'. They all agreed that a course of sermons would be excellent even if this raised the question yet again of the BBC's initiative; was the BBC merely to 'reflect the average life of the churches or could it or should it give a lead in evangelism?'[1]

Welch wanted the Bible to speak in all its relevance as, he believed, it did not normally do in the congregations and certainly did not do among non-churchgoers. C. H. Dodd was invited to head a group to investigate the 'recovery of the sense of the Bible as more than "good literature", using perhaps modern translations'. But even after a couple of sessions, George MacLeod had come to a 'staggering conclusion'; that if a group of eminent clerics including W. R. Matthews and C. H. Dodd found it difficult to discern 'the essential devotional or practical message in a short passage, what do we expect the laity to do when we give them a lectionary?!' It was a paradox indeed. If the taxi-driver or postman did actually read the Bible, should the group regrettably assume that 'it is closed to him unless he has our background in biblical scholarship'?[2] Welch wanted even more: not only should the BBC do more than simply reflect the shoddy performance of the churches in liturgy, apologia, lesson and sermon; it should undertake a full-blown National Mission – it should act for the churches. His report on the group's meeting concluded with a tone of lament that whilst the churches should have taken the initiative, they had not. Perhaps they would support and 'undergird the work of broadcasting by better worship'. Welch was to develop a grand plan for a National Mission which gained him considerable support within the Corporation but finally amounted to an initiative of the Religious Broadcasting Department (henceforth the RBD) on its own.[3] To overcome the popular prejudice against all things parsonic, Jack C. Winslow, a well-known Anglican, had been to see Lang at Lambeth and suggested that the BBC should side-step the clerical preachers and engage eminent laymen whose names would carry weight. Lang warmly approved, particularly as the Oxford Group movement[4] embraced a number of eminent laymen who were speaking out on the questions of the day, and the moral heritage which should be exploited to meet today's challenges. Welch told Lang in June that each should be chosen on his merits, 'and not merely to tell the world that Buchman has got all the best men'.[5] Welch was anxious to have advice from a more sympathetic group than the too 'official' CRAC, and was convinced that the task of any religious initiative in broadcasting was to lead: Christianity itself should lead both church and nation towards deeper commitment.

With the outbreak of hostilities, long-standing preparations for a single programme for the whole nation without regional alternatives were put into force.[6] War conditions began on 1 September and the Religious Department moved to Bristol where, in October, CRAC was to meet for the only time in its history without any member of the administrative hierarchy present. The Department was now increased by the addition of Rev. Eric Fenn, a Presbyterian, responsible particularly for talks, and Cyril V. Taylor, an Anglican and an accomplished musician, for services. In November Welch wrote to Nicolls that 'we are broadcasting under ideal conditions from the Lady Chapel of Bristol Cathedral', and that the services had gained in atmosphere and quality. The Daily Service, evening weekday service and the Epilogue all came from this chapel and were signal evidence for Welch that the best BBC 'studio' was a church.

With the growing Polish crisis in late August the contribution of the Religious Department had begun to increase; short intercessions were offered following the 9 o'clock News. By the outbreak of war there were three evening services during the week. In addition to the three Sunday services, the Thursday evening service from Elliott's church, and the 'fixed point' of the Daily Service, there were now services on Tuesday and Saturday evenings. CRAC wanted this increased to a service every weekday, with special emphasis upon the interpretation of biblical material to encourage hope and fortitude. Welch himself was not keen on this and did not support the Committee – one of the early indications of his divergence from his advisers. He would only want such a regular weekday space if or when there were massive casualties and widespread suffering. (As is well known, notwithstanding the declaration of war, the country enjoyed in large measure a 'lull before the storm' until the following May, when the *Blitzkrieg* began in earnest.)

In addition to services, the number of religious talks increased and notable divines such as William Temple and J. H. Oldham gave talks on aspects of the war. Religion, they claimed, was a crucial ingredient in understanding the tasks and objectives now facing the nation. These talks were designed to evoke the responses of those who listened so that they might conceive the conflict in the perspectives of ideology and history.

During December, Nicolls offered Welch a space for a religious talk to 'compensate' for the loss of one period on Sunday afternoon. It was agreed that these should be quite distinct from the Sunday afternoon 'church' talks which anticipated an audience drawn from the committed. Welch believed that 'the sheer relentless logic of deep thinking about our present situation leads inevitably – and it must be inevitable if this is God's world – to the Christian solution'.[7] The example was set by the writer and rather well-known Marxist/Pacifist, John Middleton Murry, who gave the first group in the Friday series of talks on *Europe in Travail* but did not mention the Christian solution until the sixth and final talk![8]

By December, outside broadcasts had been generally resumed[9] and religious services gained in popular repute; there had been a definite distaste for the studio service. The Protestant emphasis predictably remained very strong, and became even stronger with the onset of the first winter of the war and the problems of blackout.

A. Roman Catholics

In view of the difficulty of 'blacking-out' churches for use at night, Hinsley asked Ogilvie for a broadcast Midnight Mass for Christmas 1939 from Downside Abbey in Somerset. It was agreed, even by Garbett, who was set against any sacramental broadcasting! Many Catholics, however, wondered if the broadcast Mass was 'efficacious in all respects including the gaining of indulgences', as one correspondent put it.[10] The Cardinal replied that as long as the church required bodily presence even more than the ability to hear, presence was crucial. Even if people were prevented for 'grave reasons', still no alternative was allowed. If listening to the wireless assisted in uniting people in spirit with their parish church, all to the good – an ecclesiastical pronouncement to this effect was not necessary. Such a positive pronouncement, the Cardinal feared, would do harm to 'ill-instructed Catholics who might imagine that they fulfilled their obligation merely by listening-in'.[11]

Whilst Welch was delighted with the Mass from Downside, he was aware that there would be an 'ugly outburst' from the Protestant underworld. The Protestant Truth Society complained that the BBC was giving 'facilities to the emasculated Italian religion', and reminded the new Director-General, Frederick Ogilvie, that 'the men from the bulldog British breed come not from priestly incantations but from the Bible'. 'Would the Italian Broadcasting Authorities broadcast an English Nonconformist service?', they asked. The BBC emphasized that at midnight only the deeply committed would actually listen, and average Protestants would benefit from a musical experience which they would not readily associate with their own forms of worship.

With an authentic Latin broadcast for Roman Catholics given in the spirit of a concession from both the sacramental and the engineering points of view, CRAC could now emphasize the problem of the single wavelength in wartime and that 'all other' Roman Catholic services should make 'a more general contribution to the broadcasting of the Christian religion in these times of stress', as Welch wrote to John Murray, SJ, of Farm Street, who had recently become D'Arcy's second on CRAC. Welch explained the new situation; the regular Roman Catholic broadcast services (both regional and national) were to be reduced from thirty to six. They would have one full forty-five minute Sunday service in English from a studio, and a twenty-minute service 'by and for Roman Catholics only' on one Friday in each month; and lastly, once in every six weeks the Roman Catholics would supply a preacher for the midweek service (hitherto Elliott's preserve) from Bristol Cathedral Lady Chapel. (Hinsley regarded this as an 'elegant studio'.)[12] Welch wanted the regular Catholic afternoon service to be Vespers – he thought it would be a great opportunity through broadcasting to educate Catholics into Catholic liturgical renewal. The war, however, made things difficult for the Catholics who, on their side, pressed for increases in broadcasting time.

The BBC refused on the grounds that denominational broadcasting was to be encouraged even less than in peacetime. Roman Catholics were credited with little patriotic fervour and when, in a news item in early 1939, this seemed to be implied, the BBC had had to apologize to Cardinal Hinsley in *The Universe*, and thus drew the teeth of the Protestant Truth Society.

Before very long, however, Hinsley lobbied the Director-General on the proportion of broadcasts given to Roman Catholics. He was aware that the BBC would go on calculating this proportion on the basis of three million out of 42 million and thus seven or eight per cent of the broadcast services. Welch and Nicolls recommended to Ogilvie that the calcuation should be based on the listening figures and above all on 'good broadcasts with a message'. Welch admitted that it was difficult to find good Catholic preachers, and they had to use the stars such as Martindale who attracted a comparable listening figure to W. H. Elliott during the midweek service. Furthermore, these services by the stars were not recognizably Roman Catholic – only the Midnight Mass was not in English and only the monthly Friday service was explicitly for Roman Catholics. Welch was decisive and confident of the Director-General's reply to the Cardinal:

> I hope we shall not discuss this question on the basis of figures; if the Cardinal can supply prophets who can (a) broadcast well, (b) give us services in English which will help all listeners and (c) say prayers properly and not gabble through them, . . . we shall use them.[13]

In other words, the country now at war was Christian and fighting for a Christian ideal, and no matter how persuasively the Cardinal and the Catholic press might lobby for a calculation based on church membership numbers, the BBC would not admit of this distinction.

Hinsley's other argument from numbers claimed strength from the Roman Catholics in the British Empire, especially Australia. This cut no ice with the Corporation. Since neither the Roman Catholics or CRAC nor the Nonconformists had complained, Welch thought the matter should rest. From the beginning, the Roman Catholics had complained of censorship and that the 'production' of services, sermons and talks was perilously close to censorship or at least the chipping away of the cutting edge of the Roman Catholic message. Since the war, the emphasis had been upon broadcasting the Christian religion, and thus paying rather less regard to the pressures for denominational chracteristics and confessional identities. As for bringing priests together to discuss the broadcasting of Catholic services, D'Arcy's resistance was simply that in view of the immense criticism by Roman Catholics of BBC policy, nothing should be done to suggest that the BBC was making covert attempts to recruit priests for the microphone and force a BBC discipline upon the 'matter and method' of religious broadcasting, no matter how poorly it was thought many Roman Catholic preachers performed at the microphone.

D'Arcy was aware of the constant fear of 'broadsides against Catholic doctrine' by the Protestants within or stimulated by the BBC. D'Arcy recalled later to Welch in September 1943 how things had improved since Stobart's day, when Martindale had to manoeuvre for position and obtain the best Catholic interests in programmes. He thought the situation was excellent under Welch and not the least because of the firm support of Cardinal Hinsley. D'Arcy knew that if services other than the Mass were broadcast, the emphasis would be upon preachers and sermons – as with the Protestants – and that raised another problem of balancing the speakers and not having one 'party' within the church 'cornering the wireless', as he put it. The regular Friday services for Roman Catholics were not altogether satisfactory, and the *Catholic Herald* was running a campaign for the regular broadcasting of the Mass. Friday afternoons were not worth the licence money, they thought. The paper complained that English language was insisted upon, yet did not the Welsh have their own language? Above all, Roman Catholics wanted the Mass – the allocation of the Friday afternoon was hardly fair when the Protestants dominated most Sundays. Welch held the same view of the Catholic Friday as the Protestant Sunday. There should be some system and teaching, and not merely a random sermon by one priest after another; they were a hit-and-miss affair. D'Arcy agreed with him.

A. C. F. Beales, a Roman Catholic formerly on the staff of King's College, London, joined the RBD in 1941; he was appointed by Welch to organize talks programmes in view of the greatly increased number of religious talks in wartime. Welch was not unhappy that he was a Roman Catholic, but it was irrelevant from his point of view. Cardinal Hinsley and other Roman Catholics, however, not surprisingly regarded Beales as their representative and somehow their adviser to the Department on Catholic affairs.[14] He was based in London, whereas Welch was now in Bedford.[15] Once the Friday services had got under way, Beales played a significant part in organizing the Catholic preachers. He put Welch in touch with Dom Bernard McElligott of Ampleforth, in Yorkshire, and a meeting took place between him, Welch, D'Arcy and Beales just as pressure was increasing to improve Catholic interests. Beales' conclusion was that the BBC would have to steer a 'careful course along a channel marked by the predilections of bishops and by the fact that when we go to a church we may lose control through the priest deciding to arrange it all himself'. The meeting decided on a new policy for Fridays: to have six studio sermons and six services from churches. In this way the RBD could maintain its influence over production and get the men whom both they and such as

D'Arcy would approve and often actually nominate. McElligott would organize the best outside services and D'Arcy the studio preachers who, McElligott thought, would be more concerned with Catholic doctrine: 'We need preachers who will talk theology in good English whereas the services would be for Catholics.' McElligott and D'Arcy were not, however, exactly at one over broadcasting policy. D'Arcy was much more the 'evangelical' and shared Welch's understanding of the value of broadcasting for Christianity. McElligott and others were rather more concerned with the rights of Catholics to take part in the broadcast operation, and therefore the objectives of Christianity via the radio. In the north, however, the Archbishop of Liverpool regarded Fr Lane, his chaplain, who was a member of CRAC, as responsible for any broadcasts from his diocese. D'Arcy had to steer a devious route around the bishops and did much to prevent Welch from training Roman Catholic priests (as he had Protestants) for the microphone and getting them to understand the influence of broadcasting in general. Welch recognized D'Arcy's 'toughness and suspicion' as 'our safeguard against BBC religion'; he thought that the 'more the clergy feel they are doing the work of the church through the microphone and not the work of the BBC, the better.'[16]

By early 1945 the situation would develop to a stage in which Fr D'Arcy was virtually to become an unpaid member of the Department. He was charged by all the staff to find good Roman Catholic broadcasters; the final approval and veto would lie with D'Arcy and no script would be broadcast without his seeing it. Welch wanted both the voice of Roman Catholicism and its liturgical heritage to be broadcast in all its excellence for the benefit and the education of Protestants, not to mention Catholics themselves. Eventually the number of Roman Catholic broadcasts increased as a result of pressure. Towards the end of the war there were more liturgical services and more talks. Welch thought that the good relations that had been sustained were due to the attitude of Martin D'Arcy, who had always exhibited the utmost courtesy, even when one of his own sermons had been banned in 1944 under the terms of the Concordat.[17]

It was not all sweetness and light by any means. The hierarchy was convinced that Roman Catholic broadcasts were too few and that the BBC was forced by the Protestant establishment to discriminate against Roman Catholic dogma in religious broadcasts. D'Arcy recognized the need for such broadcasts to have the widest appeal, but at the same time knew that any interference would be greatly resented by the majority of his fellow Catholics. It was not helped by his being away from the country a good deal so that his work of choosing speakers and churches, vetting scripts, etc. was often done by his substitute, Father John Murray, also of Farm Street. The *Catholic Herald* had often complained[18] that the Roman Catholic audience was being duped: priests were broadcasting 'pooled Christianity' simply because of the BBC insistence on broadcasts making a sensible utterance to the widest audience. Murray, the Editor of the radical Catholic paper *The Month*, told Beales that it was an unfortunate matter that Roman Catholic sermons had to be submitted to scrutiny: 'Every Catholic broadcast would be tied to every Catholic bishop.'[19] With the war and the single wavelength, any unduly overt Roman Catholic presence on the air or connected with the BBC would raise Protestant opposition. After Ogilvie's resignation in 1942, the storm over the appointment of the Roman Catholic Cecil Graves as Joint Director-General with Robert Foot encouraged the bigots out of their burrows.[20] Graves, in self-defence, told Nicolls to avoid overloading Fridays with Catholic broadcasts![21] Bracken had said in the House in January 1942: 'Religious bigotry is un-English, undemocratic and wholly harmful' ... this prejudice against Graves was 'a monstrous injury to our public life'.[22]

In the meantime, Welch had to tread a most delicate path between the hierarchies of the Corporation, the Church of England and the Roman Catholics: he thought they ought to be co-operating and learning from each other. If the influence of Christianity was to be felt in radio, Christians must learn to use the medium properly and that must mean more 'production'.[23] One of his difficulties was that calls for unity and co-operation could easily lead to charges of compromise. In effect what co-operation Welch had so far managed was entirely Protestant. When Catholic theology was mobilized, Catholic identity would be strengthened. 'If co-operation is to be lawful', wrote William Butterfield in 1942,[24] 'it must not injure the purity of the faith; it must not lead to the error of fundamentalism; it must be in obedience to the Church.' Those who co-operate must be 'specially trained to think, and act in accordance with Catholic principles'. Within this 'legal' framework, co-operation could be encouraged. Too many explicitly Roman Catholic broadcasts would encourage a Protestant outcry; too many Roman Catholic broadcasts of the more discreet kind would provoke a Roman Catholic outcry. The BBC could not win.

The Roman Catholics bore a distinct identity within the community and from the beginning would not subject themselves to a Protestant Corporation and its urge to synthesize the formation of the broadcast Christian dogma. Moreover, the hierarchical structure forbade the sort of innovation by priests which in some measure was enjoyed by Anglicans and Free Churchmen; a Roman priest was simply not permitted to write his own prayers for a broadcast or any other formal liturgical event.[25] Above all, as we have noted, the Mass was central to this identity and the place of Latin was immutable: it was the essence of Roman Catholic faith, utterance and pride and was all the more strenuously maintained in the light of the anti-Catholic feeling in these islands. Broadcasting in a real and marked way tended to put the clock back, notwithstanding all the programme correspondence which expressed strong appreciation for the articulation of clearly defined credal and dogmatic statements.

B. The removal of W. H. Elliott

As has already been noted, the establishment of a single wavelength removed a large number of people from the microphone. Whatever loss of staff there was within the Corporation as a result, the RBD needed more on account of the increase in religious programmes. Whereas the churches had obtained a recognized place in the broadcast output, the emphasis now moved from the churches as institutions to churchmen who were able exponents and protagonists of that faith which stood at the foundation of English culture. Welch was quite clear that, in the crisis, the whole notion of representation was defunct and the strong and confident articulation of Christianity was all-important. There was to be no right to the microphone based on any sort of denominational allocation. For the most part the churches represented by CRAC, apart from the Roman Catholics, accepted this impetus from Welch and Fenn, both of whom were committed to some idea of Christian unity and co-operation, Fenn particularly. He had been involved at the SCM with the development of the World Council of Churches, then in the process of formation, and was in touch with European leaders, including W. A. Visser 't Hooft, and people in America. In London, his close associate on the International Missionary Council was its secretary, William Paton, who would be called upon to give a number of controversial talks in the early part of the war.

Welch wanted the single Christian message, however difficult to define, plainly broadcast without the suggestion of a species of 'BBC religion' which was but a spurious mixture of the simplest Protestant ethic. The Catholics, as we have seen, wanted no part of it and indeed got their way, not without a struggle. They could broadcast Catholic doctrine provided that it did not provoke uglier Protestant reactions. At a CRAC meeting in 1940, Canon Guy Rogers suggested that the broadcast utterance should have three aims: (1) 'a prophetic interpretation of our situation' (here he quoted Isaiah as an example); (2) some measure of consolation, and (3) creation of hope and expectation in the language of reconstruction after the war.[26] If Welch was to bring 'prophets' to the microphone, he must first find them, then train them for broadcasting and, in addition, remove those obstacles which threatened to muffle the single voice of Christianity in the crisis.

Of the pre-war programmes which survived after 1939, the Daily Service remained untouched and was to continue uninterrupted. In no way did it seek to teach, still less to be provocative. Almost as popular had been the midweek Thursday service from St Michael's, Chester Square, London, by W. H. Elliott. In early September 1939, Nicolls with Welch decided that this regular broadcast could no longer continue and nor, indeed, could the services from St Martin's. Elliott and McCormick, in Welch's view, were giving the wrong sort of message. They were both popular, but for Welch this was no criterion. Popularity was subordinate to prophetic utterance. Elliott had become a stereotype and to this Nicolls particularly objected.

Elliott, however, had been in touch with Lang who in turn wrote to Ogilvie to 'urge rather strongly that at the present time [Elliott] happens to have a position of usefulness which may be of great value in the community.' Elliott, claimed the Archbishop, had the power to 'reach those who need steadying most in time of war'. Ogilvie agreed and averred that 'religious broadcasting is obviously even more important than it was before'. Welch was obliged to use Elliott on two occasions each month; he did not deny his command of microphone technique. Welch told Lang that in fact Elliott's broadcasts were scheduled for reduction before the war had started. He politely assured His Grace that it was time other preachers had Elliott's chances. To have had the microphone for so many years without a course of sustained teaching was to have missed a great opportunity. Welch had only met Elliott once, when he tried to persuade him to make his addresses (which lasted only about five minutes) 'deal with the great central truths of Christianity and the gospel', urging him to use his chance to 'introduce finer and greater hymns to his listeners'. Elliott refused; his listeners would switch off if he tried. Welch told Lang that it was a terrible waste to have such a vast audience simply told to be brave week after week, and no real regard paid to the Reithian objective of education. In February 1940 Welch told Melville Dinwiddie:

> The trouble with men like Elliott is that they give tabloids of comfort and moral advice but not sound dogmatic teaching and little forceful presentation of the gospel. It would be fatal to use men like Elliott and McCormick as prophets in the new age that is coming; they have

done fine work but they belong to a dying civilization. It is dangerous as we know to our cost to keep on pushing men like Elliott before the microphone, whether they have a message or not. Personality and technique can be acquired; a prophetic message cannot be.

Welch made Elliott travel to Bristol twice each month, but he could not persuade him to work his material into any sort of system; he was popular in high places and knew it. Welch thought he was a 'spent force' and quite 'incapable of preaching a consecutive and consistent message', which is what Welch wanted above all.

Elliott, however, had been listened to by thousands and Welch did not have things entirely his own way. Some in high places had their eyes on Elliott's war and propaganda value. He had developed an enormous following; from his broadcasts he had become a household name. He provided what many churchmen could not – a simple, comforting word to the simplest mind – and he reminded people of dimensions which were easily lost and forgotten in the critical late thirties. In 1936, against a background of the German occupation of the Rhineland, Elliott had formed the League of Prayer for Peace and by the beginning of the war some five and a half million members had joined Elliott in praying for peace. There were packed meetings in the Albert Hall. Elliott (with two members of CRAC, Aubrey and Berry) toured the country and had a similar if short-lived popularity.

Elliott was the product of a Reithian and perhaps Oxford Group outlook which believed that no matter how complex were the discussions about faith and politics, the Christian heritage and utterance could be made simple and engaging for ordinary people outside any formal relation with the churches. The League of Prayer drew on vast numbers in the churches and many whose religious convictions were vague but who recognized the important role of the church within the life of the nation. Since the beginning of the war, Elliott much regretted that he had not been used much more to support the nation's morale in the war effort. One of his supporters was Mrs Neville Chamberlain; others were some members of the army establishment, who thought the broadcast war bulletins were rather more frightening than was good for the morale of the rank and file.

Elliott, moreover, had a good friend in Admiral Sir Michael Hodge who on his behalf had approached Lord Chatsfield, a friend of Reith; he in turn approached both Reith and Sir Samuel Hoare, the Lord Privy Seal, on the question of public morale. Chatsfield discussed the issue in the Cabinet and told Reith that Churchill did not wish the matter to be pursued from a Cabinet initiative.[27] Graves had told Reith of Welch's view of Elliott; Chatsfield appreciated their view but confessed notwithstanding, that 'BBC religious broadcasts are not altogether stimulating but rather of the "Love your enemy" type which is difficult to swallow at this time, however sound it may be morally'. Chatsfield did not expect Elliott to change those whom he had encouraged for so long to pray for peace into warriors suddenly overnight: 'Some means to raise their fortitude from the religious side does seem important.' But he feared that Elliott's following were too close to the pacifist position[28] and thought he should be invited by the Corporation to help 'swing them over to the national effort'. Reith was also sorry that Graves would not accede to his own hope that Elliott could be used by the BBC to 'induced a bellicose rather than pacifist spirit among his many followers'.[29] Graves consulted Welch through Nicolls, who was quite convinced that the BBC should not bow to this pressure, notwithstanding Reith's close association with his longstanding friend, now the Deputy Director-General. Nicolls supported the view that 'our religious broadcasting is a Christian activity which operates from a Christian standpoint . . . and the Christian church, as represented by the BBC and the Director of Religious Broadcasting, could not accept a mandate from the Government to stir up bellicosity or to preach hatred of the enemy.'[30] Both Nicolls and Welch could see this as another attempt to give Elliott back his protected position at the microphone.

In March 1940 Elliott at last had his coveted meeting with Ogilvie, who recorded that Elliott now recognized that he could not recapture his dominant and privileged place within the religious broadcasting output. Welch offered him a fairly recently established 'popular', i.e. short talk, now entitled *Lift Up Your Hearts*,[31] at five minutes before eight each morning. But Welch feared the consequences of morale- boosting talks on 'the lovely things that remain unchanged, such as the country and the children and the like', and 'talking about crocuses when the world was going up in flames'; he was also vexed by his continual whining appeal to the Director-General. Elliott on his side lamented his loss of reputation as what he believed was the 'Radio Parson'.

The disappearance of Elliott marked Welch's victory over a style of Christian utterance which he regarded as sentimental and grossly oversimplified.[32] A very considerable obstacle and even embarrassment was removed.

C. The 'broadcast Angelus'

We have seen the pressure brought upon Ogilvie, Graves and Welch to have W. H. Elliott used in broadcasting to sustain morale and have the depressed uplifted. The concept of national interest was all the easier to define now that the nation was actively at war. In May 1940 it became clear that the situation for the British troops trapped on the shores of Northern France was critical, and George VI personally supported the establishment of a National Day of Prayer involving all Christians, including of course the Roman Catholics, and also the Jewish community. It was planned to coincide with the evacuation of the British Expeditionary Force from Dunkirk.[33] Because the King had asked that Sunday 26 May should be kept as a day of prayer Welch thought this should be reflected in all the programmes and not only the religious material.

It was quite clear that the responses to the war crisis of the main Christian institutions were being shaped and sharpened by the BBC. Those who saw a clear connection between God and country would recognize the value of broadcasting as a unique means of sustaining and inculcating their special religious world view. The war threatened King, people and church. The church was the custodian and transmitter of the poetry by which men and women popularly construed and expressed the non-material character of their personal and corporate destiny and even the national character. The National Day of Prayer was firmly instituted in May and was to be followed by many more; they would cause Welch not a little anxiety on theological as well as ecumenical grounds. He had slowly tried to remove those denominational factors which would militate against the notion of a single voice being uppermost on these national occasions. Not surprisingly the Free Churches and the Roman Catholics were consistently at the BBC's throat for drawing out too explicitly the concept of Britain as a Protestant nation in general and an Anglican one in particular. They objected to any notion of 'BBC religion'. Welch, on his part, in his enthusiasm for the BBC's Christian initiative had not foreseen the significance that would be attached to the Big Ben chimes at 9 o'clock which not only brought the ears of the nation to the radio for the News: at home and in the Empire they symbolized the heart of the nation at Westminster and indeed of the free world fighting the Nazis. With so much 'energy' evoked, this was surely a special, even 'liturgical', moment which should and could be used to good effect: it might even summon the nation to prayer.

The idea was not new; there had been a number of overtures to Reith and Iremonger to use the opportunity of the King's speech at Christmas 1934; Ramsay MacDonald was asked in the House if he would inaugurate a two-minute silence for prayer after the King had spoken.[34] Reith refused. In 1940, however, there was increasing pressure from the establishment, for example, Mrs J. B. Priestley, who argued in a note to Ogilvie that the crisis was grave and should not only be seen as the concern of the churches: it was the burden of Christian Britain, and therefore everyone should be given both the opportunity and the encouragement to pray when they were – in a real way – gathered together in this manner for the wireless news. Admiral Sir Sidney Drury-Lowe, a one-time member of the League of Nations Union, told Ogilvie that 'the mass of our people should realize that this war is on the spiritual plane as well as the material' and thus the main purpose of the wireless should be to 'canalize the thoughts of the nation, listening in on this spiritual note', into the spearhead of an immense power'. This power thus generated 'would be greatly used'. By this he reflected a notion of prayer which Welch and the BBC would rather not promulgate. Welch disapproved of 'panic prayers'.[35]

The National Day of Prayer, however, had sparked off a massive drive which soon had the support of members from both Houses and others including bishops and leaders of the denominations. There was soon money enough to finance a campaign staff and its offices. In June 1940, the 'campaign' took a variety of forms. In a letter to *The Times* on 20 June, Lord Davidson and others suggested that with Government support the BBC should devote two minutes to public prayer every evening at 9 o'clock and in the same paper retired Admiral James Startin thought this suggestion would have the support of 'most naval men'. Later in June, in a journal of the British Israel World Federation, *National Message*, W. Tudor-Pole, a bankers' agent in the West End, suggested a 'Dedicated Moment Daily': an announcement at 9 o'clock every evening should call for 'the complete dedication of our every thought, word and deed . . . as a national crusade . . . through the BBC . . . The Dunkirk miracle would become still greater.' Tudor-Pole asked people to write to the BBC and issued a printed letter form to encourage this. 350 replies were sent direct and included many establishment figures. In July, the *Daily Telegraph* carried a joint statement from Lang and Temple asking for a 'momentary act of remembrance and prayer' every day at noon. Lang had telephoned through his chaplain, Alan Don, to ask for a reference in the news to this joint archiepiscopal statement. Temple preferred 9 o'clock.

With all this pressure the Home Board discussed the issues and decided to leave the question open and consider an evening religious service every day.[36] This was exactly what Tudor-Pole did *not* want, and he emphasized to Fenn that this would 'alienate completely the man in the street whom it is most important to reach'. Ogilvie consulted the Ministry of Information and Duff Cooper, the Minister (to whom Tudor-Pole had written along with Anthony Eden and the Prime Minister). Ogilvie saw that the only possibility was to allow an extra religious service or services. Silence was impossible on security grounds: the Germans would surely fill those sixty seconds with some terse propaganda. Ogilvie regarded with great suspicion Tudor-Pole's suggested prayer: 'I dedicate myself anew in every thought . . . to the service of my country and the Empire to vanquish darkness and evil and to establish righteousness and freedom everywhere. So help me God.' Ogilvie remarked of this: 'There is a touch of fascism which is somewhat unpleasant.' He felt that if such a campaign was to be effective it ought to be supported by the churches: 'If the churches organized a kind of Angelus (as well they might if they knew their business) I think the whole picture would look different.'[37] This was a sound Reithian view: had the churches wanted the BBC to do the special thing (that of course only broadcasting could do) the Corporation would have complied. Welch, for his part, opposed Tudor-Pole, but at the same time wanted the churches to proclaim the Christian message to a wartorn nation: and things, he knew, would yet get much worse. Fenn could not conceive of any 'generally acceptable spiritual observance which could at present be uncompromisingly Christian without arousing intense opposition'. Ogilvie wanted Silvey's research department to procure an opinion before making any decision.

In the meantime, Tudor-Pole furthered the campaign on two fronts – the BBC and the churches. Doubtless he was right about more services, which was the only way Ogilvie and the Ministry of Information felt a response could be made to the joint statement of Lang and Temple, both of whom had supported the Tudor-Pole campaign: odd bedfellows perhaps. Silvey produced his figures: 'Only 34 per cent said "Yes" to an evening service every day, with 26 per cent saying "No" and 40 per cent not minding! The "yes" answers were slightly greater in the upper income groups than the lower.' Silvey reckoned that it would be the older people who would be the most faithful listeners.[38] On this information Ogilvie informed Duff-Cooper that the honest and logical thing to do would be to broadcast an evening service daily. Tudor-Pole would not give up, and Ogilvie finally agreed to meet him in mid- August. Tudor-Pole gave him a list of notable supporters including the headmasters of Wellington and Winchester, Cardinal Hinsley and even General de Gaulle! Ogilvie then attended a meeting of MPs at the Commons, organized by Captain David Margesson, the Tory Chief Whip, later Secretary of State for War. The meeting left him totally confused, although he had emphasized that 'broadcasting could only operate on a reasonably clear objective' and that the BBC would not simply provide a signal; besides it was not proper to 'force religion or non-religion upon people queuing up for the news'. Ogilvie thought Tudor-Pole's material their main inspiration.[39] Ogilvie then checked up on the alleged supporters, including de Gaulle, with whom he spoke on 29 August: 'He knew little about the project and nothing whatever about its broadcasting aspect.'[40] The Boy Scouts' President, Lord Hampton, thought the church should take the lead and not the BBC. Lord Halifax told Ogilvie emphatically that Tudor-Pole had no ground for suggesting he was in any way interested. From Buckingham Palace, Sir Alexander Hardinge reported that the King had always refused Tudor-Pole's request for support. Hinsley and Lang both firmly disassociated themselves from the Big Ben Silent Minute and from Tudor-Pole. Lang told Ogilvie that he had 'never gone so far as advocating its adoption by the BBC in the form adopted by Tudor-Pole'.[41] Tudor-Pole might have asked 'What's in a name?', but could hardly have complained: he was after all quite adamant that his was not a Christian notion: he was concerned to have all religions united and all creeds in concord. Not surprisingly, he was feared by some churchmen as being yet another offshoot of the Oxford Group Movement, but rather more extreme and somewhat less than Christian. The idea of silence so favoured by churchmen as an element of private as well as corporate observance, was attractive in theory as a part of religion on the wireless, but many failed to realize the nature of the technicalities involved. Temple had been told that Duff Cooper was not against the idea, and so put it to Ogilvie, who carefully explained that silence was simply not possible for three reasons: the quality of most sets could only 'provide' silence if they were switched off; secondly, 'wave-band drift' meant encroachment from other stations, and, thirdly, the enemy would undoubtedly use such a time for propaganda. Temple fully agreed and left it to the BBC: 'Whatever you do, do not give us exhortation to dedication!'[42]

Welch had spoken privately to Lang and Temple and asked them not to press for any further comment upon their July statement in the newspapers. He made the same appeal to Cardinal Hinsley. The Cardinal told Ogilvie that he was very much opposed to 'anything which savoured of mesmerism'! Not surprisingly, all the notables who might have given the general idea some support in the interests of the war effort and national morale, were quick to extricate themselves when questioned by the Director-General. Welch told Nicolls that he thought 'some of the birds in the Tudor-Pole bush are about to take flight'. Ogilvie meanwhile was at a loss and confessed to Lord Halifax,

It's a hard life! At the moment we are being told from some quarters that we are 'throwing spanners in the works of God' – when of course our only anxiety is to serve the cause of religion, the country, and other good causes to the fullest possible extent.[43]

In September, however, the Board of Governors decided not to co-operate: there was no consistent notion or objective in the 'dedicated moment'; there should be no increase in religious broadcasting and the 'dedicated moment' did look like thrusting religion down people's throats. Welch and Fenn, however, disagreed with the complete dismissal of Tudor-Pole's intentions: his motives were good, they thought, and he was 'surely on the side of the angels'. Welch thought perhaps the movement should be made the subject of a talk, but made it quite clear to Nicolls that 'since the movement is not obviously religious, the decision lies with you and the Director-General'.[44]

The BBC had to make a decision. But that was by no means easy: Churchill wanted the Board decision reconsidered and conveyed his message through Captain Margesson, who had encouraged the Prime Minister to re-open the discussion. Ogilvie arranged to see Anthony Bevir, Private Secretary to Churchill, on 7 October and told him that he feared 'a sordid underworld' which attached to the movement and that if the decision by the Governors was to be reversed 'by a mere fiat from No 10', there were serious consequences for the constitution of the BBC; political interference in religious matters might go on in Germany, but not here! The Ministry of Information had discussed it in July and August and left it to the BBC to make the decision. 'Did the Prime Minister wish to be involved in all this?', Ogilvie asked, with an appropriate sense of dramatic implication! The next day Ogilvie managed to see Duff Cooper and complained to him that the procedure of Margesson in going direct to Churchill, i.e. in providing the movement with access to No 10, was improper. The BBC, he said, was anxious to act constitutionally and hoped the Prime Minister could understand this. Ogilvie then decided to see Margesson without revealing that he had already talked to Bevir. Ogilvie stood firm and for the first time, Margesson agreed that the matter was finally to be left to the BBC. The Corporation would take Welch's advice and arrange a talk, but not have the BBC taking a technical initiative by leaving the period from 8.59–9.0 silent – or rather, without broadcast material which (as we have seen) was not quite the same thing. Ogilvie at least showed that he took Churchill's alleged request seriously: the BBC would form a committee including Temple, who had shown interest, Major Astor, Dame Meriel Talbot and naturally, Ogilvie himself. Margesson was invited to join it, and he agreed.

The Committee met on 28 October; to Welch's surprise, he was included in it. Since his intention had been to keep this 'crazy religious movement' well away from the BBC's religious work, he told Temple that he had no desire 'to have religious broadcasting linked with telepathy and to give people a false idea of prayer'. Welch urged Temple to oppose it.[45]

Ogilvie prepared a note for the Committee suggesting that the BBC should not co-operate in the movement but consider the extending of religious broadcasts to a daily evening epilogue. Sir Allan Powell, the Chairman of the Governors, returned to the suggestion of the Big Ben chimes – live or recorded – and Margesson welcomed this as entirely satisfactory. Nicolls suggested the chimes should signal the time for listeners to think etc. Temple strongly supported this idea: the BBC 'Angelus' would call men and women to think of the cause for which we were all fighting.[46] Ogilvie for the Corporation wanted the BBC's initiative to remain simply the broadcasting of the chimes with no 'official prescript' from within the Corporation. Welch was asked to suggest a speaker for a talk, and eventually Howard Marshall was chosen to give a talk just prior to the first broadcast of the chimes, appropriately on the eve of Armistice Day, 10 November. The Committee was then asked, somewhat to Welch's amazement, how it regarded religious broadcasting in general. Powell wanted a view about the amount. Temple was content with the time allowed and would not ask the BBC for more. Did they want a regular Epilogue at the end of the news/talk broadcast each evening? The Committee thought it would be welcomed and should be tried. The Committee approved the prayers now proposed for Children's Hour, and also before the news at 8.0 a.m. Ogilvie was sickened by the whole thing and confessed to Lord Macmillan (whom he had hoped would have been present):

> Sixty seconds charged with *odium theologicum* and *anti-theologicum* of a somewhat lurid kind, raising issues of politics and religion which have roughened our rough island story many a time . . . the BBC refused to bow the knee to God or Baal or No 10.

The Board of Governors agreed, as did the Home Board, that Big Ben should be live whenever possible even at the risk of gunfire being heard. All the more authentic, it was thought.[47]

The Radio Times on 8 November announced that the chimes would signal a moment for 'consecration to the land they love and the success of its cause' – Big Ben at 9.0 was a cue. On 9 November, Howard Marshall made his careful introduction at 9.15. It was a time for thought or prayer and might be for some 'the most important minute of the day . . . There's been a demand for this minute and the BBC have met it. If you don't need it yourself, then at least there's no harm in hearing the friendly voice of Big Ben.' Tudor-Pole agreed: the BBC had met the demand. Soon enough, however, the Big Ben Movement would be demanding more: talks and more pertinently an explicit indication why the chimes were broadcast. The chimes might, as the *Listener* leader suggested,[48] be an 'inspiration' but that was not quite enough for Tudor-Pole or Margesson. They wanted the Marshall talk repeated every month and also wanted the *Radio Times* to carry explicit mention of the use to which the chimes should be put: dedication. Hugh Martin, in charge of Religious Affairs at the Ministry of Information, was besieged with requests to organize a campaign about the Silent Minute. People ought to be told more precisely how and what to think during the chimes: Ogilvie said no: it was just a signal – an 'Angelus' for people to do with as they wished. The Bishop of Lincoln asked Welch to have the BBC suggest to listeners they should say the Lord's Prayer.[49] Welch could only give the official reply: the BBC decided to offer 'time but not advice' as to how the chimes should be used. In *The Times* the policy had been to advertise in the Broadcast Programmes: '9 – News and "Dedicated Moment" ', and Sir Waldron Smithers[50] wanted the *Radio Times* to be as explicit. The pressure continued, and the discussion dragged on into 1941. Ogilvie met Smithers at the end of April and 'was not encouraging' – he wanted postscripts by members of the forces – which was a way of getting Margesson to the microphone and the chance for greater explicit promulgation of the movement – now organized from Tudor-Pole's office under the heading of the 'Big Ben Silent Minute Council'. Sir Waldron Smithers then saw Duff Cooper at the Ministry of Information on 14 May. Cooper agreed with him that the BBC announcers could say 'Dedicated Minute' and this should be printed in the *Radio Times*. Why not? – asked Cooper. Cooper thought, however, that Sir Waldron Smithers was 'very nearly mad but not quite',[51] particularly as he wanted the corporation to promote the song 'When Big Ben Chimes' written by a movement devotee, Helen Taylor:

> When Big Ben chimes
> He seems to say
> Be silent all, and pause
> And pray O Lord our God
> Make strife to cease
> In Thy good time
> Grant us Thy peace.

Ogilvie told Cooper that the Governors had yet again[52] decided that their original decision should stand. However, Ogilvie was forced to compromise because of Cooper's promise to Waldron Smithers. Since the Committee had agreed in October 1940 to an occasional talk, the Director-General recommended that this should be quarterly. When consulted, Welch would not decide – he would only advise on scripts.

By the end of December, Tudor-Pole's Council decided to circularize its supporters on the progress of the movement and claimed considerable support at home and overseas. In the Dominions, radio stations used recordings of the chimes at noon local time in Australia and 9 p.m. local time in New Zealand when the Bishop of Wellington had given a broadcast in support.[53] In the New Zealand Parliament, proceedings were stopped at 9 p.m. and the chimes were heard over loudspeakers. In 1942, the Big Ben Council had a new chairman in the indefatigable Major-General L. L. Hoare; he lobbied the new Minister of Information, Brendan Bracken, who was soon demanding an answer from Graves.[54] It was yet another refusal, and Welch was anxious to support Graves and keep the churches and the BBC well away from this movement. Welch told Hoare that the churches would certainly not support him unless his prayers were specifically Christian. He would not have the movement a subject of the prayers before the 8.0 a.m. news, as had been suggested at a Programme Planners' Meeting. For their part the churches and the Chief Rabbi published small booklets[55] in response to the somewhat confused appeals in the national and church press that these chimes were a signal for prayers and the churches should advise on its use – as indeed Ogilvie had always said they should have done from the beginning. The Methodist, W. J. Noble, told Temple he hoped the churches would produce a combined interdenominational booklet; but he was too late. Temple had been asked already by Hoare to produce one for the Church of England.[56]

With the coming in 1942 of two joint Directors-General in Foot and Graves, Hoare hoped for a change in BBC policy. He met Graves in November 1943 and heard him more sympathetically affirm the BBC's commitment; the Directors-General were not being 'obstructive' and 'in no way hostile' and indeed that they 'shared in common with the Council the wish for a spiritual motive'. Graves assured Hoare that 'the BBC was prepared to collaborate on any proposals of Major Tudor-Pole'.[57] Hoare was, as the King's Secretary, Hardinge, noted, 'certainly very persistent'; but the King would not mention the Big Ben movement in his Christmas broadcast!

With the war now approaching 'its critical phase' Hoare and the Council decided to step up its campaign to have the BBC do its bidding. Hoare complained afresh to Graves that the BBC was not honouring its earliest 1940 agreement: i.e. extra seconds prior to the chimes, a mention in the *Radio Times* and more talks. Foot would have none of it, and reminded Hoare of the talks given since Marshall's first in November 1940: they would try to keep the chimes free and distinct from previous immediate announcements but there would be no 'buffer' seconds and no explicit mention by announcers or in the publications. Hoare was afraid that the chimes were increasingly regarded as a time signal – a neat piece of argument: none of his other claims were based on any objective evidence. On Hoare's suggestion, the new Archbishop of Canterbury, Temple, wrote to Graves that perhaps the BBC should after all remind the public of the reasons why the chimes were introduced; he was surprised that Graves gave the standard reply. Hoare particularly wanted Temple to urge Foot to have the chimes and not simply the Greenwich time-signal, on the Forces programme. Temple, however, would not sign Tudor-Pole's circular letter to MPs in March 1943.

By that circular letter, the Big Ben Movement had gained sufficient support among MPs and members of the Lords to fire a hefty salvo at the Corporation through the Ministry of Information and the Prime Minister. They thus forwarded their 'evidence' again to Brendan Bracken in mid-April; this included a substantial number of churchmen who along with the MPs 'had given us a mandate to approach the Prime Minister'.[58] Nearly seventy from the Lower House (but not including Harold Nicolson, who strongly felt that the circular had deliberately misrepresented the BBC's attitude) were joined by eighty peers, ten bishops plus Lang of Lambeth, ten Deans, a handful of clerics and, rather surprisingly, J. H. Oldham and Maude Royden. Sir Adrian Boult signed, as did Middleton Murry, Joseph Rank and Dame Laura Knight. This was a formidable line-up and the Board responded with a clever compromise which showed that they could respond to an initiative but still take an initiative within it. In the *Radio Times*, the billing would simply read 'Big Ben Minute' but without any reference to the movement or to any debatable notions of 'dedication'. The *Radio Times* mention on 12 April prompted the Bishop of Coventry, Neville Gorton, to write to Brendan Bracken urging him to have the BBC 'tap the submerged public that needed concrete symbolism for any imaginative ideas'. For people outside the churches, prayer was natural 'once they get a context . . . We want a spiritual focus for the ordinary chap right now – they are asking for it.' Did the Bishop have evidence from real examination or was he playing on a hunch? Either way, he thought the church could not tap this source; it was for the BBC. Bracken thought Foot should see this and both agreed that no further action should be taken and the Bishop would have to settle for an acknowledgement. Welch agreed: he saw no sense in 'asking unbelievers to pray'. He did think the Bishop of Coventry might be a good man to give the talk and put the dedication idea into a Christian perspective. But he would not have the BBC Religious Broadcasting Department brought into this tedious discussion and hoped that the Corporation would not be further pushed by the Tudor-Pole set. Again in November 1943, the *Radio Times* carried an approved note which simply drew attention to the appreciation in Britain and around the world at the sounds of Big Ben, now billed since Easter 1943 as 'Big Ben Minute'. Nicolls had suggested adding 'signal' but Foot thought it would invite yet more enquiry.

Yet more enquiry, however, was forthcoming – this time over the change from the Forces Programme to the General Forces Programme in February 1944. The old Forces Programme, which had eventually carried the chimes at 9.0 p.m., was now closed, and the BBC could save time and money with just two programmes and not three: the Forces Programme was merged into and superseded by the General Forces Programme which would forge a clear link with Forces wherever they were and the listeners at home. Briggs quotes a note from Frank Gillard (then a war correspondent in Italy) to Haley pleading for the men who 'strain their sets to hear a Home Service News Bulletin' and who would not be satisfied until they heard Stuart Hibberd or another well-known voice reading the news.[59] Against this background it is surprising that Haley, Editor in Chief, told Hoare that since the Forces programme had gone there was no point in the movement complaining that the chimes were not now broadcast; there was no programme – it had gone. In fact, the new programme was not to be shackled by a fixed point in the evening and thus the chimes could not be scheduled. This Haley did not admit, and not surprisingly the campaign continued. Haley undermined Nicolls' notion of a signal by simply telling Hoare that if 'your members' want the chimes they should retune to the Home Service.[60] He did not think the chimes had a place in the General Forces Programme, even though a large section of the audience abroad apparently craved links with home and notwithstanding the absence of a news bulletin at 9.0 p.m. Air Chief Marshal Dowding implored Haley to reinstate it: 'The fact remains that the forces have been denied a spiritual link'.[61] *The Times*, as expected, carried more letters and Haley rebuked Hoare sharply: 'The BBC must retain its independence of judgment . . . and it cannot allow that judgment to be ruled by outside bodies, even though they may have become identified with some item in its broadcasts.' This had implications for the RBD which would not be fully noticed until after the war.

From Lambeth, Temple complained that the omission of the chimes was 'extremely regrettable'.[62] They were finally not to do with 9 o'clock or even the news: they were a signal to thought whenever they chimed at home or overseas. He wanted the chimes reintroduced 'for a common, united act of recollection which for some is a remembrance of unity and others a dedication and prayer'. This was rather serious and Temple was asked to meet Welch in April.[63] Temple fully accepted Welch's explanations about the General Forces Programme now being autonomous whereas the old Forces Programme had only had the chimes because the two programmes merged at 9.0 p.m. The old overseas programme heard odd chimes but not the complete set. Temple's unease, like Hoare's, was that the new programme was off on its own free of chimes. Haley was determined to reverse the forward march of this movement and if possible remove the billing in the *Radio Times* of which he strongly disapproved. Just before the European peace was declared, the movement tried to come even closer to the RBD and couched most of its propaganda in rather more recognizably Christian language than had been seen earlier when it spoke rather more syncretistically.[64]

In November 1944, Haley told Welch he hoped to drop the Silent Minute from *Radio Times* and asked him to prepare the new incumbent of Lambeth to resist the campaign to call for his support when the billing was changed. Welch knew that support would soon fade, and indeed it did – the chimes of Big Ben gradually became simply a time signal, and only a recollection of darker days for the generation who had survived them. When the Light Programme emerged from the General Forces Programme in 1945, Norman Collins, the Controller, would not have such a rigid schedule and Hoare was told firmly that the chimes would not be broadcast. The movement would continue into peace time but gradually fade from significance, at least in broadcasting policy.

The single wartime wavelength animated the notion for many that this was the voice of the nation, which of course it was. It was consequently a means towards the winning of the war, and in this setting the Corporation was constantly in danger of having its cherished independence dismantled. Ogilvie had detected a discreet strain of fascism in the outlook of the leaders of the Big Ben Movement and he was right. Hoare, Tudor-Pole and Margesson, the impetus behind the movement were inspired by primitive quasi-religious notions which identified a totem around which the nation could gather to offer prayers for its survival in time of crisis. The chimes of Big Ben offered just such an identification: 'If we approach the observance of the Silent Minute united in spiritual intent and the will to good, the power needed to establish the Kingdom of God on earth will be made available.'[65] Such language could easily beguile the rank and file and particularly those with a modest stock of religious language, which in 1940 was all the more interlaced with pessimism.

It was even more beguiling to churchmen who, understandably, saw in the proposed silence the traditional basis for contemplation. In a time of crisis it was proper for the nation to pray to the Christian God as enjoined by its Christian leaders. Archbishops Davidson, Lang and Temple were all supporters of the movement to link the chimes of Big Ben at 9.0 to silence and prayer. They would not have supported Tudor-Pole, had they heard his confession to Ogilvie that the movement was not religious, that silence was the only way of uniting all creeds and races, and that keeping silence at 8.59 each evening 'was like letting a jinn out of a bottle in order to let the light in'.[66] Such mechanisms belonged to the east; Welch wanted no part in this and regretted that church leaders had not been more united and articulate at a time of panic, when considerable numbers of powerful people could find comfort and even succour in the word associations conjured by the sombre tones of Big Ben.

For Welch and the Department, the right use of the silent minute was to say the Lord's Prayer. 'The whole theology of prayer taught by the movement is dangerous.'[67] This was not a Christian nation fighting for its life; it was a secular nation fighting for Christianity – a distinction that the Department would have more successfully maintained had the churches been less ponderous and more responsive and spoken with one voice to the growing Big Ben Movement whose language was misleadingly simple, yet optimistic and universal. Few people in the churches saw the naïvety with which the movement propounded its theories about silence in general and broadcast silence in particular. Ogilvie, moreover, was anxious that the Corporation should not be bullied by those of the movement's supporters who identified God with nation. A distilled, residual stock of Christian image and creed could too easily fall prey to nationalism and the notions of national survival and national righteousness. For Fenn more than Welch, any idea that the Christian creed somehow laminated the nation's heritage with a gloss of righteousness was to be opposed; any idea that there could be an effortless salvation if only mankind would be silent was a fraud.

Perhaps Foot was quite right in early 1940: the churches should have provided a united and explicitly Christian guideline which called people not only to hope but to repentance. As it was, the churches were either led by the nose, so that they joined the Silent Minute in the belief that any style of prayerful thought was better than none, or they spurned the movement altogether. W. J. Noble, the Methodist, could for example put his weight behind Tudor-Pole and yet lament to Temple that the Roman Catholics were calling for their particular observations at 8.59 just as the Jews and the Protestants were calling for theirs. The churches' behaviour was only too predictable.

D. Preachers and pacifists

Since the beginning of Iremonger's time, the BBC had brought to the microphone those whom both church and Corporation deemed both worthy and capable of addressing themselves to the mass audience. The BBC also took the microphone to the churches on their home ground, with the result that the mass audience became aware of the church speaking both to itself and to them. The great bulk of religious broadcasting before the war was on Sundays. As it became increasingly necessary for the Corporation to wean the British away from foreign stations and their popular appeal to the Sunday audiences, Reith had no choice but to accept that the puritan Sunday could not survive the changes in social conditions and the increasing need for Sunday leisure to be reflected in broadcasting policy.

As we have seen, when Welch took over, he immediately called together a few influential minds to ask how Sunday could be used for the service of the kingdom of God within the British nation.[68] The idea of the 'nation' in broadcasting policy was heightened at the outset of war by the reduction of the wavelengths and the resultant concept of one broadcasting centre from which to address the nation.

One consequence was the difficulty of relating the interests of minorities to the majority preoccupation with the war effort. Throughout the war, the relation of the BBC to the Government was to be questioned again and again in Parliament and within its own power structures. There were to be times when the BBC spoke for the Government and, by the nature of things, there were times when air time might have to be given for a contrasting and even contrary view. In religious broadcasting, the whole notion of what was regarded as 'controversy' had been debated for years within the decision-making sections of the Corporation and also within CRAC. Controversial broadcasting was not permitted; there was to be no propaganda by any group or denomination – all had to contribute to the provision of a broad statement of Christian conviction, belief and application. Those outside the mainstream Christian institutions were not permitted to broadcast at all; but even those within the mainstream were not allowed to emphasize their confessional identities and so arouse controversy – or, as others preferred to call it, debate. The former, of course, were the non-Christian groups such as rationalists and free thinkers who regarded the BBC's unswerving maintenance of Christian utterance as highly propagandist, undemocratic and very controversial. For the BBC, it was not controversial that Britain was a Christian country nor that the BBC was committed to maintain that conviction and, in so doing, give special preference to all the 'accredited' churches who advised them how that conviction should be translated into programmes.[69] Only the Roman Catholics had special restrictions and were prevented from making their identity quite clear. This compulsion on the churches demanded from them the most imaginative form, style and content of utterance so that the essential content of the Christian faith might be broadcast intelligibly to the mass audience, which in turn was defined with a measurably greater precision as broadcasting developed.

With the deepening of the European crisis in the mid-thirties, the BBC naturally expected the churches to examine the issues involved in principle, if not in detail. At the same time, Iremonger, CRAC and the hierarchy of the Corporation were all agreed that controversy must be avoided. And if the churches were to speak, whilst there were myriad preachers, there were not, as we have seen, many who could broadcast with skill and authority. Two of these, however, had been William Temple, Archbishop of York, and Dick Sheppard, both close friends of Iremonger and, at the same time, widely divided on the increasingly discussed question of Christianity and the war in general and the pacifist issue in particular. This is not the place to chart the history of the pacifist debate in church and nation.[70] In 1935, both Temple and Sheppard (now Canon of Canterbury) were brought to the microphone and within the Corporation a profoundly controversial debate began which was to continue well into the post-war era; it was to raise as never before the relationship of the churches to the BBC and in particular, the shape of that relationship as identified in the work and authority of the RBD and its personnel. It was to clarify not only the conception which church leaders had of the Corporation but also the role which the broadcasters should be taking in relation to the established authority of Government and Parliament, influenced itself by issues of a religious, ecclesial and theological kind.

As the Abyssinian crisis gathered pace, William Temple was asked by Iremonger to give a talk on 'The Christian and the World Situation'.[71] In it he stated his own non-pacifist outlook and thus in effect became the first speaker in the controversial issue of the use of force. In an ideal world, he said, Christians and Christian nations, i.e. Italy and Abyssinia, would not be at war and the way of peace would be the norm. Since self-interest prevails and men will not recognize law, 'the law and its sanctions help us to resist temptations which would otherwise be too strong for us.' Temple saw the law operating via the League of Nations and the necessity of making the League effective; 'if this involves the use of armed forces, we ought to be prepared to use them.' Italy was threatening the unity of the League and to employ force in its support was 'no more war in the proper sense of the word than a baton-charge by the police on a mob engaged in destruction is a riot on the part of the police'. This concept enraged some and encouraged others. *The Listener* approved of Temple's 'thorough and cogent analysis . . . of the factors which must govern the attitude of Christian England towards the Italo-Abyssinian dispute.'[72] The Council of Christian Pacifist Groups immediately lobbied Iremonger for a broadcast and the chance to refute the Archbishop. Iremonger advised CRAC against allowing any such debate on the air; it was not edifying for 'one of the most influential leaders of religious thought to be contradicted by another.'[73] Furthermore, few could cope with the subtleties of the debate; 'unreflective listeners are not careful to weigh differences and discriminate between positions which shade off into one another.'[74] Iremonger wanted no debate regarding Christian principles at all. Later, Welch, on the other hand, wanted debate but, like Iremonger before him, not between Christian speakers in a propagandist way. This would threaten the whole objective of a united presentation of Christian faith and interpretation which, now in retrospect, seems a hopeless dream; nevertheless it was pursued with deep and enlightened conviction.

The other factor in Temple's broadcast of great significance for the RBD was his admission that it was not his business as an Archbishop to say exactly what men ought to do. He had simply 'tried to set out the principles that call for application'.[75] This was a fine point hardly appreciated by his pacifist opponents who had a good deal less optimism and faith in the future of the League. The Society of Friends virtually accused Temple of not being able to discern what was just because the introduction of weapons and force clouded the issue. By simply 'pointing to the things of peace' Mussolini, they added, might surely be restrained. In the same year, the debate became more aggressive: Temple called pacifists 'heretical though noble' and Charles Raven, the Cambridge don,[76] regarded Temple as apostate. Both were to modify their language between 1935 and 1939. Speakers on both sides of the debate sought to advise men what to think and how to argue a particular case for pacifist or non-pacifist action. Within two years both government and the BBC would decide formally just how far this could be allowed. For the moment, Temple had set the ball rolling and others wanted the right of reply. In 1936, Reith agreed to a series to be called *Christianity and War* and Canon S. D. Morris of Birmingham had opportunity for putting the opposite case.

The clergy were not the only ones with opinions. Parliamentarians also shared the pacifist outlook and clamoured for air time. The Peace Pledge Union (Dick Sheppard's initiative) had considerable support from the Pacifist Parliamentary Group, one member of which was Dr J. Alfred Salter who was President of the PPU. The Talks Department arranged a debate between him and Wickham Steed, the journalist and broadcaster, in the *Way of Peace* series in the spring of 1938.[77]

With the outbreak of war in September 1939, Sir Richard Maconachie as Director of Talks was, in effect, the censor of all these, and this included sermons. Whereas for the seventeen years before September 1939 the Director of Talks had sought to exercise some control over what was said over the air from the pulpit, this was really only effective for studio sermons and talks where the Corporation could legitimately ask to see the script in advance. With the coming of war and censorship, every sermon had to be scripted and scrutinized. Many a time a preacher who wished to add a spontaneous off-the-cuff remark was forcefully prevented.[78] Thus the voice of preacher was subjected to the authority and scrutiny of an institution which until then had given virtual freedom to the churches to proclaim their gospel and had merely intervened to prevent bickering and improve quality. With the coming of war, the Corporation was to control the churches just as it was itself to be subject to nation and Government.

The underlying question was one of interpretation; in what ways should broadcasting serve the interests of the nation and support the war effort? What would become of free speech, at least as far as the clergy had enjoyed it when from their pulpits they had addressed the nation? What of profound questions in moral philosophy which, when proclaimed by theologians and churchmen, became matters of faith? Could a clergyman, though an avowed patriot, be allowed to preach convictions which others might construe as against the national interest? Could the same man be allowed to preach other things, even if he promised to keep quiet on those particular convictions? Once the war had begun, could pacifism in any shape or form be promulgated over the air? The answer was not easily found and had serious consequences for the churches and the broadcasters thereafter. The pacifist issue would forever disengage the churches from their special hold on the administration of broadcasting, however strongly they would continue to fight for that hold through RBD and CRAC.

Welch, as we have seen, wanted to shift the weight of religious broadcasting from its Sunday context to the weekday; from a liturgical and homiletical to what he called a 'practical, weekday Christianity.' Welch wanted the lost Sunday talk compensated for on a weekday by talks on the application of Christianity in the time of national crisis; he wanted Christianity to have its broadest compass of conviction proclaimed on the air. He had asked J. Middleton Murry to broadcast a series on *Europe in Travail*. In October 1939, Welch knew that a principle was at stake; Murry was, as Fenn told Welch, 'at least fifty per cent Marxist and one hundred per cent pacifist', and both men knew it was more than likely that this very first series of weekday talks would come to an untimely end. Welch told Murry that 'a good deal of the future work of this department depends on the result and success of these six talks'.[79]

Maconachie would not have anything to do with them. Welch's view was that, as censor, Maconachie was 'only responsible for the technique of drafting and speaking.' He was soon to discover otherwise! Maconachie thought them 'poor in style and content' and Lindsay Wellington realized the growing delicacy of the situation between him and Welch. Had Welch both the authority and competence to arrange such a series when the Director of Talks was out of sympathy with them? Murry's talks read better than they sounded, and would not appeal to the non-reading public, and for this reason the Adult Education Department would not support him. This weakened Welch's position. (The Central Council for Group Listening did, however, take the talks.) Then Welch received a note from the Director of the War Office Public Relations which curtly warned that Murry's views were 'hardly suitable for consumption by the soldier in wartime.' Was this because the ideas were bad for morale or because Murry's style would not encourage soldiers to listen? Either way, Murry was mostly known for his pacifism and his left-wing political views and rather less for the Christianity which he had only lately espoused. Welch defended him: he was the 'forerunner of a widespread return to Christianity – the prophetic note such as he strikes is most urgently necessary today.'[80] Furthermore, as a layman he would carry more conviction, notwithstanding his close association with the Peace Pledge Union. The fact remained that Murry was known as a pacifist and for some this disqualified him from the microphone.[81] Welch thought the War Office should support the talks as very suitable for soldiers who, he believed, 'questioned the fundamentals of society and church' and hoped that listening groups would be formed in all the Commands!

As Fenn has explained,[82] after September 1939 the Corporation was in a measure of panic, worrying over possible violence and bombing attacks and also over the measure of freedom of utterance it would be allowed by the Government. On sensitive questions of conscientious objection and pacifist convictions, the broadcasters had to tread very carefully. Laurence Gilliam, for example, thought in his imaginative way that the subject should perhaps be given his documentary feature treatment in order to allay misunderstandings and the sort of hostility which such convictions evoked. On 18 November 1939 the Home Board turned him down in favour of a talk or discussion which would place overall control in Maconachie's hand. Fenn had already seen the danger signs. Sir Richard regarded the Corporation simply as a servant of the Government and thought that it should broadly do as it was told in the national interest. Gilliam's suggestion was brought to the Talks meeting and Maconachie squashed it on the grounds that pacifism was a matter of religious conviction and therefore not arguable; besides, such a talk might contravene the censorship rule and would 'prejudice sections of the population against the successful prosecution of the war.'[83] Gilliam wanted to illustrate the liberal character of the present Government towards conscientious objectors. Welch and Fenn realized that there would be harder times ahead if the Christian message was to be heard. For Maconachie it was one thing to have the spiritual and moral issues of the war examined and in particular to have churchmen calling for a critical look at the basis of our society; it was quite another to broadcast the donnish debates and drawing-room conversations of the intelligentsia. The power of broadcasting, he rightly thought, was being undervalued; the very utterance of contentious issues could lead the undiscerning to think that the BBC was in support of conscientious objection. Welch wanted quality and breadth in Christian preaching, and later told Aubrey that religious broadcasting must be regarded

> . . . as leaven in the general BBC output . . . keeping the fact of God and the truths of religion strongly before the mind of listeners. I only wish the quality of our broadcasting were as good as the quantity; but here we are limited by personnel and by the poverty in the churches, for prophets are few and far between and the real corporate work, thinking and routine of the churches does not make spectacular broadcasting.[84]

Indeed, what made spectacular broadcasting were most often events and personalities, and only occasionally spoken words when they were simple and liturgical events when they were sublime.

One such personality was, of course, Temple, to whom Welch was close and for whom he had the highest regard. But from the Corporation's point of view, Temple, though reputedly wise and even, according to many, prophetic, was also highly controversial. In Scotland George MacLeod of the community of Iona was similarly regarded. He had a long and outstanding record in broadcasting since 1926 when he was at St Cuthbert's, Edinburgh.[85] MacLeod was a pacifist and everyone, especially in Scotland, knew it; indeed, he himself thought that his pacifism and his association with the Fellowship of Reconciliation cost him a great deal of financial support for his work on Iona. Welch wanted both Temple and MacLeod at the microphone, and not merely to offer the public the required balanced view consistent with BBC editorial policy. Welch knew that both men could proclaim support for the war effort and speak in the national interest from theological convictions which were not so much above political discourse but rather moving in similar directions on a parallel track.

Temple himself recognized the suffering that resulted from maintaining the law by force; this was costly to servicemen and civilians alike. MacLeod represented and articulated a view which on one level was quite the opposite of Temple's. For MacLeod (as for many others, especially Anglicans),[86] a pacifist too was serving the nation and should expect to suffer, not only because of the traditional opprobrium attached to pacifism. MacLeod told a Scottish Fellowship of Reconciliation meeting in 1939 that pacifists 'should join a corps to serve the state in the most dangerous job that the state could give them consistent with their principles: such a corps should have a stricter discipline and shinier buttons than the Guards.'[87] In the light of this, Melville Dinwiddie (the Scottish Director) might well think that one of MacLeod's defects was his 'reluctance to think things through'. Welch, however, thought he was 'alpha +', and once the Murry series was over, he wanted MacLeod for yet another series planned to bring the Christian gospel to bear systematically on the contemporary crisis. This was to be *The Christian Looks at the World*. Welch told MacLeod that his being a pacifist might be an advantage: 'In this department we are most anxious to preserve complete freedom of speech during the wave of propaganda that is even now slowly gathering.'[88] But to Welch's consternation, MacLeod had no desire to speak as a well-known pacifist: the gospel could be proclaimed in realistic, practical and down-to-earth ways (MacLeod was known for his directness) without any sort of pacifist reductionism: 'I do not think pacifism is the gospel from which all else springs; the gospel is that from which, for me at any rate, pacifism springs.' (This crucial and pithy epigram was to encourage Welch time and again when he was defending his convictions before the hierachy of the BBC.) Welch was sufficiently realistic to recognize that MacLeod's reputation was rather more for his pacifism than for his Christian ministry, and that if he went on the air to answer any listeners' questions at the end of the *Christian Looks at the World* series, people would be bound to ask him about pacifism. This, Welch reassured Dinwiddie, might overshadow the whole series to the detriment of what he regarded as more important questions of wartime Christian attitudes.

During the early months of war, both Temple and MacLeod broadcast talks and sermons and represented the two major opinions towards the conflict. The concept of a Christian society was uppermost in the broadcasts of most clergy. The need to defend Christian civilization was the purpose of the war, they proclaimed. There could be no retreat, said Berry of the Congregational Union. Welch's friend, F. A. Cockin, a Canon of St Paul's Cathedral, proclaimed that a victory for Germany or Russia in their present frame of mind would be a disaster for humanity.[89] Cardinal Hinsley thought Britain was fighting for a Christian civilization, a notion also at the centre of a broadcast by E. S. Woods, the Bishop of Lichfield, from his cathedral in October: 'Christian tradition . . . still has a mighty potency and . . . reasserted by the church might yet make our nation Christian in fact as well as in name.'[90] The church's fundamental task, despite the limitations of wartime, was 'making God real to men . . . and so bringing the ideal of a Christian England within the realm of possibility.' All such sentiments were perfectly acceptable to the BBC in particular and the nation at large; in practical terms they implied support for the war effort and backed up Temple's blunt and rather less poetic utterance: 'We should make no terms with Herr Hitler or his Government.'[91]

On the other hand, when Charles Raven preached during Advent 1939, a few discerning listeners might have been forgiven for seeing in his references to the figure of Jesus veiled signals of his own pacifist position and his convictions elsewhere expressed.[92] Jesus refused weapons and was ready to 'surrender every single worldly support'.[93] Unlike MacLeod, Raven was not a national figure and besides, had a reputation as a scientist, a field in which pacifism hardly features.[94] He was, of course, well-known as a pacifist among churchmen. His publications were widespread and his position had been the subject of considerable controversy. Welch nevertheless had no reason to hesitate in bringing Raven to the microphone once the war had started.

Less well known but notable for his declared pacifism was Leyton Richards, formerly of Carrs Lane Congregational Church in Birmingham, a leading Nonconformist church in the region, from which broadcasts were frequently made.[95] Richards had made his position clear before the war started.[96] Welch, who thought him the best Congregationalist preacher in the Midlands, engaged him to preach on 12 November 1939. When in October Archbishop Lang announced that that day would be kept as 'Armistice Sunday', Welch, having ascertained that Richards intended to preach on pacifism, asked him to postpone the broadcast until 11 February 1940; he felt that a pacifist sermon on Armistice Sunday would be inappropriate and hurtful. In January Richards submitted the text of his sermon, on 'Christ Triumphant over the Power of Evil'. Welch, who knew he would be held responsible for it, asked him to modify what he had said about non-pacifists like Temple, whom he accused of 'collapsing onto the side of a sub-Christian world order'. Welch, himself a non-pacifist, thought that Richards ought to respect the integrity of his opponents' convictions.

Richards readily agreed to rewrite the sermon, but to Welch's surprise the second version was still explicitly pacifist. He had expected of Richards the same theological breadth and discretion he had found in Raven, Donald Soper, and MacLeod, all of whom had broadcast since the war began, but had avoided articulating their pacifist views so clearly. But was a preacher to 'trim his sails to the political wind', asked Richards. Welch, who felt strongly that in any controversy both sides should have access to the microphone, felt unable to withdraw his invitation to Richards simply because he had chosen to preach pacifism in such an outspoken way.

Richards gave his sermon; he preached 'a more excellent way'; as Jesus met his foes unarmed, so should we; 'he persisted only in loving and forgiving his enemies who sought to do him harm.' War is the best answer to evil the world knows, but the Christian reading the gospel is faced with a choice between two ways: 'In the light of his triumph we pacifists have a right to assert that victory over the power of evil belongs only to those who fight with the weaponless love of Jesus Christ.'

The immediate reaction, inevitably, took the form of angry telephone calls; but out of some four hundred letters which Richards received, only a few were abusive; the majority, he told Welch, were not so much hostile as 'honestly bewildered as to how to translate the Christian way into practical effect at this present time'. The press, however, accused the BBC of allowing the Fifth Column to the microphone, and of offending millions of fighting men and their relatives by broadcasting prayer for conscientious objectors.

Welch defended Richards to Nicolls and was 'entirely convinced that such a sermon in war time must have rendered the church a great service. If the Corporation should be criticized he would accept full and public responsibility.' Ogilvie, for his part, supported Welch when he was criticized by H. G. Strauss, MP, who asked Sir Stephen Tallents, the Director of Public Relations, for a copy of Richards' sermon. Tallents spoke of free speech and said that, like literature, broadcasting should be a 'perpetual encounter between truth and error.' Such noble concepts of broadcasting were a luxury not permitted in wartime, but Ogilvie stoutly defended Nicolls' decision to have both sides of a divisive issue examined: 'We did right to allow him to speak according to his conscience.'[97]

Notwithstanding Churchill's remark in the House that the nation was fighting for freedom of conscience,[98] the Chairman of the Governors, Sir Allan Powell, thought otherwise, as did Reith and the Minister of Information. Reith had met with a number of clergy and church dignitaries who were against Welch's policy, and who had complained to Reith that he banned broadcast sermons on the subject of war. Ogilvie told Reith that this was plainly not true; war was neither banned nor promoted. Richards' sermon was itself one of a course on 'Christ Triumphant', and Richards had chosen pacifism for his subject.[99] Welch was now under pressure from both CRAC and Powell, and he felt he should make a full statement of the aims of the RBD, in order to give the Committee at its next meeting the fullest chance to discuss the issue and reaffirm his and Ogilvie's policy. Ogilvie told Welch that, in his view, the Governors and Powell had acted 'on their own in this whole conscientious objection business and very precipitately and determinedly too.'[100] Ogilvie had been 'waging war on this internal front and was reasonably confident of winning but the battle can't be hurried'. Welch was an impatient man.

When CRAC met on 7 March, Powell, Ogilvie, Tallents and Nicolls were all present to watch Welch tread a delicate path. He accepted full responsibility for his support of free speech, though he did point out that the fact that the RBD was in Bristol caused practical problems and made negotiation difficult. He had invited Richards to broadcast; he had not asked for a pacifist sermon, but once the invitation had been issued, events had been set in motion which could not easily be stopped. In all sermons so far, broadcasters had taken the line that 'our nation's cause is righteous, that we fight against evil and that we may rightly pray for victory'.[101] In inviting Richards, he assumed he would preach a sermon appropriate to the first Sunday in Lent, on some such subject as 'The Conquest of Evil in Individual Lives'. But once the invitation had been issued, there could be no withdrawal, otherwise the Corporation would be accused of 'denying free speech to ministers'. (C. V. Taylor remembers that at this Powell shifted uneasily.[102]) This was to be the area of contention: who gave the invitation, the BBC or the RBD? It was clear that Powell wanted to distance himself from the Department over this issue; the Corporation was already under pressure from Parliament, and this was no time to have pacifism at the forefront of broadcasting policy.

Characteristically, Welch enumerated five ways in which broadcasting in general and the BBC in particular had gained from the episode: (1) freedom of speech had been upheld; (2) the BBC had gained the gratitude and praise of pacifists; (3) the episode illustrated Churchill's statement that we were fighting for freedom of conscience; (4) the pacifist statement had been a 'necessary reminder to the church of that "more excellent way" which would lead to a more Christian society' (echoes of Temple and J. H. Oldham); (5) listeners were reminded that war required moral choices – an important element in democracy. Welch asserted what he saw as the BBC's relationship with the RBD: from the beginning of broadcasting the rule had been that every minister was responsible for what he said.

He then went on to outline four principles of religious broadcasting during war which bore on the present crisis: (1) patriotism is a part of religion but religion can never be merely a part of patriotism without ceasing to be Christian; (2) Christians are bound by Christ to pray for their enemies; (3) their intercessions must be for the whole world and not merely for themselves, and (4) it was right to pray for victory. The Committee was presented with the thinking of Welch and Fenn, who had drawn up this statement with Garbett's approval. The meeting heartily supported Welch and his invitation to Richards, even though to a man they declared their profound disagreement with what Richards had said. It was all the more irksome for Welch that Richards was a rather dashing Congregationalist, and not an Anglican. Even Richards' close friend, Berry (formerly of Carrs Lane), could not support him in this. The Commitee diplomatically expressed the warmest thanks to the Corporation for making the invitation and C. S. Woodward, the Bishop of Bristol, hoped that more broadcasts would take place on the theology of pacifism for the benefit of 'church people'. After the meeting, Powell made himself quite clear: 'Thank you for a most interesting meeting, Welch. But remember if there is any more preaching of pacifism, there will be trouble!'[103] Welch had been warned – soon enough principles would be translated into personalities and the Governors would become even more sensitive. This issue underlined the divergence between Welch, who was a theologian, and Maconachie who was not. Powell, moreover, could not understand how a theologian who held pacifist views could make a religious utterance without referring to his pacifism.

A week after Richards' sermon, Welch had invited Raven to preach a series of four sermons in the autumn of 1940 so that the pacifist position should occasionally be heard 'to prevent the church from becoming more and more nationalistic and Old Testament' and so that pacifists could come to the microphone and show their unity with other leading Christians. 'They may split on the pacifist issue but must really unite on those other fundamental issues of Christian faith.'[104] This was too subtle for Powell and the Governors – they thought it hypocritical. They met on 6 June and took CRAC to task for the minutes of the meeting on 7 March, which implied that the *BBC* had invited Mr Richards to preach a pacifist sermon on 11 February. They all but washed their hands of the RBD and its director: CRAC's assumption was quite wrong.[105] CRAC had given 'warm approval to the Corporation to allow freedom to Mr Richards' but it had done no such thing. Dr Welch had issued the invitation and, in effect, the Governors thought he should have known better than to invite a man who not only was a publicly declared pacifist but would seize any opportunity to proclaim his position. Welch's views on what the broadcast had achieved were not in accord with Corporation policy and should not appear in the Minutes.[106] Powell met Garbett in mid-May to assure him that the Governors appreciated all that Welch had done and to discuss the question of CRAC's relation with the Corporation.[107] The directive which was to come should be given as little publicity as possible and not sent to all members, but merely noted at the next meeting. At the end of May the issue was again raised in Parliament.[108]

Although Garbett had reassured Powell that he had no doubt about the 'righteousness of our cause' and that he was 'strongly opposed to the wireless being used for any kind of propaganda which would weaken the national resolve',[109] the Governors regarded the gains of the broadcast of which Welch had spoken at the March meeting as entirely a church interpretation, and not the views of the Corporation.[110] On 6 June they issued their directive: there could not after all be complete freedom of speech in wartime and 'Christian ministers cannot be given a position of exceptional privilege in this regard. Religious broadcasting should . . . be in full accord with the national effort.' So far, Welch could agree and the invitation sent to Raven for his four sermons could stand. But the Governors further directed that no invitation could be sent to 'any known member of an organization or any individual who does not hold these views'. Did this open the door to inquisition and requests for declarations that potential preachers did not belong to some organization or other with pacifist aims but about which no one knew? Welch was ready for a fight. He had accepted the ruling, but with Garbett's support he would fight the notion which the Governors now evolved of a 'disability', even though Garbett later thought Welch, in this matter, had 'no sense of proportion'.[111] Powell recognized his difference of opinion with Garbett but stood firm; since there were plenty of non-pacifists who could proclaim the gospel there was no need to use people who were known to be somehow involved with pacifism and thus 'disabled'; the Governors could not 'separate the individuality of the speaker from his outside association and from what he may have said or written elsewhere.' Raven had made himself quite clear in his publications.

In July, the question of conscientious objection came into the troubled area between the RBD and the hierarchy. Up till now it had hardly featured in any practical way since few, if any, laymen who were eligible for military service were invited to the microphone for religious talks or sermons. However, Welch was shown a document marked 'secret' which was passed to all departments and regional executives from the Programme Contracts Executive, the Department responsible for booking of artists and the agreement of fees, etc. It contained a ruling from the Director-General that artists who had registered as conscientious objectors should not be booked by the Corporation. Any artist who should ask why he had been refused should be told verbally that the Corporation had decided not to book conscientious objectors for broadcasting or take them on to its staff. The document stressed that nothing should be put in writing. Welch and Fenn immediately set to work on an appeal against the ruling.

If its effect was only to exclude conscientious objectors from giving religious broadcasts, there was no practical problem. But if the intention was to exclude those holding pacifist views, then the situation was serious. Welch, supported by Nicolls, thought it was time to challenge both the Governors' ruling of 6 June and this one as they applied to religious broadcasting. He expressed his views in a memorable essay to Ogilvie; he hoped Powell would receive a copy, and Ogilvie reluctantly passed it on. It was sent on 2 August, appropriately the very day on which the Home Secretary published his advice to local authorities that no one should be penalized for the mere holding of an opinion.

Welch distinguished between three groups of pacifist motivation: political, humanitarian and christological, i.e. 'those who feel directly called of God to follow the example of our Lord in meeting evil only by love even to the point of death'. Both Archbishops had told their Convocations that pacifist priests should be allowed to exercise their ministry. Welch drove home the point. If the churches and the state did not forbid pacifist clergy from speaking and preaching, and if furthermore the BBC itself had never since the beginning claimed official control or censorship over the clergy and their broadcast sermons, it could not do so now. The church leaders, however, had counselled the clergy not to use their pulpits for propaganda, and by the same token, CRAC had always regarded any explicit pursuit of sectarian identities as 'propaganda' to be contrasted with its common agreement over 'mainstream Christianity'. Welch was concerned about the ban because it excluded men known for their pacifist views from doing any other broadcasting. For the BBC to 'excommunicate' such men would be to 'upset the whole basis of religious broadcasting in this country'. The BBC was both a 'secular organization' and 'Christian Corporation', but it had no authority to make judgments which were in the end theological; that privilege belonged to the RBD.[112] Such a ban was out of step with both the Government and the churches. The BBC should not allow pacifism to be broadcast – with that Welch fully agreed. But this should not exclude men such as Soper, MacLeod and Raven, who were three of Welch's best broadcasters and could be relied upon to produce good material which would in no way explicitly promulgate a pacifist view.

A week later the Governors met; they were not moved by Welch's appeal of 2 August, and affirmed that their ruling of 6 June stood; the three men were accordingly 'disabled'. Powell had the support of Duff Cooper, who fully agreed with the ruling and particularly felt that the radio should be seen to be regarded as 'the most important war weapon after the armed forces'. Duff Cooper thought that no special privilege could be given to Christian ministers who belonged, and were known to belong, to organizations opposed to the war effort, and who had conscientious objection to military service. The relevant papers were sent to Wellington, now in the Ministry of Information, so that Duff Cooper would be prepared for any question in the House.

Ogilvie then met Welch in London and tried to make the directive of 6 June quite clear; the issue was not finally about theology, nor was the BBC stepping into areas beyond its competence. The main issue was about politics, government and the role and effectiveness of broadcasting in the national crisis. People known to hold pacifist opinions would not be well received, whatever else they might wish to convey. 'The Governors held,' Ogilvie told Welch, 'that a known pacifist . . . suffered from a "civil disability" which inevitably prejudiced the reception of his broadcasts by listeners.'[113] The Governors did not wish Welch to conduct any sort of 'inquisition' – it was enough that these men were known to have views that were not fully in accord with the national effort.

Welch had appealed to the Governors and they had made their pronouncement much to the irritation of Ogilvie and Nicolls, who were fully behind him. The Director-General regretted that Welch had sent this appeal at all and wanted more subtlety: 'Tactics are not irrelevant to the attainment of our objectives.' Another of Welch's tactics would also not help the cause; Ogilvie advised Welch not to appeal to see Duff Cooper who was, anyway, doing his best to protect the BBC from those who wished it to be even more subject to Government control. Powell knew well that an appeal by Welch to Duff Cooper would drive a wedge between the BBC Governors and the RBD, and so bring the Department into closer relationship with the churches. Welch's only consolation was in Powell's suggestion that the situation might change and that the matter might be reviewed after three months, when the emotions surrounding Dunkirk would have subsided. Furthermore, if they could obtain a recantation of some kind from George MacLeod to the effect that the war could only be won by force of arms, then he might be approved! Raven could certainly not broadcast and was naturally sad about it. He told Welch that he honestly believed he had something to say which men like Temple and Oldham had not said in, for example, *The Christian Newsletter*[114] and that this could be said without raising the pacifist issue. While it was no new thing for a minister of the gospel to be an 'ambassador in bonds', for the BBC to refuse every pacifist meant that the RBD ceased to represent the churches. Religious broadcasting should be different from all other broadcasting; its primary loyalty, thought Raven, was to the church; it was 'an extension of God's work in a Christian country'. Welch was saddened by the exclusion of Raven, and for his part Raven never forgave the Department for bending under the Governors' ruling.[115] But as Welch knew, the BBC, for all its Christianity, was a secular organization and responsible for all its output to the nation and thus to Parliament.

Welch suffered a conflict of loyalties and confessed his 'troubled position' to Powell in the autumn. He wanted the BBC to come out of the war with honour, clear of the charge of intolerance which was characteristic of the Nazism against which the nation was fighting. He wanted to manifest the unity of the gospel, particularly as the churches were so divided over pacifism. He wanted the BBC to show itself clearly to be above the charge of propaganda by broadcasting both a publicly known pacifist alongside an equally well-known supporter of the war effort in perhaps a single evening programme. Welch suggested a broadcast by Raven with Temple or W. R. Matthews, but it was not allowed. He appealed to Powell that they should understand each other and 'was desperately anxious that we should come out of this war with clean hands and our loyalty to God and his church which I serve, untarnished'. Welch's second appeal was that the directive of 6 June should be interpreted by his Department on the advice of the Director-General, the Controllers, and the Advisory Committees and not be subject to a ministerial blanket ruling via the Governors. The Director-General was equally as keen.

The battle Welch confessed to be fighting moved even further out of his control when the issues involved the Scottish Regional Director, Dinwiddie, never a great friend of A. C. Craig, who had been working in London with J. H. Oldham on *the Christian Newsletter* since the war began. In Scotland Craig was well known as a pacifist. Welch had not known this when inviting him to preach at a service the coming December. Fenn knew him closely as a devout Christian who 'accepted the whole of the Sermon on the Mount'[116] but had never translated the injunctions against violence into political action; he did not belong to any pacifist organization and nor did he encourage any to oppose the war effort. Dinwiddie's view was quite simply that in Scotland a broadcast by Archie Craig would arouse considerable opposition. The matter was further complicated by the public reputation of Sir Hugh Roberton, the Conductor of the Glasgow Orpheus Choir, who was also well known for his articulate opposition to the war and his participation in 'The People's Convention', a well-known pacifist organization with a galaxy of supporters from the world of politics, the arts and entertainment. In November 1940 Powell and Graves, the Deputy Director-General, went to Scotland and met Dinwiddie, to discover that in the latter's view any broadcast by Roberton would raise considerable opposition and if Craig was allowed to broadcast, Roberton in turn would make 'a dickens of a row' – as Welch reported to Craig in cancelling his invitation for December. Much to Welch's annoyance, the Governors preferred the advice of the Scottish authorities including Dinwiddie to that of the Director of Religious Broadcasting in London. Both he and Fenn were very angry and even considered resignation.[117] CRAC was due to meet on 21 November and Welch, anticipating trouble, appealed yet again to Powell for leave to interpret the June ruling as he had previously asked. After all, the three months mentioned in August had now gone by and perhaps the matter might be looked at again. He wanted to reassure CRAC, who had maintained support for the Corporation over their general religious policy. Powell was unmoved; Craig, it was agreed, was a well-known pacifist; there could not be complete freedom of broadcast speech in wartime and Christian ministers could not be privileged. Moreover, Powell argued that there was a fundamental dishonesty in inviting a pacifist to broadcast and then forbidding him to broadcast on the very subject closest to his heart and conscience. Welch argued in vain that this was as if to say that Raven *qua* scientist could not speak with authority on the behaviour of birds without mentioning the war effort! Powell feared that the BBC would be exposed to questions in Parliament and other complaints if invitations to pacifists were construed as meaning that the BBC endorsed their thinking on everything. Fenn enlisted the support of men like Nathaniel Micklem, the Principal of Mansfield College, Oxford,[118] and William Paton both of whom made forceful appeals to Powell. Paton even uttered a threat: if the BBC could not allow a pacifist minister to preach whilst not mentioning pacifism, 'the churches will be honour bound to protest against something they regard as an invasion of religious freedom wholly out of keeping with the traditions of our Christian country'.[119]

CRAC met on 21 November and broadly supported Welch in opposing the ban on MacLeod and Craig.[120] Its thinking was not quite consistent; while it appreciated the problems of the Corporation at a critical time, it still wanted freedom for the churches to appoint or invite men to broadcast through the machinery of the BBC and its RBD. Woodward, the Bishop of Bristol, argued that religious services could hardly be put into the category of broadcasts which 'deal with the war' as the Governors had ruled. 'Religion', he said, 'transcended all political divisions.'[121] In broadcasting it most certainly did not, as Richards' sermon had shown. Ogilvie pointed out that when Middleton Murry had broadcast his quite non-pacifist talks, there was an outcry for censorship – not because of what he had actually said but because *he* had been given leave by a public corporation to say anything at all at this time and so implicate the Corporation in a charge of undermining the national effort. The obvious thing to do, in his view, was to choose broadcasters from the 99 per cent of ordained men who supported the national effort and simply not invite the others. That was what the policy had been; Ogilvie called for CRAC to show a little humility and recognize that the leaders of the Corporation could also be credited with principles as deeply held as their own which enabled them to 'have the Christ-Caesar relationship as clearly defined' as the clergy. Powell supported Ogilvie's remarks, adding only that the Committee should note one implication of inviting a man to broadcast: 'We are not able to separate the speaker from his reputation.'

Finally, Cyril Garbett, by then Bishop of Winchester, suggested that it would be 'wiser not to pass any resolution in this matter. The minutes would bear out the fact that there was a difference of opinion.' So said the official minutes; the majority of the Committee and its Chairman understood the situation of the Corporation but did not agree over these men.[122] The Government would not have pacifists undermining the war effort and Garbett was forced to agree with the Corporation at least by implication. But Welch and Fenn were not prepared to let the matter rest, and William Temple at York also intended to continue the struggle and prepared a motion for consideration by his bishops.

Sir Hugh Roberton, meanwhile, had made himself quite clear over the pacifist issue and had a reputation at the BBC as a 'rather talkative interpolator at the microphone', at least according to the Director of the BBC Secretariat. Roberton had been asked by Dinwiddie those same questions as had been asked of MacLeod and Craig: would he agree that the national cause could only be won by the use of arms? Roberton could not answer affirmatively and thus Dinwiddie recommended to Powell that the ban should also embrace the celebrated conductor. 'As Sir Hugh Roberton had reaffirmed views already publicly expressed . . . the BBC could not invite him to the microphone with the Glasgow Orpheus Choir.'[123] Notwithstanding a hostile response in the press to this statement, only about two hundred and fifty letters of protest were received. In the House, the Minister of Information, in reply to a question, said that it was his intention to 'exercise as little control as possible over the entertainment programme of the BBC'.[124] Nevertheless there were growing signs of disquiet from some Labour members. Vaughan Williams withdrew his symphony.

In the new year the press made much of the ban on the three heroes of pacifist principles. Hugh Redwood in the *News Chronicle*[125] supported them and rather scorned Powell's insistence not upon their pacifism but their reputation as pacifists; Canon Raven 'will not be allowed to talk even about birds'.[126] Whilst the National Council for Civil Liberties was preparing a petition to the BBC on all those banned with special reference to Sir Hugh, William Temple pleaded in public[127] as Welch had already done in private, to have the BBC broadcast sermons wherein those who differed on the question of armed force should 'maintain their spiritual fellowship in the bond of charity'. No pacifist should be excluded from the microphone provided he promised not to advocate his pacifism. Powell might well recognize these phrases. Welch, as Harold Nicolson noted, was a 'fervent adherent of William Temple'.[128]

Garbett, however, thought that Temple's letter, about which he had no advance knowledge, had got everything 'out of proportion'. Before replying to Temple, Powell consulted Garbett,[129] who assured him that he had resisted pressure from Welch (and from within CRAC) to make public the deep disagreement of the Department and the Committee with the Governors.[130] He did not agree with those who seemed to think that the BBC was part of the church; it was, if anything, part of the Government. A compromise was reached which marks a turning-point in the Governors' policy: pacifists might be invited, but only those who were not known as such; at the same time there should be no inquisition. In effect, Garbett supported the BBC; perhaps as Chairman of CRAC he had no choice. After all, Raven and Soper were recognized members of the Peace Pledge Union and this for Powell was a form of 'public agitation.'[131] Powell's reply to Temple was predictably evasive: in practice the issue involved less than a dozen preachers and had Temple not written that the British pacifist 'was weakening the British capacity to fight and increasing Hitler's chances'?[132] Powell had an excellent secretariat.

In the House the debate continued. In his reply to George Strauss, MP for Lambeth, Duff Cooper expressed the intention to 'keep the BBC as a public forum . . . where all opinions could be freely voiced . . . just so long as it does not interfere with the prosecution of the war'. But in practice as it was with preachers so with artists; there were sufficient in favour of the war to fill the programmes. Cooper asserted that if pacifists were 'notorious' they were 'enemies of the country'.[133]

Temple recognized that broadcasting had been entrusted to the BBC and was grateful for the opportunity it gave to the church. He told Powell: 'Religion cannot become part of anything purely national without forfeiting its distinctively Christian character.'[134] Temple, with Welch, wanted the RBD recognized as the churches' place in the broadcasting institution; it should be regarded by the BBC as finally the responsibility of the church itself, and the BBC 'activity in this respect stands on a different footing from anything else the BBC may undertake'. The pacifist issue had pushed him into an extreme position. Powell would entertain no such ideas;[135] his case was overwhelming so long as the notion of broadcasting as a weapon of war was maintained. In peacetime the control exercised over religious broadcasting had been largely an agreed discipline on churches and individual broadcasters exercised by the Department through Iremonger and the hierarchy up to Reith. The church had its officer in the Corporation. In war, not even the churches could claim such privilege.

Opposition was now mounting: it was a scandal that eminent persons were barred from the microphone and the public denied contributions from artists of all kinds. Duff Cooper was asked if he would set up a committee of enquiry into the BBC's anti-pacifist policy. He refused. Noel-Baker put another interpretation on events: the ban brought this minority view into publicity, and 'gave advertisement to an opinion which has no national support'. Duff Cooper stated that 'Everybody has the right of free speech but not everybody has the right to . . . exercise (it) through the BBC.'[136]

Subsequently, on 20 March, Winston Churchill made a significant statement which reflected the change of policy in respect to clerical broadcasters as well as musicians and other performers, especially those connected with the People's Convention. Churchill told the House that the connection between opinions 'calculated to hamper the nation in its struggle for life . . . and dramatic and musical events' is 'not apparent' and the relation not worth making. Mr Neil Maclean, MP, asked Churchill on behalf of Sir Hugh Roberton if he would now be free of the ban. Churchill saw 'no reason to suppose that the holding of pacifist views would make him play flat . . . my endeavour is to make him play up!'[137] William Paton thought there was no real threat to the freedom of the Christian gospel, an issue over which Fenn and Welch had been prepared to risk their jobs; nor was there any real parallel between the ban on musicians and that on the pacifist clergy. Nevertheless, Paton was prepared for an 'all-out confrontation with the Home Office'.[138]

Garbett wasted no time in asking Powell whether in the light of this, the ruling could be changed; he could now firmly support Welch. Powell hoped that after the Prime Minister's statement, the situation might very well change, but 'it might take a week or two'. The Corporation was under considerable pressure and ordained pacifists were mentioned explicitly in the petition to the Board by the National Council for Civil Liberties which hoped each case would be reviewed. The change in policy took only a month: the People's Convention adherents were the first to be freed from the 'civil disability' clause and about the end of April 1941, the Governors agreed that the ban should relate only to those who opposed the war effort and who were indeed known for that attitude. Welch had gained half a victory. Early in May, Ogilvie wrote to Welch informing him that he was now free to invite George MacLeod and Archie Craig to broadcast. Neither of them had ever made any statement which could be construed as opposition to the present war. Welch wasted no time; MacLeod was on the air within another month, and was soon talking specifically to soldiers!

Soper and Raven, however, were both well known for their opposition to the war – the latter particularly in print. It was perhaps inevitable that such an eminent Cambridge don should still be ineligible after all this discussion. Welch, however, persisted in his efforts on behalf of both of them, and also of Joseph McCulloch.[139] Despite Nicolls' support, the Board's ruling remained: 'When in doubt, don't.' In 1942, Garbett made another formal overture to Powell on behalf of Raven and again they met to discuss it. The appeal on Raven's behalf was based on his being in no way against the war effort, whatever he might have written on the theology of pacifism. Powell and the Governors were mostly conscious of his relations with the Peace Pledge Union, which had frequently been in trouble with the law and gained some public attention and even had its premises raided. Raven remained a PPU sponsor and that was enough for the Governors. Garbett told Powell that he would not press the matter 'under present circumstances'. Raven was, however, asked to write a number of scripts on British naturalists for translation into Arabic to be broadcast on the Near Eastern service – he was contracted as an 'artist'.

In May 1944 Welch appealed yet again for Raven and Soper on the grounds that the original ban had been during the collapse of France and when an invasion by the Germans was feared imminent. Welch reminded the new Director-General, Haley, that the whole trouble had come about through Leyton Richards. Many pacifists, including Raven, had written to express their regret that he had used the microphone for pacifist propaganda. The Director-General and Programme Planning only made a final decision eighteen months later when the war was over and the ban on pacifists removed.[140]

An ironic footnote to the pacifist dispute attached to the figure of Dick Sheppard, who had been influential in the first years of the development of BBC religious policy. Sheppard had founded the Peace Pledge Union and had been one of the most passionately outspoken pacifist figures until his death in 1937. Iremonger had maintained his links with broadcasting from Lichfield and had a regular book review on Sundays under the title *From a Deanery Window*. These were so successful that Maconachie once told a Home Board meeting in September 1941 that he thought these reviews the best the BBC was doing. Iremonger had been an intimate of Sheppard, and not surprisingly awaited with some eagerness his biography by Ellis Roberts published early in 1942. Iremonger prepared to review it and submitted his script for censorship as usual. He himself was no pacifist, had little sympathy for pacifists and could be very harsh.[141] In his review, he wanted to show Dick Sheppard as a pacifist and how, had he lived, he would now be in prison for his non-violent convictions and his involvement with the Peace Pledge Union. Powell was shown the script by Robert Foot and the broadcast was cancelled. Iremonger was furious; it was an 'insult to my friend'. Powell explained that there was no ban on the mention of the PPU, but that he would rather nothing should be said at this time which would 'give outstanding importance or any sense of great achievement to a movement such as the PPU'. Powell, Foot and Graves thought it unwise to allow Iremonger to enunciate the sentence: 'The issue was quite simple: war or no war; Dick Sheppard's answer was "We say no!" ' They preferred not to admit that Dick Sheppard's greatest expression was through the PPU.

The wrangle went on. Iremonger was doubly irked because Powell had written 'Private and Confidential' on his letters, which forbade him taking any formal advice or going to CRAC, of which he had been a member since 1941. Powell believed that it would have been 'improper for the Committee to arbitrate between the BBC and any individual'.[142] At CRAC's meeting in October 1942 there was considerable and heated debate as to whether the issue could be raised there. Finally Iremonger, on hearing that the Committee 'could express no opinion', walked out in a fury. Fenn considered resigning but was persuaded not to. Such a decision would have forced Welch to consider a similar course, and Nicoll's opinion prevailed: the BBC was, after all, only exercising its editorial responsibility. Notwithstanding Garbett's appeal to both him and Powell, Iremonger resigned from CRAC, and Powell told Garbett they had no choice but to accept his resignation. In future book reviews would not be left in the hands of one man, he added – as if that had any relevance to the immediate issue. Foot and Graves told Iremonger late in October that they were sorry that his association with the Corporation should have been severed by a misunderstanding; but for Iremonger it was a matter of conscience. He might have heeded the advice to his successor and recognized the need to play a much more subtle hand against Powell.

E. Talkers and radicals

Over the pacifist issue, a compromise had been reached, and however much Welch regretted that Raven and others would not be allowed to the microphone throughout the duration of the war, the compromise worked in his favour. The BBC could be seen to uphold the practice of free speech governed by principles which revolved around the concept of the 'national interest'. Those invited to the microphone were not to be subject to an inquisition – at least not formally! They would naturally not be invited unless it was clear to someone that they had something to say and that they had not said anything which would have gravely implicated the Corporation in anti-war propaganda.

The pacifist issue focused more clearly than any other the church's self-conscious struggle for freedom of speech and in particular William Temple's concept of the unity of the gospel and his belief in the responsibility of the Christian Corporation to share in and promote expression of that unity. This pressure worked in support of Welch and his initiatives during the early part of the war. There were also those in Parliament who supported such notions. Aneurin Bevan was anxious that the BBC should not be guilty of the very crimes against which the country was now fighting across the Channel; the Government through the Minister of Information was identified with the policy of the BBC and thus 'great harm has been done to the reputation of this country'.[143] The BBC must be committed to a policy of giving a balanced presentation of any controversial issue. Once war had begun, there was no doubt that the cause for which the nation now fought must be made explicit. Pacifists were by definition committed to non-violence and, with the country in arms, it was naturally difficult for the Corporation to uphold free speech for Christian pacifists who were, it could be argued, more of a thorn in the side of the mainstream churches than the considerable number of Christian sects which had been banned from the microphone for somewhat less provocative beliefs. Though Ogilvie had failed to wrest the issue away from the dangerous orbit of Government and the Chairman of Governors, Sir Allan Powell, his initial reaction at the time of Leyton Richards' sermon in 1940, had been 'since the church is divided . . . it seems right that the other side should also be presented'.[144] Powell had represented the less liberal view that the BBC should simply serve the Government's propaganda interests in time of crisis.

There were two important men who did not agree and in their quite separate ways they helped to sustain a real measure of independence for the BBC: James Welch and Sir Richard Maconachie. The latter at the time of Dunkirk was Director of Talks, and therefore responsible for the censorship of the spoken word in that area. Welch was responsible for a more subtle form of the spoken word in the broadcast sermon. On the pacifist issue, Sir Richard regarded a sermon simply as a talk, particularly when such utterance stepped out of its allotted field and presumed to tackle issues which could hardly, in his view, be any longer regarded as religious. Such sermons were talks, albeit by ordained men; they implied an ideology.

In January 1941 a rather haphazardly organized conference of some three hundred clergy met in Malvern under the chairmanship of William Temple to 'think out the general implications of fundamental Christian principles in relation to contemporary needs, so supplying

. . . maxims for conduct which mediate between fundamental principles and the tangle of particular problems'.[145] Welch freely confessed this was the 'Magna Carta of this Department . . . religious broadcasting is concerned with the moral and religious principles which Christians believe should test and govern the political and economic activities of man in society.' If the Malvern Conference had, as Temple believed, helped to 'put the church on the map again for many who had ceased to regard it as having any relevance for these problems', it was the task of religious broadcasting to pursue these same objectives and present a balanced discussion and analysis of such issues in the regular weekly religious talks period which distinguished this aspect of the BBC's religious output from the Sunday programmes. Temple, however, was not popular in certain quarters of the hierarchy and in particular with Maconachie, who had never been in agreement with that Religious Talks policy which had allowed Welch a measure of autonomy and protection from scrutiny under the auspices of CRAC and the churches. By the beginning of 1941, Maconachie, as Director of Talks and acting Controller of the Home Programme, was not only concerned that Welch was overworked but also was unsure of his competence to make judgments over religious talks, of whose content and bias he disapproved. He was 'out of sympathy with the general policy of such talks'. He was not alone; as we have seen, the Chairman of the Governors shared this view. The BBC, Welch believed, was committed to the church's mission for a Christian society. T. S. Eliot had said as much in a widely-received series of lectures before the war; his ambition was for a Christian society 'not of saints but of ordinary men whose Christianity is communal before being individual . . . a community of men and women not individually better than they are now except for the capital difference of holding the Christian faith'.[146] Temple and his Malvern colleagues – and notably V. A. Demant[147] – recognized that the church no longer represented all citizens and that it must recognize Demant's claim that political theory was heavily dominated by economics and finance and thus the church must have part in this discourse. However much broadcast religion had concentrated in pre-war days on the individual and his religion, Welch was determined to see that the hard-won weekday talk was given to the examination of such issues.

Maconachie's expression of disquiet issued in a call for discussion with Welch and the hierarchy: R. H. Eckersley, Godfrey Adams, Director of Programme Planning, the Director-General and Maconachie himself. They were to meet in February 1941 'to discuss the treatment of secular matters in talks arranged by the Director of

Religious Broadcasting'. Three major changes resulted from this meeting. Between them, Welch and Maconachie were to have the assistance of a trained producer to straddle the two departments and link Welch in Bristol to Maconachie in London. Secondly, on the policy question, the churches were not permitted to deal with political and economic issues which were plainly controversial unless this was part of a balanced presentation. Finally, all such scripts 'with a policy angle' would be sent to Nicolls, the Controller of Programmes, 'who in turn would refer to Sir Richard any points of which he remained doubtful'.[148]

SUNDAY BRIDGE
"Do you mind if we have the Archbishop during this rubber?"

Welch recognized and indeed shared Maconachie's concern not to have religious talks simply state both sides of a controversy in any point-for-point fashion. Maconachie was well aware that such a presentation, simply leaving the listener to make a judgment on the evidence, undermined the authority and freedom of the churches to say, for example, that 'evil slums must be abolished and houses built in accordance with the principles of the Sermon on the Mount, which are . . .'. He objected quite simply to shallow one-sidedness, which he associated with many religious speakers whose interpretation of events was open to considerable qualification. Many of these talks dwelt upon the causes of the war and proposed historical perspectives which were highly controversial, and such talks went beyond Temple's maxims for conduct defined somewhere between principle and actuality. A compromise was reached: if an ordained man spoke his opinion on housing or rationing or whatever, he should declare it as his opinion and not only be fair to opposing views but be sure to present them in sufficient substance to indicate their seriousness. The Christian churches, in whatever mission they believed themselves to be undertaking in broadcasting, must proclaim those Christian principles necessary for the upholding of a Christian nation. This compromise embodied both notions: that the BBC would support the invitation of Christian speakers to elucidate Christian theological principles on social issues of all kinds; and that these talks would be subject to BBC scrutiny and some degree of censorship for which (unlike the broadcast sermon, for which Welch was responsible as 'censor') the BBC hierarchy would be directly responsible.

A month before the Malvern Conference, a joint statement on 'Foundations of Peace' was published by Cosmo Lang of Canterbury, Cardinal Hinsley of Westminster, Walter Armstrong of the Free Church Federal Council and William Temple of York.[149] The statement referred to Pius XII's Five Peace Points of Christmas 1939 and added 'five standards by which economic situations and proposals might be tested'.[150] These ten principles, the statement ran, must be 'made the foundation of national policy and all social life'. This was an extraordinary piece of ecumenical co-operation by the mainstream Christian leadership, which was to call forth a strong response from Welch. He had a plan to bring a high-powered group of speakers, in a series on *The Church Looks Ahead*, to examine the presuppositions of this remarkable ecumenical text. (He had been forced by Maconachie to change the title from *Foundations of Peace*.) J. H. Oldham, T. S. Eliot, Dorothy L. Sayers and Maurice Reckitt were among the speakers, and these important talks focused a serious threat to the independence of the religious output by the Talks Department.

For almost a year Welch had been thinking that the BBC could take a unique initiative in a quite remarkable service to a nation now at war — indeed it would be more than a service; it would be a 'mission'. He described it as a 'spiritual call to the nation'. The Corporation could not easily appeal to non-Anglican denominational leaders, as they would be sure to raise questions about their proper representation in the scheme. Nor could Welch be too explicit in his approach to the Church of England, though it should have been the obvious body with which to discuss this exercise. With Lang's tacit support, however, Welch felt confident that the RBD might rightly issue a challenge to those who had little or no connection with the church. He hoped John Maud would do this, but he refused. Welch canvassed the heads of the various departments for their support for a week of broadcasts 'designed to make the spiritual issues of this war live for the ordinary listener'. Sir Adrian Boult, for example, was all for it. Welch wanted the series entitled *The BBC Speaks to Britain*, but was soon to have his aspirations considerably reduced. There were many constructive responses; for example, Val Gielgud, offered T. S. Eliot's *Murder in the Cathedral*, and the Director of Variety, Eric Maschwitz, suggested 'Scrapbooks'! Welch's hopes to have the BBC broadcast a 'message' embodied in drama and features in addition to religious broadcasts were soon to be dashed. Adams, as Director of Programme Planning, was not prepared for this wide-scale thematic approach to the organization of programmes. It became a series of discussions which held the air during peak listening on four consecutive evenings.

The series *Three Men and a Parson*, subjected clerical utterance to penetrating lay scrutiny, and was the first broadcast venture of its kind. Welch was forever hoping that the BBC would allow the kind of discussion that would force the clergy to listen to the serious questions of the 'non-churched'. F. A. Cockin chaired the talks, which were backed up not by drama or whatever might have 'spoken' in support (Boult had offered a recital of John Ireland's setting of 'These Things Shall Be') but, that week, by an early morning series called *Lift Up Your Hearts* which had originated in Scotland as a five-minute programme of thought and prayer before the news.

Three Men and a Parson won considerable notoriety and the Talks Department might well have been jealous of the twenty minutes of prime time Welch had coaxed out of the Home Board. The series was arranged for the week of 24 February to 1 March 1941, with two special Sunday services to follow. Predictably, the subject of the final talk was the 'Ten Points' and the Joint Statement. The central issues discussed were wealth, inequality, family, education and work – matters which many thought were not quite appropriate for the beginning of Lent. Scripts had been scrutinized by Duff Cooper, who was anxious to avoid giving any possible ammunition to critics, especially those in Parliament. A. P. Ryan, the newly appointed Home Adviser, regarded this series as indicative of the RBD going beyond traditional bounds and told Duff Cooper that 'this affair has shown that the BBC Religion Department cannot continue in future to function as it has up till now, free from full policy control over lay talks'.[151] That week Welch had told *Radio Times* readers that 'whenever the Christian church has offered only comfort and consolation it has failed.'

Unfortunately a technical failure in the English transmitters occurred on Saturday 1 March, and hardly anyone in England heard the fourth talk and the references to the 'Ten Points'.[152] Welch decided to give the *Lift Up Your Hearts* series himself for the following week and elucidate the 'Ten Points' again for the benefit of the English listeners who had missed them. In each five-minute session, Welch merely spoke of the 'point' with a brief comment which expanded the significance of each. This was enough to provoke a parliamentary question from M. R. Hely-Hutchinson, the MP for Hastings, who objected strongly to the 'injury to our united war effort', because of 'the propagation . . . of highly controversial political doctrines.'[153] The programme had been a misuse of broadcasting time by 'anonymous speakers' claiming the support of high authority in the church. On 11 March Duff Cooper had issued a directive that 'all scripts of the Religious Broadcast Department were to be subject to the same scrutiny as other talks'. He repeated this in the House, adding: 'It is not considered desirable that politics should enter into religious broadcasts and the point of supervision is to ensure that they do not.'[154] Welch, naturally concerned, sought some further elucidation of this. The Board met that day and approved both the Minister's directive and his parliamentary reply. Maconachie raised the question as to how politics should be understood. 'Politics', in the view of Harold Nicolson, meant 'political controversy or party politics and nothing more'.[155] Welch thought it a serious blow to his work.

During April and May attempts were made to agree on a formula which could put the proposed Concordat into words. Garbett was convinced of its need; his championing of family allowances in the Lords was, Welch thought, a good example. Ogilvie was not convinced and wanted no examples cited in the wording; he thought it 'un-Christian' to use the microphone to advocate a one-sided policy. Draft statements went back and forth between Nicolls, Welch and Maconachie, and a text was finally agreed in August; its protection of the Christian position owed as much to Nicolls as to Welch. The Corporation, through the RBD, invited speakers to begin from a Christian premise but did not require them to defend or justiy the truth of Christian revelation. This policy was not to preclude 'self-criticism by Christian thinkers' or 'the perplexities of the sincere enquirer'. In this way, the two thorny questions of controversy and mainstream Christianity were avoided. Nicolls was fond of the notion of the BBC as a Christian institution which, through the RBD, allowed the churches to examine themselves over the air. Here he was at variance with Maconachie, whose friend Harold Nicolson wanted the Christian foundations during wartime supported rather more than threatened.[156] The Concordat accepted that politics and economics would not be excluded from religious talks, but recognized that ordained men had no special competence and were concerned with principle, and not detail, and required that a clerical or lay expert competent in both theology and politics should make clear in which capacity he was speaking, both recognizing the controversial nature of the subject and encouraging opposite views to be discussed.[157] CRAC at its October meeting agreed that the ruling was 'clear and acceptable'.[158]

For the next four years the Department had to tread very delicately in the conception and production of talks. Scripts of sermons and talks were to be subject to the scrutiny of Maconachie who, until 1944, was increasingly concerned with the trend in religious broadcasting away from services and utterances more traditionally associated with Christian piety towards talks on a variety of social issues about which growing numbers of Christians wanted guidance. In a Christian nation this extended to the whole population, no matter how vocal were those who criticized the Christian monopoly in the Corporation's policy. From this basic conviction Welch and the Department sought to organize courses of talks which expressed as clearly and eloquently as possible the united Christian attitude towards any given issue. As we have noted, the first major consecutive series of talks was *Three Men and a Parson*,[159] not regarded even by Welch as a great success. It did, however, begin a tradition of self-examination and self-criticism which in turn was a prelude to deep discussion and culminated in proposals to open religious broadcasting to scrutiny not merely by the Corporation but by the churches themselves. By the Concordat between the two Departments, Talks and Religion, the stage, if not the scene, was set for the Corporation to exercise a measure of control as to how questions of theology and philosophy were to be debated.

In the early forties, limits were established on how radically the church could assess or criticize itself and also assess political and economic questions. In both cases the BBC resisted initiatives by the RBD to enter the arena of sociology, notwithstanding Temple's dicta in *Christianity and the Social Order*,[160] which compared *ex cathedra* utterances by an archbishop with his opinions as a citizen. Maconachie thought this distinction an excellent guide and was only sorry that the RBD could not apply the principle more consistently. It was one thing to have the Department enter into political and sociological detail as if they were experts, and quite another to convey opinions thus expressed in the context of news reporting. Maconachie constantly complained that, notwithstanding the Concordat, the Department would not apply the rule to potential speakers with sufficient force. Between the two Departments and the two opposing forces stood CRAC and Garbett, who himself represented both worlds – the church at worship and the church involved, as he was, in social affairs. He naturally approved the Concordat, just as he approved the compromise over pacifists. But he would not support Welch so readily when the latter attempted to apply sociological analysis to the church itself.

In 1940–41 a series was planned to 'play a return match', as Welch told Garbett, following the series *The Christian Looks at the World*. This time he wanted *The World Looks at the Christian*, with such men as Stephen Spender and C. E. M. Joad to organize the attack. No one liked it at all. Harold Nicolson, in a fine judicial tone befitting one of the Governors, told Ogilvie that 'as a pagan who has always been convinced of the value of religion, I am not happy about this series'. He thought the clergy were too proud and that the Christian faith could resist every argument. He feared it would shake the faith of religious people who were not absolutely convinced or to whom religion appealed on an emotional rather than an intellectual level. Either way, he 'hated to feel that anything put out by the BBC had disturbed the faith of anybody'.[161] Welch was disappointed at this refusal to allow 'the church to discuss itself', as Nicolls had understood the series. This was the 'real follow-up to the "mission" (*Three Men and a Parson*) and a straightforward piece of evangelism', as Welch argued to Nicolls. Maconachie thought it would contravene a pre-war CRAC decision against controversial broadcasts, which these most certainly were. Garbett told Welch quite frankly that it was not 'our business to go out of our way to arrange what are really attacks on the Christian faith; . . . with so little time available there is so much we should set forward in definite positive Christian teaching.'[162] Welch knew very well that a good proportion of the time allotted to his Department on Sundays was given to 'definite Christian teaching', but this did not reach those outside or on the fringe. Such teaching simply did not convince. In April, the Director-General rejected the suggestion, as the hierarchy was simply not prepared to have the Corporation involved in a scheme which to them undermined the faith of the churches. Welch's idea was quite the opposite; he was entirely persuaded that 'if the church would come out into the open and meet honest criticism, we should commend it and the Christian religion to many listeners who think of it only as privileged and obscurantist'. The Corporation and CRAC did not agree. A concept of the Christian religion prevailed which in wartime the BBC was committed to sustain, and which gave this impression of a closed mind; many believed that an enormous number of the regular religious programmes were devoid of any serious intellectual content. There were some exceptions, however; for instance, in July 1942 William Paton of the International Missionary Council broadcast four talks on *The Church and World Order*, but they caused great difficulty from the policy angle, and had to be approved by the Home Office. The last talk, on 'International Reconciliation', included the statement:

> The economic life of Europe is tied up with that of Germany, . . . so that a pulverized Germany would mean the lowering of the standard of life in the whole of Europe. . . . Germany remains a great community of human beings . . . for whom God cares and who will desperately want healing.[163]

The series had the approval of both Archbishops, the Cardinal, and the Moderators of the Church of Scotland and the Federal Free Church Council.

The new policy was an uphill struggle for Welch and the RBD. He was proud to boast to all and sundry that notwithstanding the reduction of the Home Programme to one wavelength at the outset of war, the Department's output had increased dramatically, not the least in the number of weekday talk periods for which he was responsible. They went out daily at 7.55 a.m., and on Wednesday evenings, Thursday (lunchtime and evenings) and Friday evenings. The difficulty, which Welch fully realized, was one of production; the quality of both speakers and material was not always up to the standard expected by the Talks Department, particularly when a clear ideological gulf existed between personnel as in the case of Guy Burgess,[164] the producer of *Three Men and a Parson*.

As a broadcaster, however, C. S. Lewis was the notable exception. Welch had approached him in 1941, having read *The Problem of Pain*. He wanted 'something like *The Christian Faith as I See it* – by a layman'.[165] It was this initiative which culminated in the series later published as *Mere Christianity*, which added not a little prestige to the BBC's religious output; not however, without vigorous debate in the religious and secular press.[166]

In autumn 1942 the issue came to a head. Foot, the Joint Director-General, raised the question whether the increase in religious talks was

12. Sir Richard Maconachie

13. William Temple

14. John Williams

15. Mary Somerville

16. J. W. Welch (*left*) and Ronald Selby Wright

leading to inferior production. George Barnes, now Director of Talks, was also concerned with quality; he thought that the RBD was handling non-religious subjects with insufficient skill to avoid the charge of partiality. Harold Nicolson, in a policy broadcast in October, had made it clear that 'the middle way . . . is the only way along which the Corporation can discharge its public duty'. And outside News, this was nowhere more crucial than in the Talks Department. Barnes rightly argued that the listener would not and could not distinguish between material from various departments. The RBD should not handle 'lay' subjects. It emerged that the number of talks in 1942 was just about double the 1938 figure. Notwithstanding Foot's clear commitment to a policy of the BBC contributing to the 'Christianizing of the nation' (as he said to Welch after his Cambridge sermon in November 1942), it was also clear that he had to take note of the increasing murmurings against the religious talks policy in the Home Board and Programme Policy meetings. Maconachie was responsible for seeing that the RBD managed to abide by the Concordat. Fenn was sure that Maconachie had no real understanding of Christian theology, and thought that Christianity was simply a matter of sermons and good works. He was an agnostic, but on the Talks for which he was finally responsible Fenn found him 'scrupulously fair'.[167] The Concordat had made it clear that Christianity, i.e. the churches, would be expected to pronounce on questions of principle in other areas of discourse which Maconachie recognized as non-religious. The churches could enter these paddocks as equestrians but not as jockeys: the Ten Peace Points in 1940 had been the focus of a major effort to have Christianity speak to a Christian culture at war and their reception had been welcomed. *The Times Literary Supplement* wanted to know how exactly they would work and Welch believed the BBC should help that elucidation just as the SCM Press had tried to do in a published comment on the Ten Points.[168]

In November 1942 Welch was invited to give the Cambridge University sermon. He chose the text 'A sower went forth to sow' and dealt at length with the principles of religious broadcasting, the churches and the BBC.[169] Religious broadcasting, he said, must not only reflect what the churches were doing and thinking, it must lead, just as indeed did William Temple, who 'bestrode this nation' and gave such a tremendous lead to Christian thinking about almost every aspect of Christian life within the nation at war. Welch extolled the Corporation, elucidated the various audiences for religious broadcasting, and gave a measured tribute to the BBC's wartime hierarchy with a side glance at the Concordat, by putting on record that 'there has been no real interference with the broadcasting of the Christian gospel in this country since the war began'. He also declared the purpose of religious broadcasting to be propagandist, although he was always reluctant to use the word, which reminded him of 'Malet Street' (the headquarters of the Ministry of Information). This important sermon, given quite wide publicity, was the first detailed public statement on the aims and philosophy of religion in broadcasting that Welch had yet made. The penultimate sentence of his sermon, paying the warmest tribute to the BBC, proudly recalled that since the war and the single wavelength, religious broadcasting had increased threefold.[170]

This statistic troubled the Talks Department, and Maconachie regarded it as almost sinister. In January 1943 he wrote a detailed analysis of the increase in the number of talks organized by Welch's Department; he regarded this increase as a 'pincer movement' upon an area of talks which was, by his meticulous design, to be free from propaganda, particularly in respect of the prosecution of the war. Maconachie's complaint to Foot and Graves (now Joint Directors-General) was that the BBC's concern with impartiality and the difficulty, even impossibility, of maintaining impartiality in respect of the crisis, was not helped by an increase in religious talks which reflected a partially approved, exclusive Christian standpoint – that of Temple. One side of the pincers had been checked by the Concordat in restricting political and economic statements to matters of principle. Maconachie was worried by the other side: talks put out by the RBD on scientific and philosophical subjects by those whose qualifications are 'religious rather than intellectual' and which 'reach – as listeners know that they are of course bound to do – the Christian conclusion'. It was becoming more and more difficult for the 'casual listener to recognize a "religious broadcast" as such' and Maconachie thought that a tendency 'seems to be developing by which the religious element is deliberately played down or disguised'.[171]

Welch was beside himself with fury[172] over this sudden, unexpected and quite tendentious attack. He replied immediately with a well-argued, albeit almost spontaneous, statement which described every category of religious broadcasting as deriving from a specifically Christian premise. It was the Corporation, he emphasized, which provided a privileged position for the Christian churches. Hence when the Department wanted to organize a series on *The World Looks at the Christian* it was those outside the Department, Maconachie, Ogilvie and Nicolls, who were opposed to it. Not all religious broadcasts were concerned to persuade and convert. The scientific and philosophical talks such as a series for parents on the religious life of children, a series on the meaning of the universe by C. S. Lewis,[173] a series on scientific method and its limits – all these, claimed Welch, arose because Christianity is concerned with patterns of the truth and cannot be silent about them. Maconachie disagreed: in broadcasting terms, these were open to being controversial or one-sided and as partisan as the sermons broadcast on Sunday. Welch suggested there be an even wider base for the Concordat than 'political and economic'; perhaps even another Concordat for philosophic and scientific talks! Maconachie had little respect for those who sought to bring a Christian interpretation to bear on scientific questions, but he could not see the limitations of so many scientists when they similarly sought to pronounce on religious and particularly theological issues. Maconachie, like so many of his agnostic contemporaries in the BBC (Harold Nicolson was a case in point), wanted Christianity to undergird the common Christian ethic and so did not want it exposed to, for example, the criticism of the rationalists who laboured unceasingly to have time at the microphone to examine Christian claims. Predictably they sought to demolish the Christian monopoly in broadcasting on both political and philosophical grounds. The BBC was against cheap polemic.[174] Maconachie believed that 'Christianity is a matter of faith and not reason and once its apologists agree to define it as capable of logical proof, they are sunk.' He agreed with Harold Nicolson: 'The church often loses in these discussions when it imagines it has won.' The easiest way was to consult CRAC, which quite naturally did not want such exposure. The BBC could not be seen to be undermining Christianity: Nicolson had earlier told Ogilvie how much it was needed.[175]

Welch knew that any open controversial discussion would have to wait until after the war. In the meantime, the Concordat would remain a form of words to discipline the aspirations of the Department. Maconachie and Welch were charged by the Board to ensure that they observed it,[176] however ambiguously. Nevertheless, after both they and the Director General had signed it, Foot offered a definition of the BBC religion policy, perhaps to put the Department in its place.

The key notion, he claimed, was 'Christian simplicity': the Sermon on the Mount would guide the BBC's approach to religion which should remain 'fundamental and simple' – 'a simple faith for simple people all of whom know that they are not self-contained or omnipotent, but . . . there is something beyond their reach'. The Sermon on the Mount, thought Foot, 'should be enough for all . . . it corresponds so nearly to what any decent person thinks ought to be the code of life that it becomes difficult not to believe that it is all true.' Foot thought it had all been made complicated by denominations and 'offshoots of Christ's

real teaching'. Someone like Temple, 'who seemed to think that by
dealing with economics, eliminating the profit motive, he could provide
some sort of permanent cure for the ills of the world, . . . was barking up
the wrong tree. If they could only read the Sermon on the Mount, they
would realize that they were dealing with superficialities.'[177] It was
hardly surprising that Welch and Temple fought as hard against this
half-truth within the Corporation's hierarchy as against the 'protectio-
nism' of CRAC and those who objected to religious controversy on the
grounds that it weakened national morale.

Finally, in January 1944, the situation relaxed and Foot ruled that it
was no longer necessary to submit talks and sermons to any Controller;
Welch was the entrusted arbiter. He told Dinwiddie that we 'must not
fall down over this'; he wanted three weeks' notice for every sermon in
order to scrutinize every word. Religious broadcasting had in a real
way 'come of age'.

17

RESTORING OLD IMAGES: CHRISTIANITY IN THE CULTURE

A. Systems and slogans

Since Reith's days, religion in broadcasting had been seen as the unique means of bringing an authoritative expression of Christian opinion to the widest public, including the committed Christian community who either would not read or had no guidance as to what they should read in order to mature and improve their Christian understanding. Iremonger had developed the Sunday talks and groomed men like Anthony Deane and C. H. Dodd in order to educate the Christian community. The Corporation had always allotted time on Sunday for the churches to speak to themselves and any who might benefit.

Welch wanted a much broader policy: the churches must not only bring the teaching of the church to bear on critical social and national questions, it must reaffirm the centrality of the Christian faith for the survival of Christian civilization. Religious broadcasting must also recognize the gulf between faith and unfaith and make every effort to reach those who were quite outside the active life of the congregation, but who were asking serious questions of believers, whether intellectuals or ordinary church people. Cockin was convinced that the public impression of Christianity was clerical: people wanted 'a lot more plain guidance as to what being a Christian means in terms of ordinary conduct'. Cockin's reading of some of the public response to *Three Men and a Parson* was that agnostics had expressed a desire for 'quite straight instruction in the meaning of the Christian faith'.[1] It was quite clear to Fenn from the public response that the regular broadcast sermons were as 'superficial and trivial as the minds to which they are addressed'; the public was impatient with 'pretence and long, question-begging explanations', and yet at the same time that same public wanted 'short tabloid answers in yes or no style'.[2]

In December 1940, a Bristol producer, Howard Thomas, sent out a number of invitations to speakers who might participate in a new programme series 'with the purpose of providing easily assimilated knowledge and information'.[3] It was to become the most widely-listened to of all spoken word programmes apart from the News, and developed from the provision of information by a small group to an entertainment which relied upon the talents, lucidity and experience of its contributors. The first broadcast, with C. E. M. Joad, Commander Campbell and Julian Huxley, took place on 1 January 1941, anticipating a much later programme with its title *Any Questions?*[4]

The Brains Trust, as it soon became, had been going just a few months when Joad[5] made some comments which upset a great number of people. A listener had asked the question: 'Would you have designed human beings as you know them or could you have improved upon the design?' Joad replied that he would have made them 'capable of improvement' but added what many regarded as blasphemy, 'If *I* had to make human beings . . . as I think I could have done . . .' Numerous letters to Welch and to both Archbishops accused him of taking upon himself the character of God. Welch was angry because Joad could talk about religion on a Sunday (*The Brains Trust* was in those days repeated on Sunday at 4.0), but the Home Board had not allowed him to bring Joad into *The World Looks at the Christian* and have open debate. Joad would have welcomed this, provided adequate time were allowed; religious issues should not be excluded. He was, after all, a recognized and prolific authority on moral and philosophical issues. *The Brains Trust* was, he thought, trivial enough; he wanted to examine such questions, including religious ones, as might be troubling servicemen and could be answered with some degree of simplicity.

However, in June 1942 the Governors, notably Nicolson, pronounced on the matter: *The Brains Trust* was 'not the appropriate setting for the discussion of religious matter'.[6] This was largely the result of the failure of C. S. Lewis to avoid being 'eaten alive' by Huxley, as Welch put it. By spring 1942 questions about compulsory church parades and religious teaching were being asked, and Huxley's eloquent reasonableness clearly 'won the day'.[7] On this highly popular platform religion was seen to be losing: neither W. R. Matthews (as Fenn had warned Thomas) nor C. S. Lewis were skilled in this manner of discourse; tabloid answers were just not satisfactory; it had been all too embarrassing.

On Cockin's advice Welch had already gathered together his 'inner advisers' to examine the concept of a religious Brains Trust. He had spoken to Garbett who was much in favour and encouraged him to go ahead with this 'innovation in religious education'; that, after all, was the motivation, notwithstanding the clear concept of entertainment which dominated *The Brains Trust* which everyone knew so well. Could a religious version attract a comparable audience? Welch's group had met at Jordans Conference Centre in May: Henry Brooke, MP, Cockin and Rose Macaulay, the novelist, were among the minds which coined the title *The Christian Anvil* or eventually, *The Anvil*. The group was quite sure that the Governors were right that *The Brains Trust* was unsuitable for religious issues; there simply was not enough time. At the same time religious questions were submitted in great numbers and there was a call in the press for religion not to be excluded and, in the religious press, for a religious Brains Trust. As Howard Thomas notes, the popularity and influence of *The Brains Trust* was enormous in schools, societies and wherever people met for discussion. It was a new style of utterance.

Welch hoped for John Whale of Cheshunt College, Cambridge, William Temple, now Archbishop of Canterbury, Mary Trevelyan (Warden of Student Movement House in London and so in touch with younger people) and John Strachey, the left-wing thinker whom Fenn regarded as now 'nearer to the religious position than the pure Marxism of his earlier days'. In all the preliminary discussion Welch had the support of Nicolls. Maconachie approved the Brains Trust style as good broadcasting and particularly as it entertained by its authentic exposure of honest opinion by entertaining speakers. Indeed, it had been agreed by Welch's advisers that there should be no presentation of an artificial consensus; there might be fewer questions to give much longer time for each issue, but differences would not be shirked and listeners would see that 'Christians could disagree in charity'. That would not help the Governors who were committed to the policy of protection, sensitive as they were to a charge from Parliament and the church establishment that the BBC Corporation was undermining the faith of the nation, not to mention the work of the clergy.

Test recordings were being made during the summer and autumn of 1942 with a view to broadcasts in January 1943. Recording discs had to be used because of censorship. So far, two speakers were approved: Mary Trevelyan, who had a good voice and was very lucid, and 'our nice Franciscan, Friar Agnellus Andrew', whom Fenn regarded very highly. Fenn wanted Richard Crossman as chairman, but he was not willing. Maconachie thought Trevelyan the best chairman and the problem was how to find the team. Eventually, Fenn persuaded Cockin to join and Mary Trevelyan was put back in the team on the instruction of Sir Cecil Graves, who preferred not to have a woman in the chair. In the end, Victor Murray, a Cambridge don, was appointed chairman. Professor Whitehorn, a Presbyterian from Westminster College, Cambridge was also invited to take part. The producer was Hilton Brown of the Talks Department, assisted by A. C. F. Beales for the RBD based in London.

William Temple, who was deeply unhappy about eliminating religion from *The Brains Trust*, was troubled by the June decision on the development of *The Anvil*, with all it betokened in the compartmentalizing of religion: 'The Christian view should have an even chance with others in answering questions put up by the general public and not only those . . . specially interested in religion.'[8] Temple recommended John Maud as a member of the team.

The first six *Anvil* broadcasts began on 7 January 1943, following an introduction by Welch on 1 January. He invited listeners' questions and the response was immediate; within four days more than four hundred letters arrived, compared with only about thirty during the months of publicity in 1942. Following the first broadcast, almost a thousand letters were received in one week. The majority of questions (the task of scrutiny fell to Beales) were fundamentally theological and ethical, followed by those concerned with science, history, sociology and politics. Of the theological subjects, the favourites were reunion and co-operation, followed by specific dogmatic ones such as the Virgin Birth. The first programme included Whitehorn on the languages of the Bible, Cockin on gambling and Agnellus Andrew on euthanasia. Mary Trevelyan gave a lucid account of how one became a Christian. In each session about six questions were attempted and the name of the questioner given; the producers were thankful for the technological facilities of recording, which meant that the team was not confronted with questions to be answered live. Agnellus Andrew thought the level rather trivial, but the quality soon improved. The questions were simple, even if the answers had to be complex; they derived from popular conceptions to be found in and out of the pew. According to Silvey, *The Anvil* continued to be listened to by a large number, compared with the run of religious talks, during all six programmes in the opening series.[9]

The Anvil was in a real way a species of public relations exercise. Welch wanted more: he wanted Christianity to stand on its own feet and not shy away from intelligent debate. The *Catholic Herald* thought the same: Christianity should not be a 'cockshy for everyone'. But at least *The Anvil* gave the chance for a number of convinced Christians with differing points of view to 'discuss between them the real grounds of faith in answering the objections submitted by the public'.[10]

Public reception to *The Anvil* was positive: religion was again presented as open to question and the public was enfranchised through the chairman. Agnellus Andrew told Fenn from his church in Manchester that 'the working classes' were 'amazingly interested and want longer sessions'. By the end of the first series the number of requests was substantial – almost 2,500 letters with specific questions. Beales, the Catholic theologian, categorized them in order of frequency and it is noteworthy that by far the greatest number were concerned with 'the soul', and in particular 'life after death' and 'immortality'; 'war', 'science and religion', the 'Bible' and 'Christian reunion' followed in lesser numbers.

Whilst the *Catholic Herald* recognized 'the unmistakable lack-lustre atmosphere' by comparison with *The Brains Trust*, the *Church Times* complained that the answers were neither clear-cut nor comprehensible. They competed with each other; everyone seemed content with the final contrast of 'contradictory conclusions'.[11] Cockin was sensitive to the problem of the parsonic voice, about which so many complained, and suggested that 'every parish shall buy a recording machine and have it working in the church and make the parson listen to it!'

William Temple was concerned that the only people who would listen to *The Anvil* were already religious. It would do nothing 'to redress the balance for the large number of detached folk who are disposed to take what they hear from *The Brains Trust* as settling the matter'.[12] He wanted someone to put the Christian viewpoint forcefully. Graves, however, maintained his ban on religion in the *Brains Trust* – the programme was far too flippant.[13] In January 1943 *The Brains Trust* team itself sent a joint protest to Powell: 'We cannot but deplore what amounts in effect to a virtual ban on religious discussion.'[14] But the Board of Governors would not budge from their highly compartmentalized view of Christianity and what was good for it.[15] Temple held that 'So long as there is a likelihood of questions like "What's the difference between a man and a monkey?" there ought to be someone there who would give the specifically Christian answer.'[16] But his plea was in vain.

Welch was keen to ask the Board for another series, and 'to improve the technique' by a better chairman (he suggested Quentin Hogg, who in the event did not enjoy his turn in the chair),[17] and a more varied team. He wanted a pool from which guest speakers could be drawn. He yet again asked for a species of devil's advocate, 'especially one who represents the people', by which he meant the young unchurched. Welch had the programme time extended and put forward to an earlier hour. The Board approved in February: the new series was to begin in May.

As the second series progressed into May and June, both Fenn and Welch wanted the programme to include some opposition. They wanted the Department to go 'baldheaded for a group of notables and include "opposition" and thus impregnate the programme with greater cut and thrust'. Welch wanted Joad and Huxley alongside C. S. Lewis and Cockin. But Fenn knew that his 'elders and betters' would uphold the Charter and refuse controversy. They did exactly this and private discussion with Garbett and other members of CRAC in the autumn of 1943 confirmed that no such innovation could be contemplated while the war continued. (No one expected that it would last so long.) Maconachie, however, wanted someone who would watch the interests of 'ordinary and unsanctified commonsense' and comment on the replies. Much depended on the chairman. Maconachie was infuriated by bad production and bad chairmanship. He complained to Hogg for once allowing Cockin to admit that he knew nothing about the Russians and then launching into an opinion about them! He thought that *The Anvil* had failed because the chairman, whether Hogg or Murray, had allowed the speakers to waffle; he resented the team's rejection of 'production'. By the close of the second series in June 1943, the pool of speakers had provided variety and Barbara Ward, for example, made a significant contribution and received considerable correspondence. Press comment was sparse now that the novelty had worn off, but the *Church Times* continued in its critical vein about interdenominational wrangles in public. Welch himself was only half satisfied because the Corporation continued to operate a ban on controversial broadcasts largely on the strength of a negative conclusion to a CRAC discussion in 1928.[18] They would still hardly admit the existence of dirty linen, let alone allow it to be washed! Later on George Barnes, now Director of Talks, hoped to have 'entertaining' clergy on *The Brains Trust* but not to talk about religion![19] But the BBC hierarchy remained implacably against religious questions being discussed and would not have Barnes' suggestion considered. This was all the more irksome to Howard Thomas, because the questions which came in thick and fast to *The Brains Trust* were accompanied by one constantly recurring comment; that not enough answers dealt with 'controversial topics', such as politics, sex and religion.[20] But as Haley, the Editor-in-Chief, told the British Association for the Advancement of Science, 'We choose questions whose reply will be a matter of opinion rather than matters of fact.'[21] In a religious context these would be controversial and therefore inadmissible on policy grounds. The Brains

Trust genre of entertainment was not to embrace religion and *The Anvil* was not to become a religious alternative with any comparable appeal as entertainment. *The Anvil*, as Temple had feared, would simply be listened to by the committed – any idea that it would aid or convince outsiders was wishful thinking.

Welch's concept of mission in religious broadcasting derived from a churchman's understanding of the role of preaching in modern society. Most intelligent clergy were aware that religion was out of fashion among vast tracts of the population and Welch was among the first to recognize that the men[22] he had gathered together for his systematic evangelistic appeal were able to speak with an exceptional simplicity, and express theological concepts in common speech rather more ably than most clergy. He told C. H. Dodd that of his broadcasts for the BBC over the years, his three sermons on the apostolic preaching were the best he had ever done. The earliest preaching, Dodd explained to Welch's pleasure, was marked by and begun during crisis for individual, community and nation. This characterized the motivation for the whole of this and a similar course of sermons the following year which concentrated upon the crisis of the war from the angle of human rights.[23] In both courses, Welch wanted his team of preachers to carry on the tradition of his earlier years and the influence of William Temple. Through radio the best minds of the church could speak to the nation with one voice. Evangelism in broadcast religion made an appeal to the ordinary listener as best it could, in order to bring to bear a Christian interpretation of current events and to support the belief in a Christian society not only in the broad language of theology but in specific areas of national policy on which the clergy might have opinions. William Temple's were highly developed.[24]

Mission, courses of sermons[25] and *The Anvil* went hand in hand as the war continued. The last-named provided in a quite new way a means by which the Department could listen to questions from listeners, even though those questions were carefully 'filtered'; questions of a controversial nature were not allowed. Both preaching in Sunday services and the answers to listeners' questions in *The Anvil* (now significantly relegated to Sundays) were an attempt to state complex theological notions in the simplest possible language. By the nature of the coverage, Welch could never be quite sure who was listening – he sought to appeal on the one hand to the intelligent and educated outsider, and on the other to the uneducated listener whose religious knowledge was rudimentary or simply based on childhood experience of Sunday school and churchgoing with parents. Welch was well aware of these widely diverse audiences. The problem with the concept of mission in broadcasting had always been the absence of relation between speaker and listener, and the very limited opportunity for any real discourse such as might be part of a relationship between the clergyman and his congregation. Broadcasting could not structure this discourse. It was, in effect, only 'one-way' and most effective for those who wanted not discourse but recital, who understood religion in terms of the ritual utterance of Bible and Prayer Book. Religious broadcasting had served these people from the beginning. The Daily Service in particular was directed to the hospitalized and housebound who needed the comfort which it could provide; simplicity was paramount. Welch wanted broadcast religion to engage the outsider also; radio could uniquely provide a forum for debate. As we have seen, church leaders were not prepared to have religion debated; that would threaten the security of Christianity and upset the individual believer. Welch proposed a sort of 'Hyde Park on the Air' and a staff meeting at Bedford in May 1943 approved the idea; Beales saw it as a 'one man Brains Trust' and thus an improvement on *The Anvil*, since one man could speak with more authority than several, who tended inevitably towards speculative replies. Welch nevertheless wanted the agnostic and doubting listener represented and had to decide on how this listener construed his agnosticism or disbelief. The staff were ready to press forward with the acceptance of controversy. In September 1943 another important meeting took place between Welch, Nicolls, Barnes and Maconachie, who all reiterated that 'religious broadcasting should make Britain a more Christian country'.[26] The mission of 1944[27] was the outcome of this conviction; to make the gospel intelligible to the critical, contemporary mind. It was the natural follow-up to a notable initiative which had attempted to make the gospel *story* live – an initiative which Welch thought the most remarkable series of religious broadcasts which had ever taken place. For this, as for the mission in 1944, Dorothy L. Sayers had made a unique contribution.

B. Drama and dogma: radical and sacred utterance

(i) Beginnings

As early as 1924, CRAC was asking questions about appropriate religious broadcasts for children on Sundays. C. S. Woodward thought such programmes should be undertaken by experts in children's work, and the National Sunday School Union was consulted. At the same time, the Committee was being asked to consider modes of communication which were appropriate to this new medium and which might provide an alternative to the 'sermon' denoted as much by its ecclesial and sacred setting as by its content. Educational questions about intelligibility were not often asked; the emphasis was upon the 'recital' and declamation of Christian theology, no matter that some might achieve a greater degree of receptivity than others. CRAC recognized that there were possibilities with the presentation of the Bible in a variety of ways: biblical readings interlaced with music and non-biblical literature all 'featuring' religious ideas and presenting the response to religion in arts and good works – all parts presented in concert with each other: a sort of entertainment providing 'God was not depicted as a bloodthirsty personage'.[28]

The Cardiff Station Director, E. R. Appleton, was a keen Christian layman with a flair for innovation. By 1927 he had won a reputation on the strength of the vast audience for his 'Epilogue' which he called the *Silent Fellowship*. He was encouraged to produce Sunday children's programmes which would make the Bible come alive for the young. The result was *Joan and Betty's Bible Story*,[29] broadcast monthly on the National Programme, dramatized Bible stories accompanied by scripted conversations between Appleton and his daughters which sought to bring out their meaning and also their relevance. They continued from 1930 to 1933. Iremonger had ideas about drama and what were loosely called 'features' and told the Committee at his very first meeting that drama and the wireless could combine to provide an 'effective evocation of religious emotion'.[30]

The following year CRAC discussed religious drama at greater length and considered the formation of a religious drama committee; even in these early days Iremonger was convinced that the faith of the Bible could and should be conveyed through drama.[31] Martin Browne of the Religious Drama Society advised Iremonger to bring together a variety of playwrights and discuss possibilities of sponsoring plays for the RBD. E. V. Rieu, Laurence Housman, the actor Lewis Casson and Ellis Roberts met Iremonger in June 1934 and discussed plays such as those by Clemence Dane (*Naboth's Vineyard*), W. B. Yeats (*The Resurrection*) and an Easter opera by Martin Shaw. The prolific Housman offered his *The Unknown Star* and six other plays. By this time radio drama was developing by leaps and bounds; its most notable practitioner was L. du Garde Peach. It was a genre of its own and through the works of Peach, Sieveking and Gielgud, it had evolved its own special philosophy and technique. A radio play was quite different from one performed in the theatre and writing drama for the microphone demanded a new set of skills for which there were no precedents. Radio drama was shorn of almost everything except words:

at that time, sound effects were rather primitive. By 1939 Val Gielgud and his authors had experimented sufficiently to prove beyond doubt that writing for radio was a distinct technique.[32]

Sunday broadcasting, however, was subject to a whole range of restrictions, and furthermore, the RBD under Iremonger had neither staff nor skill to produce its own dramatic features. Geoffrey Dearmer[33] had joined Iremonger to be particularly responsible for children's programmes. The production of any broadcast drama in this field – religious or secular – depended upon close co-operation between the RBD and Val Gielguds' Department. Any religious play had to meet literary and artistic standards, and at the same time to reflect the religious sensitivities inherent in the Corporation's Sunday policy. The biblical drama each month was short and again based so closely upon a biblical text that Iremonger's Committee could only approve. Dramatizations of the stories of Nehemiah and Solomon were examples of what went out as a regular Sunday afternoon broadcast each month. Iremonger wanted more: he wanted drama which examined religious themes without being didactic or expository. Iremonger looked to Housman to provide him with 'live religious drama without controversy or hurt to sensitive religious feelings'. Housman replied bluntly that since there was no agreed religious dogma, as in the medieval dramas, controversy was inevitable. 'Unless religious drama can deal with our present social order as uncompromisingly as party politicians . . . it isn't going to be really alive.'[34] Housman complained that the BBC could not be a really effective educator unless it allowed real debate between Christians and non-Christians. He saw no room for a 'forward move in religious drama'. He could not bring either the kind of help or the kind of play Iremonger needed. The following year Iremonger was pleased with Robin Whitworth's *On the Third Day*, a play for Easter Day, and told Gielgud that he hoped to be ready to 'go forward a little' by October 1935, i.e. he thought CRAC would approve. In January on the Home wavelength the country listened for the first time to T. S. Eliot's *Murder in the Cathedral*, in effect the first full-length religious radio play.

In spring 1938, encouraged by Val Gielgud, Iremonger asked Dorothy L. Sayers to write something for his Department. The outcome was a most successful nativity play, *He That Should Come*. She thought most nativity plays were 'remarkable for their twadding triviality' in form and content.[35] Her starting point was axiomatic and simple: Jesus 'was born not into "the Bible" but into the world.'[36] She wanted to shock the listener into the reality of the situation in first-century Judaea and illustrate the 'tremendous irony' of the subsequent history. She was inventive and startling: her Roman legionaries sang:

> Beef and beer, beef and beer,
> Sitting at home, sweet home, boys,
> With a wench in your arm to keep you warm,
> O take me back to Rome, boys.

Sayers was not a biblical scholar but had a powerfully informed Christian conviction which would soon make itself felt in a good deal of religious broadcasting.[37] *He That Should Come* was produced by Val Gielgud on Christmas Day 1938 and was warmly received. Mrs Winston Churchill was one of those who wrote in praise.[38] Martin Browne thought it the best nativity play now in the repertoire. Through the new medium, Sayers' play and Val Gielgud's special effects had given the situation 'actuality' – a word she chose; thereby the story could be 'perhaps dangerous and possibly even blasphemous'.[39] Sayers had infused the story with her own historic-theological convictions, and the listener became aware of the infusions of 'actuality' – the sounds which could create 'presence' in the very private world of each home and fireside. Radio drama under Gielgud had been experimenting on these lines for some years and *He That Should Come* was the first major venture of Sayers and Gielgud into the area of what had been conventional religious utterance, all the more consequential because the wireless had taken it to a million and more homes. But the key notions were 'actuality' and 'blasphemy': *He That Should Come* was after all still – as Sayers admitted – essentially the familiar story, the one usually adorned with 'baby songs and bells and all the charm of complete unreality.' What if she might venture further from the first chapter of Luke to the first chapter of St Mark?

(ii) Children in home and school: catechesis or education?

Welch had been principal of a training college and had firm opinions on the place of religion in the education of the rising generation. His circle of educationalist friends included Tissington Tatlow, Basil Yeaxlee and R. E. Parsons of the Church of England's educational body, the National Society.

In his new broadcasting post, he came into contact with two sides: *Children's Hour* under Derek McCulloch, and the BBC Schools Department under Mary Somerville. Both Departments were jealous of their place in the Corporation and both heads were formidable and single-minded. The schools were represented in policy-making by the Central Council for Schools Broadcasting (CCSB), as the churches' interests were focused in CRAC. Both the Schools Department and the RBD threatened the autonomy of the Corporation and were subject to enormous professional competition.[40]

Welch believed that his work among children – at home or in school – was part and parcel of the mission of the BBC to the nation in time of war: he must do for children what his best broadcasters such as Cockin and others would do for adults. Dissatisfaction with the *Children's Hour* Sunday religious output of forty minutes led to a measure of conflict between his Department and the other two heads, concerned as each was with canons and standards of utterance appropriate to their departmental catchment. *Children's Hour* had to be entertaining and the Schools output had to be educational. With the Departments combined, Welch hoped children could look forward to this 'new Sunday regime . . . without their programmes being turned into the wrong sort of Sunday school.'[41] He told Nicolls that up to now *Children's Hour* on Sunday had been 'patchy' and 'failed to provide any continued teaching, clear objective or thought-out philosophy'.[42]

The notion of the BBC being involved in any systematic teaching was anathema to Somerville and her CCSB advisers. They included representatives from the National Union of Teachers, who were vigorously opposed to any idea of the BBC engaging in religious education or instruction and so usurping the role of the teacher. Nevertheless, there was a war on and children were being evacuated in their thousands. They were being uprooted and rehoused and in consequence coming under the scrutiny of the authorities, particularly the educationalists. The churches were deeply concerned that these displaced thousands were now severed from home and church: not only were they being deprived of regular worship but the whole evacuation had revealed the ignorance of these children: 'At the moment a professedly Christian country was staking all in the defence of Christian principles, there was a system of national education which allowed the citizens of the future to have a purely heathen upbringing.' So said a *Times* leader of 17 February 1940, written at the invitation of Dawson, the Editor, by his friend Anthony Deane. This was to focus a 'new crusade' for the teaching of religion in schools. He expressed a widespread sentiment and began a prolonged debate which animated churchmen with enthusiasm and educationalists with fury.[43] The schools broadly reminded the churches that there were simply too few teachers with the necessary expertise in teaching religion and thought it cowardly of Deane to complain that the clergy were unwelcome in the classroom. On the church side, a request came from Lang of Canterbury to Ogilvie, and also from the Mothers' Union and from

Cardinal Hinsley, that the BBC should encourage and instruct young children at home and at school in the religion which stood as the foundation of a nation at war.

Welch inherited from Iremonger ideas for a departmental provision for children: there had been talks for sixth formers and Iremonger had considered a broadcast service for elementary school children. Relationships had been made with the CCSB and Welch proposed to provide a short broadcast service of worship at the beginning of the school day once each week, and for the *Children's Hour* audience every day a five minute service at the end of the programme. In neither area could there be any explicit element of 'instruction'; any such inculcation would have to be discreet. Against a background of the Cowper-Temple discussion, and the development between the wars of the Agreed Syllabus,[44] Welch had to tread a delicate path between teachers and churchmen. He soon formed an agreeable relationship with A. C. Cameron, Secretary of the CCSB, and began negotiations for a BBC schools religious service. Any use of the Bible would be 'devotional rather than exegetical' and the purpose of the broadcast would be to provide a demonstration of how worship could be both aesthetically satisfying and appropriate to young listeners.[45]

By January 1940 Welch had negotiated for a specialist addition to the Department in John G. Williams, a young Anglican from a Rotherhithe parish in East London who already had a reputation in the field of religious education.[46] He would divide his time between *Children's Hour* and the hoped-for schools service. It was his conviction that liturgy should be more than a matter of aesthetics or contemplation. He presented a paper for Welch's June meeting with A. C. Cameron outlining the objectives. The proposed service should, of course, be free of any controversial material; it would provide 'positive and consecutive teaching in the practice of private prayer and its relation to all the activities of life'; it would provide incidental opportunities to learn what were the elements of Christian worship.

This objective was by no means easy to achieve, particularly in the light of the Schools Department's sensitivities about the church in the classroom. Introductions to the service by Williams were seen as *de facto* propaganda, or at least a discreet form of teaching if not indoctrination. So stormy a passage did the service have from conception to execution through Somerville's Department and the CCSB that the Council said it would provide facilities but not actually approve! The first experimental services began in September 1940, and Williams tried desperately to satisfy both CRAC and CCSB. The initiative, however, remained with the RBD.[47]

Mary Somerville, whilst in favour of the service, was by no means convinced that the appointment of Williams was satisfactory: he had insufficient educational experience to enable him to undertake his introductions to the biblical component in the service without being doctrinaire. Both Welch and Williams were between Scylla and Charybdis: if too diffuse, they would offend men like Anthony Deane; if too dogmatic, the teachers. Somerville, like Welch, was aware of the distinctive traditions of radio drama and introduced the idea of a dramatic component in the schools service at a CCSB meeting in July 1940.[48] Such a component would help young listeners to understand the dramatic character of biblical material – particularly the Old Testament stories.[49] There were hesitations about 'the dangers of theatricality'; there were also the immense problems of school reception. Participation (which belonged properly to worship) could be threatened by inducing passivity – a theological danger in the view of Dearmer and Fenn. After considerable debate over questions of catechesis and indoctrination, the schools broadcast service saw the birth of the so-called 'dramatic interlude' designed by Welch's department and executed by Somerville's to accord with pedagogic requirements. These were intended to 'present to the imagination . . . a picture of Jesus Christ . . . and lead to the thought "he who hath seen me hath seen the Father" '. The first set of interludes was written by a variety of Schools Department people in consultation with John Williams, and produced by a former head teacher seconded to the BBC Schools Department, Doris Starmer-Smith.

In the fields of both *Children's Hour* and schools broadcasting, Welch was engaged with drama as a medium of education. It was a remedy for what he regarded as a lack of quality within *Children's Hour* and a discipline against traditional ecclesial utterance in the schools context: entertainment and pedagogics were focused in the drama and Welch believed this to have enormous potential for broadcast religion. He told Derek McCulloch that he wanted 'more distinguished contributors' than the famous L. du Garde Peach who had already dramatized a Paul of Tarsus series.[50] He put plans in hand to approach Dorothy Sayers.

(iii) The Man Born to be King

Welch thought a dramatization of the life of Jesus would 'fulfil the obligation of the Corporation to the nation in this time' and Dorothy L. Sayers, because of her sharp and confident Christian conviction, was the one who could make the telling of this story 'fresh and vital'; the Children's Hour Department could surely serve no greater purpose than this.[51] Welch asked her for help in February 1940; there were five million children listening to Sunday *Children's Hour* – what staggering responsibilities for 'consistent Christian teaching in dramatic form'. His suggestion was 'exceedingly tempting', she replied, and insisted that her one condition would be that Jesus would be dramatized with the same realism which characterized *He That Should Come*. Christ's presence as a 'voice off or by a shaft of light, etc., suggests to people that he never was a real person at all, and this impression of unreality extends to all other people in the drama.'[52] She thought such an innovatory radio presentation would 'break through the convention of unreality which surrounds our Lord's person . . . which threatens to be lost in a kind of Apollinarian mist.' At the same time she would write with the children in mind and would not put in 'anything smart or sophisticated' such as the discussions of Greek philosophy and the rather sneering wisecrack about the paternity of Christ that appeared in *He That Should Come*. That sort of thing, she believed, was outside the scope of a child's mind.[53] Welch wanted Jesus to be the subject of that same inventive creativity that would make credible characters of the other Gospel personalities. Radio after all enjoyed a freedom not allowed to press and cinema; furthermore, he naively thought that in Children's Hour 'we can rightly ignore the prejudices of adults which are absent from the minds of children'. (He was to be proved wrong.) 'Splendid!' cried Sayers; 'between us we should be able to think out something which shall be realistic and give as little offence as possible.' Sayers believed that the Bible was meant for recital; yet the more beautiful that recital, the more unreal it sounds.[54] And were they to offer their audience a dramatic reality or would they succeed in making the Christ story 'as stereotyped and dull as ourselves'? 'If we are going to contaminate these little ones by our unimaginative lethargy, it would be better that a millstone. . . .'[55] Welch was delighted at her energy and her theological conviction: they both believed that christology could be taught by dramatization. She was 'hired' in June at £25 for each play – probably twelve, providing, she insisted, that she had full consultation over production and casting. Welch told her 'not to spare the dynamite'. She was at the time preparing a couple of talks for Fenn under the title *Creed or Chaos?*[56] She explained that without creed there was chaos and this series of plays would dramatize with the utmost reality the Christ-story of Christian dogma: it was, as it were, dogma in dramatic prose with all the imaginative invention of a proven artist. For the next two years, throughout the writing of the series, this was the central, intractable problem: how to create a realistic dramatic narrative which was both believable to an audience she regarded as essentially pagan and appropriate to the theology of the gospels. She speculated on both questions and made her own decisions.

She began work on the first in the series in July. She had experience in the nativity material and so produced her first sketched text of *Kings in Judaea* quite quickly. She submitted it to McCulloch notwithstanding the uncertainty she felt about not having Gielgud as a producer. She hardly knew of McCulloch and was determined to keep Gielgud in the picture. She told McCulloch that she looked forward to working with him. Welch and his Department, however, stood between them; he was to umpire the battle between Sayers and warring factions, first in the Children's Hour Department and later in the churches. Sayers had finally, on Welch's persuasion, agreed to have McCulloch as producer with Welch as 'theological adviser'. She sent her script to McCulloch in November 1940. At this point amity took its leave! Notwithstanding the favourable opinion both of Gielgud and McCulloch's assistant, May Jenkin, there were problems about language and understanding, over which the Children's Hour Department had firm ideas and considerable experience. McCulloch was away and Miss Jenkin thought to write on his behalf and offer a few comments: they were, she told Sayers, 'mere spots in the sun'. She agreed to the first script in principle but since there was no visual 'spectacle' in radio, essential difficulties of thought and language should not be too great. Here, in her innocence, she trod on quite the most sensitive corn by asking 'if you will allow us discreetly to edit'.[57] Sayers blazed back: 'I knew how *you* would react; it is also my business to know how my audience will react and yours to trust me to know it.' Nothing would induce her to allow editing. McCulloch tried to sooth the situation: he thought a meeting would remove all the misunderstanding but she would only agree to this if the changes were construed not in terms of the creative writer's art but the creative producer's art; she would protect her right as a playwright; he could take it or leave it. Miss Jenkin's letter was a 'blazing impertinence'; what would become of her reputation if she allowed her style to be dictated by 'little bodies of unliterary critics?'[58] She demanded another producer. Miss Jenkin's tactless letter gave her a golden opportunity to dig her heels in and insist on Val Gielgud.[59] McCulloch naturally defended his assistant. By the same post Sayers vented her spleen to Welch: 'Theatre is theatre. It is because these little committees of the Children's Hour have no experience of the theatre that they never succeed in producing theatre, but only school lessons in dialogue.' She demanded a professional producer; that meant the so-called 'Sayers-tamer', Val Gielgud.[60] She would do no more until the matter was settled: she would certainly not have McCulloch, 'who thinks it part of his business to teach me how to write!'[61] Welch tried to effect a reconciliation. She agreed to try McCulloch again, since Val

Gielgud was not willing to undertake the series unless it was the initiative of his department. (In that case Sayers might very easily have put up her fees.) She did insist on reminding Welch that when he took her on it was an 'adventurous step of cutting out the juvenile experts and trying a new experiment – giving children professional theatre'. She began work again early in December.

But May Jenkin was determined to defend her professionalism and vindicate herself. She wrote: 'You claim to know your audience, but do you know ours? Do you know what the eleven-year-old elementary child listens to?'[62] The simple answer was no; Dorothy L. Sayers mixed with or could only envisage the educated child, or at least those reared in a literary environment and in some degree exposed to the language and liturgy of the Catholic faith: hence her certainty about the widespread childhood passion for mystery rather than 'understanding' and even, as she often quoted, the delights of the Athanasian Creed! 'The normal child is not interested in being a child – he wants to grow up . . . drama, colour and mystery is their real meat.' For Sayers, dramatic narrative should be the servant of action, passion and tragedy. The Children's Hour emphasis upon intelligibility was entirely negative and untheatrical. May Jenkin's letter was the last straw; Sayers envisaged the awful possibility of being tied to this lady should McCulloch be indisposed, and therefore promptly cancelled the whole project! It was for Welch to pour yet more oil on the troubled waters and redeem the plays rather than the personalities. His whole attitude could be summed up thus: no one matters except the plays; those who work for the BBC must 'deny themselves and hope they may be used'. But he flattered too; a Sayers play on the Life of Our Lord would not only make radio history, it would be a landmark in religious education and the life of English-speaking Christianity. 'God', he told her, 'would have been working in and through you.' It was a matter of 'revealing the character of the Son of God to the younger listeners of this country', and over against such an objective, no one, Sayers, Welch or McCulloch, really mattered. He extolled May Jenkin's experience and virtues and persuaded Sayers that they were fighting over questions of production and not over her creative abilities. Finally Welch would not accept the cancellation: since the quality of the Children's Hour religious material had not been of the best, he appealed to her for something more than outstanding. The plays had to go on; they belonged to the children of this country. It was this appeal by Welch, on the penultimate day of 1940, which effectively gave broadcasting and the English-speaking world the series of plays *The Man Born to be King*.

But this did not happen without the most dramatic struggle, in which the BBC and its Religious Broadcasting Department were pitted, it seemed often to Welch, against all the powers that be in both church and nation. Welch had kept the door open to further negotiation both with Sayers and Gielgud. For her, Gielgud was steeped in the tradition of 'real' theatre.

> There isn't, as Miss Jenkin suggests, one thing called theatre and another thing called 'radio drama'. There are different kinds of media for drama . . . and the first thing a professional wants to know about any play is: 'Is it theatre?'. The second thing is: 'Is it technically right for this medium (i.e. unseen voices)?' The professional puts these things first, leaving it to the author to decide on what kind of message he wants to put over.[63]

She thought May Jenkin's attitude typical of the BBC civil service mentality, which 'prevents the saying of anything that could conceivably be unintelligible to the lowest mentality'. She put her finger on the issue which Welch had always felt most profoundly; broadcasting had to be intelligible to the widest audience and therefore, she complained, 'you must refrain from using any theological term that can't be understood by a stupid person not interested in theology so that the fairly intelligent person who is interested never gets catered for at all.' For these reasons, she would defer only to Welch and have no other third party or BBC department telling her how to write for the theatre. She was all the more confident because she had taken some pains to secure the opinions of professional schoolteachers about the first play before sending it to May Jenkin.

It was now up to Welch to maintain the delicate relationship between the dramatist and the sponsor. Nicolls was a key figure, but had been injured by a bomb on Broadcasting House. Welch too slipped on the ice, broke his collar-bone and was out of action till February. However on 13 February Gielgud agreed to the project with much enthusiasm; Welch felt sure that a meeting between the three of them would remove all ambiguities. He had his own problems at this time with *Three Men and a Parson*[64], where censorship questions were compounded by the involvement of the Ministry of Information in the RBD's talks output. Finally, however, Welch, Sayers and Gielgud came together in March and the series was set fair to go. Welch had at last succeeded in landing a big fish for the combined benefit of Children's Hour and the RBD.[65] Sayers thanked God Gielgud was going to produce her works as plays and not as disguised sermons, which she complained of in the current Children's Hour religious material. Gielgud was excited by the series and was glad that the 'ineptitude' of the Children's Hour Department was now out of it.[66] For the moment and until the end of 1941, she was free to struggle with the writing and remained in regular touch with Welch and Gielgud.

She was preoccupied with the idea of the kingdom of God as a 'suitable line now, when everybody is bothered about what sort of government the world should have'. Characterization would be difficult; there was the devil in the Temptation Story, and at the end Judas was the real difficulty – 'the man with the greatest possibilities for good and the very worst possibilities for corruption'. She was anxious not to be implausible nor to make Christ look a fool, and she would not have those cheap explanations which admitted not knowing Judas' motives but merely said that, alas, there was a bad apple in every barrel; this kind of thing 'jerks one out of the theatre into the school-room'. Thomas could be worked into earlier scenes as 'being literal-minded and stupid'. She was worried about the shortage of female parts and also of women's voices. 'Mary is the world's worst snag'; she said almost nothing; and as for Mary Magdalen, 'we skimble over her profession'. She didn't care that the biblical scholars had considered Mary of Bethany and the Magdalen to be two different people; the church tradition said they were the same and that was good enough! She admitted to Gielgud that she wanted Welch left out of discussion of production and those questions of theology which were bound to be raised in the process of translating the gospel narrative into a coherent dramatic plot; invention could be acceptable to dramatists but less so to theologians. She had to 'tamper with the text', and hoped Welch and the theologians would not mind![67]

On the figure of Jesus himself it was, she thought, extraordinarily difficult to devise a 'colloquial rendering of Christ's sayings that would make him sound like a human being and yet isn't cheap or undignified: he must be made to use the same idiom as the rest of the characters and it must not be a Bible idiom.' He should be presented, moreover, as a human being and not as a 'sort of symbolic figure doing nothing but preach in elegant periods when all the people round him are talking in everyday style'. She recognized that in making the parables intelligible she would get into trouble with those who loved the familiar text. She believed that most of Jesus' speeches in her plays had 'some kind of warrant in scripture'. Fortunately, permission had already been gained from the Lord Chamberlain, Lord Clarendon, to 'impersonate' the figure of Christ in a context of entertainment. There was neither precedent nor parallel. Clarendon had told the Director-General that if television entered the discussion, the conclusion would have been very different.[68] The first play to feature the controversial figure of Jesus, *The King's Herald*, centred on John the Baptist. Notwithstanding the exceedingly valuable assistance she gained from William Temple's recently published *Readings in St John's Gospel*,[69] she was uneasy about 'carving up the text', as she put it to Welch when submitting her manuscript for his approval. Whilst Welch constantly reiterated that his job was 'chiefly theological', he and his colleagues ventured into the lion's den when they commented on her manipulation of biblical language. None of them thought it really suitable for children! Welch, nevertheless, thought her skilful combination of disconnected gospel narratives was excellent and brought the story to life.

But the first of many profound ambiguities were brought to the surface and into the axis between Welch the broadcaster and theologian and Sayers the dramatist and apologist. Theological and biblical hermeneutics were inextricably mixed, and it was for Sayers to insinuate them into her drama and for Welch to gain acceptance for them in his religious broadcasting policy. As a parson (as were Fenn, Williams and Taylor), he was an amateur in the field of drama and he confessed: 'We are tied and bound by the biblical picture as presumably most of our listeners are.' They had been shocked e.g. by the theophany on the River Jordan at the Baptism of Jesus. But it belonged to a conception of Jesus which the Department only slowly accepted: it was 'an artist's conception governed by the necessity of character creation'. Welch believed and remained convinced through the many months of struggle over this series that the shock was not only salutary, it was the guarantee that Sayers had achieved her purpose. 'All we can do', said Welch, 'is stand on the touch-line and be prepared for trouble.'[70] In fact, he was in mid-field.

Meanwhile Sayers worked on with 'the most delicate job I've ever struck' and at every step encountered new problems. In the third play, which included the Wedding at Cana, for example, she took the liberty of having Jesus speak the parable about the wise virgins from Matthew 25, because it would have been dramatically 'unconvincing for Jesus to sit through the party without utterance except to perform the miracle'. Instead of inventing dialogue, she made him tell the parable. It clearly was not easy: she recognized the conflict between 'recital' and 'theatre'. 'I wish one of the evangelists had thought to tell us what the disciples felt about living with a person who could turn water into wine and multiply loaves and fishes.'[71] Throughout the ministry of Jesus a great many threads simply had to be 'knitted up together'. Time after time she wrote to Welch slightly apologetic for having to 'take liberties with the accepted chronology' or invent this sequence and that character in order to keep the dramatic momentum and make intelligible rationalizations about gospel incidents. She took exception to William Temple's caution over the Johannine story of Christ walking on the water. The gospels were finally sources for the story – 'transcripts from life' and their authors were recorders: 'John makes the shorthand transcript while the others produce the *précis*.'[72] The fun of this game was to create dialogue and 'reconcile as many separate versions as possible so as to make a detailed and convincing story'.[73] In this crucial and long letter to Welch Dorothy Sayers revealed her frustration with liberal biblical hermeneutics:

> If some biblical critics had more dramatic sense and less religious prejudice they might learn to treat their documents with greater respect and not dismiss so many things as 'incompatible' when a little pulling and patting would 'compat' them quite comfortably.

She would not on the other hand yield to any precious evangelical or fundamentalist squeamishness over the use of the text for dramatic purposes. She was equally cavalier with biblical scholarship: 'People called the Gospel after Matthew because he was a nice person.' He was not told the stories of the birth of Jesus, as these would have been more interesting to Luke the Physician! She worked on what was actually in the text and not the details of how it came to be there and constantly made it clear that her task was 'to make each episode have the quality of a play and not simply a scripture lesson illustrated by snatches of dialogue'.[74] She restricted the part of the Evangelist and often cut out a narrator altogether to let the drama convey all the information itself. Soon enough she confessed to Welch that small children would make very little of this material, but she intended to do her utmost to engage their attention. The Children's Hour association was, however, wearing rather thin.

During the autumn of 1941, the question of casting was raised. Welch wanted Harman Grisewood[75] as Jesus but he refused. His colleague in features, the author and actor Robert Speaight, a devout Roman Catholic, was thought by Sayers to be the best of a good many possibilities. Nicolls was obliged by the Programme Planning Committee to reduce the period from forty-five to forty minutes in spite of Welch's pleading; but he did manage to schedule these regular broadcasts to avoid the conflict with the popular *Brains Trust*. (This was just as well, since Sayers had little regard for this programme.) Programme Planning decided that the first play, *Kings in Judaea*, should be broadcast on 21 December just before Christmas – it was to be the first 'radio Oberammergau'. The BBC hierarchy, including Nicolls and Adams, Director of Publicity, expected some sensitive feelings to be touched and thought it best to forestall any criticism by arranging a press conference before the first broadcast. It would enable Sayers and Welch to give a strong personal testimony to any who would condemn the Corporation for producing a 'BBC Christ' as they had already produced a 'BBC religion'. The voice of Speaight should also be heard to disarm the extremists.

By the end of November, Sayers was halfway through, very confident and agreed to face the press on 10 December. It was a catastrophe: for all her lengthy and frank apologia, the popular press could not fail to provoke the extreme evangelical right wing of Protestant England. She admitted her problems were considerable; the playwright had to invent and not all the events in the gospels could be dramatized.

> I have invented a certain amount of ordinary conversation even for Jesus. . . . The popular representative of Christ as a mild and effeminate person who had no harsh words for anybody is a shocking travesty of the figure which spread through Judaea like a flame: such sentimental falsification is a most dangerous blasphemy.

She wanted 'no piety in the stained glass manner.'[76] Typically, the *Daily Herald* used the headline 'Gangsterisms in Bible Play' for a brief report next day by P. L. Mannock, who had pounced on the use of the words 'rake-off' and 'twister' (put into the mouth of Matthew). Jonah Barrington of the *Daily Express* admitted to Welch a few days later that 'it was a pity but inevitable that the press picked up the slang angle'. Welch agreed, but said it was not only bad press reporting: 'People are not prepared to accept the full implications of "*Incarnatus est*".' Ogilvie passed to Welch a letter saying simply: 'Two shocks broke on us this past week: Pearl Harbour and *The Man Born to be King*.' Barrington's own short piece (with a photograph of Speaight) also quoting the lines about 'rake-off' and 'sucker', somehow came into episcopal hands; Garbett was furious and sent this piece to Welch. Garbett complained that CRAC had not been adequately informed back in October when it was mostly preoccupied with the Concordat. Garbett voiced a growing popular indignation which would, however, soon go to extremes with which he would feel little sympathy. But no one, he thought, no matter how gifted, should make Jesus use words of her own invention and 'especially if they are in the nature of slang'. He told Welch in no uncertain terms that the plays would do 'grave harm and detract from the reverence due to our Lord'. Meanwhile another influential body, the Lord's Day Observance Society, met in council on the 12 December and H. H. Martin, its vigorous General Secretary, wrote straight to

Ogilvie with the Society's protest. This was 'theatrical exhibitionism'; this was the impersonation of Christ and therefore blasphemous; a 'contemplated violation of the third commandment which forbids taking the name of God in vain'. It was an added provocation that the Sabbath was being defiled, as had been done for years by the broadcasting of jazz and music hall on Sundays. They appealed to the BBC to respect the Lord's Day and – in a significantly confused phrase – to 'refrain from staging (*sic!*) on the wireless this revolting imitation of the voice of our Divine Saviour'.[77]

The hostile response of the cheap press however, was not a disaster for Welch: it was simply more publicity. He cheered Dorothy Sayers with his conviction that great numbers would listen to these plays who did not normally bother with religious programmes at all. Moreover, he was certain they would say what 'all our religious broadcasting has failed to say and in a way beyond our present powers.'[78] In other words, if the exposition of Christian belief by the churches and the clergy was no longer effective, then the 'story' at the centre of the churches' faith must be transformed by every means. Sayers would do just that; it would be innovative, contemporary and secular.

> People will be shocked, and rightly. We are prepared for our Lord to be born into the language of the Authorized Version or into stained glass or paint; we are not prepared for him to be incarnate.[79]

'This defective belief' he was sure was due to Puritanism and not to Karl Barth. The great virtue of her plays was the combination of christology and historiography: with Barth, Welch would not pursue the 'historical Jesus' uncoupled from dogmatic theology. Nevertheless, the pursuit had still to be made, as Sayers had said so often, for those who had never heard of Papias or Barth in or out of the churches. 'I love a fight', Welch told her, and he was about to have one.

Within a week of this very wide press coverage[80] opposition came thick and fast, and not only from the extreme Protestant right represented by the Lord's Day Observance Society and the Protestant Truth Society. Brendan Bracken spoke to Ogilvie on 17 December with considerable unease; he told him that the Ministry did not want to be mixed up with or organize the BBC's Religious Broadcasting Department, but there was a question down in the House from Sir Percy Hurd, the Member for Devizes, asking what he intended to do about revising the plays to avoid giving 'offence to Christian feeling?'[81] Bracken had already been approached by numerous MPs, and he thought 'the House would be dead against' the plays. Bracken regarded the *Daily Herald* as the villain of the piece, but was anxious not to have the BBC's relation with the Ministry of Information examined yet again; he wanted an assurance that the voice of Christ would not be used. He urged Ogilvie to recognize that 'war deepened people's religious feelings' and that 'gangster language would create a storm'.[82] However he agreed to answer that the matter was 'being referred again to CRAC'. On the same day Ogilvie was also assailed by the Lord Chamberlain, who in all the press publicity had been 'accused' of 'allowing' these plays: 'the BBC with the permission of the Lord Chamberlain' was everywhere, Clarendon complained.[83] He had assumed that there would be no impersonation: 'merely that the words of the part would be spoken into the microphone'. He added that the interpretation of 'audience' could raise problems if it led to the theatres pressing for permission. Bracken instructed Ernest Thurtle, his Parliamentary Secretary, to answer in the House that it was not the Minister's function to 'exercise jurisdiction over religious plays by the BBC'.[84] This remark made the situation worse: the BBC had *not* referred the plays at all to CRAC or any other committee. CRAC, like the Home Board, had only been told that Sayers intended doing these plays; indeed, the first three plays had arrived only days before the press conference on 10 December. Garbett was very angry at this situation. The Governors were due to meet on 15 December. Harold Nicolson, though somewhat uncertain, believed the BBC should experiment.

Powell wanted CRAC's advice 'once more' and had Ogilvie instruct Welch to call CRAC together speedily before 21 December when the first play was due to be broadcast. Welch tried his best but soon realized he would not get a quorum; he accepted the first two plays and sent them to members requesting their comment. Fifteen out of nineteen members replied and only one, the Provost of Guildford, strongly disapproved: he would not have our Lord speaking words which were not in the gospels. But this was Garbett's view; he told Welch in the strongest of tones, that both announcements at previous CRAC meetings had failed to make it clear that Christ would be 'impersonated and that the language would be modern'.[85] Fenn and Taylor closed ranks behind their leader. (Garbett thought it 'high-handed and discourteous' that Ogilvie had called CRAC together hastily, at a time when he could not be in the chair – and had asked for an opinion at such short notice.)

Welch met the Governors on 18 December and they all agreed that *Kings in Judaea* – effectively a nativity play and so without Speaight – should be broadcast as planned. Another meeting of CRAC was planned for 7 January with Garbett firmly in the chair. Welch had already explained the problems to him and impressed upon him in no uncertain terms the importance of these plays: they were the 'most important event in religious broadcasting we have ever undertaken – the Department was unanimous.'[86] At the Board of Governors' meetings Welch had been grateful for the Director-General's strong support. In Ogilvie's judgment these plays were 'precisely the kind of thing that religious broadcasting ought to do; . . . this was *par excellence* the mission work of radio.' He shared Welch's conviction that the plays would bring the life and teaching of Jesus to 'the great public outside the church' in a manner hitherto impossible for religious broadcasting because 'Dorothy L. Sayers combined a full belief in *"Incarnatus est"* with an advanced christology'; she also had a great talent.

The Governors asked Welch to prepare a piece for the *Radio Times*.[87] His message was as reassuring as it was radical and got to the heart of a hermeneutical discussion which neither the critics in bodies like the Lord's Day Observance Society nor ordinary church people understood. No more did Brendan Bracken! At the end of the day it was, as Welch said, a question as to how the compilation of the gospels was to be understood. The clergy, he was certain, did little to help the majority of the faithful come to terms with such questions; indeed, they kept them to themselves for fear such complexities would upset the popular and simple notions which passed for Christian belief. Miss Sayers was 'simply repeating the work of the gospel writers themselves. Their work was to paint a picture . . . of Jesus of Nazareth. . . . The gospels are a portrait in miniature. Miss Sayers' plays provide the same.'[88]

Welch, who was deeply committed, appealed again to Garbett: 'If we do not broadcast these plays we shall lose an opportunity which will never come our way again.' With only two days to spare Bracken eventually told Powell that the Ministry agreed to the broadcast subject to CRAC approving the remaining eleven plays. Garbett, still smarting over the BBC's treatment of CRAC, agreed to call an extraordinary meeting on 7 January. Gradually Welch began receiving significant messages of comfort: the Moderator of the Church of Scotland gave approval[89] and the General Secretary of the National Sunday School Union told Welch that he 'started out prejudiced in favour'. The Bishop of Derby was enthusiastic; and he said it would threaten to diminish his immense respect for the BBC if they were deflected by the protests of Mr Kensit, who had a hand in the Lord's Day Observance Society's campaign and almost every right-wing Protestant movement. The *Church Times*, however, was quite willing to print the LDOS appeal, as indeed did *The Times*.[90]

The first play was broadcast on 21 December as planned, and the press received it calmly: 'No shocks', noted the *Daily Express*; 'dignified and simple', said the *News Chronicle*. 'Bold and good' wrote Hannen Swaffer in the *Daily Herald* – and well might it make amends, since everyone blamed the *Herald* for its sensational item on 11 December. H. H. Martin of the LDOS thought it was a 'growing shame' and had no intention of letting the matter rest. The extent to which the LDOS's campaign succeeded is impossible to estimate. Within a week the Programme Correspondence section had received nearly 3000 letters, eighty-eight per cent of which were hostile. The compiler of this statistic told Welch that of all these letters only eight per cent had actually heard the first play and much of the wording of these letters derived from Martin's advertisement in *The Times* and elsewhere. Many of the letters stated that the correspondent would not be listening to the broadcast anyway. The Presbyterian Church of Ireland was influenced by the Protestant campaign and submitted the collective protests of seven presbyteries. Garbett by now had been won over; in his diocesan leaflet[91] all was forgiven; CRAC had unanimously made the right decision; the educational value of the plays was above question and he would trust the author to see that her modern language did not change the substance of the message. He used Welch's clever but specious argument that the plays were no different from Bach's *St Matthew Passion*; Christ was being 'impersonated' there too (!). Dorothy Sayers did not agree. The protest was not against a narrator repeating the words of the gospel narrative, even in modern speech. It was the combination of this with invented and colloquial modern speech which provoked the charge of blasphemy. It had quite clearly a measure of justification.

CRAC met on 7 January in the presence of Powell, who had already discussed the issue with Garbett that morning. They had reduced the problem to three questions: Should Christ be impersonated in any circumstances? Were Dorothy L. Sayers' plays a suitable vehicle? What about the protesting minority? The Committee hoped that this would not open the door to impersonation on the stage or the screen. They put their trust in Garbett and Welch as theological editors and insisted that the plays should not be removed from the *Children's Hour* context; there should be no suggestion that children should not hear them.[92] That would mean capitulation to the LDOS and possibly also the Ministry of Information. The Committee wished above all not to be associated with the fanatical Protestants and every member in turn spoke of his delight at Sayers' literary genius. The Provost of Guildford withdrew his former criticism and Welch reported that even 'the rather stuffy Guy Rogers' had pleaded that her characterizations should not be touched.

Welch confessed his surprise that it was the plays themselves that had convinced CRAC, which had been keen to clear itself of any taint of the wider criticisms voiced elsewhere in press and church. But 'full-blooded victory' though it appeared, some punches had to be pulled after all: the Committee would not give public approval to the plays unless they had power, in the person of Garbett, to withdraw the *imprimatur* if there was anything 'gravely offensive to Christian sentiment or any false doctrinal teaching'. Welch had no choice but to agree to this; he had to use more diplomacy than his nature 'happily allowed'.[93] Garbett could thus restrict the freedom given by the Corporation and by which the energies of Dorothy Sayers, Welch and Gielgud had been animated since the project began. Welch, whilst respecting Garbett as a 'fairly progressive and broad-minded Anglo-Catholic' thought him 'not a little conventional'.[94] When he threatened to withdraw the plays to protect the integrity of the author, Garbett countered with the integrity of the Committee. He was promised access to all the scripts well before production and transmission. To Sayers' annoyance, she was, after all, subject to yet another committee, and drank 'damnation to the Kensits of this world'.

During the next six months, she struggled with the writing of the next play and the production of the last, and was irked by the growing trickle of criticisms from Garbett. At the Cleansing of the Temple, Sayers saw Jesus in a 'towering rage'; if this was open to the construction that he lost his temper then it would cause offence. Bystanders in the same scene thought him 'mad as a March hare' but again Sayers had to sharpen her own blue pencil. She fought back on christological as well as literary grounds: could a bystander credibly remark 'He is beside himself'? Garbett would probably have said no but insisted that her phrase might cause offence; the 'March hare' was reluctantly excised. Garbett was similarly concerned about the domestication of Mary, the Mother of Jesus: the Roman Catholics would surely complain. Sayers was furious: she would not turn Mary into a 'plaster statuette' or be browbeaten by the Council of Trent into suggesting Mary knew more about what was happening than her own son!

> I've tried to make her a real person with human feelings and to avoid the violent extremes of making her more than human or less than intelligent; the Roman Catholics and Protestants must do a little giving and taking.[95]

Welch certainly thought that on this issue, Roman Catholic opinion, at least on CRAC, would not complain.

By the middle of February, with only the fourth play under way, Welch also became irritated by Garbett's criticisms, few and slight though they were. Welch disagreed with them but was in duty bound to pass them on. He knew that Garbett had borne many personal insults and had defended the plays against obscurantist and fanatical opposition; but at the same time, being the one man in whom CRAC had invested responsibility, he now believed himself responsible to Christians of all confessions to ensure that no irreverence was broadcast. 'It has obscured his understanding of an artist.' Sayers had to cut 'ducks and drakes' and an injunction to 'keep your eyes skinned'. Whatever view the Jewish leaders might have had of Jesus, Sayers could not express their disrespect by the phrase 'a vulgar upstart'. Welch was disappointed at such trivial comment.[96] Sayers thought the episcopal minutiae were irrational: 'ducks and drakes' was after all found in Shakespeare and was in no sense slang. Moreover Garbett's odd sensivitities simply stripped the story of its reality and cast the enemies of Jesus as perfect gentlemen who would not use an irreverent word about him. It was ludicrous, and Sayers believed it was time she dug in her toes. But she knew she could not respond to Garbett as she had to May Jenkin. She feared how it would all go when her crucifixion script was submitted. She had no wish to make trouble and withdraw her scripts, nor was she standing on any artistic dignity. She wrote to Welch:

> The scandal of the Cross was not a solemn bit of ritual symbolic of scandal. If the contemporary world is not much moved by the execution of God it is partly because pious phrases and reverent language have made it appear a more dignified crime than it was. It was a dirty piece of work, tell the Bishop.[97]

But Welch simply could not tell the Bishop: Garbett was about to be translated from Winchester to York and resign from his Chairmanship from CRAC – a position he had held since broadcasting began in 1922. Welch well knew that he would have to persuade Sayers that since Garbett had done so very much for religious broadcasting over the years, the BBC could hardly fall out with him over these plays just when everyone from the Director-General downwards would be thanking him for his efforts and saying goodbye.[98] Welch tried to be soothing; the new Chairman he hoped would be C. S. Woodward who was 'the best all-round bishop on the bench'. Perhaps Miss Sayers would discuss her innovations with him and not with Garbett.

17. Dorothy L. Sayers and J. W. Welch

18. Dorothy L. Sayers, Robert Speaight and Val Gielgud

Radio Impersonation of Christ!

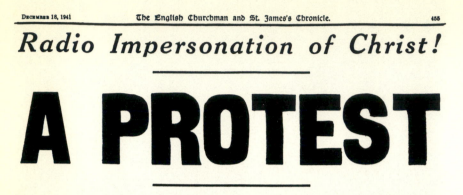

A PROTEST

Christian People were shocked during last week-end at the announcement of the proposed impersonation of our Lord Jesus Christ in a Sunday Play on the wireless. It is intended to take place during the Children's Hour on a Sunday afternoon early in the New Year. It is the first time a radio impersonation of Christ has been attempted anywhere in the world.

The Play is also to include the use of many modern slang terms in the presentation of New Testament history—which means in effect a spoliation of the beautiful language of the Holy Scriptures which have been given by inspiration of The Holy Spirit.

Following Protest has been lodged with the B.B.C.

> 108 Finchley Road
> London, N.W.3.
> 12th December, 1941.
>
> The Council of the Lord's Day Observance Society, at its meeting to-day, had under consideration the Press announcements of a radio innovation on a Sunday afternoon in the New Year of a Play entitled "The Man Who was Born to be a King," in which the voice of our Blessed Lord is to be introduced by a Shakespearian actor.
>
> My Council desire to inform the B.B.C. that this proposed theatrical exhibition will cause much pain to devout Christian people, who feel deeply that to impersonate the Divine Son of God in this way is an act of irreverence bordering on the blasphemous. It is a contemplated violation of the Third Commandment which forbids taking the Name of God in vain.
>
> The B.B.C., by its recent continentalising of Sunday Broadcasts with Music Hall and Jazz Programmes, has already distressed multitudes of good citizens. We therefore make an earnest appeal to the B.B.C. Authorities to respect what remains of the hallowed hours of the Lord's Day, and to refrain from staging on the wireless this revolting imitation of the voice of our Divine Saviour and Redeemer.
>
> Signed on behalf of the Council,
>
> **H. H. Martin,**
> *Secretary.*

Fellow Readers of "The English Churchman"! Enter your own personal Protest as well, asking the B.B.C. to ban this Christ-Dishonouring proposal. Write—in your thousands—to Director-General, British Broadcasting Corporation, Portland Place, London, W.1. It will also help if you write to the Lord's Day Observance Society, 108 Finchley Road, London, N.W.3.

19. Opposition to *The Man Born to be King*

She was increasingly troubled by the last week in the life of Jesus. Again and again she pleaded the necessity of innovation to make the story marry together. How was she to make sense of the Triumphal Entry into Jerusalem? The quotation from Zechariah 9 was a theological device by the editors of the gospels. She believed it her task to turn theological exposition into dramatic narrative and convey salvation history through mundane cause and effect. It was not easy. Jesus, she believed, was not conspiratorial and nor did he stage-manage a parade in order to fulfil the prophecy:

> The arrangement was made and the password devised by somebody else and for another reason. Somebody asked for a sign and was given a sign, and thus the prophecy was fulfilled in a perfectly natural way and so was *really* fulfilled.[99]

Sayers argued like a liberal but wished she need not do so: she feared all these obligatory explanations would undermine her efforts and exhaust her impetus to write. She felt 'little confidence about anything' and had moments of 'bishop-ridden despondency'.[100]

But not only bishops! Welch thought perhaps C. H. Dodd should be consulted on the increasingly complex exegetical questions raised by her innovations. Was, for example, Mary Magdalene in fact Mary of Bethany? She insisted that they were the same and that perhaps the evangelists muddled the whole thing. Either way she categorically refused to have any more Maries than were absolutely necessary. 'Neither Codices, nor Archbishop Gore nor Archbishop Temple nor the opinion of various correspondents who will probably object, shall move me. So there!'[101] Not quite all her acerbity had gone and she was all the more cheered by Garbett's unexpected acceptance of the sixth play without a word of complaint. Welch was sure they had turned the corner and thought perhaps Sayers should go and see him. Garbett was 'more difficult on paper than he actually is'. Welch frankly assured her that she had nothing to fear: the Bishop was neither a biblical scholar nor a theologian![102] If Dodd had been Chairman of CRAC, the plays might never have been agreed upon at all! Sure enough, the corner was turned; Garbett approved the next play and in April met with Sayers to discuss the Crucifixion.

As the story unfolded public acclaim was consistently vigorous and the opposition only marginal. The members of a CRAC sub-committee, all aged over fifty, expressed their delight to Welch and strengthened his conviction. The cycle was well over half-way through and he was now sure of his claim that drama and the so-called 'feature' programmes provided the finest weapon for the contemporary church:

the 'old-fashioned methods were done for.'[103] That was all very well, Sayers replied, but the clergy must realize that drama was the business of dramatists and not evangelists: they each had quite distinct and irreconcilable objectives. For the moment she struggled on with the eleventh play, the climax of the story in the Crucifixion. She feared that Garbett would be very troubled, but he told Welch he thought it 'quite wonderful'; however he hoped certain realisms could be cut. He accepted that harsh words were used at the time by the opponents of the Man from Nazareth. But such expressions as 'you lying crawling son of a pariah dog' and 'you rotten little ten-a-penny Messiah' would surely give grave offence to the irrational and sensitive religious sentiment which Garbett felt centred upon the figure of Christ in the church rather than in the story. Moreover, Garbett feared the response of the cheap press. Welch counselled Sayers to give him what he wanted; after all, 'he has swallowed a lot!' Neither Welch nor Sayers wanted a fight, so she complied.[104] Notwithstanding comment from Garbett and F. R. Barry, the Bishop of Southwell, the episode sustained the realism she had sought. 'It's pretty brutal and full of bad language, but you can't expect crucified robbers to talk like a Sunday School class.'[105] Garbett was warmly approving of the last play and wrote to Sayers to tell her so. He also confessed to William Paton that, notwithstanding all his caution, the figure of Christ in the series 'stood out with "numinousness" '.[106] Sayers came slowly to admire her episcopal adversary who had been prepared to face his share of criticism and after all was 'not a bad old stick really!'[107] She was, nevertheless, surprised to have his commendation.

By mid-October it was all over bar the praise. Nicolls, speaking for the Director-General, wanted to repeat the series each year: it was a 'great achievement and a landmark in broadcasting'.[108] The BBC gave her seventy-five twelve-inch records of the whole cycle! It was her magnum opus and she was quite happy to reconsider aspects of the text for re-recording. She told Nicolls that she was grateful for all the support she had had from the top, and always insisted that had it not been for Welch's vigour the plays would not have materialized. It had been the happiest production she had ever undertaken, and not the least because of Welch. William Temple had told Foot in June 1942 that the cycle was one of the great contributions to the religious life of our time.[109] The archiepiscopal seal was complete: Garbett later reflected to Foot that there must be 'multitudes who must be very grateful to the BBC'. Listener Research reported[110] that 12.2 per cent of the adult population listened to the second episode, thanks to the wide publicity afforded by the opposition. The Listener Research

Department's three hundred correspondents who sent in their replies gave an indication that the appreciation by this not inconsiderable audience was high. Welch reckoned that more than two million adults plus innumerable young people and children listened. The average over the whole cycle was something approaching 8.8 per cent of the adult population, well above the average for the adult listening figure for Sunday *Children's Hour.*

The printed text was published by Gollancz the following year. In his introduction Welch claimed that notwithstanding the very considerable – and organized – opposition 'not a single alteration was made to appease [it]'. For her part Dorothy L. Sayers expanded her concepts and convictions about theology and art and about history and liturgy.

> It is the business of the dramatist not to subordinate the drama to the theology, but to . . . trust the theology to emerge undistorted from the dramatic presentation of the story. This it can scarcely help doing, if the playwright is faithful to his material, since the history and the theology of Christ are one thing: . . . the drama of his life is dogma shown as dramatic action. . . . He is the only God who has a date in history.[111]

She acknowledged her debt to William Temple and Sir Edwyn Hoskyns, both authorities on the Fourth Gospel. The dramatist does not want to 'select and reject' like the textual critic, but rather to harmonize: thus she treated all four gospels as 'equally witnesses of truth' and recognized her debt to tradition, legend and even well-known fairytale, such as the names of the Magi – they 'remain three and remain kings'. Sayers claimed her right as a craftsman. Here was a great story which should be told as such: the 'final indignity' of pious hands had been 'to make of his story something that could neither startle, nor shock, nor terrify, nor excite, nor inspire a living soul': this was to 'crucify the Son of God afresh and put him to an open shame'. She was biting in her word to the churches: 'An honest writer would be ashamed to treat a nursery tale as you have treated the greatest drama in history.'[112] She spoke, perhaps uniquely, as an exceptionally gifted storyteller as well as an essayist who was also a confident and intelligent believer in the Catholic faith, encapsulated as it had to be for her in language and therefore dogma; history and therefore art.

> Dogma must be taken by the writer as part of the material with which he works and not as an exterior end towards which his work is directed. Dogma is the grammar and vocabulary of his art.[113]

There is, as it were, no revelation outside recollected utterance. For Dorothy Sayers, the gospels were the works of the artist and believer and theologian and her plays the work of the craftsman. Her job was to tell again a story already told to those who have not heard because of the oppressive and smothering clamour of piety. 'We have done what we could: may the Master Craftsman amend all', she concluded.[114]

Val Gielgud for his part paid tribute to the BBC and especially to James Welch, who preserved both author and producer from 'harassing outside influences' and 'maintained his faith in and his enthusiasm for the series from beginning to end'.[115] How right he was.

After the first broadcasts in 1942 the plays were repeated in the winter of 1942–3, and again at Easter 1944, 1945 and 1946. Problems arose over contracts and re-recordings. Sayers herself had doubts about using the plays year after year in a liturgical setting at successive Eastertides. Eventually the enthusiasm wore thin and with the re-emergence of television in the 1950s there was talk of translating the whole concept into a visual experience.[116] In 1950 she vowed to Gielgud that she would never permit the cycle on commercial television and 'the feeding of the five thousand by Hovis and MacFisheries!' After the war the series was recorded for the transcription service of the BBC and was sent on disc to every continent, including Palestine and the member nations of the Commonwealth. In the Department, there was considerable division later on as to how the cycle should be used: simply the Passion episodes at successive Easters or in its entirety? There were attempts to use the cycle in connection with Sunday services and courses of sermons, especially for young people. With the post-war construction of radio in the stratification of audiences it was in great danger of being mutilated from a cycle of plays which cohered in one large canvas to a repository of illustrative material to be used in conjunction with preaching or other teaching.

The Man Born to be King was significant for religious broadcasting policy in three ways:

(1) The hierarchy of the BBC, the Government and church leaders were initially alarmed by press coverage which saw in these plays an attack on the sacred. It was an attack on the foundation of religion, on those sacred texts which focused the nation's relation with Christian institutions. Initial fears were overcome in the reading and in the broadcasting of the cycle which made all other criticism irrelevant. Garbett was won over, as were very many. The press can take little credit for bringing the project near to catastrophe; at the same time it brought publicity to a series which might otherwise not have been listened to by nearly as many. As the series proceeded the numbers listening fell.[117]

(2) Evangelicalism on the extreme right showed its insecurity and lack of intelligence. Since the very beginning of broadcasting, church-men had expressed their initial reserve at the offence done to Christian preaching and liturgy by casting pearls before swine and exposing the inner courts to scrutiny or even question. Controversial broadcasting, as we have seen, was not permitted. The protests against Sayers' cycle were not only from the LDOS (of which Iremonger was a member!). They came from mainstream churchmen who objected to the implica-tion of a theological conviction which was summed up in *'incarnatus est'* and which stood at the heart of Sayers' motivation to write, i.e. that Jesus was a historical figure. The cycle desacralized the world of Jesus of Nazareth rather too distinctly. Sayers throughout managed to hold together the proclamatory post-Easter posture of the gospels them-selves with the historicism of Temple's position on time and event. For many Catholics, including John (later Cardinal) Heenan, the mixture of 'historicism and gospel authority was not permitted.[118] Nothing should be included in any aid to teaching the New Testament which was apocryphal or imaginative; everything had to be 'recogniz-ably biblical'.[119]

(3) The motivation for these plays had been in the provision of material for children in the setting of the BBC's pre-war Sunday policy. Before the war McCulloch and *Children's Hour* had no part in Sunday broadcasting. Welch knew there was nothing attractive to vast numbers of children, including evacuees, in the traditional Sunday services. Hence Geoffrey Dearmer's appointment and eventual transfer to *Children's Hour*. Welch conceived his young audience for these plays, like his adult audience, as those who had little knowledge of the gospel story. The cycle provided for both children and adult listeners a vehicle for education and 'knowing about' the Christian faith in a manner which all but a tiny minority, e.g. Bell at Chichester and the Religious Drama Group under Martin Browne, also based at Chichester, were unwilling, unmotivated or unprepared to attempt. The theological colleges showed little or no interest, although Welch had tried to animate diocesan conferences. His message to them was that his work in the BBC was a supplement to that of the clergy. The Sayers cycle rooted the lectionary of the Church of England in storytelling and theatre. It was rejected by many in the churches because it stood in opposition to the liturgical drama to which fewer and fewer were committed. It was welcomed warmly by many more who thought that its captivating eloquence would win back deserters. As it was, two million people were excited and entertained because Dorothy L. Sayers had decided from the outset that this would not be 'church' speaking to

nation, but Christian tradition speaking to each fireside listener. That had not quite happened to the gospel story ever before. It was colloquial and perhaps convincing: above all it was popular, and the common people heard it gladly.

That it was the most astonishing and far-reaching innovation in all religious broadcasting so far is beyond dispute. The cycle belonged to radio and the medium of a profound entertainment. Unlike the lectionary, repetitive recital would only defeat the object. As soon as the war was over, the cycle began to date.

(iv) Drama and the schools

As the dramatic element in the schools religious service developed, it became increasingly difficult to find suitable written material. Somerville and Welch both took note that the schools were strongly against constant repetition but recognized the hard fact that these dramatic interludes were not in unlimited supply. In her search for writers Somerville confessed her desperation. Since the beginning, the construction of scripts and the translation of these into the drama or feature programmes had been a hand-to-mouth existence. 'We shall have to cast the net wider . . . I am beginning to dread the thought of 1943–4,' she confessed to Welch. Where were the clergy who were good at children's services? Would not Dorothy L. Sayers oblige? Welch promised to ask her, but she would not. *The Man Born to be King* had been traumatic enough from every angle, and she would not venture into the realm of schools programmes. Welch had already toyed with the idea of dropping the schools service in favour of episodes from the cycle. Somerville hoped for a series of interludes on the life of Christ and, with the shortage of material causing so much anxiety, this was a course she hoped Welch would pursue.

Welch had always seen the immense possibilities of radio in the service of teaching theology and the Bible to the committed as well as to the lapsed. His objectives were missionary and educational: there could be no future for our culture without a quite new understanding of the Christian religion being put before the adult world in general and the rising generation in particular. His schools policy was dominated by the sure knowledge that religious education in schools was poor or almost non-existent; that there were only a handful of qualified teachers who understood the relationships between religion and pedagogics. (He frequently admitted his earlier reluctance to leave the training of teachers for the BBC.) With the advent of the schools service, Welch's constant search for dramatists within the leadership of the church took an even more urgent turn. His most outstanding discovery had been Joseph McCulloch who, however, could not provide quite the material to satisfy the Schools Department. Welch knew that he had to produce material which had to satisfy pedagogic sensitivities firmly embodied and eagerly articulated by the CCSB Committee under Sir Henry Richards. The pedagogic vetoes and objectives were vested in Mary Somerville and once the beguiling dramatic component had moved beyond the experimental stage and been approved by the teachers, Welch and Somerville between them had to find writers – all the more difficult a task against the background of the very successful Sayers.

In December 1940 Welch had visited the Anglican Community of St Mary the Virgin at Wantage to meet Sister Penelope, whom the RBD had commissioned for some Lenten talks for the following year.[120] She was an Old Testament scholar and teacher and had invited Welch to talk about radio and its possibilities: she was euphoric in her vision of how radio would help re-establish Christianity in the nation. Welch certainly believed her to be quite talented.

As he talked with Sister Penelope, Welch expressed his convictions that no recovery of the moral and ethical fibre of our national life could be hoped for unless the Bible became again a book known and understood by the British people. People read it as literature but had no real idea as to how and what to believe of it. He had had to start on the ground floor, as he later told Lindsay Wellington, the Controller of Programmes. Only in the schools could the key to its total message be most fruitful for future generations.[121] Welch wanted to bring together the fruits of modern scholarship, textual criticism and the teaching of the church: he believed in a 'central message' which was free from sectarianism and profoundly ecumenical. Sister Penelope was animated by Welch's idea and began work on a project which aimed at the dramatization of the biblical message to cover some twenty hours in half-hour sections. Welch was delighted and drew in Somerville. In March 1943 a gruelling and rather unfortunate series of negotiations began between the writer and two or even three BBC departments: Welch, Somerville and Val Gielgud.

With the submission of the first eight of Sister Penelope's plays, Welch in a commendatory note to Mary Somerville was cautiously enthusiastic: this was a 'bigger venture even than *The Man Born to be King* – dramatically not nearly so good', he admitted, 'but as scholarship, even better'.[122] Sayers had seen the text and was quite approving.[123] The Schools Department was not impressed: Somerville was clear that Sister Penelope's series *People of God* belonged, if anywhere in radio, to Welch's output and not to hers. Whilst the head of Schools was not unmoved, she was sure that Sister Penelope had not really thought specifically enough about her audience – their ages and how much (if at all) they knew of the Bible already.

The possibilities of Sister Penelope's plays being broadcast became more and more remote and, whilst she agreed to be helped, she wanted to retain the last word on the broadcast script as she believed Sayers had. The fact that the plays were taking 'so much out of me is proof that they were commissioned by the Lord': the BBC Schools Department did not seem to appreciate this, she rather sadly told Welch. The CCSB were the heathen opposition; the broadcasting authorities were hell-bent on 'watering down the Bible': 'she was not doing it to please the BBC'. This remark brought from Welch his most thorough analysis of his position as both priest and Director of Religious Broadcasting. It is worth quoting in full:

> You are not writing for the BBC, you are writing for the church; the five of us in this Department . . . have all been sent to this job by the church, seconded by the church and commissioned by the Archbishop. And when you realize that the church has been excluded from the enormously powerful world of the cinema, but that the church really has a chance of working inside the world of broadcasting, then it is surely right for the church to second us to baptize this incredibly powerful instrument of the microphone . . . The BBC allows the church to commission these plays and their work is essentially the work of the church. We could not as priests work for the BBC; we can only as priests work for the church . . . we have to study our medium and the church must master this medium . . . the canons which govern the work of the church in other fields have to be altered when the church invades the medium of broadcasting. All the time we are conscious that we are doing the work of the church and one of the saddest things about our work is that some members of the church will not realize this.[124]

Notwithstanding Sister Penelope's confusions, Welch was still convinced that there were real possibilities provided her scripts could get through 'the narrow doors of (1) pedagogics; (2) drama and (3) the radio'.[125] She had vast experience of teaching the children of the committed and indeed a good many others, but did not reckon on a schools audience conceived on a national scale. Welch still thought this was the biggest thing yet tackled by both his and Somerville's Departments. Somerville was not so sure; the plays were scholarly but did not comprise a 'golden thread', as Welch had assumed: 'the woman is neither a dramatist nor a poet'.[126] The Corporation paid Sister

Penelope off with £50 and Welch admitted that perhaps she had been led 'up the garden path' as much by her own approach as by the BBC. Ironically just as Sayers was not prepared to have her authority as an artist compromised with McCulloch's *Children's Hour* colleagues, Sister Penelope and her Mother General would not permit her theological authority to be compromised by the Schools Department.

Welch remained convinced that the dramatization of a biblical 'key' was possible. He turned his attention towards another writer – Hugh Ross Williamson, a gifted young Anglican priest ordained in 1943 and spotted by William Temple who encouraged him to respond to Welch's invitations to write for radio.[127] He had been invited to a CCSB meeting which altogether approved the dramatic interludes for summer 1943, particularly as there was concrete evidence from the schools that the construction was improving and children were understanding them better.[128] Williamson was commissioned to write a four-part play on St Paul[129] for the Home Service, and he agreed to produce a cycle of forty-two interludes on the life of Christ based on Mark's Gospel with St Peter as a 'story-teller' forming a link between episodes.[130] Welch had made it clear that the series was 'in no sense a syllabus of instruction', but that in the New Testament material, there was the basis of a ready-made script.

Williamson struggled with his scripts of the interludes and, like Sayers, immediately found himself in deep waters of theological and biblical interpretation. He insisted upon using the Gospel of John for his source and chronology. How briefly and convincingly to dramatize, for example, the 'dove' narrative of the baptism of Jesus was a problem of language as well as theology. Williamson wanted to include the sounds of a real dove, but Welch said simply that this 'went beyond the evidence'. Williamson also wanted to have Peter's wife out of the way early, and so had written in her death as reverently as possible. He found yet more difficulty in dealing with miracles and was tempted to translate the biblical notion of *thaumaturgos* into narrative both descriptive and propositional. He had to risk encouraging children to accept the presentation of such data as believable in the way other historical data might be similarly believed – for instance in the work of Rhoda Power in schools history drama broadcasts.[131] Apart from one simple but signficant difference from most drama in school broadcasts, namely, that the children broadly knew the end of Williamson's story, there was underlying his whole effort the discreet suggestion that the biblical and gospel narrative was not after all narrative and was thus not open to dramatic treatment.

His dramatized interludes on the life of Christ began in January 1944 and were variously received. Some schools thought they lacked a sense of dramatic vitality, but others – whose teachers commented rather more from a curriculum angle than on the actual observed responses of the children listening – believed they served a useful purpose in furthering an understanding of the Jesus story. The CCSB thought the experimental series had only been justified in that it appealed to children 'of higher than average intelligence'. Significantly the Committee agreed that – as Welch had hoped with Sister Penelope – consideration might be given not to a sequential dramatization of the life of Christ so much as 'a selection of incidents to illuminate the child's general grasp of the New Testament story'.[132] The emphasis therefore shifted from history to theology. This was out of step with the policy on teaching. The same meeting agreed to yet another significant shift which would widen the scope of material available and appropriate for the schools service. John Williams had made the point that whilst God should 'be kept at the centre of attention', the series should also express the human interest which the schools clearly wanted. They agreed that the interludes could now 'illustrate Christ-like behaviour but that this behaviour need not have originated from conscious Christian action'. All manner of biographical material containing examples of natural virtues would, agreed the Committee, 'invite a Christian interpretation'.

At the close of 1944 there was one further impetus to Williamson's work. The Butler Act was now law and its radical provisions in respect to religious education in schools made the teaching of religion through broadcast drama an even more exciting and powerful possibility. The Act stipulated that there should be a compulsory act of worship in all maintained schools and this, coupled with the conscience clause allowing teachers to withdraw, made a broadcast service all the more appropriate. Moreover, the non-denominational or supra-confessional character of the religious instruction required by the Act coincided with the longstanding preoccupation within the RBD to embody and define a species of Christian utterance which was not beset by denominationalism. Against the setting of the debate about religion in the schools, undertaken feverishly and passionately since the turn of the century, one can more readily appreciate Welch's passionate commitment to a Christian proclamation 'grounded but not shaped by the dispersion of the Catholic faith'.[133]

With the passing of the Butler Act, to much of which he was privy through William Temple, Welch was all the more animated by the idea to which he had set his mind when taking up the BBC task in 1939:

reaching the young. In January 1945 he set about getting off the ground a mammoth Williamson series of thirty half-hour plays on the whole Bible: 'The BBC should take the initiative in producing a key to the whole Bible which will rehabilitate the Bible in the minds of our children and their teachers'.[134] He wanted it broadcast once each year, so that each intake of children would have the Bible presented to them, and followed up in classwork with the aid of a BBC Handbook to the series. Welch had the support of Nicolls (before his transfer to the position of Senior Controller) and naturally of CRAC. Somerville, too, was keen: 'Broadcasting is *par excellence* a medium for the telling of stories.' Serialized broadcast drama was perhaps a 'successor to the medieval mystery cycles and was now, as then, particularly appropriate for the intellectually less able'.[135] Drama – it had been agreed and firmly maintained by the CCSB Religious Service Committee all along – was much to be preferred to mere 'narration'.

The Corporation agreed to Welch's plan but insisted on making a final decision and apportioning the £5000 to pay for it only when the CCSB Committee had approved a sample episode. Williamson chose Jeremiah, an Old Testament figure singularly congenial to being dramatized on account of the not inconsiderable material in the Old Testament book of that name, which some scholars construed as biographical.[136] The whole scheme depended upon the success of this one play. It had to be approved by Somerville as appropriate for schools broadcasting before money would be made available for production.

By June 1945, there were plans for a major reorganization in the Corporation, and in particular for the placing of Welch's Department alongside Somerville's under the Director of the Spoken Word. Moreover, the CCSB, as a result of the Butler Education Act, had decided to accept full responsibility for the schools religious broadcasts.[137] This was exceedingly significant, if at the time rather more so in theory than in practice. For the moment the relation between Welch, Somerville and the CCSB would continue as hitherto, with Welch able to take initiatives in respect of the BBC, and Somerville in respect of the teachers and the CCSB. In the reorganization, it looked increasingly as if the proposed cycle of plays for schools would be the final responsibility of Somerville's Department: it would fall to her and not Welch to ask for the finance. Somerville, for her part, was becoming increasingly uneasy about Williamson's interludes on the life of Jesus: they raised too many questions about education and cognition. She thought Williamson had made a crucially erroneous assumption about his audience, and was too ready to assume a background of 'the faith of the church'. In his Jeremiah play, too, he thought that a biographical treatment was adequate, and did not see the need for any 'elucidation of theological, religious and political data which alone makes the figure of Jeremiah intelligible but which involves a consecutive scheme of "teaching" '. 'Adjustment to the child is essential', said Somerville.[138] Her own consultative group wondered 'whether *anyone* could bring alive the story of Jeremiah for children while also keeping hold of the historical and religious significance of the material'.

Jeremiah represented the failure of an attempt to teach through a medium of entertainment. If Sayers had succeeded in teaching it was because her cycle held the interest of the adult and to some extent a young audience on the basis of some knowledge of or sympathy with the story. Williamson was in a similar position with the Life of Jesus interludes: some knowledge, however scant, could be taken for granted in many school children around eleven years old. This was not the case, however, with the Old Testament. Welch wanted the lectionary dramatized with sufficient intelligibility for a 'golden thread' of biblical theology to be 'taught' to the uninitiated. The 'emerging' biblical conception of God could not, however, be taught to junior children. Welch only reluctantly accepted Somerville's veto.

(v) Sixth-form religion

As we have seen, the talks for sixth forms had a rather less turbulent passage on to the air. Before the war, Iremonger had secured the church history talks which, notwithstanding Somerville's objection that they stopped at the Reformation, went ahead. The war, however, brought them to a close.

In autumn 1941, a two-year series began, as Welch had hoped and for which he had struggled, on *The Making and Content of the Bible*. This was largely the initiative of Alan Richardson, a young and prolific scholar who had already brought out an important book on biblical criticism. Welch wanted men who were not only scholars but who had ability, actual or potential, as broadcasters or teachers or both. Herein lay the foundation for yet another unending dispute between the BBC and the CCSB: the 'dons and beaks' debate. It raised the question whether either group could assess their ability to speak to children in schools.

With the end of the series on *The Making and Content of the Bible* in sight, Welch wanted to pursue a complementary series of talks which would do for Christian doctrine what the talks had done for the Bible – a dispassionate and objective analysis of the grounds and content of Christian doctrinal belief. In 1942 the Ten Propositions published by

Temple, Hinsley and the Free Churches had provoked considerable discussion in the BBC on the place and policy of religious broadcasting. Welch had been particularly involved.[139] He wanted Christian doctrine discussed by the rising generation just as much as by their elders; the country was at war and traditions embedded in a Christian society were gravely threatened. Why not have an *Anvil* for schools, in which questions of faith could be discussed with an agenda imposed not by teachers or clerics but arising naturally from sixth-formers themselves? The Schools Department said a firm 'No'. Welch was overruled. He had suggested the most eminent of dogmatic theologians, John S. Whale of Cambridge, but Somerville feared that the idea simply would not pass the Home Board, sensitive as it was to the questions of controversy. Sir Richard Maconachie was convinced that an 'arranged *Brains Trust*' would be tumbled by sixth-formers and would therefore be no *Brains Trust* as the public now hugely enjoyed it. A. C. Cameron of the CCSB, like Somerville, thought that it was educationally unsound. Cameron, however, went further. He thought the teachers would baulk at the notion of having doctrine taught in any style.

The CCSB had made a request for comparative religion.[140] They had a perfect right to ask for this, and the RBD had an obligation to respond, but it was a significant departure from what had till now been a consistent presentation of the viewpoint of the mainstream churches. In any case, Welch was sure that this was impossible, on pedagogic even more than on theological grounds. Talks on other religions could not be on the same level of scholarship as those on Christianity; he did not believe that scholars able to put Buddhism, Confucianism and Islam across were available. An objective presentation of the non-Christian religions would take an enormous amount of time; it would raise major issues of policy; and an academic approach would render the enterprise useless. His six years of research in Africa had taught him, if nothing else, that a detached academic study of indigenous religion got nowhere: 'Only when I was allowed to be present at the worship of the ancestors, I began to understand the thing I was studying.'[141] Any attempt at such talks by the Schools Department would amount merely to a programme on what Christians know and think about Buddhism, etc. Such talks could, of course, be attempted, but certainly not within the ambience of a philosophy of religious education.

As an alternative to comparative religion, Welch had suggested that next year's series be on the Life of Christ. He wanted it to be scholarly and objective; 'doctrinal questions would emerge naturally and rightly from the study of our source book . . .' He was clear about indoctrination: 'unhesitatingly I want to avoid anything which savours of preaching, propaganda or proselytizing'.[142] Cameron, for the CCSB, accepted this; the proposal for a series on the *Great Religions of the World* on the Home Service could be regarded as supplying what the CCSB wanted in that field.[143] Subsequent courses concentrated upon scholarly introductions to the world of the Old Testament and the New.

When the war ended, the Schools Department returned to London, as did the RBD from Bedford, and liaison was considerably easier. The Schools Department was now in a better position and more determined to find out the audience for these talks and the extent to which they were appreciated. A postal survey was organized for the spring term 1946 to estimate the size of the audience and 'as far as possible' the wishes of the audience for future courses. The proposal was for Old Testament and New Testament series for the three terms from summer 1945 to spring 1946. Less than 150 grammar schools were listening and the vast majority of the audience were girls, Protestant and aged sixteen or seventeen. Forty per cent of schools used the talks as a basis for their religious instruction syllabus. The total number of students listening was around 3,000. There were inevitably problems about the time of the broadcasts and the relation of the broadcast to the amount of time in the curriculum given to the subject. Less than half of the listening schools followed the broadcasts regularly throughout the three terms. Comments made it quite clear that after a particularly difficult or problematic talk, the teacher would either skip a week in order to elaborate on that talk or simply abandon the series from then on. There seemed to be a case therefore, for fortnightly broadcasts. Schools which only allocated a single period for religious education would only take the broadcasts now and then, since to do otherwise would put the Corporation in the role of a substitute teacher. Whilst there was slightly more adverse than favourable comment, there was certainly appreciation. The survey had no way of assessing the ability of teachers to integrate the broadcasts into other teaching. From Welch's point of view, one particular comment was troublesome: 'The criticism is less of the talks than of their suitability for boys and girls of sixth forms, for whom they were "too academic", "overloaded", with "too much background knowledge assumed".'[144] It was the 'dons and beaks' debate over again and all the more acutely since Welch was in effect introducing biblical scholarship into the curriculum in a way that even the few good agreed syllabuses were not doing. Biblical scholarship was a species of science and neither the schools nor even the churches were quite ready for it. T. W. Manson was one of the scholars who were not willing to undertake such simplification. The postal report made it clear that those schools which took the programmes seriously hoped that the Corporation would do what they themselves could not: provide a species of substitute teaching. A Schools Department summer conference for teachers had produced the same conclusion. The schools, as the report had shown, were simply not teaching the subject. The head teachers wanted scholarly authority but the ordinary form teachers wanted the teaching material itself. No matter how good the speakers were, the sixth-formers' response was 'Why on earth does this matter to us?' Kenneth Grayston, who had succeeded Fenn as Assistant Director of Religious Broadcasting, concluded what mattered to them was not Christian origins etc., but the very nature and place of religion itself:

> Speakers assume that their listeners accept the Christian assumptions which the speakers themselves bring to their subjects; . . . on the whole they do not give weight to the inevitable influence of popular versions of the rationalist and scientific attitudes; . . . the talks are too much like the traditional scripture syllabuses throughout the schools.

The BBC was committed to using 'dons' but it began to look seriously as if they should be using 'beaks'. Grayston's suggested syllabus for the 1947–8 Bible talks was designed to widen the scope to include the issues which were concerning the sixth-formers. He thought that a third of the time should be devoted to 'the relation of religion to the life of man'.[145]

R. C. Steele of the Schools Department knew of the SCM Sixth Form Religious Conferences and was in touch with Robert C. Walton, a Baptist minister who had set up 'SCM in Schools'; he was much in favour of the BBC broadcasts and was glad to have the BBC interest. Steele was also in touch with Tissington Tatlow of the Institute of Religious Education, who urged the appointment in the Schools Department of an 'expert who might be both pedagogically and theologically trained': a schoolmaster rather than a don! Richmond Postgate, who had by now succeeded Mary Somerville as head of the Schools Department, was confident that the Corporation should be concentrating on providing programmes to assist those schools unable to provide adequate religious instruction, rather than supplementing the provision in the very schools already well catered for.

Steele also consulted the Ministry of Education Religious Instruction Panel, which rather hesitantly confirmed Tissington Tatlow's pessimistic report on the school situation.[146] Above all, the panel, chaired by R. E. Williams, the Senior Staff Inspector of Religious Instruction, encouraged the BBC to widen the scope of the Schools

Broadcasting Council (the CCSB had just been reconstituted under this name) as soon as possible so that it might strike out beyond biblical courses and take an unparalleled initiative in providing for sixth formers the structured teaching of religion which would involve discussion of the deepest questions of life. Steel quoted a head teacher of a Stockport school: 'Sixth formers are not interested in the moves already made in this game of chess but why the game is being played at all.'[147] At a conference of Home Counties teachers organized by J. A. Scupham, the Home Counties Education Officer, this same point was emphasized: the sixth-form pupil wanted to ask fundamental questions about the nature of 'being', irrespective of any particular or necessary religious prerequisite. Steele's intention was to plan some fundamentally different courses for 1949 and 1950. He was aware of the small but significant number of teachers who requested talks for 'modern' schools in addition to those for the grammar schools. The idea was confirmed by yet another consultation with the Ministry of Education Broadcasting Panel in January 1949. HMIs requested the BBC to consider the possibility of talks for thirteen- and fourteen-year-olds, particularly as modern schools in their opinion 'tended to give more time to the subject.'[148]

The Schools Broadcasting Council reported in autumn 1948 and formally requested the Executive of the Council to approve a fundamentally new policy: to provide a new series entitled *Religion and Philosophy*, which was to 'supplement' religious instruction. The series – as all the evidence suggested – must assume no prior biblical or ecclesial knowledge gained from either school or church.[149] Above all, the Council supported the Schools Department's conclusions from their extensive evidence[150] that the courses must deal with 'the general philosophical presuppositions of religious beliefs'. The Christian faith must also be subjected to a similar 'scholarly and ordered exposition'. Whilst the number of listening schools was constantly on the increase (in 1947 it was around 16,500), the percentage taking the new sixth-form religion and philosophy series remained very low. Forty-seven per cent of all grammar schools were taking broadcasts in one or more subjects, but in England and Wales the number of schools taking the sixth-form religious talks amounted to only around two hundred. If the BBC was to be recognized as offering a major curriculum component, an increase in the number of schools listening would only be achieved by an improvement both in the material itself and the way in which it was presented. Constitutionally the relations between production and presentation had always been difficult. Because they were religious, the responsibility for the talks lay with the RBD. Because they were talks to schools they had to be filtered through the educational and pedagogic sensitivities of the teachers in the Schools Department. Not that the projected talks suddenly abandoned the 'dons' for the 'beaks'. The course for 1950–51, for example, examined the question of moral choice and examined arguments for the case that 'there is a God whose nature is such that the life of man can be bound to him'.[151] Speakers included Herbert Butterfield and F. A. Cockin, by now Bishop of Bristol. Out of ten speakers, seven were established theologians including John S. Whale, an experienced broadcaster who was now head of Mill Hill School.

Whereas in Welch's time the centre of gravity for religious education had been in the RBD, with the Schools Department assisting, the situation had now changed; the initiative was now with the Schools Department, in closer co-operation than hitherto with the world of education, particularly since the reconstitution of the Council in 1947. It was a most significant structural change.

(vi) Youth club religion

By the beginning of the war the BBC had made enormous progress in its programmes for the young which centred on *Children's Hour* and the Schools Department. In both departments the place of religion was always accompanied by controversy and dispute; there was always suspicion of any form of preaching which was not at any rate subject to the canons of entertainment and pedagogics. The churches, who believed that they had a right to an outlet in these areas, were resisted by Corporation producers who would not allow their work to be suddenly and arbitrarily upset by a style of programme which looked like preaching dressed up in an acceptable disguise.

The RBD was always in search of new forms appropriate to an increasingly diverse audience: different styles reached different groups. Broadcasting was naturally preoccupied with the adult listener except when numbers justified a policy which would cater for a younger group exclusively. The Schools Department and the RBD were the most concerned here, and were subject to similar outside constraints; the CCSB and CRAC had in common a commitment to objectives not by any means always at one with those of the broadcasters. The Director of Religious Broadcasting had a relationship with all four parties.

During the thirties the Schools Department had continued to grow, but it had become clear that for all its efforts for the child in school, little was being done for young adults, particularly those who left school at the minimum age. There were issues to be taught that would only attract this youth club audience if the style was obviously adult: there could be no smack of 'schooling' or these young adults would switch off; they had learned how from older adults! In school they had to listen; at home they need not.

In the late thirties, the CCSB and the Central Committee for Group Listening both suggested that the BBC should be concerned with adolescents and with providing suitable programmes which would aid the development of knowledge and citizenship. These early programmes were careful not to cultivate a style reminiscent of school. From the beginning it was clear that programmes for the post-school adolescent must avoid any suggestion of authority figures and the transmission of knowledge by bookish talks received by a predominantly passive audience: there had to be 'discussion, not dissemination'.[152] Only by encouraging and respecting the opinions of the adolescent could any programme hope to succeed.

The first experimental series was devised and organized by Mary Somerville and broadcast in 1938–9 under the title *The Under Twenty Club*; it had in mind an audience aged seventeen to twenty 'and the more intelligent and vocal among them at that'.[153] She had been one of the growing number of educationalists who recognized the importance of debate and discussion for the training of young citizens and had spent considerable time particularly in those schools where Schools Department programmes were received. It was clear that if these programmes were to have their counterpart after school age, the content must not only embrace the interests of the middle class but extend from subjects of a moral and philosophical kind to sport, parents and even BBC programmes!

With the coming of war, controversial elements were immediately suppressed, as for example, a programme which examined the Government's policy on refugees. Moreover, people complained enough about encouraging the young to 'talk "blah" about political matters'[154] and once the war-time single programme had begun any such experiments had to take care not to enrage too many adults! After *The Under Twenty Club* came *The Armstrongs*, a serial in which discussion took place with the young and not so young in a lower-middle class family. Each episode was devised by Somerville and the dramatist Ronald Gow. This programme was well received by adults and dealt with issues somewhat nearer home such as family relationships and various moral and social questions: housing, post-war planning, employment and the arts. The greatest difficulty was in making young people in discussion express themselves in a way entertaining both to adults and to other young people. It was a problem at the base of broadasting policy. There were soon requests particularly from the youth organizations for more 'educative' programmes which would appeal to youth clubs and be heard by young people in groups who would then discuss such issues together. This impetus gave rise to the series *To Start You Talking* which, after a few preliminary experiments, finally went on the air in 1942. Throughout all these preparations, two things were clear: such programmes would be heard also by the adults; young people in their clubs wanted to hear not only experts being quizzed but the opinions of those like themselves. Discussion and debate dominated; no matter how much the adult input, it had to remain clearly and honestly a discussion for teenagers.

In spring 1942, Welch and Fenn were hopeful for some part in this series and for a contribution by their department to youth and youth clubs, especially perhaps some form of broadcast service. Welch and Fenn had been approached by the Standing Conference of Juvenile Organizations for some part to be played by the BBC in getting youth clubs to participate in religious discussions. Welch wanted a scheme of broadcasts in Somerville's series in which young people between sixteen and twenty put their questions on church and religion to a parson. He wanted nurses, clerks, university students, refugees and members of the Forces asking straight questions about evil and Christian ideals, about the existence of God and about the church.

Somerville thought this all too erudite and, above all, that it assumed young people had the basic theological data to be able to appreciate such questions. They were more ignorant of and untroubled by such issues: 'Our job is to see that they are given a clear picture of what Christianity means to the Christian – and then invite them to evaluate it.'[155] As an educationalist she assumed that whatever knowledge these young people actually possessed was of little real use in debate: only the educated classes possessed such data and the programmes had to embrace a wider youth audience. Somerville, like Welch was fully aware of the general policy restriction on religious discussion at the microphone and the pressure from the Rationalist Press Association and others to participate in any debate which raised issues on which they would rightly claim authority and competence. Talks were the only means by which the Christian position could be put; discussion would have to be entirely local and domestic and not to be broadcast.

Discussions continued between Fenn and Somerville but without concrete results. Plans for a fourfold series on religion were postponed in the hope that C. S. Lewis would undertake the task. Somerville approved and hoped that something could be done for the spring of 1943. A. C. F. Beales, the Catholic, prepared a series of scripts, and a series appeared under the title *About Christianity*: it was to be essentially descriptive and the statements by the Christian expert would be 'tripped' by the expressions of doubt from the young participants. A good deal of preparation was undertaken with youth clubs and Fenn met stimulating response from young people quite outside the orbit of formal Christianity as well as from among the committed. The young, it was clear, wanted discussions: they wanted the cut and thrust between the so-called expert and his opponent, the unbeliever. But it was not allowed by the Governors. Somerville hoped the answers of the 'well-informed Christian' could be presented in a sufficiently dramatic situation such as a prisoner-of-war camp 'to lessen the resentment which might be felt in the absence of a Rationalist'.[156]

The series *About Christianity* went out in March 1943. As far as Silvey's Listener Research Department and the Schools Department's Education officers around the country could ascertain, the responses were average. The four sessions had tackled the Bible, morality, faith and 'the possibility of brotherhood', and brought together four boys including a Roman Catholic Czech, all of them very articulate. Nancy Hussey, the producer, feared that a sense of the discussion being rigged would not go unnoticed. It did not. There were two main criticisms: first, that too much knowledge was assumed in the audience and, secondly, that the parson 'had all the ammunition' and his case was presented more as proven fact than as a point of view.[157]

The series did, however, prompt the Bishop of Coventry, Neville Talbot, to ask Welch to think again about the youth clubs: too little was being done, particularly as the rising generation were sceptical of the clergy who did not, by and large, understand 'youth psychology'. They were looking to the BBC for 'guidance and help' he thought, and Welch should be making some provision. The Church of England's Central Youth Council, as represented by Charles Claxton, was also concerned about the appalling state of religion in the nation's youth clubs, especially those not connected with churches.

It was an address in St Martin's-in-the-Fields by the Bishop of London, J. W. C. Wand, which gave impetus to the Corporation's provision for the non-uniformed youth clubs. Wand had been invited to preach at the Boys' Brigade Jubilee Service, which was being broadcast, and it went disastrously wrong. The Department was criticized for 'producing' broadcasts in which the speaker felt obliged to address himself to the broadcast audience rather more directly than the one in front of him. The Boys' Brigade wanted publicity themselves; the Corporation wanted relevance to the wider audience. In effect, said Cyril Taylor, the adult audience had a reasoned academic lecture, but the boys of the Brigade, and any young ones who might have been stimulated to listen by this special occasion, were hopelessly put off.[158] Something should specially be done for those youths who did not normally listen to the 'middle-brow' Sunday evening services, and the non-church youth organizations should advise.

After consultation between the BBC and such bodies as the YMCA, YWCA and the National Association of Boys' and Girls' Clubs, it was clear that there would be qualified co-operation. Welch took his cue from Selby Wright, the Radio Padre,[159] who suggested that services should be broadcast from youth clubs to youth clubs, rather on the model of the services broadcast to anti-aircraft units. Welch and Selby Wright got together their team including the Rev. Berners Wilson, who had just joined the National Association of Boys' Clubs. He helped design the first series to run monthly from October 1943 to March 1944.

By this time Somerville and Fenn were struggling to evolve a new series on Christianity in *To Start You Talking*: 'Is Christianity right about (i) Believing in God? (ii) Going to Church? (iii) Sex Morality?'[160] Somerville was committed to discussion as a basis for the programme and sought to devise the Christian-Rationalist axis without offending Corporation policy. Canon Cockin would state the Christian position in a recording at the outset of the programme and the discussion would be entirely by teenagers across the Christian-Rationalist divide; 'experts' would therefore be excluded. But Haley, now Director-General, rejected the whole scheme.

CRAC had upheld the PMG's ban on controversy since 1928 and the wartime situation had simply agitated other quasi-religious movements as well as the churches themselves to see that Christianity was not subjected to any more ideological stress than was already focused in the conflict. Welch, for his part, most certainly wanted religious debate brought into the market place,[161] and by this time was preparing the Governors, the Director-General and CRAC for a profound change of direction in the policy of broadcast religion.[162] But Somerville's series on Christianity had no real chance so long as the Corporation was effectively forced to comply with the decision of the churches in particular and the Christian establishment in society at large. The long-standing lobby by the Rationalist Press Association met with strenuous resistance by the Governors as well as the RBD. They firmly believed that the Association was not requesting discussion and open debate, but rather a regular slot for propaganda, which they would not provide. Such an innovation as Somerville now proposed was doomed to failure, despite Welch's support. Haley maintained his opposition to such an innovation in a youth or schools context – a ruling that would persist to the fifties.[163]

It was clear, therefore, that any initiative from the RBD for youth clubs would have to take a liturgical rather than an educative form with as much information or stimulation as possible – even under the watchful eye of Somerville, whose Department maintained partial control over these operations. The immediate model was the service for schools: a liturgical framework, however attenuated, within which a dramatic interlude of some kind could secure attention and carry the message. The series began in October 1944 and continued monthly until April 1945. The aim was to provide a service to those youth clubs which were without one. After the first four broadcasts there was deep dissatisfaction from the youth organizations and from some churches: the services were, in a word, too conventional – the same hymns as in church, interspersed with prayers and the inevitable talk. Cyril Taylor believed that radio was again being wasted: the schools service was the obvious model – it could do what the churches could not.[164] By the end of the first series this style was too much for the National Association of Mixed Clubs; young people in the open non-church clubs 'hardly know what religion is, much less are ready to join in true worship'.[165] If religion was to be presented in this context, it must be in some context akin to the series *To Start You Talking*. Welch had to refuse, because the style of *To Start You Talking* was forbidden. The central truths of the Christian faith could only be transmitted through worship. Taylor therefore wanted good liturgy and good radio; there was an acute danger that the Department was producing neither.

Berners Wilson of the National Association of Boys' Clubs conducted the next series almost single-handed from a variety of churches around Britain accompanied by an extensive publicity campaign. Scotland meanwhile was developing its own series, *Youth Seeks the Answer*.[166] Involved in the preparations were now twenty-eight youth organizations committed to fostering the life of both the church and non-church groups. Taylor always maintained that these services should be designed for non-church goers. The churches, however, did not always agree: 'Our present policy does not have the confidence of the churches', Saxon in the North complained.[167] The reason was clear: the churches were not satisfied that the services were actually recruiting. Evangelistic motivations were not spelled out, but at the North Region RAC it was the general conviction that 'our task is to win people not so much to belief in Christianity in general but to be members of the church'.[168] The services for youth should be linked more closely with the church youth organizations than the non-church ones. Saxon lamented what many would not recognize – that the clergy find it 'difficult to work with outside bodies and doubt the wisdom of co-operating with the state; the 1944 Education Act will continue the process of divorcing Christianity from the church itself'.[169] A few far-sighted clergy such as Edward Patey insisted that *To Start You Talking* was the obvious way to get the unchurched exposed to and involved in religious thinking.

During the spring of 1947, more Standing Committee consultations took place and the non-church youth organizations made it abundantly plain that they did not approve the preoccupation with liturgy and 'club-styled' services: they were patronizing.[170] The 1947–48 series was conducted by the talented Berners Wilson, whose manner and style was mostly appreciated. Again, the complaints focused on the churchiness: all the services came from Anglican centres. The 1948–49 series roughly replicated the previous ones, but were this time from non-Anglican churches and conducted by a Methodist, Douglas Griffiths of the Methodist Association of Youth Clubs. The nonconformist buildings at least proved more congenial to broadcasting since the pulpit was in the centre and the proceedings could be controlled more efficiently!

The next innovation, first used in Scotland, was to insert a dramatized broadcast interlude into a church service. At the appropriate moment it had to be relayed via a public address system into the church from which the broadcast was made. It was a tricky problem for the engineers, but it succeeded! The interludes were produced by the Schools Department. The preacher would speak to the dramatized human situation and questions would be taken unscripted from the youth participants, but be so prepared as to avoid all controversial material![171] With the youth clubs wanting to revert to services from clubs and others, mostly the church youth people, wanting broadcasts from churches, this might prove an effective compromise. R. A. Rendall, the Controller of Talks, thought otherwise: the questions would appear rigged and anyway belonged to a club rather than a church context. Scotland had by far the easier time since a vastly larger proportion of young people were found to be attracted both to the church context and the 'dramatized' sermon component which the engineers in Glasgow had 'brought to a fine art'.[172]

The Scottish scheme had dramatized the parables and had a good response from the listening groups. About four hundred youth groups listened to *Youth Seeks an Answer* in the winter of 1949–50, and the 'large majority of these were church groups'.[173] Falconer was confident indeed: 'The 96 per cent of these 400 groups wishing to listen again next year would indicate that in this respect our youth religious broadcasts would seem to fulfil our intention of being the handmaid of the church.'[174]

The English series, this time conducted by Bryan Reed of Westhill College, Birmingham, were modestly successful; 'adverse comment', according to Listener Research, was negligible.[175] The general press response was favourable and encouraged Reed to consider a further series but Taylor had sufficient evidence to conclude that these services were being taken mostly by church youth groups. Taylor thought the summer meeting of the Youth Broadcasting Committee should have more representatives from the British Council of Churches and the mainstream churches. At this meeting Bryan Reed's style of service was definitely not approved; it was appealing not to the older teenager but rather to the older schoolchild. The non-church youth bodies in particular wanted something less like a modified church service, but rather something more explicit such as the service for schools.[176] The days of a Sunday evening broadcast service to youth on the Home Service were numbered: the responses were generally marginal and the Department concluded that the Light Programme was the more widely appreciated setting. *Sunday Half Hour* could take a youth group format; this was approved by Richmond Postgate in spring 1951, and Taylor reported it to the youth organizations. Some regretted the shift from a service to community hymn singing, but this did appear to be more popular. The RBD initiative among this age group finally petered out and was superseded by a half-hearted arrangement with the Schools Department and a Light Programme initiative, *The Younger Generation*, a highly successful series which followed on from Forces Educational broadcasting.[177] By the summer of 1951 the notion of a special service for the post-school age group was effectively abandoned.

It had become clear that if the BBC had the ear of the young in the pre-war period and subsequently until around the early fifties, the churches were not able to comply with the demand for discussion and debate and the exposure of Christianity to such scrutiny as the young seemed to demand. The emphasis was upon the asking of questions. In Scotland the young were asking questions about the nature of the faith, which seemed to be accepted very much more widely there than in England. South of the border the young seemed to demand more radical explanations.

Discussion and questioning were the obvious ways by which young adults could learn. The identity of the Christian believer would not be received on trust; it was as difficult to speak to the sceptical and untutored teenager (who need not listen) as to the captive school pupil who was obliged to. The idea of worship outside the committed congregational circle was resented. It reflected two assumptions by both churchmen (including CRAC) and teachers: (1) that the school and secular youth club could undertake this liturgical activity as something appropriate to the concept of citizenship in a Christian culture; and (2) that the liturgical repository of Christendom in an attenuated form could provide a vehicle for evangelism and recruitment. The churches ultimately wanted adherence or conversion; the educationalists wanted analysis or stimulation in the search for religious truth. The problems were replicated in the schools: the rising generation questioned the authenticity of Christian claims and the presentation of Christian lifestyles. Religious education was masked by confessionalism, and the educators were not quite prepared for the radical dismantling which the rising generation wanted. This reluctance perhaps led to the mechanisms of religious belief being dismantled whether the churches liked it or not. The pity of it is that in the schools, a generation passed not caring if the pieces were ever put back together or not. The young wanted questions; the churches offered assertions; both were disappointed.

C. Schools religion: post-war developments

In the immediate post-war era, it was clear that the regular religious services which began on Welch's initiative in 1940 and the dramatic element which developed later were to become regular features of school broadcasting as the number of schools listening increased.[178]

With the reorganization in the Corporation, the main issues involved in providing a religious service for schools were (*a*) constitutional: who and which department was actually responsible for the broadcast, in the light of the Schools Council's overall acceptance following the Butler Act; (*b*) the problems of production and the pursuit of suitable material, particularly for the dramatic interlude; and (*c*) the responses of the schools, teachers and pupils. The Schools Department and the RBD continued to debate all three issues, and by 1951 it was possible to produce the most detailed report so far on the value and scope of the religious service.

On the constitutional issue there was a tug-of-war between the two Departments over how responsibility should be defined. It was important to Grayston and Williams – as Welch had always maintained – that the service was seen as an act of worship and – as indeed the Teachers' Advisory Committee had strongly emphasized – *not* a teaching device. It was not a component in the curriculum.[179] On the other side, the CCSB commissioned the BBC Schools Department to produce it in a manner satisfactory to schools. Williams agreed with Somerville on the need for definition, but the sector in the BBC which had brought the service to birth wanted most strenuously to maintain control over it. Williams had always been conscious of pressure by the CCSB and the Schools Department to 'water down the Christian content of the prayers'. In 1947 Williams and Grayston were fighting for ultimate control on the strength of their definition of the event as an act of worship offered to God and not simply an aesthetic and emotional exposure to humanitarian and quasi-Christian virtues. In that year, the two Departments formally agreed to share the production as indeed they had done from the outset: the service to be produced by the Director of Religious Broadcasting with 'advice from the Director of Schools Broadcasting as to audience suitability'; the interlude by the latter 'subject to religious advice and editorial supervision by the former.'[180] Plans were soon in hand to appoint a production assistant to be responsible for the production and presentation of the service. The new Head of Religious Broadcasting, Francis House, placed enormous importance on the wider work of his Department but was unable to provide a children's specialist who in turn would have so minimal a responsibility in the RBD. In 1949, Postgate and House, the two heads, met and agreed to the new relationship: 'the services and interludes should be planned and produced by the Head of Schools Broadcasting, subject to religious advice and religious editorial supervision by the Head of Religious Broadcasting'.[181]

The morning service for schools was now to be a Schools Department operation. The Department which had originated the broadcast had been motivated by a concept of Christian culture and the importance of presenting worship in a manner sufficiently compelling to lay foundations for possible Christian commitment later. However, this new agreement shifted the emphasis distinctly; the Butler Act and later the decision by the CCSB to take full responsibility for the service as a 'schools' broadcast both tended to shift the service into the field of moral education and character building. Not surprisingly, the teachers in the schools were concerned about deep questions of intelligibility as well as the more practical questions of participation. There were problems over reception, as the technicians had constantly pointed out.[182] Efforts to produce a selection of one hundred hymns suitable for schools went some way towards standardizing the available books.[183] There was always a good deal of complaint from the schools and an SBC Conference in December 1948[184] left the BBC in no doubt that hymns were the main obstacle to successful participation by schools. A schools hymnbook was the answer, if only the LEAs would buy it. A meeting in May 1949 between the two Departments and the SBC decided that however distant the prospect of a school hymnbook might be, the schools should at least be informed of the hymns well in advance through a termly leaflet instead of the present arrangements via the *Radio Times*. This compromise was not improved upon till the eventual publication of a small hymn book supplement to the BBC Hymn Book in the mid-fifties.

In 1949 the Schools Department acquired a new member of the production team, fulfilling the hopes that Somerville had expressed in 1947. The Rev. Robert Walton, secretary of SCM in Schools, took up his duties in the autumn and had the qualifications in both education and theology which the position demanded. The RBD remained advisory, but the responsibility for the religious service and the talks for sixth forms was now securely based in the Schools Department. Walton had problems with both, but the service was all the more complicated by the commitment to the dramatizing of biblical material. The scripts of Hugh Ross Williamson had formed the basis of the interludes since 1944, with several theological and schematic changes. The device of using Peter to give a consecutive narrative was replaced by a series of incidental stories chosen to present the essential message of the New Testament. According to the SBC Commission of 1949, the interludes should provide 'a subject for meditation' in a dramatized story without a narrator, and a means to 'bring the New Testament to life'.[85] Each interlude should be followed by a prayer taking up the theme of the interlude or a prayer which could be repeated by the class (for example the Lord's Prayer). The Advisory Committee had always strenuously enjoined the producers to avoid any catechetical infringements in these sections: it was so easy to 'preach'.

Walton, like Williams[86] and Notcutt-Green who were producers before him, faced the schools themselves over questions of both pedagogics and theology: the interludes had to have 'action and dramatic incident', said the Commission.[87] In the Life of Jesus series, miracles should be presented as historical reality and not merely as a valuable insight into or a 'sign' of his ministry. Two distinct attitudes were evident here: on the one hand, the approach of contemporary theologians like Temple and Richardson, who argued the acceptability of the concept in a philosophical arena; and on the other, those who took a traditional view and regarded the 'accounts' in the New Testament as comparable to descriptive material by which modern scientific man construes the world. This discussion between theologians in the RBD and educationalists in the Schools Department was profoundly disturbing. Many of the latter were, of course, practising, devout but frequently untutored believers. Could the biblical material be dramatized without raising historical questions which neither encouraged meditation nor belonged to an act of worship? Walton asked why the stories of Joseph, for example, should never be told in a religious service on the grounds that some scholars have some reservations about their historicity?[188] As stories they had something to say without the need of explanation. Williams represented the other view: Old Testament stories were in a way 'pre-Christian and have no more spiritual weight than those culled from Hindu or Buddhist sources'. Perhaps Dean Inge was right: the Old Testament was only for Christian graduates! Williams represented the mainstream churches and the many Christian teachers who themselves had been brought up to believe that the Old Testament was preparatory and that it should not be imbued with a Christian content which it did not possess; the Department as always was 'up against our old friend the natural virtues'.[189] Dramatizing the gospels remained for Walton as exasperating a task as it had been for previous Schools Department producers. The schools complained of the difficulties of interludes which dealt, for example, with the Temptation story; they could not be appreciated by eleven-year-olds. Walton's view was that naturally some stories, for instance the nature miracles, could not be dramatized. However, the 'story as a whole must not be falsified', as he told the SBC: to have omitted the Temptation would have been to 'distort the gospel story'. In the end, Walton, like Williams, had no alternative but to present the Life of Jesus in the manner of biography rather than catechesis. The gospel stories served, in an act of worship, as ingredients in an expression of spiritual or inner commitment: social, spiritual and intellectual. In a schools broadcast, the interlude had to make the raw materials of the churches' lectionary intelligible not only to the uncommitted but also the untutored.

Five years after the end of the war, and at the point of policy change, the Council decided to test the waters once again and discover the extent to which the schools were taking the service and any other information which would guide the development of policy. Another postal survey was mounted in 1951 and reported on the listening situation for the previous year. The survey was made in six hundred schools, secondary modern, all-age and primary being represented in equal numbers. In each of the three age ranges, schools were chosen from both urban and rural areas and the overall response to the questionnaire was encouraging – around three-quarters replied. From the numbers of schools it was possible on the basis of the SBC's directory of registered schools to estimate both the number of schools and the children who would be listening to the schools service.

It was clear that in addition to those who tuned in occasionally, the schools listening regularly were about eighty per cent of the sample. These were drawn equally from town and rural schools, except for the all-age schools, the majority of which were in rural areas. The report provided firm evidence that the largest number of children listening were aged between eleven and thirteen. What was also alarmingly clear, however, was the number of primary school children listening, particularly those in the nine- to ten-year-old age range.[190] On the basis of regular listening, the report estimated that 'the total audience for the religious service was 6860 schools'. Allowing a margin for error, that figure could have been as many as 8000 or as few as 5700 schools. In secondary modern schools the estimated number of children listening in a potential 2677 schools was just under 280,000; in all-age schools, 182,000 children from a potential 4226 schools; and in 8393 potential primary schools, an audience of almost 480,000 children. The remarkable observation was that of an estimated audience of almost a million children just about half of those listening, occasionally or regularly, were in primary schools and therefore were below the age for which the religious service had originally been designed.[191]

On less statistical questions, the report could only affirm that around half of the secondary modern and all-age schools were able to say that the service as a whole was appreciated. The questionnaires, it must be remembered, were directed to the teachers and not to the children! Somewhat less than half of the schools (excluding the primary) affirmed their appreciation of the interludes. A persistent note was the request for a special primary school service for children under eleven.

The 1951 postal survey marked the end of a decade of bi-partisan action by two Departments in the Corporation, governed and advised by two outside professional institutions, the SBC and CRAC. The debates between the two Departments focused upon the central philosophical issues which revolved around religious utterance. The motivation of Welch and the RBD at the outbreak of war was, of course, ecclesial. The schools act of worship should provide a notion of ordinary church services and thus the best idea of what children might expect when they attended for themselves. The same principle operated in the wider Home Service output, and any innovation which stemmed from and belonged to the medium of radio itself was in danger of widening a credibility gap between the BBC experience itself and that of the 'local' church. By the same token, the teachers were anxious for the broadcasters not to behave as surrogate educators or to mount a broad catechetic operation only appropriate to the children who came within the orbit of the active and committed Christian community, and not the nation's schools.

By 1955 it was clear that the Schools Council initiative could achieve results among the young that were not easily possible in the churches. The Corporation was obliged to recognize one salient fact: however distinct was the clerical resistance which stood between the broadcasters and the congregations, in the schools there were very few specialist teachers. The sixth forms were potentially the most fertile soil for equipping the rising generation with the philosophical and exegetical tools with which belief of any kind could be constructed. The Schools Council made it quite clear to Robert Walton that there was a challenge to belief inherent in any presentation of Christianity, and, as far as the schools religious programmes were concerned, broadcasts must be addressed 'primarily to the understanding by means of a systematic structure of fact and argument'. Moreover, methods appropriate to liturgical activities were simply unsuited to schools.[192] The churches might have taken more heed; in 1954, over a third of all grammar schools in the United Kingdom were taking the *Religion and Philosophy* Series.[193] The churches quite understandably were rather more concerned with falling numbers in the Sunday schools among the younger age groups. The Corporation and Schools Broadcasting Council were no less anxious about fourteen-year-olds. One experiment was *The Bible and Life*, which after an encouraging pilot scheme began in spring 1956 with dramatized investigations of *How the Gospels were Written*. Similar techniques were used for discussions on moral issues. For this age, there was now an alternative to the religious service as the traditional vehicle for religious education.[194]

Notwithstanding the dearth of skilled and qualified teachers revealed by the preparation and publication of the Butler Act in 1944, vast numbers of teachers were themselves committed Christians or belonged to the ranks of the 'half-churched' or even the lapsed. They represented a strong lobby in favour of teaching Christianity and laying foundations for moral behaviour and the inculcation of sound ideas about society and democracy, both of which were gravely under threat in 1939 and in the period up to 1950. After the war, the shift in emphasis towards discussion and the questioning of established patterns of belief was considerably hampered by the restrictions which the Governors of the BBC and CRAC placed upon controversial religious programmes. They were certainly only permitted for the adult listener. The very considerable support for the school services by the teachers, in spite of their constant review and criticism, arose from either distinctly ecclesial and Christian or distinctly educational motivations, or, in many cases, from both. The humanist, Mary Somerville, though favouring the latter, was keen to pursue both, providing educational criteria were met. Here lay the philosophical dispute. For Welch and later House, the greatest and most complex question was how to turn the utterance of faith and commitment into an intelligible and provocative discourse for a given age-range. In practical terms, how could the faith of Albert Schweitzer be an example to the children of Doncaster or Devizes? How could the Feeding of the Five Thousand be turned into a credible and imaginative narrative understandable to eleven-year-olds, as well as to those who were three forms up the school? What prior knowledge could be assumed? None, in the opinion of the educationalists. And moreover, there were the rank-and-file teachers with liberal ideas about teaching the Bible as part of the heritage of a Christian culture but who were self-confessedly unprepared to teach the subject with any scholarly integrity. Religion belonged more to the clergy at the beginning of the school day than to the teacher in a recognized place on the timetable.

For almost a decade teachers, dons, theologians and the clergy struggled to delineate boundaries between so-called secular schooling and the catechesis proper to a minority who belonged to the church. There was a danger that the dramatic form would be more subject to æsthetic than didactic considerations, and that the sound effects of storms and boats would divert the attention rather than stimulate the imagination; that the 'point' of the stilling of the storm narrative would be lost. The dons, too, feared that modern scholarship and scientific method in biblical exegesis would be excluded simply because it questioned profoundly the simple assumptions of untutored Christians, both teachers and clergy! In 1952, the Corporation brought together under Basil Yeaxlee the largest gathering of clergy and educators yet consulted to investigate this vexed issue: was the dramatic and æsthetic element in the schools service conducive to faith or simply educational? If the former, it did not belong in school and if the latter, it was not properly worship. It was clear that such attempts to present the miraculous content of New Testament narrative as had been undertaken in the dramatic interludes were only valid if they emphasized insights into the words of the gospels. Anything else was strictly educational and did not belong to an act of worship. The Director of Education for Nottingham believed that such services could only be justified if the local churches and the parents took the trouble to put the interludes into a wider context. The interludes should not diminish commitment or belief. The clergy present were understandably concerned that the purpose of any dramatic element should be to shed more light on the gospels.[195] They approved the conferences's commitment to churchgoing as expressed in the stated motivation behind the schools service: it was not only to provide occasion for children to worship, it was also 'the last chance of encouraging seniors to attend church after they left school'.[196]

The educationalists for their part were becoming more and more child-centred and rightly preoccupied with questions of intelligibility and knowledge. How could an eleven- or even fourteen-year-old, without any experience of church or Sunday school, have the faintest notion of the real significance and meaning of the man who fell among thieves? Even a Director-General had reminded Williams that the dispute between first-century Jews and Samaritans was not self-evident. It would only be familiar to children who had been to Sunday school or church and who had been 'within earshot' of this crucial piece of imagery, used so frequently as a powerful motif in contemporary preaching. In schools it would simply have to be taught and learned; and strictly there was no place for this in an act of worship.

In 1951, however, the long struggle ended with a victory for the SBC, and the RBD resigned itself to the fact. The problem became one for Robert Walton, who might well have exchanged his dog-collar for a mortarboard. CRAC no longer performed an advisory function; this now fell to House and was all that formally remained of his Department's involvement.

18

THE AUDIENCE ACROSS THE CHANNEL

A. The Empire

In *Let Truth Be Told* Gerard Mansell has traced in great detail the astonishing shortsightedness and parsimony of the Government in the mid-thirties; it saw no special significance or value in a venture upon which Reith had been working since the mid-twenties with, as Briggs says, 'vision and enterprise' and 'wholehearted support'.[1] This was to have the BBC broadcast programmes to the Colonies and Dominions. Not until the early thirties was this vision realized. A *Listener* leader was sure that if this service could succeed, it 'could not but be a comfort and solace to the dweller in the remoter parts of the Empire and a means of strengthening the link which binds together all of us who share the heritage of a common tongue and origin.'[2] The development of short-wave transmission would bring a signal from the mother country to the remotest parts of the Pacific and Australasia and to the Americas, Africa, India and the Middle East – wherever there were Britons and wherever English was spoken. In characteristic style, Reith wanted the hard-won service opened by royalty: in November 1932 George V spoke to the Empire from his desk in Buckingham Palace. This was for Reith the 'most spectacular success in BBC history so far'.[3] Letters began to arrive in great quantities congratulating the Corporation, notwithstanding the poor quality of reception in many parts of the world.

If the Crown was an instinctively recognized focus of national identity for the vast majority of Britons in the Dominions, the national churches were not far behind; English, Scottish and Welsh communities in the USA, as well as fraternities around the world, were soon to express a need not only to be kept in touch with news of home but for some sense of remembrance and participation through church services from the various denominations to be found at home and in some measure replicated in the Colonies. At first, however, there was little concern for programmes other than entertainment and news. But once Frederick Iremonger was in charge of religion, various schemes were discussed for broadcasting religious services. Eric Southam of Bournemouth, a very old friend of Iremonger's, suggested that whereas in the Home programmes it was hard to prevent the clergy from having their turn, in the new service one man could develop an identity and thus forge a regular link with the overseas listener. Iremonger had discussions with Cecil Graves, who was keen as was Reith. Reith agreed in principle to the broadcasting of a regular service to the Empire provided that it was 'inter-denominational in ritual and teaching, as much as and I think more so than St Martin's.'[4] Reith impressed on Iremonger that the broadcast should be world-wide and aimed – as Iremonger recounted later – 'at countrymen in the dominions who value all possible contacts with the old country, not the least that of religion.'

If the audience, however, was so broadly defined, sermons and services were not so easily devised. There were fundamental differences which were to mark the whole development of broadcasting overseas and distinguish it clearly from the aims of religious broadcasting at home. There would be no evangelistic objective; the aim was to be anecdotal and nostalgic and use such elements as Big Ben chiming from Westminster.

A technical issue brought a subtle theological question to bear on policy both now and much later: the ability to record programmes. Ultimately with the invention of the Blattnerphone metal tape recording machine, a religious service could be recorded following the original transmission and replayed several times across the time zones of the Empire service. For the purposes of broadcasting, the geographical zones were dropped in favour of time zones: broadcasting was from 9.30 a.m. GMT until 3.0 a.m. GMT.[5] Not surprisingly, the first service came on New Year's Day 1933 (following the King's speech) from St Martin's, with Pat McCormick preaching. Services were broadcast from Westminster Abbey and York Minster and messages from Empire listeners soon expressed the appreciation which Iremonger and Reith had expected. So impressive were the Anglicans that a report by an Australian Broadcasting Commission manager could not but praise them for their freedom from 'traditional ecclesiastical intonation'. He wanted every clergyman in Australia to furnish himself with a short wave receiver to hear the sermons 'as preached by the modern clergy in England'.[6] Iremonger was not so sanguine. He wanted to shift the regular service from St Martin's. Considerable correspondence from around the world and particularly from Australia and India showed that one particular cathedral was associated with the United Kingdom – St Paul's. Ellis Roberts and W. R. Matthews have outlined the difficulties which Sheppard encountered on becoming a canon in 1932.[7] St Paul's Chapter was particularly leaden, as Dean Inge had complained. Iremonger wanted to install regular services to the Empire from this most British of places of private and public worship: great men were buried there and great men were remembered there. The Chapter, however, for some time would not agree to broadcasting services to the Empire. (They had refused permission for their organ to be used for 'secular' purposes in the late twenties, when the BBC had planned an evocation of Sir Christopher Wren.) Supported by W. H. Elliott, a former Precentor, now at St Michael's, Chester Square, W. R. Matthews prevailed on his Chapter and a regular service began on 9 June 1935, to be broadcast on the second Sunday of each month from 'the Parish Church of the Empire'. It was the climax of a great variety of broadcast services which specially appealed to English speakers abroad and particularly Britons: services for Boy Scouts from Windsor, Easter Day from Palestine and 'Anzac' day from St Clement Danes in London. The Roman Catholic Cardinal Archbishop Hinsley broadcast from Westminster Cathedral and the inclusion of the traditional Jewish ex-servicemen's parade in Whitehall gave the widest confessional and religious embrace to these broadcasts. With the development of recording techniques, it was possible for the Sunday epilogue to be recorded and transmitted the following Sunday. The Church of England naturally had half of these services, contrary to Reith's earlier notion of a completely interdenominational approach. Iremonger soon discovered that overseas exiles wanted a fair representation of denominations – this was reflected in the proportion of Anglicans to the rest. The Christian Year was acknowledged by special services at Christmas 1937 and Easter 1938. Elliott's midweek service from St Michael's, Chester Square, was broadcast monthly. There had been considerable discussion between Iremonger and the Overseas Director about what actually comprised a church service, a debate which would assume a serious and critical importance for the Department before long. The exiles wanted more than the liturgical sounds of home: they wanted a lively preacher to provide a personal link.

Overseas religious broadcasting developed without any great innovation until the war loomed on the horizon. So long as broadcasts and relays of religious broadcasts were conceived in terms of an audience of British exiles, the nostalgic and associative characteristics of church services were a comparatively simple matter. The regular St Paul's services and other special services seemed obviously appropriate. The emphasis was upon renowned preachers or personalities speaking to Britons who happened to be abroad. Rubrics governing such broadcasts were mostly restricted to matters of time: it was no use celebrating the morning sunshine when listeners in Asia would be hearing the service around 7.30 in the evening. There was a good deal of discussion about the complexity of timing as a result of broadcasting into the various time zones. J. B. Clark, the Director of the Empire Service feared that in India, the exiles would be having their whisky and soda after their exercise just as the religious services came on! Mansell tells of Lionel Fielden, whom Reith had sent there to develop broadcasting, urging that the Corporation concentrate on the highest quality; and that meant, in this context, philosophers and preachers.

In April 1939, Welch became aware that the task he faced could not be undertaken alone: he wanted Eric Fenn, the English Presbyterian whom he had come to know when working with him at Sidney Sussex College, Cambridge, in the twenties. Fenn was in the SCM and well acquainted with the ecumenical developments of the thirties which were coalescing into an institutional formation of a Protestant World Council of Churches; it was Protestant without being anti-Catholic.[8] Overseas broadcasting of religion involved modest production and was somewhat neglected. In Welch's view it was all far too 'easy'; it had been couched in terms of nostalgia and association and coupled with the influence of W. H. Elliott. It all tended towards a sentimental religious outlook characterized more by patriotism than Christian belief. He was happy neither about St Paul's nor about the 'canning of English services' to be sent out willy-nilly. In July 1939 he told Clark that there was too much work in preparation for *The Christian Looks at the World* to spend time on anything original for overseas. The staff of the Overseas Service were also concerned about what was being said and what should be said to its increasingly diverse audiences: since 1938 the Corporation had begun to speak other languages than English and indeed the notion of 'Empire' or 'Imperial' broadcasting, which headed memoranda prior to 1938, raised questions also about 'native' audiences which understood English: overseas broadcasting was no longer to expatriates alone. The war brought the issue into a distinctly European and political arena and forced the Corporation into yet another language, soon enough to be associated entirely with the enemy. British troops were also part of the diverse overseas audience. Very soon this audience assumed important dimensions for the Corporation's religious policy.

B. The Forces

(i) An alternative wavelength

As we have seen, with the outbreak of war, the BBC was reduced to a single Home Programme. Before the war it had also been much concerned about the penetration of foreign commercial stations, notably Luxembourg.[9] As Professor Briggs has explained, the attraction of these foreign stations was considerable, especially among that sector of the BBC audience which was not given to highbrow selective listening, particularly serious music and talks. Indeed, the emphasis in the French programme from Fècamp was entirely upon entertainment. Once the war had begun and vast numbers of troops were over the Channel on French soil, the question arose about the development of an alternative programme on the Fècamp model to attract the Forces and, more importantly, for the military leadership to raise and sustain morale.[10]

The Board of Governors soon resolved that there should be a 'special wavelength programme' for the Forces[11] and before the end of December 1939 decided that entertainment should be the keynote. On Sundays 'variety should be broadcast with discretion'. The decision once made, Nicolls invited every departmental head for suggestions; the hierarchy assumed not without reason that the demand for religion would be minimal and since the armed Forces had their chaplains, the need was even less. Since the Home Programme could so easily be received in France, the new programme need only occasionally carry a religious service.

Welch was ready for this and brought to the discussion questions of principle which he believed were glaringly absent from much of the thinking. Briggs acknowledges that Welch 'was the only man who looked far ahead and drew out the logic of what was happening'. [12] After all, the Corporation realized the implications for commercial broadcasting of the presence of troops overseas, particularly as they were not yet fighting but settling down to a rather artificial existence as 'displaced persons'. If the Corporation did not act soon, commercial operations might not only win the ears but also affect the morale of the fighting serviceman.

Welch realized that the success of any new broadcasts would depend on listening conditions. Nor would he bracket all soldiers together as a species: 'the young soldier really is asking searching questions about this war, our civilization and a philosophy to live by.'[13] He wanted to talk to chaplains and hoped he could get to France to see for himself. Above all, the programmes should be designed entirely for the British Expeditionary Forces (BEF): most Home religious broadcasts, he thought, were unsuitable for the troops, taking into account (*a*) listening conditions in billets, etc.; (*b*) the fact of compulsory church parades and (*c*) the remoteness of the average soldier from a live church involvement. The lesson had been learned before.[14]

Welch, for his part, recognized that the new 'popular' programme would mark the beginning of a development of an alternative and ambiguous output which would have enormous implications for broadcasting in the United Kingdom; it would lead to the notion of stratification of audience and listener and to the concept of competition in the Home Services which would be discussed after the war in the context of a 'light programme'. It might even be said to have prepared the ground for the post-war institutions of competitive broadcasting and commercial television in the mid-fifties. The alternative programme would attract vast numbers away from the Home programme and provide for the RBD the challenge of an enormous listening figure for a religious programme the popularity of which, in the event, would surprise even Welch. He quickly submitted his concrete proposals: daily prayers, a Saturday epilogue and a weekly talk; on Sundays a special short service for troops, and on Sunday evening community hymn singing led by Sir Walford Davies, plus an epilogue. Welch wanted only two hours out of the BEF's projected 84 hours. He took it for granted that there would be no major change to the Corporation's Sunday policy, notwithstanding general agreement within the Department that there was no future for the 'puritan' Sunday. But he was wrong: the Governors and the Home Board had decided that the Sunday policy should not apply to the BEF programme and that Welch should square the issue with the churches through Garbett and CRAC.[15] Welch was furious: he owed allegiance to both camps; as a priest of the Church of England he would be accused of 'selling the pass' and abandoning all the achievements for which Iremonger had fought so hard. CRAC should have been consulted, he claimed: the work of the churches would certainly be adversely affected, and above all they would construe the BBC decision as based on expediency and not borne of principle. It was indeed a principle, but one which Welch and many others were not prepared to recognize: i.e. the principle of competition in giving the public what it wanted, especially as it seemed to be getting some of it from elsewhere! Welch did not want a merely negative attitude to apply to the new programme: he wanted rather a 'positive and enlightened policy justified by certain accepted principles'. He was loyal to his employer and did not want the BBC accused of doing in wartime what it agreed not to do in peacetime. The Corporation should not abandon its standard; if Fècamp was giving what the soldiers wanted, this did not mean that we should simply abandon the religious principle behind Sunday policy: 'because a few listeners have put on uniform and crossed the Channel, why should they be considered different persons religiously?'[16] The day's broadcasting on the BEF should not replicate or suggest a weekday. As Briggs notes, only Welch realized that this was the end of the BBC Sunday policy, which simply would not be resumed after the war or ever. Again commensurate with his profound convictions about the Christian civilization for which the troops were fighting (irrespective of exactly how aware the troops were) Welch reminded Nicolls and the hierarchy of what was at stake: the existence of a Christian civilization. 'Why should we assume that the BEF cares less about the thing for which it is fighting?' This was taking a cosmic view of the task which of course the planners could not so easily consider when all manner of political and financial issues were threatened; the Corporation believed it must succeed in gaining the confidence of the troops with this programme.

Events moved quickly: no one had clear ideas as to how long the BEF would be 'living alongside Frenchmen rather than fighting Germans'.[17] A. P. Ryan was the BBC liaison with the forces and reported in January 1940 on the situation in France for listening and programme possibilities. Above all, as he told Sir Cecil Graves, the Deputy Director-General, the clergy/chaplains at the front reported no requests for any religious content in this programme. Listening conditions were 'communal' and wherever a wireless was on, it was always amid a group; private listening was a virtual impossibility. The rank and file mostly wanted something as 'background' and Ryan gathered that 'cheerful church services would be well received'. It was 'idle to hope for serious listening . . . the troops will accept good serious stuff as one of the facts of life: they won't mind and they won't listen.'[18] Nevertheless, the new programme provided a chance for the BBC to improve its image abroad and win more public affection at home where, of course, the programme would be welcomed. History would prove Ryan to be right. Welch, moreover, had strong convictions about the broadcasting potential of the new programme which would prepare the soldier for the world he would face when the war was over.

The wrangle over the abandonment of the Sunday policy upset Garbett, who was set to protest to Ogilvie that CRAC had not been consulted. Welch prepared a full statement of principles which, he submitted, should govern the approach to Sunday programmes. The emphasis was that Sunday programmes should be valued as significantly different from other days; the quality should therefore be of the highest order which would 'nourish the spirit after a week of starvation'.[19] It should 'defend the person in a technological civiliz-ation'. Sport and dance music should be allowed but questionable jokes 'in the Garrison Theatre' (radio variety shows) should *not* be. We must have a Sunday policy of some kind, insisted Welch: it was the duty of the Corporation to interest and entertain even if it had to find quite radical ways of 'working-up' the audience (rather than the 'listener' in this context). To date, such procedures were regarded with suspicion. Even Ryan had noted that the men's reaction to the 'chatty style of Fècamp' was out of accord with the image of the Corporation: 'the men want to be talked to by a gentleman.'[20]

Welch hoped to assess the French situation for himself; for the moment he sought to substantiate his policy theories by consulting the principals in the field, the chaplains. He asked 1500 chaplains and received some revealing replies. Most saw religion as out of place in the 'light' material of the Forces Programme; the church was its own worst enemy: 'incalculable harm is done by the clerical voice'. The chaplain of a destroyer, HMS Sikh, was J. Stanton-Jeans who took the trouble to canvass his ship for opinion; he deserves a full mention. 'For sermons, more please from chaplains to the forces or people like Dom Bernard Clements.[21] News is the most popular and more listen to Winston Churchill than to any other talk programme.' Stanton-Jeans offered his interpretation of what his company wanted:

> We aren't barbarians and we are not heroes (could you tell the politicians that!). We can't walk on grass or see flowers; we can't get mud on our shoes or see the earth swishing away from the plough; we can't see our homes, our mothers, our sweethearts or any of the things or people we love. Please let our contact with the outside world be something in the nature of sound and less of noises: the vast empty noises of defeated spirits.

Welch saw in this letter a confirmation of his diagnosis: the programme must be of high quality, no matter how unused the non-religious mind might be to certain elements. There could be talks which were about the human condition without being liturgical or parsonic; they could reveal and even teach without lapsing into a preaching style, which the chaplains recognized almost unanimously as counterproductive and bad public relations for the faith, for which just a few – and not only officers – knew clearly they were fighting. Welch's optimistic view was that the planners of the BEF programme underestimated the integrity and even the wit of most fighting soldiers – not all aesthetic values were lost by the donning of khaki.

In January, Welch's request for a twenty-minute service on Sunday evening was approved by the Home Board. He planned the first for 18 February, and immediately received an exasperating caution from Dinwiddie in Scotland that 7.0 p.m. was an inconvenient time for 'live' services: it would be difficult to cut into twenty minutes of services beginning at 6.30 p.m. Studio services would be just as difficult as all their singers would be in church! What about a recording, he asked. Welch was impatient: 'They must put the men first and not their own ecclesiastic comforts.' He wanted no bodged-up outside broadcasts, nor did he want studio services: they were artificial and no reminder of the world back home which the men wanted so badly. Nicolls tried to help: he feared that the churches generally could not or would not adapt their cherished routines and thought the studio would be much the best. Welch insisted on actual churches and was already inviting his own specially selected group of preachers whom he knew would comply – the congregations would hopefully follow. 'The men want the hearty congregational services they would get at home' – if they ever went, he added. This insight was to have crucial implications for the very long-term future policy of religious broadcasting: the most popular religious broadcasting would in one way or another involve the singing of hymns. Welch knew that the straight outside broadcast of church services, for all their adaptability, was finally designed for the physical congregation present. That was the 'company', the players who made the broadcast valuable to others who, like the house-bound, would be bodily present but for their infirmity. The preacher was above all to address himself to the unseen audience: the Department had been telling that to preachers since the very beginning: the physical congregation must forego its privilege and gain whatever inspiration it could as if it too were part of that 'unseen' public. Many were pleased to do just this: some felt they gained enormous *kudos* from a visit from the BBC for an outside broadcast; others again had neither the standards to qualify nor the inclination to comply.

The other crucial factor in this discussion between Welch, Nicolls and Dinwiddie was simply that hymns were a popular and recognizable focus of religious recollection and utterance: they belonged to home and childhood and were free of the complexities of language and association which characterized liturgical services and sermons. Hymns made little or no demands beyond the ability to sing them. Whilst he would not pander to the lowest tastes, Welch accepted the importance of this common cultural element which he recognized as belonging to Protestant Britain. The home audience, he soon discovered, would be happier with the provision for the Forces in which it could join than would the Forces be joining in with the Home programme when this could actually be received across the Channel. Roger Wilson from the Listener Research Department soon confirmed that the short BEF services are 'much preferred to a full service from the Home programme which is simply too long for the troops; they want community hymn-singing.'[22]

Welch wanted to see for himself: Ryan and Ogilvie had both been to the BEF in France together with the Listener Research people.[23] He was assisted by C. D. Symons, the Chaplain-General in London, and chaplains in France. It was agreed by Ogilvie and Nicolls that he should go in mid-April and make his own assessment. The most crucial question was the timing of broadcasts and, since the various armed services had various routines, it was virtually impossible to determine with any accuracy when the vast majority would best benefit from religious talks: services were rather easier. Welch wanted just as much for the Forces as for the Home listener. In five days Welch visited chaplains, officers and men in great numbers and in a variety of places. His conclusions were far-reaching, and above all he was convinced of the enormous opportunity offered to the BBC. These half a million men 'deprived of home, interests and friends . . . form the most homogenous audience the BBC has ever been offered. . . . The homogeneity, the sense of fellowship and the passionate interest in home are the three data about this forces audience which must affect religious broadcasting in the new programme.'[24] The BEF was trained but largely inert and Welch observed that soon enough the diversions in France wore off: men spent most of their leisure time in billets and in these conditions, he was surprised to find that the BEF 'does *not* work on Sundays!' Thus they wanted church services just as they had them at home – no special wrapping and as different from their church parades as possible. Time and again, reports from the Listener Research Department would declare that 'compulsory church parades were so much disliked that they caused a widespread prejudice against religious broadcasts . . . young men who have never been required to go to church at home, resent a compulsion to do so in manhood.'[25]

What Welch proposed in the light of his visit was to begin in July: it would concentrate particularly on Sunday: a morning service from Bristol Cathedral for ten minutes, 'complete in itself'; a ten-minute talk after lunch at rest times; the combination of the present fortnightly community hymn-singing and evening service into a weekly half hour comprising twenty minutes of hymn singing, and a one and a half minute thought for the day with prayers for those at home. Sunday would close with a five minute Epilogue which might be simultaneously broadcast on the Home. On Wednesday there should be a simple quarter-hour Epilogue which could combine hymns and psalms with comment and interpretation. By the end of May, Welch's proposals were approved. The Dean of Bristol, Harry Blackburn, was asked to take the first of the Sunday morning services. In the First World War he had been the first British padre to win the MC for bravery and was an excellent choice: he had long experience among troops.[26] Welch 'instructed' the regional directors and significantly concentrated on the Sunday evening service, now called *Sunday Half Hour*. It must be able to be broadcast 'without embarrassment to any listener in large canteens and should be as different as possible from church parades' – men should enjoy it! He wanted the organ and women's voices, evening hymns and 'home atmosphere'. He told the Northern Ireland Director the programme was not exactly a hymn-recital so much as 'an incitement for Forces listeners to recognize and join in; this invitatory aspect is important'. Welch recognized, however, that the quality of the reception and the primitive and poor quality loudspeakers made participation rather more difficult particularly as soldiers in this war, as in perhaps all wars, were given to singing together – not because of war but because men were together.[27]

In general, Welch felt 'it would be dangerous to leave such a programme in the hands of a parson', and furthermore he insisted on being consulted before any parson was invited. The regions would contribute once each six weeks but the final authority for the speaker would be with Welch and Broadcasting House. The Department kept a card-index with the name of every parson who had ever broadcast and a considerable proportion had 'N/A' on their card: 'Never again!' The Chaplain-General, Symons, was delighted with it all and thought Welch's provisions would be deeply appreciated by the BEF. Welch believed there was no shortage of hymns which men would recognize from their peacetime experience and this in itself would afford a profound, if also a saddening, recollection to men away from home. Nevertheless, Welch wanted quality: the hymns should 'satisfy the criteria of good poetry, theology and music', a notion promulgated by Dr Stanton, the Director of Music for the Midland Region. Walford Davies had collected together a list of a hundred hymns which was distributed to potential arrangers of the *Sunday Half Hour*: it did not pretend to indicate a BBC selection of the best hundred hymns but rather those familiar to serving men. Stanton (with Walford Davies) had criticized Welch for insisting on such hymns as 'Abide with me' as unworthy of the BBC, especially at this time when at home the 'mission' was under way. Welch knew that the Forces listener was 'conservative in hymn-association' and he was not to be the target of the 'mission' broadcasters.[28] Whatever could be said to the serving soldier must follow on appropriately whatever could arrest his attention: familiar hymns were to speak for themselves and not be subsidiary to the endeavour to 'plug our mission'. It was consonant with his belief that the BBC had a special task to produce programmes specifically for the BEF and mostly to provide cheer.

Before long Welch had devloped other ideas for the Forces which derived from his unease with the too traditional material of the midweek service: he wanted something to 'feed the spirit at the end of the news bulletin'. There had already been an epilogue of an unconventional style broadcast in the overseas programme, and Welch wanted this model developed for the Home listener. *Think on These Things* was the outcome; a series of experimental programmes, presented by Eric Fenn, began in autumn 1940. They would consist of music and readings; the readings were to be non-biblical and non-ecclesiastical. The programme was not a service, not even a traditional epilogue; Welch's aim was 'to utter through music and fine reading some simple truths to draw the mind to beautiful and lasting things and thus to give food for the spirit'.[29] Both readings and music were chosen from an enormously wide range – the former by Dorothy L. Sayers, Walter de la Mare, David Davis (later of *Children's Hour*), Stuart Hibberd and Adam Fox, at that time the Oxford Professor of Poetry. The choice of the music was the responsibility of Walford Davies, but much of the searching out was done by Alec Robertson and Trevor Hervey, and suggestions were also made by Adrian Boult and Vaughan Williams.

The first programmes went out after the Nine o'clock News and Postscript, so commanded a huge audience; Listener Research reported that of five million people who listened to the News, three and a half million were staying on for *Think on These Things*. The Ministry of Information had to be placated; it wanted more direct morale-boosting, and thought the programmes too highbrow; fewer people would be comforted by Beethoven's Fourth Piano Concerto than Welch and Taylor imagined. (The producer, Robin Whitworth, was also aware of this danger.) The Ministry feared that the readings were an attempt to soothe the news away.[30] Welch's reply was that there might be death and destruction all round, but people should be reminded that there is also courage, resolution and hope: 'It does not obliterate the news but puts it in perspective.'[31]

Despite Welch's pleas, the Home Board decided in January 1941 that the programme must be dropped from the Home Service and replaced by a traditional epilogue at the traditional time – the end of the day. The programme did however continue on the Forces Programme, though on a more modest scale and to a much smaller audience. It followed the Nine o'clock News there, and for Welch was as important as the News itself; if that spoke of war and struggle, *Think on These Things* should speak of peace and courage, and not only in words, but with a contrast of form as well as substance. Hence his concern to have music eloquent in itself, and not subordinated to any religious text associated with hymns. Speakers had a free hand to extol the virtues of courage and endurance and to focus upon the nation and its more worthy characteristics in countryside and tradition. David Davis spoke on gardens, Thalben-Ball on the Temple Church, and Philip Cox on the Rig Veda. As Taylor explained, 'the programme should have a spiritual background, but the last thing we want is that it should be ecclesiastical'.[32] He saw two classes of programme, informal talks and poetic/musical mosaics; he wanted the former, as he knew too well that the BEF found the latter 'remote and arty crafty'. Fenn and Welch realized that unless they made the religious content of these programmes obvious and explicit, the talks would be taken away from the Department. Even Taylor had thought they might be better produced by Val Gielgud. The solution was to sustain the notion of spirituality without piety, or religion without church: it was 'vitally necessary that somewhere in the Forces programme, there should be a space for the really beautiful'.[33] Fenn believed, as did all in the Department, that this was essentially a religious aesthetic which transcended the forms of piety and utterance which belonged to diverse 'congregationalist' styles and thus to the public images of church. Nevertheless, Fenn insisted that if specifically religious music was included occasionally, the Department's hold on the programme would be secure. It was not easy: the Department received sharp criticism for 'using' poetic and musical material (particularly the former) for 'secondary' ends: in a programme on Housman, for example, Trevor Harvey used 'The Shropshire Lad' to illustrate notions of friendship in a simple straightforward way. Nicolls was horrified: it reminded him of the abuses in broadcasting during the twenties. The Director of Programme Planning, Godfrey Adams, felt strongly that this sort of programme belonged to Gielgud and not to Welch at all. Adams articulated the specifically BBC outlook that wanted religious broadcasting to remain thoroughly consistent with popular concepts of religion and not be organized by Welch's Department according to canons of overall programme planning: it was not for him to decide how much and what sort of religious programme should provide a break in the spate of entertainment material. Besides, Welch had no 'production' experience which Adams regarded as crucial to this sort of amalgam; he should develop 'production' only as it related to the presentation of religious programmes of a predictable kind designed for radio. The Forces midweek slot was now in jeopardy.

(ii) The 'Radio Padre'

Welch's creativity turned elsewhere. In the early summer of 1941 he had a visit from Silvey of Listener Research and a certain Corporal Newcombe, the Press and Entertainments Officer for the 8th Anti-Aircraft (AA) Division. The men in these Divisions, Newcombe explained, were the most lonely and bored in the Forces today: small clusters of men isolated from their homes, manning guns and searchlights. AA chaplains had an almost impossible task: each one was responsible for nearly 2000 men on scattered gunsites. A radio link was obvious. The men overseas had the Forces programme; what of these isolated remnants? Welch met Sir Frederick Pile, the officer commanding the AA units, who supported his request for an army padre to be seconded to the BBC. He would visit homes and units and be given the midweek service/epilogue slot in the Forces programme. Welch had mooted the idea to Dinwiddie during the midweek epilogue crisis, and at a party which Dinwiddie gave in June 1941 he met Ronald Selby Wright, a chaplain to an Edinburgh unit and well known in Scotland for his pre-war talks to boys' clubs.[34] He had broadcast on ten successive Sundays on the model of his own boys' club at the Canongate Church, Edinburgh. He had been minister there since 1937.

Early in July Welch was at the War Office in consultation with Symons, the Chaplain-General, who was in support of Selby Wright's secondment to religious broadcasting. Symons told Welch he was anxious for the well-being of these men, especially those on sites with women personnel: he wanted this padre to broadcast to maintain not only morale but fidelity. These men and women needed a service in which they could participate and the Corporation could provide uniquely what the chaplain could not – the elements of Christian worship in which, with no more than a hymn book, the men could take part there and then. Welch agreed with Sir Frederick Pile that ideally the services should be broadcast each week in the epilogue period – 9.20 on Thursday evening: the day before pay day, Welch thought, would make for more agreeable reception! Also he should encourage the men to write in with problems, and these letters would in turn be passed to the resident chaplain: the radio padre would retain a pastoral function. Selby Wright was anxious not to lose touch with this group of men; thus it was written into his secondment that he should travel and spend large amounts of time with various sites around the country. It was an exceedingly exhausting assignment. He gave four talks in November 1941, *Let's Ask the Padre*, which were sufficiently well received by the Corporation and the Chaplain General to encourage his secondment for six months beginning in February 1942. Dinwiddie, himself a former soldier, had prepared the way and Welch managed to assure the heads of the churches that there were no denominational issues at risk; Selby Wright was, after all, from the Church of Scotland.[35] Certainly Garbett and Matthews were convinced that there should be no question of denominationalism considered. Symons told Selby Wright that this secondment might lead to even greater co-operation between the BBC and the Royal Army Chaplains Department. The War Office finally agreed in February 1942: Selby Wright would not draw pay.[36]

Selby Wright worked tirelessly for his six months' secondment and was regarded as a success. Notwithstanding the continued pessimism in Silvey's reports on Forces listening to religious broadcasts, Selby Wright's talks were consistently well received. Silvey's report in July 1942[37] prior to the Radio Padre's series in November, declared in no uncertain terms that religious items were deeply resented – simply because of the compulsion of church parades in the King's Regulations. The interest in religious talks was minimal and, of course, the listening conditions proved an insurmountable obstacle which no amount of 'radio-genic' attraction could scale. Selby Wright was direct and simple if somewhat patronizing: when asked whether compulsory church parades were right or wrong, he could only extol the views of the War Office:

> Church parade is part of the whole set-up of the army. You don't attend it only as an individual; you attend it as part of the whole corporate life of your regiment – as part of 'service' in a real sense, that is on a higher plane than cleaning brasses.[38]

The *Listener* critic W. E. Williams focused a good deal of the criticism that these programmes were shallow or full of rather too many aphorisms which were never quite explained. Williams was irritated for example, by a serious programme on the issue of post-war reconstruction: there were no real answers to the heartfelt questions of the soldiers sitting opposite the Radio Padre as to how it would be for them after the war was over. Williams was not sure why anyone should ask the padre at all![39]

Notwithstanding Selby Wright's predictably 'establishment' outlook, his broadcasts were virtually the most popular of almost all BBC religious broadcasts.[40] His audience eventually numbered around seven million with, ironically, the greatest proportion from Home listeners. Welch had been prophetic in January 1940: the Forces programme would provide an attractive alternative which would shake the foundations of Home broadcasting long before the war ended. Welch later compared Selby Wright's broadcasting with the success of

Sayers' cycle of plays: the Roman Catholic Beales wrote in *The Universe* that the Radio Padre was the greatest thing religious broadcasting had ever done. Apart from Selby Wright's broadcasts, the religious programme directed to and listened to by the Forces with the greatest success was the *Sunday Half Hour* of hymn singing.[41]

A sequel to Selby Wright's secondment is told by him in *Another Home*.[42] His talks were heard so widely in occupied territory that eventually prisoners-of-war were helped.[43] His talks continued into 1944 and became increasingly popular in both broadcast and printed form.[44]

(iii) The General Forces network

As Professor Briggs explains,[45] the BBC by 1943 had three programmes and an increasing number of Home listeners tuned to the programmes in the General Overseas service designed for the Forces beyond northern Europe. Far flung troops wanted to be kept in touch with events at home just as much as formerly lonely AA soldiers in Gunnersbury wanted their 'Radio Padre'. During 1943 the Forces Programme was scrapped and the General Overseas Service became the parent network for all the Forces wherever they were. Broadcasting was a lifeline: as the Home Service faded on land, sea or aircraft apparatus, the men wanted contact with home maintained – indeed a 'Home Service' for mainland inhabitants, as it were, now overseas. It was, as Briggs says, 'a quest for nostalgia' and from Welch's point of view there were two programmes which he could readily provide: the short talks on the lines of the Radio Padre and the never-failing *Sunday Half Hour* of hymn singing. Norman Collins took charge of the new service and encouraged Welch to engage William Temple to do a regular five-minute talk. The series was planned for February 1944; Collins thought it the 'biggest forward step we have yet taken' and wanted speakers of prestige to follow this impressive beginning.

Collins, meanwhile, had taken a trip to the Middle East and returned with new ideas about policy. Listeners to religious programmes were themselves a species of 'isolated units', and attempts to arrange programmes for groups listening in canteens should no longer apply. Morale boosting was crucial: the Forces listener wanted 'authentic' church services and not hybrids doctored for the troops. That meant cathedrals and ordered liturgical styles reminiscent of home. The emphasis under Collins would now be on quality rather than popularity. This applied as much to *Sunday Half Hour* as to Sunday services: community singing was not always choral! Cathedral choirs and the BBC singers were to be preferred. The emphasis was upon 'eavesdropping' by the General Forces Programme listener into the affairs at home. Services on Sundays thereafter included broadcasts from the great cathedrals: St Paul's, Winchester, Manchester, etc. The morning service for Sunday was organized by Francis House, from 200 Oxford Street, the studio from which overseas broadcasts were organized. It was to be directed to the ninety per cent of the population – forces or civilians – who were only occasionally in a place of worship. It was to unite serving men and women with their families at home: it had to combine 'reverence with legitimate inducements to listen'. House was faced with an almost impossible task: to produce a service which could be received 'without irreverence in canteens' which might well be busy or crowded. It would go out to India, Egypt and the Middle East.

By the time of the invasion in June 1944, yet another forces programme had been prepared; it went on the air on 7 June,[46] directed to the Allied Expeditionary Forces. House had organized a meeting in April between the Chaplain-General, Symons, and a number of Canadian, American and British chaplains who would co-operate in the provision of the General Forces Network morning service. Welch had been deeply disturbed over the possibilities of enforced co-operation on the part of the BBC, so that Sunday services alternated with the American 'Radio Chapel'. He would not countenance the 'appalling mush' of these programmes and refused to have anything to do with them. They were, as Professor Briggs notes, 'a travesty of religious broadcasting'. But it was more than a question of sentimentality and superficiality. Welch saw ahead with sharp perception as ever: the American style was also pluralistic and such a free-for-all had characterized American religious broadcasting from the beginning.[47] American Christianity, Welch believed, was full of 'fancy religions', by which he meant Christian Science, Mormonism and Spiritualism: the very bodies who would continue to batter at the doors of Broadcasting House for access to the microphone. It was, as Welch told Maurice Gorham, 'the thin end of the wedge' which would have serious repercussions on BBC religious policy after the war. Even worse, it was shocking that at the most striking moment of danger, men of the invasion forces should be offered such a projection of the Christian faith. Welch was not only a broadcaster but a priest: 'it may be the only Christianity they hear at such an important and critical time of their life'.[48]

As we have noted, the response of Welch and his Department to the invitation at the outbreak of war to provide a religious programme for serving men had serious consequences for the post-war religious broadcasting policy. Assumptions were made about the traditions of a

Christian society and the extent to which religion in day school and Sunday school had a bearing on the concepts of religion in the minds of those to whom the broadcasters addressed themselves. As we have seen, again and again, religious activity among non-church attenders was a response of some kind to the simpler elements of Protestant piety – in particular hymn-singing. Those for whom the liturgy of Catholic Christianity meant anything were few.

Broadcasting to fighting men, in contrast to the home audience, was undermined by conditions both in the listening apparatus and the social environment: the concept of addressing the small committed homogenous group was out of place. Broadcasting to the Forces was casting bread upon very troubled water: the very nature of the war and the surrounding conditions of combat encouraged a cynical response both from the ranks and from officers. Chaplains frequently reported the attitude of troops towards the clergy from home who had the temerity to pronounce on questions of love and hate but who were a long way from the uncongenial theatre of fighting wherein men behaved less like men in the struggle to stay alive. Fighting men listened to the Radio Padre more readily than to bishops simply because he was with them or at least, reputed to be. Perhaps for these reasons, the most popular broadcasters at the outset of the Second World War had been those who had survived the First World War as chaplains and had developed an ear for the language styles and thought-forms of the serving soldier.

Of the programmes, those involving the singing of hymns whether by large or small forces, were the most appreciated. The whole gamut of talks and Sunday services were popularized in order to attract listeners and keep them. It was no easy task: distractions militated against attention to religious utterance, especially when this depended upon sequences of abstract thought rather than anecdote, dramatic narrative or lively illustration. Broadcasting to the Forces endowed religious programmes with a manifestly successful style in congregational singing which encouraged an active response and evoked memories of childhood, youth and home. Richard Longland, a major in the Royal Engineers who became the BBC Army Liaison Officer in 1940, quoted soldiers' liking of crooners: 'they help us to learn the words'. Longland noted the obvious: if soldiers who now travel by motor no longer need marching songs, they certainly want songs to sing.[49] The most that could be done on this foundation was done in the series *Think on These Things* which began again in peacetime under Eric Fenn. Hymns and religious music were accompanied by explanation and illustration. Preaching as the churches understood the term was only possible in the context of hymns and simple prayers: music enabled word to persevere. At the close of war, the Light Programme took over from the General Forces Programme and was the setting for the hymn-singing services known as the *People's Service* and the long established *Sunday Half Hour*. These two 'Forces' programmes bequeathed to the post-war Religious Broadcasting Department a concern with listening figures and a challenge perhaps more theoretical than real to get through to millions of people whose motivation to listen was marked either by the domestic timetable or the sacred memory of school and youth.

At the close of the war, W. E. Franklin, the Director of Overseas Audience Research, submitted the fruits of his biggest ever audience investigation[50] involving the responses of around a thousand correspondents. It was the clearest picture Welch had received and it was not encouraging. It mostly confirmed what he already knew. Religious broadcasting to the Forces only appealed to the committed six per cent who were prepared to listen, however difficult the listening conditions, however attractive the alternative. Seventy-seven per cent were polite enough to say that they had no strong feelings against religion but they had no positive feelings either. The six per cent who were in favour wanted above all a diversion from the war by way of a reminder of home and the familiar hymns. Predictably, the most popular regular programme was *Sunday Half Hour* and the most memorable series Sayers' *The Man Born to be King*. Moreover, the enthusiasm for the Sunday hymn singing was qualified: only two-thirds of those who were prepared to sing with the hymns would tolerate the Epilogue. The determining factor was simply whether the set was left on or whether there was sufficient irritation from the programme to force it to be changed over! After five years on the same ship throughout the whole of the war, a fleet chaplain told Welch that in those five years it was only to *Sunday Half Hour* that his ship ever listened. That would eventually be true for a vast number of civilians.[51]

C. The Germans

After the Munich crisis of September 1938, The Corporation began broadcasting in German. It started with news and soon expanded into other programmes involving comment and opinion. As the crisis developed, the question of propaganda was raised. Talks in the series *Sonderbericht* gradually moved from attitudes of appeasement to rather more 'plain speaking'.[52] When the war began, the situation changed further. In no area of broadcasting policy was the BBC, as the voice of Britain, left to itself. Briggs and Mansell have shown how the autonomy of the Corporation in wartime was seriously threatened, and how very close were the links between the various departments of Government and the divisions of the Corporation, especially those responsible for broadcasting outside these islands.

In the RBD, it was clear that the rebroadcasting or direct relay of religious services conceived for an English-speaking audience, distinguished from the Home listener merely by being abroad, was no longer adequate.

The churches of Germany were not all diehard supporters of Hitler; the Confessional Church and the Barmen Declaration of 1934 were evidence of that, well known to churchmen in Britain and the USA. Eric Fenn had been in touch with the official German Church hierarchy through the Ministry for Church Affairs in Berlin, and one of its officers, Bishop Haeckli. But he had other contacts with the German churches, particularly through Nathaniel Micklem,[53] a Congregationalist who knew more than most the shape of German church life under the Nazis, and also through the Lutheran Pastor J. Rieger, who was in charge of the German Lutheran congregation in East London, and whose curate was Pastor Franz Hildebrandt. Rieger had met leaders of the Confessional Church in Berlin, and reported to Fenn that the churches badly wanted a service in German on Sundays. Fenn had seen in Hans Lilje yet a third section of German Protestantism who stood, he said, 'midway between Niemöller and the "German Christians" in their attitude to the state'. All three groups wanted religious broadcasts, including talks to Germany by English clergy who could speak German rather than by Germans who might be regarded with suspicion. Fenn gained yet more support from Visser 't Hooft, the General Secretary of the WCC (in formation) in Geneva and also from William Paton at the International Missionary Council and William Temple. Welch and Fenn together submitted these proposals to Ogilvie and Wellington at the end of July 1939. The accumulated evidence told them that 'all sections of German Protestantism except extreme "German Christians" would welcome services broadcast in German provided they were wholly free from political intention.'[54] Wellington and Graves were 'fearful' of the propaganda element and Graves' Foreign Languages Committee said no – notwithstanding Ogilvie's wistful regret that it should even be asked whether 'the Christian message is a suitable matter for international broadcasting – what a commentary on the state of the world!', he lamented.[55] Despite all Fenn's efforts, the outcome was simply permission for the broadcasting of ordinary outside broadcasts of services in English from English churches.

What was at stake for Fenn and the Department, and also for Temple, Paton and Micklem, was the principle of the universality of Christendom which in turn was the antidote to the 'Vansittart' outlook which tarred every German with the same Nazi brush. The other rather less abstract motivation was the lack of any reliable religious broadcasting in Germany.[56] Gerstenmaier, from the radical German Christian wing, thought the propaganda ministry in Berlin might be less intransigent on this if it knew that comfort for the sick and housebound had to come from the enemy![57] Welch asked simply for a service in German on Sunday evenings, similar in liturgical shape to the Daily Service, and without a sermon. For the moment the hierarchy still refused. Visser 't Hooft claimed that there were millions of Germans outside Germany who would be impressed by a demonstration of the universality of Christendom beyond the confines of the nation-state. He told Fenn he wanted the broadcast services as 'nearly as possible identical with those in English'.[58] The fact that no explicit political ideas would be allowed to intrude into a religious service would itself be a form of propaganda. Visser 't Hooft, however, wanted more; he urgently wanted news and comment in German. Information about the church struggle could be broadcast; the necessary documentation could be smuggled into the country by diverse means. Above all he wanted to lessen the growing isolation of the German churches; but this really amounted to a species of propaganda.

After war was declared the policy of strict scrutiny on all scripts became a matter of even greater sensitivity. But this did not always work. A particular example was a talk which William Temple was to give on 2 October 1939 on 'The Spirit and Aim of Britain'. It included critical references to the Treaty of Versailles: while some clauses in the Treaty were 'admirable', the 'total effect' created a 'sense of genuine grievance'.[59] Ogilvie sent Maconachie all the way to Bishopthorpe in York to discuss changes to the script; on 28 September Maconachie commented to Ogilvie that 'If Goebbels doesn't make some very useful capital out of this, he must be getting past his job.' However R. A. Butler saw Temple at the end of September and assured Ogilvie that Temple had been willing to make the changes.[60] Nevertheless the talk went out unaltered, not only in Britain but also in a German translation on the European Service. Welch later told Bishop Bell (on 27 November) that it had clearly been 'conceived and written for broadcasting to Germany'.

Broadcasting to Germany was discussed by CRAC in October 1939, but to Welch's annoyance it decided to shelve the issue pending more information. Notwithstanding all Fenn's efforts so far, the Committee were open to but not convinced of the need.[61] Welch, Fenn and Hugh Martin (in charge of the Protestant desk at the Ministry of Information) were baulked by both CRAC and the Home Office. Moreover, the BBC was under pressure from the Government via the Department of Enemy Propaganda (part of the Foreign Office which was at Electra House), the Ministry of Information and the Political Warfare Executive, all of whom were concerned with establishing precedent and authority in propaganda. The possibility that the BBC might be taken over completely was a cause of anxiety to the leadership, and decisions in this very sensitive area could not be made without reference to these Government departments.[62]

Martin, for the Ministry of Information, wanted J. B. Clark, the Director of Overseas Services, to provide items of 'religious news' in German; as a close friend of Fenn he also supported Fenn's request for religious services. Fenn and Paton had gathered together a group of churchmen, including Garbett, to study the German church struggle; one result of this was a 'Committee for Non-Aryan Christians' which organized services in St John's, Smith Square, for Confessing Church refugees and their friends.[63] Bishop Bell had preached at one of these in October 1939. Why not, asked Fenn, use this as a model? Visser 't Hooft had meanwhile again requested broadcasts which should not, of course, be politically aggressive or even 'too directly anti-Nazi' otherwise the general Christian public in Germany would only become more pro-government and anti-English. That was the crucial propaganda issue: only the BBC could mount such a service in an objective way without embroiling a religious activity explicitly in political warfare: could it be 'innocent'? When Martin forwarded these requests, Clark could only say no.[64] A religious service might be misrepresented and 'jeopardize our success in other fields'. News broadcasts had been established; it would be difficult to insert a religious service without giving the Nazis grounds for being extra suspicious and so distorting the motivations of the BBC. Welch simply asked if that mattered, since the Germans were suspicious anyway, and besides 'an act of united worship, sincerely offered, will achieve what sincerity always – and alone – can achieve.'[65]

Nicolls was naturally sympathetic and Ogilvie, on seeing this request together with yet another from George Bell, agreed to raise the matter with the Overseas Service Board at the end of December: it agreed then in principle.[66] The BBC could now discuss the issue within certain limits and it was, of course, also a matter of persuading others. Welch was asked for his thinking on the services. He stressed to Clark that they should not include a sermon and should be broadcast at a time not normally associated with propaganda. Welch was a churchman first, a broadcaster second; he made a subtle but important distinction. The intention was not to provide services for those who were deprived of them but 'to use international broadcasting to make the ecumenical church more real . . . this movement gives organized expression to the fact that membership in the church is above national differences.'[67] This international fellowship could – in time of war – only be strengthened by international broadcasting, and thus the BBC would be laying the foundation of peace in the most practical way. This was a prophetic insight, and events after the war were to prove just how right Welch and his advisers had been. Welch suggested a small committee to advise on these services, including Bell, Micklem and either Rieger or Hildebrandt. Perhaps the form might resemble the occasional Anglo-German services at Holy Trinity Church, Cambridge, in which Hildebrandt spoke in English and a British speaker in German. Clark refused both suggestions. The Governors, furthermore, were not impressed by the ecumenical aims:[68] such broadcasts should not be directed to such objectives, particularly as the German churches were by no means committed to them.[69] The Board could only recommend services in English to emanate from a national church like York or St Martin's, and similar to those for Empire broadcasts. All that would be allowed were hymn tunes 'familiar to the audiences in non-British countries'. Did the Governors imagine that the average Lutheran was as familiar with Wesley as the average Anglican was with Bach? The idea was unworkable, as Welch and Fenn both sadly recognized.

Behind Clark's decision, however, was the decision of Electra House (specifically R. J. Shaw of the Department of Enemy Propaganda) with whom Ogilvie had exchanged ideas. The Department was in agreement with the idea of services as part of the 'world programme of the BBC'.[70] But if they were given a 'propaganda' flavour, with special German hymn tunes so that Germans might recognize a measure of 'appeal' to them in particular, 'we should be opposed to the idea.' Ogilvie, astonishingly, told Shaw that he was 'glad to know that your views and ours are alike on this point'.[71] Poor Welch thought otherwise and told Bell that he had spent a month on nothing but pleading for services in German; he was convinced that his colleagues were 'wholeheartedly with us', though on 'expert advice' the services could not be in German only. Clark had also met Martin and told him (and his Church Advisory Group at the Ministry) that the problem was at Electra House: Shaw feared simply that religious broadcasts in German to Germans would 'create an impression of insincerity'.[72] Martin wanted to put the matter straight: 'We are certainly not proposing to use the service as a means of preaching to the German church.' Welch had told him of Temple's talk broadcast in German, which had been unquestionably political. Martin asked why such a provocative talk (such as his group was *not* proposing) could go into Germany but not a service *without* any such address! Martin and Welch were in full agreement with Martin's own Church Advisory Group, which included eminent leaders committed to a greater or lesser degree to ecumenical co-operation: Cockin of St Paul's, Bernard Clements, Oliver Tomkins of the SCM, Aubrey of the Baptist Union and Hutchinson-Cockburn of the Church of Scotland – hardly a coterie of ecumenical fanatics! They said in their report:

> If ever a stable and reasonable peace is to arise it can only be by the growth among the nations of the world of common spiritual and moral standards. It is therefore a Christian and national concern to encourage in any way possible those in Germany who stand for such ideas and to let them feel that there are those in Britain who share them.[73]

On somewhat shakier ground, Martin claimed that some of the German church leaders had been misled by the absence of accurate information. If Germany was not to be singled out, then let such services go out in other European languages. But it was his Committee's feeling that 'the very fact that the Germans are our enemies is the reason for the institution of such services on purely religious grounds': the English language international service did 'not in the very least meet the needs we have in view'.[74] T. F. Burns and Rev. Philip Usher, Martin's counterparts in the Roman Catholic and Orthodox sections respectively, backed up this report with similar vehemence. Indeed, Burns for the Roman Catholics had already discussed it with Harman Grisewood and Fr Muckermann, a well-known German Roman Catholic, before 1939.[75] There was agreement that the ecumenical intention was uppermost: talks such as that given by Temple in October should 'breathe the spirit of the gospels', and should remind Catholics of the freedom they had once had and had now lost and show how much they were shut out from the religious life of the world. Burns wanted full scale anti-Nazi propaganda and the use of 'great and popular German writers as a witness against Hitler'.[76]

Shaw at Electra House was surprised to receive these bulky documents from Martin and Burns and even more irked that they in effect complained that Electra House was responsible for the decision not to allow such services. Shaw was quick to express his concern to Ogilvie, especially on Martin's accusation that 'the BBC have not been entirely in accord with us in this matter'. Shaw asked if Ogilvie had forgotten his letter of agreement only two weeks earlier, and concluded rather curtly that Martin and Burns of the Ministry should rather complain to the BBC and not to Electra House! He suspected that the BBC was simply blaming Electra House for its reluctance to undertake these broadcasts. Ogilvie, however, defended his position: the BBC did not wish to hide behind Electra House nor act as an intermediary between Shaw and the Ministry of Information.[77] Clearly Electra House had not thought the matter out; as a department of the Foreign Office it reflected the increasingly popular attitude that there were no really good Germans. Martin's Advisory Group stuck to its convictions, despite the fact that Ogilvie had again committed the Corporation to an agreement with Electra House. The Corporation had taken the decision after 'weighing all the evidence internal and external', which was a way of saying that since the Foreign Office had expressed its opinion, the BBC had no choice but to obey. Shaw disliked being blamed for it! He had, after all, supported a policy of exposing National Socialism as a false religion, particularly by news coverage of the sad fortunes of religious minorities in Germany. It is perhaps too simple for Jackson to affirm that the real problem for Welch was to 'wear down the BBC's objections'.[78] It was rather the objections of the Foreign Office. Welch had told Bell in January 1940 that 'in justice to the Corporation, the officials are wholeheartedly with us. . . . On the expert advice they receive, they do not feel justified in broadcasting services in German only.'

The campaign which Welch had fought so hard effectively ceased. There were requests from several English clergy for such broadcasts. On 17 December 1939 Lord Elton, a familiar and accomplished broadcaster, had written a stern note to Sir Walter Monckton which was passed to Ogilvie; he blamed the Ministry of Information, 'very largely staffed by cultured agnostics and atheists . . . to whom the religious outlook is unintelligible'. There were many sincere Christians in Germany who did not deserve 'this terrible Nazi fate', and someone should say so. The BBC had to prepare a reply; Leonard Miall, who was responsible for talks in German, told the Controller (Overseas), Sir Stephen Tallents, that 'we should do more harm than good if we broadcast anything which might be interpreted as implying a British God'. There was the evidence of Radio Strasbourg which regularly broadcast a Catholic and Lutheran service as indeed did Paris Radio. One suggestion was for simple readings from the Luther version of the Bible: more 'effective than half a Beethoven sonata', one Dutch emigrè wrote.

Through the indefatigable efforts of the very vocal Bishop Bell, meetings were arranged between himself and Ivone Kirkpatrick,[79] the BBC's Foreign Adviser, and Martin of the Ministry of Information. During July and August 1941 he presented (on the authority of several German pastors in Britain) the urgent need for religious services in German, and not merely the present English service relayed from various churches, as Electra House had suggested. Bell had the support of Temple, who was now convinced that such broadcasts exercised a 'pastoral ministry' and thus could only be conducted in German by Lutheran pastors.[80] By July 1941 both Electra House and the Ministry believed that the fundamental disparity between Christianity and National Socialism should be the objective of religious broadcasts to Germany. Welch's ecumenical objectives were not appreciated.

In early August, both the BBC and a German Religious Advisory Committee set up at Electra House by R. H. Crossman discussed the issues and both rejected any suggestion of 'sermons of devotional or exhortatory character'.[81] Only religious news and the occasional outside broadcast in English could be contemplated. Welch was somewhat irked that he was not on this committee, the BBC being represented by two others,[82] though he was somewhat consoled by the presence of both Bell and Martin. In effect, Crossman's Committee construed all aspects of religious propaganda in terms of what could be conveyed by the spoken word in talks and news. A speaker might declare his opinions as a 'Christian' or a 'believer'; there could be quotations from German classics and constant reminders of the German religious calendar. Christian issues might be raised directly in plays or obliquely by the choice of certain music, but, to Welch's distress, services were excluded. Unlike the Home programme, the European Service made a distinction between broadcasting religious services and religious talks; on the former 'propaganda' for the cause of Christian civilization, to which Welch and Temple were so keenly committed, was conveyed by broadcast services, and by the sermons they contained, as much as anywhere. It might not be the worship of a 'British God',[83] but Welch was quite clear that 'we use the Christian religion to strengthen our propaganda'.[84]

The relationship between religion and propaganda had already been debated by the RBD and the European Service in a different context. Religious services in English for European listeners had begun on Easter Day 1940. If such services and sermons had the English nationals in mind, then the notion of propaganda was very much in the background, but if they were directed to English-speaking continentals, then the element of propaganda could not be ignored. The only safe approach, Taylor was told, was to have a world audience in mind, but this was too simple an answer. English nationals stranded abroad in Europe would need encouragement and some knowledge of how the Christian churches were responding to the crisis. It was thus not simply a matter of broadcasting choral Evensong or studio services without a sermon. Taylor, upon whom fell the contrivance of such services, was troubled by the problem of producing services which, if bereft of the sermon, would have to find other ways of being explicit: the personal link of the Englishman abroad with his native land and his home church would have to rely upon liturgical and other elements rather than the exhortatory character of the traditional sermon.

This is not the place to examine in detail the development of the complex propaganda debate between the BBC and the Government Departments.[85] By the spring of 1941, however, the Ministry of Information and the BBC European organizers were asking why religion could not be used in propaganda to Europe. J. Tudor Jones wondered why the acceptance of the Pope's Five Points[86] had not been used; they were surely a 'starting point' of universal appeal for Europe 'including the Reich, whose leaders had betrayed the reputation of the Germans as second to none, champions of Christendom'.[87] Welch replied that the Five Points were by no means widely accepted; moreover Christian opinion was very sensitive about the use of religion in this way; 'we ought to walk warily if we are calling in religion as a weapon against Nazism'.[88]

In the Ministry, there was concern that the propaganda took little account of the moral perspectives in the cause to which the allies were committed. The Foreign Adviser to the BBC was Ivone Kirkpatrick, who happened to be a Catholic. He and Noel Newsome, the man for whom – as European News Editor – propaganda was a daily preoccupation, began a discussion which directly contributed to the growing belief that religion should play a part in broadcast propaganda.

Newsome had no time for religious broadcasting as it operated at home: it was usually disappointing, and only exceptionally beautiful or moving. He doubted if the BBC Religious Department could produce anyone of the eminence and calibre to 'awaken the dormant forces of Christian opinion', a phrase he had borrowed from the Catholic author Christopher Dawson. The religious broadcasting of the Home output belonged to the past: Christianity, he believed, was outstripping these outworn modes. Welch broadly accepted this view. He also agreed that much of the Ministry's output was morally equivocal, notwithstanding the influence of people like Hugh Martin. Newsome was hoping to correct this.

In a memorandum dated 5 May 1941 Newsome wrote: 'If our propaganda is to have any force at all, it must include a convincing projection of the part played by Christianity in our history'. But the problem was the form it should take: religious services such as dominate the Home output would not do. It was not merely that the churches insisted on being seen as the custodians of the nation's religious heritage; we must show that 'we are so attached to our religion that we shall fight for twenty years rather than submit to Nazi persecution.'

This notion appealed to Welch. It drew a distinction which allowed for a conception of the national Christian identity being the consequence of Christian foundations laid and built upon by church and other institutions. Newsome believed that this notion of civilization was invested with an ethical integrity drawn most powerfully from Christianity. It was this Christian 'seeding' whose fruits were not only often ignored by the churches but even rejected by churchmen who would not accept the fact that the kingdom of Adam could be slowly or cumulatively redeemed and recognized as such in the outworkings of the institutions of British law, education and now, broadcasting – particularly in time of war.

The churches for their part, Newsome maintained, were not the institutions to which the BBC should turn for an expression of this propaganda. They were divided, sectarian and incoherent: while not unimposing as national institutions, the churches in this condition could hardly be regarded as a 'suitable vehicle for conveying to Europeans our oneness with them in religion'. A 'hotch-potch of services representing all the churches of Europe would be wasteful and harmful.' Welch wrote his agreement in the margin of this eloquent memorandum. He recognized that whatever services could be contrived, other than national religious ceremonies from the great London cathedrals, they would have to transcend the churches' divisions and articulate a common core of national Christianity which was not thoroughly entrenched in conservatism nor focused in the fast-growing but reactionary 'Big Ben Silent Minute Movement'.[89] Notwithstanding his wariness of promoting the oft-abused 'BBC Religion', Welch believed that only the BBC could instigate and design such propaganda. The whole concept animated both his ecumenical objectives and his conviction that there should be a special service and a very special man to organize it.

It was naturally difficult for Welch to be in touch with all the machinery of relations between the Corporation, the Ministry and Electra House. The RBD was in Bedford and the staff were rarely in London, notwithstanding Welch's tireless willingness to travel as often as possible. In the midst of the German religious services discussion, he began to think that the Department was still too small and that there was work enough in the increasing overseas responsibilities for another man. He had not been invited to join Crossman's Committee, and he told Nicolls that this was cause enough 'for getting a first class Director of Overseas Religious Broadcasting appointed as soon as possible'.[90] Welch was able, however, to attend the fourth meeting of Crossman's Committee and then came the turning point: Crossman gave an 'unequivocal' approval to a suggestion pressed hard by Welch himself, that 'the Christian church in this country be allowed the opportunity of praying and worshipping with their fellow Christians in Germany'. Crossman's only stipulation was that such services should have no political content or bias: there was to be no sermon. Welch had won the Committee over by not attempting to go beyond limited propaganda objectives and by his belief that the Christian faith was of 'immense propaganda value' without in any way being distorted to achieve subsidiary ends: 'The very nature of the Christian message is itself propaganda for a cause which we believe to be right against a cause which we believe to be evil.' He wasted no time, with the assurance from Crossman still in his ears, in going to J. S. A. Salt, the Director of European Services, with a request for a ten-minute service – a 'simple act of Christian worship' to include Lutheran hymns, Luther's Bible, Bach chorales and a blessing. He could think of no propaganda 'which would be so powerful in support of our cause as the sharing of a Christian act of worship . . . no measure would more quickly strengthen the Christian and anti-Nazi forces in Germany.'[91] Newsome, European News Editor, agreed: 'Such broadcasts would powerfully benefit our cause.'[92] The first broadcasts took place during Christmastide 1941 and catered for both Protestants and Catholics: a twenty-minute Lutheran service conducted by Pastor Franz Hildebrandt, and Midnight Mass from Ampleforth, such as Germans had been accustomed to hear in peacetime. The question of a regular service was yet to be settled, as also the question of ultimate responsibility, whether with the Crossman Committee or the Controller of the European Service.

From Welch's point of view, staffing was now an even more acute problem: he wanted an overseas assistant not simply for the German broadcast religious services but for the whole range of overseas broadcasts. In September 1941 Welch had told Garbett he was hoping John Baillie of the Church of Scotland would be appointed. Welch realized that he was aiming high, but Baillie was after all 'among the first six Christian thinkers of this country'. Baillie showed a deep interest but concluded that his work in Scotland was more important. Welch then turned his attention to Nathaniel Micklem of Mansfield College, Oxford, and again was told that perhaps he was aiming too high. The matter was crucial to the RBD, the Empire and Overseas Divisions and the highest executive levels of the Corporation. Since so much foreign and particularly European broadcasting was subject to Foreign Office influence (as represented by Electra House), and also that of the Political Warfare Executive and the Ministry of Information, any consideration of staffing had to be very subtle indeed. Welch saw the new position as akin to his own; the man should be an innovator; 'there's work waiting to be done and work waiting to be made.' The Overseas RBD would be comparable to the Home one. What he was looking for derived as much from his conviction about Christian civilization as from his standards of professional competence: 'We are fighting this war for Christian ideals and to make possible the creation of a Christian society in Europe and the world' – with characteristic passion he couched his memorandum to Nicolls in the poetry of Christian idealism.[93] The Control Board for Overseas on 6 November agreed that Micklem should be invited as one of Welch's 'chief assistants to give specialized guidance in overseas religious matters'.[94] But Micklem turned the post down notwithstanding Welch's characteristically emotive appeal later in the month: 'I have no hesitation in saying that the work of religious broadcasting in our overseas division is both more important and more difficult than anything we are tackling in our Home Programme.'[95] Judging by the struggle he was having for the German language religious service, this was no mere rhetoric. Welch feared the appointment of 'a well intentioned but immature parson who might be "used" without realizing the increasing tension between church and state as this war advances and who might unwittingly sell the pass'. Correspondence between the two men proceeded for a month; Micklem was very much attracted by the offer, but finally had to refuse; his college came first.

In January Clark expressed his disquiet. Welch's enthusiasm for a specialist organizer for religious broadcasting smacked of a missionary approach. It could also have been a threat to the overseas autonomy in this area: 'I regard religious broadcasting as a natural element in the Empire Services radiated from this Christian country; it should be kept within fairly modest bounds.'[96] Welch met the Empire Service Directors in late February 1942 and was strengthened in his conviction that the Department was producing overseas programmes *in vacuo*, with neither intelligence reports nor listeners' correspondence to assist. The work simply could not be done properly until a man had been appointed. The meeting decided that, however much such a style might have stuck in Welch's throat, these overseas services must emphasize nostalgia for exiles who clearly could not be educated in the 'Home' manner: they deserved therefore the finest services that could be found around the country – and for the RBD this meant the exasperating denominational policy. Meanwhile, the extra staff member was still being sought; Ogilvie had agreed that no appointment would take place without full consultation with the Ministry of Information. However Fenn met Martin in mid-July to find him astonished that the BBC was going ahead with a departmental appointment. This had to be a BBC initiative and thus the left hand could not always know what the right was doing.

During the summer of 1942, Visser 't Hooft came to London and met Welch in respect to broadcasts to Germany. They both believed in the importance of these for the sake of ecumenical relations between the British and German churches. They agreed that there should be a man in the Corporation in London responsible for the overseas and particularly the German task. Visser 't Hooft recommended the 33-year-old Francis House, then curate of Leeds, who had for two and a half years before the war been his assistant. Francis House was asked to London, and met Salt, who took an immediate liking to him – he had 'just the right kind of personality and approach'. He took up the appointment on 1 October 1942. He was responsible for the Empire services, daily and weekly; European services in English and the presently occasional service in German at Christmas and Easter. He was to collaborate with Hugh Martin at the Ministry and would attend the monthly meeting there. The weight of responsibility for the organizing of Empire and European broadcasts was firmly with the RBD and not, as Fenn had feared, with the Ministry. For Welch this was a crucial advance. It was the church's task to take initiatives in this field, no matter how much the government were preoccupied over such material with a view to propaganda: the church was in the BBC as it was not in the Ministry. For Welch this was of theological importance, as he constantly reaffirmed to Nicolls and the Controllers of the Overseas Division. In Francis House, Welch had secured a special ecumenical perspective in the Department. He only regretted that on policy questions the hierarchies in the BBC and Ministry regarded his ecumenism with some suspicion: the churches as a whole did broadly the same, at least judging by the attitude of CRAC. Without Temple, Welch and Fenn could simply not have maintained this line for so long and, indeed, with such considerable success.

19

ECUMENICAL INITIATIVES

At his enthronement in Canterbury Cathedral in April 1942, which was broadcast, William Temple declared 'one great hope for the coming days – this world-wide Christian fellowship, this ecumenical movement.'[1] Within a few months he preached the inaugural sermon at the launching of the British Council of Churches in St Paul's Cathedral. Perhaps rather diplomatically, he spoke of ecumenism as 'more a matter of adjustment than substantial innovation'. Action was nevertheless crucial now that Christianity was no longer unchallenged and was even repudiated. The primary need, Temple declared, was for a 'clear and united testimony' to Christianity itself. The difference between Catholic and Protestant, he stated with singular courage, was very small compared with the difference between Christian and non-Christian. That meant co-operation not only between Christians themselves but also with those who 'live by the principles we claim as Christian who are as yet unable to accept the faith in which we are persuaded that those principles are grounded'.

Welch shared the same objectives in broadcast religious policy; Temple's second group who 'shared the principles' were those to whom Welch directed a considerable sector of broadcast religious programmes. Even more profoundly did Welch share Temple's ecumenical convictions. His urge to have the BBC speak with one voice was all the more animated by listener research. In 1941 Silvey had carried out a mammoth investigation to assess the numerical strength of those listening to religious broadcasts. He had developed a radical technique for this enquiry – only the second of its kind.[2] The sample consisted of 5000 adults with wireless sets at home. It was a retrospective enquiry, and the results were based on programmes actually and deliberately listened to.[3]

For Welch and the Department the quarter of the sample 'favourably disposed' was rather more significant than the sixteen per cent who were 'very enthusiastic' and who, he assumed, were probably active churchgoers. The 'favourable' were listening increasingly to Forces programmes and the bulk of these were aged over fifty. Silvey sounded the alarm: 'The proportion of listeners who are interested in religious services is bound to diminish with the passing of time.'[4] Whilst five million were 'very enthusiastic', another seven and a half million were 'favourably disposed'; these were much younger and contained a greater proportion of men. They were probably rarely in church but, for Welch and the Department, they were open to the influence of religious broadcasts and a distinctive Christian voice. Welch, as Iremonger before him, had no illusions: the BBC had severe limitations placed upon it from within and without. Furthermore it was, of course, easier to speak of ecumenical co-operation than union.[5] He had also to counter the opposition to 'BBC religion' to which he was always exposed.

As we have seen, Welch finally secured an overseas assistant in Francis House, himself equipped with a background in ecumenical European church life. Broadcasting could do an immense amount for the life of those European churches who could neither preach nor worship freely, much less broadcast their own religious services.[6]

By late summer 1942, Crossman had agreed on the broadcasts to Germany in German, and George Bell and William Paton very largely organized the speakers; they were mostly German. Anthony Eden personally indicated that he was strongly in favour, and these long sought-after broadcasts went out every Wednesday from 2 November 1942. Welch had established a fact: the RBD was committed first to the churches, and would recognize only to a degree the limits, boundaries and divisions created by war. It was an ecumenical objective of particular significance; it would bind together the same church in two countries by the service of the German pastors here to the German congregations under such stress at home. Welch told House he was to be responsible for the 'most important piece of religious broadcasting we can possibly undertake in wartime'. In Britain, ecumenical objectives were not so easily realized.

A. National Days of Prayer

At home, however, Welch had other very significant ecumenical objectives which again derived from the role of broadcasting to a nation at war. Since 1939 his preoccupation had been with the quality of broadcast religion and finding the best preachers and speakers, but particularly the former for an emerging species of broadcasts – the sermon series. They would present Christianity to the public on a united front. But Welch also wanted to educate the churches; and the

Sunday series of talks were designed to bring the best in scholarship to the widest possible church audience. In spring 1942 Fenn put on twelve talks on *How Christians Worship* with the object of answering the simple question of the man in the street: why do people go to church? More particularly, it was designed to break down the insulation of parochial denominational attitudes among the churches themselves. Predictably Temple gave the first two and Iremonger the last (on broadcasting and worship). The exercise was backed up by the British Council of Churches, whose Youth Department issued a twelve-page study outline for use in church youth clubs. The talks were designed to enable Christians of different traditions to understand one another better. Fenn wanted ecumenical action: people needed to meet and worship together.[7] Even the editor of *The Listener* in a leader hoped that the series would help people grasp the 'common elements' in the received historic faith and help people to 'enter more sympathetically into the worship of churches other than their own'.[8] The Eucharist was the problem: Garbett could not conceive the series without it; with it the series would be controversial.[9]

1942 saw the third in an important series of annual broadcast rituals which marked the church and state connection in time of war. Armistice services had almost since the beginning of broadcasting been broadcast to the nation notwithstanding early resistance to Reith's initiative by the Home Office.[10] In May 1940, as France fell, George VI had called the nation to a National Day of Prayer. There was a specially interlinked broadcast, a service from the City Temple with a sermon by William Temple direct from York Minster. In the earliest of these successive National Days Welch was in a position to counsel that the whole BBC output on that day should reflect the solemnity of the times; Britain stood alone: it was the time of Dunkirk. For the broadcast on 8 September, however, the obvious choice of a churchman to speak for the nation was Lang of Canterbury. Welch had no choice, even though Lang's talk from Bristol at the outbreak of war had been trivial and disastrous. Fenn and Welch had sat horrified as Lang toyed with odd notions which in their opinion quite missed the gravity of the situation.[11] Maconachie too thought that Lang provoked 'unChristian reactions'. 'To have the head of the national church is officially correct but official correctness is not enough.'[12] Welch could only agree.

Welch knew that given the invitation to the Archbishop of Canterbury, on this second Day of Prayer there would have to be invitations to all other church leaders at the very moment when he wanted to have the churches speak with one 'co-operating' voice. However, the broadcasting day and all available religious services had to be shared out between the Archbishops of Canterbury and Westminster, the Church of Scotland and the Free Church Federal Council, which latter body was not at all happy that the Cardinal Archbishop should have so pronounced a place in the middle of the morning all to himself. That he did not even mention the National Day of Prayer gave grounds for Nicolls' contention that his talk bore a 'not very distant resemblance to Roman Catholic propaganda'.[13]

Welch was convinced that the BBC could and should be doing a great deal more to unite Christians in an act of prayer for peace. In planning his schedule of services for 1941, he recognized the clear dilemma which Iremonger had known and Stobart before him: the BBC could obviously mount such occasions much better than the local congregations, and yet on such a day could not be seen to be encouraging the faithful to stay away from churches in favour of the broadcasts. He believed, however, that this predominantly Protestant nation ought, at some point, to hear the voice of the Cardinal Archbishop, even though the Corporation had received a mountain of letters in September 1940 following the address in which he had spoken of Britain being the 'dowry of Our Lady'.[14]

In his preparation for the September 1941 National Day of Prayer, Welch put an innovative suggestion to the Archbishop: he wanted the bishops of the Church of England to sanction the installation of loudspeakers in all their churches. Cosmo Lang would preach in a service broadcast from a studio and with him, those in the churches up and down the land would pray and worship 'with one voice'. Listeners in the churches would participate and be told the details or at least 'conducted' through the services. It was to be an 'important development in religious broadcasting'. It would provide an example to the nation – not only would the public and the general listener be asked to pray but they would know that those in the churches would be responding to the same invitation. He told Garbett he thought the *Ecclesia Anglicana* could be realized in a quite unique way; throughout the world not only would people listen, they would take part in singing and praying, etc. It would be a rediffusion on a grand scale. To Welch's regret, Lang was hesitant: 'The clergy', he said, 'do not like their ordinary services being interfered with and not all would be able to install loudspeakers. . . . You know how difficult it is to get the clergy to combine in any movement of that kind.' Predictably, perhaps, the Bishops' Committee turned it down:

> Though they fully appreciated the point about securing the greatest possible unity on such a day . . . they did not think it was advisable to

recommend churches generally to suspend their own services in order to listen to, or even take part in, a service sent from the BBC.[15]

Welch had already prepared his ecumenical 'plan B': he wanted to have the Church of Scotland and the Church of England interlinked and cross-connected. Would Lang preach at St Giles' Cathedral, Edinburgh? No – this would involve a return invitation to a Presbyterian to preach in St Paul's or the Abbey, and this reciprocation might not be so easily agreed by the Chapters! Temple, however, did agree and Welch planned for a Free Churchman to occupy the 'reciprocal' Anglican pulpit. W. R. Matthews of St Paul's was not keen on the idea at all; St Paul's Cathedral could not be used! Then began a lengthy correspondence between Welch and the Episcopalian hierarchy in Edinburgh. Welch asked for a service from St Giles; the Moderator would give a welcome, the Minister would lead the service and Temple would preach. It was not to be. Opposition came from E. D. L. Danson, the Bishop of Edinburgh:

> Such a proceeding would be harmful to our church, seeing that the Church of Scotland is not in communion with the Anglicans. . . . The national day of prayer is not a suitable occasion for a joint religious service; it suggests that the state connection of two religious bodies is more important than episcopacy . . . such a suggestion would grievously offend . . . and call forth a host of protests from our faithful people.[16]

He would accept the Moderator of the Church of Scotland to preach, but not William Temple. Dinwiddie regretted Welch's urge to obtain Danson's approval, and told Archibald Main of SRAC that Charles Warr, the Minister of St Giles', regarded it as a 'gross impertinence to prevent an Anglican clergyman from preaching in the Church of Scotland's St Giles' Cathedral'.[17] Temple, for his part, told Welch he would not 'upset already problematic relations' but thought 'how tiresome it all is', particularly as Danson had complained directly to him: Scotland, after all, was as 'national' as Wales. Temple agreed, therefore, to preach from Bedford. Welch confessed to Dinwiddie his emotions of both anger and sadness: 'It really is shocking that on a National Day of Prayer the Bishop of Edinburgh should refuse [to allow] the Archbishop of York to preach the gospel in a House of God across the border.'[18] It was all the more lamentable, he told Temple, because so much 'unexpected cooperation' had developed between the Corporation and the Roman Catholics in the context of the Day of Prayer. He told Danson rather icily that his only hope had been to 'manifest to a large listening public the union of Christians in both countries on a day on which the nation is called in prayer to God', and to use the opportunity which broadcasting provided for the divided churches: he regretted that when the King called the nation to prayer 'we cannot close our ranks and worship together'. Yet another blow fell in July; Welch was summoned to Lambeth by Lang, who was about to have lunch with Winston Churchill. They had been in correspondence over the question of national occasions. Churchill thought Lang ought to be more 'obvious as head of the Anglican church; he should speak more frequently.'[19] He confessed his embarrassment to Welch, particularly as Temple had already been invited for the National Day of Prayer in September. Lang was to broadcast to the Empire; the Prime Minister and the Government, however, wanted him to address the home audience. Temple, notwithstanding the respect he commanded from Winston Churchill,[20] was too political a figure in a manner that Lang certainly was not; Temple as the focal point of the national church on such a day would suggest political notions that the Government might prefer to be rather less explicit! In the event, it was a 'trinitarian galaxy' – for the first occasion on radio when three bishops spoke together in one service: the Archbishops of Armagh, Wales and Canterbury with special prayers by the Moderator of the Free Church Federal Council, Sydney Berry. Typical of the sensitivity of the Ministry of Information was their unease over Welch's choice of the hymn 'God the All-terrible'.[21] The Foreign Office regarded it as having 'associations with the Tsarist regime'; Soviet listeners must not be offended! It was changed.

In 1942 the Day of Prayer was fixed for a weekday and the War Cabinet demanded an 'undenominational' service. The Ministry of Labour authorized that factories should cease work for the duration of the service which began at 11 a.m. The churches naturally organized local services; but Welch thought the broadcast received more serious attention than any National Day of Prayer on a Sunday. To his astonishment something like seven million people listened to the service following the 9 p.m. news and just under six million at 11 a.m. Again all the churches were represented on the broadcasting platform; however the ecumenism for which Welch had worked in vain in 1941 was not attempted in this ceremony again.[22]

B. Sermon courses

In 1943 Welch was fired to answer an observation by a correspondent in Cornwall. She had heard sermons on social issues of all kinds, but what exactly, she asked, was meant by 'the gospel'? At this time the Department was increasingly uneasy about two isolated sermons Sunday by Sunday and wanted to introduce more co-ordination of good broadcasters. Welch brought together Dodd and Iremonger, James Stewart of Edinburgh, Rowntree Clifford and Cockin each to contribute to a series of special sermons, subsequently published as *Man's Dilemma and God's Answer*. Welch noted in the preface that the motivation of sermon courses was to match the BBC to the urgency of the days.[23] This series was to be a major test: Silvey mounted an enormous operation to test responses and opinion from a special sample committed to listen to a series over three months. Welch was encouraged when Silvey's panel of people agreed that the series had presented a united front to the world.[24] At the same time it provided a good deal of complex data which reaffirmed the general request for services from the listener's own denominational base. Most significant of all, however, was the response to Dodd's talk on the Bible and the apostolic preaching. Welch thought this was Dodd's best ever broadcasting contribution, and it provoked a good deal of correspondence which called for Bible study and more detailed teaching on the life and times of Jesus. It was crucial to the overall thesis behind the series. If Christ was central to the Christian, there should be further opportunity to appraise the culture from which he derived. The series was criticized by the *Church Times*[25] for its interdenominationalism.

In 1945 another series to cover three months was planned. *People Matter* dealt with the biblical concept of justice. It was a theme which had 'too lightly engaged the minds of Christians', thought Cockin, who helped to plan the series: 'Victory must establish justice in every relationship.' In 1946 yet another series was planned on the subject of Christian responsibility: *Am I My Brother's Keeper?* Mervyn Stockwood, Daniel Jenkins and Canon L. John Collins began to establish a presence in the broadcast programmes. It was not enough, however, to have these series broadcast without some response from the churches. Welch's object had been to use connected series of broadcast services with preachers who agreed to participate in a scheme of extended sermons designed to declare the essential Christian faith within a certain framework. He had always hoped that the old traditions of pre-war group listening in churches would operate in order to inform the Christian community as well as the uncommitted. It was, moreover, a well constructed public relations exercise which brought the theological élite from the universities and the churches into the orbit of the ordinary listener – both churched and non-churched. With the increasing influence of the *Brains Trust* and the urge towards discussion, the post-war interest in teaching through group discussions favoured innovation in broadcasting technique.

An initiative of the North Region and the new religious programmes organizer, Eric Saxon, in this adult educational arena was the long-running series *The Creed of a Christian*. The first series in the autumn of 1946 was launched with a good deal of publicity paid for by the Corporation, particularly aimed at the churches: the series was 'designed to answer some of the questions Christians ask about their faith'.[26] Saxon had been animated by the suggestion of the Livingstone Report on *The Church and Adult Education*,[27] and by the hopeful beginning of Mary Somerville's series of discussion programmes for teenagers entitled *To Start You Talking*.[28] *The Creed of a Christian* was, however, for adults in the congregations, and was designed to deepen the ordinary layman's understanding of basic Christian credal statements. Policy considerations excluded what would be deemed 'controversial', so Welch was concerned that the six programmes for the first series in 1946 be broadcast to Christian congregations.

An innovation was that the teaching sermon was quite distinct from the act of worship preceding it. Moreover, it gave the opportunity for churchgoers around the country to get back from Evensong in time to hear the sermon at the end of the liturgical service. Not everyone liked this arrangement!

The tone of the Livingstone Report had been somewhat provocative, and sure that the BBC could educate congregations by exposing them to a level of competence beyond the expertise or initiative of the local clergy:

> Some closer liaison between the work of the church in broadcasting and in the parishes seems to be necessary; . . . there is still . . . insufficient recognition of the immense work for the church which can be done through the medium of broadcasting.[29]

The first series, on *The Nature and Work of God*, had a favourable reception nationwide: there were around two hundred groups in the regions, forty in the Liverpool diocese alone. Moreover, with the burgeoning of the Light Programme and the popularity of *Sunday Half Hour*, there were clear signs that the place of the Sunday evening service was threatened, and innovation was essential. Silvey reported to Saxon in December that the overall response to the series showed a clear demand for an evening service.[30] It had proved to Saxon that the evening service on the Home waveband could at least attract the churchgoing public notwithstanding a good deal of criticism that as the sermon followed the liturgical worship section people would switch off thinking perhaps it was a service without a sermon.

The series continued monthly into 1948 and for the autumn of that year became much more adventurous in tackling the questions increasingly asked about the nature of the church: all the major confessions were represented including the Roman Catholics. 'Each talk would contain a positive statement of the doctrine of the church and raise the questions which each denomination asks of the other churches'.[31] By 1951 the organization of these series became more efficient and had the co-operation of most of the Protestant denominations. The Church of England Adult Education Council circularized all the dioceses in England and Wales and eventually 36,000 leaflets were distributed, this time with booklists related to each talk. The 1950 series on *The Modern Man* featured F. A. Cockin, by then Bishop of Bristol, and John Marsh, Professor of Theology at Nottingham – a keen advocate of the BBC's religious work.

There was a good correspondence: 750 letters of appreciation gave a sufficient picture to show that the responses were patchy and sometimes marginal. Saxon was astonished to find that many of the clergy simply had no idea of the scheme; he knew that the opposition, as usual, came from those who resented this BBC competition. Saxon thought that at least the series on the Catholic Church had helped to answer criticism of the BBC's religious policy. Putting the most optimistic interpretation on the very few statistics available, Saxon reckoned that there were between 200 and 1,000 listening groups! Put against the number of substantial congregations in the region, this was disappointing.[32] Such intelligence as Silvey had managed to glean on listening figures together with Saxon's own investigations did, however, offer interesting observations about religion in the churches. There was a clear demand not only for the credal foundations of Christianity but for Christian ethics and their practical implications for everyday life: marriage, politics, gambling and Communism. Saxon considered an approach to extend the series beyond Christian belief to Christian behaviour.[33] Edwin H. Robertson, House's assistant, confirmed from his own information (which appeared in the official reports) that for considerable numbers the talks assumed too great a knowledge.

The series called *The Creed of a Christian* demonstrated that the potential for the education of the churches and the body of committed churchgoers could only be realized with the co-operation of the central and regional church authorities. These were only at best half-hearted. The clergy would not readily install systems in their churches nor would they willingly interfere with the order of evening services in favour of the broadcasts. Notwithstanding the complexity of these talks for great numbers who heard them, it was a means by which the churches might have made the use of Sunday evening services into something of a movement, as for example sectors within Anglicanism were influencing profound changes in the mornings. The growing influence of television would bring the reorganization of radio in such a way as to reduce even further the hold of the churches over the prime period of evening services. It was an ecumenical opportunity lost.

C. The *Christian News-Letter*

But the most significant ecumenical initiative during Welch's period was without a doubt the genesis of a radio species of the later *Ecumenical Press Service*, of the World Council of Churches, an enterprise to bring the churches in touch with each other and in particular to inform and comment upon major movements within Christendom. It was the beginning of a religious news and current affairs output to inform and educate if not to comfort.

With the formal establishment of the British Council of Churches in September 1942, Oldham and Fenn met to discuss the possibility of a series of programmes under the umbrella of the BCC to disseminate ideas and information about the churches to a wider audience but in particular to the churches themselves, and especially to the clergy. Oldham was hard of hearing and was not easy at the microphone. He wanted Fenn to do these programmes. Fenn, however, as a member of the Corporation, was ineligible. It was critical that the Department find the right man. Fenn was in touch with a very wide ecumenical spectrum, Oldham's newly formed 'Christian Frontier' and William Paton's international group which had produced the main line of thought in his series of talks given in July 1942 on *The Church and World Order*.[34] Beales, the Department's talks producer in London, was a Roman Catholic and shared Fenn's concern that the programme must have a 'point of view' and one which, coming from the right man, would obviate any unease among church leaders lest their particular confessional and ecclesial attitudes or actions might be dealt with in any prejudiced way. It was to be Oldham's *Christian Newsletter* on the air.[35] Fenn had further meetings with Paton, Oldham and Craig. They almost insisted that if the British Council of Churches was the 'supporting agent' then there should be a BCC sub-committee to clarify its own interests and offer advice on questions of a critical nature – of which there were many! Paton and Oldham wanted the BBC to provide a 'critical survey of the religious situation in its broadest sense' and 'take a critical line in putting ecclesiastic matters in their wider setting of events in the community at large'.[36] The Corporation, however, as

Welch realized, could not have a point of view – it could only be a channel. The hierarchy, Welch feared, would surely veto any suggestion that the Corporation stood behind the BCC in 'criticizing' the churches through this new programme. Fenn thought there was a mountain of material to make a 'very good story' and with William Paton, knew Nathaniel Micklem to be the man who had reputation and respect enough with the churches and with the Corporation to mount such a programme. If, hitherto, Welch had tried very hard (as had Iremonger to a much lesser degree) to interpret current events according to Christian criteria, the new venture would do much more; it would encourage 'comment' on the utterances and actions of the churches and expose such material to a critique derived from an ecumenical viewpoint focused in the BCC.

Fenn conceived the new programme as including a regular review of books by Iremonger, who would explain what Christians were writing and ought to be reading, coupled with what Christians were doing and perhaps should be thinking.[37] Iremonger was by no means convinced; for him religious broadcasting was moving in the wrong direction. It was aimed, he thought, 'a bit too high'. 'The churches are in grave danger of being swamped with movements and institutions' which appear as the 'end of, rather than promoting, the Kingdom of God.' He doubted if Fenn's syllabus would appeal to the middlebrow and 'certainly not to the lowbrow'. Iremonger recognized at least these distinctions within the life of congregational Christianity, both Protestant and Catholic, notwithstanding Oldham's insistence that the BBC should be educating the new post-war culture in the Christianity of the twentieth century which might best be called ecumenical. It was, at any rate, one of the clearest ways in which the Department gave support to the thinking of William Temple, now at Canterbury. Fenn wanted the BBC to show just how widely the main churches supported Temple's approach to political and economic issues, notwithstanding his over-estimations.

For the Corporation, Welch was under much pressure to do the opposite of Fenn's intention and reduce the amount of comment: 'The element of news should be uppermost', Howgill in BBC News told Welch. The programme had been authorized on that basis. At any rate, comment must be explanatory rather than critical for fear that the BBC's policy on religious controversy should be compromised.[38]

The Editorial Committee of Paton, Cockin and Fr John Murray for the Roman Catholics sat under Oldham's chairmanship and tried hard to steer a course between news and comment. *Christian News* programmes began on Sunday 1 November 1942 and continued until June 1943.

After only eight weeks the title was changed by Nicolls to *Christian News and Commentary*: he thought there was rather more comment than news! The first programme gave background – explanations of 'Religion and Life' and 'Sword of the Spirit' movements and the church situation in the occupied countries. Subsequent programmes dealt with China, the Jews, prisoners of war and the Scottish missions at home. Iremonger gave his review of books. It was, as Iremonger had suggested, all rather erudite. The series ended with a general summing up by Micklem of the twenty-three bulletins which balanced foreign material in twelve programmes against home and domestic material in eleven; general opinion thought the balance was fair. But the listening figure was low – roughly half of the audience for a straight talk. At the close of the first series Welch was all the more convinced that to speak to the rank and file in the churches, including the clergy, the programme should deal more with 'persons – not movements, tendencies, masses or ideas'. He wanted to examine the whole content and treatment of modern missions and get the churches to examine such questions on the air. He wanted to send Micklem out as 'our man from Mars' for a month's tour of British churches and then to give some sort of talk on the style of Priestley's *English Journey*.

As the series resumed and continued through 1944, Beales became increasingly uneasy; it was not, as its title suggested, a 'news' programme – only rarely did it report what he called 'hot' news – information provided through the *Christian News and Commentary* as a primary source to the United Kingdom listener. He wanted the series so administered that the Christian listener would not feel certain of any opinion until he had heard 'what Micklem will have to say about it next Sunday!' He wanted up-to-date reporting, for which, of course, Micklem was hardly equipped; he wanted a real news service without which the 'up-to-date Christian could not endure!'. No such concept had so far entered the thinking of the Department: i.e. that it might provide a news agency for the BCC in particular and the wider interests of Christendom in general. Fenn was troubled by the whole question of balance between views and comment. In 1945 Micklem was replaced by John Foster, the historian, generally agreed to be a better broadcaster. Fenn was worried, however, that the 'hotting up' gave the material the character of propaganda; it was impossible to make this into 'attractive' broadcasting in an atmosphere of listening figures and audience-catching without suggesting that the material was of wider interest than the figures showed that it actually was. By this time the 'news' character of the series had been so emphasized that it might now be said to have a wider than minority appeal.

After the war the whole issue of the policy of the BBC Talks Department came under review.[39] The new series under Foster, now entitled *What Are the Churches Doing?*, was designed to appeal 'to a wider range of listeners than clergy or churchgoer'.[40] But it did not appeal widely enough – in spite of all Welch's efforts to have the church press encourage the clergy to listen. Foster also pressed the SCM to advise secretaries in universities to encourage students to listen at lunchtime (the programme went out at 1.10 in the regions).[41] The listening figures were very low and two other aspects troubled the Controller of the Home Service, Lindsay Wellington. He told Welch that there were too many fixed religious points and he wanted them reduced and that the long-running midweek service on Thursday was 'incongruous and uneasy in the context of main evening listening on a weekday'. The fact that the churches were monopolizing a weekday segment of airtime, and for talks rather than sermons, slowly became less and less acceptable to the hierarchy.[42]

Welch, however, had initiated the series under Fenn's control, which focused the objectives of the Department upon connecting the widest possible Christian audience with radical Christian movements in the world-wide church. It brought continental personalities to the British audience, particularly Karl Barth[43] and Emil Brunner. It would eventually merge into a talks policy which no longer allowed the churches' interests represented by Welch to have quite such freedom as war conditions had allowed. Moreover, the heaviest blow to Welch's initiative in this area had come in October 1944 with the death of William Temple. Within six months of that event the war ended; the single home wavelength and the notion of the BBC's mission for Christianity ended with it. The coming of the peace disengaged the nation from its intense preoccupation with ideological objectives which had animated the morale and been so congenial to Welch's hopes.

20

THE CONCEPT OF MISSION

Whereas Iremonger believed that Christianity had a place in broadcasting, Welch believed that the BBC was the spearhead of the churches' mission. The single wartime wavelength would match the single utterance of nation to people. Halfway through his time as Director of Religious Broadcasting, he focused his conviction in a sermon to the University of Cambridge.[1] Broadcast religion, he declared, was not simply a component in the general output to serve the Christian minority: it was 'to proclaim Good News to all'. The BBC was 'committed' to Christianity and 'Broadcasting House is a parable of modern civilization.' Broadcasting could do for the churches what the churches could not do for themselves: it could serve the committed housebound, and it could reflect the very best in liturgy and scholarship. Welch knew well that whilst the BBC hierarchy were concerned to avoid giving offence to the churches, there was considerable resentment that the Corporation should be formally subject to an outside committee, namely the Central Religious Advisory Committee.

Religious broadcasting, however, 'must not only reflect, it must lead'. As Harman Grisewood has observed,[2] CRAC, unlike Horatio at the bridge, was determined to stand watch over the BBC religious policy instead of facing out to the churches and defending the Corporation's initiative on their behalf from which they stood only to benefit. For example, Welch wanted to have the BBC purchase the war-damaged church of All Souls, Langham Place, to extend the arena of experiment and so assist the wider parochial ministry. The Church of England was obstructive and timid: it was needed to maintain the Evangelical balance with the Anglo-Catholic All Saints, Margaret Street. The answer was no.[3]

There were three categories of listener, Welch believed, to whom the BBC religious policy directed this so-called 'mission': first, there were committed Christians who would benefit from exposure to the widest range of confessional identity within the mainstream churches. Broadcast religion was manifestly ecumenical. It was also educational: the churches had the opportunity to build themselves up. The second category was much more interesting: the 'half-churched'. To these, the churches 'had failed to speak effectively a saving word for man in society'. To this group, Welch believed, came the BBC's most outstanding contribution to the mission: Dorothy L. Sayers' cycle of plays, *The Man Born to be King*.[4] There was in this group a sufficiently widespread acquaintance with the gospels as a 'synthetic' story and with it a notion about the founder of Christianity derived from piety and construed as biography. However unstable this 'acquaintance', Welch believed, Sayers' plays would rescue the figure of Jesus from the arcane language of liturgical recital and provide for these vast audiences a real historical personality.[5] Welch's commitment to drama was tenacious: he wanted to extend its influence into the broadcast liturgical setting: radio must appeal to the imagination even in worship. In 1945–46 he experimented with broadcast services: instead of a sermon, a 'dramatic interlude', these were written by the very few writers who understood his intentions; Wilfrid Grantham was one.[6] The experiments provoked opposition, although in this instance CRAC was in favour. Many clergy, however, were against it: it turned worship into entertainment: the BBC should not come between a man and his God, said a correspondent. The BBC hierarchy objected on departmental grounds: the RBD was doing what properly belonged to Val Gielgud. The Governors also heard complaints from the very people the BBC should serve above all in its religious policy: the housebound. Listener Research reported seventy-five per cent of correspondents against it.[7]

In Welch's third category were the Forces: the greatest challenge; if the ears of Category Two were half-closed, theirs were quite closed. What this group needed was 'nothing less than the intellectual rehabilitation of the Christian faith in the minds not of scholars but of ordinary thinking men'. He blamed the clergy: 'These men have rejected the version of Christianity they have seen in the army and church.' Herein the BBC mission had not been successful. There should be more laymen; Welch knew how the public had complained of clericalism since Iremonger's day. The 'thought for the day' programme *Lift Up Your Hearts*, begun by the Scottish Director, Dinwiddie, was designed by him to begin a 'new spiritual movement in Scotland', to give 'a tonic talk with a religious background'.[8] Notwithstanding the immense popularity of many of his Forces speakers, Welch eventually recognized the impossibility of reaching the complete outsider and the 'artisan and blackcoated working classes'. It was a painful admission. Perhaps the totally 'unclerical' Christian could build up some vestige of the Christian contribution to contemporary life: *My Faith and My Job* was an attempt to engage the layman. Welch believed, theoretically at least, that Christian belief could be distilled through a 'lay intelligence', however uninformed in theology. The response was marginal.

To the churches, Welch challenged the frequent criticism that the very excellence of broadcast liturgy and spoken word put the parochial clergy and the local church at a decided disadvantage with the reply: 'Discontent is the spur to progress.' Broadcasting provided ecumenical opportunities: it prepared the way for that measure of co-operation that might 'keep open the possibility of a Christian civilization'. He hoped the churches would accept the idea of rediffusion. He tried to persuade Lang that there was an unimaginable potential, particularly in the light of the forthcoming 1948 Lambeth Conference: the whole of the Anglican Church might listen to one voice – his – at the opening service. Lang said no. Welch's 'mission' called the churches to recognize that millions were no longer participants: committed in some measure, perhaps, but not active. Broadcasting could prepare the way. In 1943, Temple's Committee on Evangelism had recognized the value of the medium.[9] Welch's constant message to the churches was that the mission of his BBC department was to 'plough up some fallow land and sow seed'. Radio could open the way for a Christian utterance preparatory to potential commitment and participation: church services alone on the air were a waste; the key was in dramatic 'radiogenic' forms which penetrated the imagination and enlivened the spirit.

With the end of the war, the mission in a real way was over. The righteous struggle had been victorious, and if some were dreaming of reconstruction, others were asking questions about democracy and freedom of speech. It would be time for all assumptions to be tested. In broadcasting policy, the religion of Britain would have to be looked at afresh. Welch wondered if in the enormous struggle the churches had really learned the lessons.[10] Others wondered whether Welch had learned his lessons: with Temple replaced by Fisher, Welch knew that the impetus would now be impoverished. He had not lost his radical flair, and knew that with his Department's victory programmes over and the operation now back in Langham Place there would be just as great a challenge in doing now what could not be done during the war: bringing the traditions of Christian creed and belief into the 'market place'.

PART FOUR

THE CLAMOUR OF VOICES:
THE CHRISTIAN MONOPOLY AT RISK
1945–1951

21

POST-WAR REORGANIZATION

If the wartime religious output was marked by the hoped-for single voice of Christianity to a nation at war, the peace brought an expansion of regional identity and the freedom to develop it. If the single wavelength at home had carried the single voice of Christian tradition to a Christian nation, the peace would be marked by plurality and the clamour for free speech. If the war had heard the portentous sounds of Christian self-examination, the peace brought diversity and polarity, as had already to some extent become clear in the utterances of the committed to those who had ears to hear and those who did not. Broadcasting placed importance upon response in understanding, appreciation and benefit. If in wartime the 'Christian Word' was free to be broadcast to whoever might be listening, in peacetime it had to justify its very existence in the broadcast output. Welch wondered if the wartime radio broadcasts would 'bear the scrutiny of an impartial Christian mind when peace has set out work in a wider context'.[1] However vigorously he had fought for the 'testimony of one faith to one people', with the arrival of victory he was faced with diversity even as he prepared the programmes for the Sunday after VE [Victory in Europe] Day; centrality and singularity could no longer be a realistic objective. The Head of Religious Broadcasting was no longer in sole charge as wartime had allowed.

A. The Department and the Regions

(i) *The wartime background*

The war had severely curtailed the initiative of the regions, notwithstanding the intention by the Corporation hierarchy to give them as much freedom as possible. Briggs quotes Foot's concern, as Director-General, that the BBC was in danger of looking at its policy too much 'through the eyes of a Londoner'.[2] There had been considerable resistance to centralization ever since the transmitters were able to provide a signal for the whole country,[3] but it increased alongside the regional initiatives during the thirties. Once Iremonger had joined the Corporation and set up his Department, the 'centre' gained in establishment, first with Geoffrey Dearmer and others, but by the beginning of the war he had prepared the ground for an executive assistant. He had actually sought an assistant from within the Corporation and the only two replies were from staff in the equipment section!

With the outbreak of war and the single wavelength, the ground was even better prepared for a unique role for the Corporation as a servant to the Christian faith, above both denominational and regional boundaries. All ears turned towards the metropolis for a variety of subjects, and churchmen naturally wanted access to the one programme which reached the nation as a whole. Foot was anxious to give the regions as much latitude as was possible in wartime, and thus instituted a monthly meeting in London of all the Regional Directors with all the Controllers of the Corporation's principal functions. As the importance of the news increased, it was focused on the sound of Big Ben striking at 9 p.m. For Welch the output of his Department was now the voice of one church to one nation through one wavelength.

No sooner had war begun than Welch had issued his unofficial directives about the quality of sermons: there should be no 'indifferent sermons at this time. We want fewer but better words if we are to preserve the integrity of the spoken word'.[4] Religious broadcasting had a great part to play, but not unless the quality of religious broadcasting improved. Melville Dinwiddie was a committed member of the Church of Scotland, who would not take easily to Anglican instructions. Dinwiddie was not exactly a member of the RBD, but was its equivalent in the Scottish Region. By January 1940 Welch's staff consisted of Fenn for talks, Cyril Taylor for services, and John Williams for the service to schools,[5] a formidable array of talent. (Beales and Selby Wright came later.) Elsewhere in the country there were only part-time specialists; in Wales and similarly in Northern Ireland, it was the Regional Director and his staff who organized the religious services. Welch had every intention of exercising considerable control from the centre, notwithstanding his confessed reliance upon regional intelligence – BBC or otherwise – for the best material, places and people.

Soon enough there was dissatisfaction expressed at the February Regional Directors' Meeting, notably by Dinwiddie. Welch was called to answer. For the three national regions, Scotland, Northern Ireland and Wales, the regular services were arranged by the Directors. Welch had just come from the north so had less reason to worry – he knew the situation well and had many friends there. Cyril Taylor knew the West similarly. Northern Ireland was scheduled to provide one service a year and Wales four. Scotland would give twelve; Welch thought that this was sufficient especially as they had a monthly Thursday evening service.[6] Welch defended this allotment and the control focused in London which it betokened: 'We cannot afford in a single programme to broadcast poor services and poor sermons even to satisfy regions.' He had asked the North to produce a service and a preacher and neither were good enough. Wales presented the same problem; the Bishop of Monmouth produced a platitudinous sermon which he would not change. Welch appealed to precedent: in pre-war days, Iremonger had been under no compulsion to consult the regional directors for the national programme. They were entirely responsible for their own regional services. Why change now, particularly with one wavelength? Religious broadcasting 'ought not to reflect either regions or denominations'.[7] 'Our services have got to be less and less ecclesiastical in form, content and phraseology.' Dinwiddie in Scotland was not content with such a severe restriction of his autonomy and, by the same token, the reduction in the importance of Scotland as a nation rather than a region. Welch wanted George MacLeod to have all three of Scotland's allocation for the next quarter, and the Home Board supported him.[8] Dinwiddie believed Scotland had special needs and was particularly at home in theological discourse. Sermons without solid doctrine would not do. Metrical psalms, which were peculiar to Scotland, would now be rarely heard. The proposed schools service, Dinwiddie thought, was an Anglican construction and could hardly be recommended by the Scottish Advisory Committee. Dinwiddie did believe the times were urgent and that a panel of the best men should be deployed time and again. He wanted James S. Stewart as one. But Dinwiddie had appealed to figures and yet Scotland was outnumbered eight to one by the rest of the country.[9] Now was the time for Scottish Presbyterians to hear Anglican or English Presbyterian services. Dinwiddie had to admit that Scotland preferred to hear more of its own voice more of the time. Welch repeated his plea over and over: the BBC should strike out on its own and instead of reflecting the church life in general, make a clear bid to lead the religious life and thought of the nation.[10] For his part, Dinwiddie tried to convince his Anglican colleague that it was delusion to think that people would listen to the services of other denominations than their own. Dinwiddie believed that the non-committed outsider possessed sufficient ecclesial background to recognize the differences between the denominations. The concept of 'outsider' was in dispute. Welch believed that the outsider was indeed quite outside the orbit of the churches. Dinwiddie knew his 'outsider' to be a Scottish product who, whether attached to a church or not, would be in some remote way familiar with the approximate contours of the Christian faith. It was a dispute which recognized the relative strength of Scottish Presbyterianism. Welch could only suggest that Dinwiddie use his three services each quarter for the national Church of Scotland – the Romans, Anglicans and Nonconformists would all be catered for from England!

In August 1940 a compromise was reached between Welch and the regional directors. The Directors for Wales, Scotland and Northern Ireland would be entirely responsible for services in English (and on occasions in Welsh and Gaelic), but they did agree to send all sermons to Welch for his final approval. He also wanted copies of correspondence. For the North, Midland and West regions, Welch was entirely responsible; the regions were themselves only responsible for the engineering.[11] He had won a partial victory, but the struggle with Scotland would continue. (There were also expressions of dissatisfaction in the North region but they were more muted.) The General Assembly of the Church of Scotland in May 1941 discussed a motion which expressed resentment at the Archbishop of Canterbury speaking for the nation in the crisis. A report in *The Scotsman* asserted that in Scotland the Archbishop had 'no more standing than the Grand Lama of Tibet'.[12] The motion was defeated with the support of John Baillie. Soon enough, however, Welch became exasperated with the generality of the Scottish contribution to the Home programme and hoped that Nicolls, the Controller of Programmes, would see the sense of a scheme in which the regions were obliged to submit their proposals for broadcast services to the Director of Religious Broadcasting in London, who would decide whether any given service was 'worth taking'. Dinwiddie was furious, and saw storms on the horizon if the limitation on national allocations was sustained. The two men met in June and Welch was convinced that after all, Dinwiddie had a case: the Church of Scotland was a national church and must be free to evolve its own version of St Martin's style interconfessionalism within mainstream Scottish Presbyterianism.[13] Scotland was given another 'British' church service each quarter and Dinwiddie promised he would step up efforts at training the clergy.

The acrimony between Welch and Dinwiddie touched a deep and sensitive nerve in the relation of London to the rest of the country. Welch had visited Manchester in order to clarify the relationship. Coatman, the Director, had an assistant who looked after religion and both resented the heavy hand of London. The simple fact was that on the single wavelength each region wanted a larger slice of the national programme cake. The number of services (*all* talks were Welch's responsibility entirely) which each region could produce for its own local consumption was substantial. Welch had no complaint to make at this situation. But the Home Service carried prestige, and, whilst each region knew its own prestigious churches and preachers, Welch was intent upon regularizing the many conflicting sources of advice between and within the regions. He was for example, appalled by the suggestion of the North Region Programme Director that when a series of sermons was proposed, the title should be circularized round the regions with a request for volunteers. Moreover, each region had its own special requests for anniversaries and similar celebrations. Welch had always refused: every Sunday could easily have been filled with special services for the Scouts or Toc H or whatever. The Scots took this all the worse because Welch insisted on the central importance of the Christian year and would not allow any but the most nationally prestigious event to interfere with the BBC's celebration of the Anglican calendar.

As the war continued, the Corporation under Haley, the new Director-General, began planning the post-war re-establishment of the regional operations. Haley was committed to regionalization and its concomitant notion, competition – the very thing that Welch did not want. By the end of 1943 and the spring of 1944 when the regionalization issue was being discussed by the BBC hierarchy, Welch felt a review of the situation was needed: regional identities in the religious output would be re-established, come what may, when the war ended. Welch was looking out for a replacement for Fenn who was about to leave. Dinwiddie put forward David H. C. Read, a Church of Scotland padre, now a prisoner of war. In the event, the Methodist Kenneth Grayston took over from Fenn; he was later Acting Director between the departure of Welch and the arrival of Francis House in 1946.

(ii) *Post-war expansion*

As the war ended, regional identity for religious broadcasting was much expanded. Welch had secured in the North an 'alpha plus Anglican' in Eric Saxon, whose bishop hoped he would be primed for a theological college.[14] In Wales, Glyn Parry-Jones, a Presbyterian, took over from the 75-year-old Major Jones; whilst not an SCM Secretary as Fenn had hoped, he won Fenn's approval. The West Region RAC also rejected an SCM Secretary. A single post for the Midlands and the West Region combined went to an Anglican priest, Martin Willson, who had been a chaplain in North Africa, on the recommendation of C. S. Woodward, now Bishop of Gloucester and Chairman of CRAC.

(The Midland Region did not get its own Religious Broadcasting Organizer until 1947.) There was some conflict over Cyril Taylor, who had come to the Department in wartime from being Precentor at Bristol Cathedral, but he remained with the Department and Welch in London: Welch thought Taylor's return to the West would be a 'serious misuse . . . his great gifts are bound to be largely wasted there'.[15]

Dinwiddie told the Scottish Advisory Committee that whilst he was reluctant to give up his work as Religious Broadcasting Organizer it was now time to have an assistant.[16] A Presbyterian minister, Ronald Falconer, was appointed. Dinwiddie would have liked a chaplain, but one refused the post and another could not be released from the Army soon enough. Scotland now had an indefatigable patriot.[17] He too would be overworked before long. George MacLeod later told Dinwiddie it was a wrong decision and 'a waste of a man who should be in the parish'.[18] It was an odd remark from such a good broadcaster.

In Scotland as in other regions, the local identity was to be expressed through the religious output and the policy of pursuing such distinctions was complex. At the time of regional expansion and self-consciousness, the tension between the centre and the periphery remained acute, and not only in Scotland.

Francis House for his part undertook a radical change of policy when he succeeded Welch in late 1946. No more the objective of presenting a single image of Christianity; the regional momentum was too strong. There was a serious danger that the status of the centre and House's authority would be undermined. He inherited Welch's post-war responsibilities, which covered almost every aspect of the religious output. How to exercise control was crucial. House developed the 'long' staff conferences begun by Welch wherein all the Regional Religious Broadcasting Organizers met to thrash out the issues. House wanted more systematic planning and, as with Welch, wanted sermons preached in the setting of consecutive courses involving the best broadcasters in the country who would be heard by all. He was also committed to regional development, and for Scotland knew that the fanatical Falconer, as many including House regarded him, had the authority of the Church of Scotland behind him in a country where the rest of the Protestants were few and considerably sectarian. Above all, House was concerned to secure the maximum participation of all members of the Department staff in the planning of broadcasts of 'common concern'. One peculiarity of religious broadcasting, unlike any other department in the Corporation was that the best resources were not concentrated in London; only by 'drawing on the resources of the whole country could the gospel be proclaimed most effectively'.[19]

Imaginative and innovative ideas were not confined to London, but London nevertheless needed a concentration of expertise: the resources of the centre could not be replicated in all the regions, albeit Saxon in the North had a specially incisive understanding of radio to make him exceptional among the Organizers.[20] Saxon was fond of the expression 'radiogenic' – an utterance which belonged in style, format and substance to the medium. Radio, as House was constantly saying, could do what the churches could not do for themselves. Welch, too, had thought the day would come when eavesdropping on church services would cease. In the regions this argument was not so easily carried. It all depended upon how the audience was defined in respect of its religious consciousness, education and upbringing. Hymn-singing in England was popular and sermons in Scotland just as much. Pressure by the 'local men' who were pushing or being pushed to the microphone did not – House tactfully told his 1950 staff conference –always give the best result. House wanted the aesthetic and imaginative elements in radio brought into the service of religion, and in particular dramatic utterance as radio had quite uniquely developed it under Val Gielgud.

In 1950 House gained another member of staff in London, Ormerod Greenwood, an educationalist and a Quaker whose concern was to find good writers of drama, especially radio drama. He was there to find 'fresh methods for expressing theological thought in order to reach deeper levels of thought and devotion'.[21] He firmly believed with House that religious broadcasting could not succeed if it relied only upon the policy of reflecting the faith of the churches around the country. It was obliged to do that, otherwise the BBC would be constantly under attack. Greenwood believed the churches to be preoccupied with one objective: that radio should 'speak' as they themselves were accustomed to speaking and moreover to being heard. Dorothy Sayers' cycle of plays and the more recent experiments in 'dramatic radio sermons' had not been altogether well received. The broadcast cycle was applauded because it put the churches' story prestigiously into an 'entertainment' context; the dramatic sermons and even extracts from her cycle in broadcast services were not heartily approved because it all looked 'contrived' and in any event did not belong in a liturgical context. T. S. Eliot had encouraged Greenwood in seeing the close relation of drama to liturgy; the latter springs from the former, but the churches were broadly not prepared for such a notion.[22] Greenwood tried to organize a conference for scriptwriters in 1952; House regretted that nothing came of it.

By the end of 1952, Scotland had yet another religious assistant in Stanley Pritchard. In the North, R. T. Brooks, a Congregationalist, joined Eric Saxon, and House had acquired another Anglican, Richard Tatlock, to be responsible for the Light Programme output.

It was clear that by the end of 1952 the regional output in religious broadcasting concentrated on reflecting the churches to the churches. Scotland, for example, contributed few Sunday services to the basic national Home service and took the fewest from that output into its regular Sunday output.

Not surprisingly the appeal of Church of Scotland services was rather low in England; only three per cent of Sunday services were from north of the border. The North of England provided an enormous output, thanks to Saxon's initiatives which House was pleased to deploy nationwide. The remaining regions however relied heavily on the London output. In denominational terms, the Scottish output contributed most to interdenominational services but there were more Church of Scotland Sunday services than there were Anglican services in England! Dinwiddie always maintained that the BBC should reflect the indigenous rather than the imported: the Church of Scotland was established, the others were not. In the complex and protracted debates about controversial broadcasting, both Scotland and the North were cautious and baulked at their obligation to take these London initiatives into their regional outputs. Haley had little choice but to let each region decide.[23]

Scotland for example was straining at the leash to reflect and stimulate the increasingly well organized missionary enterprises of the Church of Scotland and its various schemes to recapture the war-torn commitment of Scottish Christians up and down the country. Here the energetic Falconer and Dinwiddie were in close sympathy with the General Assembly.

The enterprising Falconer was always in pursuit of new forms to appeal to the fringe and those 'totally' outside the church. He was also in pursuit of closer liaison with the local presbyteries. In 1948 the Church of Scotland had encouraged the development of 'liaison officers' who would stimulate co-operation at the local level. In order to challenge listeners to attend their church, Falconer worked on a substantial initiative for 1950 – a 'radio mission'. It all depended upon the local church co-operation, and policy dictated that the BBC could not run its own 'mission' independent of the local support. Falconer found the lay interest more fervent than the clerical. The Scottish RAC approved and CRAC likewise.

The 'mission' was planned over five weeks with about sixty broadcasts designed to 'challenge the careless, recover the lapsed and strengthen the faithful'.[24] It was set against a background of substantial evangelical and interdenominational post-war activity particularly in the densely populated areas around Glasgow. Enormous publicity embraced every minister of the mainstream churches, and the scheme of broadcasts involved tried and tested clergy, mostly from the parishes but some like Archie Craig of *Christian News-Letter* and James S. Stewart of New College, Edinburgh. The mission involved complex organization: conferences and liaison meetings, questionnaires and reports: it was designed to animate the churches and particularly the clergy into vitalizing the non-clerical energies into action directed at those whose loyalty to church and nation still had a spark. Falconer believed that it entirely depended upon the mobilization of the laity.

Falconer rallied the most articulate minds in the Scottish churches and the speakers were slotted into the various normal religious programmes: Sunday quite naturally saw most of the action in the morning and evening services on the Scottish Home Service. The weekday talks in the *Lift Up Your Hearts* series deployed the people most highly regarded by Falconer: George MacLeod, Archie Craig and George Duncan of Corstorphine. In the weekday talks, episodes from the life of Jesus were dramatized, and in *Sunday Half Hour* combined choirs backed up the words of George MacLeod, Selby Wright and those like them who could combine brevity with profundity.

Falconer had no doubt that the enterprise had 'strengthened the faithful' – the churches wanted more. The second aim, to 'reclaim the lapsed', gave the most encouraging results; church attendance increased, largely from the recently disenchanted or, as Selby Wright had said in a *People's Service*, those who had accustomed themselves to the religion of the armchair.[25] Falconer believed that the lapsed would be energized by traditional services raised to new eloquence by expert preachers like MacLeod. Otherwise church services were a barrier; not surprisingly these were received most favourably by the churches and particularly the laity. Silvey's research had made this clear. The restraints by the Corporation disallowed any extension of religious broadcasting outside the traditional (and therefore mostly Sunday) contexts, and thus innovation in strictly broadcasting terms was limited. The dramatic elements in the weekly programmes were again designed to appeal to those who had some knowledge of and loyalty to the biblical witness: it was a key to the re-awakening of the lapsed conscience. Listener research provided evidence that these programmes were good radio and even – as Falconer was quite ready to concede – 'entertaining'.[26]

It was clear that the efforts of Falconer to animate the General Assembly to approve the presbytery 'liaison officer' as distinct from the clergy did much to allay the fears of the clergy about 'BBC Religion' and all that the notion provoked. In his report to the BBC and the SRAC Falconer said bluntly that the churches had approved the idea but had done little about it. The clergy for their part took little trouble and above all 'did not use their own faithful people adequately'.[27] The most they managed was to relay the BBC's information, but they were not committed, it seemed, to preparing lay members for a concerted co-operative involvement. The number of congregations where there was any conscious attempt to work this out in practice, Falconer concluded, was 'terrifyingly small'.[28] The grand response to the mission which was expected simply did not happen. But it was by no means a complete failure: there was evidence of expansion and recruiting success. Where the clergy did recognize the potential of religious broadcasting, the laity were animated into concentrated effort. But more education of the latter and even the former was imperative. The 1950 mission, Falconer concluded, served as the 'Dieppe raid of this particular technique'. It would serve as a preliminary sortie for further enterprise in another year. He hoped the next attempt would do more. Falconer accepted the fact that those who would hear these broadcasts were finally the faithful, and in 1952 it was to this group first that the 'mission' would be aimed. He also accepted the notion that the 'lapsed' were both inside and outside the active congregational life of the national church. The Corporation could only travel at the rate to which the churches were committed.

The radio mission was a regional experiment all the more possible in Scotland because the country was small and the churches more homogenously related. Falconer from his 'dominion' north of the border had set the most complete example for the rest of the nation, and not the least for the centre; Francis House considered this a useful model.

But as the regional organizers developed their own styles and discovered their own people, it became increasingly difficult for House to control and co-ordinate the output. Above all he had to keep a close watch on the denominational balance throughout the country. It was managed with remarkable skill. Most pressure came, as we have seen, from the Roman Catholics whose members were half those of the Anglicans in Northern Ireland but less than a quarter nationally. At the other end were the Plymouth Brethren who had consistently been refused airtime sinced the beginning and were only approved at last by CRAC in 1947; even then they failed to provide acceptable preachers who were neither 'unctuous [nor] Americanized'. House told his men that the department would have to be on its guard against 'marginal Christian bodies'. He was now under compulsion to provide choices, and the increasing pressure on the Corporation to embrace minorities did at least provide an impetus to the Department nationwide so to order itself that not only would each know what the other was doing, but that the choices for the listening public could be so adjusted that the mainstream Christian utterances should be heard the loudest; the Corporation would not undermine this commitment.

CRAC was marginally reconstituted at the close of the war simply by the introduction of the three-year term for the membership. Garbett resigned the chair in 1945 and was replaced by C. S. Woodward, by then the Bishop of Gloucester and Welch's staunch supporter.[29] The Committee, both established and non-Anglican, formed a powerful group. Each Regional Committee sent a representative, usually the Anglican Chairman.

B. Roman Catholics

By the summer of 1945 Beales had left the Corporation. He was a layman and therefore could not in any real way 'represent' the hierarchy. Nevertheless, Griffin was concerned at his departure; he had regarded Beales as in some way 'our representative to date'. At the same time, D'Arcy was appointed Provincial of the Society of Jesus and decided that he ought to resign, not only because of extra work but because of the difficulties of maintaining his precarious position as the Roman Catholic member of CRAC in the face of Beales' more radical influence over broadcasting policy. D'Arcy had always insisted that Beales had no official standing as a Catholic and that it was in every way improper for the Department or the Corporation to defer to him on any official or even unofficial matter. He was decidedly left-wing and had a way of inviting left-wing Catholic opinion onto the air. Barbara Ward had been invited on to *The Anvil* without any consultation with D'Arcy; Beales' advice had been accepted instead.

Thus D'Arcy withdrew his services and the whole delicate question of Roman Catholic representation was raised afresh. The more aggressive and vigorous Cardinal Archbishop Griffin was capable of a somewhat more formidable expression of opinion. Welch by the end of the war, was convinced that Catholics by and large thought him prejudiced and unfair, albeit he tried his best to do for them what he attempted with slightly more success to do for Protestants: to train them for the microphone on the assumption that their sermons and talks, if not their liturgy, should in a real way be intelligible to other Christians. Moreover, every observant Roman Catholic was aware of the trouble that could easily be stirred up by extreme Protestants in the person of J. A. Kensit, secretary of the Protestant Truth Society, whose executive had instructed him to ensure that the Corporation was never in doubt about wounded Protestant feelings following Roman Catholic broadcasts.

With the departure of both Beales and D'Arcy, the way was open for Roman Catholics to think out a policy for a replacement. The whole affair came to a head in the autumn. D'Arcy had constantly complained to his fellow Catholics that in his opinion and that of the RBD there was only a handful of good Roman Catholic broadcasters able to reach across the great divide and speak to Protestants without frightening them away or offending their sensibilities, while at the same time retaining the good will of fervent Catholics. Welch wanted more than a handful, and tried to set up 'training days' for Roman Catholics to come to Broadcasting House for a working session to aid their microphone technique. D'Arcy had consistently told him that this would be seen not only as interference but as a fundamental refusal to afford Roman Catholics their 'rights' at the microphone to speak to their own people as they would and abuse the Reformation if they so wished! Conflict was inevitable.

When the war was over, Welch tried hard to placate the Catholic anger against his own conviction that most Roman Catholic broadcasts were poor. He offered them more Sunday services, in English of course, which would satisfy those who complained of too little space in the prime sector of the religious output. However he also offered them the opportunity once a quarter to be at their best in a liturgical service in Latin, replacing the Anglican Evensong. It would educate the listening public and could do nothing but good – except, of course, in the eyes of the Protestant Truth Society and its supporters. The emphasis for most Roman Catholics was upon recital: 'the truth and nothing but the truth ... take it or leave it',[30] and no matter how appealing or convincing many like D'Arcy and McElligott thought such recital should be, what mattered to most was the protection of Roman Catholic culture in a hostile environment. Welch recognized that in view of the limits imposed upon Catholic broadcast services, the weight of Catholic broadcasts must be borne by talks; there should be more of these. D'Arcy was in agreement provided there was no attempt by the Corporation to put Catholic against Catholic, as he felt had happened in his conflict with Beales. It was this fear as much as his new post which prompted his resignation.[31]

With Beales and D'Arcy both gone there were two gaping cavities in the Corporation's Roman Catholic policy: the representation which Griffin believed he had in Beales on the inside of the productive enterprise and that of D'Arcy on CRAC. Griffin believed there were two places 'free' for him to fill. Haley and Welch for their part were adamant that there was no possibility of the appointment of a Catholic to the staff simply because he was a Catholic. Haley did want a dignitary on CRAC and hoped Griffin would send a bishop. There was, in addition, an obvious place for some regularly structured Roman Catholic advice to be offered to the Department akin to what D'Arcy – notwithstanding the relative informality of the arrangement – had undertaken. The idea would not go away, particularly as the Romans, among their 'handful' of good men, including the celebrated Dom Bernard Clements, had one exceptional broadcaster in Father Agnellus Andrew. He had been an outstanding contributor to *The Anvil* and a regular broadcaster of talks and in studio services. He was a Franciscan Friar in Gorton, near Manchester; he had a wide understanding of the British Catholic presence, and travelled a great deal as a teacher. Griffin thought he might succeed Beales, since this reputedly 'Catholic' place was now vacant.

Welch met with Andrew late in September 1945 to discuss the possibility. Whilst there was no doubt that there must be a hierarch to replace D'Arcy on CRAC, this should be quite distinct from any advisory task for the Department. Haley wanted no programme finance going to such a man. Andrew and Welch had always managed to work together and whilst he realized the job would not be 'altogether comfortable' in view of the politics, he was willing to be trained, perhaps as a producer, or at least acquire the knowledge of technique inherent in the advisory task. Welch and Andrew then talked with Griffin, who agreed to the scheme in principle. In November, Griffin met Haley and it was agreed that CRAC should get a second dignitary in addition to Mgr Masterson of Salford (from the North Region RAC), while Agnellus Andrew was to be engaged on a special BBC contract to do more diligently and effectively what D'Arcy, regrettably, had only been able to do rather piecemeal. Andrew, at any rate, recognized that in terms of educating the Roman Catholic clergy there was a great deal to do. He thought their addresses were poor and that the 'general level was appalling and sometimes mischievous . . . and did no good to Catholics . . . our services were shapeless and uninspiring'.[32]

Andrew set about the task with vigour: he was one of the few Catholics in Britain who recognized the potential of radio, and realized that if they were not involved in it, a considerable opportunity would be lost. The principal difficulty was that most clergy had little conception of this and even less compulsion to take it very seriously; broadcasting was, after all, what Protestants did. Andrew as peacemaker, and rather beyond his brief, initiated the building of bridges particularly where Roman Catholics were in great numbers: the North and in Ulster. In 1946, for example, the Northern Ireland RAC had at last persuaded Mgr H. Ryan to serve. He had the idea that the Mass would be broadcast. As in Scotland, however, this most certainly was not considered, and the Catholics were told to adapt. Since this was not possible Ryan resigned. It was Andrew who managed to retrieve the situation.

The situation which faced Andrew was increasingly complicated by the new regional policy and the centrifugal movement towards the wider recognition of the nation's diverse identities.[33] Power was being claimed, and nowhere more forcefully than in Scotland where the notion of region had been rejected in favour of 'nationhood'. Andrew's vigour frequently came up against the new Religious Broadcasting Organizer appointed in effect by the General Assembly of the Church of Scotland, just as the Head of Religious Broadcasting had been by the Church of England. The power struggle was serious now that the Corporation had appointed Andrew to put Catholic broadcasting in order. The Roman Catholics, like the others, were anxious to establish their position on the regional RACs.

His first year was spent in preparing for dialogue and the organizing of a conference for the Catholics to speak to the BBC: not a little would be gained if the staff of the Corporation would listen. The Bishop of Nottingham chaired the first of such conferences in Manchester in October 1946. There were six Catholic divines including John Heenan of Manor Park in East London, already a skilled broadcaster. Welch and Agnellus Andrew represented the BBC in London. Welch defended the policy of the Corporation and was delighted, if sceptical, at the outcome of a pre-conference meeting: Andrew had clearly convinced them. They told Welch:

> Roman Catholic broadcasts would not be directed exclusively or even mainly to Roman Catholics. Our ideal therefore would be to give Catholic doctrine in a Catholic form but in manner and in language likely to prove useful to the great mass of non-religious listeners.[34]

It was an astonishing piece of double-think when it was quite clear to all that most of the criticism against the BBC was that it denied the three and a half million Catholics their true identity in the Mass and that broadcasting watered down their dogma. The conference spent a good deal of time on criticisms that there were too few services, too many from studios, and certainly too few Catholic broadcasts around Easter; the clergy were vetoed and censored; and the RACs were unashamedly Protestant. Welch replied that it was not a matter of numbers alone but quality, and above all, a willingness by broadcasters to accept some 'production' with a view to making themselves understood. At least he could say that, now that he had a Franciscan on the staff, all these complaints would not go unnoticed!

Indeed not. From now on Andrew would be a direct link between the BBC and the Bishops through Cardinal Griffin, who called for a report of the situation for presentation to the Bishops during their Low Week meetings. Andrew presented the first in 1947: 'Relations between ourselves and the BBC are good', he told their Lordships, 'but it is clear that in spite of some progress we are still in the experimental stage of Catholic broadcasting and much remains to be done before we can feel that we are making the fullest possible use of apostolic opportunities.'[35] Cardinal Griffin might have gone along with notions about broadcasting to non-Catholics, but was understandably more concerned with fair shares to begin with. He had told Andrew the year before:

> It is time we refused to receive the crumbs from the rich man's table and either got out of broadcasting altogether or [had] what are our proper rights. The more pressure we can exert on the Religious Advisory Committee the better.[36]

With the departure of Welch and a new Director, Francis House, the situation looked considerably brighter for the Romans. The key notion in religious policy was 'reflection': the BBC's task was to present as faithfully as possible the wide diversity of the Christian church presence in British culture and society. In 1948 House was beginning to think about the broadcasting of the Eucharist and the Roman Catholic Mass: broadcasting must accurately reflect what was going on in the mainstream churches.[37] Agnellus was naturally pleased and the confidence of the hierarchy was secured – at least in part. There were the occasional disputes between the Corporation and the Catholic authorities. In 1948, for example, Westminster Cathedral would not give permission for a Third Programme broadcast of Elgar's *Dream of Gerontius* – presumably not because of Newman's hesitation before converting to Catholicism! It was because secular broadcasting did not belong in the sacred space of a cathedral.

In 1949 Andrew was taken up with the vexed question of teaching new scientific theories to children in the schools output. A dispute between the Corporation and the fundamentalists had simmered since well before the war and had involved a discreet lobby by both Catholics and Protestants together. *How Things Began* was a series for schools which tried to explain the theory of evolution. Barbara Ward had entered the campaign, and told Arnold Lunn that the Roman Catholic position was getting a better voice now that Andrew had more than a toe-hold in broadcasting policy. Ward objected to evolution being taught not as a theory but as proven facts; Andrew had to keep the *Catholic Herald* informed, particularly as it was prepared to carry letters from angry Protestants: he told House that these broadcasts were 'disturbing to many of our child listeners'.[38] The Corporation persisted all the more confidently because the CCSB had firmly endorsed the series, particularly as the objective was to explain and elucidate the theory and not teach it as a fact. A good deal of protest was muted for this reason.[39]

Another principal cause for dispute between the hierarchy and the Corporation itself was the issue of birth control. It too had a long history, going back to Iremonger's time. The Catholics were not the only protesters, but were forcefully committed to oppose any promulgation of the subject in the talks output. Andrew's energy was directed against the Corporation's Talks Department, aided by the sympathetic opinions of such as Harman Grisewood and Barbara Ward (a Governor since 1946).

Andrew's effort was directed mostly towards the religious policy and gaining an increase of Catholic broadcasts. He recognized the reputation that Catholics had developed as bad broadcasters, and expended great energies to 'produce' as many such people as he could visit. He was also committed to the argument from numbers which had been opposed by the Corporation since Reithian days. He had a particularly difficult time in Scotland, although he always appreciated the good relations he enjoyed with the BBC staff there. In Scotland there were roughly one and a quarter million fully paid-up members of the Kirk and nearly half a million Roman Catholics, with the Episcopalians and others trailing far behind. In 1948, however, out of just over one hundred Sunday broadcasts on the Scottish Home Service, only five were Roman Catholic. Andrew's energies were indefatigable: field work was necessary to counteract the lack of enthusiasm among Scottish Roman Catholics, who generally believed that they had no future in Scottish broadcasting.[40] He felt the situation was not being helped by the rather young Roman Catholic member of the Scottish

RAC, who opposed the broadcasting of the sacrament just as did his Presbyterian fellows.

House and the Advisory Committee could only reply that notwithstanding such inequity in the proportion of time, Roman Catholics had a distinctly sectarian and often bombastic approach to broadcasting: they wanted to present what they saw as the truth and the whole truth. House counselled Andrew to urge his colleagues to resist the temptation to pursue their identity so vigorously in their broadcasts. It would only provoke controversy. The emphasis was upon training in order to bring the best people to the microphone and assist their utterance: they must be subtle. There was no censorship, Andrew told the hierarchy: he was there now to help a broadcaster 'say what he wants to say as effectively as possible to this audience in this medium'.[41]

As the audience for the Light Programme increased, it was clear that Catholics would have to participate in this programme along lines that Andrew admitted to the hierarchy would not be 'altogether congenial to us'. Any traditional and distinctly Roman Catholic utterance would raise considerable resentment; there was enough already. It was not only the Protestant right wing which complained. The more that the policy of reflecting the church at its widest continued, the more this Protestant sector expressed its opposition. Suddenly 'our Catholic friends appear to have more than their fair share of programmes'.[42] As the regions expanded, House replied, the Catholic presence in the broadcast religion output increased. Archbishop Geoffrey Fisher was equally concerned that the Roman Catholics were 'exploiting their positions in the BBC as they try to do everywhere' and, along with the Free Churches, were undermining the dominance of the Church of England in the broadcast output: 'The great majority of listeners should hear Church of England services.'[43]

In preparation for the Festival of Britain 1951, House wanted a strong ecumenical witness over the air, and suggested that all the Protestant churches combine in a special service from St John's, Waterloo Road (the church nearest to the main Festival site), and that the Roman Catholics broadcast Mass from Westminster Cathedral. Both Fisher[44] and Garbett complained indignantly that this would give the Catholics a premier position in their own cathedral, while the Church of England would have to 'muddle in' with the Church of Scotland and the Free Churches. House was obliged to yield to these protests; apart from the opening service from St Paul's Cathedral, at which Fisher preached, on the first Sunday of the Festival each of the three churches had its own separate place. The preacher at the Roman Catholic High Mass was Mgr Ronald Knox, and Scotland too had a fitting Presbyterian counterpart. In connection with another state occasion, the death of George VI, House reported later on 22 April 1952 that Fisher had refused to take part in any evening interdenominational service unless the BBC would broadcast 'a fully representative Anglican service in the morning'.

Andrew went on diligently collecting statistics to support his case for more services. The Catholic appeal to numbers should have been convincing,[45] but neither the Corporation nor CRAC was prepared to be convinced. What did pay dividends, however, was his whole-time involvement in the training of new talent. Catholic programmes were on the increase, and the number of acceptable Roman Catholic broadcasters had grown in a few years from a handful to almost a hundred. In 1950 another conference of the BBC and the Roman Catholics was organized, this time to increase the flow of ideas between the Corporation and the Roman Catholic members of the RACs around the country. The policy, everyone knew, had been made clear time and again; it was a chance for these men to recognize its implications for the dissemination of Roman Catholic teaching. Archbishop Masterson of Birmingham could not but agree to the bald statement that 'BBC religious broadcasting was designed for the outsider: it was evangelistic'. He recognized that this end could only be achieved by sacrificing or compromising the Catholic position. It was an irresolvable dilemma, although not thought to be so at the time.

In the broadcasting of the Mass, for example, it was crucial to make what would otherwise be a musical performance into an intelligible broadcast with the aid of a commentary. Bishop Ellis of Nottingham insisted that only with a substantial commentary could the event be described, in all its significance, to a non-Roman church audience. House explained that he only aimed at a commentary which would enable the untutored listener to know what others were doing at any given moment; such a listener could hardly be expected to enter into the experience.

The conference was mostly concerned with the question of how to sustain integrity in Catholic teaching without arousing the wrath of the majority. Andrew felt able to draw a distinction between (a) the provision of the full Catholic teaching over a period, in such a way as to be intelligible and even persuasive; and (b) only providing that teaching which would be acceptable to those outside the church. He rejected the latter as a betrayal and totally dishonest. It was a question of tactics: Catholic teaching should be diffused and interlaced with the teaching common to the mainstream churches. In this way, ordinary listeners would become in some measure familiar with Catholic thinking. There was enough programme correspondence to support this.

The 1950 conference marked a significant move forward in relations between the BBC and the Roman Catholic leadership. House was prepared to have a policy *aide memoire* submitted to the members which would interpret clearly the Catholic response to the policy laid down earlier.[46] The BBC policy, as defined in his Policy Document of 1948, was to broadcast the Christian faith 'as it is found in the Bible and living traditions of different Christian denominations'. According to the new statement, Roman Catholic broadcasters were 'in principle expected to transmit the full depositum of Catholic teaching' and there was to be no ban on doctrine that would 'provoke antagonisms'.[47] Certain subjects however required 'special handling': it was a question of tactics.

Agnellus Andrew made it clear that there was a long way to go before Roman Catholic teaching gained its rightful place in the nationwide output. He was now working full time in pursuit of these objectives but needed assistance. Soon he was given an assistant and finally transferred to London from his base in Manchester as a full member of staff of the RBD. This satisfied the hierarchy that their interests were at last being fully protected.

It was now the task of the Roman Catholic church to educate itself and its clergy to make Catholic dogma intelligible to the unschooled audience. By the end of the decade it would become clear that the Catholics, like the Protestants – if they talked dogma – were talking to their own, as did other acceptable minorities.[48] 1951 at any rate was the most profitable year since the war, Andrew assured the Cardinal; he had convinced two bishops, Ellis of Nottingham and Masterson of Birmingham, who were now working hard for religious broadcasting, and through them he had put hierarchical weight behind the co-operation of Catholics with the BBC. Things had never been better.

C. 'Home', 'Light' and 'Third'

Professor Asa Briggs has outlined the genesis of the immediate post-war innovations in programme and audience definitions.[49] For their part, CRAC and the department were immediately encouraged to pursue possible programme ideas and were concerned with the intermix of mission, education and evangelism. The Home programme had always been for the broadest possible audience and Welch's talks and services had to keep to Maconachie's strict demands. With only one wavelength at home, religious broadcasting had been under strain to produce programmes which would appeal to the various sectors of the population without any overt educational preparation. The programmes thus ranged from five minutes before the news to the weekday talks to which Welch still had virtually a prescriptive right.

For the new Light Programme, the constraints were similar to those that had applied to the Forces Programme. As Briggs explains, it was to be an entertainment programme. CRAC saw it differently; in setting up the new programme, the Corporation should be just as much obliged to provide a place for an appropriate religious utterance in time of peace as it had to the troops for their welfare in time of war. CRAC wanted a 'daily service'. Gorham, former editor of the *Radio Times* (now Controller of the new programme) would accept religion only on Sunday where it would be seen to belong by the bulk of the audience. Welch was predictably impatient; religious broadcasting would only suffer by this traditional pre-war separation from normal weekday broadcasting.[50] He wanted a short weekday talk by Professor Norman Snaith and was passionately confident in the appeal of such a talk: 'three and a half minutes of humanity and one minute of sting in the tail.' Haley, the Director-General, agreed with Gorham in not wanting religion on the Light Programme during the week. It was for entertainment of high quality, and the presence of religion would only serve to cheapen the religious contribution in such an explicitly non-erudite and non-reflective atmosphere. Welch presented the case for some form of Daily Service on the Light Programme, particularly as this wavelength served the large numbers confined to hospital beds with radio centrally tuned to the Light. People naturally wanted to be entertained and some form of daily service would be to their benefit. Subsequent Controllers (Collins and later Chalmers) accepted a five-minute service each morning, *Five to Ten*.

The other staple items on the Light Programme were *Sunday Half-Hour*, the *People's Service*, and a hymn programme organized by Eric Fenn, *Think On These Things*. All three programmes were designed to teach the Christian faith with the greatest simplicity and as a preparation for evangelism: this was a new idea. *Sunday Half Hour* had been built for the Forces in 1940 and had gone out ever since as an evening service on the overseas wavelength. At the close of Welch's term, the department was divided over just how 'radiogenic' this programme could be. They all agreed that it must be popular. Successive audience research reports showed an audience of around six million,[51] and yet Welch remained troubled by the easy presentation of hymns and the temptation for preachers to broadcast what he called 'sermonettes', a brief amalgam of dilute theology. The comparable morning service in the Light Programme was the *People's Service*, with hymns and popular preaching.

Discussions had begun during the war on the so-called 'arts' programme. Welch was animated by the idea of religious programmes quite unlike those on either of the other two services where standards could be sustained without the problem of 'selling' the substance or devising measures to either attract or retain the audience. He wanted discussions like *The Anvil*, and more drama, church music from a strictly liturgical angle, and perhaps University sermons or the sermons of great preachers of the past. Here was the opportunity for sustained adult education in biblical exposition and detailed series of talks on strictly pastoral issues. George Barnes, the first Programme Director, straightforwardly told Welch that even though there might be religion on the new wavelength his department had 'no right to a place in the programme'. In short, he didn't want religion 'isolated like an infectious disease, but rather let it be the common cold which is always with us'.[52] Barnes wanted new church music and in respect to drama was suspicious of the label 'religious' in connection, for example, with the Sayers cycle. Drama would have to deal with matters of life and death and issues of faith and philosophy. As to whether there could be a revival of the *Anvil* discussion and talks or debates on issues of faith and scientific thought, it would all depend upon the advice of CRAC on the issue of controversial broadcasting. Barnes wanted talks by Karl Barth and world figures in theology and church. But in no sense was he prepared to admit the style of sermon which campaigned or lobbied for any kind of commitment. Welch had hoped for an appointment of 'chaplain' to the Third Programme. The names of F. A. Cockin, James S. Stewart, C. H. Dodd and Austin Farrer had been mentioned. The department was eventually to appoint the Assistant Director of Religious Broadcasting to be particularly responsible for talks specially in the Third Programme. One of Welch's last reports on the extent and scope of routine religious broadcasting made no mention of the contribution of the Department to the new programme.[53]

22

PRESSURE ON THE CHRISTIAN CARTEL

With the post-war reorganization and the development of the three wavelengths, religious broadcasting was under increasing pressure over fixed points in the schedule and in respect to audience figures. CRAC was to be challenged with two major problems: the timing of the Sunday evening service and more consequentially, the breaking of the monopoly which CRAC in the name of Christianity, and not of 'religion' *per se*, had effectively enjoyed since the very outset of broadcasting in 1922. For questions about access to the microphone by non- Christian religions, the fringe sects and the Humanist (Rationalist) lobby, CRAC had simply informed the Corporation that either they could not offer advice or that any attack on Christianity could not be tolerated; this 'non-advice' amounted to a veto on the fringe bodies who, though not part of the mainstream, constantly claimed their Christian orthodoxy as did the Christian Scientists. The Rationalist Press Association constantly claimed a democratic right to question the Christian bias and monopoly in the programmes. But when CRAC thus 'advised' the Corporation fell into line.

A. Sunday policy

Before the end of hostilities, with the arrival of Haley as Director-General, it was made clear that the RBD could no longer claim its right to a fixed place in the centre of the most popular period in Sunday broadcasting: the one hour preceding and following the 9 p.m. news, itself sacrosanct and highly regarded by Haley. On St George's Day 1944, for example, Maconachie wanted Shakespeare's *Richard II* in two parts (from 8.0–9.0 and then 9.30 to 10.30). The writing was on the wall; there was a request for the evening service to be moved to the earlier time of 7.15–7.55, the hour when the nation was or should be at its evening worship. The broadcast this particular day was from St

Martin's, now under Eric Loveday who would not allow a broadcast from an Anglican church during service hours; a well established principle as well as a tradition was at stake. Welch was keenly aware of the division of loyalty. He appealed to Temple: 'I don't honestly think it is unreasonable of the Corporation to make this special request in view of all that they have done for religious broadcasting since the war began – not to mention the expenditure of £30,000 on religious broadcasts – I don't feel I can press my objection any more.'[1] Temple was fully aware of the implications, he recognized the BBC's generosity, but if *Richard II* was to go out instead of the service it would be 'the thin end of what would be a very damaging wedge'; he would say no more, but would 'resist that wedge being driven home'. The issue would have to go before CRAC in October. A compromise was devised, and the evening service was broadcast from 7.45 to 8.25. Welch had consulted his CRAC sub-committee, Eric Southam, Martin D'Arcy and Sydney Berry. Two issues were in debate: the notion of Sunday broadcasting (the Reithian notion of Sabbath 'seriousness') and the predominance of the church-going public among the listeners to the evening service; they would face what Welch knew would be a conflict of loyalty and would 'raise up a crop of trouble for us with the clergy'.[2] Already as the broadcast addresses and sermons gained in reputation, particularly through the new sermon courses, the clergy were becoming increasingly critical of and even more embarrassed by the competition of broadcast services; let the broadcast service overlap the local church service hour and people would stay away unless their loyalty was very strong. Southam advised Welch that as long as the churchgoing public could get back for the address, 7.45 was acceptable. D'Arcy had no opinion on what he considered a particularly Protestant squabble. CRAC was firmly against the competition implied by the change of time and wanted its mind clearly recorded. The new time drove a wedge between the churchgoer and religious broadcasting and would discourage those who wanted both to listen and to attend church. Moreover, 'it seemed unfortunate that the work of religious broadcasting should fight against the work of the parson in his church'.[3] Welch was appalled by this ungracious and hypocritical view, particularly as the Committee at the very same meeting could discuss the Sunday morning *People's Service* on the Forces Programme, which coincided precisely with church morning service hours, and conclude that 'invalids and those who could not attend church might join in worship with their fellow Christians'.[4] This was not a question of principle; the evening service was a straight broadcast from an outside church. The clergy would resent the competition and the loss of a potential congregation among the Home Service audience, rather more desirable than the Forces audience who, it could be assumed, would be quite outside the boundaries of the 'committed' and would have to be enticed to listen. There was no certainty that they could be encouraged to attend in any reckoning.

The Committee pressed the issue yet again in the context of post-war reorganization. Sunday was more than ever regarded by Haley as the 'quality' broadcasting day. Welch knew the wedge was being driven home. He had been doing his utmost to educate and prepare the clergy through diocesan conferences and nonconformist assemblies.[5] Haley decided that the disputed 'clash was not outrageous'[6] and agreed with Nicolls that 'the quiet classic is the right thing for Sunday night' to follow the service. CRAC raised the issue again in 1946; the Dean of Manchester, chairman of the North Region RAC, led the attack. The broadcast service should be later or shorter but certainly should not begin before 7.45. Haley was determined to preserve for the classics the 'hard won half-hour before the 9 p.m. News' and asked Silvey for statistics. His reply included the crucial observation that by spring 1946, the Light Programme audience had gone from thirteen per cent to thirty per cent.[7] Thus the evening service was under much more severe competition from the dramatic serial or *Grand Hotel* or even *ITMA*. The change to 8.0 would not remove this competition (unless, of course, no churchgoers, potential or actual, listened to such programmes). Silvey told Haley simply that a service from 8.0 to 8.40 'would please far fewer listeners than would be disappointed by the disappearance of the serial'.[8] Lindsay Wellington, Controller of Programmes, told CRAC that the earlier time was 'best calculated' to serve the interests of the general body of listeners.[9] (Ironically, Wellington could not be present at this meeting of CRAC and asked poor Welch to read the statement for him.) The BBC's concern was the general public; the churches were concerned about their congregational numbers. But the Corporation was no longer quite in the service of the churches as in pre-war days: Wellington's statement marked a significant break with the Reithian tradition.

B. Controversy: policy change, 1947

Ever since the series *God and the World through Christian Eyes* in 1931 Iremonger and the Department had hoped for a measure of debate between Christians and non-believers. Controversy, however, remained forbidden by the churches. Welch had planned the successful series *The Christian Looks at the World* in 1940 and hoped for a 'return match' – *The World Looks at the Christian*. It was rejected by the Home Board, which did not approve his objective: to 'air the convictions of the sincere critic and doubter of Christian dogma and to allow the church to answer'.[10] The BBC was coming increasingly under fire from the Rationalist Press Association (RPA), the Radio Freedom League and *The Freethinker*. All had kept up a vigorous campaign since the twenties and regarded the BBC as the most 'dangerous instrument of misdirection in this country'.[11] The Corporation remained firm; Kenneth Adam told the Managing Director of the RPA, F. C. C. Watts, that the Christians were a minority of some substance and were thus allotted 'one-thirteenth' of its broadcasting time.[12] More letters of protest began to flow into the corporation as a result of Welch's broadcast, 'Religious Broadcasting in 1942', which was predictably 'mainstream' in orientation. C. E. M. Joad in *The New Statesman*[13] thought the RPA lobby would now prove a test case of the BBC's policy: 'It is to the BBC we must increasingly look to circulate ideas . . . and not only the official and majority opinions – of a people fighting for liberty.' The RPA stepped up the campaign with a fifty-page pamphlet, *BBC Religion* by 'Clericus', and canvassed Conservative Party HQ, which resulted in the War Cabinet Office requesting the Minister of Information for a statement of the relevant facts. In an exchange in the Commons, the Minister, Brendan Bracken in reply to a question, said, 'I am in favour of controversy on the BBC – of course I am.'[14] He would not be pressed further to question the BBC on religious discussion.

In 1943 Fenn and Welch had managed to persuade Maconachie (Controller of the Home Service) to mount a series of six talks on *Great Religions of the World*. The attempt to include a rationalist speaker was not successful and it was left to Nathaniel Micklem to give the final talk on Christianity. As a result of this series Julian Huxley asked Barnes, the Director of Talks, for a series on Humanism; Maconachie, with what he thought proper regard for the opinion of CRAC, simply told him that the most he could expect would be 'factual exposition free from any suggestion of propaganda'.[15]

Maconachie was irked that Huxley's text went automatically to Welch who, for his part, notwithstanding his reservations about the ban on the Rationalists, was nevertheless unhappy with Huxley giving this one isolated talk; he wanted a consecutive presentation. Maconachie thought it quite irrelevant whether or not Welch agreed with Huxley's paper: the question was whether it was fair and accurate. Welch, with Nicolls, believed that CRAC's ban on controversy in 1928 applied to all the BBC talks output and not only to those of the RBD. Maconachie disagreed, although he accepted that care should be taken to see that Huxley did not proselytize. Welch had his doubts: 'If the dykes [of the 1928 ban] are breached by this talk, we must be ready for the flood.'[16] The upshot was a series of three talks on Humanism, with Huxley, Gilbert Murray (the Greek scholar and League of Nations enthusiast) and J. H. Oldham, who had the last word.[17]

In an important appeal to the Director-General in February 1944, Welch formally requested leave to move further away from the 'mere reflection' of church services and the 'orthodox presentation of Christian claims'.[18] Rationalists and Unitarians were pressing their claims, and the church, like religious broadcasting, could no longer expect to shoot and not be shot at. 'Whilst the old CRAC assumption was that calling Christianity into question on the air would be to give offence', the time had now come for free discussion so that the Corporation could take an initiative in which 'basic issues on which religion rests may be shown to be worthy of debate by competent minds.' This was the crux of the suggestion; Welch and the Department had no intention of allowing Christianity simply to be a target at the microphone. There would be discussion by serious highly qualified, and recognized philosophers or theologians. In particular, it would look at Christian dogma, how bridges could be built between its area of discourse and those such as science and technology, and the popular philosophical assumptions beneath various popular notions; there was as much a popular misunderstanding of science as there was of theology. 'The Christian must take his chance with the rest.' But Welch's paramount concern was respect for truth. Against the background of the Nazi and Soviet domination of their media and the state machinery for control of propaganda on both sides, debate in Britain must at all costs be free of propaganda, slogan and half-truth. 'But in one important field' Welch lamented, 'broadcasting gives the impression of one-sided dogmatism – that of religion.'

Thus it was as a priest of the established church as well as a servant of the BBC that Welch sought to bring Christianity to the 'Areopagus' of radio so that the Christian could take his chance along with the rest. He had the integrity of the Corporation in mind: it gained nothing from protecting Christianity from intellectual ruffians and only gave the impression that Christianity was a matter of 'emotion rather than truth'. 'A faith which dare not defend itself is unworthy of the times and remote from authentic Christianity.' The Corporation had a duty to the public; there was an area of discussion 'still hidden from the multitude' and it was the Corporation's task to refute the common half-truth that Christianity was intellectually disreputable. There was also an incompatibility of utterance: pulpit exposition was out of reach of the critics, and was usually in a declamatory or didactic style not amenable to a seminar-styled analysis which asked penetrating questions. The clergy were, in effect, hiding the faith; the BBC should now expose it.

> The true climate of Christianity is free discussion, not protection, and its worst enemy is indifference and not antagonism. . . . BBC religious broadcasting will fail its purpose and our people if it does not meet this critical situation by abandoning its sheltered position and coming out into the market place for free discussion – for that is where most of our listeners are.[19]

Haley, still Editor-in-Chief, was entirely in agreement. CRAC should not only discuss the question but recognize a few salient facts: Christianity 'cannot pick and choose its critics', and if, in such discussion, arguments are to be real, things may have to be said that are wounding to the deepest Christian susceptibilities. Haley was a journalist and was not tolerant of any sort of sham or 'staged' discussion; it would be a 'disservice and a violation of truth'. The proposal should first be approved by CRAC; Haley hoped that these proposals of Welch could, if properly handled, 'prove a great advance in the service which wireless can perform for religion'.[20]

CRAC was asked to discuss the issue at its meeting in February 1946, for which Welch prepared a well thought-out statement. He made it clear that Christianity might in future have to be defended by the 'use of reason alone', but at least Christians, whether ordained or not, would not be asked by the Corporation to organize an attack upon themselves. The practical outcome would be threefold: debates between, for example, Huxley and C. S. Lewis; discussions on the subjects of reason and rationality; and programmes which analysed the variety of religious belief through the testimony of various believers. CRAC called an extraordinary meeting for June 1946 and the outcome for religion in the BBC programme was profoundly significant.

Woodward rightly warned the meeting that it was the 'most important and serious subject upon which we have had to deliberate during the whole time of the Religious Advisory Committee'.[21] The presence of Powell and Haley made it clear, as Woodward indicated, that they both wanted to take as much account of the committee as possible. Perhaps unfortunately, even Woodward in the opening discussion immediately construed the central issue in terms of the broadcasting of 'anti-Christian' views, which was not exactly what Welch envisaged. The issue was not merely about an attack on Christianity so much as a greater freedom of discussion. Welch had made it abundantly clear, however, in his preparatory statement of

February that anti-Christian broadcasts were the problem. Woodward also made it quite clear that the issue was, in effect, whether they supported or were opposed to Welch's claim that freedom of discussion was desirable; did they think it was harmful to the Christian faith? If it had value, then what of those Christian propagandists outside of the mainstream groups – Christian Scientists, Spiritualists and others? The two issues were part of the one major question which they now had to face.

Haley explained that the Corporation was under pressure from a Parliamentary group of RPA enthusiasts which hoped for change in policy and had applied continuous pressure.[22] But CRAC was, in a word, against any substantial change; it was particularly resistant to any kind of attack on Christianity. The Committee was broadly in favour of allowing 'sincere statements of non-orthodox beliefs'. That, Welch claimed, and the Committee accepted, was, in effect, the *status quo*; there had been a series on Humanism and one on the World's Great Religions. Bishop Wand of London thought that opponents of Christianity had space and facility enough in press and publications, and that there were so few who were openly hostile that space in broadcasting time was unjustified; the population as a whole would not care for it. John Baillie thought there was some evangelical possibility in the opening up of broadcasting to alternative views, and particularly to atheists and rationalists: 'by giving them a little more rope they might hang themselves.'[23] He thought that there were simply too few who followed the thinking of Huxley. The vast majority may have a vague religiosity 'but would not recognize themselves at all if they heard Huxley speaking'. The Roman Catholic Bishop of Birmingham, Masterson, believed that it was quite out of the question to allow a public utility to attack the roots of a Christian country: if the opponents of Christianity were denied the use of radio, that was 'surely a thing to thank God for'.

The Committee was not prepared to support Welch as he had hoped. By and large, all wanted more serious discussion but, at the same time, they wanted the Corporation to control and organize any discussion so that the Christian position was not subject to any attack. Furthermore, they wondered how Haley could expect churchmen to advise him how to organize opposition to the teaching of the church when, as Welch assured them, the RBD would not actually be taking the decisions about the programmes: that belonged to the Talks Department. The Committee was prepared to allow discussion only if it were conceived in terms rather more of recital than rapport. They realised that the question of who would decide and 'umpire' the discussion would lie with the Talks Department; they would doubtless consult the RBD whose advice would not, however, be binding. CRAC believed that the BBC should no more grant a prescriptive right to anti-Christians than to anti-monarchists. Baillie did however say, 'A faith by which a man lives, whether he is Julian Huxley or anybody else, is something to be respected.' Wand, on the other hand, thought some would make capital out of the notoriety which went with public attacks on established positions: 'If we open the door, we should be very careful how far we open it.' Wand was not in favour of opening the door at all.

The Committee recognized the power of radio over the young and the 'untutored' who would, perhaps, have no real chance to hear a considered reply. It would be important for the BBC to mount a discussion in which the interests of Christianity were properly protected by programmes arranged in such a way as to present a balanced view. But even so they feared such exposure to untrained ears. This was precisely Welch's point: 'We are failing in our work and not helping people to meet the arguments they are meeting every day on the air.' Remarkably, it was only Aubrey, the Baptist, who fully supported Welch; he argued that the greatest obstacle to Christian proclamation was not hostility but indifference; and there was no way of gaining people's interest comparable to strong controversy. There must be no attacks on the person holding the belief, but Christianity itself must come under attack on the air just as it did increasingly in contemporary published discourse:

> If we get the attack and if we have got the answers, the BBC might create so much interest in the religion of this country that all the churches would find such opportunities as they have not had for a long time.

Aubrey concluded that they would do more harm than good by not allowing 'much fuller freedom' than the BBC had done up to that time.

Aubrey's was the lone voice; the Committee endorsed a proposition drawn up by Baillie and Woodward:

> The Committee do not feel able to advise a general opening of broadcasting facilities to anti-Christian speakers, but are of the opinion that some further experiments should be tried in giving opportunities for the sincere representatives of non-Christian views to explain their views.[24]

It was a vindication of the *status quo* and a clear index of CRAC's underlying assumption that the Corporation was a public utility in service to both Christianity and the churches; however vigorous the discussion between Christian and non-Christian belief, ideology and moral philosophy, however fast changing the substance of that discussion, however shallow and slogan-ridden it might be among the various age-groups and educational levels – all these factors were subordinate to the commitment which the Corporation surely had to maintaining the Christian and thus the church lobby, notwithstanding all the arguments about freedom and democracy which had so often figured in religious dicussion during the war.

At the close of the meeting, Welch officially announced his resignation to take effect from the coming October. He had set in motion a policy which would profoundly alter the relationships of the churches to the BBC; but he would not participate in its implementation. To his disappointment, the Committee also decided that the pressure from Christian 'sects' though strong, was insufficiently significant for the BBC to use broadcasters outside the mainstream churches.[25] Woodward as Chairman urged his view that the Department was committed to Christianity and should not invite people outside the mainstream churches. As in the pre-war discussion it was, of course, for the Corporation to decide whom it would use to broadcast on religious (as contrasted with distinctly Christian) subjects. Here CRAC refused to advise; this would, in effect, be to have the Christians structure their own downfall. In short, CRAC's attitude was rather negative.

The question was passed on to the Board of Governors at whose meeting in November Haley presented a document in the light of the CRAC meetings and the deputation of Rationalist MPs. Had the Rationalists and others a 'prescriptive' right to the microphone, he asked. Whilst the Corporation could not cater for every minority, he believed that the BBC had always aimed to widen the opportunity for freedom of speech, and now it was time 'to widen this freedom further'.

As to whether controversial broadcasting would wound Christian susceptibilities, he believed that various series so far had allowed the utterance of non-Christian views without propagandist fanaticism; he did however, fear this from the RPA; he thought they would probably never be satisfied. On the BBC and its relation to the so-called 'Christian Country' debate, Haley reminded the Governors that whilst it had constantly been the policy of the Corporation to spread Christianity – as CRAC had emphasized in June – his own view was that 'there could be no higher duty than the search for the truth'.[26]

In October, Haley had received the Parliamentary deputation from the RPA including Bertrand Russell and Alderman Joseph Reeves of Greenwich. They had asked for free discussion of religious issues in order to stem the apathy on the subject. More to the point, they wanted broadcasts provided for people 'on the other side of the line' between Christian believers and non-believers of all kinds. Haley realized that it was a thorny issue; Welch and the RPA were in effect ranged against CRAC. The BBC, Haley told them, had to govern the pace at which progress in the search for truth could be undertaken. Moreover it had a variety of responsibilities and not only this one. Somehow it had to keep within the climate of contemporary thought and retain that which was most vital to all its actions: 'the respect of public opinion'. For Haley that public opinion was impregnated with a sufficiently powerful Christian sensitivity as to be prescriptive for the Corporation's approach to religious controversy. The RPA might well ask for its share of broadcasting time to reply to the Christians, but it was not the only minority group. The Corporation had to choose between one and another, and there were advocates of all manner of opinion perhaps by no means as sophisticated as the RPA. Controversy could degenerate into crude attacks or mere recital. The Governors could not risk the loss of public goodwill, however, tenuous its relation to formal Christianity.[27]

The Board of Governors decided to 'hasten slowly'; against CRAC, controversy should be confined to 'round table' discussions where challenging statements could be taken up and countered immediately. Nevertheless, there was to be no suggestion of representation or the prescriptive right of any sect to the microphone. The Governors seemed timid in the face of CRAC's influence. They instructed Haley to present to CRAC the practical implications in terms of critical programmes, and more immediately to develop the policy concepts more distinctly.[28] This he did in March 1947. He stressed that the Corporation's highest duty was to 'search for truth', and this could not be done without controversy. The BBC would act as censor and be 'prepared not only to be accused of behaving in an arbitrary manner but actually to do so'. CRAC had little to say, except that it would watch the experiment with interest and it understood the motives which had prompted it.[29] The decision was made public that same month.[30] Haley was determined to find a new arena where religious questions could be argued.

Following the public statement in March 1947 a series of affirmation and discussion programmes were mounted by Anthony Rendall, Controller of Talks, and the RBD, although its contribution was advisory only. In the summer of 1947 *Why I Believe* had a variety of speakers affirm their belief. The series included J. B. S. Haldane and Bertrand Russell, who spoke of the faith of a Rationalist.[31] It was made clear to each speaker that in no sense were they to regard themselves as representatives of minorities. The Christian Scientists, who were constantly hammering on the BBC door, would not take part, as they would accept nothing less than a programme to themselves, as in the USA. A more complex series of discussion under the general title *Belief and Unbelief* followed in the autumn of 1947, and attempted some structured debate between Christians and non-Christians. The producer, Robert Waller, felt that the whole series was rather better than the previous one, but nevertheless suffered from the dampening spirit of the Governors' policy statement. It was negative and even oppressive; people were frightened to participate without enormous preparation – the time for which they simply could not afford. T. S. Eliot turned down the invitation for this reason. Looking back on various attempts between 1947 and 1950, Somerville believed that the series were not so successful as could be hoped for two principal reasons: time and resources; the Talks Department had insufficient people and, moreover, thirty minutes was simply too little time in which to conduct an intelligent discussion ostensibly free from contrivance and, what Haley wanted above all, to avoid humbug![32]

During the years following Haley's policy change, the notion of controversy would be restructured into what became known as 'fundamental debate'. By this terminology the Corporation not only retained the initiative but created a conceptual framework in which, it was believed, any such discussion should take place, and avoided the problems of democratizing the air waves by providing spaces for Rationalists and others who clamoured to say what they pleased, rather in the style of the party political broadcasts.

The CRAC response had been protective and lacking in imagination at a crucial moment in post-war history when it was becoming quite obvious that the broadcasting monopoly of the Christian 'mainstream' churches could no longer be justified. Pre-war fears of giving offence to the majority and later the single wavelength had both ensured the inviolability of the establishment mainstream influence with both the Governors and the Heads of Departments: Christian Britain had to be reflected, supported and inculcated in broadcasting policy. But change was now inevitable.

The extraordinary meeting of CRAC in June 1946 had shown just how suspicious the churches were of broadcasting and the BBC. Whatever the Corporation's commitment to 'Christian Britain', broadcasting could not remain the private reserve of the Christian establishment. Haley, for the first time since Reith's days, moved the Corporation away from this position towards a more democratic attitude, greater freedom in the exchange of ideas, and the questioning of belief. Rather than support the initiative of Welch and Temple,

CRAC decided that since it could no longer retain complete control, it could hardly advise the Corporation on an approach to religious and particularly the theological issues which could only weaken the mission to which CRAC believed the Corporation itself was committed. Against Welch's advice, the Committee clung to the notion that the Corporation should protect what it saw as the faith of Britain from the newly enfranchised inheritors of the post-war culture. After the meeting of June 1946, the initiative to bring Christianity into the centre of contemporary debate was lost to the Christian establishment and would not be regained, not, at least, in British broadcasting policy.

c. Talks policy

As we have seen, when Welch succeeded Iremonger, he was determined to wrest the Christian output away from Sunday and onto weekdays where it could articulate more vigorously what Christianity could say to the nation at war.[33] Welch had fought hard for and won two fixed talks slots on weekdays, in addition to the midweek service and the daily *Lift Up Your Hearts*. In a vivid way and notwithstanding the criticism of Maconachie and others, Welch succeeded with his available force of articulate exponents. The Tuesday evening talk was the pivot of the various mission series of talks, *The Anvil* and discussions; it was virtually the 'property' of the RBD. Notwithstanding Welch's ability to ward off his critics, religious talks came increasingly under fire, in particular from Rendall and the Talks Department, concerned as they were with standards of spoken word and its production.

With the war over, the compulsion to maintain an orthodox Christian utterance gave over to increased questioning of the Christian monopoly and its hold over certain spaces in the schedule, even on Sundays. With an alarming drift of the Home audience to the new Light Programme[34] Haley gave Wellington, as Controller (Home Service), encouragement to make the best of the Sunday programmes; it was after all 'the BBC's best day of the week from the point of view of professionalism and distinction'.[35] Welch wanted above all to educate the churchgoing Christian as well as that sector of the non-churchgoing public favourably disposed towards Christianity. In a ten-page enquiry following a series of mission sermons (*Man's Dilemma and God's Answer*) five thousand listeners were asked for their suggestions for future 'educational' talks on subjects where their knowledge was uncertain. The list was almost endless: people were as much puzzled by theological and biblical language as by the state of the nation and complex moral issues. This survey was by no means only drawn from churchgoers.[36]

When peace returned, Welch had the benefit of two regular weekday evening times, for the midweek service on Thursday and the religious talk on Tuesdays. Several series had been organized involving international affairs, biblical history and a particularly provocative series, *What is a Christian Country?*, with such eminent thinkers as John Maud, R. H. Tawney and Gordon Rupp. Early in 1946, however, Welch was under pressure from Wellington; the regular, fixed slot on Tuesday would no longer be protected and predictable; the post-war situation demanded greater flexibility and no one department had a prescriptive right to programme time. By spring 1946 Welch had devised a series with the broad and ambitious title: *What is Happening to Us? – A Christian Interpretation of Civilization.* He persuaded Wellington that it would 'show what resources there are in Christian faith for coping with the situation'.[37] However Wellington told Welch that he could not assume this 10 p.m. Tuesday slot would be his of right; after September, the Talks Department would be making its claim. This was bad news for Welch, particularly as the regular Sunday series, *Christian News and Commentary*, by Micklem had been replaced by a weekday talk in a more popular reportage style by John Foster, entitled *What are the Churches Doing?* Fenn was profoundly unhappy about the pressure to make the doings of the churches more 'popular'; he was all the more concerned because Foster himself was acknowledged – not least by Wellington – to be a more acceptable broadcaster than Micklem. Fenn was sure that such popularizing trivialized the fundamental issues and thus created an unwelcome form of propaganda.[38]

In August 1946 the Home Board decided that this programme too could no longer continue in the regular weekday slot. In the post-war period there were pressures upon broadcasting time from industry and commerce, and the churches simply could not expect to maintain what many producers regarded as a propaganda programme at the very time when the BBC seemed increasingly to be taking a journalistic approach to questions of balance in the presentation of diverse opinions. Welch's response was to decide that the midweek service should give way to a programme which might reach a much wider audience, and not only one of churchgoers. Fifteen minutes of Christian comment on Thursday evenings would be of much more value than nine minutes at an earlier time on Monday evenings.

Both Wellington and Welch expected volumes of protest from the churches, and not least from CRAC; the midweek service was a long-established tradition, going back to 1931. However the Committee was sufficiently impressed by Welch's arguments to agree to the change. He was about to leave his post, and wanted to secure this principle for his successor.

The change from a service to a 'reportage' programme represented an 'important conviction', he told Wellington the day after the CRAC meeting: 'It would be a retrograde step if we were to incline, however slightly, to the restriction of religious broadcasts to the broadcasting of church or studio services.'[39] It marked the first attempt by the RBD to venture away from recital and argument (services and straight talk) into 'talking about' – the explication of various church and Christian motivations, initiatives and enterprises from a somewhat more 'objective' position. Welch intended to mobilize a regular body of listeners through the press, diocesan bishops, clergy and ministers. He encouraged CRAC to spread the word.

Wellington, meanwhile, was considering other radical departures from the Christian monopoly; he suggested that the regular religious talk on Tuesday should be the responsibility not of the RBD but the Home Division which, of course, embraced Rendall's Talks Department. Welch had to comply in order to keep the one regular Thursday evening fifteen-minute period for his Department. The Tuesday programme would be run by the Talks Department. It was agreed that Tuesday evening would be for the 'serious treatment of philosophical, ethical and religious thinking' and Thursday for 'reportage'.[40] However much advice the RBD might give, the Tuesday talk had now been removed from its orbit of control. The first series was to be by Professor H. A. Hodges of Reading, on *Philosophy and its Relevance*.

By the close of 1946, Welch had gone and his place was temporarily taken by the Methodist Kenneth Grayston. He was highly regarded by Grisewood and Wellington and both sides recognized the rules of the contest. During the interregnum, Grayston was left to negotiate for the Christian interest both on the Thursday (midweek service) time and the Tuesday 'values' space. He told the rest of the Department that Christian talks programmes would only get on the air if Lindsay Wellington could say: 'This is a good and welcome pressure on programme space.'[41] Whilst Wellington accepted Grayston's contention that a balanced religion output must include talks as well as services, the talks programmes were those over which the hierarchy would exercise considerably more control. Indeed, there were producers in the Talks Department who firmly believed that religious programmes, if they must be broadcast, could be tolerated only on Sundays. This lobby was very strong. Grayston and the Department were forced even more keenly into the discussions about objectivity in reporting.[42] Grayston maintained that religious talks were to be distinguished from sermons (which could only be properly understood in the context of an act of worship). There were three classifications: the first was exposition of Christian truth, apologetics and its relation to other viewpoints. This class usually belonged to the Tuesday evening 'values and controversy' space. The second category was the application of Christian principles to contemporary affairs and everyday life. Again this belonged to Tuesdays but would be heard now only occasionally. The third category was reportage of Christian activity at home and abroad. This belonged to Thursdays, and by spring 1947 Wellington told Grayston that he was 'not disposed' to continue anything like *Christian News* here; the Department had to produce a more attractive programme, relevant and appealing to a bigger slice of the listening audience. Foster's programme had again appealed to a 'minority of a minority'.

During 1947 Foster left for the Selly Oak Colleges and the Department evolved a new programme – *Christian Commentary* – which aimed to help listeners develop standards of judgment in political and social affairs on the basis of the Christian faith – not by direct exposition of Christian principles but by examples from current events on which the formation of judgments by Christians was required. It was a significant shift from the church's holding a place in the schedule to talk to itself and to others about itself. It was a Christian view of current events. It was now clear that in the Home Service's serious output, Christian talking was not going to have the opportunity it formerly enjoyed; it would have to make its contribution within the wider service of broadcasting. Instead of one presenter as in previous schemes, there was now to be a team of four: Oliver Tomkins, Kathleen Bliss, A. C. F. Beales and F. A. Cockin. Grayston defined the aims as the examination of fundamental Christian issues against a background of contemporary events together with new trends in Christian opinion and action.[43] By the close of 1947, moreover, it was increasingly clear that the Home Service was losing considerable numbers to the Light Programme where serious talks of the type modelled for the former would not be acceptable. Whatever adaptations could be contrived for this audience, the Department now as never before had to compete for the ears of the Home audience. If it was going to talk at all, it would have to be intelligible, not simply for fear people would switch off their sets – that was nothing new – but because of the danger that the hierarchy would withdraw the microphone.

23

FRANCIS HOUSE AND WILLIAM HALEY: NEW POLICIES

A. Oxford discussions, 1947

In autumn 1947, Francis House joined the Corporation for the second time, this time from the World Council of Churches. He shared the Catholic emphasis within Anglicanism and was fully aware of one important aspect of his task at the BBC: to bring the leaders of the churches as closely in touch with the BBC hierarchy as possible. In Geneva, House had rubbed shoulders with Christians from every part of the world church. Whereas Welch had sought for the articulation of a central Christian 'message' above confessional and denominational boundaries, House recognized the dangers of a 'vague undenominational Christianity without dogmatic basis' – as he told CRAC at his first meeting after taking office. He was adamant that there could be no return to the 'emotionalism' of the 'radio personalities', pressure for which Welch had resisted so vigorously. But nor could there be any more of Welch's supra-confessional Christianity beyond the bounds of the denominations. Professor Briggs' view of the change of Director is rather too simple; far from there being 'no major change of direction', the differences were fundamental; it was not merely a question of 'a certain change of emphasis'.[1] Welch had known only too well that without a tenacious and unswerving BBC commitment to an as yet untried ecumenical utterance, broadcasting would simply encourage a species of 'free-for-all' between the Christian confessions, determined, as they might so easily become, to see that the balanced plurality which obtained in the country at large was duly replicated in the BBC output. He would be proved right.[2]

On taking up his post, House wasted no time; he visited various RACs and also consolidated the thinking of a conference on religious broadcasting which Grayston had convened at Oxford. As well as the Department staff and House himself, Majorie Reeves, Kathleen Bliss and Frank Gillard had been among those who met in June to examine the state of the world to which religious broadcasting should address itself. House was also motivated by *Puzzled People*, a study of popular attitudes to religion which had been conducted by Mass Observation for the Ethical Union. While it did not claim to be typical of the whole population, it did represent a significant sample of urban attitudes. In his preface the Ethical Union General Secretary spoke of the disturbing findings of the report: the ignorance and confusion of those who call themselves Christians and the disintegration of orthodox belief: it had left a vacuum 'which will be filled by worse if it is not soon filled by better'. And there was worse to come: 'The principles of Christianity have failed to save the masses from desultory living.' Churchgoing was much reduced and ordinary people, including some churchgoers, were ignorant of the Christian faith. Whatever its limitations, House thought *Puzzled People* was impressive and worrying.

Like his predecessor Kenneth Grayston, House lamented the success of a popular technological mentality which attacked what was in effect a spurious sort of Christian dogma which in turn defended itself with the weapons of the last century. Fr Martindale had been one who constantly complained that the BBC supported a style of hollow liberalism which encouraged scientists to speak on theological issues with little respect for the canons of theological utterance. Scientists like Huxley and Hoyle had a reputation for attacking the claims of Christianity in a way that angered theologians and those who wanted such men to conduct the debate according to at least some sort of equivalent of the Queensberry Rules. Some opponents thought such rules were written more often than not by theologians rather than philosophers; it was a clash of unsharpened wits wherein the contestants came out of their respective corners but missed each other by yards, while the onlookers – or listeners – were left merely confused. The BBC, said House, should be educating them.[3]

House shared the widespread concern at the post-war lack of improvement of social conditions, the threat of atomic conflict – not to mention the coldest and most prolonged winter since well before the war; all conspired to bring the nation 'face to face with a breakdown of public morale'.[4] The ordinary man, House's conference believed, wanted meaning rather than proof and thus the RBD must take a threefold theological initiative in re-laying the foundations of Christian dogma at all levels: the affirmation of the fact of God, the Christian concept of a moral universe and the Being of God against the background of tragedy and fear.[5]

It was further clear to House's Conference that of those who listened to or were exposed to the BBC's religious output, the large majority heard it on the Light Programme.[6] It was clear, as *Puzzled People* had said, that far fewer than these were actually in church. The whole Department was well aware of this striking but safe assumption, and believed that, however superficial might be the listening and whatever the motivation – intellect, sentiment or nostalgia – this vast audience must above all be taught. House insisted, as Welch had before him: 'We cannot afford a policy of merely going round one church after another trying to find good broadcasters.' Against the increasing pressure to have the Department's microphones in every church in the country, House wanted tried and tested men for this new initiative; the regions would have to accept them. It was not enough, as Welch had wanted, to mount the controversial debates in the market-place; House believed there could be no such debate so long as the nation remained in ignorance of the Christian fundamentals. House's 1947 Oxford Conference had recognized that the new 'deep concern' about human life was 'not at home in Christian jargon' and was 'set on edge by the missionary desire to exploit this perplexity in the interest of speedy conversion'. The nation had above all to be taught the essential nature of that Christian faith represented by the Christian denominations – there could be no suggestion as there often had been by Welch, of supradenominationalism. The Department was agreed, moreover, that whatever else it did, it had a responsibility to 'proclaim the gospel unequivocally'.

B. Clamouring sects

House inherited CRAC's decision of 1946 on 'mainstream' Christianity and also the increasing clamour from other Christian bodies regarded to a greater or lesser degree as 'orthodox'. The three most important, or perhaps most formidable, bodies were Moral Re-armament (MRA), the Spiritualist National Union and the Christian Scientists. These three, as opposed to the more widespread Rationalist lobby, had made formal request to the corporation for space on the air for talks and 'services' with a view, naturally enough, to putting their own case and propagating their claims to Christian orthodoxy. During the thirties each of these three groups had formidable supporters of whom the Corporation was obliged to take note. For MRA there had been the Earl of Athlone, for the Spiritualists Lord Dowding, and for the Christian Scientists Lord Lothian and the Astors; the Christian Scientists had maintained the most persistent pressure on the BBC on grounds of religious orthodoxy rather than of the BBC's duty to democracy and to allow open access. The policy of CRAC remained as it had since the earlier days of Unitarian pressure; any groups not regarded as 'mainstream' were invited at the corporation's somewhat theoretical discretion. CRAC was bound to say that the Corporation was free to invite whom it wished to the microphone, but in fact the BBC usually withheld invitations, either from fear of CRAC censure or for other reasons – including perhaps the importunity of the groups in question!

On the Spiritualists, the BBC followed the ruling of the Church of England as expressed by the Archbishops' Committee and its Report on Spiritualism of 1938, which in turn had been influenced by an investigation in the USA by Herbert Thurston, SJ.[7] In 1948, the Spiritualist National Union, which was celebrating its centenary, requested a series of talks but was refused. Barnes and the Home Service Committee agreed to some discussion at a future date, but stipulated that this celebration should not be marked by a programme devoted either to the Report or to elucidation of sectarian propaganda.[8]

Moral Re-armament also celebrated an anniversary in 1948 – its tenth – and wanted to broadcast. Its celebrated founder, Frank Buchman, reached the age of seventy that year. House had sufficiently convinced both Barnes and Haley that the MRA was not a religion nor a denomination and that, apart from Buchman, there was not one representative suitable to be invited to give a talk on the MRA's coming conference in Caux in Switzerland. After ten years House was sure that the MRA had ceased to be an 'exclusively' Christian movement. Buchman's recent speeches, House observed, contained no explicitly Christian content – there was no mention of Christ or the church or any fragment of Judaeo-Christian tradition, but merely a call to change.[9] MRA was offered a part in some discussion-style programme in which other views and questions would be put. Barnes and Haley were influenced by T. S. Eliot's castigation of the movement in *The Idea of a Christian Society* (1939), in which he had described it as an abuse both of Christianity and of the English language. Haley on this advice decided that such a broadcast might provoke widespread complaint from the churches; moreover 'we ourselves would be acting as MRA publicity agents'.[10]

The Christian Scientists had contended since 1923 that on the basis of both numbers and orthodoxy they had a justified claim to a place in the schedule of broadcast religious services.[11] But CRAC had, predictably, refused, and the Governors had tactfully supported them. In 1941, however, they accepted Barnes' judgment that though the existing ban on services should remain, Christian Science was now one world view among others which might deserve a place in a series such as *What I Believe*.[12] The Christian Scientists declined this invitation on the grounds that it diminished their status; they wanted a place for a 'service'. After the war the Board encouraged further discussion between Lord Astor and Haley.[13] Notwithstanding a somewhat frantic appeal by Lady Astor to Haley in March 1949, the 'mainstream' churches were secure in the programmes allotted to the RBD. Christian Science did, however, renew the challenge to the churches when giving evidence to the Beveridge Committee in 1950.

C. 'The Aims and Achievements of Religious Broadcasting': Francis House

In 1948, the lobbying of myriad groups[14] in pursuit of a place on the air called into serious question the Corporation's attitude to its historical commitment to the Christian churches the plurality of which considerably concerned the Director-General. Haley himself examined some issues of broadcasting policy in his Lewis Fry Memorial Lecture to the University of Bristol, *The Responsibilities of Broadcasting*, in May 1948. An important task of broadcasting was, he claimed, 'education in the field of citizenship' and that 'the educational responsibility of broadcasting towards all spheres of the individual's and of society's development shall not be diluted.' Moral responsibility transcended all others and 'in every point of its contact with the community, it can seek to establish standards and values and to show that the search for truth is endless and an end in itself.' 'The search for truth' had become almost a slogan. The publication of this speech had significant repercussions. The Secretary of the British Council of Churches (henceforth the BCC), David Say, invited Haley to elucidate this point further at the Council's November meeting. C. S. Woodward, now Chairman of both CRAC and the BCC, wanted Haley to examine the 'moral responsibility' more fully and the BCC to examine the whole issue of broadcasting: it might even appoint a commission, particularly in the light of the forthcoming charter.

As House took up his post, Lord Simon of Wythenshawe became Chairman of the Governors and, to House's surprise, took a particular interest in the religious affairs of the Corporation. In February 1948, Simon addressed CRAC and raised questions about religious policy which he hoped might be investigated afresh. House wanted a new approach to policy and furthermore the BCC Commission, Woodward had intimated, would require an accurate statement of any new BBC policy in respect to Christianity. The outcome was a substantial report prepared by House and Silvey, 'The Aims and Achievements of Religious Broadcasting: 1922–1948', which examined the extent and character of the programmes, the audience listening and, for the first time, a picture of clergy attitudes.[15] The report would be presented to CRAC in October 1948.

In Part I of his report, House reviewed the pre-war and wartime policy, quoting BBC handbooks and in particular the thinking of exceptional men like Sheppard and the Bishop of Ely's Report of 1931.[16] There had been a significant shift from Sunday to weekday activities: by 1948, out of twenty-four regular programmes, eighteen were on weekdays. The major difference was, of course, the policy change of 1946/7 which admitted controversial programmes; it represented for House 'a challenge to the Christian churches to substantiate the claim of Christianity to be true'.[17] It recognized that the persistent claims by Rationalists, churches outside the mainstream, opponents of Christian claims on philosophical grounds and many others opposed to the Christian monopoly in broadcasting policy had to be taken seriously and that churchmen were no longer able to hide behind the pre-war and wartime protections upheld by the Board of Governors. Now at last, said House, religious broadcasting can 'carry out the critical side of the Christian apologetic which otherwise goes by default'. He recognized, as some in CRAC certainly would not, that the initiative for the broadcasting of philosophic views and those of minority religions would move further away from the RBD towards the Talks Department under the policy direction of Barnes and later Harman Grisewood, Director of the Spoken Word. House predicted (accurately and somewhat to his regret) that whilst this policy would not affect the general output of his Department, it might well 'affect the climate in which the Department does its work'.[18] It was a subtle and crucial observation.

As we have shown, House was aware that for all Welch's prophetic innovation and his struggle to extend religious broadcasting, the war had protected Christianity against attack in a way which Welch had regretted. One positive effect was that the Corporation spoke – as did Parliament – of the country being Christian at root, and said that the war had been a fight for a righteous Christian cause which underpinned aspects of British politics. House was aware that Haley was impressed by the notion of a Christian heritage and that he wanted the RBD to concentrate on a single mainstream line of church utterance which would enter the arena of controversy without fear. House, on the other hand, wanted both some reflection of denominationalism in religious broadcasting and also respect for the vast majority who might be outside the churches but not outside the influence of Haley's 'Christian heritage': there had to be debate and attacks on established positions as well as chances for the churches outside the mainstream to air their views. For House, education was crucial: at the least it was putting the record straight and removing false but popular notions of the Christian faith; at best it was preparing the ground for the keenest utterance of Christian dogma in its most simplistic form: this would be done by the clergy. House also had to contend with the growing autonomy in the regions and in Scotland.

House was impressed by Haley's Lewis Fry Lecture, and his concept of a 'cultural pyramid aspiring upward'.[19] The listener would be induced . . . to discriminate in favour of the more worthwhile. Haley had spoken proudly of the Light Programme, which had decreased its variety programmes by a quarter with a resultant increase in the audience: 'Each programme must be ahead of its public' to afford a compelling inducement 'but not so much as to lose their confidence.' In terms of religious programmes, the bridging moved from the Light Programme, with the vast number listening to *Sunday Half Hour* and the *People's Service*, through services and talks on the Home Service to the Third Programme and its 'highly specialized mission to the intelligentsia'. In this way, religious broadcasting could achieve its principal aim: 'to make Britain a more Christian country'. House noted that it had far too long neglected the interests of the churches themselves: it must be linked more directly to the churches as they actually were; he wanted the non-churchgoer to recognize that Christian commitment involved active congregational and denominational participation. This was peace time. Nowhere had Welch called for a response in quite this way. Religious broadcasting must now, said House, 'reflect and proclaim the faith of the churches'.[20] (Agnellus Andrew and the Roman Catholics were specially delighted to hear this.[21]) It must concentrate on the creed and beware of 'fostering a kind of disembodied Christianity or "radio religion".' This could be achieved by innovation, experiment and teamwork. Religious broadcasting had to give a lead by putting out what the churches intended to do at any critical moment, in a way which assisted the churches in doing what they intended.[22] It was for his Department to become fully and increasingly aware of what was about to happen in the churches. Above all, House concluded, religious broadcasting was 'a continuous teaching mission . . . its intention is evangelistic and its methods must be mostly educational.' By courses and well-planned series, broadcast over long periods, each denomination could have its 'crack of the whip' and need incur no loss of prestige or identity in the broadcasting schedule. However, when the minorities were given space to 'make positive statements of their distinctive convictions', the mainstream churches must express deeper commitment to denominational balance. Welch's visionary ecumenism was superseded.

Part II of House's report was concerned with listener research statistics based on comparative figures for two 'typical' Sundays in 1948, and were the results of 6000 interviews. Silvey's figures showed clearly: (1) that there had been an enormous shift from the Home Service to the Light Programme and a serious decline in the weekday audience for Home Service religion programmes; (2) that churchgoers formed a small minority of those who listened to religious broadcasts; (3) the total Sunday audience for religious programmes amounted to something approaching 13 million, whereas only around 2–4 million were in churches;[23] (4) most listeners on Sunday were working class and most were women. However fragile these findings (and House recognized their methodological limitations) they tended to confirm what he had for long believed.

House had also made use of a BBC clergy mailing list. Out of 500 questionnaires sent out in August 1948, only 140 were received with any useful reply.[24] The predominantly Anglican results of the clergy questionnaire showed that the influence of broadcast religion was regarded positively by the 140 who replied. A considerable proportion thought broadcasts gave the greatest help to Christians on political, social and international issues. Fifty per cent recognized the place of religious broadcasting for parochial work and the value of making a link between them. A larger proportion had the rather vague hunch that religious broadcasts helped 'maintain the religious consciousness of the listening public' but by way of criticism believed that there was a serious lack of any clear link with the churches. Religious broadcasts were otherwise too academic and parsonic.[25]

House had his own beliefs confirmed and to some extent elucidated: above all that there was a vast audience, perhaps as many as seven million, which listened to one or both of the major Light Programme 'hymn-based' liturgical hybrids: the *People's Service* and *Sunday Half Hour*. The churches, furthermore, must above all be enrolled or dragooned into greater co-operation with the broadcasters in the teaching of the fundamentals of the Christian faith in these broadcast spaces: an evangelical objective through an educational method. The nation must be taught the rudiments of the faith. House believed he must attempt in the general output what the Schools Department was doing with sixth formers: to lay a foundation of Christian 'course work'. Unlike the pre-war Sunday lectures for the committed, the general audience would now have to be induced, enticed and encouraged to remain: this enormous listenership would have to be entertained; dogma would have to be made 'popular'.

CRAC, however, received 'Aims and Achievements' with guarded enthusiasm and recognized the dangers not only of complexity and 'SCM religion' but also (in the light of House's preoccupation with the Light Programme) over-simplification.[26] Archbishop Masterson of Birmingham joined with Mervyn Stockwood in wanting both simplicity and complexity: simplification meant broadcasting to the vast Light Programme audience in platitudes. They also wanted 'definite dogmatic teaching' which would attack and challenge the directly prevailing anti-Christian philosophies such as Marxism. Mervyn Stockwood clamoured for more time to examine the Marxist claim from a Christian point of view.[27] House defended his insistence on the importance of the large Light Programme audience and told CRAC quite simply that it was a question of finding the right men who could communicate Christian dogma with the necessary simplicity whilst retaining the integrity of the churches' belief. Dogma, he knew, was not simply explained.

House had been invited to discussions with the hierarchy before Haley's lecture to the BCC, *Moral Values in Broadcasting*, in November 1948. The future religious policy of the corporation was about to be hammered out, and would last more or less intact for about a decade. House recognized that whilst religious broadcasting (like schools and political broadcasting) was purposive, the Corporation must ask to what extent it was obliged to support that objective. He reflected to Barnes and Somerville that whereas the BBC had, from the beginning, been committed to the maintenance of the Christian faith, that objective had been considerably modified by the wartime problems and the work of Welch. Welch had believed that all broadcasting should support a Christian world view. A discipline had been imposed by the establishment and BBC hierarchy upon Welch and his churchmen.[28] It also entailed a similar 'discipline' imposed upon the BBC by the churches, who were not prepared to tolerate any encroachment by those outside the mainstream. In 1948, the pre-war safeguards on the Christian place in the schedules were under considerable strain not only from opponents of the Christian monopoly but from within the Talks Department and other programme departments. Ironically, Wellington and Nicolls had fought against the radicalism of Welch to protect the notion of a Christian heritage as Haley would do against House's convictions about pluralism. Haley wanted the Christian tradition in Britain to speak with one voice, whereas House knew that CRAC would only remain co-operative if it knew that the BBC was not committed to pursuing further the special 'BBC religion' associated with his predecessor. And it was not only CRAC that was restive. The Regional Committees were somewhat surprised that House had not given them notice of his intention to review the 'Aims and Achievements'. The most vocal disquiet came from Scotland and the North Region. Regions were no longer 'colonies' as they were in Welch's wartime 'emergency'; they were now 'dominions' and had their own autonomy in planning. The nations and the regions must reflect their local ethos, temperament and denominational character. For CRAC not to realize that the local Religious Broadcasting Organizers were employed to serve their religion first and foremost was an illusion. R. W. Falconer put the case for all in no uncertain terms: had House consulted the regions, the information in his policy document would have been all the more definite.[29]

In the 1928 *BBC Handbook* a piece by Dick Sheppard had spoken of constructive idealism, standards of values and the prevention of any 'decay of Christianity in a nominally Christian country' almost in one breath. Welch had consistently taken a radical view of this tradition in his discreet promotion of the Reithian view that Christian values were not the custody of the churches alone and that the BBC had a duty to pursue this constructive idealism which rested finally upon a Christian foundation. House believed that the purposive broadcasting by his Department should reflect more accurately the plurality of the faith as it was believed by the 'mainstream' churches and others. His ecumenical background had made him acutely aware of the diversity of the worldwide church and, consequently, that the broadcasting of religion by the BBC had not only to 'commend the faith' but allow the many churches to do it each in their own way. There should, however, be no bellicose sectarian propaganda: the denominations at least deserved their identities.

House also recognized that the BBC itself was no longer committed to making the country more Christian. He was aware, however, that there was now considerable goodwill among the leaders of the churches and particularly that sector active in the relatively new British Council of Churches.[30] They also recognized that in House they had a 'churchman' who would encourage them to enlist their constituencies towards a greater co-operation with the Department. David Say, General Secretary of the BCC, told House that if the BCC were to commission an investigation, it would 'ultimately be of use to your department'. The 1947 policy change on controversial broadcasting had provoked some tentative 'debate'; in this area the BBC in its commitment to the 'search for truth' tried hard to regulate the conflict between rival propagandists and ideologists. Kathleen Bliss, the Editor of the *Christian News-Letter*, was employed to do just this. In Talks policy, the Corporation remained nominally committed to Christian values, although House complained vigorously and repeatedly that he did not get enough of the 'values' space to which the 1948 policy 'entitled' him.[31] Grisewood and Somerville, for their part, complained that the churches simply could not produce good enough speakers who could resist the temptation to be propagandist; the churches were doing too little in any concerted way to purvey and disseminate the values of that sort of broadcasting which had been designed to present the church to the churches. *What are the Churches Doing?* was soon replaced by Grayston's programme, *The Christian Outlook*[32] and yet remained the programme with the smallest listening figure in the Department's output. Designed for the churches, it became the symbol of the Department's struggle for a regular commitment not wanted by the Talks Department. House claimed it was not even parallel to the 'service' of the Corporation to other minorities such as farmers! It had all to do with a concept of Christian Britain and the BBC's part in its promotion.

House wanted guidance and this was why Bishop Woodward had invited Haley to address the BCC in November. Woodward was concerned that the ecumenical aspect of broadcasting policy should not only take the form of the well publicized protest of the Churches' Committee on Gambling of July 1948. It had embraced all the churches and also the BCC but Woodward regarded it as negative and question-begging. The BBC's responsibility to Christianity and to the interests of the churches was not at all straightforward and clarification was now urgent: simple protest was not enough.

D. *Moral Values in Broadcasting:* William Haley

In his address in November 1948, Haley left the British Council of Churches in no doubt of his commitment to Reith's standards to a degree which would have delighted Welch.[33] *Moral Values in Broadcasting* was the most considered analysis by a Director-General since Reith. The Corporation, he said, had an overall duty to do the 'right thing', and whilst this duty devolved upon every member of staff, it was finally the duty of the seven Governors to 'distinguish right from wrong'. This duty was embedded in the moral traditions of Christian Europe which animated the Corporation's search for truth and its concomitant quest for editorial impartiality. This applied to Christianity; hence the policy change of the post-war years and the BBC's commitment to controversial broadcasting. Haley asked the churches to accept the rough with the smooth. Doubtless to the relief of his audience, the BBC was not neutral where 'Christian values' were concerned:

> We are citizens of a Christian country, and the BBC – an institution set up by the state – bases its policy on a positive attitude towards Christian values. It seeks to safeguard those values and to foster acceptance of them. The whole preponderant weight of its programmes is directed to this end.

This was disputable, to say the least: House, and Welch before him, had been besieged by protests from Christian individuals and groups against the explicit and implicit attack on Christianity and Christian values, above all in the BBC's drama output.[34] House was on shaky ground: it was impossible to have every broadcast play or feature cast into a dogmatic 'Hollywood' mode with the 'moral' tacked on to the end. The churches feared the effects of broadcasting plays which presented alternative moral postures. House demanded not that he might act as censor for the churches but that the Corporation should take account of the 'possibility of negative effects on listeners' observance of moral standard' in respect of any particular dramatic production. Otherwise what could the Corporation possibly mean by its commitment to 'high moral responsibilities'?[35]

Haley's assurance to the churches was in the context of the search for truth: some of the world's greatest drama and literature which could be regarded as anti-Christian would 'certainly' be broadcast but 'our regard for Christian values would "regulate" the number of such plays broadcast'. He put it to the churches that any control or censorship of the general output was quite unworkable; it would only lead to clericalism: conviction and tolerance must co-exist and the Corporation must provide the 'best in all aspects of life' with which it is concerned; it must never 'fail to put the Christian point of view wherever it is relevant'. It was not the duty of the BBC 'in everything it does' to make people accept the Christian faith; that was the duty of religious broadcasting, and Haley vowed that part of his duty was to do 'everything we reasonably can to foster and strengthen religious broadcasting'. He concluded by asking the churches – if they seriously intended to set up their Commission – to look wider than simply the broadcasting of religion and even to answer the widespread complaint that the BBC was leading the nation by a short, sharp route to moral ruin. The churches should look at the broadcasting of information and news; at its encouragement of social services and at educational broadcasting. How can broadcasting enable people to become more committed and better citizens? Haley promised formally to extend the discussions he had already had with House and Fenn to the churches through the special assistance of key figures in the corporation, notably Barnes and Grisewood.

Haley told the BCC that the Corporation would continue to maintain the idea of a Religious Department within the Programme Division and provide a place in the schedule for regular worship. His speech accepted the relationship of the RBD to any possible audience for its programmes. It was to be the area of Christian propaganda or, as the churches would naturally prefer it, 'evangelism'. The churches, however, could no longer expect the Corporation to make the Christian faith 'the criterion for everything it does'; this fact had to be faced. Haley had given the churches a strategy for enquiry and House had provided the data.[36] The BCC decided thereafter to go ahead with its commission, particularly in the light of the forthcoming revision of the BBC Charter by the Government.

The Commission was the outcome of Cockin's commitment and vision; it marked the starting-point of close co-operation between the BCC and the BBC.

Haley, Cockin and House believed the churches should be looking at the issues beyond the horizons of the RBD to the wider questions of broadcasting in society. There were predictably to be two sections dealing with the two main areas: Cockin chaired Section One on the responsibility of the BBC: 'What are the standards and can it be claimed that they should be Christian?'. The members included Kathleen Bliss, Marjorie Reeves and Richard Crossman (as a consulting member). Section Two was more directly concerned with religious broadcasting, and the questions were: 'Who listens and how?' 'What does it do for the churches?' 'Is it efficient?' These were not easily answered, still less so without the co-operation of the BBC and in particular, Silvey's Audience Research Department. The Corporation agreed to make statistics and personnel available and the Council provided secretarial help to make sense of all Silvey's figures. Professor John Marsh was the chairman of this section with Ronald Selby Wright, Kenneth Grubb and others including, this time, a bishop. It is interesting that Section One included Eric Fenn and Section Two Selby Wright, both Presbyterians and both active in broadcasting, but distinctly diverse in their concepts of what broadcasting should be doing.

Cockin was deeply aware of the public relations problem inherent in the disparity between the relatively few broadcasts and the countless examples of the Christian presence in the community at large; the

Commission was to look particularly at this area. In his own section, the uppermost question that had to be answered was the extent to which Britain was a Christian country, and whether Christians could take part in any genuine search for truth, especially in a controversial setting, when it was clear to some that Christians started from certain base points which 'we may not alter or deny'.[37]

Cockin was also concerned to have the churches informed by more than prejudice. It was common knowledge, which had frustrated House and others before him, that the churches in general and the clergy in particular were not greatly committed to listening since so much took place when they were in pew and stall. A good deal of their knowledge of what the broadcasting hierarchy believed was gleaned from press reports. Cockin wanted the co-operation of the Corporation's executive, and because of his own outstanding commitment there was little doubt he would get it. Haley's speech in 1948 had been in effect the stimulus of the Commission, but the obvious authority to be consulted was Harman Grisewood: he had just published his incisive *Broadcasting and Society* which above all had taken Haley's philosophy into a Christian environment and examined the problems of broadcasting in a liberal culture from a Christian angle. Fenn, now assistant editor to Hugh Martin at SCM Press, had asked him to do it.

Grisewood met Cockin, Fenn, Bliss and G. A. Coulson in November; the question uppermost in their minds was how far Christian values could be assailed by opposing views and remain Christian? How tolerant could a 'disintegrating' society, as Grisewood had called it, be of opposition to authority, particularly in relation to Christian tradition. The BBC had an enormous responsibility to show tolerance, but he was troubled by the notion which arose out of it – impartiality. Whilst the Corporation had tried to disseminate the faith, the Christian could not 'debase the hard currency of doctrinal definition'.[38] Grisewood shared the belief that concepts of tolerance and impartiality led almost inevitably to indifferentism: impartiality betokened a divesting of authority and the BBC was in danger of heading that way. Not all the staff were Christian and not many of them had read his book![39] The Committee was equally confused over the notions of impartiality and tolerance: without its traditional and hard won autonomy in relation to the establishment, whether in the church, Parliament, education or the arts, the Corporation could only act as custodians of the liberal motivation that would encourage the freedom to speak for whoever wished it. The BBC, Grisewood hoped, would maintain its firm commitment to Christianity. Yet how? This powerful instrument was not an agency 'directly operating for Christian ends . . .

but insofar as they are good ends, we are concerned to cherish them and protect them from degeneration, even when this effort seems to take us no step further towards a Christian order.'[40]

This last sentence was crucial to the future character of broadcasting: the Corporation's commitment to Christianity might not be intelligible to the clerical mind, or commensurate with an ecclesial passion for the refurbishment of belief, particularly as the churches seemed to be declining. It was not a commitment to that 'sectional' interest denoted even by the established churches. That the Corporation acknowledged that it had a duty to protect society could only encourage the churches to look beyond what appeared to some as a threat to faith and therefore to the church. In practical terms, Grisewood reminded the Committee that for the moment the Corporation would be going too far and confusing tolerance with impartiality if it put Christian, Marxist and Humanist propaganda into programme juxtaposition with the suggestion that the audience could 'choose for themselves'. Any insistence on impartiality would simply 'further the work of the disintegrating forces'. The public could not choose for itself, and thus the Corporation was firmly in the business of educating those vast tracts of the population unfamiliar with such propaganda, and quite ignorant of the social, philosophic and linguistic origins of such utterances. The churches were bound to prepare at least their own constituencies to face these issues for fear that they would construe such propagandist utterance in terms of an attack on Christianity and moreover, lay the blame at the door of the Corporation. Grisewood amplified to the churches his caution to society at large; broadcasting could only do so much but must at any rate be in the vanguard of society; and the churches should do more to prepare themselves to face what he believed was the increasing heresy of the times: that the process of repudiating traditional Christianity was itself evolutionary. Such a view could only issue in a free-for-all and the BBC could not be party to this. It was, above all, Grisewood's meticulous thinking which animated the Corporation's commitment to a philosophy of controversial broadcasting which issued in what it preferred to call the Fundamental Debate.[41]

Cockin's Committee examined this very sensitive area once again with the Controller of Talks, Anthony Rendall, who was finally responsible for translating the 'search for truth' into programme terms. He had to admit that the 1947 policy had so far failed.[42] A free-for-all could not be successful: people were simply not prepared to change their minds, and in effect there had been no real 'encounter of belief'. Rendall felt the lack of an intelligent broadcasting philosophy outside the Corporation: too many saw it simply as a platform for recital – the churches no less than others. Rendall, however, believed the malaise was due to the enormous size of the Corporation and the increasing isolation of the output departments. Religion, moreover, was resented by many because of its protected position; furthermore, few others either were aware of or cared about the view of 'high culture' shared by Haley and Grisewood. It was during this exchange that Cockin's Committee decided that the Commission's final report should make it quite clear that Haley's Victorian liberal Christian ethic showed that he 'appeared to have little conception of how the ground had been cut from under his feet'.[43] The Commission sounded pessimistic: 'The past can provide little guidance for the problems of a large-scale industrial society.'[44] Not surprisingly, Haley profoundly disagreed.

The Committee also examined rather less erudite issues, including the overseas output with Ian Jacob, and Scottish affairs with Melville Dinwiddie, who produced statistics to suggest that the Light Programme was beneath the average Scottish listener: many programmes were 'too slick and too topical for them to follow'.[45]

By Easter 1950 the Commission had Eric Fenn's draft, and wanted to hear the views of Haley as Director-General and George Barnes as Director of the Spoken Word. Whilst Haley was deeply grateful that the BCC should have mounted such an enquiry, particularly as he lamented that few had previously been attempted on broadcasting, he was irked by what he read in the draft. The Commission wanted Christians on the staff, but not Marxists; it wanted higher standards; it wanted Haley and his editors to maintain the highest view of what should pass for sound discussion and serious enquiry. Haley told them several times that there were people in powerful places in the establishment and among intellectuals who strongly believed the BBC was intolerant: the Commission seemed to want it both ways, i.e. tolerant exposure of all positions but based somehow in Christian belief. Haley was sensitive to the criticism that the BBC had weakened what was essential to the maintenance of moral values, namely the Christian faith. There was a call on the one hand for the recognition of a pluralist culture, on the other for the centrality of Christian faith.

It was this meeting which convinced Cockin, Fenn and Bliss that the Corporation was in a real dilemma. Haley had made the point firmly: the staff were frustrated by pluralism and themselves suffered from the 'malaise of the times': they were expected to be tolerant and to direct propagandists from disputation to discourse. The problem was, as Haley recognized, bound to notions of democratic broadcasting and the clamour of variant opinions which, until the coming of broad-

casting, had had little or limited dissemination. Broadcasting enfranchised without educating. Bliss believed the Corporation could not
act without the cultural landscape being tilled in readiness for the
broadcast utterance; but this had to be done by others.

Without this meeting with Haley, the Commission might have
sounded quite foolish. He had convinced them that the churches could
no longer be protected in the general output: they should take their own
initiatives, all the more urgently now, since the Corporation would
soon be forced to satisfy wider democratic demands: there would
certainly be more prejudice and over-reaction, not the least by the
churches. The Commission at least avoided this and called for the
churches to 'foster an intelligent and critical interest in broadcasting',
not only to assist themselves but to help the Corporation. With all
Haley's talk about levels of cultural interest in the Light, Home and
Third Programmes, the Commission, not surprisingly, called the BBC
to educate people into being 'better listeners at various levels'.[46] It was,
of course, asking a great deal of the churches too; it would depend on a
whole class of leading clergy being committed to a widespread
educational programme which would involve helping ordinary Christians to grapple with or at least recognize with some clarity the character
and scope of the contemporary intellectual malaise. The Commission
saw religious broadcasting itself as being designed to reach the outsider
quite as much as the churchgoer: there was insufficient recognition of
the need (seen by Bliss and Oldham) for the churches to 'pre-educate
the faithful', at the same time as broadcasting used its opportunity to
'pre-evangelize the faithless'. Section Two, concentrating on religious
broadcasting, had called upon the churches to 'enlarge their own
channels of adult education' if they were to make 'more effective use' of
the BBC material. As Bliss had said in Section One, such material was
in effect the culmination of an analytical and educational process and
untutored Christians should be helped at an earlier stage; such help
was the indispensable prerequisite of lay training. It was quite clear,
however, that the clergy were capable only of the more traditional
forms of construction: they were on the whole not trained in the
analytical methods of modern education.

The churches were now being warned: they had conspicuously failed
to reach the working classes who, it was believed, were nevertheless
listening to popular religious programmes. It was, however, a 'sand-
bag wall' with neither commitment nor participation on the part of an
increasingly non-churchgoing population; it would not hold for long.
The BBC was becoming a channel for diverse, variant opinion. Lord
Beveridge himself would soon be calling for equality and democracy

and even suggesting how the BBC was to conduct its religious business. The central place of Christianity in broadcasting policy would soon be challenged by egalitarianism. But for Haley, the BCC might have failed to face this issue. Whatever course the Corporation might soon have to take, there was now 'fruitful ground between the Corporation and churches',[47] however liberal and heterodox the former might appear to the vocal champions of the old orthodoxies.

24

POST-WAR INNOVATIONS

Since the first broadcast service in January 1924, the Corporation had been particularly sensitive to the charge by the clergy that their authority was being usurped: broadcast religion should be doing for the churches what they could not do for themselves. This was particularly clear in education and in the endeavours of Stobart and Iremonger during the thirties to bring the most eminent scholars to the microphone and so into contact with ordinary church people. Broadcasting was of unique value to the housebound. The other regular services added the attraction of a preacher and so an evangelical opportunity, reaching a wider audience than the clergy could hope to do.

But such broadcast services were not only designed to evangelize; they might also educate. During the war the Roman Catholic Mass was remarkably well received by Protestant Britain. Church of England clergy, however, were not a little anxious that Anglican worship suffered a 'disability' without the sacramental dimension. It was an innovation which would concentrate the debate and emphasize the gap between those who believed that radio enabled like to address like and those who construed it as a species of public relations: reputations were at stake especially when people at worship could be overheard. The churches and the public at large generally rejected the 'service' designed for radio; the Daily Service for the housebound was the exception.

The clergy and the RACs, for their part, mostly resented any innovation which kept people from participating in congregational activity; they rarely faced the fact that fewer and fewer were inclined to do so. Religious broadcasting would have to change and thus become more popular or concentrate more on what the medium could achieve unique to itself. In his review in the *BBC Year Book* of 1946, Cyril Garbett, in his parting remarks on vacating the chair of CRAC, claimed that the broadcasting of *The Man Born to Be King* was 'the most far-reaching and influential evangelical method ever used.'[1] It had been an outstanding use of the medium. Welch had wanted more: the churches and broadcasters should strive for a co-operation which would put the clergy in touch with those who talked back – the thousands who responded to broadcast preachers with requests for help. There was not a popular preacher who did not receive hundreds of such letters. The BBC it, was suggested, could surely innovate and direct anonymous correspondents into an orbit of pastoral care. With the wartime growth of the popular services on the Light Programme, the acceptance of such broadcasts by increasing numbers of homes touched greater numbers who were not remotely given to churchgoing and yet were open to 'pastoral' assistance. No working relationship ever entered the CRAC's discussions; the Department made its own attempt to provide what, by and large, the churches did not: pastoral care for the unchurched and uncommitted.

A. 'Light' and Pastoral

In the Light Programme 'we have to guard against too much speech', C. V. Taylor told the Department at the end of the war, with reference to the long-running Forces programme of hymn singing, *Sunday Half Hour*. It was the most widely heard programme the Department produced, and almost every Sunday evening 'completely overshadowed the alternative Home Service programme'.[2] Welch told the Department in 1946 that *Sunday Half Hour* was definitely not a service – it was 'punctuated hymn-signing', and there should therefore be no 'hortatory sermonettes'. The clergy and the producers had to realize that this was a religious and not a music programme; the essential material lay in the text of the hymns which should simply be explicated by the clergy; otherwise the programme turned religious material into sentimental diversion and sustained the doubtful but widespread view that the RBD exploited the national desire to sing in general and to sing hymns in particular. Or it simply turned the principal component of congregational Christianity into a form of mass entertainment. House's concept of the popular Sunday morning *People's Service* was distinctly apologetic; he thought it dealt with 'the popularly held half-truths prominent in the mental furniture of most.'[3] Richard Tatlock, an Anglican newly recruited to the Department to be responsible for the growing Light Programme output in religion, wanted to bring congregations together to listen and have their clergy preach on the same theme at their evening services. Among the best preachers were William Purcell (later to join the BBC staff), George MacLeod, William Barclay, the Roman Catholic McNarney and Ronald Selby

Wright. Against a canvas of hymn singing, the simple word was designed with varying degrees of success to slip in the apologetics almost unnoticed. Nevertheless, listener research spoke constantly of too much speech, despite the fact that there were usually little more than seven or eight minutes out of thirty!

From the Music Departments in London and in the Regions there were constant complaints that the singing was simply not good enough for BBC standards. But everyone was aware that in this one programme, the BBC – whether Music or Religious – Departments had little or no control over who and which churches were chosen. It was usually difficult to match a good man with a good choir in a good building: engineering, music and regional religious departments were rarely in agreement over the stature of many broadcasts. The great attraction of the programme was that ordinary churchgoers sang hymns to ordinary listeners, and every Listener Research report said over and over again that the seven millions who listened preferred the programme to the Home Sunday evening service over which CRAC had deliberated so intently. The possibilities for a concerted policy in the 'spoken word' of the Light Programme's hymn-singing were limited.

In 1947, discussions began about an altogether more practical programme which might offer the one ingredient particularly associated with the work of the clergy: pastoral care. In all the policy deliberations during the war, Welch's defence against criticism from the church press (in particular that coming from the clergy who were being undermined by the BBC) was that religious broadcasting could not do nor should it attempt to do what the churches could do for themselves.[4] The post-war Department began to shift the emphasis more distinctly towards the churches. Welch had always talked of cooperation with the clergy but had admitted to Dinwiddie in January 1943 that 'religious broadcasting in this country has developed independently of the churches, except for the "unofficial" Advisory Committees . . . the gulf between our work and that of the parochial clergy is too wide.'[5] Nevertheless, the vast number of letters received by popular broadcasters included in some cases requests for enlightenment on an intellectual plane and in most cases assistance with personal problems. John Williams had tried to encourage the clergy to find ways to meet this need. The better the broadcaster the more the letters and the less time he had to reply to them. Those like Weatherhead, who had his own staff, were better equipped than others. In earlier days of the war, John S. Whale received shoals of letters asking for advice on diverse matters which he had little hope of being able to give.[6] In the North Region, the immensely popular programme, *The Parson Calls*, featured the Anglican Wilfrid Garlick who, with Eric Saxon, had organized a programme which sought to answer popular spiritual questions. Garlick was troubled by the vast correspondence he received asking for specific help with particular personal problems. The task was beyond him. Later on William Barclay would receive up to one thousand and more 'from people with heartbreaking problems', as he lamented to House.

The new programme would deal at least with one widespread pastoral problem which constantly featured in the letters to preachers: ageing and dying. There was evidence to suggest that there were problems which might be addressed *via* the impersonal medium of the radio voice. The National Corporation for the Care of Old People when consulted, however, resented being segregated for entertainment and educational purposes but approved the idea of programmes of particular interest to older people. Stuart Hibberd, the announcer, was recruited as the 'sponsor' or 'compère' of talk, song and advice for the sick who were elderly and the elderly who were ageing. In time, Stuart Hibberd was to focus the reassurance of the programme's intention and to become an indispensable part. Tom Chalmers, later the Controller of the Light Programme, wanted mostly, for this weakened group in the population, talks which would bring 'positive comfort without preaching resignation . . . it need not be clerical nor need it be always specifically Christian'.[7] Chalmers, a man of profound Christian belief, wanted straight talks, and not the 'magazine' ideas of the RBD; the programme must be 'pastoral' in that the subjects chosen for the talks would arise from unsolicited correspondence. At a meeting in October 1948 between Chalmers, House and Williams, the question of how to reply to correspondence arose: was there not a measure of pretence in responding to heartfelt cries with a standard BBC acknowledgment? Williams insisted they be answered personally and was told simply that he as a broadcaster was not in business to run a parochial pastoral service for the BBC: it was a painfully crucial question at the centre of broadcasting philosophy. The programme eventually gained its title and began in January 1949 as *Silver Lining*. Within six months, Silvey's Department had produced figures to show conclusively that *Silver Lining* was listened to by a majority of working class women.[8] Silvey was sure that it fulfilled a real pastoral need: a mass of letters to one contributor convinced him of a 'great mass of utterly unhelped misery for which neither the medical profession nor the churches are providing the answers . . . there is no true understanding by either of the relation of religion to emotional problems.' The staple fare of the programmes were simple prayers and 'comfortable words'; for these the Controller of the Light Programme tried to restrain the 'sermonizing instincts' of several – and particularly the lay speakers. The BBC was, after all, doing what the clergy by repute did better.

The emergence of the *Silver Lining* was all the more interesting because the Talks Department from the beginning had no wish to be involved: discussion proceeded entirely between the Light Programme and the RBD. Much of it revolved around the extent of the Christian content of the talks and what was meant by the policy directive that the talks did not need to be always 'overtly Christian'.[9] As the programme continued, there developed four principal styles of talks which it is interesting to compare with Grayston's analysis of Home Service talks on religion.[10] House identified the following : those given by sufferers to other sufferers with no specific Christian reference; talks by doctors and psychiatrists, seldom with direct religious reference; talks on personal relationships on a Christian basis with no explicit Christian moral teaching; finally, specifically Christian devotional talks on subjects such as bereavement and grief, etc. Notwithstanding the exclusive production of this series by the RBD , Anthony Rendall, and later Mary Somerville, who succeeded him as Head of Talks, were concerned to avoid cliché and muddled thinking and in particular, wanted some 'one hundred per cent Christian' talks as well as others which it was agreed should be neither anti-Christian nor 'controversial' in the 1947 policy sense. By 1951 House could confidently boast to Haley that notwithstanding its devotional and 'populist' approach, and notwithstanding a somewhat diffuse or discreetly Christian approach, the listening public, as represented by 4,000 letters, regarded it as a Christian broadcast, and Haley should not admit *Silver Lining* into the arena of 'controversy'; he should not allow invitations to members of the Ethical Union, who were clamouring to be allowed to present alternatives to what they regarded as a one-sided presentation of the world as seen by a receding sector of the population. In this they were wrong; the very considerable audience, mostly over fifty, would not be usefully served if an afternoon Light Programme series became an arena for disputation well beyond the education and the receptivity of this audience.

The programme focused upon an audience not served by the Talks output of the Home or Third Programmes, and enabled the RBD to appeal to that very sector of the population to whom broadcast religious services were aimed at the very outset in 1924; the housebound, and those who because of sickness or frailty were unable to worship with others. *Silver Lining* did more; it distilled a species of Christian utterance which 'whilst reflecting Christian values and experience . . . should not take the form of sermons or apologetics'. Opponents in and out of the churches dismissed it as giving the advice of 'Old Aunty' – the BBC. Others complained of its lack of 'teaching'. It nevertheless succeeded because its 'distilled Christianity without apologetics' deployed the poetry and prose of human example; it focused upon those who had developed faith out of suffering. Professor Emile Cammaerts was a particular favourite for his talks on bereavement, on science and on religion – a subject not normally acceptable as such into the *Silver Lining* arena.

There was, however, always a good deal of pressure against the Christian exclusivism: Tom Chalmers, the Controller, was not happy with the overt Christian bias. By the end of 1950, after two years of the programme, the clergy (including Weatherhead and Selby Wright) had the lion's share of the talks. Chalmers handed the Light Programme over to Kenneth Adam in 1950 and hoped his successor would bring in more lay opinion and biography: 'this talk is not a platform for evangelism; the spiritual comfort afforded by the church is not the only or necessarily the most acceptable remedy.' It was the language of clericalism which could so easily dominate and even 'overpower' the language of comfort which Chalmers eagerly hoped would be penetrating, poetic but without propaganda. The Department clung on hard; whilst House was prepared for a distilled, discreet or even hidden 'metaphysical position', it should remain Christian; he hoped it would not become Freudian, for example! Above all, whatever the speaker's conviction, he must 'respect the claim of the Christian faith to be true'.[11] It was as Tatlock rightly claimed, a programme in which Haley's policy of preserving liberal values was maintained 'under the influence of Christianity'.[12] Gradually the clerical emphasis eased, and under Somerville's watchful eye, the scope of interest widened. Speakers included a T.B. sufferer, and the Chairman of the National Association for Mental Health, a doctor himself suffering from disseminated sclerosis, and a paralysed girl; Dr Gilbert Russell was introduced in later series.

The growth of *Silver Lining* highlighted an argument between the churchmen and the broadcasters over the extent to which preachers could preach in the context of a programme which set out deliberately to provide advice and comfort in specific areas of human behaviour to a specific audience. As in the Home Service, so also in the Light Programme, the RBD was increasingly obliged 'to speak of religion without mentioning it' – a phrase which Welch used of another Light Programme series, *Think on These Things*. Wellington forced the Department's producers to evolve a style of utterance which could be squared with their Christian conscience and at the same time touch various levels of consciousness and meaning in their audiences. Selby Wright had done this supremely well for the Forces. On populist levels, *Silver Lining* spoke personally, and above all to those whose intellectual grasp of a complex analysis and whose education in the formal language of Christian utterance was very limited indeed. It was the product – as Williams had always stressed – of Christian compassion which characterized so little of the BBC's religious output. *Silver Lining* was popular without being sentimental. For Norman Collins, the first Controller of the Light Programme, sentimentality had been the essential character of religious material for this audience. Against this notion, the Department fought to have the bare bones of the Christian faith 'taught' in a framework of popular music, by means of *Sunday Half Hour* and the *People's Service*. The aim was to 'preach through hymns' and 'as far as possible avoid sentimentality, pricking bubbles at times to make people think', as Fenn put it. The RBD believed that sentimentality was fraudulent, and to be resisted at all costs. That was not easy, with Advisory Committees pressing on all sides for a discreetly protectionist policy. The broadcasters, too, were acutely aware of the needs of the sick, elderly and frail listener. Some of them were in hospital, and some provision was made for them by Sandy Macpherson, the cinema organist, with his series *Silver Chords*, from which the RBD made unobtrusive efforts to disassociate itself. It had originated from a Welsh Region programme in 1948, and was produced by Mai Jones as a 'Sunday programme with a slightly sacred touch'.[13] House and the Department had no liking for what they saw as the deliberate sentimentality which prevailed in its choice of both music and hymns.

Another long-standing Light Programme success was Fenn's *Think on These Things*,[14] which formed a Sunday epilogue. Fenn needed at least a summer break, and the Department was looking for a change, and in 1951, after various other ideas had been mooted, House suggested a species of hymn request programme accompanied by brief biographical pieces from those who sent in the requests. It would be called *Sacred Memories*, and would be compèred by the evangelical preacher Tom Rees. Haley was not at all impressed; he recognized the problem of *Silver Chords* and the need to counter it which House felt so strongly, but he also feared the danger of what he called 'sob stories'. There had to be safeguards: 'The BBC should maintain its reputation for austerity and a certain sparingness where the inner things are concerned'.[15] House was confident that he could guard sufficiently against sentimentality and what Haley called 'tabernacle evangelism'.

Kenneth Adam, now Controller of the Light Programme, was totally in agreement; he thought House incapable of an 'offensive or tasteless mishandling' of such a programme but did not care for *Sacred Memories*. Somerville would have none of it and, much to Haley's relief, the title was dropped in favour of *Hymns that have helped me*. However *Think on These Things* returned after the summer interlude and continued until 1960.

The more popular programme of Sandy Macpherson, *Chapel in the Valley*, was a post-war Light Programme innovation and depended a great deal upon sentimentality and the personality of Macpherson himself. House and the Department objected vigorously to the suggestion that the programme was a 'service' and House complained that inevitably the unsuspecting listener would not distinguish between a church and a studio; he believed many were deceived and shocked to discover that the programme was not from a church but from the Hoxton Cinema![16] It was agreed in 1950 that the Methodist hymnologist Dr Leslie Church was to be 'adviser' to Macpherson in the choice of hymns.

Some thought the BBC should not be providing this sort of programme, however well presented, as it could be by producers like Tatlock who believed that sentiment could be used for much more sophisticated objectives. The somewhat reticent Haley knew he had in Francis House a sufficiently conservative safeguard against vulgarity; the *People's Service* and *Sunday Half Hour* were evidence of this. The serious purpose of these 'popular' programmes was to teach the Christian faith.

B. The sacraments and the Mass

In the autumn number of the Anglo-Catholic quarterly *Ascension* in 1948 House and his Department were severely criticized as 'the worst enemy of the clergy'. House answered this criticism with a four-page press release. It was not his fault that listeners preferred church services to those from studios nor that the Light Programme services were popular and well received. Whatever the limitations of all these broadcast services and however likely it was that Light Programme listeners would listen at home and not be seen in church, the most important thing – argued House rather cleverly – was that 'week by week and year by year, the listening public are reminded that there is a "worshipping community" in their midst and that they get the best of it on the wireless.'[17] House here reflected his feelings for Eastern Orthodoxy and the notion of the 'liturgical presence', irrespective of lay participation. If, however, people were encouraged to imagine that they could worship by listening and not acting, House declared that one enormously significant innovation would counter such a belief: the broadcasting of the sacrament of Holy Eucharist. In July of that year the Governors had been persuaded to allow the broadcasting of the sacrament, against all Haley's instincts to keep out of this most provocative and sometimes 'acrimonious' debate.[18]

The discussion on the propriety of broadcasting the Eucharist raised the most serious conflict between the BBC and the churches that had yet taken place. It touched the churches at their most sensitive point; and although the question had hovered for years on the edge of the Corporation's policy, it had not, as yet, come into the open. It raised both theological and constitutional questions and, more than any previous broadcasting innovation, provoked the churches into furious debate which revealed their considerable ignorance both of the nature of broadcasting and of the relations of the Corporation to the churches themselves. Between 1948 and 1950 House attempted to allay the fears of the churches that such broadcasts would, for example, desacralize the ritual or undermine the authority of the priest or, most seriously, promote a concept of 'non-attending' and non-participating communication, a notion which went against the thinking of all the churches without exception.

The Corporation's policy had been relatively clear, if not elucidated since the time of Reith, who ruled simply that Holy Communion would not be broadcast.[19] In 1937 the whole of the Coronation service of George VI was broadcast, including the sacrament, except that at the Consecration and Communion, Iremonger had the listeners switched to St Margaret's for 'suitable' sacred music. As we have noted, Hinsley had requested Midnight Mass for the duration of the war only because of the blackout regulations; churches could not easily be darkened and thus the radio expedient overcame the theological scruple.[20] The issue was vigorously raised at the North Regional RAC in 1945 and after some discussion, the Committee agreed with Mgr A. H. Ryan that 'it is no more possible to broadcast a sacrament than to photograph it!'[21] Anglicans did not have quite this notion of *mysterium*: it was a question of example and – at the very least – of public relations. Iremonger had remained convinced that in the face of the Roman emphasis upon the centrality of the Mass, the Protestant churches as a whole and the Church of England in particular suffered in broadcasting from a growing impression that Protestantism was non-sacramental and bore none of the authoritative marks of the received sacramental faith as Roman Catholicism did. Protestants could play fast and loose with the ritual to suit the BBC. Welch had not agreed with the traditional ban but made no effort to change it. Garbett, however, was much in favour of change.[22]

In 1946 Radiodiffusion Française, which spoke of 'Our Lady of the Ether', published a report in response to criticism by the more orthodox French Catholics.

> We are no longer in Christendom, and so the broadcasting of the Mass has the paradoxical result of making available to all the echoes of the supreme Christian mystery . . . comfort is now given to all those people whom a materialist society deprives of the mainspring of their lives.[23]

House was attracted by precisely this idea: the provision of the sacred mystery for those who might not by inclination make any effort to search for it. In a Christian culture, the established means of mobilizing this experience through broadcasting must be deployed in every way to ensure that society was not deprived.

In October 1947 the vicar of a parish church in Workington made an impassioned appeal to the Corporation for the broadcasting of his Harvest Festival: quite by accident the whole service was broadcast including the Prayer of Consecration and the Communion of the congregation. The broadcast from Workington evoked considerable correspondence which was consistently in favour. Geoffrey Fisher was approached by both clergy and lay people; as many were in favour as were vigorously in opposition. The Workington broadcast was followed by another from St Mary's, Chatham, under Joseph McCulloch, this time, instead of the celebrant giving a 'commentary', John Williams gave both explanation as to what was happening and a declaration of its meaning. Again, reactions were mixed. House sought for a policy guideline and on 24 February 1948 asked CRAC: 'Should not the whole Eucharist be broadcast?' Should it be only in part, omitting the central and sacred Consecration and Communion, or the whole service without restriction? CRAC was remarkably enthusiastic, and particularly stressed its value for the sick and housebound: it decided there should be broadcasts 'from time to time' without omissions.[24] Fr Andrew believed that this was because the Protestants recognized that under House, the Catholics would stand to gain in his policy of denominational recognition. This meant that the Mass would be granted and the Church of England would be under greater pressure to compete.[25]

House prepared his case for Haley and the Governors. His difficulty was the Scottish churches: Waddell of the Presbyterian Church in Ireland was certainly enthusiastic but undoubtedly did not represent the

Scottish Presbyterians; the Scottish RAC would have to decide for itself – as eventually would the Welsh and the Northern Irish committees: CRAC was regarded regionally as a southern and 'centralist' body, and this February decision would not be taken as binding on all the rest, particularly as the Chairman of SRAC, Professor John Baillie, had not been present at the February meeting. On no such matter in the whole history of religious broadcasting had there been such concern with regional autonomy. Until there had been a ruling from Scotland, House's proposals could only be experimental and in turn encourage further discussion in the churches. CRAC had discussed the possibility of twelve such broadcasts per annum, and predictably Catholic Christianity would have the lion's share. The Roman Catholics would want a Midnight Mass, as in wartime; the 'other' churches between them would have a total of three. The Governors were afraid people would 'have their radios on as background'.[26] Publicly, they agreed with CRAC provided that 'special care be taken to help listeners understand'.[27] House and Bishop Woodward worked on the 'safeguards' requested by the Governors, particularly by the Roman Catholic Barbara Ward. There must be an absolute limit of twelve services, and for two years from Christmas 1948, no broadcast was to be arranged by any region without consultation from the outset with the Head of the RBD – this was the hardest to accept, particularly for the least compliant members of House's team, Eric Saxon in the North Region and Ronald Falconer in Scotland. Saxon was concerned that House and the London CRAC had no real knowledge of the preferences of the North Region, where Nonconformity and Catholicism looked quite different. Saxon had trouble particularly with the divided opinions of the Free Churchmen. The President of the Methodist Conference for 1948 was E. Benson-Perkins; he was also a member of Northern RAC. He was deeply opposed to the proposal; he belonged to the 'pearls before swine' school; the service would be received by those outside the discipline of the church. To all the regional criticism, House replied with two arguments: first, that the experiment was for the housebound (a key concept of religious broadcasting since the beginning) and, secondly, that to broadcast Holy Communion would reinforce the notion of corporate worship and the 'inadequacy of mere listening'. The question of the sacred, however, was much more powerful and trailed not far behind issues of both denominational and regional identities. Free Churchmen were acutely aware that the act of communion for them was essentially silence, whereas for Catholic Christianity it was linked to 'recital' – the spoken or sung text which provided a canopy by which 'communication' was hidden or en-shadowed – even obscured – for the bystander or eavesdropper.

It was no real surprise to House that the press got wind of CRAC's decision and the Scots were understandably aggrieved. Benson-Perkins also raised the constitutional issue which CRAC had certainly not anticipated: he thought the BBC should consult the church leaders: it was too important an issue to be decided by CRAC alone, particularly as CRAC was advisory. It rather looked as if the BBC had simply done as CRAC had advised: Archbishop Fisher thought similarly; he was annoyed at not being consulted. House and Woodward decided that the Corporation should not refer the matter, officially or otherwise, to Archbishops[28] or Moderators or Presidents. House had to turn CRAC's whole-hearted support into practical steps which would be seen to be 'experimental'. He asked for regional opinion; Falconer found the Presbyteries hostile; in Wales there was acceptance of two such broadcasts but they would not originate any for themselves.[29]

The 'experimental' plan was eventually outlined in the *Radio Times*,[30] and whilst the various regional committees were still mulling over the proposals, the Department went ahead with the first round of broadcasts around Christmas 1948. In Scotland, Falconer reported that there simply was 'not one gleam of hope': seven out of the nine Presbyteries had voted unanimously against the Corporation decision. Dinwiddie was convinced that the Corporation must meet a challenge to its public relations; all would depend on convincing the Presbyteries before the General Assembly of the Church of Scotland made its own decision.

In England, the Baptists set up a three-man commission consisting of R. L. Child, M. E. Aubrey and P. W. Evans of Spurgeon's College and prepared a statement for the Baptist Union Council General Purposes Committee in March 1949. The broadcasting of Holy Communion was 'ill-advised' and they would not recommend Baptist churches to take part in any such broadcast: 'no broadcast can transmit the characteristic actions of the Lord's Supper'; the private 'pastoral' actions would have to be omitted and this would be detrimental. House thought that the Nonconformist objections were finally political rather than theological: the Free Churches had most to lose since their liturgical style made their services least amenable to broadcasting.

Fr John Heenan was to conduct Low Mass from St Chad's Cathedral, Birmingham, and was tactfully asked by House to make it quite clear in his commentary that this service was directed to 'his own people'; House, as always, feared the Protestant reaction. In this way Heenan could be didactic in the context of a broadcast which was uniquely 'propagandist'. It reflected the constant problem for the Roman Catholics, who for comparable political reasons supported the broadcasting of the Mass as vigorously as some Presbyterians opposed it. It had been understood that there should always be an alternative programme to enable people to move off the waveband.

One very vociferous argument against these broadcasts was that by ancient tradition only the initiated actually communicated. The opposition feared that the arcane environment of the participants would be desacralized by the presence of the 'lapsed' or the non-committed via the radio. During the broadcast from Bradford Cathedral at Easter 1949, Saxon gave the commentary and addressed himself to an audience which was committed, though unable to be present. At the communion itself, Saxon simply remarked: 'Those who listen cannot share this central act but we can remind ourselves that the risen Lord is present where two or three are gathered together in his name and we can worship with the church of God.'[31] In Heenan's Low Mass, there was concern for the English-speaking audience, so all the Latin was translated. The Nicene creed was replaced by the Apostles' Creed: 'You'll probably know it better', he told his listeners. Heenan further stressed that worship was directed first to God rather than 'something for the listener'. House declared confidently that all the preparation had been done with Roman Catholics who were unable to attend church in mind. It was, he said, the best that any confession could provide, not only for their own devotees but for the broader Christian community. Hence his constantly declared conviction that since the sacrament was – to a greater or lesser degree – at the centre of each confession's liturgical life and identity, to broadcast it served one of the cherished objectives of religious broadcasting policy: ecumenical education. The correspondence supported this claim only to a limited extent. For Roman Catholics, the broadcast was mainly for the faithful; for the Protestants it was at least for the faithless.

There was more opposition: in May 1949 the Convocation of Canterbury debated a motion put by Percy Harthill, the Archdeacon of Stoke, a well-known figure and a pacifist; he wanted the Archbishop to 'take steps to discourage the broadcasting of such services in the Canterbury province'.[32] Lack of interest was such that only 71 were present, and a small majority of 52 per cent voted that the motion be not put.[33] Haley took this debate as grounds for going again to the Governors on the basis of a completely new CRAC request. There was stronger opposition however, from the General Assembly of the Presbyterian Church of England which debated the matter at the same time. T. W. Manson furiously opposed these broadcasts and his view carried the day; the Assembly opposed it . . . 'inasmuch as personal participation in the sacrament is an essential part of it'.[34] Manson was concerned with the concept of physical participation: to broadcast the act of communion was to present the sacrament as essentially non-participatory.

Further broadcasts of the sacrament took place during the spring and summer of 1949, including the first Methodist service, conducted by the formerly hostile Benson-Perkins, who thereafter had nothing but praise for the BBC initiative. In September 1949 the Methodists decided that the choice of any congregation for a BBC broadcast should be organized centrally and not remain with the initiative of the local circuit.[35] The first Baptist-style service eventually came from a 'Union' church (combined Congregational and Baptist) in Mill Hill, London. Professor John Marsh gave the 'commentary' and spoke of the listener 'overhearing'. The preacher, Maurice Watts, however, spoke of the broadcasting of the sacrament to 'show the Lord's death till He comes'.[36] R. L. Child, the principal of Regents Park College, Oxford, was troubled; he felt that Watts was quite wrong. The sacrament was not a 'memorial'; the Pauline assertion was rather the result of the sacrament. The broadcast itself must be either for the insider or the outsider, but not both:

> I cannot imagine a Christian invalid feeling otherwise than frustrated by the descriptive words of the commentary which would prevent rather than assist the mental concentration necessary if one is to imaginatively associate oneself with what is taking place.[37]

In the Mill Hill service all that reached the listener were spoken words and silence. The Baptist Union of Scotland for its part remained hesitant, neither protesting nor approving: 'since the central act in the communion service is one of silent spiritual communion between the soul and God it would seem that no known technique of broadcasting could overcome that difficulty.'[38] Broadcasting would only be possible if the 'conditions' in the church were exactly recreated in the home where the 'elements are in the presence of the assembly'. It was an extreme and somewhat bizarre Protestant view but accorded in some measure with a North American approach wherein 'pre-blessed' elements were 'reserved' in the home and were consecrated by the priest during the broadcast.[39] The theological issue did not evaporate and would later become profoundly contentious. Broadcasting could not easily cope with silence and nor could the listener only be an 'initiated eavesdropper': House and his committee had to make this service somehow intelligible to the 'interested non-attender' and thus a commentary would be in a real way 'even more than the eyes of the listener'.[40]

Regrettably, perhaps, with the advent of TV, the notion of participation through the imagination was profoundly reduced by the diversion of the 'picture'. The sound commentary which House had struggled to perfect could at least significantly control the 'outside broadcast' element in favour of those aural aesthetic considerations inextricably woven into the celebration of the sacrament. On the question of the silence considered indispensable by conservative Nonconformists, Dakin the Baptist could only encourage the Department to keep experimenting. *The Christian World* suggested that a clock should be heard during the silence![41] Authenticity was a troublesome concept.

At the meeting of CRAC in March 1950, a decision would have to be made: the experiment was ending. House tactfully asked Harthill and Manson for their considered views and brought together the thinking of the RACs and the churches. Outlining the findings of Listener Research, correspondence and press comment as broadly as possible, he said that the general comment was 'favourable to the continuation of these broadcasts' although not decisive evidence for the BBC now to move from experiment into normalcy. The axis of the CRAC debate reflected the polarity of the positions held by two Presbyterians, John Baillie in Scotland and T. W. Manson in England! For the Roman Catholics, the 'public relations' value overshadowed all such Presbyterian scruples and indicated how well their leaders understood the advantages of broadcasting the Mass: the French had overcome all such troubles. Manson and Harthill believed that such programmes 'cast pearls before swine'; they both argued that in the pre-Constantinian Church, catechumens had been permitted only at the first part of the service; the '*missa fidelium*' then followed. Manson was uncompromising:

> The sacrament is only for church members and no invitation is extended to any others; those who do want to participate need only join some branch of the Christian Church. If they are not prepared to do so they are outsiders and in this matter have no rights or privileges whatever.[42]

Baillie was impassioned in opposition to Manson. The remaining CRAC Free Churchmen believed that their own sacramental form was sufficiently intelligible for an uncommitted or casual listener actually to 'learn' something. The Anglicans valued the broadcasts for the housebound notwithstanding the question of non-participation. Woodward, Stockwood and Cockin all agreed that the objections to the

'sacred offence' which were still considerable, were effectively undermined by the disinclination of the uncommitted to continue listening.
Indeed, the Governors would eventually recommend that the continuity announcers would present a formal encouragement for the
uncommitted to listen elsewhere! House and the Department won the
day: the experiment should become normal, subject to a variety of
safeguards in respect to the number of broadcasts and the regional
allocation. (The General Assembly of the Church of Scotland finally
ratified the earlier decision of its Public Worship Committee without
discussion.[43] Such broadcasts should be 'infrequent'; this half-hearted
approval reflected the hesitancy of the Presbyteries.) Apart from the
English Presbyterians and the Baptists, the mainstream churches
agreed both in fact and principle that the social and theological
sensitivities which had been widely expressed were subservient to the
overall advantages of public relations, education, ecumenism and
evangelism. House, however, had but slender evidence of all these
aspects within the very limited observations which Silvey had undertaken.[44]

House presented this generally positive picture to the Board of
Governors in May 1950.[45] They were concerned, however, with the
question of balance: the heavy 'Catholic' interest was obvious and
House made it clear that it was simply that the Church of England and
the Romans were more interested than the others: they wanted the
broadcasts 'regularly' as against 'occasionally'. (The two-year experiment had involved twenty-three broadcasts, eighteen of which were
'Catholic' and only five shared between the Free Churches.) The Board
approved further experiment as CRAC suggested.[46]

At the Convocation of York in autumn 1950 an attempt was made by
the Provost of Newcastle to have both Archbishops summon a
theological committee to advise the clergy. House was understably
indignant, particularly in the light of so much publicity during the
whole two years of experiment. Haley was worried by the proposal,
which raised questions about the authority of the BBC. The proposal
was finally defeated in June 1951 and Haley thought the sacramental
discussions had proved satisfactory and that the Corporation had in
very large measure gained the approval of the major churches. House
and his team had created a new genre of liturgical broadcast in such a
manner as to allay the fears of almost all the leaders that broadcasting
would promote non-participation. On the contrary, the well received
'commentary' by such men as Taylor, Agnellus Andrew and John
Williams, had turned an 'outside broadcast' into an event for radio in
which the esoteric, mysterious and arcane activities were explained as

well as described to the various sectors of the audience. The overall concern was for the committed housebound listeners. In the event, comment became less and less as the Department gained greater co-operation from interested churches which were prepared to see proposed broadcasts more in terms of a 'sound' experience for the wider audience than merely for those present. Televising the sacrament, however, was to remain a long way off.

C. The BBC Hymn Book

Debate about the BBC's policy in respect to hymns had begun with the beginning of broadcast services. It revolved at first around the Daily Service and the 'performance' of hymns by the 'Wireless (later, the BBC) Singers' – a group of eight voices whose objective was to make the words of the hymns easily discernible against the jostling of all manner of interference in the air waves. There was appreciation, criticism and even abuse of this special Daily Service 'use' of hymns; it was a quite new devotional style to which vast numbers outside the churches were exposed each day. They wanted more: hymns must be more 'entertaining' and should be better presented: they should 'appeal'!

From the beginning of broadcasting it had been obvious to Reith and Stobart, and later to Iremonger that hymns made good entertainment, especially in Wales![47] The Ely Report had called the churches to task on the quality of music and hymn-singing[48]. The BBC had set an example to the churches. The clergy often complained that their own standards were being shown up as lacking in quality and precision. Others welcomed the educative opportunities of the Corporation to enlighten both sectors: the churchgoing public who sang hymns, as it were, on a regular confessional basis, and the non-attending public who appreciated hymnody as part of the heritage of Christian Britain. With the coming of war, this aspect was heightened and Welch was aware of the educative and public service opportunities which broadcasting could provide. Nevertheless, the complaint against the BBC continued: there were either too many new hymns or not enough. The local churches were resistant to innovations and thus the same genre of hymn was broadcast time and again. Another sector of the audience claimed that such broadcast services were dull and unimaginative; yet another sector wanted the very few favourite hymns broadcast more often. This latter notion had been behind the development of *Sunday Half Hour*: 'it was intended primarily to be (sanctified?) entertainment depending upon its appeal to association and emotion'.[49]

With the advent of the single programme and Welch's belief in the

BBC's mission to the nation, he was in touch with a great many outside his Department, not the least the musicians and notably Alec Robertson and Trevor Hervey alongside Walford Davies and Adrian Boult. The musicians were as much concerned with aesthetics as theology, as indeed was Welch. Since it became increasingly difficult for him to innovate in the raw materials of other Departments, he turned more and more towards the raw materials of his own: hymns. Hervey, Thalben-Ball and Stanton, the Director of Music for the Midland Region, were all convinced that the BBC ought to be teaching the churches how to sing and to some extent, what to sing. The tradition after all, was there in Walford Davies' *Melodies of Christendom* – an attempt to train choirs through broadcasting.[50] There had already been hymn programmes, recitals by large choirs and small for the general listener and the housebound, but now, it was thought, was the time to re-educate the custodians of British hymnody – the churches. However diligent had been the attempt through the Daily Service (and there were always complaints against innovations in this sacred space) to introduce new words and new tunes, it was now time to do something fresh, particularly as the increasingly successful *Sunday Half Hour* was – as some thought – doing the cause of new hymnody no good at all.

The BBC had achieved a great deal. Trevor Hervey believed the popularity of many new tunes was due entirely to broadcasting. 'Dear Lord and Father of Mankind' was a good example; Vaughan Williams' tune had appeared first in *Songs of Praise*. But he wanted more. Why not revive *Melodies of Christendom* in another form, not this time to educate choirs but rather the general church-going listener? Welch and his advisers in the Department came up with *Hymns Old and New* – Stanton was asked to espouse the cause and set up a regular programme every four weeks or even two. (Welch was aware that there were people in the Corporation 'a little restive' at the great amount of time being given to religion.)[51]

People in high places in the Corporation approved the scheme all the more keenly as it sought to educate and would help perhaps to still the constant stream of criticism against BBC religion from the two ends of the church and nation axis. Welch thought the programme should show why bad, popular hymns were bad and how good unpopular hymns could be sung and perhaps become popular. After a while the Department could then add to its list of popular hymns, always somewhat thin. Such additions to the hymns sung regularly might be welcomed by the clergy rather than resented; so often it was said that the BBC's intervention led to their competence being questioned! The new programme would expose the listener to the three agreed components of a sound hymn: good theology, good poetry and good music. Whatever the merits of the myriad available hymn books, few entries were justified on all three counts.

Nicolls agreed to it and the first programme in a series of ten was planned for 5 October 1941. Welch had the support of the School of English Church Music, Canon Adam Fox and a Cathedral Precentor, James Ferguson of Salisbury. The new programme would be congregational with an organ and not with the BBC Singers nor with string accompaniments. Since Hervey was preparing the BBC Psalter, programmes on the Psalms would perhaps alternate. Welch told Nicolls; 'We shall try to teach listeners something about intelligent and enjoyable hymn-singing . . . and to commend hymns which satisfy the three criteria of good poetry, theology and music and deal with the difficulties facing average congregations',[52] whose ears, he told the *Radio Times* Editor, 'we would hope to open'. Perhaps above all, the programme would prepare the way for the *BBC Hymn Book*.[53] Whatever the merits of all the books from which they had to choose, the BBC with the right advice could at last produce a hymn book which satisfied all three criteria.

A BBC Hymn Book had been mooted more than once during the thirties, and considerable work had been done between 1937 and 1939,[54] but during the first year of the war the project had hardly touched Welch and his busy Department. But then he was brought reluctantly into it and could hardly leave it all to Iremonger, now Dean of Lichfield. It was clear to Iremonger and others that progress could be made, but at the same time there were problems to be resolved; the politics of sacred music were delicate and not always harmonious. Iremonger advised Welch to call the music committee together as soon as possible. The next stage in the production of the Hymn Book was now on Welch's desk and faced him with an ecumenical challenge he would rather have done without.[55]

By the end of 1940, Iremonger was increasingly involved with his Cathedral and handed over his part, that of collating the suggestions of the original 'church' committee, to Stanton.[56] Welch moreover was still unsure of the agreement of the Oxford University Press which meant, effectively, Vaughan Williams. Iremonger believed that Walford Davies could get Vaughan Williams to agree to almost anything, but that did not finally commit the Press, which was naturally concerned to protect its copyright holders. A further problem was that the influential G. W. Briggs of Worcester was hoping for a second edition of *Songs of Praise* from the Press before the BBC book was ready. In December, it was agreed that the Press would allow the BBC to use tunes from *Songs of Praise* for other words and would not insist on Vaughan Williams' tunes for any hymns they used from that same book.

With Welch now collaborating with Iremonger, the differences began to appear as they shared the task of approving Stanton's draft list. Welch, while constantly confessing his incompetence in the matter, nevertheless resisted, albeit with tact and guile, the Dean's charitable reluctance to reject the selection made by the churchmen in 1939 of the best hymns from their respective denominational books. The Baptists were a cause of dispute: Welch doubted whether they would give their goodwill to the book: 'Still less would the inclusion of twenty hymns of moderate quality persuade Baptists to buy the book.'[57] Welch wanted the denominational selections subjected to BBC advice, scrutiny and, finally, decision. There was no point in trying to placate all the denominations: 'We must be ruthless in applying the three criteria of good theology, poetry and music.' He wanted reassurance particularly now because, as the new Director of Religious Broadcasting, he would take the opprobrium when the book eventually came out. For the moment he felt no great anxiety: he and Iremonger were working steadily through Stanton's draft. He expected no great problems for roughly two thirds of the tunes. For the remaining one hundred and fifty tunes, there would have to be approval by the not yet appointed music committee.

In July 1941, the so called BBC Hymn Book Committee met to review the situation. It was drawn from the publications, music and religion departments, together with Nicolls, who from the beginning had shown considerable interest in the project; he was anxious to please the churches and regretted the Committee's admission that 'the original attempt to include hymns from all important denominational hymn books had failed'.[58] Nicolls told the Home Board, which finally had to approve the whole scheme, that the new book would be an anthology, and not a compendium in any way giving proportional representation to the denominations. Welch had struggled for this notion to be made perfectly clear.[59] Nicolls naturally concurred that the criterion should be 'artistic', but both Iremonger and Welch insisted that this aesthetic concept should extend both to the words and the theology; there could be no theology without language, and language which must be subject to canons of poetic style as well as content and thus aesthetically sublime. 'The avowed intention of the committee was to produce "the best book ever".'[60]

Oxford University Press was now ready to publish words and music together, but doubted whether paper would be made available. This was rather disappointing to Iremonger and Welch, who both firmly believed that as the war was prolonged, the need for the new book was all the greater. At least however Vaughan Williams had expressed his willingness to check the music: he had told Walford Davies (who died in the spring of 1941) that he would be unlikely to exercise his veto except in what he called 'extreme cases' over a good music committee. For this co-operative goodwill between the Corporation and the music advisers to Oxford University Press the ground had been prepared almost entirely by Walford Davies only a few months before he died. His loss was incalculable.[61] The Music Committee should be chaired by his friend Sir Hugh Allen, Director of the Royal School of Music, and Welch for his part would have Adam Fox as consultant. Allen had insisted on this BBC relationship to the Press through Vaughan Williams. When music and words were ready, all the drafts would have to go to Vaughan Williams for his approval. It was a costly arrangement, not least because Vaughan Williams had not wanted the BBC book to be edited by Walford Davies, whose musical taste he distrusted, and had told him so. He claimed moreover that he was protecting the interests of Martin Shaw and Mrs Dearmer. Not surprisingly, Vaughan Williams feared that the BBC book would drown the two books which he had launched in earlier days, the *English Hymnal* and *Songs of Praise*, and perhaps all his work would be wasted. With the death of Walford Davies, W. K. Stanton had the closest connexion with Vaughan Williams and was the link for the BBC Committee. It was a delicate situation: if Vaughan Williams rejected the draft or refused his blessing, the Corporation could hardly appoint another consultant, since the Press would consult him anyway.

The drafting continued into the spring of 1942 and the end began to look as if it might be in sight. Stanton had a 'difficult' meeting with Vaughan Williams in March; he agreed the tentative terms of his 'consultancy', which the Press in the person of Sir Henry Milford also accepted. Stanton did not think Vaughan Williams would 'go out of his way to be difficult'.[62] Before the draft could go to the music committee, however, there was the problem of a number of hymns with several tunes available but none suitable; there was neither time nor talent available to commission other tunes. Stanton would not go to the Shaws and could hardly ask Vaughan Williams himself. There was one hymn with twenty-four verses[63] – when would it be used and by whom, asked Stanton. Notwithstanding all the work so far, Welch had still 'great doubts'. He was much influenced by Cyril Taylor and convinced that the anthology should be set alphabetically and not according to the church's year; that was to suggest a compendium and would not do.

This unusual treatment would also be given to the metrical psalms, included for the benefit of Scottish listeners. The Scottish advisers were

Professor W. T. Cairns and Dr G. Millar Patrick of Kelso, who was particularly helpful to the music committee; Dinwiddie regarded him as 'the best hymnologist in Scotland'. He was pleased to be consulted on what he regarded as an Anglican venture.[64] His advice was simply that the metrical psalms should be scattered throughout the book and not form a special section on their own. Welch had little optimism about the use of the proposed book north of the border and Iremonger anyway had always seen it as an English anthology.

In the summer of 1943, Welch confidently told Nicolls that the whole thing should be ready to go to the Press by January 1944. He had not envisaged the sensitivities of their eminent consultant Vaughan Williams. Furthermore the differences between the approaches of Iremonger with his 'compendium' and Taylor with his 'anthology' began to show; Iremonger was appalled by the emphasis on the alphabetical list and the sweeping away of the seasonal blocks as in most other books. (The issue would finally be resolved with a comprehensive index including seasonal classifications.)

The Music Committee met at last in November 1943 under the stage of the Prince of Wales Theatre in London, upon which, ironically, the current show was a tap-dance revue entitled 'Strike a New Note'! It deliberated for three days and thereafter the draft was effectively ready for the BBC Hymn Book Committee. Nevertheless, the revisions continued in the hands of a 'tidying up committee', R. S. Thatcher, Stanton and Thalben-Ball. Welch consulted the Hymn Society and was fully aware that the problem of drafting and redesigning pushed the publication date yet further back. He wanted the words looked at by yet another advisory team, including Fox. He knew that the Congregationalists were working on their new book and that new editions of both *Hymns Ancient and Modern* and *Songs of Praise* were in progress; the situation became all the more urgent. By the summer of 1944, just as the Music Committee were about to meet again, a serious cleavage of opinion was in evidence: Taylor on the side of the congregations, Welch on that of the radio listener.

Welch reluctantly agreed that Taylor might circulate the BBC Hymn Book Committee with a two-page letter stressing in no uncertain terms the danger of the committee approach and its 'inevitably academic atmosphere'.[65] The book must be 'used', and a good piece of musical workmanship would not necessarily have that 'something' which made it a good congregational hymn tune. There was a danger in having superior tunes imposed on unwilling congregations. Taylor was evidently assuming that the new BBC Book would be used widely by congregations; he was perhaps a little over-optimistic. Welch for his part recognized Taylor's musical superiority but maintained that the BBC Book was not only to be 'the best ever', as the BBC Hymn Book Committee had hoped; it was to be used for broadcasting and thus had an ecumenical function which somehow stood above all the others. He told the Music Committee that the Congregationalist editors had asked to see the BBC draft and had been refused.[66] These editors were concerned with congregational 'effectiveness', whilst the BBC was not: 'Our primary object in publishing this book is that we may use it in our broadcast services and so set a standard of hymnody which will be listened to by the nation'.[67] The BBC, thought Welch, had no right to produce a book which would not differ greatly from the new *Hymns Ancient and Modern*, *Songs of Praise* or *Congregational Praise*; the editors of the latter had gone to great pains to obtain the views of 'denominational opinion'.[68] In a word, Welch urged the committee to regard the *BBC Hymn Book* as 'setting a new standard of hymnody because we are free of the governing circumstances which control the contents of other hymn books'. If there was a dispute about two available tunes – one familiar and the other not – the criterion was musical quality and not present usage in congregational Christianity. By the BBC broadcast example, what might not be familiar today would doubtless become so tomorrow.

The Music Committee worked on in September 1944 and met again for three more days in April 1945; the task was getting more and more wearisome. Welch decided the draft should be looked at by outsiders and sent it this time to Eric Milner-White, the Dean of York.[69] His views were both depressing and challenging. Iremonger's insistence on the book being in some measure 'representative' in order to avoid falling into what he believed was the '*Songs of Praise* onesidedness' meant that Stanton's draft included a large number of hymns described by Milner-White as 'salvational', emphasising the subjective. There were too few seasonal and doctrinal hymns; there was an acute theological issue at stake here. The best standard of verse obtainable was 'pedestrian with perhaps fifty exceptions'.[70] Hymns should concentrate on the primary truths of the Christian faith and therefore any definitive book would be bound to concentrate on the church calendar; such hymns were 'Godward', more objective and less likely to get lost in the 'sea of personal piety'. They would moreover contribute to the 'consecrating of time to God by the Christian Year'.[71] Thus Christmas, Easter and Ascension hymns should comprise the largest proportion: these are uniquely educative; 'pietistic hymns are regrettably introvert'. Millar Patrick, the other consultant, was equally helpful. Welch wanted John Betjeman involved, but Nicolls refused to expand the committee's consultative net any further. Welch wanted such advisers precisely because the book was in danger of being so obviously a committee product.

As the war ended, Welch anticipated that the draft would be ready for printing by Easter 1946, although Vaughan Williams himself had still not seen it. One major cause of delay was that with the exception of Stanton and Taylor no member of the Music Committee could find time enough for sustained application. Stanton and Taylor were the only ones who managed to do so. The other factor was the methodology of the Music Committee: it sought not only to find tunes for good hymns but hymns for good tunes. By now Stanton was about to leave the BBC and Iremonger was taken up with his biography of William Temple and wanted to be relieved of his involvement. Welch pressed him into a compromise: he would pass judgment on the finished draft, but need not attend any meetings! Welch wanted Iremonger's *imprimatur* at all costs.

The revision problems dragged on: the metrical psalms were the subject of a good deal of rancour. Millar Patrick accused Milner-White of being out of touch with Scotland; he wanted more psalms; the Committee had so far refused even the 23rd! Unfortunately, as Welch confessed to Dinwiddie, Scotsmen and Sassenachs judge metrical psalms by different standards: 'they are part of your religious life; they are not part of ours.'[72] As a result of consultations between the Scotsmen Millar Patrick and Dinwiddie it was decided that there should be a separate section for metrical psalms, although Welch had no illusions about the book being used north of the border.

During the summer of 1946, Welch was also preoccupied with the issue of broadcast religious controversy and was preparing CRAC for a radical change of policy.[73] Relations between the Corporation and the churches were about to take a slight turn for the worse: the new policy would subject the faith to some not altogether acceptable scrutiny. Nicolls wondered if it was a mistake to upset the churches by yet another radical BBC initiative which looked like going ahead without consultation with CRAC – something which Welch was determined to avoid, just as Iremonger had been over *New Every Morning*. Nicolls was also somewhat anxious about the omission of a good number of popular hymns. Among these were favourites like 'Onward, Christian Soldiers', 'Nearer, My God, to Thee' and 'Lo, He Comes with Clouds Descending'. By now, moreover, the Oxford University Press was negotiating with the BBC publications manager and it seemed that preparations for printing were on the verge of completion. In June 1946, Welch announced that he was leaving the Corporation. Since he was no longer to be in the forefront of negotiations, Taylor's views were now likely to carry greater weight. Nicolls believed CRAC should be consulted on the popular hymns which had been omitted. Welch's successor, Grayston, was horrified; this would raise grave difficulties and he could not see why CRAC should have any say at all in the choice of hymns; CRAC, unlike the special committees, was not competent. In January 1947, it was formally decided at a meeting chaired by Nicolls and attended by Grayston and Taylor that the members of CRAC be given rough proofs of the galley sheets for consideration in March. It was a preposterous notion.[74] Nicolls felt strongly that CRAC should approve the *Hymn Book* for fear that the Corporation production would be 'aesthetically perfect but with many of the necessary vitamins lacking . . . our religion would suffer'.[75] CRAC set up a subcommittee, consisting of Aubrey, Eric Southam and Guy Rogers. They met with Taylor and in effect opened the selection to the scrutiny of the churches.[76] It was clear that the BBC initiative as Welch had conceived it was under threat. It was particularly ironical that the Church of Scotland complained that religious broadcasting would suffer if it were confined to relatively few metrical psalms when Scottish religious services would not rely upon this or any other book. The Scottish Psalter and the *Church Hymnary,* as Dinwiddie had told Welch, could not be undermined by the BBC. Dr Davidson felt 'we ought to press for more Psalms not as a region but as a country'.[77] The Welsh programme director thought the inclusion of a proposed section of twenty Welsh hymns would serve no useful purpose. In the middle of March, Stanton visited Vaughan Williams and finally delivered the draft.[78]

Throughout the summer the suggestions of the CRAC subcommittee had to be considered by the Words Committee, i.e. Iremonger, Welch, Stanton and Taylor. The CRAC committee wanted 'Onward, Christian Soldiers', 'Beneath the Cross of Jesus' and 'O Love that Wilt not let me Go'; there were calls for others including 'There were Ninety and Nine that Safely Lay'. Iremonger thought such hymns were unintelligible, and also too extravagant in their confession of the results of personal conversion.[79] He wrote furiously to Nicolls in July, distressed that years of planning could be

> . . . upset by three backwoodsmen like Aubrey, Southam and Rogers . . . Most of all it would be wrong to be guided by John Reith. There is very little left in the poor man's soul and he is simply talking from old Church of Scotland reminiscences which do not matter one iota to the present generation.

He feared the BBC would, after all the labour, give way to these 'four old-timers'.[80] Welch had no objection to four more metrical psalms but these extra hymns would mean spoliation: 'It is fatal to think of the BBC book as popular . . . only the BBC was free of vested interests.' CRAC had simply not fully understood the objectives of this book, he thought, and he would not wish to be associated with these extras already considered at length by the BBC committees.[81] Stanton would fight hard against such 'introspective morbidity': however far from fine the present book, the inclusion of such hymns he thought would make it 'less fine' and he begged that no additions would be made.[82] Taylor thought these hymns were 'not at home' in the new book.

By the end of May, however, everyone involved had been given even more to think about than CRAC's banal requests: Vaughan Williams had given Stanton a thirty-seven page report on the draft. 'He has pulled all of us to pieces fairly drastically,' was Stanton's comment.[83] He condemned the Music Committee; 'they seem to have no courage'; and the methods of the Words Committee passed his comprehension. The book however was likely to 'win on points' – Vaughan Williams said 'yes' to 261 hymns; 'yes if amended' to 75; 'doubtful yes' to 61; 'doubtful no' to 34 and 'certainly no' to 55. 'I shall be obliged to condemn the book as a whole unless certain omissions and commissions are rectified.' Then followed a detailed list which made it quite clear to Stanton that Vaughan Williams believed nothing could supersede *Songs of Praise* and the *English Hymnal*. Stanton told Taylor:

> I wish, oh, how I wish we had never bothered about him . . . the truth is that we are at cross purposes fundamentally and I do not see anyone moving Vaughan Williams from his impregnable position.[84]

By the autumn of 1947, the Corporation was caught between Vaughan Williams on one side and CRAC on the other; progress was even slower than before. Nicolls managed to organize a consultation between the old BBC Hymn Book General Committee which brought Iremonger, Welch, Stanton and Taylor together with Grayston and the Director of Talks, Rendall, under whose direct control the RBD was now set. Nicolls got some of his way and Welch some of his: the CRAC hymns were conceded and several requests by Taylor for omissions were refused. R. S. Thatcher's request for 'Holy Father, Cheer our Way' to be dropped was refused. Nicolls had got his way and the Corporation would be at peace with its advisers! However much Taylor, Stanton and Welch might be disppointed, all other considerations were now dwarfed by the Vaughan Williams' report. The key intermediary had to be the Oxford Press.

Since by now the Music Committee had adopted many of Vaughan Williams' revisions, it looked, according to the Press, as if his attitude was softening and that the Music Committee's revision might be accepted.[85] Stanton was in touch with Vaughan Williams and with the representative of the Press, and managed to obtain a working approval. By the turn of the year, the text of the Hymn Book had at last gone to the Press and at the February meeting of the Hymn Book Committee, Taylor was authorized to say that the difficulties with Vaughan Williams were now resolved. Nicolls told Iremonger that he hoped the words would be out by December 1949 ready for the Christmas market; the music would be out at Easter. Stanton, however, objected strongly; after all this time, to put a words edition on the market would simply encourage organists, clergy and congregations to put the old tunes to the new words. What was Nicolls thinking of after the years and years of struggle by the Music Committee to bring new tunes within arm's length of the old words so often buried deep in the bosom of congregational Christianity? The words and music *must* come out together.

And so began a new phase in the struggle to bring the anthology to life. Iremonger took up the cudgels against Nicolls, who was sternly reminded that every member of the Music Committee was against this philistine and inartistic device.[86] Nicolls soon agreed: if the BBC hymns and tunes were to be broadcast, organists and choirmasters would need the music or they would otherwise take little notice. In May the copy went to the printers; the Press assured Nicolls that there was no question of the two editions being prepared separately. The new Director of Religious Broadcasting, Francis House, thought quite the simplest arrangement would be to hold the words in stock until the music was ready and publish both together around Easter 1950. Nicolls wanted them to come out in December 1949.

In the summer of 1949 however, another calamity befell; Iremonger pulled out. He had just finished his biography of Temple, and told Stanton in August that he wanted to be relieved of proof reading and all the rest. Stanton was fearful of the bad reception he thought the book would get, and now, without Iremonger, he was going to insist for all he was worth that every detail be checked before publication, and resist any more changes. By Christmas, the proofs were arriving and there was now no real committee to check them.[87] House believed the Corporation must put all its faith in Stanton, who had all the drafts and all the wherewithal to check every necessary revision. Taylor and

Thalben-Ball, however, were pressing for more revisions and these were costly in terms of the manufacture of music plates by the printers. Nicolls decided the BBC would simply have to accept the extra cost and that therefore delay was inevitable. Any future meetings of the revisers would give Stanton the casting vote.[88] By February, 'everything was going as smoothly as can be expected when musicians meet'.[89] The Oxford Press did not agree and Geoffrey Cumberlege himself entered the debate: he knew that Stanton was being continually assailed by Thalben-Ball and Taylor on revisions and alterations: the BBC could not go on making alterations forever. Would Nicolls please 'ask the members of Stanton's committee to restrain their last-minute ardour for radical reform!'[90] This was hardly fair and primarily a commercial view: perfection could not be arrived at. But Taylor, the longest surviving BBC participant in the project, had not lost sight of Welch's objective: 'the best ever'.

Stanton too wanted the task completed. Taylor and Thalben-Ball believed their requested revisions were hardly 'radical reform'. When they saw their collection in book proof form for the first time, there were changes to chords and keys and the necessary adjustment of some settings for congregational use. Oxford wanted the words out of the way, but Taylor resisted Nicoll's urge to accommodate Cumberlege and the Press. A hymn book is – as he kept saying – a book of hymns with music and not an 'anthology of mediocre religious lyrics', as they would certainly be judged if the words came first without their musical counterpart. Taylor rejected the gnostic heresy which regarded hymns as first a set of words or first a tune. A hymn was not one without the other; it was a genre of aesthetic utterance which taken as an inextricable whole could allow for imperfection in one or other of its parts but only as an aesthetic whole. The BBC, anxious to avoid extra costs and embarrassments with the Press, was prepared to throw this crucial notion to the wind.

However on 1 July 1949, Nicolls agreed to simultaneous publication around Easter 1950. Iremonger was delighted and Taylor and Stanton had simply to agree to greater speed; but the music was still being minutely examined in October and the Press was none too hopeful and could not envisage the music being ready before the end of 1950.[91] Meanwhile Iremonger was asked to write a preface. Vaughan Williams forbade the BBC to refer to him at all; so he has no mention except in the index! Delays in the music production meant that Easter 1950 became totally impracticable. Nicolls, House and the publications manager, Strode, hoped that the Press could manage publication in time for the Festival of Britain celebration on 3 May 1951.[92] The Press

said that this too was out of the question and blamed Stanton and
Taylor, although not in so many words; there were simply too many
revisions and the music plate engravers were not actually employees of
the Press, which had to wait its turn. It might be ready in July but
probably October was more realistic. In January 1951 the Corporation
began to talk of publicity; and in February the Press produced the first
trial copies and Nicolls sent one to Iremonger: 'as much as I regret the
title, I have only myself to blame for not being able to suggest a better
one.' *The BBC Hymn Book* was published on 2 October 1951 and
launched by CRAC not only with a dedication in the Daily Service but
with suitably varied treatment on the three wavelengths: a 'critical
analysis' on the Third, an 'illustrated presentation' on the Home, and
Sunday Half Hour on the Light Programme.[93] Haley sent a copy to Reith
and hoped he would 'accept it as something very personal from us to
you . . . if only people will think on these things we may yet see a nobler
and more sanguine world.'[94] It was characteristic of Haley.

The churches thus had a new hymn book. In *The Christian World* the
previous December, John Marsh had hoped that 'some hymn book
common to all churches might get into circulation' and even be
discussed by church leaders. The BBC had provided just that book, but
not for church leaders; they were rather busily discussing their own. In
1951, the Congregationalists produced *Congregational Praise* (in preparation since 1939); the new edition of *Hymns Ancient and Modern* had
already appeared in 1950. The reception however was encouraging.
Eric Routley thought it would be valuable for adventurous congregations.[95] The *Church Times* was not so generous: the new book was
'infected with the *Songs of Praise* virus', the so-called 'religious lyric'.
The fact that a whole group of penitential hymns for the Lenten season
had been omitted was to be regretted. It appreciated the sense of
integrity about the original words of many hymns. Dean Inge in the
Evening Standard thought the BBC should be complimented and that the
churches should be grateful.[96] The *Methodist Recorder* hoped it would
serve to teach the churches; and the *Friend* hoped it would unite them.[97]
The most prestigious journal to comment was *English Church Music*.[98]
There were 'tiresome' harmonizations and 'serious disfigurements' to
some tunes. The book also tended to look backwards, but its
outstanding merit was simply that it 'puts into the hands of the vast
BBC congregation an anthology which is, in the main, representative of
the best views on hymnody in the first half of the twentieth century'.
Henry Havergal, Director of Music at Winchester College, hoped that
the subject group classification would have a 'refreshing effect on
repertoire in the Established Church'. Leslie Hunter, Bishop of

Sheffield, told Iremonger he thought it a hymn book of the Catholic church, but there was too much music from the Music Committee!

By November 1953 twenty-three and a half thousand word copies had been sold and nearly twenty thousand music copies. This was disappointing and compared most unfavourably with early sales of the very popular BBC service book, *New Every Morning*. The 'vast BBC congregation' might be attracted to a book which served the isolated piety of those who worshipped at home and who could in some sense 'participate' in the Daily Service through the words of *New Every Morning*. They would hardly be expected to sing quite so animatedly. Besides, most congregationally committed Christians had a hymn book in the house. The *Journal of Education* however thought otherwise – it 'fills a very obvious gap for the individual listener'[99] and would serve a useful purpose in schools and colleges.[100] The emphasis of course was in England and Wales: House was rather disappointed to learn that in Scotland the truth of the matter was that BBC policy had for a long while been to try to accustom the kirk audience to the new (i.e. 1928!) *Church Hymnary*. If it could have had its way, Scotland would have opted out of the Daily Service altogether – new hymn book and all!

Cyril Taylor has since declared that the whole convoluted saga of the *BBC Hymn Book* represented a conflict between the BBC and its advisers (in and out of the Corporation) on one side and congregational Christianity on the other. It was 'a tension between authentic liturgical art and authentic congregational participation'.[101] The *BBC Hymn Book* was animated by aesthetic and ecclesial considerations, both in the context of broadcasting. There was no single book which could always be used satisfactorily and, as in the schools situation, several books had an equal claim in the broadcast programmes. A new book by the BBC would provide both a standard and a source of education. It was a wildly ambitious and optimistic objective and Welch fought hard and unpopularly to keep the notion of 'anthology' uppermost; it could not but be useful in broadcasting.

The notion of a hymnary was equally powerful: hymn books belong to congregations and not individuals, hence each major specimen in the English language reflects a social organism and a religious identity. The BBC had no axe to grind in this area, and Welch indeed had hopes that the BBC could provide a collection that would reflect the new ecumenical thinking of wartime Christianity. However only about ten per cent of the collection derived from authors whose life and work was grounded in the twentieth century. As in other books, the substantial period of hymn writing was clearly the nineteenth century and accounted for more than sixty per cent of the whole anthology, with the eighteenth century some way behind. The religion of the *BBC Hymn Book* was grounded in the piety of the nineteenth century, no matter how strenuously the Words Committee had sought to excise what were now glaring anachronisms. There had been talk of preparing an anthology for the younger generation but it would be the BBC schools initiative which would make the only significant advance, as far as broadcasting could do so: a stringent selection from this anthology to form a hymn book for schools.

Congregational Christianity was moreover at its most sectarian when around its altars or communion tables: its hymn books reveal its theological priorities and passions. A central core of inherited commitment hinges on the source books of self-conscious recital. Even numbers are remembered, and nuances of tunes and texts become part of a distinctive liturgical parlance. The BBC could finally insist on the use of its own book only in those broadcasts over which it had direct control: the Daily Service and Sunday services from studios. House told his regional colleagues, including the Scots, that 'the weightiest reasons must exist before there is any departure from this rule'.[102] The Corporation had abandoned the notion that the mainstream churches would adopt the book not long after work resumed in 1940.

The agony over the production of the BBC book reflected a belief by Iremonger and Welch and many others in the Corporation that there was a body of Christian commitment within the nation as a whole which was not however to be found in the churches. The Corporation had a special duty to this group, and if programmes should deal in a new way with philosophical and ethical issues arising in the welter of debate in a Christian culture, aesthetic artefacts must also be considered; a hymn book was, as Iremonger conceived it from the beginning, an adjunct to the BBC service books and psalter. The churches effectively ignored it, not only because they each had their own; they had simply not been consulted about the hymn book to any real degree.

At various stages since 1927, the Corporation had considered a hymn book for broadcasting. To have suggested to CRAC that the churches and the Corporation collaborate on a new hymn book to be the best of them all, and to expect a commitment to have it adopted by the churches to supersede all the others, would have been to ask the Protestant churches to unite at a stroke. When such notions were soon abandoned, the Corporation could only produce one more anthology which looked so much like yet another hymn book as to warrant scant consideration by churchgoers and suspicion by church publishers.

One cathedral in England did replace its *Hymns Ancient and Modern* with the *BBC Hymn Book* – Lichfield!

D. Television and religion

The other major policy issue facing House on taking office was television.[103] Welch had discussed it with CRAC,[104] and they all agreed that 'there was not much religion could rightly contribute' except perhaps ceremonies, plays and documentaries. Welch told Garbett that whilst there was not much to be done during wartime, within twenty years television would be available for everybody and 'the churches must do some real thinking about it before it is upon us'.[105] A nativity play was broadcast at Christmas 1947 and Donald Soper gave the first televised religious talk, lasting seven minutes, the following New Year's Eve. House visited Alexandra Palace in the autumn of 1947 and was enthusiastic. Haley wanted him to prepare CRAC for a positive decision not on programme material 'but exploring if TV can decorously help the churches'.[106] CRAC said an emphatic yes.[107] Bishop Wand proposed that the Corporation be given the freeest possible hand in experimenting with types of worship, and all thought TV could properly be used to evangelize. Haley, however, was more interested in non-liturgical material than church services and did not want it spread abroad that the Corporation was eager for the latter; apart from policy factors, there were simply not the mobile units available. More problematic was the denominational issue, as Welch had realized: television would make explicit aspects which the spoken word and sound broadcast could obscure of the denominational characteristic of a given church: it was painfully evident to House that the common ground between the denominations could only be achieved in the studio.[108] CRAC had been aware of this, as well as the problem of Sunday televised services keeping people away from churches and children away from Sunday schools. Television would inevitably encourage and exacerbate the denominational variations and therefore religious material should be developed quite outside the scope of liturgical services and more designed to exploit the visual medium. CRAC feared a 'stunt' reputation for televised church worship.[109]

Not until the beginning of 1950 did televised religious programmes become more frequent: there simply were not the facilities, finance and opportunities to make experiments: earlier plans were only on paper. House was anxious that religious programmes should not get left behind in the expansion and floated a plan of action in the summer of

1949. He was in touch with the young secretary of the British Churches Film Council, Colin Beale, also with the Baptist Professor of Old Testament at Bristol Baptist College, Henton Davies, who had used a variety of visual aids to teach his subject. House pressed for programmes; he also pressed for staff and envisaged Beale as a TV staff producer (it would be two years before he got him). House wanted services in church and studio and perhaps a series of films: above all he wanted action. George Barnes happily agreed, notwithstanding the growing autonomy of the television structure. He wanted a policy for religion in television as for every other part of the service.[110] House was also conscious of how far behind was the BBC initiative – the French, Canadians and Americans were televising the Roman Catholic Mass: there were films, chapel services, interfaith programmes and religious education. The great differences were in both politics and costing; the churches in America, for example, had considerable part in financing.[111]

Notwithstanding the reluctance of the Corporation, the first outside broadcast of a church service was on Christmas Day 1949 from the Royal Hospital, Chelsea – full of ceremony and movement; it was no ordinary church service, and fully accorded with the intention of Norman Collins, now Head of the Television Service, to restrict any such programmes to 'major festivals – they would be the chief occasions'. There were simply not enough studios, and even though planning had begun for the new White City broadcasting centre, there were no plans to replicate any tradition such as had produced the religious 3E studio in Langham Place.[112] House knew, nevertheless, that he had to stake a claim and produce a good programme for the Governors and for CRAC. The television programmes would have to help 'viewers in general' to enter into the religious significance (in this case) of Christmas Day. It would be evensong. House saw no point in evading the denominational nettle in view of the very obvious fact that television favoured sacramental and ceremonial liturgical forms. It would at least force the Department to develop non-liturgical religious programmes. House, Haley and Collins had agreed that the same policies would apply to television as to sound and House had to scotch rumours that television was to 'invade the sanctuary'. Collins was not a religious man and certainly made no secret of his view that religion had no place in the entertainment medium he believed television to be.[113] House told the Department that at any rate the Christian contribution would be accepted as an 'integral part of the programmes; its evangelistic intention is recognized and it must represent the faith of the mainstream churches'.[114]

"Your sermon was good enough for television, vicar."

There was a good deal of anxiety over this first outside televised service, but afterwards there was general approval; Garbett saw it and was sure that 'the fullest use of television should be made for religion'.[115] The next service was from St George's, Windsor, after the King had inspected the Boy Scouts; the third, on Easter Sunday morning, was from the Chapel Royal at the Tower of London; both were full of movement, ceremonial and spectacle – but not the stuff of normal services.

House had invited the Dean of Westminster, Alan Don, to have a Whitsunday service televised. He felt that the Abbey authorities would surely wish to 'make their contribution to this new medium in the cause of Christ'; there could be no better occasion than this. He tried to make it clear that the cameras etc. would be almost totally unnoticed. (He himself was determined to avoid St Martin's-in-the-Fields on this occasion; he wanted the 'national shrine'.) However the Chapter would not agree: 'There was a reluctance', said Don, 'to introduce this new form of publicity into our public worship.'[116]

In spring 1950, House urged the consideration by the Television Executive of religious programmes other than church services: he was convinced there was considerable potential and Barnes agreed. A meeting took place in March and to House's surprise McGivern, TV Programme Director, himself a churchman, agreed that the Corporation must evolve a specific religious policy and not have religion merely produce random items. Henton Davies, Beale and Edwin H. Robertson between them produced a mass of ideas which convinced McGivern that 'it was obvious that there was a very great deal of programme material and that television could give a great deal towards the cause of religion and teaching and spreading the Christian way of life.'[117] It could even involve a staff assistant and a separate section in television. It did not mean, however, that House could expect a studio in White City. Maurice Gorham wanted a 'first sketch' of possible contributions; House pushed complex notions of 'experimentation' – an expensive activity in television unlike radio. There had been a variety of programmes so far to suggest the new directions: outside broadcast church services, religious drama and magazine feature programmes, e.g. a life of Christ in famous paintings, *The Eye of the Artist*, which went out in March 1948. House suggested a possible form of daily service and *Christian News and Commentary* for television.

The Board of Governors discussed the issue in July: Barnes, the Director of the Spoken Word, simplified the television possibilities into worship, address and a children's service (the Corporation was aware of the lobby from the Sunday school movement that television should not distract children from their regular attendance). Barnes explained to the Governors[118] that any experimentation implied the provision of a religious assistant at Alexandra Palace (the first home of TV). The Board agreed to an experiment of four religious services per annum for two years and asked for a report on the implications of a regular television religious contribution: this was House's opportunity. In October, CRAC watched a film of the first televised evening service from a parish church – a Harvest evensong from Warlingham in Surrey. The broadcast had confirmed House in his view that televised Church of England services were best able to retain the interest of the general public and allow the committed to share in an act of worship. Haley thought it a 'valuable experiment'. House made it quite clear to CRAC that the Board of Governors would await their advice in 1951: they should consider in relation to television all those factors which had earlier come into sound broadcasting: timing, frequency, denominational balance, sacramental services and the figure of Jesus in televised plays. House was sent to Alexandra Palace for some weeks to report on potentialities, and gained immensely from producers, technicians and announcers; each professional practice involved issues for religious broadcasting.

His lengthy report, 'Religious Programmes on Television', produced in December 1950, called for immediate action in the procuring of an assistant; he wanted Colin Beale from the British Churches Film Council. CRAC was aware of the march of television but as yet there was no regular religious item: programmes were all rather *ad hoc* and this worried various members, particularly the Roman Catholics, who were anxious to have Midnight Mass broadcast regularly on Christmas Eve. House wanted his 'specialist' to get to work (albeit part-time) before CRAC pronounced on the subject in response to the Board's request. He was convinced that there should not be a separate religion department created in the television structure: any suggestion of a separate department surely implied regular time committed to religion. House wanted regularity in the total output and believed that the difference in the character of the content of religious programmes did not involve the development of 'radically different methods of production'. He was also quite convinced that the rise of television would lead to a drop in the Light Programme audiences, that those looking for participation in a religious service would not turn to television and probably would not approve of the marriage between religion and entertainment (any more than they had done on the Light Programme), and that the vast majority of viewers were non-churchgoers, an even greater proportion than listened to the Light Programme. There was little doubt that television would increase and House planned to have his 'expert' in the system just as soon as he could.

At first, Haley was not convinced about the need for extra staff – he thought the present forces could somehow be 'redeployed'. House insisted: there was a serious principle at stake and the loss of even one man would seriously impair the sound output. Besides, there was no one with the skills – he wanted Beale. Haley finally agreed and by August 1951 Beale was appointed part-time to the Department based at Alexandra Palace. House had won a victory: religion could be conceived in professional terms as having part in this visual revolution in broadcasting. Lotbinière, the Head of Outside Broadcasts, told all his producers: 'We neglect Mr Beale's advice at our peril.'[119]

In the appointment of Beale, House established religious broadcasting in the television service and emphasized the thoroughly distinctive character of the visual. He had secured religion a place in the general output and had the advice of a professional outside the RBD to research the potential of religious programmes and present the case both to the broadcasters themselves and to CRAC.[120] He had also taken the churches a step towards the door of religious programmes on television which the British Council of Churches Commission believed was 'wide open'. Its conviction was that the door 'must be entered'.[121] Beale was to guide CRAC and the churches further in.

25

THE BEVERIDGE ENQUIRY:
CLAMOUR AND REPRIEVE, 1949–1951

In his chronicle of the emergence of the Beveridge Committee of Enquiry in early 1949, Professor Briggs makes two points which are pertinent to the religious issue in broadcasting policy: the importance which the Government and Beveridge placed upon encouraging submissions, and the question of the monopoly. Briggs notes that only one headline in the sparse initial press comment included the word 'monopoly'.[1] Moreover, whilst *Tribune*[2] complained that too much power in 'the hands of a small but isolated group' determines 'what listeners shall hear', the more specific religious issue was uppermost in the minds of those on both sides of the party political divide. In Briggs' view the Committee was not fully representative. It did, however, include the Labour MP for Greenwich, Joseph Reeves, a vigorous and militant humanist who had helped co-ordinate the Rationalist Press Association Parliamentary lobby against the BBC in 1948.[3] Reeves had campaigned not only for the RPA but for the Ethical Union and the Christian Scientists; his parliamentary colleagues had called not only for greater freedom broadcast talks but, more significantly, that 'the treatment should remain not merely historical and doctrinal but embrace ceremonies . . . and social influence of the various religions.'[4] Haley replied that the Corporation was progressing with 'deliberation and care', and was determined 'to aid the general search for truth'.[5]

Reeves and the groups clamouring for a voice saw the notions of free speech about to be translated into BBC policy. Haley was realistic about the search for truth and the part broadcasting should be playing in the religious debate. He had hitherto encouraged Welch in his conviction that the Christian faith should be open to scrutiny, notwithstanding his own convictions that the Corporation had a special commitment to Christian values. Proceeding – as he told Reeves – 'with deliberation and care' he construed in terms of talks and talking.

He believed that whatever should be the expansion of religious discourse, debate or dialogue, the sensitive area of cult and ceremony could not so easily be democratized – nor did he wish it.

In January 1949 Lord Astor once more pressed for the admission of the Christian Scientists into the protected 'liturgical' spaces: Sunday services and the morning programme *Lift Up Your Hearts*. Though it might sound like a talk, House and CRAC regarded the latter as a species of small sermon, and this was one reason for refusing the Christian Scientists access.[6] *Lift Up Your Hearts* had been designed not only for that 'Christian' audience which could not benefit from the Daily Service, but 'listeners who are interested in, but not definitely committed to, the Christian faith; it may be their only real contact with Christianity during the day.'[7] CRAC and the Department had no intention of allowing the controversial Christian Scientists into this domain. The search for truth must be undertaken in the 'Talks' output; 'Service' times were 'sacred', whatever their place in the schedules.

House and Woodward were determined that this unofficial pressure on Haley should not succeed; notwithstanding division within the Board of Governors, no decision would indeed be made without recourse to CRAC and the Department.[8] In 1950 Haley decided that it was now time to ask CRAC to consider its position again, particularly in the light of the many radical submissions being made by all manner of groups with one motive in common – breaking the Christian monopoly, although he was sure the Board would not support Astor against CRAC.

Haley decided that on the broadcasting of services there were three questions CRAC should be asked:

1. Does CRAC still advise the BBC to confine religious services to the 'mainstream' churches?

2. If so, on what grounds?

3. If the Corporation wished to widen the bounds of the 'mainstream', could CRAC suggest an alternative 'definition'?[9]

CRAC discussed the matter in October 1950. It opposed the 'statistics' argument, partly because there could be no adequate method of ascertaining and measuring 'adherence', but more crucially because it failed to take account of the Corporation's public service and educational responsibilities to a Christian culture. T. W. Manson, now on CRAC, suggested an alternative criterion – the only acts of worship broadcast should be those 'addressed to the God of the Old and New Testament'.[10] Theological considerations, said Woodward, were not quite the same as ecclesiastical and social ones; he preferred the BBC's 'Christian nation' definition, which the Roman Catholic Masterson regarded as distinctly Protestant but accepted. This was a valid point; the notion of 'Christian Britain' and the BBC's responsibilities to the 'Christian public' tended to keep Roman Catholics at a discreet distance from much policy-making discussion. Their designation as 'mainstream' was controversial and not wholeheartedly accepted outside CRAC. This dominantly Protestant body invited Masterson together with three other members, Kathleen Bliss, T. W. Manson and Leslie Cooke, to form yet another sub-committee to answer Haley's 'Three Questions'.

In the meantime Astor visited Lord Simon and urged his request even more strongly.[11] Those who made submissions to the Beveridge Committee could be divided into two groups, the monopolists and the pluralists.

A. The monopolists

During 1949, the challengers to the Christian monopoly were busy preparing their submissions for the arbitration of Lord Beveridge's Committee.[12] The principal religious bodies included the British Council of Churches, the Roman Catholics and most mainstream Protestant bodies except, surprisingly, the Church of England; its own views were embodied in the CRAC submission.

(i) The British Council of Churches submitted Part I of its Commission[13] which examined the influence of broadcasting on society and the general BBC output. The BCC wanted to add a fourth objective to information, education and entertainment: 'the rehabilitation of conviction'. In the current climate, the BCC wistfully believed that the churches were 'now more than ever' committed to toleration 'even for those who most bitterly oppose the Christian faith'.[14] Conflicting interpretations should be brought out into the open and 'the resulting contradictions honestly faced'. The BCC supported the CRAC view that the only alternative to the traditional 'mainstream' policy would be a commercial 'free for all', and therefore some criterion could not be avoided. The Corporation would have to decide whether it was committed to 'some kind of "preferential treatment" for the Christian view'.[15] The Commission believed in the notion of moral stability for which all men were searching, and that the Corporation had a duty to take an initiative to organize a 'radical re-examination of the Christian conception of man's life'. Christian 'forces had no more powerful instrument and ally' than the Corporation. The Commission recognized the educational facilities it afforded, particularly in the light of the 1944 Butler Act. The BBC . . . should 'provide full opportunity for the expression of the Christian faith and way of life'.[16] The BCC had a difficult conceptual task: to accept plurality and alternative systems of thought which denied the Christian presuppositions and, at the same time, support Haley's search for truth against a background of moral values which the Commission could not divorce from 'Christianity [as] a whole, in which faith and ethics, conviction and values are held together'.[17] Whilst leaving aside the question as to whether the BBC should afford 'preferential treatment' to the Christian view, it hoped that in any debate 'as touching all matters involved in the right ordering of society ... the Christian ... contribution should be heard.'[18]

In spring 1950 Beveridge accepted oral evidence from a BCC delegation, comprising Cockin, Bliss, Coulson and Fenn from Section I of the Commission, with John Marsh from Section II and David Say, the BCC General Secretary.

Beveridge thought their report a 'very interesting, carefully reasoned and moving' memorandum. He wanted to know the Commission's view of the BBC's monopoly and the concomitant orthodoxy of Broadcasting House: what about the 'refreshing rebels'?[19] Cockin argued that the real conflict at the base of civilization was insufficiently exposed; indeed, there should be a 'very radical and realistic clash of opinions not only on the air but in the minds of the Corporation'.[20] Kathleen Bliss articulated the dilemma which Haley had presented a month before: the BBC had to decide who would have a say, and the need for cohesion and leadership would easily be lost in the attempt to do justice to the tiniest minorities. But that was precisely what Beveridge wanted: the BBC should give a voice to everyone, provided they were not advocating crime![21]

The Director of Education for Lancashire, A. E. Binns, asked if they would accept a free and vigorous attack on Christianity? Kathleen Bliss replied confidently that in a 'life and death' situation for civilization the BBC had a duty to raise the debate above the trivial and marginal issues of astrology, faith healing and the return of spirits – a hard swipe at the Spritualists and Christian Scientists who were battering on the doors of Portland Place for a chance at the microphone. 'We are not prepared to bring our big batteries to shoot at those little pip-squeak targets.' There must be serious debate, added Cockin, and not mud-slinging.

Mr Binns went further: if broadcast material came upon vast tracts of the population like a thief in the night would not the faithful be shocked – to say the least? This was a valid point: such broadcasting could and did arouse considerable public notice, and misconceptions would inevitably abound. There was a real risk, Fenn confessed, and one which the churches had to face but were not doing so: overt attack would come as a 'terrific shock to the under-resilient'. He at any rate was 'prepared to risk the damage'.[22] Cockin was pushed even further: would he allow the non-liberal his voice on the air, especially one who resists freedom of thought? The question was close to home: too many in the churches, including CRAC, regarded the BBC as properly committed to Christianity and thought attacks on the latter were not admissible. Cockin reiterated the Commission's liberal commitment: issues which concern 'man's truth about himself' must come into the open, notwithstanding the Christian's affirmation that 'this truth is expressed in the Christian's view of man's life'. The issue must be brought out and fought out and not 'coupled up with licence'. It would be a long job! Cockin could only see the BBC as a species of University taking the initiative in guiding the evolving shape of a public seminar. It was the Corporation's task to choose the most competent minds in each field and have them spend considerable time together in order to demonstrate how their minds could be seen to change in the light of their considered interplay. The 'bugbear', he concluded, was triviality.[23]

Beveridge himself was anxious about Haley's influence over certain sections of the report, in particular concerning regionalism. Cockin as Bishop of Bristol had close connections with the West Region and had gathered a good deal of information from the BBC in Bristol. The influence of Scottish religious affairs under Dinwiddie and Falconer was formidable and the Commission had heard the regional lobby loud and clear. There was a good case for emphasizing the value of the regional group, particularly as there were complaints about the Corporation being top heavy and over-centralized. Haley however had signalled that he disagreed with such a view and in effect the BCC had fundamentally redrafted its views on this point. Beveridge wanted assurance that the Commission was not simply discreetly submitting a BBC view by another route. Beveridge said that he would have been sorry not to have known that the draft had been discussed by Haley and Barnes. Cockin and his colleagues found it difficult to make Beveridge understand their position and were thus astonished at his eventual report.[24]

(ii) The Roman Catholics were by no means ready to put so much faith in what for them was a state institution deciding for the church. They believed that a principle was being discreetly ignored, notwithstanding their support for House and the Department. Cardinal Griffin had supported the CRAC Roman Catholic members who consistently believed that they were being discriminated against and had thus been forced to invoke the numerical strength of the nation's Catholic adherents. In their submission[25] they compared their numbers with those of the Free Churches (as given in the *Christian Year Book* for 1950). They outnumbered the latter by more than two to one. This state of affairs was not reflected in the programmes or the structure of the Department. The Anglican Head of the Department should have not one assistant but two – one each from the Catholic and Free Churches. They wanted religious broadcasting to be made 'dependent to a greater extent upon the organized Christian bodies in the country', and at the same time they wanted the Head of Religious Broadcasting to 'be made directly responsible to the Director-General'. They complained because the RBD was not bound to be guided by the advice of the churches. This was not an argument likely to appeal to Beveridge. On the basis of numbers, however, the position was 'fantastic'. The BBC was plainly being unfair and even prejudiced; the distribution of posts as well as programmes was discriminatory; the Roman Catholics were not getting their fair share. They demanded 'sufficient Catholic producers to deal competently with all Catholic work'.[26] Since they could not accept in principle the notion of a secular body acting for the church, they could only appeal to a liberal idea of 'fair play' on the basis of numbers.[27] Masterson had convinced the Bishop of London of the equity of the argument. It was unlikely to convince Beveridge, who was not anxious to have the BBC authority dissipated by either politics or religion.

(iii) The BBC had submitted its own very lengthy statement to the Enquiry.[28] Three paragraphs on religious policy were drafted by the secretariat and approved by House.[29] The justification for the 'mainstream' ruling assumed that its message would be most likely to be 'acceptable to the overwhelming majority of listeners to religious broadcasts whatever their denomination'. Paragraph 67 quoted from House's 'Aims and Achievements', that more than one in three of the adult population heard at least one such broadcast and that religious broadcasting had helped to maintain the 'religious consciousness' of large sections of the population and educated Christians themselves. They were a comfort to the housebound. Religious broadcasts were, in a word, 'successful'. CRAC intended to amplify these paragraphs and moreover present its case against a background of the sort of criticism which it knew it would be getting from various quarters opposed to the 'mainstream' policy and the Christian monopoly. House and Woodward were convinced that Beveridge himself had little grasp of the relation of the Corporation to that very large group for whom religious broadcasts were already, or could be made, intelligible and useful. House feared Beveridge would be swayed more by the very small minorities who would argue rather loudly in terms of liberty and freedom of speech. CRAC wasted little time in preparing its case.

The CRAC submission[30] was based squarely on Haley's belief in the connection between the BBC and the Christian faith: religious broadcasting had a particular duty to the churches and should explore new techniques of presenting the message to the outsider. In reply to those who complained that there were too many Christian religious programmes, the time allocation 'bears a due relation to the actual membership of the Christian churches in Britain'.[31] In addition, a third of the adult population was listening to one religious programme or another; were as many listening to serious music? The cause of religion was better served by speakers of whatever denomination who could use the microphone with effect than by observing a strict proportion between the many existing denominations.[32]

CRAC broadly argued that so long as the BBC was committed to serve and reflect the faith of the churches to which collectively most Britons belonged (or had belonged!), and so long as representative preachers kept away from interdenominational bickering, the 'mainstream' churches were justifiably the avenue of advice on questions of religion to the BBC.

> The result of this policy is that the overwhelming majority of those who wish to listen to religious broadcasts can tune in . . . without fear of violation of their consciences or fundamental convictions.[33]

It was this argument which House strongly believed Beveridge and the secularist lobby would either not understand or the methodology of which they would reject. It was a faithful reading of Christian Britain, notwithstanding *Puzzled People* and the statistics in the *Christian Year Book*. The CRAC submission was anxious to relate this assertion to the broadcasting of services. It put its weight behind controversial discussions, albeit rather pompously; who, after all, was to decide which 'relevant and sincerely held convictions' can be 'expressed' in controversial broadcasts?[34] CRAC was not going to accede to any dismantling of its power.

In the notion of a 'Christian Britain' which it used without embarrassment, it appealed to Beveridge as if with a datum almost beyond dispute. CRAC played somewhat fast and loose with the language, talking of the Christian minority as far exceeding those who listen to serious music and the BBC's religion policy as 'serving the cause of religion',[35] when it really meant denominational Christianity in general and the 'mainstream' in particular. It was the protection of Protestant Britain: acts of worship must be 'mainstream'. Unorthodox, i.e. 'controversial' expressions of 'sincerely held convictions on religious questions' were encouraged in the Talks output. Ritual was the uneasy preserve of the 'mainstream'; the 'fringe' might speak its mind, but the Sunday spaces and the ceremonial which filled them belonged to the 'mainstream' churches. The Reithian concept was not dead. Many construed popular religious programmes as a species of 'Variety' rather than the ceremonial of traditional Christianity: it was part of the price the churches were prepared to pay.

B. The pluralists

(i) The Unitarian submission[36] represented the non-orthodox Christian position and was understandably plaintive. It quoted Haley and House: 'Manifestly the BBC is not being true to its aim to "search for truth".' If the BBC was catering for non-churchgoers, could it be, they asked, that 'orthodox' Christian presentation had failed them? The Unitarians pleaded for a place in the mainstream; they wanted their publications recognized in the periodical review of books; they wanted more Sunday services and, most provocative of all, a place on CRAC. The vast majority, they claimed, were no longer 'touched by the traditional expressions of revelation'. The argument was terse and logical, but ineffective against the long-standing power of CRAC which had 'refused to advise' the Corporation on such broadcasts. The BBC had in fact included the Unitarians (along with Jewish broadcasts) in a policy of 'mainstream with two exceptions'. Beveridge would no doubt be moved by such arguments, particularly as the Unitarian influence, as Professor Briggs has observed,[37] was historically certainly more significant than their numbers.

(ii) The Christian Scientists,[38] with more eminent support, and the Spiritualist National Union,[39] were further away from orthodoxy than the Unitarians. The Spiritualists did not only appeal to Beveridge on the basis of influence and numbers but also claimed that they were 'more in the mainstream' than many others, 'as evidenced during the early years of the Christian Era'. Whilst Beveridge was hardly likely to be moved by such undemonstrable claims, he would perhaps be moved by their appeal to human rights: 'the public cannot fully enjoy the religious freedom referred to in the Atlantic Charter.'

(iii) The Ethical Union plainly objected to the BBC being 'an instrument of Christian propaganda'.[40] The Rationalist Press Association took the same line.[41] Haley's contention that Britain was a

"Ladies and gentlemen, please! Save your differences until we are on the air."

Christian country was vigorously contested. How could this assertion square with the findings of the report *Towards the Conversion of England*? If, as this report had claimed, 'A whole generation has been suckled in agnosticism', surely the BBC must proceed not on the basis of a Christian country but 'on the fact that only a minority . . . can be ranked as Christian'. How otherwise could Haley's 'search for truth' be undertaken? How could it be reconciled with the assertion that 'Christianity is the supreme embodiment of truth'?[42] Christian propaganda should be abandoned in favour of 'an impartial treatment of all forms of belief'. There could be no search for truth when, as Haley said, the BBC was seeking to 'foster acceptance' of Christian moral values, and when even the churches themselves declared that religious broadcasters were 'the servants of the church in Broadcasting House'?

It was a compelling and logical argument, if far too intellectual for the vast mass of people who, as House rightly claimed, would register their 'civic' adhesion to the 'C of E' when marrying, entering hospital or dying. Regrettably for the RPA and the Ethical Union, their numbers were pitifully small notwithstanding their erudition.[43]

C. Reprieve: a new Government, 1951

During 1950, the opposing forces, as it were, slowly gathered. The Governors were challenged by the Christian Scientists and CRAC finally submitted to Beveridge. House gave evidence to the BCC as it put the final touches to its report.[44] CRAC was still considering its answer to Haley's 'Three Questions'. The Beveridge Report was published in January 1951. CRAC met in March and had to reply both to Haley and to the Report. It had the BCC Commission before it and agreed that the 'root questions' confronting society were 'questions of faith . . . on which any values must rest, whether Christian or not'.[45] It also had before it the draft answers to Haley's 'Three Questions' offered by the Bliss-Manson subcommittee. The question of statistics was raised again by Wand and Masterson, who were both strongly against the present 'mainstream' policy; they thought it was 'untenable, illogical and unlikely to achieve the desired end of equity'.[46] House's rejoinder to the statistical argument was that the notion of the 'nominal' Christian would have to be abandoned in favour of, e.g., baptismal candidates. The churches and particularly the Roman Catholics would surely refuse to have such lines drawn. Who would define the 'nominal'? Neither would House abandon the long-standing conviction of his Department that the Corporation could bear witness to the Christian faith above denominational divisions; he believed he had 'historical, sociological and doctrinal' support for his policy.[47] The religious faith of the overwhelming majority was a species of Christianity somewhere within the mainstream, and the BBC must 'protect' the liturgical precedence of the mainstream traditions and in so doing, facilitate the worship of God as something rightly to be undertaken by the Corporation itself.[48] Regular times of 'worship offered to God' were not the place for any such relativizing; the issue, as Rowntree Clifford asserted, was between 'faith and unfaith'.[49] Controversial broadcasting belonged to the Talks context, even though Somerville would assure them that attacks by one group upon another would be resisted even in this 'open' environment.[50] The statistical lobby was strong but there was an impasse.

House and Woodward produced, therefore, a three-tier alternative somewhat more logical than the 'mainstream with two named exceptions'.[51] The first was the mainstream CRAC churches controlling Sunday and other 'liturgical times'; the second, other religious groups including the Jews, Unitarians and Christian sects. The criteria here would be statistical and objective: number of adherents, degree of public interest and dissemination of publications; contributions to public debate on philosophical and ethical issues; accordance with the Charter of the BBC and institutional stability. It should 'not just be an American mission or a constantly dissolving collections of sects'.[52] Above all, these second-tier groups were obliged to 'address the general public as well as their own members'.[53] The Corporation was not, as House consistently maintained, providing a means of communication to any propagandist sect. For their part, the Roman Catholics had to show great tact in the broadcasting of the Mass by addressing themselves to their own.

House's third tier involved controversial and debating programmes, which would have to be produced by the Talks Department, as questions of conscience would inevitably arise if the ordained staff members of the RBD were asked to promote an attack on Christianity – even if only apparently. This separation was not acceptable to Haley. CRAC took the view that 'non-churchgoing listeners insofar as they are religious at all, are Christians'.[54]

Thus the churches constructed a rationale for 'preferential treatment' by the Corporation. Masterson, Wand, Cockin and Woodward all noted that there would be 'protest from the churches' if the mainstream represented by CRAC was in any way diluted by others outside – even the Unitarians, over whom there was still serious divison in the Committee. The Corporation was expected to defer to the churches on all religious, theological and doctrinal matters. Haley, in his lecture on *Moral Values in Broadcasting*, had been effectively the first to challenge this view; it was not the task of the Corporation to 'sustain the Christian faith or recruit for Christian churches' – so he told the Committee yet again quite bluntly during the March debate.

Over the Beveridge Report, CRAC, in a word, was scandalized – by its theological and ecclesial ambiguities and its recommendation that the RBD should promote Christian values as distinct from the Christian faith. It was a political conflict; the churches were determined to hold fast to their hard-won tradition no matter how much it had lately been challenged. For the second time in its history, CRAC decided to hold an extraordinary meeting in June and present its findings to the Governors on the two issues – Haley's 'Three Questions' and the Beveridge Report.

As soon as he had read it, Wand informed House that the Beveridge Report would encourage the growth of undenominationalism or a 'theosophic amalgamation' of all religions.[55] The church leaders were immediately critical; the Church of England Men's Society considered a campaign to prevent the recommendations of Beveridge being approved by Parliament. House was not unduly anxious – he thought that some of the more dangerous wording could be satisfactorily explained; he believed there was 'a general tendency to suggest that religious broadcasting ought to be undogmatic in a sense which an agnostic might use the term but which no instructed Christian would accept'.[56] House wanted the Governors left in no doubt that CRAC and the churches would not tolerate the Beveridge suggestion[57] that the objective of religious broadcasting 'should be conceived, not as that of seeking converts to one particular church but as that of maintaining the common element in all religious bodies.' CRAC thought that Beveridge had simply not understood either Haley's concept of 'moral values' nor its own submission, both of which made the clear distinction between Christian faith and Christian moral values, a distinction which the BCC report had taken pains to preserve.[58]

Beveridge's rejection of the chimera of complete editorial objectivity demolished the arguments of the Ethical Union and RPA which wanted the Corporation to regard Christianity with complete impartiality. There must certainly be teaching, but this would mean 'taking a broad view of the teaching of Christian values rather than a narrow doctrinal view'. To this, CRAC objected most strongly; it could only lead to diminishment and a religion without belief, as Wand had said. The BCC had insisted that Christians had a dogmatic basis for their Christian values. CRAC was relieved to read of Beveridge's deference to the initiative and authority of the Governors, but rejected the notion that religious broadcasting should continue 'to emphasize spiritual values as illustrated in the teaching of all who call themselves Christian'. They found this hard to take seriously; it was essentially humanist in outlook: dogma and tradition, it seemed, were dispensable.

When CRAC met on 19 June it was in no mood to compromise. Cockin believed the BBC's religious policy would fall into complete disarray if the Beveridge suggestions were taken seriously. CRAC's appeal to the Governors against Beveridge again sought to exclude the Unitarians.[59] Beveridge was aware of CRAC's division of opinion on the matter. Had there been a compromise 'for the sake of fellowship', as W. G. Moore, a Congregationalist member wanted, then the Roman Catholics would have washed their hands of CRAC, just as many of their leading members would have wished. Woodward insisted that he was only prepared to accept the Unitarians as members of CRAC if they changed their name![60] The Roman Catholic submission also received comment in the Report, and the notion of 'mechanical adjustment' on the basis of numbers was firmly rejected. Agnellus Andrew was sorry that CRAC could not rise to discuss the principle of church affairs under state control. He might have guessed that the principle would be buried beneath the more pressing question of statistics which had side-tracked the Committee so many times before. Masterson understandably feared that the Head of Religious Broadcasting 'might become very much a BBC official over whom the churches concerned had no authority'.[61] They had to be satisfied that the principle had been stated and was now in the minute book. CRAC's recommendations were fiercely conservative: any adoption of the Beveridge approach would upset the churches and make for far less effective religious broadcasting as a result. Essentially it demanded: 'Retain the present system!'

In July, the Report was debated in Parliament, but the religious issue was not touched. Woodward told Haley that Wand was reliably informed that the Government 'deliberately kept religious broadcasting out of the White Paper; they were content to leave CRAC to deal directly with the Governors.'[62] In the event, it was raised by the Church of England Men's Society, and Patrick Gordon Walker, for the Government, passed the whole question back to the Governors. Haley was quite sure that the Government had no intention of saying anything to the Governors, and there was no mention of religion in the White Paper[63] at all. Haley told Woodward it would all be coming to the Governors in October. Of the Lords' debate Woodward reported:

> I sat through three and a half hours of the Lords' debate yesterday . . . the speeches were dreary beyond words; they would have emptied any church. The only reference to religion while I was there was a remark by Woolton that he found *Lift Up Your Hearts* dull . . . 'not half so dull as we are finding your speech'.[64]

It looked as if all was set fair to have everything remain as before.

Parliament was dissolved in September and by the time the Governors considered the question, Churchill was back; the Beveridge Report 'ceased to count in anyone's calculation'.[65] For CRAC at least, there was reprieve and relief; it had no doubt the Governors would leave all as it was; they did! Religious broadcasting should 'continue as at present' and in November they succeeded in calming the troubled waters.[66] The 'mainstream' churches remained as before – in control; except for an increase in the number of broadcasts for the Unitarians. Beveridge would not be accepted, but the Governors hoped that there might be more programmes on secular moral values.

The interdenominational, even ecumenical, ship had weathered the Beveridge rapids, but not without a fortuitous change of direction in the political winds; however the Conservatives were not expected to rock the boat in the unpredictable waters of religious sensitivity.[67] If the RBD was now bound by Haley's policy, House knew that this must issue in greater co-operation between his Department and the churches themselves. The ways had parted, and it was for the churches to recognize that they no longer had the Corporation behind them as in 1931.[68] Since there were so many of them, the BBC would at any rate continue to act as umpire.

PART FIVE

MORALS AND MISSIONS:
THE PARTING OF THE WAYS
1951–55

26

MORAL VALUES: CORPORATION
INITIATIVES

A. After Beveridge

In a lecture to the English Society in January 1952, G. M. Trevelyan, the historian, concluded: 'Even if the future civilization proves better than the old . . . it will at best be deficient in many things of value that were there in the past'.[1] The Governors of the BBC would have concurred as they met to discuss the Corporation's religious output in the wake of the Beveridge Report and, in particular, the increasing pressure from various bodies to have fundamental changes made to the present policy. In autumn 1951 Haley had managed to concentrate the debate on the questions which he had examined years before.[2] The Corporation could clearly no longer regard CRAC as the only repository of advice on the religious questions raised both within and outside the RBD. Francis House had repeated time and again that CRAC could only advise on the Christian content of programmes. Indeed, the Sunday Committee had stated from the beginning that it would not advise the Corporation on, for example, Jewish programmes.[3] In 1950 House had said quite clearly: 'At the practical level, I do not consider that CRAC is the kind of body from which it is reasonable to expect that the Corporation can obtain useful advice except on the subject of Christian broadcasts'.[4] In the Beveridge Report there had been calls for consistency: either change CRAC to the Central *Christian* Advisory body, or have the constituency extended to justify the word 'religious' or, indeed, have yet another Committee. In effect, the Governors had to advise themselves, and this they did: they considered that the Corporation had a responsibility to those who looked outside Christianity for a basis for moral behaviour. Let there be some species of 'Hyde Park Corner' on the air.

Most notable among the *non*-Christians were the supporters of the Rationalist Press Association who wanted yet another meeting with Haley in the light of the Beveridge Report. C. Bradlaugh Bonner, the

Secretary of the Parliamentary Committee for Freedom of Religious Controversy, discussed hoped-for schemes with a producer on the Third Programme Staff. His proposals were intensely erudite and involved mostly professors of philosophy and the behavioural sciences. With the exception of J. Z. Young of University College, London, Mary Somerville later thought them all 'dim academics whom we would not wish to use'.[5] In autumn 1951, Haley, with Barbara Wootton and Lord Tedder, two of the Governors, met Lord Dowding, Bradlaugh Bonner, Alderman Reeves and Lord Chorley, representing the Committee. It was a formidable lobby. They wanted a 'minority sects advisory committee' of some kind, and talks of a controversial kind in which debate could take place without the Christians always having the last word. Bonner had complained of an eight-part series, *Man Without God*, broadcast in January 1951, in which Lord Elton had, he believed, misrepresented the non-Christian case and in particular had assumed that God was the deepest need of every man, 'as even the atheist knows in his heart of hearts'.[6] Lord Dowding, representing the interests of the Spiritualists, hoped that any new minority advisory committee would invite submissions from the widest spectrum.[7] House predictably thought this was difficult to take seriously and, besides, he had little respect for the methods, not to mention the thinking, of this group.

The Board of Governors met again in November, but postponed the debate until after Christmas in order to 'gather up the strands of the discussions' which would then be presented for the consideration of CRAC. In January 1952 it was clear to Haley that the BBC's commitment to religious programmes was now pluriform. Its commitment to the churches was explicit: Beveridge's species of 'free-for-all' had been rejected and the 'mainstream' churches had an effective monopoly of broadcast services. These were unambiguously Christian and thus the Governors conceded that the amount of religious broadcasting of this kind was 'about right'.[8] The distinction between Christian values and Christian faith made by Haley and the BCC was to be the basis of Corporation policy and, as we have seen, it marked the point of departure not only in conceptual but in practical, institutional terms. There would be programmes which would reflect this polarity.

For House and CRAC it was quite obvious that broadcast services would be the particular arena for innovation, not the least in the popular programmes on the Light wavelength. Anything other than popular material was not acceptable. In 1950 Tom Chalmers, the Controller, had made it quite clear to House and Edwin Robertson that whilst the Light might be the context for a sort of 'Hyde Park Corner of the Air' (which had been tried without success during wartime and

20. Melville Dinwiddie

21. Agnellus Andrew

22. Francis House

23. William Haley

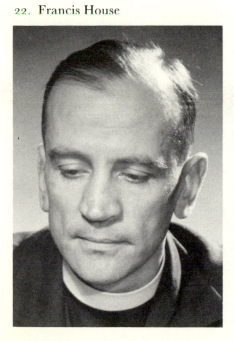

24. Harman Grisewood

25. E. H. Robertson

26. J. W. Welch (*left*) and Cyril Taylor

later recommended by Beveridge), any serious level of discussion was beyond his audience, whatever Haley might be hoping for in his bid to improve its standards and at the same time keep the audience away from the independent stations.[9]

The second element in the Board's policy concerned the implications of the 1947 statement:[10] how to put 'the search for truth' into operation. There had been a number of talks series on World Religions (1948), Spiritualism (1948), *The Right Thing to Do* (1948), scientific humanism under the general title *The Pattern of the Future* (1949) and the prestigious series *Man Without God* in 1950/51. Several had been on the Third Programme and others on the Home. Haley had to tread carefully not only because of the powerful resistance by the churches to any widespread attack on Christianity; he was cautious of wounding public sentiments and yet was strongly committed to the search for truth: critics of the BBC such as Bertrand Russell, Julian Huxley and Fred Hoyle were powerful voices.

In order to implement the 1947 policy, Haley, Somerville (in charge of Talks) and Harman Grisewood had conversations with several notably radical churchmen, and in particular J. H. Oldham. The BBC, they decided, was not in business to organize a slanging match: 'controversy' was too emotive and even old-fashioned a term. Could not the BBC take the initiative in setting out an agenda of public debate which would itself be an educative process, and not simply a response to those like Bradlaugh Bonner who wanted a similar space for 'recital' such as he and others believed the churches were hanging on to for dear life. His case was further strengthened by the regular provision of talks spaces for which Edwin Robertson was now responsible. Robertson was a prodigious reader and was very close to new as well as established theological thinking, particularly in the growing ecumenical atmosphere.[11] His endeavour was to educate the clergy and laity alike and particularly, on the new Third Programme, examine theological issues in greater depth than could be done in Sunday sermons. In many areas, he later concluded, the 'churches on the whole have not helped us . . . we have practically nothing to reflect . . . we have to initiate creative thinking.'[12] Karl Barth, Reinhold Niebuhr and Emil Brunner were brought to the Third Programme: it was the only context in which such profundity could survive. To the humanist and rationalist lobby, this all contributed to the overall impression that the Christians had all the running. Controversial programmes since the policy change had not all been easy. The programme efforts between 1947 and 1950 had been disappointing, not least because of lack of time, but also because considerable numbers of atheist and rationalist speakers either were reluctant to reopen the old religion-versus-science wrangle on any sort of popular level or simply departed too far from their programme brief. House and Somerville also thought that their combined resources in staff and expertise was simply not adequate. There needed to be someone especially competent to observe the intellectual climate with time and insight to ascertain the principal contours of contemporary debates. Oldham had suggested Kathleen Bliss, his partner in the *Christian News-Letter*.[13] It was a 'field-work' task and Mary Somerville was delighted at the prospect of having Kathleen Bliss as a part-time seconded member of her staff; she was 'the right chap for the job'.[14]

Bliss was taken on in February 1951, first to examine what the BBC had already done about the Governors' directive of March 1947, secondly, to consult with her advisers on the direction of appropriate controversial discussion for broadcasting, and thirdly, to define the area of debate for the future.[15] The BCC had convened a meeting arising from Haley's request to their Commission for more detailed suggestions; Haley had wanted the debate extended to all listening levels. In March 1951 F. A. Cockin chaired this 'think-tank'. Bliss and Oldham were augmented by Marjorie Reeves, Eric Fenn, David Say (the BCC General Secretary), Professor C. A. Coulson and Richard Crossman. The outcome, in September, was a report of about twenty-five thousand words produced by Oldham and Bliss. Rather than 'Controversial Religious Broadcasting' they preferred 'Fundamental Debate'. In six months she had discussed, read, lunched and corresponded with almost a hundred people. There were weekends and myriad group discussions with a vast cross section of British intellectual life. It is regrettable that this report was never published. It was a diagnosis of contemporary culture and was exceedingly complex when seen as a basis for programmes, although Bliss and Oldham had gone to considerable lengths to relate the material to ordinary human experience. George Barnes, however, said bluntly that he found it hard to read and thought it would only be useful to broadcasting if the idea within it could be 'reduced to the dramatist's simplicity'.[16] It was a prophetic remark. The 'prime difficulty', Bliss confessed to Mary Somerville, was 'getting A and B using different language to agree that they were talking about the same thing . . . the first thing to find was a formulation which enabled those whose differences lie at the root of our popular confusions to begin to understand each other.'[17] It would take a long time, and the BBC could guard against the 'ill effects' of controversial religious broadcasts by conceiving its tasks in long-term educational patterns. It might not, however, content the rationalists who, like the churches, were not easily herded together for discussion.

But as Cockin insisted to Lord Simon, over the last fifty years Christian and humanist thought had drifted so far apart as to be out of earshot of each other. If the attempt was not made on the right lines, however, 'the consequences will be worse than the present'.[18] In January 1952, the Governors accepted that something had to be done by the Talks Division, and – as the policy statement of 1947 had said – 'with good taste'![19] The BCC had almost got what it wanted.

B. The 'Question Mark' Series

The third area considered by the Governors centred on Haley's belief in moral values. They thus asked CRAC to consider programmes especially for younger people who were 'disposed to reject moral values put forward in a purely Christian context'.[20] Haley wanted programmes about moral postures as reflected and focused in the lives of notable figures who had found their own philosophies and particularly those outside formal Christianity. Somerville and the Schools Department had been developing such biographical programmes, and Robert Walton, now responsible for religion in the schools output, knew this to be a persuasive method of teaching. Haley made the point explicit: these programmes, perhaps with such a title as 'Values in Living', would be quite outside 'mainstream' broadcasts. They would also be quite separate from controversy and the so-called 'fundamental debate': they had to be 'very simple'.

CRAC was predictably cautious and rejected Haley's tripartite division into straight religious broadcasting, Fundamental Debate and non-Christian moral talks. It believed that Christians must have a part to play in moral teaching, but somehow controversy, i.e. Fundamental Debate, must be avoided. It had grave doubts about Haley's notion of 'commonly agreed' ethical precepts; how could such a list be drawn up and by whom? Moreover, how could this problem be resolved in programme terms without discussion, debate and therefore controversy?

Mary Somerville had no doubt that Haley was asking for the almost impossible: there would only be a very small sum of commonly agreed values. And furthermore, since the young to whom these talks were to be directed listened at best to the Light Programme and at worst to Luxembourg in search of light entertainment, it was hardly any use for the Governors to insist on radio being the obvious route to the adolescents of the nation. Professor Barbara Wootton had a great deal to say on the Board but made it quite clear that the whole business was exceedingly complex and by no means as simple as they expected the talks themselves to be.[21] Mary Somerville would have to get them on the air and could only conceive of their succeeding, if anywhere, at the 'popular "hero" level'.[22]

The Governors, notwithstanding, agreed to Haley's initiative:[23] the talks would state and not discuss; assumptions would neither be questioned nor attacked. They should deal with 'the kind of behaviour which has come to be respected and admired in our civilization: kindliness, consideration for others, courage, truthfulness, justice, honesty, faithfulness, social responsibility and all forms of dependability. The series should aim at showing that such standards are held in common to be the guides for a good life.'[24] The BBC had articulated its own natural theology and its own belief in morals without (or irrespective of) religious sanction. It was the inevitable outcome of Haley's reading of the climate of 1951 and his belief that the Corporation had a growing responsibility to those without what he called the 'antecedent models' which a religious education or upbringing provided. In Grisewood's view the BBC had a duty to the 'world of disbelief and doubt and the world of reason as opposed to faith', areas far more 'populous, ancient and dignified than Mr Bradlaugh Bonner and his friends would have us believe'.[25] It was crucial for any proposed series that whilst a number of speakers should rightly be Christians, the balance would be in favour of those without a religious sanction for their moral code.

Michael Stephens, a talks producer, provided a definition for Somerville:

> Not those at the forefront of ethical controversy [but] those whose personal integrity and social responsibility [are combined] with imagination and intelligence enough to formulate a persuasive (though personal) ethic while having nothing to do with Christianity and who can expound their own beliefs in terms which make them acceptable to others.[26]

Speakers, however, were not easy to find. Barbara Wootton, who was strongly behind the scheme, had little idea how to translate complex notions involving sociological, political and anthropological data into simple ten-minute programme material! The other Governors wanted 'parables rather than Gifford Lectures in miniature'.[27] The Rationalist Press Association and other Humanist bodies failed to suggest any good broadcasters who would avoid the sort of presentation which Haley feared would look like sermons in a secular guise. CRAC at any rate had preferred the notion of talks being secular in order to disengage ideas of an eclectic moral philosophy from the realm of theology which most members believed was not amenable to notions about a common sum of moral values.[28] By the autumn, Somerville and Kathleen Bliss had gathered twelve speakers of whom seven were Christian. People prepared to give straight talks were not difficult to find. Each was asked to select one quality which was essential to civilized life. The series entitled *Question Mark*, had to be attractive and secure the audience: Somerville decided to begin with the lawyer Edgar Lustgarten, who spoke on 'Keeping One's Word', followed by Lord Hailsham on 'Chastity'. George Cansdale, the Superintendent of London Zoo, spoke on 'Faith', and Elliot Dodds, the editor of a Huddersfield newspaper, on 'Tolerance'. The series ran from October to December and the Corporation was anxious to have as clear a picture as Silvey's research department could provide. It seemed that a good proportion of the audience listened because they were waiting for *The Archers* to start at 6.45, these talks occupied the preceding ten minutes![29] There was little evidence that any apathy had been disturbed. The producer Ronald Lewin, who had considerable reservations about straight talks on the Light Programme, thought that by and large these were good, but from the correspondence to the speakers he was sure that 'those listeners whose interest was most actively aroused were either already believers or who – lacking a faith – were looking for one'. It was a worthy experiment but next time they should not be talks.[30] Somerville wanted story, discussion, and dramatization; in a word – she told CRAC – she wanted a more appropriate and attractive use of the medium. Discussion, however, sounded too much like controversy for CRAC; it suggested 'Fundamental Debate'. Kathleen Bliss had said again and again that whatever else could be said about this new area of broadcasting policy, it was certainly not simple and even less did it belong on the Light Programme. As we have seen, Haley was determined to raise the tone of the Light Programme.

The Home Service was the obvious place for such material, and the post-war reorganization had included provision for regular talks of particular concern to House and Robertson, who with other contenders knew it as the 'values' space: it was open to competition. Some suggestions were taken and others were refused. House frequently complained that notwithstanding the BBC's commitment to the Christian faith, there had been a serious diminution in the number of talks series offered by the Department, and notably from Edwin Robertson, which had been accepted. House wanted a regular weekly place for a religious talk and eventually got it, but not without a struggle. But he did not want the Department's contribution discriminated against by the overall heading of 'A Christian View' thus relegating his output to a corner in the schedules which exploited popular prejudices against religion.[31] Notwithstanding the most imaginative and creative efforts of Robertson to produce all manner of interesting schemes of talks on subjects like Church and State, the Jewish problem, and Pacifism, there was inevitably resistance from the Home Service planners. Wellington, the Controller, complained constantly of the 'hand to mouth approach' and resisted any request for a regular commitment of space to the RBD; it had to be on merit. However, Robertson's commitment to the Third Programme gave opportunity for the seriousness and erudition of his schemes to be all the more enthusiastically discussed: there also everything was on merit! There could be arcane meditations and theological discourses for the non-specialist which need not be shaped for the Home listener. (House later lamented that he was the only one in the Corporation who was prepared to make a case for meditations.[32] But the Third Programme would not accept them; Grisewood thought them no substitute for normal church services, which the Third did not take anyway, except occasionally on major church feasts, where both the liturgical setting and the sermon were acceptable, primarily on aesthetic grounds.)

In 1952, for example, Robertson planned for the Home Service a series of conversations between young scientists and young Christians. Lindsay Wellington thought little of it: '. . . no hard thought, no conclusions, nothing but a vague awareness that there may be a reality different from and more important than science . . . so what?'[33] Somerville yet again feared the problem of controversy and the demands of the Rationalist Press Association. By the middle of summer 1952, things began to improve when Kenneth Adam took over the Home Service and was committed to seeing that the Department was given a fairer crack of the whip.

C. 'Fundamental Debate'

Kathleen Bliss had been against Robertson's scheme simply because the proposed participants were not, in her view, sufficiently weighty to make a significant contribution, particularly as she was struggling with the Fundamental Debate. The young scientists would not be 'fundamental' enough and this would undermine the quite new thing the BBC was trying to do. The post-war democratizing of the airwaves had in her view 'atomized' subjects of debate and thus increased the general confusion. The BBC had a new task in the explication of fundamental questions; this was quite distinct from being the platform for the expression of minority opinions. The Governors were committed to help the millions 'hungering after information on spiritual issues', and thus the objectives of the Corporation's initiative, as Bliss saw them, were fourfold:

(i) to keep before the mind of the public serious questions of human life and its purposes and motivations;
(ii) to provide material pertinent to these questions;
(iii) to provide alternatives to those holding rigid convictions; and
(iv) to demonstrate the possibility of moderate, sincere and informative debates between persons who disagree.[34]

Above all, she was aware of the futility of controversial broadcasting which was by nature and perhaps inevitably a 'slanging match'. She was convinced that the Corporation could provide a medium in which the heavyweight thinkers could not only converse in public but could do so in a way intelligible to a serious, albeit inexpert, audience. It was an ecumenical and even reconciling task which must inform the public as to the nature of the debate without being destructive: diverse insights into the great 'human, cultural and religious questions which no one person or group can answer' should be 'heard and related to each other'.[35] Bliss precisely clarified Haley's hope that the BBC would be positive: 'A constructive debate should help the listener to build on what faith he has' and moreover engage the minds of those in the universities and elsewhere who were bound by a 'common sense of urgency' to be distinguished from their introverted contemporaries who were far less worried about the problems of the day. She believed the BBC played a responsible role in world history, as she had told the Beveridge Committee: 'It has got not only to reflect and to represent but it has in some sense to lead because many people believe that Western culture has got its back to the wall.'[36]

Within a year, Bliss from her travels had reduced the Fundamental Debate to four aspects of what she wanted to call 'The Human Prospect', and believed she had found people sufficiently committed to the Corporation's endeavour. They must be sincere, so that the Home Service audience which might not understand the first time round would at least by their sincerity be carried on to the next stage of the discussion. There were four questions:

(i) Can human behaviour be explained in terms of heredity and environment?
(ii) What is the human prospect on secular humanist assumptions?
(iii) Is man the maker or the product of history?
(iv) What relevance have the claims of religion?[37]

After all her consultations, Bliss moved from the original idea of examining beliefs to the wider assumptions beneath beliefs. There were thus four fundamental attitudes: Humanism, Behaviourism, Marxism and Christianity. Each would have two programmes and the advocates of each 'attitude' would be assessed and criticized by 'outsiders' rather than opponents. It was a way of avoiding the confrontation of opposing recitals and indicating as clearly as was possible the subtleties of debate in such a manner that aggression would be precluded. It had not been an easy concept for the Governors to grasp, and it was clear that Haley's earlier initiatives had been rushed through with unsatisfactory results. With Bliss now effectively on the staff it was important that they understood her objectives. Cockin, now Chairman of CRAC, had a meeting with Sir Philip Morris, a Governor of the Corporation and Vice-Chancellor of Bristol University, after which he felt confident that Morris at least had grasped what was aimed at. It was not a matter of air space for all who claimed Christian orthodoxy but a 'quite independent issue on which churches as such had no particular right to speak'. Cockin agreed to make it plain to CRAC that 'the churches as such had no business to interfere with Fundamental Debate'.[38] When CRAC met in October 1952, Bliss had powerful support from Cockin and Grisewood, who told the Committee that Fundamental Debate was not only of major importance but 'ought to be a continuing element in broadcasting'.[39] It was a significant moment in the development of the BBC's policies in the educational field. Bliss reassured the Committee that the aim of the debate was 'not to shake people out of the beliefs they hold but to show them what other points of view there are'.[40]

By the close of 1952 she and J. H. Oldham had brought numerous people together for conferences and weekends. They sought a means of providing both a market for those with ethical and religious cures to peddle their wares, and also a platform on which the BBC would present a new-found synthesis in which conflicting views were seemingly harmonized. For their part, the participants were mostly academics with a reputation to consider, both professional and private. The temptation had been to cast the debate in the terms of the scientific approach to ethical questions. Bliss had been much influenced by Karl Heim whose two books, *Christian Faith and Natural Science* and *The Transformation of the Scientific World View*, had been published (in German) in Tübingen in 1949 and 1951 respectively.[41] Both Bliss and Oldham thought, however, that this would be too technical for the Home Service audience. The first series should examine the more general attitudes which would be of interest to those people who might be concerned to widen and inform their opinions and could cope with a few basic technicalities.

Invitations were sent out to a variety of behavioural scientists, philosophers and theologians to attend a weekend conference at St Julian's in Sussex in July 1952. Four papers were circulated on the four chosen 'attitudes': Humanism, Behaviourism, Marxism and Christianity. Participants admitted later that they found themselves alongside people with whom they would not normally expect to converse in any depth. The weekend brought together Karl Popper of the LSE, John Baillie, the Principal of New College, Edinburgh;[42] James Drever, Professor of Psychology, also at Edinburgh; Harold Blackham, the Secretary of the Ethical Society and Alasdair MacIntyre, a philosopher from the University of Manchester. Bliss had been in touch with other notable scholars including Michael Polanyi, Stephen Toulmin and V. A. Demant, along with others who had had a similar meeting the year before. The preparations had been exhaustive and the resultant discussions over almost three days were intense and disciplined. Much of the success was due to Oldham's grasp of the four major perspectives and their inter-relatedness: Professor Medawar of University College, London, believed there would have been no real debate without his wizardry in the conduct of the discussion. Karl Popper thought it one of the best meetings of this kind he had ever attended. Alasdair MacIntyre, however, thought that the meeting reflected an interesting axis between the rationalism of the Christians and of Karl Popper and of 'the scientists in general' on the one hand, and the 'kind of thinking which Communists do, on the other hand'.[43] The key questions for MacIntyre were rationality in faith and in the context of the Christian apologia. Baillie regarded Popper's concepts as being closer to the Christian position than those of any other non-Christian present; moreover, like Demant, Baillie was impatient with the prevailing lack of any theological depth among the participants generally. It had been a long-standing complaint among those who had resisted controversial broadcasting that the 'opposition' had little real understanding of the Christian apologia and consequently set up their own quite false 'Aunt Sallies' which they then proceeded to demolish. The purpose and value of the projected series was to have people listen to the echoes behind the slogans: 'People who habitually listen to sermons don't hear atheists giving a reasoned account of their position; those who accept the behaviourist account of the origin of religious belief as all there is to it do not take easily to exploring the mind of a rational theologian.'[44] The weekend at St Julian's set the tone and encouraged Bliss and Oldham to proceed towards the next stage of the programme-building process: getting the contributors to speak not only to each other but to the Home Service audience! Blackham recognized the problem and put his finger on it when he told Bliss that the key to the success of the weekend was the 'allusiveness and background unexpressed but understood'; but this, as everyone realized, could not be assumed to be present in the

Home Service audience. The July debates, however, did move the notion of the Fundamental Debate a further stage towards the series of programmes called *Encounters of Belief*.

By the end of the year Bliss and Oldham had secured three of the four principal advocates: Blackham for the Humanists, Drever for the Behaviourists and Roy Pascal, Professor of German at the University of Birmingham, for the Marxists. The most difficult to find, she later confessed, was the Christian advocate;[45] Professor H. A. Hodges of Reading eventually agreed. The advocates were each asked to produce a paper stating their position, and the next problem was to find those commentators who were clearly distinguishable from each other and also sufficiently able as broadcasters. Pascal's paper was the most problematic: it had to be on the Marxist view of man in history: 'Does man make history or is man shaped by historical and social forces?' This was Oldham's formulation, and he suggested Edward Crankshaw as one of the Christian advocates in reply, the other being Martin Wight, an historian from the LSE. The four 'advocating' papers were sent round to the critics and commentators, each of whom could privately – or to Bliss and Oldham – vent their impatience with what they regarded as not worth taking seriously. Sir Herbert Read, for example, found in Blackham's paper 'a bleak kind of Humanism without subtlety and without depth'.[46] Vincent Turner of Campion Hall thought it naive. V. A. Demant thought James Drever's paper showed that he had not the 'faintest idea of the intellectual side of Christianity'.[47]

Early in 1953 Bliss became aware that the Christian responses in the final pair of broadcasts were the most difficult to organize. She had consulted such eminent men as E. H. Carr, Professor of International Politics at Aberystwyth, Arnold Toynbee and Isaiah Berlin. Finally theology, philosophy and sociology were all represented in Hodges, Stephen Toulmin and Patrick Nowell-Smith (both of Oxford), and Martin Wight. But complexities also remained unsolved in the two programmes in which the Christians had the first major say; Bliss, after the event, thought that the Christians did better as critics than exponents! By the end of January the order was decided and the four pairs of programmes on the four major themes were all ready with exponents, supporters and critics. This scheme provided each exponent with comment from his own side, while critics would express two different points of view on the opposite side – a two-way discourse shared by four! Notwithstanding enormous preparations and voluminous letters from J. H. Oldham, Bliss found these 'interdisciplinary' conversations preoccupied with definitions, even for the eirenic

Blackham; he wanted more – perhaps rather too much more – taken as understood than was appropriate to the audience. It was not enough to bring these people together and let them expound their own views and answer their critics. Bliss was reluctant to act in any way as a chairman of these discussions – she feared it would invade their integrity. She collected and collated masses of comment and sought thereafter to put together something resembling a script which each participant would speak like characters in a morality play. This was the complaint of Drever, whose pair of programmes on Behaviourism and Naturalism Bliss actually regarded as the best of the eight.

Drever had focused on a difficulty: how to allow highly articulate, yet naturally cautious, academics to inter-relate across linguistic and knowledge boundaries towards others who were unacquainted with their ways of speaking. Thanks to both Oldham and Bliss and their perception of the four areas of investigation (or 'ways of believing in the world', as she regarded them), the participants did make progress in debate and self-analysis alongside each other. Bliss had to get them to achieve more than profitable discussion; they must realize that the end product was broadcasting – moulding the subtle and complex materials of their discussion into shapes of meaning intelligible to men and women who might also be asking questions about science, humanism, Christianity and the Soviets, but without the intellectual background and perspectives of these specialists. If they had ever felt any obligation to these people, they had long since forgotten it and could only say what they had to say to those who spoke the same language.

It was, as Drever had complained, like 'writing a play with the actors having the last word on their parts',[48] and all the more complex for Bliss as she was not in fact the producer of the series for the Corporation. Somerville had recruited a young Anglican, Lorna Moore, for the series, and naturally there was a conflict of functions, although certainly not of personalities. She complained that Bliss as adviser to the series 'looked away from the BBC in her planning and discussions and this prevented the producer having a confident overall view'.[49] Moreover, as the participants continued their discussion, they became convinced that any material for a programme could only be arrived at after yet more discussion; for this, however, there was simply insufficient time. The discussion to date had to supply the raw materials for the programme, and it fell to Bliss and Moore to do the best scissors-and-paste job possible. Without Moore's skill in bringing the participants into some disciplined order, the series would never have gone on the air.[50] Drever had been right: each participant had to

speak his 'part', *not* as he had spoken it but as these two had edited it for
the microphone. In the event each participant was happy to do so,
provided the editors did not make the concord too obvious. Drever and
others wanted the programmes to be unscripted, but at this stage in the
history of controversial broadcasting this was simply not permitted.[51]
Had the participants each produced a series such as Michael Polanyi's
1951 Gifford Lectures,[52] Bliss and Oldham might have together
produced their 'morality play' and created both sides of all the inter-
related debates from previously written material. It would have been
anything but debate, and further consultation with the 'contributors'
would doubtless have provoked resistance to the alterations and the
butchering of their texts for broadcasting purposes. In the event, at no
point was Bliss satisfied with the final texts of the broadcasts: changes
and refinements were being introduced almost up to the last minute.
Moreover, at the very moment when the most important consultations
were coming to fruition, the Corporation had a new Director-General
and the Fundamental Debate initiative was now left without that
special support that Haley had given since the earlier wartime
discussions with Welch. Haley went to *The Times* and was replaced by
the former soldier Ian Jacob, who had been Director of External
Services.[53] In his reply to CRAC's good wishes Haley stressed that
what he termed 'the deeper issues in religious broadcasting' were
among 'the most serious responsibilities of the BBC'.[54] Apart from
Reith, Haley took the deliberations of CRAC more seriously than any
other Director-General of the period.

On 30 January 1953, the *Radio Times* was to carry Bliss's introduction
to the series on the 'four main attitudes to living' which would make
'certain demands on the indulgence of the listener who is unlikely to
find here any ready made answers'. It was exactly according to the
policy of the Corporation: no 'confessions'. The press was pleased at the
announcement and looked forward eagerly to the series.[55] By the time
the *Radio Times* actually appeared, the bottom had fallen out of Bliss's
scheme: the principal Marxist, Roy Pascal from Birmingham,
threatened to withdraw from the enterprise. Pascal, a member of the
Communist Party, had been suggested by Alasdair MacIntyre.
Pascal's second was another of his generation, Benjamin Farrington,
Professor of Classics at University College, Swansea. As deliberations
proceeded during January for finding the two Christian critics,
Oldham had been convinced that one of them at least must have a
sympathetic appreciation of the Marxist position: MacIntyre was that
man. Oldham's other earlier recommendation was Edward Crankshaw, the journalist and broadcaster, who contributed the column

'Inside Russia' to *The Observer*. He was an opponent of everything Marxist. Pascal had been worried by the choice of MacIntyre: he thought him too sympathetic to Marxism to put up a strong case. He objected even more strongly to Crankshaw because he 'enjoys no prestige in the intellectual world as a thinker'.[56] He feared the discussion would embrace the more practical aspects of contemporary Communism and thus move away from the arena of the philosophy of history with which the third pair of programmes was concerned. Moreover, Pascal was convinced that Crankshaw would not be taken note of in academic circles and thus bring the debate into disrepute. He complained that Bliss had, by inviting Crankshaw, changed the character of the broadcast. He suggested Hyman Levy, Professor of Mathematics at the Imperial College of Science and Technology, who he believed would be willing to take his place.[57]

Meanwhile, the first programme, on Humanism, was broadcast on 3 February and with the series off the ground it was all the more urgent to get a replacement for Pascal. Bliss believed that the Marxist pair of programmes was in a real way the most important. The first two pairs, on Humanism and Behaviourism, would inevitably give an impression that we were all living in 'an intellectually stable world in which we solemnly decide whether or not we can go on believing'.[58] The Marxist and Christian discussions were integrally bound together. The Marxist programme was intended not to give the Christians the opportunity as the only real opponents of the Communists but to widen the debate. She believed that the Fundamental Debate series made just as many demands on the Christians as on the others to avoid a simple and protective exposition of their case for Christianity and the church. She wanted the Christians to show that their faith understood the ranges of the human spirit hidden from their opponents, and thus to display its relationship to Western culture.

Pascal had withdrawn the day after the first programme, and Bliss and Oldham began frantic negotiations with Levy on the one hand and the maligned Edward Crankshaw on the other. Pascal's original source paper for the programme was one which Oldham regarded somewhat contemptuously as having little with which a liberal democrat need quarrel.[59] To make up for this exposition of Goethe rather than Marx, the Corporation had invited another member of the Communist Party, Professor Benjamin Farrington. Meanwhile, Crankshaw had generously agreed to withdraw for fear of wrecking this pair of discussions. But he was furious: he was certain that pressure from the Communist Party was the reason why Pascal withdrew. Oldham after much deliberation and conversation with Levy came to believe that Crankshaw was right and that Pascal had played an underhand game, 'purely self-regarding with no trace of public obligation'.[60] Oldham agreed with Crankshaw that the scheme would collapse if the latter would not withdraw. Crankshaw lamented that he could not take part in a serious discussion of Marxism 'without point-scoring and outside the ambit of the Cold War'.[61]

Kathleen Bliss now had the problem of staging the discussion with two new participants and no time for them to meet together and discuss each other's papers. Levy was certainly not prepared to speak Pascal's 'part'. Moreover, who would take Crankshaw's part? Bliss invited the historian Hugh Trevor-Roper of Christ Church, Oxford and boldly told him that Pascal had withdrawn not because of the substance of the programme but because 'recent events in the Communist world have made him very anxious not to appear in public'.[62] Unfortunately, Farrington and Levy's last-minute contributions could not be discussed at sufficient length and Trevor-Roper was impatient with an obvious shift in Farrington's contribution away from the assumptions of Marxism towards the achievements of Communism. Unlike the other three pairs of programmes, the Marxist debates would have significant policy repercussions if there was any suggestion in the final broadcasts that the established view was under-represented or distinctly weaker. Both Somerville and Grisewood had severe misgivings about the programmes scheduled for 3 and 10 March. By mid-February there was still no script ready and Somerville would have been ready to cancel the programmes but for her faith in Bliss and Oldham. Moreover, Levy's further contributions to some extent made nonsense of MacIntyre's previous responses to Pascal and so made Bliss's scissors-and-paste operation all the more difficult. Whilst Farrington was able to work more alterations into his material, Trevor-Roper had no time to do so, and thus refused to alter his. It was a regrettable index of the academic disregard for broadcasting on the one hand and the critical importance of this particular facet of these four discussions on the other. Meanwhile, Bliss was still working on her patchwork for programmes seven and eight for the end of March at the very moment that the Marxist programme was due to go out. It could not be done. Aware of Grisewood's misgiving, Kathleen Bliss took upon herself to cancel the programmes with just twenty-four hours to spare. The BBC accepted responsibility, and the accompanying opprobrium which the *Daily Worker* meted out the following day. At the allotted moment, and notwithstanding the *Radio Times* billing, the expectant public heard the voice of Stephen Spender reading a selection of poems. There were around one hundred calls of complaint.

Bliss and Oldham were profoundly disappointed, not the least because of the sequential importance of the Marxist discussions to be followed by the pair concentrating particularly upon Christianity.

> The kind of Christianity I wanted to see presented was the kind that led Dostoievsky to make his radical break with Russian nihilism and Berdyaev to proclaim the spiritual emptiness of the communism which sprang from it . . . the future of Christianity depends more on whether it can meet the need for an assurance of love than whether it can answer Stephen Toulmin's cosmological posers.[63]

Bliss was sure that the prevailing assumptions of secularism, by which she meant a distilled form of Marxist historicism, were fundamentally at variance with Christianity and that, moreover, Christianity could not be proved on the basis of those assumptions. She lamented to Somerville that the Christians were in a bad position to take issue with the 'secularists', since for so long from pulpits and in religious broadcasting Christian preaching had been protective and self-conscious. It was mainly an exposition of Christian beliefs by means of assertion and a contradiction of what was popularly regarded as opposition by those who proclaimed the loudest that the opposition was devilish – by which they meant anti-church. Some of the criticis of *Encounters of Belief* complained either that Christian dogma was not scrutinized at any depth or that the Christian exponents were not good enough.

It was also partly a question about conventional definitions of what was controversial in religious debate. Edwin H. Robertson, the Assistant Head of Religious Broadcasting, was pushing for initiatives on the Third Programme. But it was no easy task against the resistance of Mary Somerville, who did not believe that the RBD was fully capable of mounting an objective series, particularly outside a strictly Christian subject area. Robertson had, however, succeeded in his series on world religions; it had been the first major departure from a policy which invariably had these being discussed exclusively by Christians. Some of his radical schemes, however, needed higher authority than the Controller of Talks. The Governors had to approve his suggestions for a series of talks on the theology of Rudolf Bultmann of Marburg, a subject that would be certain to raise profound unease in large numbers of people. It naturally depended upon the style of utterance, the audience envisaged, and the wavelength. Robertson believed that the churches by and large did not listen to the Third Programme. The questions raised by religious controversy in the broadcast output were all the more combustible when in conjunction with anything that spoke about Communism in almost any form. *Encounters of Belief* was designed for the Home Service, and planners could not assume a great deal of knowledge in its audience. This was a special difficulty for Kathleen Bliss; no less than sixty people whom she invited to take part simply would not have anything to do with it. Her objectives could not be realized, because each felt that his position was so profoundly at variance with the rest that the generality of Home Service listeners could not even begin to grasp the premises of the debate. Moreover, the debate itself could not be reduced in the carefully prepared scripted form to anything resembling real discussion. Unscripted talks or discussions by Marxists were certainly not permitted.

The gaping hole in *Encounters of Belief* caused by Pascal was more than unfortunate. Oldham reflected that it might have been foreseen: there was a distinct and basic difference of approach upon which Alasdair MacIntyre had put his finger. He had made the point at the St Julian's gathering in July 1952 that 'rational discussion is only possible on liberal presuppositions'.[64] Bliss, perhaps the more committed apologist, agreed that the churches were unable to undertake the attempt not only because of their protectiveness but because their constituency was powerless to command a hearing outside its own boundaries. Moreover, the marked reluctance of very many dons to take part in the series was an index of the academic snobbery which set up a barrier against anything 'popular'. Bliss wanted to build bridges between formidably variant methodological positions. The churches, she was sure, could not and would not: 'No one else but the BBC is prepared to do a comparable service to society.'[65] Oldham was less sanguine. 'The BBC could not, in the state of public opinion in this country, accept a debate in which the Marxists were not routed; the Marxists in that case would not play.'[66] The time had not yet come when there could be a real debate in public between Communists and their opponents: the methods were fundamentally discordant.

Haley's view, around the end of his time as Director-General, was that Communists by and large could not be trusted for an objective view. He had told the General Advisory Committee that when an objective view of any subject is required, 'a contributor who is a Communist should not be chosen'.[67] The *Encounters* series came at a time when increasing numbers of people – politicians, journalists and other delegations – were travelling to Russia and on their return wanting space on the air to talk about their visits. The BBC had deliberated on the subject. The Chairman, Sir Alexander Cadogan, had no doubt in his own mind that it would be a 'misuse of the facilities' to allow these people on the air, particularly to deliver an uncritical monologue. Ian Jacob feared for the 'gullibility of the liberal-minded man, of whom a sprinkling usually gets included in most delegations to Russia'. He believed such people were being 'consciously used as a weapon by Communists in their efforts to undermine the country'. Jacob believed that there could not be freedom of speech on issues relating to Marxism and particularly Soviet Communism unless and until there was freedom given in Russia to these otherwise inevitably unreliable witnesses.[68] For this reason Jacob claimed that the *Encounters* programmes had been cancelled because the Communists had been devious and because the opposition was 'extremely inadequate'. This was precisely Somerville's view. Notwithstanding this BBC caution about the Communists, Kathleen Bliss was still optimistic, albeit sharing Somerville's view that the Marxism programmes failed because the historians would not 'bite the challenge'; there should be a new attempt now to plan a new series arising from the first, in which Marxist historicism would be examined.

Whilst Jacob sought the views of the General Advisory Committee, the press tossed the merits of the series back and forth; it was quite clear that the churches were not altogether in favour. Julian Huxley, who had suffered from BBC strictures against open debate, felt that the Corporation deserved the thanks of all liberal-minded persons for its initiative in this valuable series. *The Universe,* however, thought it was bound to confuse the majority; with customary protectiveness, it regarded the Christian religion 'as something to be taught, not an open question to be argued about'.[69] As far as Silvey's audience research could discover, there was average appreciation for the series: many thought 'logical reasoning was irrelevant where questions of belief were concerned . . . professing Christians were inclined to think the case for Christianity was poorly served'.[70] The Secretary of the Christian Evidence Society contended that only 'qualified apologists' should have been deployed, perhaps reflecting the widespread impatience with academic theologians in general and philosophers of religion in particular. This was partly the motivation for the series. Bliss and Oldham believed that whilst the Corporation was bound to reflect aspects of the wider debate within society, it was clear it could only proceed on the basis of what forces were available. They had made the point at the outset of the discussion in their original document for the Governors[71] that there was simply not enough good debate going on outside for broadcasting to rely upon it. In a word, it had to be created, and this was beyond the normal task of a BBC producer, notwithstanding Robertson's departmental initiatives.

From the very outset, the combined vision of Bliss and Oldham had been not merely a set of discussion programmes tailored to comply with Haley's 'definition of controversy'. After their first report had been circulated they had extended discussions with many of the leading minds in the English-speaking world – T. S. Eliot, Dick Crossman, Isaiah Berlin, Meyer Ffortes, Paul Tillich, Patrick Nowell-Smith and Herbert Read, to name only a few. Fundamental Debate was visualized as a very long-term project which only the BBC could stage before that cross-section of society which virtually all of these people believed to be asking questions about man in nature and history. Bliss and Oldham were convinced that the Debate could not be carried through in one year or even two; at least five were needed. Oldham envisaged a group of thirty or forty minds, 'all with something of a creative gift', who would be kept in touch with each other by Bliss as mediator. It was important above all to encourage their willingness to meet together for weeks, weekends and evenings to monitor the developments. Various series of programmes would animate a regular and growing number of 'specially attached' listeners. They would be found not merely among intellectuals but, Oldham believed, in quite appreciable numbers among the working class.[72] Bliss's overriding faith was that the BBC, 'by far the most important national medium of intercommunication', should 'not abandon too easily the idea that it can make a positive contribution'.[73] The RBD had now what was called the 'values' space and Francis House very much hoped that Bliss would join the staff of the Corporation and produce talks and discussions for his department. Her contract with the BBC had ended in March; if she were a producer on the staff, she could relieve Robertson and reconsider the BBC commitment to the Marxist-Christian debate still outstanding. But the long-term vision was beginning to fade.

In April 1953 negotiations began for taking Bliss into the Corporation for another stint of Fundamental Debate. She wanted to be, in effect, the producer of the next stage in the initiative, but not as the concept of producer was normally construed. She and Somerville disagreed somewhat as to the extent of the necessary commitment to the BBC's administration. Bliss was sure that only by a single-minded effort could any BBC initiative come to useful fruition; the discussion had to be created by a much more inventive 'middle-mind' than she had allowed herself to be hitherto. Such a debate demanded exceptional knowledge and insight in the producer, and no one had this as she now had, especially as Lorna Moore had resolved not to be part of the *Encounters* team.[74] Bliss therefore pursued the idea of becoming a talks producer herself, with the firm support of House and Grisewood, the Director of the Spoken Word. Meanwhile, she hoped Allen and

Unwin might publish the scripts of *Encounters* in one form or another, but Philip Unwin could only record that they would be interested in any book she might produce but could not publish the radio programmes, 'wonderful material' as they were.[75]

Bliss hoped she could be attached to a producer for a three-month apprenticeship, and the Talks Department were happy to oblige. She envisaged a series on Marxism for the coming autumn, but the Home Service Board turned it down; it should be the province of the Talks Department and their own producers (in this case Michael Stephens). Somerville thought the subject needed further exploration and was, moreover, increasingly concerned about the shift of Bliss's thinking. In one way Bliss was relieved at not having to endure the tribulations of the previous January all over again. Instead she joined J. A. Scupham, Head of Schools Department, in the autumn for two weeks of intensive exposure to production and script preparation – not that she needed much practice on the latter.[76]

One question (notwithstanding her singular genius for editing other people's remarks) being examined in Talks policy was the unscripted discussion. It had been done time and again but not with this sort of material and personnel. Her conclusion after this experience was that it was well worth trying, particularly as the facility for editing sound recordings became more efficient. As Briggs notes, new post-war styles favoured conversation rather than the lecture; there was a growing demand for 'spontaneous chat and sharp dissent'.[77] *Encounters of Belief* had been a preparation for further unscripted, albeit not uncontrolled, discourse. In the future Bliss resolved to take a firmer hand as the chairman of various discussion groups; with recording facilities, the notion of spontaneity would be better sustained. It would still, however, be stylized; scripted discussion could sound unscripted and retain the greater weight of the material. Above all she wanted to avoid placing a microphone in between debaters who were free to air their opinions and respond to each other without any preparation. The sort of contribution to the Fundamental Debate which she believed that she and her contributors could provide was the result of hours of thrashing out problems in discussion, finally reduced to a stylized form of exchange of views which made complexity intelligible. It was a problem for academics as well as broadcasters.

Her view of debate was also much informed by Robert Walton's Schools Series, *Religion and Philosophy for Sixth Forms*: there was a clear demand, as Walton had shown, for more than one view to be elucidated.[78] This was particularly relevant in the vexed history of two Schools series on evolution which went back to 1941: *Man's Place in*

Nature and *How Things Began*. In a remarkable way, the BBC had managed to keep these programmes away from their own formal connotation of what was controversial, notwithstanding the vigorous Evangelical and Roman Catholic criticism. This debate had been in full swing as Bliss was preparing her *Encounters* series. Grisewood had been in pursuit of her concept of Fundamental Debate so as to avoid the head-on clashes between antithetic positions such as prevailed between the creationists and the evolutionists. Such clashes would be likely to 'degrade the discussion and confuse the mind'.[79] It was not the first time that the conflict between religion and science had caused considerable anxiety to the BBC. Fred Hoyle, for example, had given a talk in 1950 in which he boldly asserted that religion was 'but a blind attempt to find an escape from the truly dreadful situation in which we find ourselves'.[80] There were violent reactions; Somerville was even sent to placate a very puzzled RAC in the North of England. Iremonger had complained to House and Reith to Haley. CRAC had been concerned that Christian interests were not being served by this aggressively provocative approach. Haley had assured Reith that he was as anxious as he (Reith) to have a 'high and serious and moral system of broadcasting in this country . . . within the concept of an agreed serious body of opinion and not by means of purely personal predilection'.[81]

Somerville and her assistant, James Thornton (later her successor), were happy to have the Bliss/Oldham concept of the BBC's initiative in the Fundamental Debate pursued further. Bliss was contracted for two further years, up to August 1955. In September 1953 she immediately called another group together to examine the contribution of Polanyi's Riddell Lectures on *Science, Faith and Society*.[82] She was at pains in her report for Somerville to show that the thinking men and women with whom she was in conversation were committed to making the seriousness of the situation intelligible to a wide but untutored audience. Polanyi, she reported, was anxious for the general audience to see the continuity between science and ordinary experience.[83] Somerville, for her part, was anxious that Bliss not only keep her mind upon the thinking among scientists and philosophers but also keep her ear to the ground and inform the BBC as to what is actually 'biting people puzzled and befogged about religious issues'. Moreover, the Fundamental Debate must find a context in which ordinary people, and not only intellectuals, can speak about religion without being frightened or pressured into a display of conviction. This distinguished the operation clearly from the initiatives of the RBD.

Bliss made various suggestions for programmes and in particular a series on the ethical and religious implications of the population explosion and the pressure on natural resources. Somerville said no to this – it was not as 'biting' as the religion and science issue: the very basis of culture was bound up with the ways in which scientists differed from theologians in their approach to and definitions of reality. By the end of summer 1954, Thornton feared that, in programme terms, there was very little sign of life except suggestions for a couple of short talks entitled *Keywords*. Bliss however was soon planning another conference which would again concentrate the debate between Humanists and Christians: it was an issue at the very base of the culture. Somerville approved it and wanted programmes to be ready for concrete planning by Easter 1955. The Home Service Board approved the idea.[84] The same meeting also approved a series of talks on ethics and religion which was the initiative of the Talks Department but not, it appeared, in any relation to Bliss's enterprise: two talks on *Morals without Religion*, to be given by Mrs Margaret Knight, a lecturer in philosophy from Aberdeen, early in 1955. It would all but take the roof off Broadcasting House!

D. *Morals Without Religion*

By the summer of 1954, sound broadcasting was increasingly over-shadowed by the progress of television broadcasting and the Talks Department was as conscious as any in Broadcasting House that there had to be new initiatives. Grisewood prepared a paper for the Board of Governors based on Silvey's research. He made the point unequivoc-ally that as the Home Service had lost both prestige and authority with the advent of the Light Programme, the number of Home Service listeners declined and the audiences for talks 'shrank in sympathy'.[85] Somerville's assistant, Thornton, lamented that there was a desperate shortage of new speakers;[86] and Margaret Knight was thought to be a good performer. She had been on the Scottish Advisory Council for the BBC and with her husband Rex Knight had published an introduction to modern psychology in 1948. She was a friend of Barbara Wootton and much interested in juvenile behaviour and problems of deviance.

In early 1954 she had submitted a script to a Talks Department producer on the subject of ethics and humanism, and this was passed to Edwin Robertson on account of its close relationship with the Fundamental Debate background and the 'values' spaces in the Home Service output for which he was responsible. Robertson felt that he could not use it; both he and Lorna Moore, who had produced

Encounters of Belief, regarded her script as negative and not the proper way 'to present a worthwhile philosophical standpoint'.[87] As the Talks Department lost interest in the Bliss/Oldham scheme of the Fundamental Debate, it was now a question of getting other exciting people to the microphone. Barbara Wootton thought Margaret Knight was good material for the Third Programme. The Talks Department was also anxious lest any impression might be given to Mrs Knight that the RBD had the power to reject her scripts as unsuitable for their own reasons.

In any event, she wanted to broadcast on the Home Service and chose a new subject, since her original idea of discussing humanism with Anthony Flew had come to naught. Joseph Weltman of the Talks Department construed her scheme of broadcasts on religion and conduct as something akin to Fundamental Debate. It was soon quite obvious to Kathleen Bliss that Mrs Knight's proposals did not come within that orbit. Bliss, for her part, was planning a further conference for January 1955 to consider the next stage of the enquiry. The Talks Department in the person of Thornton made it rather ominously clear, however, that there would be no broadcasting commitment as a result of this conference.[88] It was a significant disclosure. Mary Somerville was getting impatient: yet another conference would mean at best programmes delayed until the spring. Moreover, there was a growing pressure against scripted discussions; and Somerville thought it 'high time we let the Humanists have a say on their own',[89] and leave any discussion till later. Grisewood as Director of the Spoken Word felt the same way. The BBC initiative was beginning to slip. Matters were complicated by Somerville's illness.

Margaret Knight submitted her scripts on religion and morality in the autumn. Almost everyone involved thought them hackneyed, negative and relying too heavily on assumption and ridicule. Even these were not her first attempt. Her first scripts had arrived in November 1953 and been rejected quite simply because they had been scrutinized by the RBD. Agnellus Andrew for the Roman Catholics knew that the hierarchy would take a very dim view of these attacks on the Christian position. Her producer, Weltman, realized that she held strong anti-religious views and that she regarded the BBC as a 'citadel of an archaic and dogmatic theology'.[90] House thought there was ground for good discussion here, but was unhappy with the anti-religious slanging that accompanied her treatment of the crucial issue of how unbelieving parents bring up their children. No such issue had been broadcast before, but House thought it was a pity that her passionate anti-religious diatribe was so naive; some of her points were being made in other ways by all manner of people, even 'in the remarks of Archbishops and evangelists'.[91] He thought Mrs Knight's script for her first talk philistine in places; it in no way did justice to any sensible concept of what religion actually is. A similar complaint had been made by the Christians in *Encounters of Belief*; the 'opposition', no matter how erudite in their own fields, had a less than competent grasp of what they were attacking and indeed reflected their own lack of training, their prejudice and their inherited misconceptions largely informed by half-truths. The source of such half-truths, as House admitted 'with penitence', was doubtless the clergy! Mrs Knight, however, like so many, might have been expected to consider the issues more seriously and not remain an uncritical entrepreneur of half-truths. Mrs Knight did take account of House's observations and made some alterations accordingly.

On the suggestion of Kathleen Bliss, Somerville invited Mrs Jenny Morton, the wife of Ralph Morton of the Iona Community and a former missionary in China, to give a Christian reply. Mrs Knight would give two talks, and the third of the series would be a discussion with Mrs Morton. The first talk went out on 5 January 1955. Oddly enough, her most contentious remarks went almost unnoticed.

> People will say: 'Children are not literal-minded. . . . It is no use giving the child cold-blooded lessons in ethics – moral teaching has got to have colour and warmth and interest. So why not give him that by the means that lie ready to hand – the myths of religion and the moving and beautiful ceremonies of the church? The child will cease to believe in the myths as he grows older, but that won't matter – they will have served their purpose.'[92]

This could mean, said Mrs Knight, that if he threw over religion he would throw over morals too, and be a ready prey to Communist propaganda; 'Tying up morals with religion could help to drive people into its arms.'[93]

The *Daily Express* and *Daily Telegraph* predictably took this all rather badly; they reported that the Archbishop had not heard it so could not comment; nor could House, for this was not a 'religious broadcast'. The call yet again was for discussion: Mrs Knight should not have been allowed to make this utterance free of the constraints of establishment control. It was the very old debate among the broadcasters which went back to the twenties: if a view contrary to the interests and convictions of the Christian establishment was to be expressed, these must, as it were, be 'hedged about' with a protective netting through which contentions or threatening assertion would pass with the greatest difficulty. In 1951 the series *Man Without God* had involved eight talks on separate evenings in the Home Service organized by Somerville and not by House.[94] It was not debate: it was 'recital': each of eight views put in an irenic presentation without reference to each other. Scripted discussion was the next stage pursued by Kathleen Bliss in *Encounters*, where prosaic assertion could be responded to in similar vein but without any notion of rancour or abuse. When Bliss sounded out Mrs Morton, she lamented that the possibility of getting really constructive discussion between Christians and those whose assumptions are broadly humanist 'does not increase with time'.[95]

By the time of Mrs Knight's second talk, the Press was ready for her and made enormous capital out of it. The Corporation had a vast correspondence and the usual telephone calls. 'The general trend of the calls' the Duty Officer reported,[96] 'was that the BBC should *not* have allowed her to express her views on the air.' The public, it was clear, was not ready to be told that whilst the real Jesus who preached to the Jews was crucified, 'we do not now believe that he was the son of God and of a virgin nor that he rose from the dead'.[97] Unlike the *Encounters* series, Mrs Knight's talks were in effect heard only in the south: outside London the regions had other programmes and so the response was somewhat muted. Nevertheless, the churches were generally resistant and critical although few would have gone to the lengths of the coarse indignation of the *Daily Sketch* or the *Sunday Graphic* whose Terence Feely spoke of the BBC allowing a 'fanatic to go on the rampage beating up Christianity. She may be hot stuff on what makes small boys steal jam, but on religion she is just about as useful as a barker at a sideshow.'[98] When the series was over, the upmarket press weighed in more sedately and complained almost in unison that whatever the broadcasters might say, the BBC should not provide a 'free-for-all forum': it was part of a national institution and should recognize inherited conventions.[99] *The Times* thought the issues were too complex for broadcasting and for public consumption in this form. Nevertheless, the Corporation was still judged to be out of order in giving too much license to sceptics.[100] Curiously, one of the BBC Governors, Lady Rhys Williams, asked whether the talks had been a form of seditious libel. She also raised the question of Jacob's supervision of programme policy and complained that she had known about the Knight talks only after the event. The other Governors however, stood firm behind the Director-General and rejected her plea for 'more adequate supervision of policy'.[101] Thornton, Director of Talks, had to obtain advice from the BBC's solicitor, who thought the offence was anyway now practically obsolete. He also could see no grounds for the accusation of blasphemous libel and thus no case to alter the controversy policy of 1947.[102]

Broadly the response from leading churchmen was negative: Roman Catholics including John Heenan, Archbishop of Liverpool, and the Anglican Bishop of Coventry, Neville Gorton, complained bitterly. Gorton wrote to Churchill and forced him to complain to Jacob and, as Briggs notes, 'all Churchill's distaste for broadcasting came to the surface'.[103] Briggs rightly says that the voices of calm were few. One of them however was that of W. R. Matthews, Dean of St Paul's; he thought that Scientific Humanism had perhaps been presented in 'a courteous manner' and 'in the long run would be of great benefit to the church by awakening it to the real situation'.[104] F. A. Cockin, Chairman of CRAC, came to Mrs Knight's defence in *The Observer*: he had no sympathy with the hysterical outburst; the upholders of the Christian faith had no right 'to feel aggrieved when those unable to accept its claim state their case in public'.[105] In Scotland the churches actually came to her defence against the abuse of the *Sunday Graphic*. Dorothy L. Sayers, however, complained that people like Knight 'seldom show signs of having read any Christian apologetic that is less than fifty years out of date', and did not think her 'dismay and indignation' were at all 'useful for any fruitful discussions'.[106]

It was clear from the correspondence to the Corporation and to Margaret Knight herself that there were those who believed she had said what many had been thinking and in so doing provided an identifiable focus of support for those who knew themselves to be alienated from formal, participant Christian commitment.[107] On the other hand there were many who protested at any attack on the notion of Christian Britain and the BBC's part in its maintenance. The Press reports of the comments of Bishops and Free Church leaders made it clear that they thought that while the principle of free speech should underlie BBC's policies, there were 'Queensberry Rules', so to speak, for which Mrs Knight cared little. A wide variety of Roman Catholic and Protestant evangelical bodies – all politically conservative – wrote strongly in condemnation of the broadcasts.

CRAC was divided: some, with the *Church of England Newspaper*, recognized that those who shared Mrs Knight's views probably outnumbered those who did not, and this discussion would be beneficial to all; these issues would be aired before the public because of the nature of the medium. Nevertheless, CRAC thought that 'direct attacks on the Christian faith were objectionable'.[108] As House read the Committee's mind it could no more be responsible for giving advice on the continuation of this series than it did in 1946 when the controversial broadcasts were first contemplated.[109] It demonstrated yet again that the Corporation could hardly expect CRAC to plot its own downfall by giving its blessing to what were reputedly 'anti-Christian' broadcasts. CRAC wanted serious discussion and did not think the Knight programmes were in this category.[110]

CRAC was discreetly paternalistic and based its views upon a reasonable belief that any entry into these delicate and troubled areas demanded not merely intelligence but knowledge and at least some modest background in theology, church history or philosophical method, which, as church leaders knew well, the rank and file in the churches simply did not possess – probably through no fault of their own. The manner in which large tracts of the population 'believed' in Christianity was akin, for Mrs Knight, to Churchill's complaint to Ian Jacob that it was 'inhumane to brush away even a crumb of comfort from young or old in their journey through this hard world or quench a gleam of hope in an aching heart'.[111] There was thus a correlation between the familiar elements of the Christian religion (which some might have called clichés) and the national identity focused in Crown, Church and Parliament. Thus Arthur Bryant wrote in *The Illustrated London News*:[112] 'Our Monarchy, Parliament, our ideas of right and wrong, all grew out of a belief in God and in what the BBC's lady lecturer dismissed as the antiquated and childlike Christian myth.' Margaret Knight had made a public attack through an 'establishment' institution upon the commonly regarded substructures of civic Christianity which bore all the obvious characteristics of tradition and which, moreover, sustained what many would have agreed were the deeply ingrained if hardly noticed religious images in which somehow all reality cohered. The vigorous reactions by the churches showed no awareness that the 'offence' of Mrs Knight was in a real way against the clergy by whom the ordinary churchgoer had been largely 'protected' from such issues.

CRAC now insisted on serious discussion on the lines of the Fundamental Debate. Ian Jacob wanted something similar, and summoned Somerville to have House produce a Christian series by way of controversial broadcasts from a Christian point of view. 'Now at last there is some hope of reaching a wider audience.'[113] The Talks Department were keen to use Mrs Knight again, although Grisewood cautioned that it would be 'a mistake for the BBC to build up Mrs Knight as the spokesman for the humanist point of view'.[114] As a result of the enormous response to these broadcasts which continued through the summer of 1955,[115] Mrs Knight now claimed that as she had been attacked by the Christian and Tory press, she deserved the right to reply at the microphone, particularly as *The Listener* had carried similar rebukes in its letters. By the end of the year she had a polite but definite refusal from Weltman: 'We must give the chance to other humanists of making their contribution.'[116]

In the meantime, with all the talk of Mrs Knight 'clearing the air', the Corporation pundits were trying to examine what to do next: more series to give the Christians the next crack of the whip, or more Fundamental Debate? The former choice would be comparatively straightforward – each should have his turn provided he promised to speak with good manners! The latter demanded a depth of patient commitment which after all, was not perhaps the duty of the Corporation as Kathleen Bliss and J. H. Oldham had understood it. Bliss was at any rate planning another series for the following year, *Keywords*, in which Christians and Humanists discussed certain fundamental notions.[117]

Grisewood's view of Mrs Knight's broadcasts was that the Corporation was 'at fault in allowing a teaching element in the broadcasts . . . where we put on a teacher we underwrite the authority of the speaker to teach as distinct from a right to express an opinion.' It was as much a matter of production as content.[118] His response to this incident marked a significant shift of emphasis, and indeed an advance in broadcasting philosophy, as the Corporation became more and more preoccupied with visual affairs and television. Times were changing, he thought, and the Corporation should allow a speaker to develop his view 'free from any obligation to meet a challenger . . . ; later on, differing views could be put with equal freedom.'[119] It was a signal change and Grisewood reached this conclusion notwithstanding his fellow Catholic Agnellus Andrew (now Roman Catholic Adviser to the BBC), who had complained, after the Knight series, that the BBC should always present both sides in close conjunction.[120] Grisewood said no to this: the BBC was committed to educating the audience, but this was a long-term enterprise, and each programme space was an environment in which a speaker was free to recite and argue his belief which should stand by itself and not warrant any 'answer'. Otherwise, thought Grisewood, the programmes would suffer.

Margaret Knight, meanwhile pursued with the Corporation her right to reply to the Christians. Kathleen Bliss's Fundamental Debate, however, was on the wane. Somerville complained that she had been 'a great talker but an indifferent doer' and felt that Bliss's opposition to the Knight talks had not been 'entirely disinterested'.[121] Bliss believed Margaret Knight to be among the 'destroyers' of unity: 'unconsciously she was mainly actuated to destroy a tyranny of her youth.' The churches could not accept that people like Margaret Knight had no other concept of the Christianity they were now opposing. Bliss regarded the RBD (now becoming gradually larger) as increasingly committed to protection. 'Like the great majority of churchmen', she later wrote to Thornton,[122] 'they assume too easily that they know the objections to Christianity and the answers.' The BBC, she counselled, must be warned against such assumptions and should not add to the national disintegration by supporting them. The BBC was the one institution in a powerful position to seek 'some common ground even among opposites'.

Somerville, meanwhile, was moving on to other large projects, one of which was a series in the early summer of 1955, *Foundations of Western Values*.[123] She was less and less interested in the wide span envisaged by Bliss and Oldham who had fought almost singlehanded for their cause and had had little support from CRAC in particular or the churches in general, notwithstanding House's affirmation to the contrary in his response to Mrs Knight's original talks. Somerville lamented that 'the times seem to have passed for the large general statements that were found inspiring in earlier days.'[124] Discussions and self-contained, well-argued exchanges were now increasingly demanded. Margaret Knight was used again from time to time.

By the end of 1955, however, it looked as if the Fundamental Debate was being forgotten.[125] Whilst it had been a Talks Department initiative, Bliss and Oldham represented in broadcasting perhaps the most eloquent and radical corner of British Christianity, which had derived from the *Christian News-Letter*. The tradition of James Welch and his efforts to have Christianity meet the challenge of popular opposition 'in the market place' were vested by the Corporation in the Bliss and Oldham team. The Fundamental Debate implied a measure of dismantling of the received creed and text, and not surprisingly the churches took little notice. House believed the Corporation could only undertake the rather modest task of selecting the best of the independent thinking outside the BBC. Bliss thought otherwise, as we have seen. House did agree, however, that occasionally the BBC could 'step outside its normal role and stimulate some new thinking'. He lamented to R. S. Lee, the vicar of St Mary's, Oxford, that the Fundamental Debate had not been successful. He differed from Welch before him and from Roy McKay, his successor, in his view of the BBC's initiative: 'Unless the churches through their best minds are really grappling seriously with Christianity in the modern world, I cannot see that we in the BBC can do very much about it.'[126] The lack of success of the Fundamental Debate was, he thought, due to an understandable lack of support in the churches. CRAC had said often that it was not in business to advise the broadcasters how to attack Christianity or church; it had other interests. There were also distinct differences of outlook between the Talks and the Religious Departments and predictably, the Fundamental Debate fitted better into the latter than the former. On other fronts the churches were still profoundly suspicious of broadcasting as tending to draw people out of the churches or at any rate keep them away; television was slowly becoming a Sunday reality!

Mrs Knight's series and the 'aftermath' coincided with the departure of Francis House for the World Council of Churches in Geneva. His successor, Roy MacKay,[127] saw the implications quite clearly: if hitherto the RBD had managed in a real way to keep out of this area, notwithstanding the efforts of Edwin Robertson,[128] and if the Talks policy of the Corporation was moving more and more towards Grisewood's notion of 'freedom to speak without answer', then any new initiative for radical discourse between Christians and Scientific Humanists, whether Margaret Knight or others, would perhaps have to come from the RBD, whatever CRAC might say. Haley's speech to the British Council of Churches in 1951 was still the operative policy guide. He had distinguished, as we have seen, between moral values, which the BBC was committed to uphold as belonging to a Christian country, and on the other hand the Christian faith as such, to which the BBC was not committed; that was the province of the RBD. House rather expected the churches to provide his Department with the new thinking not only in the Christian-Humanist and other debates, but particularly at that moment when the thinking 'gets to the point of consolidation and clarity at which broadcasting becomes a possibility.'[129] In effect, that left the initiative with the churches; both his predecessor and successor knew the initiatives to lie with the Corporation. It was the broadcasters' job to discern when 'broadcasting becomes a possibility' – even a necessity.

As McKay settled into his new task and considered the reactions to Mrs Knight, he took up the issue, so to speak, where Welch had left off: if it was the duty of religious broadcasting, as Haley had said, to make people join the Christian faith, 'one of the ways of doing this is to allow the Christian and the actively hostile Humanist to debate their differences on the air.' He went even further: 'If religious broadcasting is not doing this it is neglecting one of the most pressing challenges in the contemporary world.' Such a bold policy would be of 'fundamental assistance to Christianity' and, whether or not Mrs Knight was the best representative of the Humanist opposition, McKay certainly regarded her as the Humanists' protagonist in the popular mind. He nailed his colours to the mast: 'There are times when the Christian must be ready to give an answer in a context which is less than Christian' (by which he meant, in the face of misrepresented claims for Christian belief, etc.). 'If we believe in the truth of our faith we can both defeat our opponents' arguments and redeem their bad manners.'[130] Before very long church leaders would say otherwise; for the moment, however, the new arena for such enterprise was television – all the more challenging and all the more beguiling, as McKay would eventually discover to his cost.[131]

27

MISSIONS:
DEPARTMENTAL EXPERIMENTS

A. Drama and scriptwriters' conference, 1952

In 1945 Welch had written to J. H. Oldham:

> We are communicating Christian truth to the mass of ordinary
> people in this country – not to the ten per cent who think and read
> seriously. We are communicating to the ninety per cent who are not
> weekly attenders at church: in other words, we feel the church must
> speak to the nation, to society and not only to the gathered people.
> These two points govern practically all our work of religious
> broadcasting which must always be an addition to, an outreach of,
> the normal work of the church. With cinema, etc., they are a
> *preparatio evangelica*, they are to plough up secular land and sow good
> seed; the church in its parochial aspect has to tend and gather in.[1]

Welch had always seen drama as a valuable and significant part of the
preparatio evangelica. House too was committed to the exploitation of
broadcast drama for religious objectives, and since it seemed to be the
consensus of opinion at the 1950 departmental conference that drama
was the key to the broadcasting of religion both to the non-churchgoer
and to the unschooled churchgoer, someone ought to be specially
commissioned in this area.[2] J. Ormerod Greenwood, an educationalist
and a Quaker, was appointed to the Department in 1950 with a view to
examining the potential for dramatic utterance in the religious output.
Up to then the greatest success had been Sayers' *Man Born to be King*.
Greenwood consulted Martin Browne of the Religious Drama Society
and concluded that a major conference should be convened simply
'with an eye to finding good scriptwriters for religious programmes'.[3]
This raised the question of departmental rivalries; the Corporation had
an enormously prestigious Drama Department led by Val Gielgud who
of course would be a major contributor. What they were after,
Greenwood told him, was not 'the occasional work of genius' but

standards of professional competence in the various fields of 'purposive' broadcasting which, apart from the Third Programme, the whole
religious output in effect comprised. Most 'religious' dramas, Greenwood believed, could be detected a mile off: scriptwriters were fearful of
unorthodox language or even heresy; some were over-earnest, some
shallow. The Authorized Version of the Bible was a strait-jacket for any
writer on religious themes and above all, as Greenwood saw it, there
was little hope unless it was recognized by the clergy that drama and
language were not inert servants of dogma: 'Good sermons are written
by people who are sure that they are right; good plays by people who
are not. A sermon demands jargon – the enemy of drama.' Greenwood
grasped almost immediately (on scrutinizing batches of both unsolicited and requested scripts) that purposive broadcasting could not have
to do with the profound unknowing and the confessed agnosticism of
even believers. That belonged to the arena of debate, perhaps even to
the Fundamental Debate, not to the single voice of recital. By the time
the conference met, Greenwood was preoccupied with aesthetic forms
which could express theological thought in such a way as to reach
deeper levels of response.[4]

Over thirty people attended, including Louis MacNeice, Rose
Macaulay, Wynyard Browne and Noel Streatfield. There were actors,
poets and producers – called together to determine in what way they
could assist the cause of purposive broadcasting. Val Gielgud, in a
lecture on writing for radio, made it clear that it could not be handled
'under a halo'. Gielgud had commissioned James L. Forsyth to write a
radio nativity play in 1949. As Sayers had done, Forsyth used his
imagination and predictably conflated the narratives in Luke and
Matthew and cast Mary and Joseph in a rather more romantic light
than was usual. Forsyth insisted that the play was not 'religious drama
– except that its subject is of religion and its stuff is of drama'.[5] It was,
moreover, a 'faithful part of the infinity of accounts'. Herein was the
clue to a major problem of BBC religion: speculation was not welcomed
by either the faithful or the 'outsider'. It could so easily lead to
demythologizing. The problem went back to Iremonger, who had
himself rejected R. F. Delderfield's *A Spark in Judaea* because of its
'realistic content'.[6] There was a fundamental division in the conference
between those who saw broadcasting as an instrument for expanding
the orbit in which an inevitably conventional religious or dogmatic
utterance took place; and those whose passion and talent compelled
them to examine character and situation in which questions were
certainly asked and frequently answered, but not in the manner
appropriate to religion, which was accustomed to issue finally in a

27. Margaret Knight

28. Kathleen Bliss

29. Colin Beale

30. Roy McKay

31. *Jesus of Nazareth*: Jesus preaching in the synagogue

prescribed and preconceived form. Gielgud thought, moreover, that the Light Programme was inaccessible to religion; dramatic situation could not be so simplified and retain its integrity.[7] The RBD, on the other hand, believed that drama was the only means of expounding religious truths to this audience.

House was quite unashamed of having invited this very special group of people to 'contribute to an enterprise properly described as the propagation of the faith' – this was not propaganda in the bad sense. Gielgud and the conference generally did not agree; 'purposive' drama was in a profound way 'fraudulent'; it did just what the Rationalists complained that the clergy did – they proposed an 'analysis' of the human condition and provided their 'solutions' in one attenuated dogmatic form or another. The conference itself confirmed the belief of House and his colleagues that most clergy did this rather badly. There must be other ways, and drama was still the most obvious of these. The 'entertainment' value was obvious: it made for better radio. Robert Walton made the point that in the schools output dramatic presentations were already good broadcasting; they could be both provocative and informative, but drama by its very nature could not be dogmatic; it would then turn into the 'bad propaganda' which House was at pains at the conference to eschew.[8] Animated by Bernard Shaw's preface to *Back to Methuselah*, House appealed to the group to consider the importance of biography and story-telling (increasingly the raw materials of schools programmes). As Shaw had claimed, 'All the sweetness of religion is conveyed by the hands of storytellers.' House believed this; he thought contemporary preaching was profoundly unimaginative.[9]

For this reason much of the thinking in the Department had significantly been animated by a species of anticlericalism which discreetly condemned the clergy for being not merely exhortatory and intellectual, but unimaginative as well. They appeared to be (even if they were not actually) too far distant from the experience of ordinary people. The Department turned therefore more and more towards laymen. There had been a long running series, *My Faith and My Job*, which was biographical as well as dogmatic in the sense that it tried to relate Christian faith to widely divergent experience in industry and common life in a changing culture. The trend in this movement was away from the clergy in general towards the few prized clergy who were skilled broadcasters. But not only so: in the context of *Sunday Half Hour* for example, the movement was towards BBC laymen who were already 'personalities' of the microphone: Richard Dimbleby and Franklyn Engelmann were two in question.

B. The Light Programme

Here the hymn singing programmes were always regarded as one of the most popular means of teaching the fundamentals of the faith to the vast numbers drawn in some cases by nostalgia and also by association with their present or past religious involvement. The *People's Service* was even more the means to 'proclaim the common ground' of Christianity. It was a 'preparation for the gospel and not an occasion for exploring denominational differences' – or indeed presumably any others; it was, after all, on the Light Programme! One of House's major difficulties was that he was under considerable pressure from churches and their clergy to have 'their turn' at the *People's Service* or *Sunday Half Hour*, both of which gave a not inconsiderable boost to local morale and to congregational numbers. The difficulties became acute when the Light Programme music experts complained of execrable singing and poor acoustics, and when Richard Tatlock said almost the same of the preacher – as he often did. R. T. Brooks in Manchester tried his hardest to persuade churches to recognize that *Sunday Half Hour* was essentially a music programme and that the hymns were the real channel of the broadcast message. C. V. Taylor agreed with the Variety Department's music specialist that the programme as a whole should have variety: it was not merely a hymn relay, as the churches so often seemed to think. Stanley Pritchard from Scotland counselled his clergy to see it as 'nostalgia translated into action', a 'sermon in sound and a missionary act'.[10] Tatlock, however, believed that the programme was doing the churches more harm than good, notwithstanding his insistence on greater collaboration between local churches and denominations. It nevertheless maintained the largest audience for any single RBD programme and confirmed Tatlock in his opinion that 'the clergy taken by and large really *are* a boring lot and incapable of delivering themselves of anything but intangible and unreal cliches'.[11] This might have been true, but was hardly fair. The clergy 'by and large' had, after all, no training or preparation for this kind of specialist speaking; but Tatlock believed they only had themselves to blame for not seeking it. House, in spite of various invitations to theological colleges, felt that there was no real enthusiasm being shown towards the enormous possibilities of broadcasting on such a scale. Tatlock was encouraged by many clergy who were happy to have a Franklyn Engelmann or a David Dunhill read RBD scripts. Such deference and humility, however, was rare: to the great majority they represented the 'usurping Corporation'.

The debate raged on, mostly turning on the Tatlock-Falconer axis. Scotland and some of the regions didn't care for the centralist 'gentry' and the decisions about policy which made the churches' utterance subject to BBC authority and particularly Kenneth Adam, the Controller of the Light Programme, not to mention the dominating Falconer himself. Adam was appalled at some 'performances' which passed for an evangelistic endeavour. Whatever banalities the churches might be prepared to accept, he was most certainly not. He now insisted on 'putting in our own chaps', and in autumn 1951 it was agreed that three out of five programmes would be by 'tried and tested' broadcasters from the churches, the other two by BBC announcers and/or 'personalities'.[12] When House circulated the ruling, Falconer predictably cried 'BBC religion'! Against all that House had proposed to help broadcasting to reflect the churches as they were, Falconer now complained that the Corporation was coming between the church and its conscience. He sulkily suggested that the whole programme be handed over to the Music Department: how could the BBC say to the churches 'We want your choirs but we do not want your ministers'?[13] Falconer reflected the prejudices of many: whatever benefit broadcasting could confer on the churches in their expansionist endeavours, the BBC had finally no business to pronounce on the churches' own conviction about the aesthetics of their own proclamatory forms. It was not a matter of entertainment but of evangelism. To the local church *Sunday Half Hour* was an act of worship; to the BBC it was a programme. Tatlock believed that it was amateur and destructive, simply because 'by and large' the clergy could not submit to what he publicly called 'production'; privately he believed that the Department and its 'tried and tested servants' should write the scripts for the local clergy to speak.[14]

Tatlock was asking too much of the clergy. Another factor was the strong conviction which House maintained about recordings; even *Sunday Half Hour* should be authentic; he believed that any liturgical element, but prayer in particular, should not be recorded. Immediacy betokened confidence; this would be shaken if the audience discovered that an act of worship was artificially presented. When William Purcell joined the staff in the North Region, House was encouraged by the response of the head of the BBC Presentation Department, John Snagge. Purcell had produced a most acceptably styled broadcast: 'more like this forthright virile preacher, and religious broadcasting would soon become significant'.[15]

In the Home Service thinking, evangelism would hardly feature. However much the Light Programme style might encourage and enlist the most vigorous and innovative evangelical initiatives, especially in

Scotland, the Home Service, House believed, should be free of the growing influences from across the Atlantic, not least that of Billy Graham, whose British campaign had stimulated numbers of British copyists.[16] The Home Service listener was clearly more selective now; the audience for the Sunday morning service was half of what it was in 1948! This was the place to educate the committed and those who chose to listen. This was the location for eminent men like John Wolfenden, the Vice-Chancellor of Reading University, to preach on education and Visser 't Hooft on the World Council of Churches. House tried a measure of biblical exposition in the Daily Service: it was not appreciated.

C. The English churches' mission: 'pre-evangelistic' broadcasting

On the basis of the Scottish experience in co-operative enterprise between the Corporation and the Church of Scotland, interest was growing in similar possibilities outside Scotland. During Lent 1952 Scotland had planned yet another mission which had the firm support of all the mainstream churches north of the border, though the national church naturally took a leading part. In Falconer and Dinwiddie the Church of Scotland had ready co-operation; as we have seen, Falconer's rallying cry, clearly appreciated by the clergy, was that broadcasting should be the 'handmaid of the churches'. Falconer demanded a great deal in exchange: the notion of mission could no longer be a single disconnected event: it must be an ongoing initiative of the local presbyteries into whose operations the broadcasters would fit. Broadcasting would be supportive and corroborative. Falconer told the clergy in no uncertain terms that not only was the licence fee in a real way paying the churches' bills but broadcasting provided enormous publicity. The local clergy in the proposed 1952 mission[17] were asked to 'tackle their local situations imaginatively' before, during and after the broadcasts. There is no doubt that this co-operation between the BBC and the churches not only reflected increasing local evangelistic initiatives; it helped to publicize these initiatives and provide a basis of ongoing missionary activity well after the broadcasts were over. Group listening became a modest feature in some churches and within a year, the joint BBC and churches working committee, supported by the churches through the Scottish RAC, set up what they called the *Tell Scotland* Movement and employed Tom Allan of Glasgow as a full-time co-ordinator. By the close of the 1952 mission, Falconer was confident that a foundation had been laid: the churches had begun to understand a pattern of 'recurrent' mission based on a simple model of preparation, mission (i.e. broadcasts, etc.) and follow-up.[18] In every church there had to be a committed nucleus to follow the preparatory broadcasts in groups with or without the clergy. Falconer was so confident that he put together a tape-recorded series of talks on Radio Missions for the New Zealand and Canadian broadcasting authorities. Tom Allan, the Chief Missioner, shared the common evangelical belief that the mission had demonstrated a 'widespread' interest, even 'hunger', for religion aimed at what he called the 'proletariat', while at the same time, it revealed a 'shattering indifference to the church'. He was also quite certain that notwithstanding the successes, the local churches in Scotland were only dimly aware of the possibilities of broadcast religion. Perhaps most extraordinary of all was Allan's remarkable conviction in 1952 that rejection of Christian faith on what he called 'intellectual' grounds appeared to be 'much less common than it was twenty or thirty years ago. We must be more concerned with proclamation than with apologetics.'[19] It was an antithesis which House rejected, particularly at the very time when Kathleen Bliss was struggling with the Fundamental Debate. Falconer however spearheaded this concept of religion in the broadcast output (at any rate in Scotland) by his warnings about complexity in utterance which reflected a certain disparagement of theology and an impatience with those rather more reticent in their approach to Christian affirmation. Concentration seemed to rest in terms of broadcasting on that audience attracted by Radio Luxembourg and its increasingly heard *Revival Hour*.[20]

House and Robertson had been much animated by the Scottish initiatives: there was enough evidence that the broadcasting potential for the churches in their evangelistic enterprise was significant. House thought that whereas the churches had been 'benevolently neutral' they were now potentially co-operative.[21] But he also believed that the number of clergy and congregations who recognized the evangelistic need of the times were very few. In the English regions the denominational situation was quite different from that in Scotland; Taylor insisted that the problem lay with the widespread clerical suspicion of the BBC and the 'BBC Christians' – a species of 'fifth column'! They could hardly counsel their congregations to hear what they themselves did not or would not hear. Notwithstanding this antipathy, House was buoyed up by the vast dimensions of the audience for Sunday religious broadcasts and told the BCC that in any missionary enterprise the people he had in mind were 'far more likely to be listeners to the Light Programme'.[22] The concept of the Radio Mission, however, could only be construed in the context of the initiatives of the churches in England just as had been the case in Scotland. It was another way of enhancing the possibilities of broadcast religion in the eyes of the churches, who were showing few signs that they supported the call of the Archbishops' Commission in 1945 to recognize that the Christian laity was the priesthood of the church.[23]

The organizing of the English Mission marked a significant turning point in BBC and church relations, if only on a theoretical level. CRAC had almost since the beginning of broadcasting put not a little emphasis on broadcasting being somehow 'evangelistic'. The churches, however on 'political' grounds, had refused to accept the BBC as a serious instrument, as indeed Tom Allan had observed in Scotland. In late 1952, as a result of the Scottish Mission, the notion of 'radio evangelism' was further qualified by the insistence of CRAC that any BBC initiative must wait for the churches.[24] House told the Department that the emphasis must be on the strategic plans for closer relationships between the religion organizers around the country and their personal relationship with the local church leaders at various levels. The other crucial perspective was ecumenical: a mission to Royal Air Force personnel in autumn 1952 had provided statistical evidence that the biggest stumbling-block to 'waverers' was the divisions of the churches.[25] E. H. Robertson had undertaken a modest collaboration between the BBC and local churches in Hendon. It was clear that any such enterprise on a major scale must involve substantial co-operation between the mainstream churches. The Anglicans were the hardest to convince. Thus the more that the context of broadcast evangelism was construed in the terms of local co-operation, the more House had carefully to discipline his own objectives. The churches were increasingly aware that numbers were falling, and just a few saw working connections between the local Christian presence and broadcasting. The BBC's religious initiative at least in view of the great expanse of the unchurched working classes listening to the Light, was preparatory: it was pre-evangelistic. House was emphatic that religious broadcasting must reflect what was going on in the churches and would thus tend to follow rather than lead.

Hugh Gough, the evangelical Bishop of Barking, met with a number of Free Churchmen including Paul Rowntree Clifford, the Baptist on CRAC. Gough was enthusiastic about the possibilities of a radio mission, as were many others. In the diocese of Chelmsford, a three-year mission was about to end and Gough was keen to deploy the radio in such a context. House felt obliged to defuse romantic notions about the value of radio at the very time when he had to extol its potential to a vastly larger and more suspicious clergy. House told Gough that any mission must be related to an existing local enterprise and accompanied by house to house visitation; it must be ecumenical.[26] All things being equal the BBC would provide a series of the *People's Service* or *Sunday Half Hour* over perhaps a month. But the smaller the scale of ecumenism or visitation, the smaller would be the commitment of broadcasting. It was the way in which House protected the BBC from the charges of propaganda. He regretted that the Roman Catholics did not agree to take part.

As preparation for the 1954 Mission to 'London in Essex' continued, CRAC began to look at this new concept of 'pre-evangelism': did the distinction between pre-evangelism and evangelism *per se* correspond to natural and revealed theology? Should the stress fall on the moral law or on the preaching of the gospel? It was a subject which warranted further debate, particularly as the Essex mission would provide additional data to that already gathered from Scotland where further missions for 1955 and 1956 were being planned.[27] House, on CRAC's initiative, organized a conference in May 1954 alongside the negotiations for the 'London in Essex' programmes in the forthcoming September and October. He had meanwhile announced his resignation as from summer 1955, and was anxious to have the vexed issues and assumptions about the audience for religious broadcasts finally and fully analysed, not least in the light of his previous intiative which had around 1950 and 1951 marked a clear change of direction in religious policy. As we have seen, Kathleen Bliss was responsible at this time for the other major policy thrust in religious broadcasting; she was therefore called to the conference, together with Robert Walton of the Schools Department, the Roman Catholic Gordon Dwyer, Leslie Paul, Douglas Stewart (later to join the Department) and members of House's London staff. Cockin was Chairman. The aim of the conference was to 'define the target, and to explore the mental, moral and spiritual state of people on the fringe and outside the churches'.[28] The question House had examined in various ways was if and how broadcast programmes could be directed beyond the traditional categories focused upon by the Scottish and now the London Mission: the outsider or non-churched, the lapsed or half-churched and the faithful. Since the Beveridge Enquiry there had been complaints that most of the BBC religious output favoured the latter group, albeit the overwhelming number of broadcast services were 'evangelistic', and all the more successful when the tried and tested preachers were used again and again. Apart from that for the Fundamental Debate the other most recognizable audience was the sixth forms in schools; audience research had evidence that their programmes were highly appreciated outside schools by the general Home Service audience. It was disturbing.

The conference isolated three main groups within the broad category of non-churchgoers: 'the ignorant, the aggrieved and the inert'. It was a tremendous struggle to come to any sensible definition when so much of the debate inextricably intertwined theological and sociological categories. Walton was animated by his experience of sixth forms; he saw the almost total indifference of the rising generation which derived partly from ignorance of the language of belief itself. The Bonhoeffer theology of 'Man Come of Age' was uppermost in the thinking of many who lamented that modern man was now happy to rely on expert technology, etc. Men were 'disappointed' with the church on grounds of its class connections and others were anyway committed to rival ideologies. Cockin thought that perhaps increased longevity now meant that the 'hedonistic view' had replaced the 'ethical view' of life. The conference was an interchange of guesswork and hearsay, but at the same time seriously attempted to grapple with the relationship in the minds of many Christians between the malaise in contemporary life and the manifest decline in mainstream church attendances. There was, moreover, a further unease brought about by the London campaigns of Billy Graham. There were arguments for and against. The BBC hierarchy in general was quite opposed to this style of utterance and there was also deep division between CRAC and the Scottish Advisory Committee. The BBC had put itself quite out of favour with the Billy Graham Organization which, in American tradition, expected that the opportunity to purchase BBC air time would be available. Whatever else he had done, Graham had brought the language of evangelism into the light of publicity. Ian Jacob had always preferred that the BBC should be cautious: 'Austerity should be the watchword in religious broadcasting.'[29]

The conference met again in July to draw together its findings and organize its address both to CRAC and the Department. There was clearly a cultural divide between the Light and the Third Programmes; this meant that much greater audience definition was needed, even after the concept of 'non-churchgoer' had been agreed as a starting point for the discussion. Amid strenuous attempts to be concise about the condition of a decreasingly Christian society and the psychology of contemporary anxiety about the bomb and science etc., Cockin cut through these analyses and upheld the polarity between religion and church: modern men, he thought, 'see no connection between gaiters and gospel'. Religious broadcasting must therefore build upon those foundations already laid in church and school and now manifest in much contemporary moral awareness which expressed a discreet pro-Christian but an anti-church bias. Were the churches in their evangelistic zeal prepared for the same recognition? It looked very doubtful, if the Essex churches were any guide.

Cockin's 'pre-evangelism' group put considerable emphasis upon education and indeed even 're-education' with a view to correcting inherited errors which the vast majority maintained through no real fault of their own. The Fundamental Debate also gave a clue: could the churches and the churchmen behave in religious broadcasting in the way that was hoped for by others such as the humanists who clamoured at Broadcasting House for their right to have a say? Could the churchmen resist the temptation to launch into their theological recitatives, and instead (as the Fundamental Debate philosophy had outlined) engage in discourse? Not only had there to be sermons of a strong propagandist type aiming, as in Falconer's Missions, for 'decisions'; there had to be places where contemporary questions in religion could be examined: myth, gospel, tradition, etc. were not only to be the preserve of ordinands and the clergy. Intelligent but theologically uneducated people outside the churches were asking questions about faith and moral issues, and above all, the greater proportion of them held the tacit conviction that whatever the state of the churches or the popularity of the clergy, Christianity remained the repository from which moral leadership might come. Christian speaking, however, must be rid of its bland assumptions and its immediate resort to self-justification and, what to many was the most exasperating, its deployment in discussion of dogmatic language used as a substitute for argument. In such ways Christian 'recital' suppressed the genuine questions of the half-churched and tried in effect to rid them of their doubts.

As for those who were disenchanted with Christianity because of their negative views of the church, new programmes must be devised to repair the damaged 'public relations' image of the church by greater use of lay people so as to restore confidence that the church was, if nothing else, socially relevant. Programmes should investigate the Christian faith of notable non-churchgoers such as Simone Weil and should demonstrate the church at work responding to new problems, for example in housing estates. They should bring to the microphone personalities who could restore credibility, people like Mervyn Stockwood, J. B. Phillips, Molly Batten and David Jenkins. In this way the arcane activities of the church at worship would be eloquently corroborated by the clear evidence of Christian care and concern in very modern contexts. Not the least important were George MacLeod and his Iona Community. He was a well-known figure and his commitment to Christian leadership in social affairs was coupled with his pacifist background. C. V. Taylor thought he 'bestrode Scotland just as Temple did England'; he was the first non-Anglican to preach in St Paul's Cathedral. But he was firmly against the evangelistic effort focused in and, for many, symbolized by Billy Graham; many in the churches therefore regarded him with some hostility. MacLeod was nevertheless one who could help to restore the image of the churches' obligation to 'save souls and to transform society'.[30] As regards Graham himself, Cockin's group thought that so long as he continued to emphasize the relationship of his campaign to the local churches, the mainstream churches had broadly been in support. If he were to come to England or Scotland again, he must be allowed to broadcast direct and not – as in his Harringay Arena Mission – only be reported.[31]

Notwithstanding the Corporation's unease about the actual term 'Radio Mission', the scheme went ahead in October 1954 with four connected Sunday morning services in the Home Service from various churches, *Lift Up Your Hearts* for two weeks, and four *People's Services*, all four conducted by one man – Cuthbert Bardsley, Bishop of Croydon; there were also two *Sunday Half Hour* programmes. There was a good deal of printed publicity, all of which bore an emblem of a cross against radiating 'ether' circles and the inevitable term 'Radio Mission'. Nearly 8,000 posters, 18,000 window cards and a quarter of a million handbills assisted the promotion. Notwithstanding the general eminence of the broadcasters, and particularly the Bishop of Croydon, Silvey's research indicated a rather dismal response outside the orbit of churchgoers. Churches, for their part, gave rather inconclusive evidence for the effect of the broadcasts on church attendance; half reported no change at all. A large number however indicated increased co-operation between the denominations. As House reviewed the evidence, it appeared that the Mission had above all stimulated the house-to-house visitation by the congregations, but that the clergy expected too much from the broadcasts and were disappointed because the broadcasts were directed neither to the people of Essex in general nor – as some of them most certainly wanted – to the church members of Essex in particular. The clergy wanted the broadcasts to deal much more with church attendance: it was an age-old longing which regarded broadcasting almost exclusively in terms of promoting church attendance. More analytic or critical approaches were seen as evidence of the BBC indulging yet again in anti-Christian activities.[32] CRAC for its part hoped that any future missions organized by the churches together might have the BBC's support. CRAC was smarting at the

Corporation's decision not to allow the expression 'Radio Mission' to be used in the *Radio Times* billing.[33] Grisewood and Somerville were determined to avoid any unnecessary provocation of some influential non-Christian voices which complained at the BBC's 'para-church' initiatives.

Grisewood later came to the conclusion that the energy expended on the radio mission had been misplaced. He saw the problems of disparity between the 'life of the church as it is' and what he called the 'adaptive methods of professional ingenuity' which broadcasting had provided. The churches were now beguiled by them; indeed, even duped into thinking that its special 'adaptive' radio utterance in the missions would be received somehow in isolation from their traditional and historically construed 'routines'. Such endeavour was finally negative; it drove a wedge between the faith and the order of institutional Christianity. The broadcast missions had given an impression of 'a merely fashionable version of Christianity in an age where the profound and the trivial coexisted' – an age which, in the opinion of Grisewood and the growing breed of broadcasting journalists, could detect the differences between the two – not least in religion.[34]

D. Rationalists and Humanists

The Rationalist Press Association and the Humanist Council were asking for admission to *Lift Up Your Hearts*; this was unthinkable even for Mary Somerville, who feared that very propagandist vigour which the Fundamental Debate had tried so hard to dissolve into more fruitful 'encounter'. Grisewood updated the 'mainstream' policy of 1951 approved by the Governors[35] by explaining to the Humanists that *Lift Up Your Hearts* was completely the 'property' of the RBD, not least because CRAC and the Department regarded it as belonging more appropriately to an act of worship than to a talk.[36] It was not therefore 'an appropriate context' for humanist and somewhat esoteric subjects of the kind suggested by the Council.[37] CRAC, however, failed to grasp the enormous advantage that broadcasting had provided for the 'London in Essex' Organizing Committee. The Corporation was doing its utmost to raise the tone of encounter and discussion. The initiative of Kathleen Bliss and J. H. Oldham, for all its somewhat top-heavy and even lumbering progress, was trying to implement the Governors' policy directive of 1947 without leaving the air waves open for a free-for-all. Since the churches broadly regarded the Rationalist lobby as anti-Christian and pandering to left wing influence, it was difficult to find subjects which Humanists and Christians might talk about without resort to recital, propaganda or slanging matches. Moreover, the constant talk of the unchurched millions listening to religious broadcasts on Sundays understandably animated all their energies for evangelistic enterprise. What with Scotland's effort on a local level, the Anglican initiative in Chelmsford was in a practical way a means for the BBC religious output to further the churches' expansion. Grisewood, Somerville and Jacob were naturally cautious, while the RPA and the Humanist Council not unreasonably argued that they could not see much result as yet to show for all the talk about new policy since 1947, in spite of their gratitude for Mrs Knight's series![38]

By the end of 1955 the Rationalist and Humanist lobby became more aggressive and impatient. These organizations were not, however, providing good broadcasters; they were therefore not getting the programmes. It was not enough, as the Head of Talks constantly reminded them, to speak of subjects: everyone had ideas for subjects. But as Bliss had discovered, it was quite another matter to find good broadcasters who had grasp enough to fulfil an important criterion of BBC policy: the ability to appeal to a wide audience just as – it was explicitly affirmed – the bulk of religious broadcasting had done for so long. This was far from saying that the religious output appealed to a vast audience. On the basis of an assumption that the Corporation served a Christian culture, religious broadcasting had been so devised as to appeal to the widest possible Christian audience. The RBD therefore had the control of that section of air time (notably on Sundays) which was deemed 'liturgical' and which, as Grisewood told the Humanists, was inappropriate for non-Christian utterance. Oddly enough, in 1955 the Rationalists and Humanists readily accepted this distinction: they complained rather more that there were simply insufficient discussions between Christians and their opponents. Somerville knew it was simply because the Fundamental Debate had been too slow to get off the ground; Weltman (who had produced some programmes for the Fundamental Debate) knew how immensely difficult it was to get people to speak at a 'high enough level of honesty and at a low enough level of intelligibility'.[39] Moreover, the limitation of air time for any such initiatives meant that in any middle level discussion the churches and the 'theistic faiths' would insist not so much on having their best broadcasters at the microphone as their accredited representatives. The initiative could so easily shift from the BBC's production department to areas quite outside. The Religion and Talks Departments lamented that such debates were not taking place outside, least of all in the churches themselves. Co-operation with local communities meant therefore co-operation in what the churches called mission and what the humanists called propaganda. Before very long the Humanist Association would be calling for increasing provision for straight expositions of moral propositions in order somehow to balance the Christian output: the 1947 ruling had been under enormous strain. There would soon be a demand for a special member of the Corporation staff plus an advisory committee 'responsible for non-Christian sound and TV programmes'. From now on the campaign would become somewhat more militant; when next the Humanist Association submitted a formal memorandum, it had not only the signatures of E. M. Forster, A. J. Ayer, Crossman, Huxley, Noel Annan and J. B. Priestley, but also F. A. Cockin, V. A. Demant, Alec Vidler and six other notable churchmen![40]

E. *Religious Broadcasting and the Public*: the audience in 1955

Against this conflict within the Religion and Talks output, House had trodden a delicate path to the local churches via CRAC and the 'mission operators'. Meanwhile the Department and CRAC sought to plan for the future while continuing their pursuit of a definition of pre-evangelism. In the summer of 1954 the conference chaired by Cockin not only agreed its findings but made a formal request to Silvey for a 'more thorough analysis of audiences for religious broadcasts'. The main conclusions of the conference were striking and moreover, a vindication of the Schools religious policy. Here was a clue and a guide to concentration of particular broadcasts on 'the needs of more closely defined categories of listeners'.[41] For the first time in its history CRAC had set up a radical investigation of religious broadcasting for the non-churchgoer. It would talk of a BBC initiative in evangelism only so long as that demonstrated some achievement in co-operation with the churches in this, or rather, *their* task. Scotland had provided examples and 'London in Essex' was about to; only in this light could the Corporation stave off criticism from those only too ready to point the finger at the 'BBC Christians'.

The report saw the need to bridge the gap between the Light and the Third Programmes with more provision of talks, discussions and features designed on the Schools Department model especially in the *Religion and Philosophy* series. But it was also sure that broadcast acts of worship were not the way to reach the fringe listener. Therefore the requested talks, discussions and features deserved more time in the schedules. This was not going to be readily granted, particularly in the light of the Governors' insistence that the present amount of religious broadcasting was 'about right'.[42] In effect, unless the Department could successfully compete in the so-called 'values' spaces in the Home Service there would have to be considerable modification of the regular liturgical times. It was not very likely.

However, Silvey was asked to research the audience within the limits of his sampling method. Gallup Polls actually conducted a survey on his directive. The major part of the survey was undertaken during December 1954 and the sample was precisely 1859 persons over the age of sixteen. Notwithstanding what were reckoned to be 'matters of an intimate nature', there was little difficulty in obtaining replies and people were generally helpful.[43] As Briggs has observed, 'The enquiry may well have been made near a turning point in British social history',[44] not least, perhaps, because of the growing importance of television. In some instances the enquiry simply confirmed what the Corporation already knew, notably the importance of the Light Programme and the general decline in church attendance. CRAC decided that the findings should for the moment remain confidential and it was not until the autumn that they were published in the form of a lecture exposition by Silvey in St Paul's Cathedral crypt.[45]

In answer to the question as to who was listening, the findings divided the sample into frequent, occasional and non-listeners and each group formed about a third of the sample: thirty-seven per cent described themselves as frequent listeners. It was, as Silvey said at St Paul's, an immense audience: 'Religious broadcasts are heard at one time or another by two out of every three people in this country; far, far more than ever go to church'.[46] He confirmed what House had contended in 1948 and stressed the enormous difference between the numbers 'exposed' for whatever reason to broadcast religion and those exposed in churches to comparable but distinctly *participant* religious utterance.

Most of the frequent listeners were 'housewives', as they were quaintly described; indeed they were more than half of this group. The frequency with which people listened also increased with every step up the age scale. It was disturbing to find that the survey confirmed the dreary fact that the 16–20 age group had the smallest number of listeners with the largest group being over 65. Moreover, 16–20-year-olds formed half of the non-listening group, and among frequent listeners, only about one in eight was under thirty. In terms of social class there was a tendency for listening to increase with each step down the social scale, and the largest proportion of frequent listeners lived in South-West England and Wales with, perhaps surprisingly, the greatest proportion of non-listeners living in Scotland. Because of conventional attitudes towards nominal Anglicanism, it was clear that the self-confessed 'denominational affiliation' of those who listened could not be gauged with great accuracy. Notwithstanding that many listeners actually were or said they were Anglicans, it was possible to claim that the largest proportion of frequent listeners were Free Church people and the smallest, Roman Catholics. The most striking point, Silvey believed, was that only one per cent of frequent listeners claimed no confessional identity at all.[47]

Predictably the listeners to religious programmes, whether occasional or frequent, responded mainly to the Sunday output. The sixty-eight per cent in these groups together listened either to the morning service (Home), *People's Service* (Light), *Sunday Half Hour* (Light) or evening service (Home). The proportions, however, were revealing: thirty-four per cent of the sample listened to *Sunday Half Hour*. It was also suggested that the greater part of the audience listened regularly to the Light Programme, whereas there was a good deal more random listening to the services on the Home Service, both morning and evening. When this finding was coupled with the fact that the largest proportion of the listening sixty-eight per cent were over 50, that they had been for several years in some Bible class or Sunday school and that the majority were from the least educated sector of society, the appeal of the hymn-based 'services' on the Light could be appreciated. Moreover, nearly half of the sixty-eight per cent found that these broadcasts were what they were happy to call 'comforting':

> The under 50s attach most importance to the teaching function of religious broadcasting, whereas the over 50s look to them primarily as a source of comfort.[48]

The 16–29 age-group contained the largest number which considered that religious broadcasting was a help in 'understanding what Christianity means'. It was this statistic which had been in Robert Walton's expectations as the pre-evangelism discussion had developed. If the broadcasting clergy thought simple, prosaic insights into life's problems (stripped of dogmatic complexity) would serve to teach Christianity, Walton, Bliss and others regarded these as a hindrance; there had to be more respect for the questioning of any proposition, no matter how simple. The Schools Department had been making slow headway.[49]

Least of all did listeners conceive broadcast religious programmes as a means to worship at home. No doubt they would not have admitted this, and there is good reason to presume that the notion was too subtle or complex. The clergy might complain that broadcast religion enabled or even encouraged people to opt out of their 'duty' to attend worship services in church, but it was a notion more in logic than in fact. Light Programme religious 'services' were not first and foremost regarded by the audience as acts of worship. They were a species of religious entertainment which not only appealed in a way that the churches understandably could not; they were seen to be appropriate to the radio medium rather more than to straight outside broadcasts of normal liturgical events. The survey showed that the *Sunday Half Hour* audience was between four and five times as great as that for the evening service on the Home Service. Hence for a long time the Department had been concerned to innovate on Sunday evenings and so arrange the timing that the churchgoing listener who rushed home from Evensong could take advantage at least of the sermon.

The survey was thus very particularly interested in that proportion of the sixty-eight per cent which attended church: which churches, and how often? There had always been the charge that, for all their evangelical vigour, religious broadcasts were mostly preaching to the converted. This was rather difficult to ascertain, since there was an expected degree of exaggeration which had somehow to be allowed for. Notwithstanding statistical adjustments, Silvey was confident that here too the listeners could be categorized as attending frequently, occasionally, or never. This time the salient figure was sixty-one per cent, i.e. those twenty-five per cent frequently in church together with the twelve per cent who went monthly and the twenty-four per cent who went once or twice a year. Again, among the frequent attenders most were women and in terms of age most were in the 16–20 and the over 65 groups. The smallest group among the frequent attenders were those between 21 and 50. Men between the ages of 21 and 50 were the highest non-attenders, especially those categorized as 'working-class'. Again, South-West England and Wales had most churchgoers.

Silvey was also certain that there was clear evidence that church-going not only had been diminishing for years but was still doing so.[50] This was not due, however, to intellectual convictions nor indeed to any widespread complaint at the behaviour of church attenders or even the clergy, but rather to what he called 'a vast change in contemporary values'. It was nothing new, however, to be told that churchgoing was in decline; the real question was whether religious broadcasting increased or checked the decline. Since there was yet no means whereby the effect on church attendance of religious broadcasting could be statistically proved, the Department had to rely upon House's clergy survey of 1948. Silvey cautioned against any 'wholesale generalizations such as "Only churchgoers listen to religious broadcasts" or "Listeners to religious broadcasts don't go church" '. 'Even so', he added, 'there is a marked association between churchgoing and listening to religious broadcasts.' Nevertheless, the crucial fact as he saw it was that sixty-two per cent of the frequent and occasional listeners were *non-*churchgoers. Silvey thought it was this statistic which was particularly important and significant to religious broadcasters.[51]

It was all the more important when qualified by other aspects of the survey which showed that Sunday school experience was or had been a universal component in most people's early life but that this too was diminishing. There was also a strong conviction about the importance of Sunday school for the young, even among non-churchgoers and non-listeners to religious programmes. There was substantial approval, again by the non-listener and non-attender, for religious teaching in day schools, although the people who were not prepared to insist upon their children going to Sunday school or who did not think that Sunday school attendance was desirable were far less ready than others to give unqualified approval to religious instruction in day school. There was thus no case for the day school taking over from the Sunday school. On the contrary, it was fuel for the Schools Department's contention that the BBC religious output into the day schools among sixth forms was all to do with education in religion and not with any attenuated catechesis such as properly belonged to Sunday schools in the styles and according to the objectives of the various denominations. With so few specialist teachers it was no surprise that the aims of religious education in day schools were not very different from traditional Sunday school objectives.[52]

Against the background of all the discussion of Haley's concern with moral values, the survey tried as best it could to discover the extent to which people would acknowledge a religious motive for their everyday behaviour. It was not easy to be precise: Silvey could only devise a selection of what were almost slogans or at least colloquialisms to denote a certain self-interpretation. People were shown a card on which was printed:

The reason why I myself try to be honest, truthful and kind is that:
It makes life happier for other people;
I have always been taught to be;
My religion tells me to;
It is the way to get the most out of life;
That is the way I like other people to behave towards me.

Silvey was cautious with these results but was still certain that the religious broadcasters ought to take note of one rather secure finding, that around a quarter of the sample did spontaneously testify to a religious motive behind their honesty and benevolence. How they would all have worded their further remarks cannot be known. Silvey recognized that it could all be lip-service. Nevertheless, the fact that this quarter was outside the churches' immediate influence was not without significance.[53] It was certainly such a notion that informed the policy in the *People's Service*. It made the crucial assumption that to the millions who were for any reason listening, the language of religion was still intelligible provided it was neither technical nor patronizing. House, Taylor and later Richard Tatlock who organized this programme found that very few of the clergy recognized the discipline that this 'refracted Christian knowledge' demanded of their utterance. Silvey's survey threw up just a few names of specific broadcasters such as Soper, Cuthbert Bardsley of Croydon, Leslie Weatherhead and Ronald Selby Wright – all to be found on the *People's Service* or *Silver Lining*.

Silvey finally tried valiantly to provide a few clues to what the sample thought about the Bible and in particular the usefulness of the Old Testament, about prayer, about immortality, and about the divorce law. Silvey claimed his survey suggested that Fundamentalism was held less and less strongly, albeit such a statement as 'The Old Testament may not be all true but has lessons for us today', drew from most of the sample vague but charitable agreement! And yet a substantial majority of people, whether listeners or not and whether church attenders or not, subscribed in some form to a belief about prayer. (Silvey had no brief to investigate further categories in common attitudes towards the occult or superstition.) It was held by half of non-churchgoers – yet another element in what Cockin believed to be the indigenous Christianity in the population at large. Pre-evangelism was all about this half of the population. There was rather less evidence, however, that belief in life after death was of real consequence to the non-attender. Silvey sounded a warning to the churches: the belief was either denied or doubted by more than sixty per cent of those outside the churches and by as many as a quarter of those inside! Scientific thinking was creeping ever more surely into the preserves of inherited doctrines; positivism was catching up with Christians and – as Kathleen Bliss had said in all the 'pre-evangelism' discussions – the untutored and even ill-formed questionings of the most lowly could no longer be answered by the reiteration of the simplest and most attenuated Christian dogmas. It was also as much an issue of methodology: broadcasting in general had been 'teaching' too many people for too long to question and to doubt – as if this were the proper means towards enlightenment. It had certainly been Haley's approach: searching for the truth was undertaken in the atmosphere of doubt and it was only rarely full of balm: mostly it disturbed the peace. Cockin's 'pre-evangelism' group were beginning to see the implications not merely for broadcasting but for the future of Christian belief. The clue mentioned again and again was somewhere in the Schools output and surely involved first, and perhaps above all, listening to questions put by ordinary people. So often they were told that they were questions which could not be asked.

Silvey had also endeavoured to determine the extent to which listeners to Sunday religious broadcasts had any opinions upon the non-liturgical programmes apart from *Lift Up Your Hearts*. Did people have a preference for drama, talks or discussions? He gave rather short shrift to this section but the Department was particularly interested in his observation that whereas non-churchgoers were not specially interested in plays, churchgoers were much more interested in religious drama than religious talks. This confirmed Robertson's view that by and large the churchgoer was not greatly committed to hearing talks. In the final report of the pre-evangelism committee much emphasis had been placed on discussion programmes, not least, as Silvey had said, because discussion was appreciated by the non-churchgoers somewhat significantly more than either straight talks or drama. Churchgoers wanted entertainment rather than instruction; the non-churchgoer wanted debate rather than propaganda. With this final report of Cockin's committee coupled with Silvey's findings, the ground was prepared for a shift in the Department's policy: CRAC accepted the suggestions of both and rather blithely commended them to the Corporation in the hope of obtaining more programme space.[54] The Home and Light Programme Controllers, Andrew Stewart and Kenneth Adam, made it clear that the Department would have to adapt what it already had. Cockin's rather erudite committee wanted more discussion, analysis and exposition; and a good deal less straight, unexamined pronouncement. There should above all be 'analysis and illustration of the nature and act of believing and honest consideration of the legitimate function of doubt.'[55]

It was a bold approach, particularly as it was clear that the churches were becoming increasingly preoccupied with evangelistic expansion which called for a 'rather more certain sound' than religious broadcasting now envisaged. Radical opinion on the committee was prepared to use theological categories to speak about the 'extra-ecclesial world' and wanted programmes to recognize and elucidate 'evidence of the Holy Spirit beyond the ecclesiastical sphere'.[56] This would be a hard path for the RBD to tread against the background of the increasing fervour of evangelism in the churches, especially as this placed so much emphasis upon the local congregations and untutored lay participation. House was sure that Bishop Gough of Barking rightly counselled the Department to recognize a new trembling among the churches: Billy Graham had come to town! ·

F. Billy Graham

In January 1955 the Corporation was under pressure to relay some meetings in Graham's proposed crusade in the early summer, particularly as the Scottish *Tell Scotland* operation (itself the product of Falconer's initiatives in the Radio Missions) included plans to have Graham relayed live from Kelvin Hall, Glasgow, on Good Friday. The urbane Harman Grisewood was quite happy to co-operate if CRAC agreed to it all. The Bishop of Barking, however, was not a member of the Committee. Cockin hestitated, but eventually opposed the idea, particularly as several church leaders, including Dr Leslie Cooke of the Congregational Union and Donald Soper, then Chairman of the Methodist Conference, were convinced that the campaign was – in House's words – 'doing untold harm to the Christian cause in this country by associating the Christian faith exclusively with a kind of defiant anti-intellectualism'.[57] There could be reporting of the phenomenon but as much resistance as possible to relaying Graham's actual meetings. Hugh Gough was not at all pleased and had the strong and rather belligerent support of Falconer and Dinwiddie in Scotland. The rift between CRAC and the

"*Hardly has Dr. Billy Graham left our shores than along comes Mrs. Knight.*"

Scottish RAC was deep; Falconer rather thought that the London people had 'funked' the issue, whereas he had the backing of the Church of Scotland General Assembly.[58] CRAC thought that Graham's London campaign support, unlike that in Scotland, was 'under less official auspices'.[59] It simply illustrated, as House had always maintained over the 'London in Essex' Mission, that the two situations were sociologically, liturgically and theologically profoundly different. It was an unfortunate matter, over which House suffered a good deal of criticism for taking what was deemed a high church view.

His conference on religious broadcasting and the mission of the churches in June 1954 had been equally divided: the Bishop of Barking called for programmes which began with the 'simple ABC of the Gospel' and cited Billy Graham's preoccupation with the authority of the Bible. Even the evangelical G. R. Beasley-Murray of Spurgeon's [Baptist Theological] College sounded as if he was uneasy about the over-simplifications of the Graham preaching. The practical difficulties in apprehending the 'authoritative message of the Bible' he thought, involved 'a far more intelligent and sustained study of the Bible than most laymen can be expected to give to it'.[60] This was precisely the point and precisely the animation behind the pre-evangelism thinking: how to educate the basic 'unit' of evangelistic effort, i.e. the lay member of the congregation. At the very moment when the Corporation's religious policy was beginning to enfranchise the untutored layman in listening groups, etc., the Graham phenomenon, as Falconer says, 'burst like a bombshell' upon the churches' growing preoccupations with 'locality' (to be seen in the Scottish churches on a wide scale). All the paraphernalia of the 'mass' techniques in American society were now engulfing the imaginations of all kinds of churchmen, and a good number were scandalized, not the least George MacLeod.[61] Eric Fenn, now the editorial secretary of the British and Foreign Bible Society, counselled House to reject the biblical fundamentalism of the 'Graham tribe'; the Bible could not be 'rehabilitated by mere assertion', and yet he could see little sign in pulpit or in print that much help was being given to the layman; the Corporation thus had an immense opportunity.[62]

Whilst the very remarkable Graham phenomenon had encouraged an enormous preoccupation in the churches with mass evangelism, and indeed had given rise to House's special conference in 1954, it focused upon a new factor in the discussions about hopes for broadcast religion. The 'pre-evangelism' discussion sought to stratify and redefine the audience more in terms of their 'religious' needs than their social condition; traditional classifications about the housebound or hospitalized or manual worker were less important than their supposed 'religious' needs. Perhaps they doubted the faith or were ignorant of it or disbelieved in it or even despaired of the church. These classifications would also provide clues to rather more than mere audiences – they could help define religious and pastoral needs understood finally in the language of theology and pastoral care. As we have seen, programmes like *Silver Lining* or *The Parson Calls* clearly showed that a vast tract of the population could be regarded as in need of that measure of pastoral care often given but not always expected of the local clergy and community. The BBC interest in evangelism had focused on this area and made exceptional demands on local clergy in the preparations for the so-called radio missions. Quite outside this co-operative venture, the pre-evangelism discussion simply sharpened the definition of religious broadcasting as 'finally evangelistic'.

In the period from 1951 to 1956, however, just as these subtle redefinitions betokened new forms of programme discourse for these newly defined and more subtly varied 'audiences', the churches in very large measure, for their part, were looking at the obvious success of mass evangelistic enterprise and of course not least at the Billy Graham operations. Almost a half a million had attended the Wembley meetings in May 1955, and in the 'All Scotland Crusade' during March and April well over two and a half million were either at the Kelvin Hall or Ibrox Park Stadium, or were getting the message through BBC relays.[63] What was not normally appreciated in all the enthusiasm was that the churches 'bussed' very large numbers from all around the country to the Wembley and the earlier Harringay Crusades. House and the Department were almost to a man fearful of encouraging the development of personality cults, notwithstanding the popularity of the few tried and tested preachers, particularly on the Light Programme. Mass evangelism naturally focused upon one man, and this was the very antithesis of RBD policy. House had – like Welch before him – placed enormous importance on the sermon 'course', not least in the popularly styled *People's Service* programmes: the emphasis was upon the subject. In 1955 there was even talk of a BBC lectionary which would provide the broadcaster with a pre-ordained text. The Free Churches, not surprisingly, would not co-operate.

House wanted just a handful of good microphone men who were skilled in the special artillery of the spoken word through which, since the beginning of broadcasting, the preacher had – unlike well-behaved children – been heard but not seen. The great surprise of Billy Graham's impact in Britain was that he had been a personality only by hearsay. His organization had purchased air time in the USA and his success there had encouraged British churchmen to invite him across the Atlantic and thus turn his reputation into a newsworthy fact. Mass evangelism and the central personality suddenly became a fact and, for those possessed by their commitment to the spoken word of the broadcast preacher, something of a shock. Unlike any other event in the history of religious broadcasting the central personality in the midst of this colourful appeal to the multitudes was at last seen on the air: Billy Graham, televised from Glasgow, was 'watched by more people and aroused more comment than any other religious transmission apart from the Coronation'.[64]

The new initiatives just sprouting in sound radio were about to be swamped, just at a time when the opportunities for even greater co-operation between clergy and Corporation were being developed. Just as a few clergy were moving towards co-operation in the 'radio mission' and away from their historical fears of competition, the spectre of mass evangelism was now a reality. The edifice of sound broadcasting built up over thirty years by the RBD was about to be shaken by the most beguiling competitor of all: television. It would capture not only the ear but the eye, as if to say with some irony, 'When your eyes are sound, you have light for your whole body.'[65] Casual radio listening could and did take place while people were doing other things, but television was captivating, explicit and eloquent, with little left to what radio producers like Francis House wanted to exploit so creatively – the imagination.

CRAC had not agreed on the question of their support of Billy Graham. However much they might be committed to the evangelistic objective in religious broadcasting, Billy Graham was not the answer. They preferred the philosophy of the Light Programme and attempts at popularity in religion, even if it meant the 'simple ABC of the Gospel' for the rank and file. It was not that television was altogether new. In 1955, however, just as Graham took Scotland by storm, House reported that the other aspect of competition with radio was not simply the mass audiences for BBC television evangelists but that Billy Graham's organization had found a commercial possibility after all in Independent Television – and again in Scotland! Falconer told him that the Billy Graham Organization had been in touch with Scottish Television, which was going 'flat out for popular religion'.[66] A new era had begun; but competitive television was a challenge which House would leave to his successor.

PART SIX

EXPOSURE AND COMPETITION: TELEVISION
1951–1956

28

THE NEW MEDIUM

George Barnes, the BBC Director of Television, complimented the British Council of Churches on its 1950 Report as being the first 'serious study of broadcasting in any country'. This was not exactly true, but it was a nice way of saying that the Commission, unlike very many churchmen, had begun to regard television as more than a 'local curiosity'; sure enough, it had said, television would be a nationwide medium.[1] There were distinct parallels with the emergence of radio in the twenties: it was localized and had the reputation of being trivial and something of a plaything for radio constructors. Telegraphy had been quite different; it had been useful in all manner of serious endeavours, whereas broadcasting so far as it had been defined was not specially valuable for anything; the emergence of its social significance came in 1926 during the General Strike. There had been few precedents for Reith during the four previous years and yet very quickly indeed the power of the medium was a demonstrable fact in British culture: radio provided for those who would otherwise, but for the strike, have read the newspapers.

As the television service of the BBC began again after the war there were many who regarded it with suspicion and irreverence: it was not specially valuable to those whose world was books and whose contact with the exposition of opinion meant newspapers. In his fourth volume, Professor Briggs has documented the advent of post-war television and several facts are clear: television broadcasting most certainly did have precedents and was dominated, of course, by sound radio; television, whatever else it was, seemed something akin to the cinema, which was dominantly a medium of entertainment and was not, as everyone knew, governed by those charter obligations which called on the public monopoly to educate, inform and entertain. Briggs quotes an interesting comment by Robert Silvey (head of Audience Research): 'For "people like us" the programmes themselves contain much which is of very little appeal', and not the least factor against television is the 'sheer palaver involved in having to watch it: putting out the light, moving the furniture and giving undivided attention.'[2] Coming from within the Corporation, this is an astonishing admission. Silvey, in the same piece, speaks of people like himself as 'experienced listeners' for whom listening was an intelligent, intellectual absorption of material rather than any species of diversion or amusement. Listening was only accidentally or occasionally trivial! Moreover, as Briggs explains at length, there were acute technical problems inherent in television broadcasting. Sound broadcasting was and had always been a relatively simple technical operation, notwithstanding the preoccupations of the engineering division to improve the sound quality at inception, transmission and reception. Television was reproductive of a three-dimensional image and if it involved all the paraphernalia of theatre to broadcast drama then it is not difficult to envisage the elaborate equipment needed for the vast variety of human activities which might now be covered.

Not surprisingly, the philosophy of sound broadcasting dominated early conceptions of television. With the development of mobile transmitting facilities, television moved out of the studio just as radio had done with great effect from the very early days. The unfortunate difference was the cost; sound-only mobile units involved one or two men and modest pieces of equipment; television needed up to twenty men with cameras, lighting and a good deal of ancillary equipment. As we have seen, sound broadcasts of religious services were consistently appreciated more from regular places of worship – cathedrals, parish churches and mission halls – than from studios. 'Actuality' or 'the real thing' was a communicable phenomenon notwithstanding the crucial place in radio production of devices necessary to sustain a consecutive experience in the imagination of the listener.

In the churches, early pre-war resistance soon gave way to appeals by the more prestigious to have the Corporation wire them permanently. There were costs to be borne but once done, little more than the placing of microphones was needful at such locations as King's College Chapel, Cambridge, Bristol Cathedral or the City Temple, London. They were – almost instantly – ready made 'outside studios'. The rest was left to the imagination of the listener. If it was assumed by the Corporation and the broadcaster himself that this or that environment could not but be outside the experience of most listeners, then sounds might be elucidated by commentary. If there were listeners who had never been inside a church or cathedral then the sound might have to suffice. These were few, however, and they certainly did not govern the policy. It was assumed that somewhere in most people's experience there had been an experience of churchgoing, if only to Sunday school.

A few people enjoyed choral evensong because they well knew what the broadcast sounds betokened. Many millions enjoyed *Sunday Half Hour* since they knew well some setting where favourite hymns had been sung. Spaces and sincerities could be conveyed to the imagination by voices: it was the imagination that should be exploited by sound broadcasting, and no less in religion than anywhere else. So thought Francis House just as television awakened after the war.

The other major question of policy concerned finance and thus, with it, the control of expenditure. Television demanded new people for new techniques and, moreover, people with imagination who would do for the emergent medium what others a generation before had done for radio. Television, as Briggs makes abundantly clear, demanded enormous resources in men, machinery and money – not to mention space and a good deal more than the cramped studios at Alexandra Palace. The political structures of broadcasting were well established in Langham Place. Television was new, and many feared that it would be infinitely more beguiling than the Light Programme. Resources and commitments would have to change, and having started with relatively little of both compared with sound radio, the leaders of the resurrected service would now be asking for the lion's share. At this very moment, the whole issue of the BBC's monopoly was again drifting into public view.

29

BBC EXPANSION

In December 1950 T. S. Eliot raised a flurry of indignation and assent when he voiced the fears of many, including leading churchmen, over the 'television habit'. What he had seen in America filled him with anxiety and apprehension.[1] Norman Collins accused him of 'anti-Caxtonism' and reminded him that the 'elders and betters of every generation' had always been anxious about the habits of the young. BBC Television was doing its best to produce a 'not unworthy' output.[2] But not worthy enough, thought the church press. It complained that Sunday television at least was all too trivial or secular, or both. Why were there not clearly religious programmes being broadcast on Sundays? 'Television has gravely neglected religion.' Cockin shared Eliot's view that unscrupulous broadcasting would have 'poisonous effects' if the American experience was anything to go by.[3] Others expressed caution about the consequences of the hotly sought after televised church services: the churches could not have it both ways in television, any more than they had in radio during the pre-war experimental days. Maurice Gorham, chairman of a London conference on 'TV: Help or Hindrance',[4] thought that television should not be judged by the present programmes; the service was in the position radio had been in in the twenties. House was under pressure to see that religion had a firm place; it was clear that radio provided the pattern expected by the churches in television. More programmes meant, popularly, more church services: certainly Jonah Barrington thought there should be an outside broadcast from a church every week![5]

The first televised 'normal' service was a Harvest Festival from Warlingham in Surrey: the hum of the organ motor forced the organist to use the hand-bellows! What if this should be a regular event: would not the faithful be drawn from active participation? House had heard it all before. Even more serious, thought the *London Churchman*,[6] were the implications of televising the Communion Service. In the midst of the clamour for religion to have a proper and appropriate place in the television output, the Convocation of York was talking of regulating the televising of Holy Communion. At that time no such broadcast had taken place nor did it seem likely to. The BBC policy, however, did speak of television and religion operating on the 'same principles as sound broadcasting'.[7] But, as a BBC press release in November added, 'The Corporation have not yet defined their policy.' This was why Colin Beale[8] had been appointed, but, not surprisingly, although the number of TV licences was increasing by leaps and bounds, this costly service was still in its infancy. Beale's fellow Methodists lamented that he had not been appointed in 1948;[9] they had earlier cried for the churches to awaken out of sleep and 'claim a place for God and religion' in the television service.[10]

What exactly was that 'place for God' in the television service? Broadly understood by the churches at large, it was outside broadcasts of church services, just as in sound. But Beale and House had other ideas. Notwithstanding the shortage of outside broadcasting units, it was surely possible to conceive of a variety of non-liturgical programmes which could steer a safe path between the problems of broadcasting during normal church hours and the invasion of Holy Communion by television. The Governors had agreed to a policy of experimentation decided between Harman Grisewood, George Barnes and Francis House. By the end of 1951, there had been a series of Epilogues involving the use of filmed material, short talks and interviews with an ecumenical approach and on subjects such as religious art and drama. Outside broadcasts from a United Free Church Harvest Festival and from Leeds Parish Church were both well received by church and secular press alike, notwithstanding a word of caution from the *Yorkshire Evening News*, which noted that the congregation for the occasion was around 1200, and for the following Sunday around 200! Dinwiddie reported on the discussions by the Scottish RAC: whilst recognizing that the best religious television would be from churches, they accepted that the Scottish form of worship was 'of more doubtful value for television' and thus experimental programmes should be non-liturgical in the commonly acceptable sense.[11] Dinwiddie was also trying to determine the attitude of Scottish clergy to the televising of normal services. In England, it was clear to Barnes and Cecil McGivern that Anglican and Roman Catholic forms of worship were aesthetically more appropriate to television than the Free Church and Presbyterian forms, except when there were unusual occasions, for example at Christmas and Harvest. CRAC had stipulated that there should be no more than four outside broadcasts of normal services each year and that more investigation of alternative forms should be undertaken. This was partly because Barnes could not afford to tie up outside broadcast units more than four times a year. By the end of the year House concluded that outside broadcasts of church services, however well done, should appear regularly but infrequently; he was determined to pursue alternatives notwithstanding the pressure from the church press. The potential for religion lay in the weekday output and in epilogues of a sufficiently high standard to justify their place in the schedules against a good deal of opposition in the television service, given that television itself was essentially a medium of entertainment.

By 1951, House had succumbed to the dictates of the television emphasis upon personality. The new medium demanded recognizable faces, leaders who would attract a regular audience. House had long and strenuously avoided any such promotion, not only because Haley and CRAC had opposed it (for quite different reasons) but because House considered the speaker-preacher always subordinate to the subject matter of the sermon course or series. He now wanted to develop and train a species of 'religious interviewer' for the new medium: 'We must make an intensive search.'[12] (Iremonger and Welch had once wanted the same.) House was not the only one thus convinced. J. Arthur Rank opened a Christian Film Conference and challenged the churches to find the best speakers and put them on the screen in churches during worship. 'Over fifty thousand sermons are preached every Sunday – you can't expect them all to be good!' said the famous Methodist layman. He wanted the few 'inspiring orators' put on the screen, just as Welch had wanted them brought to the microphone. Beale went to this conference and found a kindred spirit who longed for the churches to be much more committed to films and visual narrative and to the training of the clergy to use the new medium.[13]

By autumn 1951 Beale had spent some time researching the nature of television production and the implications of the departmental role in the television service. He was not a producer; he was House's representative committed to television, and it was for him to provide the basis for policy consultations with the churches. CRAC had wanted material to enable it to form a judgment and Barnes had been careful to see that the Committee came to a considered judgment without haste. Beale and House visited Paris during January 1952. The visit was set up by Haley in the context of a proposed week of exchanged programmes between Paris and London.[14] One of these would have significant consequences for the religious policy, namely the televising of High Mass from the Basilica of St Denis. Beale was impressed by the variety of the French output: whereas it had first been dominated by the broadcasting of the Mass, over the two years of experiment since 1949, all sorts of programmes had been developed to provide a more amenable balance. There were programmes of a catechetical nature on the subject of the Mass and belief; programmes on the meaning of religious art, missionary activities and on Catholic social institutions. Use was made of film-strips and models. But there was one significant structural difference between the French and British services: whilst the French service provided the technical facilities, the Roman Catholic Committee for Broadcasting in France paid the bills! Moreover, all the religious programmes were outside the normal transmission hours. The aspect of balance was important: the daily BBC transmission was only about two and a quarter hours each evening and perhaps twice that on Sundays. A whole church service was therefore an unwieldy item to televise and of disproportionate length, and Barnes was, not surprisingly, anxious to have variety and alternatives. Beale noted that in France the Roman Catholic Church was the establishment denomination as was the Church of Scotland north of the border. The Roman Catholic centre of gravity was grandly liturgical, whereas Anglicanism here might be described better as grandly ceremonial. Anglican and Roman Catholic liturgy was at its most 'televisual' when in the context of national ceremonial. Important for House perhaps above all was Beale's observation in Paris that not only was the preparation of television programmes made easier by this visual element, but the 'faithful have a general background of knowledge of the visual expression of their religion and are used to pictorial treatment of it'.[15] Presbyterianism, as Dinwiddie had said, was a long way from this! The French, however, were not only committed to the grand gesture: they had experimented with various small churches to emphasize the participation of the average congregation as compared with the representatives of the nation gathered as a congregation on national occasions in, for example, Notre Dame and other large churches. Beale reported that in effect the French were looking for regular broadcasts from a 'special TV church' rigged wholly for television transmission but able to involve the 'regular' congregation.

Barnes was eager for Beale's report to CRAC at the end of what he regarded as the first period of experiment for religious programmes on television: they should 'cause viewers to reflect upon the eternal' and church services were only one approach among others. Barnes believed that the absence of a televised religious service on the major festivals of Easter, Whitsun, Harvest and Christmas would be wrong. The television service should fulfil its obligations to the established traditions of broadcasting in a Christian country.[16] Unlike House, he did not want regular or frequent religious services. In his report to

CRAC, Beale outlined the notion of balance which he had clearly seen in France. His key concepts were evangelism and imagination: the planning and presentation of TV programmes must avoid the provision of surrogate church membership but must interest the non-churchgoer. It was the 'sound' policy all over again except in one crucial area: the imagination of the viewer could be animated in dimensions not possible in sound radio. The visual ingredient raised fundamental concepts about the communication of religious truth. In sermons, for example, the French had been experimenting with filmed, visual compositions which comprised the 'sermon'. Beale was anxious to avoid the notion of 'illustration' which was a constituent part of much thinking about visual aids. A preacher on sound radio could 'illustrate' his narrative or even his argument by further narrative. Or he could use dramatic 'effects'. As we have seen, the initiatives taken first by Welch and Joseph McCulloch in the so-called 'dramatic interlude' received in general rather short shrift from the churches and the clergy who complained at the importing of non-liturgical 'entertainment' forms which seemed out of place in sermons. Beale insisted that religious programmes including 'sermons' on television were to be 'entertaining': a 'new art form' may be created in which the sermon consists of a 'planned set of visuals'. Programmes should aim to stimulate the imaginations and 'lift them into a new world of wonder'.[17]

Beale recognized that the television religious output would have to be much more balanced. His report called for his 'TV-ABC' – it had to be 'adequate, balanced and challenging'. There should be more drama and programmes for children. Programmes should be shorter and a varied style of Epilogue in the regular output should be developed; church services were simply too long, even though for the present it was conceivable that they might remain 'outside' normal schedules. Beale knew that soon enough the normal hours would increase and that with any increase in facilities for outside broadcasting the demand for church services would increase likewise, and the churches would be concerned to protect their 'actuality' in the output. It was crucial that the churches provide ideas for new programmes: family prayers, studio services, religious art and architecture, religious newsreel and religious films. He proposed that by 1954 there should be fifty-two weekly Epilogues instead of the present twelve, twelve religious services instead of the present five, and twelve children's programmes instead of the present five. The number of items should total one hundred in 1954 contrasted with the present thirty. He was also well aware that the question of the broadcasting of Holy Communion and the Mass would doubtless arise and the same pressures would obtain in television as had done in radio.[18] Rather boldly, he declared that there seemed to be 'no essential theological differences between the sound and visual broadcasting of such services'.[19] He might have guessed, however, that CRAC, like the churches in general, were not only concerned with theology: it was a matter of ecclesiology more strictly and, indeed, more controversially. Beale wanted the churches to realize that without such broadcasts, the sacramental centre of gravity would not be seen, yet with them, the disunity of the churches would be visually emphasized almost as never before.

Notwithstanding the radical character of Beale's presentation, CRAC approved it in general and supported the call for more experiment. It saw no objection in principle to the televising of the sacrament – the Corporation could go ahead! On the question of drama, which House had pursued with vigour, the Committee saw no objection to doing on television what Dorothy L. Sayers had done on the radio: most members preferred 'a naturalistic presentation on theological grounds'.[20] Even if the members had not read between the lines or had time to discuss the implications, it was a remarkable response.

There was, however, one further item on the agenda about the times of televised religious services; protection was still a major issue. House took his opportunity to prepare the Committee on the basis of historical precedent to look rather at the audiences and viewers than to the long-established fear that broadcasting during normal service hours was anathema. Sunday evening religious services on the Home Service were largely designed to reach the churchgoer, while the *People's Service* in the morning was aimed at the non-churchgoer. There need be no bad conscience about having the latter at normal church times, particularly as there was no significant evidence that religious broadcasting kept people away from church. House thought it would have made very little difference if all the services had been broadcast in church hours![21] Therefore this was a good reason for avoiding the same morass of prejudice and half-truth in regard to televised services. These anyway were bound to be few – the major festivals – and thus the problems were minimal. The Committee agreed, and would only re-examine the issue if televised services were planned much more frequently. House had not quite got his way.

Nevertheless, the Committee gave the go-ahead for further experiment and for more Sunday services if they were 'spiritually effective'. For House this meant regular and undramatic services with as much an element of routine as in the sound output. But there would not be more than twelve religious services on Sundays without further reference to the church leaders, and up to a maximum of fifty directly religious programmes each year. Barnes and Grisewood presented their propositions to the Board of Governors based on their reading of CRAC's advice, including the provision for Beale to become a full-time member of the RBD, who would act as the advisory link with the output departments in the television service.[22] There should be a further three years of experiment and the situation should be reviewed again in 1955. The Governors agreed.[23] It was, Agnellus Andrew reported to the Roman Catholic Hierarchy, as if 'a period of some anxiety had come to an end'.[24]

It was now increasingly clear to the churches and the nation that television was expanding at a great speed. For the second half of 1952 the religious content was also expanding: more Epilogues, evening services and televised discussions. Increasingly the regular services were during normal church hours but still regarded as occasional! In the spring, the Corporation began its first venture into Schools Television and got into trouble with Archbishop Fisher who thought it would be a 'perfect disaster and nothing less'; coming from a former head of Repton, his fears were no surprise.[25] Oddly enough, for all his background in CRAC's activities, Cyril Garbett, now at York, shared a similar suspicion of television as a 'somewhat dangerous invention'.[26] Nevertheless Garbett, although he didn't have a receiver, and did not propose to get one, saw its growing importance for religion. The church ought to use any opportunity which TV afforded: 'I hope we shall not leave it too late.'[27] In Scotland there were similar hopes expressed at the opening of the Kirk o' Shotts transmitter. The first televised service from it, notwithstanding the apprehension of the Church of Scotland about television, used the Moderator of the General Assembly, White Anderson. He was delighted and Scotland was almost euphoric with the pioneering service in March from St Cuthbert's, Edinburgh.[28] Agnellus Andrew, for the Roman Catholics, was increasingly satisfied with the effect of House's broadcasting philosopy upon the growing Catholic output. 1951–52 had been 'the fullest for us since the war'.[29] Above all, Andrew had been encouraged by the sacramental breakthrough in the sound output and the implications for further Roman Catholic benefits from television as suggested by the French example; there they had a regular Low Mass every week.

30

PROTECTING THE SACRED

A. The Mass

In Anglican as well as Roman Catholic liturgical spaces the congregations are often architecturally separated from the sacred priestly activities at the altar. Westminster Abbey is an excellent example: the screen supports the organ and access through it is rather small. It is the same in many cathedrals and while this is not the place to discuss church architecture, it is important to notice that the sacred activities east of such screens cannot usually be seen by any large congregation. In Westminster Abbey the choir space is rather large and can house a substantial congregation as well as singers, but if they are in great numbers, the congregation is all placed west of the screen.

In 1952 George VI died and Elizabeth II acceded to the throne and after fifteen years, the nation anticipated another Coronation. In 1937, radio had been the medium; the coronation (but for one small part) had been conveyed to the nation with an accomplished commentary by Iremonger, who took the greatest pains to ensure that listeners 'saw' as clearly as possible what was happening. The small exception was the Eucharist – at this point the radio transferred to St Margaret's for sacred music whilst King and Queen made their Communion. In 1952 television plans began to be drawn up immediately the Garter Principal King at Arms had made the proclamation on 7 June.[1]

At this moment the Corporation was planning its week of linked broadcasts with French television which included the televising of High Mass from the Abbey of St Denis in Paris. This was scheduled for 13 July and Agnellus Andrew provided the commentary. Barnes thought it 'beautiful, moving and technically accomplished'.[2] Not so the Scots: it was the first time British television viewers – and there were now well over a million of them – had seen the Mass. Dinwiddie and the Scottish RAC had decided not to take this national relay – a decision which caused considerable outcry in the Corporation. The Scots complained that the first sacramental television programme should have been a Presbyterian Holy Communion, not a Roman Catholic Mass. The

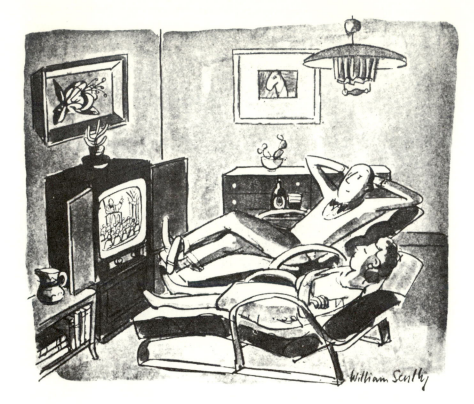

issue was both political and sacramental: the fact that it came from Paris was an additional offence. Falconer lamented that Scottish viewers were seeing more Catholic and Anglican programmes than Church of Scotland ones. The Paris broadcast would have serious repercussions.[3]

Two days before the Paris broadcast and in anticipation of it, House raised once again the issue which more than any other divided the Corporation from the churches and, more significantly, the RBD within itself. CRAC had approved the sound broadcasting of the sacrament, be it 'Mass', 'Eucharist' or 'Lord's Supper'. By 1951 CRAC regarded the sound broadcasts as no longer 'experimental', and in January 1952 were almost as positive over television. What, however, did the regions think? It was for their Religious Broadcasting Organizers to discern the feeling of their advisory committees and report. Cockin believed that CRAC not only had no objection but positively wanted the sacrament televised, if not sooner, then later. But the Department was profoundly divided; in particular Falconer of Scotland knew that his constituency was much aggrieved by Roman Catholic intrusions and a general lack of Church of

Scotland identity in the television output. House told the Department plainly that he found it 'hard to see why the sacramental sound broadcasts ought not to find a place on television from now on'.[4] He asked for further reflections following a long staff meeting at which Barnes had addressed the Department and laid much emphasis upon television as spectacle and illustration rather than 'matters of mind'. He had said the same to CRAC. Predictably there was a good deal of clerical opposition around the country to the notion of 'spectacle': it could be an opportunity for the cynic! Again, the more explicit the denominational balance the less powerful the illusion of the traditional church unity in broadcasting. Broadcasting the sacrament would heighten the divisions in Christendom without due explanation. By the same token Maurice Dean in Birmingham thought the broadcasting of Free Church and Church of Scotland sacramental services encouraged the view that these services were as important for Presbyterians as they were for Anglicans and Romans, notwithstanding the aesthetic differences which in television terms were considerable. For this reason Falconer and Stanley Pritchard from Scotland put the emphasis upon evangelism. Since the sacrament was such a profoundly eloquent token of disunity and since broadcasting television opportunities were so few, were they not putting the cart before the horse?

Opinion in favour was as much to do with ecclesial public relations as with sacramental theology or pastoral care. If all aspects of the churches' witness should be broadcast, then without the sacrament a quite wrong impression would be given. Garbett had once told Fenn in no uncertain terms that his proposed wartime series on *How Christians Worship* could not possibly be adequate without reference to the vexed question of the ban on sacramental broadcasts. Without doubt, House's commitment to a faithful presentation of the mainstream view must involve the televising of the sacrament. It was as much as anything the coupling of the pastoral care of minority interests with faithful public and indeed, ecumenical relations. Moreover, one significant sector of the audience was, as usual, in danger of getting left behind in the protracted concerns of the churches to have their rights: namely the housebound. They were of every denomination and should perhaps have the first consideration. Obviously, as House recognized, the issue was not only pastoral, as the Scottish reaction demonstrated so well: the Presbyterian housebound had no great yearning for the sacramental services to be broadcast and thus Falconer's suggestion to delay it all for five more years was consistent. Nevertheless, he was deeply concerned with this special audience. Peter Hamilton in Manchester and Cyril Taylor understood rather better the nature of the differences between the sound and visual media. Of course visual presentation could in a real way be educational or informative. To the committed, however, the visual could be a diversion and even a distraction. If the committed – and particularly the housebound – conceived the broadcast as something in which they participated, then Taylor thought television would make it much harder to worship. Taylor's thinking was backed by almost fifteen years in sound broadcasting and he was committed to the exploitation of the imagination in the way that sound broadcasting could do so well.[5] Indeed, R. T. Brooks, also in Manchester, thought the ceremonial would be 'utterly lost' on the small black and white screen. Contrary to the view of the television hierarchy, Brooks expressed the opinion of some low church members of the Department that spectacular liturgy made for bad television; Barnes, however, thought otherwise. He was sure that the informative aspect of ritual should be uppermost in the religious output, not the least for the purposes of ecumenical education. Aesthetic elements in Catholic traditions, and not the emotional appeal of hell-fire preachers, should be the stuff of imaginative producers.[6]

For the Roman Catholics, Agnellus Andrew expressed the feelings of his colleagues that television could at last remove the historical pressure upon them to produce hybrid liturgical broadcasts for the radio so as to avoid the Protestant indignation at 'broadcast popery'. Certainly he believed that the broadcast Mass could teach; but this was a secondary consideration. The first objective was the offering of worship to God by the people in their priestly representatives. Viewers stood alongside the televised congregation in the witness of this offering. Andrew was not worried by indiscriminate viewing, which had worried T. W. Manson in the earlier sound debate; after all, the Mass was first of all 'the renewal of Christ's sacrifice' and only subsequently an occasion for meditation and a course of 'spiritual formation parallel with the life of the church'.[7] As public television it was bound to be informative to those for whom the basic issues were important; it could be as valuable in ecumenical dialogue. House was strongly in agreement.

The English regional committees broadly agreed with CRAC. The Welsh would carry but not originate the televising of the sacrament, and the Scots, after considerable hesitation, decided to review the situation after first broadcasting the sacrament from their own church. This would not happen for another year. House, meanwhile, was troubled by the resistance and antipathy in the churches. The problem arose over the prospect of such programmes being regular. House wanted to go ahead but Cockin knew that the question had yet again to be considered by the churches officially. They were asked to make their opinions known to CRAC in readiness for its meeting in March 1953.

B. The Coronation

In the meantime, the television hierarchy was increasingly concerned with the preparations for the coronation. Barnes reported to CRAC that to his astonishment, television had been relegated by the Earl Marshal to positions west of the Abbey screen, whilst permission had been given to the cinema companies to produce films of the events east of the screen. CRAC was not exactly incensed but certainly hoped that, as in 1937, so in 1953 the public could witness the events at close quarters. T. W. Manson told the Committee that in the view of many listening in 1937, the religious significance of the broadcast 'fell sharply' when the listener left the Abbey for St Margaret's.[8] During the protracted sacramental debate, House tried his best to bring pressure to bear on Geoffrey Fisher. The Primates of Canterbury and York had met in June and agreed to speak to Haley. A meeting was arranged for July and Haley decided not to take House or Lotbinière with him: 'We must not be seen to be rushing the Archbishop.'[9] The encounter, however, did little to expel Fisher's fears of the television camera; he thought it was 'too enquiring'. House, meanwhile, tried to convince Alan Don, the Dean of Westminster, and his Chapter. Their combined answer was no – only the procession west of the screen could be televised. House was impatient, not the least with the general talk in the press about Her Majesty being roasted by BBC lighting. House believed that the newsreel operators, especially Warner-Pathe and Gaumont British, were 'a bunch of jackals'; television threatened their film coverage.[10] Television would show honourable members yawning, so argued the anti-TV cinema lobby, and this campaign made the BBC's task very hard indeed. Alan Don, for his part, passed House's entreaties to the Earl Marshal. House was exasperated at the lack of technical understanding of the simplest kind which was fanned by popular prejudice in favour of the cinema. In October Winston Churchill declared views in his own patronizing and somewhat irritating way: certainly 'modern mechanical arrangements' should be used to enable the public to see into the Abbey, but only what was seen by the general congregation and not what was seen by 'high ecclesiastical dignitaries and state functionaries . . . whose duties require them to be close to the Sovereign'.[11] Moreover, 'it would be unfitting if the whole ceremony should be presented as if it were a theatrical performance.' It was an astonishing piece of contrived double-think for the unsuspecting public. By October, Churchill had managed to persuade the Queen that 'television from within the Abbey should be restricted to the procession west of the screen'.[12] The Coronation Joint Committee made an announcement to this effect a week later.

Both House and CRAC wanted Her Majesty crowned before all the people and direct television would have the most powerful religious impact. Archbishop Fisher modified his opposition; he was quite happy to have cameras at the west door and what happened east of the screen seen in long distance shots. This compromise was reached in early December. The press campaign of the cinema lobby had not after all succeeded in reducing the Corporation's esteem and the Earl Marshal's Committee eventually recognized the importance of television. The extension of television east of the screen was 'approved'. Barnes was delighted; it was a great compliment to the 'high esteem in which our OB work is held'.[13] Lotbinière's reassurance about a policy of 'no close-ups' did not resolve the problem of more cameras east of the screen. House was now deputed by Jacob to see the Archbishop and put his mind at rest. It was no easy task. House did have behind him the recent unanimous recommendation of CRAC to the Governors that the Coronation should be broadcast in full, particularly now that the broadcasting of Holy Communion was well established. Fisher accepted that there would be no close-ups. But having television cameras there was a 'gross violation of the rightful intimacy of the service'.[14] Film cameras did not carry the watchful, curious eye of the public at their sets and, as for the 'religious' value, the film people could do it better in the darkness of a cinema. Film, however, could be edited later. Fisher agreed with Churchill; television viewers should not see more than the Prime Minister could see from his place in the choir stalls. Fisher wanted no cameras there at all; he did, however, agree to a demonstration.

In the new year, equipment was brought into the Abbey and a large-scale demonstration arranged for Fisher and the Duke of Norfolk. Peter Dimmock, who was in charge, was sure that it was this that eventually changed the Archbishop's views. At last he realized or accepted that cameras could be present without any intrusion.[15] The Archbishop, he thought, was prejudiced about television in general and must have been seriously misinformed.

In the event, Fisher and Don were in favour: the fears of the invasion by television of the sacred environment were overshadowed by other valuable advantages in presenting this event to the public in its full religious significance.[16] For his part, House planned a great number of broadcasts in preparation for the event, involving lectures as well as services. To his disappointment, it was clear that a combined united service from the BBC Concert Hall would not be possible on the Sunday before 2 June: each 'national' church would insist on having its own 'Coronation' service in its own region. (Welch had shared a similar disappointment over the National Days of Prayer.) House had tried hard to satisfy the instincts of the various churches in the combined Memorial Service for King George VI in the Concert Hall on 10 February 1953. There had been endless complaints: the Methodists resented the President of the Free Church Federal Council speaking for them on such an occasion; Anglicans complained that the prayers of the Moderator of the Church of Scotland were alien and too far removed from the Book of Common Prayer. The Catholic traditions were offended by the Free Church casual familiarity with scripture. Protestants in general reacted badly to the Roman Catholic hymn, 'Rest Eternal'. House had learned some sorry lessons. Once again, the BBC, it was said, was being blackmailed into giving Cardinal Griffin a special preference. He had also asked for a pre-coronation Mass to be televised from Westminster Cathedral but House told him there was little chance of this.[17]

But as Briggs well illustrates, the effect of the Coronation on the nation as a whole was enormous: the cameras had conveyed this intimate ritual to the vast majority of the population. The well publicized reservations of the church leaders tended to be buried behind the widespread esteem which television had accrued following the cluster of programmes around the great day itself. However, as far as CRAC was concerned, the televising of denominational sacramental services still belonged to the experimental stage. The discussion rambled on, marked by caution and diffidence. House and the Department were at variance and only very slowly did the churches decide that they had little objection. Cockin construed the general church outlook as fearful of the demonstrative character of denominationally arranged services. The more closely scheduled, the more did television clarify the profound differences of style and tradition, however earnest the commentators in their endeavours to play down the differences in favour of the notion that the principal denominations reflected facets of a mainstream Christian witness.

By autumn 1954, CRAC had the opportunity to appraise the first somewhat timid experiment involving four sacramental televised services: from Liverpool Parish Church, Denbarnay Church of Scotland, the Roman Catholic High Mass from Leeds Cathedral, and a Free Church in Manchester. There had predictably been a good deal of abusive anti-Catholic feeling from the National Union of Protestants and a motion at the General Assembly in Edinburgh in May 1954 to end the experiment forthwith; this had been heavily defeated, as House was pleased to point out to CRAC in October 1954. In effect, there was sufficient evidence of reluctant appreciation by all the churches. Agnellus Andrew was not so sanguine: all the furore over the Leeds High Mass convinced him, if conviction were needed, that 'to confront with our liturgy those who for four hundred years have been formed in another tradition is not instantly to compel either admiration or understanding'.[18] The route towards greater understanding was through increasing involvement of priests and laymen in the regular radio programmes including *Sunday Half Hour* and the *People's Service*. In these areas of the schedules, Andrew was sure there was less of the dark Protestant reaction which was roused to assert the illegality of the elevation of the Host.[19]

The Protestant Truth Society predictably declared itself scandalized at 'the elaborate ceremonial which was a grave offence to the conscience of Her Majesty's loyal Protestant subjects'.[20] Even a leader in the *News Chronicle* bellowed 'Call it off!' But Cardinal Heenan himself basked in an otherwise positive response from non-Catholics, and it was clear to House and the Department that the broadcast had a singularly fruitful ecumenical impact, over and above Heenan's own popularity as an accomplished talker. (House regarded him as second only to W. H. Elliott.)[21]

CRAC however, proceeded with characteristic caution and recommended another well spaced-out series of sacramental television broadcasts and a further review of this situation in spring 1956. These broadcasts would be in addition to the regular monthly services from churches, which themselves raised issues that could not wait.

C. The 'Faithful'

The policy of eight to twelve normal church services televised each year decided in the summer of 1952 was not pleasing an increasing number of clergy. Moreover the religious weeklies and notably the *Church Times* were critical. At this time preparations were also being made for the 'radio missions'.[22] The Department was under increasing pressure to avoid giving offence to the clergy, particularly as many were hoping that the radio mission would elicit the strongest possible support. The Methodist Press and Information Service had conducted a survey among its own clergy which declared that most clergy thought that there was 'no perceptible effect on church attendance'.[23] The survey warned however, that local 'extra-liturgical' activities would be considerably undermined by Sunday evening television. Falconer in Scotland undertook a similar modest piece of research among sixty of what he called 'representative and intelligent' ministers; how far were they indignant at television competition and how earnestly did they believe that these monthly services were affecting their congregations?[24] At the same time, House consulted a sample of fifty clerics in England; they seemed to have no serious objection to these twelve services but were cautious of any increase. But the Scots were decidedly hostile; they had little worry about the morning broadcasts, as it was now accepted that special services for the outsider were not greatly attractive to the committed; but there was strong feeling that any Sunday evening services televised in normal church hours would have serious effects upon the congregations.[25] CRAC decided, therefore, that the churches could 'reasonably expect' that there should be a limited number of services placed in 'the main viewing period', i.e. some time after 8.0 p.m.[26] They had no serious criticism of such services during morning church hours. The Committee also vetoed suggestions from McGivern that programmes should soon be extended, beginning on Sunday afternoons at around 3.0 p.m. House had already made the position clear; he feared the noisy criticism which would come from a sector of organized Puritanism which, whilst numerically small, was 'ably led, amply financed' and which could not be ignored. House was less anxious about sabbatarian wrath against current proposals to repeal the Lord's Day Observance Act than with the Sunday school lobby and how the churches would react to yet another invasion of their spaces by the broadcasters, even with church services.

The pressure to experiment with more popular religious programmes was now never stronger: the spectre of commercial competition made it quite impossible for Barnes to accede to CRAC's 'reasonable expectation' for normal religious services televised in the main viewing period. House thought the expectation was futile: their only hope was to produce more popular programmes which would command a respectable audience, just as the Light Programme had demonstrated with the *People's Service* and *Sunday Half Hour*. House accepted that church service outside broadcasts were 'audience losers', and counselled CRAC and the churches that they must innovate. If they did not, the commercial producers, whoever they might be, would surely find other ways of satisfying the inevitable stipulations that would govern the Sunday religious output. The Committee would have to accept that new programmes of a non-liturgical but probably hymn-orientated style would be the only ones acceptable in the main viewing period.[27] House was also aware that Beale was not a producer and was anyway still only part-time. Moreover, CRAC, he thought, would bring the Department into more disrepute by demanding somewhat artificial services arranged later on Sunday evenings during the very period when it was clear that increasing numbers of people, including churchgoers, were viewing the main output. The monthly outside broadcasts of church services were thus barely tolerable. House told Barnes that he did not support CRAC's 'expectation' but suggested all manner of outside broadcast non-liturgical programmes, including discussions, interviews and studio epilogues, many of which were being tried and tested in the experimental period.[28] House's 'expectation' of the Corporation's provision for religious protection was simply that alternatives to liturgical services should be acceptable on grounds of good broadcasting and thus, as he carefully explained, on grounds of audience statistics. If the Light Programme religious prime-time programmes could command above average audiences, so in principle could similarly popular programmes on television. Unfortunately, there were insufficient resources in machinery and budgets. Barnes thus encouraged innovation with urgency and not only because the ordinary outside broadcasts were the churches' normal offerings. He feared that they were too middle-class and that producers were doing too little to 'recreate the worship of God' for the new medium.[29] CRAC rather grudgingly agreed to the notion of a half-hour religious programme of a popular kind which was not primarily the transmission of other people at worship. But the Committee was divided: some, like Hedley Burrows, Dean of Hereford, believed that the liturgical services, whether sacramental or not, were in a real way evangelistic; others, with C. A. Martin, the Bishop of Liverpool, thought their readiness to accept innovative television programmes was the real test of whether the Committee were concerned to protect the church at its own worship from rather more attractive competition, whether sacred or secular, or whether it would accept the Corporation's willingness to broadcast good, popular religious television on its own merits.[30]

Beale thus set to work on devising a *Television People's Service*. He saw it as a great challenge, particularly as he believed that the twelve permitted church services confirmed the 'outsider' in the view that 'Christianity is completely irrelevant and definitely "not for him" '.[31] He, with a sector of church opinion, was less concerned with protection than with the exploitation of the medium: he had impressive support both on and off CRAC, notably from Cuthbert Bardsley, the Bishop of Croydon, Rowntree Clifford and William Purcell from the Midlands. It would be a half-hour programme using whatever materials were appropriate to television, especially film and dramatic reconstructions.

The aim was to show where the church is working to rebuild society, in contrast to the church services and the endemic middle-class images which Barnes felt so strongly were a barrier to worship: 'use the medium' was his injunction. The programme would 'feature' the work of selected churches such as the West Ham Central Mission in East London, the Iona Community and George Reindorp's church in Rochester Row. The programme would concentrate on the regular use of personalities, not least on chaplains of all kinds. Beale had ideas for interviews, religious current affairs and documentaries about the World Council of Churches, aid to the sick, and biblical exposition. He was encouraged by the array of television producers who actually turned his and their own ideas into television programmes. The RBD had their favourites in such people as Royston Morley, Aubrey Singer, Grace Wyndham Goldie and Mary Adams. They all believed there should be religion in the television output and used techniques learned elsewhere in their work on Beale's experimental religious programmes. Producers were free to choose techniques within the limits of their programme budgets and the available technical facilities.[32] Beale usually regarded his quarterly plans as little more than 'pious hopes' – there were too many complicated factors which prevented him from doing what he wanted.[33] House had been anxious, as had Welch before him, to see that religion was not relegated to the Sunday schedules alone. House was pressured into accepting bargains which might grant substantial times on Sunday in return for no demand being made in the weekday schedules which many felt inappropriate for religious programmes. House was not helped, however, by the seemingly constant preoccupation of CRAC, the regional RACs, and particularly the Scots, with Sunday programmes and the protection of the churchgoer. As in sound, there was an underlying belief that television religion should be evangelistic, and drama was now more than appropriate. The Corporation should take an initiative and do on the screen what Sayers did on radio.

D. *Jesus of Nazareth*

The other major problem for the churches was a decision by the Board of Management in March 1954 to begin Sunday afternoon television earlier, at 3.0 instead of 4.0 p.m. CRAC had made a protest to Barnes; House was particularly asked to minute the words 'very firm'. Listener Research had backed up the Board decision; the public seemed significantly in favour of programmes of a magazine style featuring gardening and farming subjects. The figures showed more than one third of the sample in favour of the extension, the worst time for Sunday schools and their 5–14-year-old attenders. Robertson produced counterweighted statistics which suggested that more than half the children of this age-group in the whole country attended Sunday schools 'more or less regularly'.[34] Such guesswork was futile. House believed CRAC should instead push the Corporation to begin programmes to coincide with the opening of cinemas. Cockin was furious about it and made his opinion known particularly through Harman Grisewood. H. E. Wynn, the Bishop of Ely, realized that however vigorous the BBC's public relation claim that the programmes were designed for adults, children were bound to be attracted to them and parents would be less inclined to insist on Sunday school attendance by their importuning children! Shared leisure including television would make parents more tolerant of their children's company. Wynn admitted that given a choice, children would choose the television. Sunday school was not, of course, an 'entertainment but a duty'.[35] Once again he complained, the BBC was undermining the churches' efforts to instruct the nation's children in the Christian faith at the critical time when fewer were in Sunday school. For the moment CRAC's wishes were favourably regarded: Ian Jacob wanted the question of the 3.0 to 4.0 p.m. period left open. Moreover, commercial television was becoming more and more threatening.[36]

Freda Lingstrom was the Head of Children's Television programmes and told Beale in no uncertain terms that she would not have prayers or services on children's television as McCulloch had been forced to on radio. Only infrequently were religious films and plays appropriate to television and once every six weeks was all she would consider. There was certainly no space for such things as the Moody Films (*Fact and Faith*) which had gone down so well in the context of Sunday epilogues. Lingstrom did have other more distinctly educational ideas, one of which came from one of her young producers, Joy Harington. Lingstrom wanted a group of six programmes which should introduce the young to the Holy Land so as to 'awaken interest in the origin of the most significant influence in their lives', namely Christianity.[37] By the end of the summer Harington had had conversations with House and others and the project took on a quite new objective: a televised Life of Christ. Ian Jacob, increasingly aware of the competition from independent broadcasting, had devised a special fund for innovative, creative and impressive projects. Harington had submitted her Life of Christ and it had been accepted.

Lingstrom was anxious to keep the propagandist element well away, and conceived the new project as a documentary. But Harington wanted a professional actor and was much impressed by the voice of Tom

Fleming. He had already made a mark in Scottish broadcasting at the time of the Coronation and around this time was doing a week of *Lift up Your Hearts*. There would naturally be very great problems, as Lingstrom and Harington recognized. Harington rather hoped her scripts would be 'pure gospel narrative with the very minimum of added speech if any'. She wanted the greatest visual impact to be 'testament to the words of our Lord'.[38] She was not put off by House's reasoned and carefully arranged presentation of the theological, textual, denominational and stylistic problems. He wanted a modern Bible version; the best of all, he thought, was the American Revised Standard Version. Harington thought this would be confusing to children and such modernity would cause a loss of a great deal of impact.[39]

There was a good deal of informed opinion against the project, not the least from the Schools Department which had more experience than any other in the dramatizing of the gospels. Was it narrative or poetry? Scupham, the Head of Schools Broadcasting, was sure that either way a dramatic life of Christ in sound and vision was impracticable without invented dialogue. He advised McGivern to read Sayers' Introduction. If Harington used only the Authorized Version, the whole thing would be dead and archaic; if she invented and interpreted, complaints from the faithful were inevitable.[40] Robert Walton suggested a galaxy of writers including Hugh Ross Williamson and Basil Yeaxlee. Whilst Harington was delighted to have the help of outside writers of such distinction, it remained finally Walton's special assignment and she was obliged by the weight of theological and ecclesiastical pressure in the Corporation to regard him as the final authority and guide. Because of the confusion McGivern decided to postpone the whole production and Walton was then given final authority over the scripts themselves: it was a blow to Harington, but she was relieved that Freda Lingstrom remained co-operative notwithstanding the ineluctable religious pressures. Poor Harington's first scripts had met with 'overwhelming criticism' and it looked as if, unlike the Sayers cycle, the series – whatever form it took – would be the product of a very large consultative group. Harington had little respect for Schools Department dramatizations, which she thought were oversimplified for the 'sound' classroom audience. She only hoped that Lingstrom would back up her own creativity, notwithstanding her willingness to defer to Walton on 'theological matters'.[41] She was soon exasperated by the reluctance of House and Walton to commit themselves on the scripts which by spring 1955 she had written and rewritten. Joy Harington was not Dorothy L. Sayers and could not throw her weight about as the great lady had done so dramatically; she simply had to obey. Walton felt she was not quite up to it; he got into touch with E. V. Rieu[42] and J. B. Phillips.

The consultative operation grew to enormous proportions with representatives from the Ministry of Education and from University education departments and the clergy. A symposium planned for July 1955 required documentation on miracles and space for discussion about the Markan and Johanine orders of presentation. What of the transcendental elements in the baptism and temptation stories and the inevitable Arian puzzle of the relationship between the divine and human in the manhood of Christ? The Schools Broadcasting Council was soon involved, as was the Free Church Federal Council Youth Department. There was however no invitation to a Roman Catholic! The participants raised almost every theological, textual and cate-chetic problem that could be conceived, notably that of the biblical language and how it could be simplified for the young and yet manage to teach important theological aspects. Both the clergy and the educationalists wanted to teach the 'golden thread' of biblical theology, but Walton insisted that it simply was not possible to dramatize complex prophetic Old Testament messianic expectations suitably for children: the Old Testament should be left out! Some wanted the plays to make it clear that the temptations were those of a Messiah and not of an ordinary man. But how could such an objective be realized without turning drama into instruction, asked the Principal of Westminster Training College? Harington was dumbfounded by the confusions and not the least the directive that 'the miracles should be presented as straightforwardly as possible with no emphasis on the miraculous'.[43] Little of interest emerged from this consultation except warm welcome for the project.

Walton and Harington took up the task again, this time with the help of just one new consultant, T. W. Manson. He accepted the need for invention and importation, for example allowing the triumphal entry of Christ into Jerusalem to take place on Passion Sunday rather than Palm Sunday. The new general proviso was that in production, the inventions would have to be minimized as much as possible. The vexation remained: the visual emphasis might arouse severe criticism, particularly over the elements of violence in the cleansing of the temple and the crucifixion. Walton was committed to the Markan order, and the use by Jesus of a whip was only to be found in John's gospel. Harington naturally wanted dramatic vigour but her advisers pre-vailed. Walton was concerned with biblical veracity and the problem of a 'television-authorized Jesus' which differed from the text of the

STUDIO II.

SILENCE

"The governors would be grateful, Padre, if this Christmas you could omit all that sensational stuff about the Massacre of the Innocents."

Authorized Version to which children could turn at home or in Sunday school. After much agony in writing, filming and editing, the production was eventually undertaken. Harington, Tom Fleming and a cameraman (but no sound!) travelled to Israel and Jordan, hired locals to dress up from Harington's hamper of props, and returned with exquisite footage of Jesus at the sea of Galilee, in Gethsemane and elsewhere. The sound was dubbed later at Ealing Studios and the director had the delicate task of cutting from the action in a live studio to this film as the programmes went out.[44]

The eight-part series ran each Sunday afternoon from 12 February to 1 April (Easter Day) 1956, and was enthusiastically received by both secular and church press. *The Tablet* advised parents to provide a 'corrective commentary of their own' and there was a similarly predictable objection from the *English Churchman* to the portrayal of Jesus: 'Protestants should make their fundamental objections known to the BBC.' In fact, very few did. Free Churchmen saw the series, as the Evangelicals had in 1942, as an experiment in outreach, as splendid on television as it had been on radio. Television, said Walter Bottoms proudly in the *Baptist Times*, provided the 'greatest evangelistic opportunity' to the one man who took the main part: this time a Baptist lay preacher. House reflected this widespread optimism: it was incontestable that the influence of these plays would be 'vastly greater on a whole generation than half a million sermons in forty thousand places of worship on the Sundays when the plays were screened'.[45] The hundreds of thousands watching, he noted, could not be reached by the preachers. It was a sobering thought, particularly as the churches were clearly benefiting from this licence-fee investment to the tune of £13,000 (which at 1984 values would amount to around £100,000). Literary and television critics were rather more concerned about the dragging effect of archaic language mixed with invented dialogue, and also that it was not possible to present the story for children on television with any more ease than had been done on radio. Nevertheless, the churches wanted it shown again, J. Arthur Rank wanted it put onto film for use in churches, and Geoffrey Fisher in a speech to the Church Army Annual Rally was generously positive.

As with Sayers' *The Man Born to be King*, there was considerable clamour for the television series to be repeated in successive Easter schedules: Joy Harington hoped it would be repeated year by year and improved in the process. The Church of Scotland made a formal request to have the whole thing put onto projector slides for teaching purposes. Freda Lingstrom and Walton decided against this on both broadcasting and theological grounds. As Sidney Berry had wisely remarked, however good the production might be, its fault would be to pin the presentation to a particular style, not to mention a particular biblical interpretation. Donald Soper observed that the series had failed to show the squalor of first-century Palestine.[46] As with the Sayers cycle, it was widely and generously received as evangelistically valuable entertainment, but at the same time literary opinion complained that Tom Fleming was a Sunday school Christ dispensing the Authorized Version, while religious opinion complained at Jesus' non-canonical utterances.[47] The series should not be shown repeatedly; next time, such a production should be for the adult viewer.[48] On average, fifteen per cent of the total adult population of the United Kingdom watched each episode.[49] This was thirty-five per cent of the adult television-watching public. The public esteem Silvey considered 'remarkably high' and the Corporation received more correspondence than for any other children's programme.[50]

Joy Harington won high praise, and finally received a BAFTA award for her production. Ian Jacob was warmly congratulatory: 'We are all very grateful, and this is not just a routine sentiment.'[51] So also were Barnes, McGivern and Freda Lingstrom. McGivern, like Lingstrom, however, thought that the series was well beyond the comprehension of the young. For different reasons, Walton agreed and supported Lingstrom's hopes that her original plan might be attempted in a totally adult context. Let adults ask questions about the figure of Jesus against the background of the first century, or about the troubled hermeneutic issues of the New Testament gospels, or about the language of belief compared with the language of history, or even about the diversity of contemporary Christendom in the churches. Freda Lingstrom accepted that the series had not presented credible biblical characters who over three years would have changed most profoundly. She was not happy with Fleming; she thought that, as a lay preacher, he allowed his personal reverence to take the edge off his acting. It was difficult to maintain the 'uneasy compromise' of holding the story together by interweaving colloquial English and the Authorized Version. *Jesus of Nazareth* lacked just what Dorothy L. Sayers had provided: 'an inspired script'. It was no fault of Joy Harington; she had had to contend with the churches, the scholars, and the BBC Schools Department. Believers were paranoid about additions to the canonical text of the New Testament, the biblical scholars about complex questions of historical interpretation, and the teachers about intelligibility. It was a wonder she managed it at all!

Harington, like Sayers, had struggled to show that the New Testament sources for her drama were a mosaic of a story and not a consecutive narrative. She was sure that the general audience would not know the difference and was exasperated that the clergy seemed not to know either. As with the Sayers cycle, Christians wanted it both ways: they wanted the gospel text to remain an allegedly reliable, historical and biographical record and, at the same time, to be the foundation of the churches' liturgical witness. Any attempt to translate the story into a dramatic medium was bound to stimulate questions from the 'unchurched' audience about how and why and when. They would hardly come only from children!

Almost everyone involved was soon convinced that there should be an adult project which might examine a 'divine tragedy' and present a cycle of plays in which the factuality of Jesus in his time was uppermost. Lingstrom wanted a new script writer: perhaps Eliot or Auden or even Duff Cooper. She envisaged a working party with Kathleen Kenyon (then engaged in excavating Jericho) and Hugh Schonfield, then working on the Dead Sea Scrolls. The producer, writer and these authorities would form a working party to decide the forms of the plays: it would be a partnership of 'expert knowledge, expert writing and expert television'. Let the new picture be 'a modern picture painted with bold imaginative strokes'.[52] The problem, as Walton saw it, was how to decide and define exactly which questions the 'adult' public was asking and, having done so, whether they could be answered by a television presentation. Moreover would the churches be prepared to let the BBC answer such questions in public, even if the churchmen and the theologians agreed that the questions were not only actually being asked but that they were the right questions? It was tempting to experiment with Christ in modern dress as many were doing with Shakespeare, but that would have obvious dangers. Visual information might only add to the offence or provocation which, in the Sayers cycle, had been explicit only in sound – the rest had been left to the imagination. When Jesus was set accurately against his first-century background and not obscured by catechetics or the Authorized Version, this might have disastrous consequences for belief, and for believers however earnest or ignorant. The new Head of Religious Broadcasting supposed that such a series 'would be a drama about ourselves which we should not recognize as true'.[53] It would doubtless be very expensive indeed and, if it happened at all, perhaps rather erudite. In fact, it took another twenty-two years before anything like Freda Lingstrom's project reached the rather selective public of BBC2.[54]

In 1955, however, House and the Corporation had other problems on their mind: a revolution had taken place in British broadcasting and the Corporation now had a rival in the Independent Television Authority. For all the misgivings about the Harington series, Silvey's research had shown that *Jesus of Nazareth* commanded four times as many followers as did the hero of Sherwood Forest with his band of men on Channel 9.[55] Threats to end the BBC monopoly were now, after thirty-three years, a reality; the tables of the money changers would not so easily be overturned.

31

COMPETITIVE TELEVISION:
THE END OF RADIO SUPREMACY

A. Indignation

The British Council of Churches' Commission, reporting on broadcasting in 1950, urged strongly that 'the present system of monopoly broadcasting under public corporation or some modification of it be continued as better designed to ensure freedom and initiative than either government control or commercial broadcasting.'[1] F. A. Cockin, in his speech to the BCC recommending the Commission's report, emphasized that the Corporation must do more than its charter required. It must not only inform, educate and entertain; and it must also rehabilitate conviction. This conviction dominated the policy on religious broadcasting; the Corporation had not only to educate in religious affairs but to guide and engender the formation of Christian conviction and Christian commitment in the church. Cockin told the Council that the Corporation was more than an 'honest broker'; it had a duty to take initiatives in elucidating the conflict in the culture and overseeing the debates between party and group.

The RBD, as we have seen was committed to the task within and between the denominations and the model extended to the Corporation in its educational initiative. Some Christian and other religious bodies were opposed to this monopolistic bias and complained of the BBC's partiality towards the 'mainstream' churches to the exclusion of rationalist and other minorities. To the BCC, monopoly was a positive advantage within the public corporation framework. Their opponents, however, thought it protectionist and exclusive. Discussions about the future of the monopoly were therefore animated by minority groups wanting the opportunity to have their say. The BCC saw clearly that the commercial system 'necessarily abdicates before the complexity of the problem and is content to leave things to the decision of the market'.[2]

'Commercial' broadcasting evoked in the popular imagination

images from across the Atlantic with the consequential threats to the singular and consistent broadcasting policy which the BBC had embodied since the beginning. 'Alternative' programmes, Home, Light and Third – and now television – did not detract from this. T. S. Eliot voiced the fear of a 'habitual form of entertainment'[3] on returning from America. Television was threatening enough but commercial television was a grotesque leviathan of dreadful proportions. Two years later, Geoffrey Fisher, also recently returned from America, said: 'The world would be a happier place if television had never been discovered.' (He also remarked that 'the nation could hardly afford it'.)[4] Television for the Archbishop denoted triviality; like Clement Attlee and many others, he was afraid of it. No sooner was Fisher back on British soil, but George Barnes took his chance to put the mind of the British Council of Churches at rest. The BBC would not give the public simply what it wanted but would provide each audience with what is best in every category of programme. As a monopoly, the BBC had a responsibility 'not to one audience but to many'. And he shrewdly warned the Council: 'Competitive broadcasting means more similar programmes, not more different ones.'[5] This was the crux of the debate about alternative broadcasting which had gradually gathered momentum up to the end of 1952.

Television, as Barnes reminded the BCC and indeed as everyone knew, was extremely expensive; plans for expansion had been criticized by bishops and politicians alike: the nation could not afford it. The reason the programmes were bad, claimed Gorham in a well publicized debate with Gilbert Harding, was that there simply was not enough money to pay for a better service.[6] Barnes told the Council in no uncertain terms that if the television service did not expand and experiment it would become outmoded and if the BBC was not given the means to provide alternative and diverse programmes, then private enterprise would surely do for television what Radio Luxembourg had done for pre-war radio.[7] It was too soon yet for the BBC to consider a second channel when so much energy was being expended over the first. The Corporation simply could not afford its own alternative.

The churches, for their part, were demanding more recognition; the *Methodist Recorder* lamented that Reith was not in charge, particularly of broadcast church services, and this at the very moment when the Department was trying its best to see that religion in the TV output was not relegated to Sundays only and conceived by the television moguls as inappropriate to weekdays. Notwithstanding the BCC rejection of commercial television, the churches by their impatient clamour for space in the output contributed to the increasingly vigorous calls for alternatives to the BBC monopoly. Barnes had told the BCC that in the United Kingdom, unlike America, it was the Government that made the decisions; had T. S. Eliot and the Archbishop forgotten or not noticed? If more money was not forthcoming and if the churches continued to complain, it could only fuel the energies of those who conceived alternatives to the Corporation's output in terms of the market. Raising the licence fee was not politically acceptable to the Government and thus the argument for commercial alternatives was increasingly beguiling. Moreover, the hierarchy of the BBC constantly lamented the abject ignorance revealed by its critics of the problems of television production. The churches were no exception: their disappointment at not having more broadcast services, etc. did not take account of costs, availability of equipment and manpower. If money from the viewing public was not provided by the Government for this otherwise 'much cherished' public bloom, then the alternative buds would grow independently. In the meantime, most church opinion, both Catholic and Protestant, was hostile to the Government's initial intimations about its plans for commercial broadcasting.[8] It was roundly condemned by the Society of Friends, the Welsh Baptists and Robert Speaight for the Roman Catholics. Cyril Garbett told the York Diocesan Conference that commercial television would considerably lower the high standard. The greatest hope of avoiding the misuse of television was to keep it unchanged.[9] By the following spring, it was becoming clear that television in Britain would certainly not remain unchanged: there was increasing talk of sponsorship, independent producing companies and special licences, and of raising the cost of it all through advertising.[10]

As Professor Briggs and Bernard Sendall have shown, there was a widespread and sharp division of opinion over the issue of sponsored television programmes and some church leaders took an active part. Lord Halifax had started a substantial correspondence in spring 1952, drawing support from *The Times* itself under the slogan 'Leave well alone'. Cockin also sharply condemned the suggestion of 'sponsorship', which would surely cause standards to fall.[11] A year later, however, there was growing support for a more sophisticated plan which involved a new institution alongside the BBC. Meanwhile plans were going ahead for the Coronation, but after that splendid event the controversy grew only fiercer. By the middle of June 1953, the issue had become a party one, since Attlee had declared that once in power, Labour would reverse the Churchill Government's proposals for an independent system. Earl De la Warr, the Postmaster-General, told the Upper House that a further White Paper would be issued in the autumn which would set out further details of the operation of competitive television.[12] In anticipation of his statement the BCC executive declared its mind on commercial television. Notwithstanding the implication that there would be clear indications about the control of such a system, the BCC's statement condemned the commercial scheme 'however stringent the initial controls might be'. The whole idea was fraught with danger and would imperil the BBC's achievements.[13] The statement represented the animosity of the church leadership to the whole idea. Only a week before the PMG's announcement, Fisher defended the BBC monopoly as belonging not to the state but to the people and condemned the commercial principle as irresponsible.[14] The Free Church leaders, including T. W. Manson, Hugh Martin and Donald Soper, told *The Times* that the scheme was 'unnecessary, unwanted and unwise'; when it was debated in the autumn the Government should allow a free vote in the House of Commons.[15] As Briggs suggests, the success of the Coronation simply added to the conviction of many churchmen that the BBC could not be surpassed. The National Television Council[16] had requested the support of the BCC and got it. *The Universe* declared, however, that there was 'no specifically Catholic view on sponsored television', while *The Tablet* voiced the opinion of many Catholics that the issue was one of freedom of speech: if the BBC monopoly should continue it would be the result of people being stampeded into it without any knowledge of 'fruitful alternatives'; controls would surely protect the nation from the fears felt by the Archbishops.[17] At least it was honest: as a 'religious minority' the Roman Catholic Church looked forward 'to enjoying its own means of reaching very large audiences'. Edward Ellis, the Roman Catholic Bishop of Nottingham, could see no moral principle at stake; for him, it was an open question.[18]

The debate continued through the summer, giving the popular impression that churchmen and the intellectual élite were against any form of change and that advertising was a sin! George Bell was one of the few to express doubts about monopoly without dragging the argument down to the lowest level, which *The Spectator* accused both Archbishops of doing. In November the Government took the debate a stage further with the publication of the promised White Paper.[19] The National Television Council conceded that it did represent a serious effort to meet the storm of criticism but that commercial television should be opposed, not because the nation did not want alternatives; but because it did not want advertising! The new proposals now included religion and politics, whereas Cmd. 8550 had suggested a ban on these areas so as to remove religious broadcasting from any market activity and make the purchasing of air time by richer religious groups impossible. The November White Paper suggested that religious topics should be subject to the same advisory body as the BBC, namely CRAC.[20] Coupled with the suggested 'second authority' was the inevitable implication that there could in theory be a second advisory body.

No sooner had the debates in both Houses died down, than the British Council of Churches executive was considering the further implications. The mainstream churches had consistently raged against sponsorship in any shape or form and, under the general canopy of 'aesthetic standards', rightly feared that their interests would be seriously threatened by any variation of the American system such as that promoted for example by *The Lutheran Hour* – a wealthy denominational enterprise which broadcast to British audiences through Luxembourg. Its printed organ in Britain counselled the very thing that the mainstream churches did not want, 'another outlet for reaching the masses'.[21] Whilst the notion of sponsorship was dead, the BCC executive declared in no uncertain terms that unless Fisher's suggestion of funding both the BBC and the new 'authority' from advertising were considered, there would be undoubted dangers still. He had told the House he wanted no advertising at all; but if there had to be, then the money should go into the central pool 'to fructify the whole enterprise, instead of this queer dichotomy of a BBC too pure, too highbrow, too dull or too whatsoever you please, to be contaminated by advertisement revenue'.[22] Early in December the BCC executive had reiterated the Archbishop's hopes that advertisements would be a means of subsidising the whole service.[23] There should not, moreover, be two religious advisory committees in competition with each other. The British Council of Churches was thus drawn into the debate on two secure footings and wasted no time in sending the executive statement to De la Warr.

It was the beginning of its special role in the formation of government policy respecting the place of the mainstream churches and the emerging second authority. Above all, the problems of advisory procedures would dominate the discussions over the new body. Just as crucial, advertising revenue should not be allowed to provide advantage for any religious body in its access to the mass audience. In January 1954, David Gammans, the Assistant PMG, invited the opinion of the BCC over these two issues and suggested a meeting. This fortuitously provided opportunity for the churches to make themselves clear from within the mainstream, ecumenical environment. The close proximity of CRAC and Francis House's Department to the executive of the BCC made consultation all the easier. The delegation to De la Warr was headed by Bishop Wand of London with Cockin (in his role as Chairman of the BCC Commission on Broadcasting), Hugh Martin (Baptist), Benson Perkins (Methodist), K. L. Parry (Congregational), a representative of the Church of Scotland, and David Say, the BCC General Secretary. They wanted to know who would control the religious policy and to whom a new CRAC would offer advice. Would there be two such bodies? Who would actually provide the programmes – the programme contractors or the churches? Or would the new advisory body be making programmes? It was all rather complex: Gammans was right to admit that there had been too little discussion, particularly in the Upper House.[24] The Church Assembly debated an attack on the BBC monopoly led by C. B. Mortlock, the *Daily Telegraph* churches correspondent. The Assembly was invited to welcome the November White Paper and also propose that voluntary religious broadcasts should be permitted through the new sponsoring commercial stations. Mortlock's proposal reflected the shallow, partisan and blinkered view that the BBC was a 'state sponsored monopoly'. Cockin persuaded the Assembly that the motion was somewhat premature and it was rejected.[25]

At a meeting on 17 February, the Executive Committee was almost satisfied. De la Warr assured them[26] that the Government proposed to ask CRAC to advise the new body and that there would be no question of religious bodies being allowed to 'buy time'; nor would there be any advertising within or 'nearby' religious programmes; however there was thus some doubt as to who would actually be directly responsible for such programmes, the new authority or the programme companies. On 4 March, the day that the BCC received the report of its Executive Committee, the Government published the Television Bill, which contained a substantial innovation in the provision of a grant of three quarters of a million pounds to the new Authority.[27] It was not a popular move, least of all to the constituency of the National Television Council of which both Wand and Cockin were members (as were several bishops), with Francis Pakenham (later Lord Longford) and Donald Soper. Violet Bonham Carter spoke for them and complained that the BBC was now in effect paying an 'entertainment tax' and could surely provide any required 'alternative public service television programme' without further increases such as the Bill now proposed.[28] That may have been so, but the BCC saw it differently: there was now enough money to pay for religious programmes and even employ staff to make them. Above all, the BCC wanted consultation and not competition.

Wand told the PMG that if CRAC was to advise the new body or bodies, there must be consultation at the outset in order that both religious outputs would be carefully balanced, co-operative and integrated.[29] T. W. Manson and the Roman Catholic Bishop of Plymouth were united in their commitment to CRAC as the proper advisory body to the new Authority![30] De la Warr concurred except to say that if the programme companies were 'clearly well equipped for the purpose [of making programmes] (in every sense) I do not think that anyone would want to say in advance that they should not do so'.[31] It was not altogether reassuring, particularly as it gave ready opportunity for *ad hoc* arrangements. Fisher had warned David Say of the danger of early attempts by 'one denomination or another to capture a programme company' and present CRAC with a *fait accompli* over which it could only act as censor and not adviser.[32]

On 21 January, Fisher had met Norman Collins (formerly of the BBC) and Lord Duncannon of the Associated Broadcasting Development Company, the leading protagonists in the debates about competitive television. They both agreed with Fisher that there should be no opportunity for any denomination to 'buy' time; on the contrary, Collins had assured the Archbishop that time for religious programmes should be given by the programme companies without charge.[33] It was a significant admission particularly as Collins had made no secret, during his time as Controller of the BBC Light Programme, that there were clear broadcasting possibilities for popular religious programmes on an essentially entertainment wavelength. Fisher remained uneasy; he wanted the new authority to produce the programmes, otherwise CRAC would have programmes 'fed' to it and have even less control; production must be centralized in the authority. The Church of Scotland had lobbied him in the same cause and made its mind quite clear to the Secretary of State for Scotland.[34] David Say was rather anxious that the Scots should not be taking independent action since they had attended the meeting with the PMG in February. At any rate, the General Administrative Committee of the Church of Scotland had approved the Procurator's action.[35]

On 3 June there was yet another encounter with De la Warr and with Gammans; the latter had encountered difficulties in the Committee stage on the question of buying time. By all means, he had said, keep religion and commercial interests apart but 'it would be a pity to keep our television programmes entirely secular.'[36] Gammans, like so many in and out of the churches, wondered whether religion would play much part at all in television programmes; 'it has not up to now' he declared. It was a clue to the extent he believed it would be possible in the new system. Pressed by Patrick Gordon Walker on whether the Government would allow a religious body to advertise or to buy time, Gammans was emphatic that whatever might happen in America, 'we are not going to have it here'. The PMG assured the June delegation that commercial factors would be distinctly separate from the religious output; he later told Cockin that the representatives had felt that 'almost all of their misgivings had been removed' and 'that the Authority and their advisers have both the power and the wish to ensure that religious subjects are handled in a fitting manner'. He thought that what few religious services were planned would be financed by the authority and he was 'beginning to feel that the authority will have to employ a churchman on its staff'.[37]

It was exactly what the BCC wanted, but Cockin was not at all so optimistic that the programme contractors could be 'trusted'. In the House of Lords, he expressed his fears of 'unseemly competition'.[38] Nor, with Fisher, was Cockin at all sure that all the provisions which the Authority had to sustain in children's programmes, news, etc. could be paid for from the grant and the monies that might be borrowed. David Say was sure that the PMG meant the BBC pattern to be followed and that the Authority would not encourage partiality toward those who had the money. Fisher was by no means so sure. He believed that it was imperative that all religious programmes should be produced by the Authority; otherwise CRAC could not maintain the balance.[39] He thought however, that the PMG would resist this in favour of programme contractors providing their religious programmes free of charge.[40] He was not far from the mark.

House almost agreed. Notwithstanding the acknowledged paucity of religious programmes in the BBC television output he was much concerned to see that they were not regarded separately from everything else. He did not want religious programmes – which the PMG and Gammans had construed mostly in terms of Sunday services – specially protected from the financial machinations of the programme contractors. The pressure to have the new authority make and pay for such programmes was to be resisted on religious as well as practical grounds: religion would be tarred with a protectionist brush and moreover, the authority was not seen as a programme making body. House wanted programme contractors somehow to be persuaded or encouraged to take an interest in religious programmes and therefore break the image of religious services as the norm which demanded kid-glove toleration.[41]

On 30 July the Television Act became law and the new authority was to be responsible for the securing of religious interests from advertising pressures.[42] Within a few days the new body, now officially entitled the

Independent Television Authority, had a chairman in Sir Kenneth Clark, the Director of the National Gallery and Chairman of the Arts Council. As this extraordinary year came to a close, he turned his attention to the other major aspect of the new Act, at least as far as the churches were concerned: their power and influence over the religious utterance of this rival body.

Meanwhile, CRAC reviewed the situation. Barnes hoped that there might be co-operation in this field as there had been in the engineering field, although the programme contractors would doubtless be competitors in the programme field. Therefore, Cockin agreed, competition between two rival committees would be lamentable. There was a measure of hesitation by most members, a conviction that serving two masters would create division and schizophrenia, not to mention a good deal more work! Ernest Payne, the Baptist, drew the obvious deduction: if CRAC could not find its way to advise both bodies, the ITA would turn to the churches and ask for representatives and the house would most certainly be divided. Cockin feared that such a measure would be disastrous. Grisewood made it quite clear that the Corporation wanted no changes in the way the Committee was and had always been constituted: by the BBC and not by the churches. Cockin carried the day: the difficulties would be solved in a 'typical Anglo-Saxon manner by working round them'. The Committee agreed to one advisory unit for the two bodies.[43]

In January, Clark wrote to Cockin, 'I expect you have heard of the existence of the ITA'! In view of the stipulation in section 8(2a) of the Act, would CRAC be willing to give its advice to the Authority as well as to the BBC? It was seemingly a simple question: Cockin perhaps more than most saw it rather more in terms of control than advice. If not, it would lead to competition and wherever else the BBC and ITA might be fighting to the death, it must not be in religion for fear of a house divided against itself.

B. Compromise

It would not be so easy: Clark thought CRAC was much too large and in the early stages of development of an ITA religion policy he wanted advice more readily available from a smaller committee which could meet more frequently.[44] Grisewood assured Cockin that the Governors of the BBC had approved;[45] but at all costs it should be realized that this smaller group was neither an alternative to nor a substitute for CRAC. Otherwise the BBC would not agree. Cockin put the facts before Clark at the end of March and was assured that the ITA fully

"Some of you who have been privileged to hear Canon Font-water may have been asking what makes his surplice whiter than the Archdeacon's."

realized the need for an equivalent to Francis House to be an officer of the ITA and not the companies. Clark was a 'much shrewder person' than he had expected, he told House. Meanwhile, CRAC had decided to call an extraordinary meeting in June to examine the issues in more detail. By this time Cockin was quite convinced that it was impossible to determine just how much influence the ITA would have over the companies and he would urge CRAC to co-operate with the Authority only if it was prepared to appoint its own religious staff: the one thing to be avoided was CRAC being held responsible for 'putting out deplorable stuff'.[46] House could see no way for any subcommittee to be effective unless a counterpart to himself was appointed by the ITA. It might otherwise open the way for the selection of broadcasters and other policy issues to be decided by church committees or even individual ecclesiastics. Almost everywhere in the world where this had happened, he warned 'the quality of religious broadcasting has seriously deteriorated.'[47]

At the special CRAC meeting Cockin went further: any ITA religion executive must share the convictions of the Committee and have the confidence of the churches. Oddly enough, House later declared that he would have committed much more time to the problems of television had he not been diverted by the difficulties and delays in finding his successor.[48] Finding a comparable figure for the ITA 'unknown quantity' would be harder still. There must at any rate be a religious programmes unit in the ITA, but one over which CRAC had full control. Otherwise CRAC would merely provide a facade of respectability. House wanted the Committee to consider ways of mobilizing church authorities to bring pressure on the ITA for fear it would regard CRAC's conditions as unacceptable. The Committee agreed to make the experiment provided the Authority recognized its historical commitment to 'balance, proportion, representation, standards and principles relating to all forms of religious broadcasting'. The Committee elected a subcommittee of five who met immediately with Clark who told them directly that the ITA would not be advised by a Committee chosen by others. The BBC-CRAC pressure would not be quite so readily accepted.

Sir Kenneth Clark outlined the proposals of the programme companies which were preoccupied with finding religious personalities for the cameras. Collins of the Associated Broadcasting Development Company was negotiating with Billy Graham for twenty-six filmed programmes. At the same time the companies were also negotiating with the PMG for a revision of the closed period so as to broadcast at around 7.15. There would be short programmes each evening at around 6 p.m. and an evening Epilogue. The commercial companies were anxious to disprove the 'hard things said about them', and Clark believed they were committed to see that a 'reasonable amount' of religious programmes was provided.[49] Grisewood was profoundly anxious at these obvious indications that the ITA output was taking on a character 'markedly different from our own', not the least in respect to 'personalities'. House had been under considerable pressure from some elements in the church press to exploit those who were manifestly popular preachers. His conviction about 'fewer and better' was too stringent but it was now becoming more and more obvious that the commercial companies knew that personalitites would not only draw the audiences but improve their reputations among the churches.

On the issue of the closed period, Jacob had been in touch with Sir Ben Barnett, the Chief Executive at the GPO, who favoured the companies and their request to broadcast religious programmes in the period around normal church service times and, moreover, programmes which were not church service outside broadcasts. This arrangement had only cautiously been accepted by the churches. Naturally the ITA companies wanted to 'develop the technique of presenting religious services generally' as Barnett explained. Therefore, there was hardly any question of competition.[50] 'But,' he added 'the BBC would be free to do the same as the ITA'! In any event, Barnett believed CRAC could be depended upon for 'sensible advice'. Sensible perhaps Jacob declared, but hardly powerful.[51] The new PMG, Charles Hill, he thought, had 'endorsed religious services without qualification' during the closed period. David Say had hoped that Hill would be more forceful than De la Warr but thought 'the learned doctor has a reputation for piety which may not help us in the long run'.[52] He appeared to be right. Now that Billy Graham was scheduled every Sunday, the BCC were drawn into protest: this was not co-operation; it was underhand competition!

Cockin confessed his surprise at the 'change in the whole picture' but still felt sure that the two companies so far in operation (Associated Television and Associated Rediffusion) were not only anxious to do religious broadcasting but to do it 'well and thoroughly'. The five-man

CRAC subcommittee had been offering advice and, since there was a company for the weekdays distinguished from the one on Sunday, the subcommittee believed that the moment had come to sharpen their objectives. ITA religion should be a 'missionary opportunity' for reaching the vast numbers untouched by church services. Cockin was sure that the churches could no longer stand on the principle of protection: there would have to be diverse programme expansion in the sacred hours when the faithful were at their devotions.[53] The BBC had, however, used this period for 'occasional' programmes and these were outside broadcasts of church services. The commercial companies now wanted to do it regularly. If CRAC as adviser to the ITA was seen to sanction these innovations, there would be trouble with the churches. The BCC must lend a hand in this sensitive public relations exercise. Cockin now realized that the churches were faced with an enormous challenge and 'the dog in the manger attitude just won't do!' Finally, he believed the churches were concerned either with 'keeping people in church or trying to reach the vast numbers outside'. The issue was complicated by the rumours put about by the clergy of 'BBC religion' working against the churches. In June, George Reindorp had created a stir through an extended article in the *Church Times* in which he laid the blame firmly upon the clergy who saw only threats to their autonomy in televised services: they were the 'least informed' about the BBC's work and cared even less. Reindorp hit out at those who trained them: the theological colleges were taking refuge in the old traditions.[54] Reindorp was one of the very few who understood.

Things were moving fast: commercial broadcasting was about to begin on 22 September.[55] The situation was tense, as the quarrel over Billy Graham had demonstrated; CRAC had at least managed to reduce his regular broadcasts very considerably. Cockin wanted a delay until after CRAC had discussed the new turn of events in mid-October.

Meanwhile the Authority was broadly in favour of the way that matters were developing.[56] Approval would not be given formally, however, until 18 October, and Sir Ian Fraser had no reason to doubt that all would be well.[57] On 13 October the situation was made plain to CRAC members; there was enough impetus by the companies for the new Authority to provide advice and not actually to make programmes for themselves. The ITA wanted to appoint a religion executive and a three-man panel of advisers rather more confessionally as well as regionally streamlined than CRAC: a Roman Catholic, an Anglican and a Free Churchman. If these three were drawn from CRAC the uppermost question of course was their relation to the BBC. Grisewood was firm: CRAC, and not the three-man committee, would be the statutory body in compliance with the Television Act. Without CRAC the sub-committee had neither autonomy nor authority. The Committee decided to keep the five-man team in operation until the issue had been decided at the top of both the BBC and the ITA.

Cockin's other anxiety was, as he had told the BCC, whether the churches were prepared to forgo their protection in favour of the 'vast unchurched'. The RBD historically had always fought to have the centre of gravity outside Sunday and did not now wish to be forced back into competition both with the churches at worship and with the new companies. On the other hand, other production departments in the BBC might regard the Sunday closed period as a sufficient allotment and squeeze religion out of any regular weekday times. It was a risk they had to take. Cockin proceeded very cautiously, knowing full well that the members of CRAC regarded themselves as mouthpieces of the churches who would not rush into any decision about the closed period without consultation. Whilst the general feeling was in favour of deploying the protected period for 'real missionary work', the decision might be seen as a weakening of the Committee's commitment to the BBC. It was this subtle dilemma which accounted for the timid outcome: it decided to ask the ITA and the companies to 'go slow on this for six months' in order to 'prepare the churches'. Cockin knew only too well that it would take more than half a year to get the churches to swallow the unpalatable implications.[58]

Sir Kenneth Clark, Cockin and the CRAC committee met on 21 October and the Authority made it quite clear that there was no intention of going elsewhere for advice so long as the Corporation agreed to CRAC advising them. Cockin, for CRAC, also insisted that the ITA should not rush into any announcement simply to make it appear that the new Authority had complied with the Act before Parliament reassembled. He also wondered how a CRAC subcommittee could be responsible for the religious output of ITA when there was still no sign of any executive officer to carry out the policy. Cockin complained that representation of the churches in the ITA news output under Aidan Crawley left much to be desired, not least over the affair of Princess Margaret. Kenneth Clark for his part agreed to investigate, but made it quite clear that the companies would hardly take the proposed CRAC offshoot seriously unless it was clearly an ITA committee and not a 'hangover from the BBC'.[59] Cockin hoped that the ITA would get the right man, i.e. one approved first by CRAC and then by the churches. Cockin was determined that CRAC would 'help' in the task of doing 'their level best to keep this obstreperous baby on the right lines'. Jacob had said often enough that the introduction of someone from outside CRAC would have disastrous results and Cockin could only assure the Corporation that there was no wavering of CRAC's loyalty to the Corporation; if ITA could not be controlled, the subcommittee would resign. Jacob, however, would not agree to the CRAC subcommittee being answerable only to the ITA and persuaded the Governors accordingly.[60] One of them, Sir Philip Morris, thought the idea was fundamentally unworkable: ITA would surely want its own advisory system irrespective of what the companies might do for themselves.

It fell to the cautious Grisewood to convince the ITA that they should accept the subcommittee and the supremacy of CRAC as the statutory body. He made a valiant attempt in terms of the interests of religious broadcasting as a whole. Divergent advice could only be harmful to the religious cause. In an almost lyrical essay on the value of CRAC to Corporation and religion, Grisewood hoped that the Authority would forgo its 'understandable desire for its own advisory body' in favour of CRAC with its overall concern and unanimous support for religious broadcasting by the two broadcasting institutions.[61] Cockin was convinced that despite Jacob's caution, the ITA could be helped to see more clearly the broadcasting interests of the churches through the deliberations of CRAC without it being assumed that it was a wholly BBC committee. He was right: the ITA eventually accepted a three-man CRAC subcommittee comprising Canon Eric Heaton of Salisbury for the Church of England, John Marsh of Mansfield College, Oxford, for the Free Churches, and Monsignor G. A. Tomlinson, Chaplain to the University of London, for the Roman Catholics. Tomlinson, unlike the other two, was not a member of CRAC.

The ITA agreed on 24 November and Cockin was convinced that Clark would make every effort to ensure that the scheme would work. He feared, however, that the churches would complain about the opening of the protected Sunday evening period. The Authority agreed that at each meeting of CRAC in future, time would be set aside for ITA business and the Authority's religion officer would act as secretary. Bernard Sendall made it quite clear, however, that it would be 'some time' before an ITA religious executive would be appointed so as to allow time for the scheme to take shape and time to procure one with a clear commitment to the independent cause. The ITA now agreed to what it had once regarded as a 'hangover' committee of the BBC. It did not want an executive in the same mould.[62] Objections came from the companies but more significantly, as Sendall points out,[63] the three-man committee with himself as Deputy Director-General managed it all quite well without a counterpart to House; Clark accepted it 'in good grace'.

Cockin believed that with this new arrangement he had discharged his duty; all that remained was to make the facts public.

A joint statement was issued in early January. It was, as Sendall observes, a paradox.[64] CRAC had been obliged to face a 'new factor' in the situation, namely that the new companies were eager to do religious programmes. Since no profits would be gained from advertising it might appear that they were being generous or altruistic. It was, as everyone knew, a matter of attracting an audience and maintaining it. The space between the end of the Sunday afternoon and the beginning of evening viewing was the obvious place for such programmes and the BBC had to follow. It was something of a paradox since the space had originally been designed to protect Evensong. The innovation sounded conciliatory: it was in pursuit of 'the immense missionary opportunity which religious television presents'.[65] There had been consistent complaint by the church press and now it appeared something was being done to reach the outsider. It was now clear that the use of the closed period would force both institutions towards a Bermuda Triangle in the schedules. Religion in broadcasting would be associated in large measure with what was seen to be its position in the culture: related to the times of worship. There would have to be some radical changes.

c. New leadership: Roy McKay

Another new factor in the situation as independent television came to life during 1955 was the departure of Francis House to Geneva and his replacement by a school chaplain, Roy McKay, a member of the Modern Churchmen's Union.[66] It had proved difficult to find a successor and House had complained that the months of delay had hindered the evolution of a satisfactory policy for religion in television, particularly when so many outside the Corporation thought so little was being done by those on the inside.

Various names had been suggested and there had been much discussion between Cockin and Jacob as to whether the new man ought to be a Bishop and add status to the task! Edward Wickham, Bishop of Middleton, was thought to be a suitable candidate but nothing came of it. Jacob was sorry – he rather favoured an episcopal appointment. Geoffrey Fisher, however, did not.[67] Jacob regretted that the Archbishop had no higher regard for the job and was not prepared to take much trouble about it; he began pressing House for names. Cockin favoured Mervyn Stockwood, as apparently did the Archbishop, but the Corporation most certainly did not: it was not only a question of his politics.[68] In this position the Corporation wanted able administration before charisma – that was for the broadcasters. Stockwood, Jacob believed, would have been too much tempted to do the broadcasting himself; he much preferred David Say of the BCC as the ideal figure. However Say preferred to return to the parish, notwithstanding the persuasive overtures of both Jacob and Grisewood, who regarded him as a highly desirable and trusted civil servant. Grisewood had rather hoped that E. H. Robertson could be invited, in the light of their very successful collaboration over talks for the Third Programme. But Robertson was a Free Churchman, and the Head of Religious Broadcasting was traditionally an Anglican. Approaches were made to the Ven. O. H. Gibbs-Smith, the Archdeacon of London, and to George Reindorp, Vicar of St Stephen's, Westminster. He eventually joined CRAC and according to Grisewood became one of the most conspicuously helpful members. It was finally Roy McKay who was recommended by J. H. Oldham, with whom Grisewood had substantial conversations during the period of Fundamental Debate.[69] He was appointed in March and attended the extraordinary meeting of CRAC on 17 June.

His much expanded Department comprised twenty-one people; ten in London and eleven in the regions, each of which had gained considerable independence during House's later years. It made it much more difficult for the Head of the RBD to exercise a centralist control over national policy. It was a matter of passionate dispute as to what exactly comprised a specifically regional over against a national issue. More manpower in the regions inevitably led to more initiatives and policy-making became thus the more complex.

Perhaps the most interesting staff appointment which House had secured before his departure was that of the Roman Catholic Agnellus Andrew. He had been an 'adviser' to the Department during what he admitted were the 'not altogether happy' post-war times when Haley had been told not to have a Roman Catholic on the staff. By 1954 Andrew did a great deal more than advise; he created programmes and guided policy, not least with a view to improving the standards of Roman Catholic broadcasting. By 1953 it had become clear that priests needed a good deal of training and Andrew had begun planning a Centre for this purpose; by the time of House's departure he had persuaded the hierarchy that the idea was sound enough to warrant their funding it. In due course he himself became the Resident Warden of St Gabriel's, Hatch End. (A comparable institution for Protestants, the Churches' TV Training Centre, was set up in Tooting in 1959 and funded by Lord Rank.) This greater professionalism could only in the long run be of benefit to the quality of Roman Catholic broadcasting. Andrew had a powerful ally in Harman Grisewood, and by the end of 1954 he also had an assistant, Fr McEnroe, based in Manchester and responsible for all Roman Catholic matters in the North of England and Scotland. Agnellus was no longer merely an adviser but formally a member of the Department responsible for Roman Catholic affairs.[70] It had taken more than thirty vituperative years to admit the third part of mainstream Christianity to the Corporation's executive, after a prolonged and squalid Protestant repulse.

The other major new challenge which McKay faced on his appointment was from alternative television; however he was equipped by Silvey with the most thorough audience research that had so far been undertaken in religious broadcasting.[71] He had arrived as the three-year experimental period in religious broadcasting came to an end. Barnes thought it was up to the churches in general and CRAC in particular to encourage outstanding broadcasters and innovative programmes. McKay had a great opportunity 'but only if he manages to arouse the churches' interest'.[72] Campaigns were afoot, however, to bring pressure upon both BBC and the ITA to prevent the invasion of the churches' evening service times by television. It was by no means only an Anglican lobby: the Free Churches were equally ferocious and a Methodist campaign in Stoke-on-Trent provoked McKay into declaring his mind. Silvey's *Religious Broadcasting and the Public*[73] had emphasized the significant figure of nine per cent of the population quite outside the churches who were listening to religious broadcasts and McKay was quite ready to make himself absolutely plain:

> In the end, the parish churches have got to stand on their own legs without being protected and they ought to snap their fingers at television services as alternatives to their own . . . we shall not gain in the end by fighting to protect church services against television.[74]

It was fighting talk and not so very far from the legacy of his predecessor, who after eight years concluded as politely as he could that there was a profound tension between the churches 'as they are' and the same tradition 'at their best' or as they should be. Religious broadcasting must give a lead, House had concluded, and, notwithstanding the conservative resistance, it was certain that the Department must innovate or die.[75]

McKay could see the writing on the wall: competition rather more than co-operation would characterize the BBC/ITA axis and, sooner or later, the closed period would surely disappear. Beale accepted competition as inevitable and, whilst they both hoped that there would be co-operation over Sunday religious television, Beale was sure that whilst the Corporation would 'restrict itself to the Home Service audience, commercial television would not'.[76] McKay was convinced by Silvey's findings about the 'intelligent and inquiring minority' which listened to the Home Service. This was the 'most important minority audience in this country today'; furthermore (as Silvey had also declared), those who wished to 'worship at home' were negligible. Despite the ambiguity in these statistics, they were fuel for McKay's commitment to radical innovation. Silvey had shown up the ignorance in and outside the churches: it was time for 'relevant contact'. There should be discussion, controversy and good personalities to communicate at the level set by the broadcasters and not by the churches. The Departmental religious organizers put the emphasis upon instruction: Falconer wanted a 'TV Pulpit' with the exploitation of a single personality. (It was found for him eventually in William Barclay.[77]) Edwin Robertson wanted innovations similar to his Third Programme talks, which attempted a radical examination of theological and philosophical issues and did not try to be 'popular'. McKay wanted more: it was not enough to reflect something that was already happening; religious broadcasting must 'face the issues and questions of our day' and 'meet the needs of intelligent, inquiring, sincere people, whether or not they are committed Christians'.[78]

As House had discovered, there were profound differences of conviction and passionate and widely varied opinions in the churches as to how the needs of 'intelligent and sincere people' should be met. By now, for example, Kathleen Bliss and J. H. Oldham had concluded that the churches did not much care for controversy on these lines. McKay wanted co-operation with the churches but was certainly not ready to seek approval for every innovation; he had worries enough in securing a firmer place for religion in the general television output. Whatever the commitment of Barnes and McGivern to the proper place of religion in the television service, the Department had an uphill struggle in convincing the various branches within television production that religious programmes justified on their merits had a place in weekday schedules. The churches at the same time were calling for more opportunities in television, but in a manner which sounded to McKay as if the distinctions between propaganda and enquiry were being totally ignored.[79] Such material would not reach Silvey's 'intelligent and enquiring' nine per cent. House's legacy was the Epilogue, which, seemed to be the only place for innovation. He had rightly complained to Barnes that controversy or radical talking was hardly appropriate to that reflective hour of the night!

The hours of television were gradually increasing and McKay hoped religion could increase likewise. Barnes snapped back: was it a question of prescriptive right, as the churches seemed to demand, or was it on merit? McKay's answer was clear: the time had come to make fuller use of the closed period, the disappearance of which was inevitable. Since the Postmaster-General had long since agreed that religious programmes as well as services could be broadcast between 7.0 and 7.30, it was time for religious television to devote a major proportion of its time 'to those outside the organized life of the churches'. McKay rightly argued to the Board of Management[80] that CRAC doubted whether church services would make any impact on these people and that this period should be used for 'evangelism'[81]. McGivern, however, believed that CRAC and the churches, for all their bluster, only had themselves to blame for construing television broadcasts in protective terms and in relation to normal church service times and their rights to places elsewhere in the schedules.[82] Time and again Barnes and McGivern had impressed upon the churches that television facilities were costly and limited and that non-liturgical studio programmes should be exploited with more imagination. It was clear, however, that within such limitations, religion was unlikely to be given much space unless its programmes suddenly claimed larger audiences.

Suddenly, however, everything changed and the ITA took the churches by surprise. *About Religion* went out at 7.0 pm on 8 January 1956.[83] McGivern thought it 'regrettable that the BBC allowed [sic!] ITA to start this weekly programme' and again blamed CRAC; it had 'always proceeded slowly and cautiously'. Like House and Welch before him, McKay wanted religion wrenched from its Sunday location; McGivern, understandably, was impatient that such a worthy objective obscured the possibilities for using what Sunday spaces seemed to be available. The ITA had stolen a march on the BBC, and even though McGivern regarded it as a 'talks programme thinly disguised as religion', the Panel officially thought it a 'modest beginning'[84] but in fact hardly thought that a worthy programme could be worked out on a weekly basis. John Marsh had been appalled by the idea.

The BBC Television Management encouraged suitable religious alternatives and at the end of January decided more space should be provided for religion. McKay had a measure of leverage; Barnes' and McGivern's 'far-sighted plan for religion in the television service' must provide space outside Sunday as well as the money.[85] With provision of space on a weekday, McKay could provide the religious 'alternatives to ITA' on Sunday that the Corporation now needed so badly; his *Meeting Point* was to begin in April. In March, however, the Corporation still hoped for co-operation with the ITA in their religious outputs.[86] But within a couple of months it became quite clear to McKay that it would be against the interest of the BBC 'to proceed in this direction at present'.[87] The churches and their advisers on broadcast religion no longer had the control they had enjoyed for so long. There were now others to do their bidding. It was not so much a parting of the ways as the unobtrusive beginning of rivalry; suddenly there was another audience, and the *Church Times* called for practical proof that the churches recognized 'for good or for all that this is a television age'.

32

CONCLUDING PERSPECTIVE

The end of the monopoly and the establishment of independent television marked the end of a protected species of broadcasting religion often abused by some churchmen as 'BBC Christianity' yet nevertheless appreciated by the majority as a crucially important way of bringing intelligent Christian programmes to great numbers of people. By 1956 the RBD programme staff in both radio and television had at last encouraged many of the most eminent church leaders to take broadcasting seriously, and by then, the foundations of the religious policy in public service broadcasting were firmly in place. With the advent of independent television there was now to be an alternative style of broadcast religion which, no matter how innovative its policies, would be associated with commercial interests. CRAC had now to consider how it could control the second authority just as it had done the first.

From 1922 until the Second World War, the influences of organized Christianity had enjoyed the upper hand; Reith deferred to the churches, although not without impatience at their complacency over the potential of the wireless; he thought denominational differences should surely be buried in the face of the challenge of this serious new medium. Until 1939 the churches more or less had things their own way, particularly with the arrival of Iremonger in 1933 who sought immediately for the improvement of broadcast religion and especially the pulpit performances of the many clergy brought to the microphone from all parts of the nation. He believed that the post-war prospects for Christianity were bleak, and that in broadcasting the churches had the opportunity to do something imaginative and redress what was believed to be a growing apathy towards Christianity among the mass of the population.

Nevertheless, by keeping a firm grip on the 1928 ban on controversial broadcasting, the churches prevented the considered scrutiny of Christian belief by non-believers, agnostics and fringe Christian bodies. The Corporation would by no means have allowed any form of slanging between them nor, indeed, did they allow any doctrinal dispute between the mainstream churches themselves. It is not surprising therefore, that the policy of protection increased the irritation of outside groups who soon clamoured for their right to address the nation with their own version of the truth.

With the outbreak of war James Welch tried again to bring Christianity into the market place and eventually enjoyed the support of William Temple at Lambeth Palace and William Haley in Broadcasting House. But the momentum of two decades made the initiative harder and the churches preferred to keep Christian belief well away from the positivistic atmosphere which increasingly enveloped contemporary discourse. The country, most clergy believed, was essentially Christian and it was the task of a public utility to make it more so – or at least not to be instrumental in destroying whatever Christianity could survive in the moral subsoil as new ideas took root elsewhere. The premise was right but the argument about public broadcasting was not.

Under this well-established public protection the churches supported popular preaching and some programme innovations so long as they complemented their generally understood evangelistic task which on the face of it they believed could be well served by broadcasting. Drama was one such innovation and the most notable example was Dorothy L. Sayers' *The Man Born to be King*. While immensely popular, as the enormous correspondence indicated, it nevertheless contributed to a profoundly significant shift in the popular understanding of the gospels. By presenting the christology of the churches' faith so compellingly these plays raised searching historiographical questions which cried out for investigation on the air. But they could not be debated for fear of falling foul of the ban on controversy. The more intelligible the story the more pressing the urge for answers. The churches more or less approved the translation of biblical language from its preaching environment into the arena of mundane fact and speculative causality. But this highly polished drama did more: it brought questions about the historicity of Holy Writ from those least acquainted with the arcane world of biblical studies.

Religious broadcasting, predictably, was dominated by Sunday church services, notwithstanding the efforts by the RBD to innovate. The broadcasting of services on Sundays from churches up and down the land naturally provided local kudos and also exposed the witness of faith and piety to a wide audience. CRAC had always articulated the churches' protective instincts about the sacred hours of normal services, and eventually over this issue the Committee and the BBC parted company. Until the arrival of Francis House the Roman Catholics believed there were limits to the burying of confessional identities in favour of a common core of Christian presentation. A discussion about socio-confessional identities was brought to the surface when the broadcasting of the Roman Mass touched Protestantism in its most sensitive area. Nonconformity showed its commitment to the Reformation never more fervently than in T. W. Manson, for whom the broadcasting of the sacrament was the casting of pearls before swine. Whilst the sound of Free Church and Evangelical piety made neither diverting nor aesthetic listening, Roman and Anglo-Catholic sacramental services had the edge in terms of good broadcasting. Otherwise, each appealed to his own. The BBC policy, however, was to have denominational broadcasts appeal to the widest possible Christian audience, not least to those no longer actually in the churches. But those who saw in broadcasting possibilities for ecumenical advance and a supra-confessional Christian presentation were disappointed, as the churches broadly rejected this approach as another species of 'BBC Christianity'. Ecumenical ideas should be confined to the Third Programme, to which, the RBD lamented, few committed Christians listened.

However, the popular broadcasting platform which was created, first on the Forces and then on the Light Programme, challenged Christians to greater simplicity, though they did not doubt that religion had a proper place in that output. Only reluctantly did they accept the disciplines which popular broadcasting placed upon the recital of creed and faith for the new generation. Some radical churchmen had not forgotten the dismal picture of the common soldiers' Christian understanding drawn in *The Army and Religion* in 1919. The answer was surely to simplify the faith: remove the dogma and the complex technical language of the creed which churchmen were rightly at pains to make intelligible to the committed.

Some churchmen complained that this was perverse: it was subordinating the examination of belief to shabby evangelical propaganda. The Humanists and others, they believed, had a case; the Christian monopoly of broadcasting was being abused. At the same time, broadcasting disciplined numbers of churchmen into an even greater clarity which recognized the variations of the audience. They had to speak to people in their homes where their newly found eloquence or directness would be heard, half-heard or switched off. The explanation of dogma, however, was shunted onto the Third Programme and directed to the educated, as was the lofty refinement of Christian liturgical music. Most religious broadcasting on the other hand, sought to penetrate the homely linguistic neighbourhood in which certain pennant religious concepts were recognized in their prime colours. Put another way, broadcast religion on the Light Programme tried to achieve on a grand scale what evangelists attempted more parochially: to prepare the ground for the disclosure by the churches themselves of more distinct dogmatic teaching. But the enjoyment of the Christian monopoly in the BBC by the mainstream churches provided solid fuel for critics: the licence-fee-paying public, they claimed, was being deprived of its democratic right to hear the non-Christian, agnostic or non-mainstream view. After all, who was paying the piper? . . .

It is, of course, impossible to calculate with any precision the extent of the financial investment in Christianity by the Corporation during our period. It is easy to see that television costs far outstripped broadcasts on sound only; for example, the Harington TV series Jesus of Nazareth cost around £13,000 in 1955–6. Before that, Welch estimated that the churches were benefiting to the sum of £30,000 each year; after the war the RBD increased its staff around the country and in 1950 salaries alone amounted to this figure. The costs involved in making programmes and in particular in mounting outside broadcasts and notably in television were and remain astronomical.

It is often said that the wealth of the Christian churches lies in the legacy of Victorian and Edwardian church building and the vast investment in valuable land of which twentieth-century Christianity is now custodian. This enormous heritage was the fruit of substantial sacrifice, devotion and commitment by generations of Christians who believed they were laying foundations upon which others would build. The twentieth-century church has been not a little embarrassed and even scandalized by this rich legacy. Notwithstanding significant post-war investments in new church building, the unease remains: too much wealth is tied to obsolete buildings in which congregations have long since ceased to thrive. The twentieth-century church in Britain, it is said, remains the poorer for having to maintain so many buildings at such high costs when some might be rationalized in order to service the remainder more efficiently, perhaps with more real respect to the commitment of previous generations, no matter how old-fashioned former motivations may now seem.

At the outset of broadcasting in 1922 many churchmen felt precisely this unease very deeply, not the least in the light of the dreadful war recently ended. Nevertheless, as broadcasting developed, churchgoing began a seemingly inexorable decline which some began to think might only be reversed by the new technology of mass communication. Yet had the churches been sent the bill for the growing provision of religion in the BBC's budget year after year, sooner or later they would have curtailed the operation as an expense that simply could not be met. As it was, the mainstream churches believed that the BBC had a clear duty to the Christian majority who bought their licences.

Thus vast sums of broadcasting revenue were committed week by week to servicing the established and 'mainstream' churches. What is surprising is that the churches, in their zeal to evangelize through broadcasting, were seemingly blind to the foundations they were laying in a stereo-typed utterance of an oversimplified Christian belief prepared for a largely untutored audience. The Corporation was, in effect, obliged to finance a rapport with populism; so small was the proportion spent upon debate. When radical investigations were eventually tried on a regular basis, it had come too late, Roy McKay declared in 1964. Church leaders insisted that this public utility was their servant and that this incalculable funding must not be used to undermine the faithful majority, no matter how intelligent the unbelieving minority. Perhaps the clergy who did most of the speaking in their protected times should have done more listening, not least on the air. Broadcast religion might then have equipped the committed man in the pew to be a match for his clerical mentors. Their congregations might have begun to understand Maurice Reckitt, Reinhold Niebuhr, William Temple, Charles Raven or John A. T. Robinson and all the others brought to the microphone to address the church as well as the general audience. The religious broadcasters consistently complained that the clergy as a whole did not help their flocks to listen to the leading minds who provided materials for the new dialogue between Christians and all manner of others. There was now a variety of emerging movements wherein truth, as Haley often reminded the RBD, was not only given but must be sought. The churches he thought, were speaking but not being spoken to – just when it seemed crucial that religious broadcasting now become a channel for the many new and widely overheard conversations between all shades of opinion. What was heard instead was a publicly financed monologue. The Central Religous Advisory Committee was regionally and numerically a formidable institution and the BBC hierarchy frequently lamented that the members had little idea of the problems of broadcasting and that the interests which they were invariably deputed to protect were being financed beyond the wildest dreams of ecclesiastical accountants! CRAC advised the BBC as to what the churches expected of it; only rarely did it do the reverse. There were, of course, many notable exceptions and perhaps most eminently F. A. Cockin, the Bishop of Bristol.

Broadcast religion thus contributed with unimaginable financial resources to the dissemination of Christian dogma, creed and piety. Congregational Christian ritual and the language of the Bible were conceived for and received by individuals in their most familiar and homely environments with greater or lesser degrees of reverence which may have matched or even exceeded the intensity of responses during physical presence in normal church worship. This was specially true for the housebound and hospitalized who valued broadcast religion very highly. But there were now great numbers, according to Silvey's department, whose only contact with religion was now at home. The worship of the church, no matter how attractive and 'entertaining' it could be made, in order to retain the casual listener, was, in a subtle way, being gradually desacralized; alongside the decline in church-going, religion came mainly as word and not as sight to see or ritual participation. Many churchmen, notably V. A. Demant, were increasingly uneasy. Religion was slowly but inexorably being honed into an efficient verbal communiqué with a limited dogmatic content mostly riding safely inside a hymnodic Trojan horse. Broadcast 'missions' did little to bring the lapsed back into congregational life, particularly as local churches tended to resent BBC interference. Christianity was being discreetly withdrawn from beneath its mysterious and numinous canopy. Liturgy and creed were less crucial than the speculative language of popular discourse: the poetry of religious aspiration had to be sacrificed for a supposed 'intelligibility' that the churches, rather more than the broadcasters, broadly believed would bring forth fruit or at least fill out the warp and woof of the somewhat threadbare public knowledge of Christian belief. Notwithstanding, great numbers both at home and overseas continued to listen with pleasure, particularly the middle-aged and the middle classes: but they were mostly the converted as Francis House later admitted. The churches' historic utterance at perhaps its most aesthetic was the regularly broadcast Evensong with Christmas Carols from King's College Cambridge. There was no attempt to conjure their traditions; to significant numbers listening they remain sublime. Evensong was fought for, then as now, by Christian and non-Christian alike. Sadly as religious broadcasting sought greater credibility, it became increasingly considered elitist or anachronistic.

Popular Christianity, however, during our period had little time for aesthetic or historic language or even poetry unless set to good hymn tunes. Moreover, at the end of our period, the churches were soon to be enamoured of new evangelical techniques from across the Atlantic.

For all the creative ingenuity of the Directors of the RBD, the churches in general and CRAC in particular placed too much unsubstantiated faith in the advantages of broadcasting for the restoration of faith and even the conversion of the nation. Early hesitations had given way to co-operation once the religious policy of the Corporation was consistently presented in service to the churches as 'not doing what they could best do themselves'. Successive Directors knew only too well that there was no serious or concerted effort by the majority of church leaders to take the consequences of broadcasting religion seriously enough to involve the theological colleges and the rising generation of clergy in the problems of religious utterance to a Light Programme audience which had effectively no background whatever in religious commitment, knowledge or insight.

They saw clearly that this was a culture increasingly confident in its rejection of inherited 'hand-me-down' credal formulae. To the disappointment of Iremonger, Welch, Grayston and House in turn, only a few church leaders regarded broadcasting as the most astonishing invitation of all time to twentieth-century Christianity to provide as best it could for the spirituality of a newly emerging technological and pluralist society. It was an offer to the churches to do for religion what the wireless had done so well for music: to co-operate in refining the latent faith of millions by exposing – as only radio could – excellence in the liturgical and scholarly heritage of a nominally Christian culture.

The history of religion in broadcasting policy might, of course, have been different; it might have been less paternalistic, even ecumenical; it might have been more imaginative, open-ended, self-critical and flexible. But at a critical period in the life of the British churches, they would not allow the Corporation, as Welch once put it, to 'strike out on its own and, instead of reflecting church life in general, make a clear bid to lead the religious life and thought of the nation'. With the arrival of a visual competitor in television all the more sharpened in the relation between the Corporation and the ITA, the beguiling power of radio was over and vast tracts of the population moved rapidly out of earshot. Television simply heightened the variations between the styles of the Christian denominations. By protecting their traditions almost at all costs in the post-war decade of reawakening rapport between so many new shades of contemporary thought, the churches forfeited their most golden opportunity to enhance the intellectual and aesthetic climate. However much BBC Christianity might be intelligent, cogent and even entertaining on the air, on the ground the churches made sure that Christian utterance was their affair and not the business finally, of a state corporation, for all its indigenous and even benevolent commitment to a more or less Christian nation.

APPENDICES

Appendix 1

Synopsis of *God and the World Through Christian Eyes*

Series I (1933)

God

What Does Man Know of God?
  Wm. Temple, His Grace the Lord Archbishop of York
The History of Our Knowledge of God
  Edwyn Bevan, MA, DLitt, LLD
Why Man Believes in God
  The Very Rev. W. R. Matthews, DD, Dean of Exeter
Science and the Idea of God
  J. Y. Simpson, DSC, DJUR, FRSE, Professor of Natural Science in New
  College, Edinburgh
God and the World of Art
  Miss Maude Royden, CH, DD
God and Evil
  The Rev. N. P. Williams, DD, Lady Margaret Professor of Divinity in the
  University of Oxford

Christ

Jesus of Nazareth
  The Venerable A. E. J. Rawlinson, DD, Archdeacon of Auckland
Christ, the Son of God
  The Rev. Father D'Arcy, SJ, Campion Hall, Oxford
Christ Crucified
  The Rev. C. H. Dodd, MA, DD, Rylands Professor of Biblical Criticism and
  Exegesis in the University of Manchester
Christ and Faith in God
  The Right Rev. H. R. Mackintosh, DD, DPhil, Moderator of the Church of
  Scotland
Christ and Human Conduct
  The Very Rev. W. R. Inge, DD, KCVO, Dean of St Paul's

Can We Imitate Christ?
  The Rev. F. R. Barry, MA, DSO, Canon of Westminster

Series II (1934)

Man and his World

Man and Materialism
  The Rev. R. O. P. Taylor, MA, Vicar of Ringwood, Hants.
Man and Morality
  C. C. J. Webb, DLitt, FBA, late Oriel Professor of the Philosophy of the
  Christian Religion in the University of Oxford
Man and Civilization
  Christopher Dawson
Man and Social Order
  The Rev. L. S. Thornton, BD, CR
Man and the Unseen World
  The Rev. D. M. Baillie, DD, Minister of St Columba's Church, Kilmacolm
Man's Hope of Immortality
  The Rev. J. S. Bezzant, MA, Canon of Liverpool Cathedral

Christianity

The Christian and His God
  The Very Rev. Francis Underhill, DD, Dean of Rochester
The Christian and His Neighbour
  The Rev. C. E. Raven, DD, Canon of Ely and Regius Professor of Divinity in
  the University of Cambridge
The Christian as National and International
  Sir Evelyn Wrench, CMG, LLD
Christianity and Other Religions
  The Rev. William Paton, Editor of the *International Review of Missions*
Christianity and the Hope of Immortality
  The Rev. Father C. C. Martindale, SJ
The Vision of God
  The Rev. K. E. Kirk, DD, Regius Professor of Pastoral and Moral Theology
  in the University of Oxford

W. H. Elliott, 'Christianity in Action':

Talk at a Midweek Service, 1934

What this tired old world needs more than anything else is a demonstration of Christianity in action. Let me explain what I mean. If I were suffering from a very painful and dangerous disease, I should be very anxious to find a cure. No doubt many of my friends would be sorry for me, but that would not help me very much. There would be others, I expect, who would do their best to make me realize how painful and dangerous that disease was and how often it has led to a sad end; and that certainly would not help me at all. Others, again, would come with various remedies, which they would beg me to try. But the only person who could really help me and give me new hope would be one who could say that he had suffered himself from that same disease, and that, after a certain course of treatment, he had got rid of his trouble and become well. I should be very interested in that person. I should ask him a lot of questions. And I should be very much inclined to undergo the same course of treatment myself.

Now, I think that civilization today is very much in that state of mind. It is ill, dangerously ill, and it knows it. It may pretend sometimes to be feeling a little bit better, but that pretence is not very convincing. As a matter of fact, the civilized world is feeling very depressed because it has tried so many remedies in the last few years, and tried them with such earnest hopes. Yet, so far as it can see, they have all come to nothing. Wouldn't you feel despondent and depressed, if in some acute illness your doctor had told you that such and such a remedy was absolutely the last resource, and if, after taking that remedy, you felt certain in yourself that this last resource, as your doctor called it, had failed? I think that you would.

Some of us are asking why the world in this anxious state does not try Christianity, which we believe is the one sovereign remedy for human ills. Of course, Christianity has never been tried yet. It has been tried in a diluted form, I admit. But diluted Christianity never did a scrap of good to anybody. Christ himself, the great Physician, was very definite and uncompromising. 'Do this,' he said, 'and you shall live.' He never said, 'Do a little of this when you happen to think of it or have time for it, and go on with your usual way of life.' How could He? Christianity is a way of life. None of us can walk that way and walk in the opposite direction at one and the same time. Christianity is a very exclusive religion. It is not exclusive about people, for anybody of any race can be a Christian by the grace of God. But it is exclusive about loyalties. We can't serve God and mammon. The only Christianity that is worthy of the name and that is worth talking about is a whole-hearted Christianity, which is prepared to surrender everything to the rule of Christ and to follow Him in simple faith wherever He may lead.

The world is not doing that. It is not even pretending to do that. Read the Sermon on the Mount and compare it with the aims and ideals that seem to be dominant in the minds of men today, and you will see for yourself what I mean. Yet nothing but that, the Christian rule of life and the Christian way of life, can save mankind. I am convinced of it. The world needs to be changed, radically changed, and only Christ can change it.

I wonder when we shall realize this. Will the chaos and confusion of these times drive us back to a simple religious faith? Perhaps they may. It was the sheer tragedy of his life that brought the Prodigal home in the parable. But I don't believe so much in a world driven by disaster to God as I do in a world drawn to Him by the magnetism of godliness. If only we Christian people could show the world that Christianity does work, that it can change and transform human life, that it can brace men to their duties and nerve them against their fears and ennoble them in spite of their sins and lift them up to worthier aims and link them one with another in the trustfulness and peace of a new fellowship, then I think the world would be interested, very interested. Indeed it would pause to see this great thing, and to discover the power behind it. That is why I said, when I began, that there is nothing that it needs more just now than a demonstration of Christianity at work and in action.

Appendix 3

Ronald Selby Wright, 'The Padre Asks the Archbishop':
Forces talk, 1942

Padre: We padres are naturally asked all sorts of questions, and I've been particularly struck recently as I've gone to most of the Army Commands (very nearly literally from Land's End to John o'Groats) by the fact that irrespective of where the fellows come from, or what their beliefs are, a very large number of their questions are the same. Many of them, I, quite frankly, can't answer because I just haven't got the knowledge or what might be called the technical answer. Some of these questions I was asked, you may remember, by my dear young friend Sergeant Jimmie Dalgleish, MM, who was one of the finest characters I've ever met, at a broadcast we did together a fortnight ago, just a few hours before he was killed by enemy action, and there I told him, and many of you through him, that the Archbishop of Canterbury himself might answer these questions. Well, he readily agreed to do this. So I went to Lambeth Palace – a few rooms of which he now uses for his London home – and discussed these questions with him, and here is now part of that discussion which we later had recorded, between the Archbishop and myself, and you can take my word for it that it was a perfectly spontaneous and unrehearsed discussion.

Padre: Well, it's very good of your Grace to come and answer through the wireless some of the questions which some of the fellows in our Forces so often ask me as I travel about the different Commands, or in some of the many letters they send me. The questions are always asked honestly and sincerely, and I do think that if more of these fellows in the Forces only knew the facts – as you, sir, can give them – some of the objections raised against the organized church would be removed. Now the first question is: 'Why should bishops and archbishops of the established church live in large palaces and receive such large incomes?' I know it's not the fault of the present bishops and archbishops that they have inherited these houses and incomes from the remote past, but I understand the church is now dealing with this matter. Would you be good enough to tell us, sir, and through me the Forces, what the churches propose to do about these two things?

Archbishop: Well, may we separate the houses and the incomes? The houses of course do come down from the past, and the history of them is in part an explanation of why they're there. They're both places to live in and offices for diocese administration. There is a great advantage when religious gatherings are brought together in having them in a place which is a real home, and where the leader is a host. For instance, the Lambeth Conference, which consists of bishops from all over the world, gains a great deal from the fact that the

Archbishop of Canterbury is not only the Chairman but the host, and they're all his guests; you get a personal relationship that is really very valuable, though of course it's an expensive way of doing things, and perhaps too expensive. When you turn to the money, we have to remember that this is not only a personal salary, but also a fund for keeping up the house in which such a lot of the work is done; it's a diocese office; it is also a fund for paying the staff – chaplains, secretaries, and so forth. It is just as if a bank manager were expected out of the stipend he were given to maintain the whole of the bank premises and to pay all the cashiers; or as if a general in command of a division were expected to pay the salary of his staff officers. When after this, income tax and surtax have been paid, there is very little left to live upon. The legislation we're introducing will, we hope, separate the fund from the income, and make it quite clear to the public just what each of them is, and how much the bishop is getting to live upon, himself.

Padre: Thank you, Archbishop, that makes the position much clearer. Now for another question which is always cropping up: 'Is it really true that the church, which probably means the Ecclesiastical Commissioners, draws a good part of its income from rent charged from slum property – especially in London?' Some of the men in the Forces feel that the church's voice about social reform and better housing shouldn't be listened to till the church has put its own house in order in this respect.

Archbishop: Well, it was never more than a small part of the income of the Ecclesiastical Commissioners which came from the rents of ground on which slum property did exist. The history of that is as follows. All the property of the Ecclesiastical Commissioners comes from the bishoprics, or the deans in chapter. This was all pooled and is administered centrally by the Commissioners. Part of the old property of the bishopric of London was the Paddington estate. A much earlier bishop had let it on a 999 years' lease, and he was nothing but ground landlord; it was only the ground rents that came to the Commissioners. Neither the bishop, while he had those rents, nor the Commissioners, have ever had any control over the property. It came to the Ecclesiastical Commissioners saddled with the lease. Efforts have been made to get powers to put the property right, but social reformers don't generally want to increase the powers of ground landlords, so the efforts failed. Now the Ecclesiastical Commissioners have for some time past parted with that property, and even the shadow of foundation for the charge no longer exists. Lately, the Commissioners have, in fact, been very good and public-spirited landlords. How far back they have that record I can't say, but I can say it's as long as I've ever had anything to do with them.

Padre: Thank you very much. And now for the third question: 'Has the church got any contribution to make to what we might call the social programme for the post-war world, and what is it?'

Archbishop: Well, the church can never have a precise programme, if you mean by the church the whole body acting officially. Its job is to preach the gospel and proclaim the principles that are involved in the gospel, but individual Christians ought to work these out into programmes, and there are principles that ought to be worked out from the gospel and proclaimed as widely as possible. There's no doubt that for a certain period – roughly speaking, through the sixteenth, seventeenth and eighteenth centuries – the church did very much neglect all this. Before that it had done a lot of it, and it has been beginning for some time past to do it again. We must work out these principles; we must try to make them more widely known, and then individual Christians should try to see how they can be applied in the circumstances of the day, and that leads to definite political programmes. But the making of programmes must always be the work of individuals or private groups, not of the church itself, because you come here on a number of points where there is room for plenty of difference of opinion about the wisdom of particular ways of handling the matter; the aim and the fundamental principles must be the same. I may say I tried to set out what those principles are to some extent in a Penguin book of mine called *Christianity and Social Order.*

Padre: Well, there are some people, you know, who think that providing a social programme is the most important thing the church has got to do. And now, what do you think about that, sir?

Archbishop: Oh no! The most important thing the church has got to do is to preach its own gospel – what it has to say about God and man, and the relation between them. Without its gospel it would have no social teaching of its own at all; what social teaching it has got all springs from the gospel, and another reason is that in fact men cannot follow the moral and social principles of Christ without the inspiration of the living religious faith, so the primary business of the church is always to win people to that faith. It has got to show the implications of it, partly because in days like these this will be one of the main influences, drawing people to the faith, partly because it is a real obligation upon us, and we're neglecting our duty as Christians if we don't work it out socially. But it is the faith itself with which we are concerned, trusting God whom we've learnt to know in Christ. I'm so glad you asked this, because the activity of the Press lately has given an impression that I am always talking politics. Indeed one paper said whenever I spoke it was about politics. The fact is, five-sixths of my writing and speaking is purely religious, but that doesn't get reported, and when one slips in a solitary political illustration, that is reported by itself as if it was the whole of what one said.

Padre: Well, sir, thanks very much. I'm sure you've helped to clear the air a lot, and both for myself and, I'm sure, for thousands – probably millions – of others. And now, before I go, would you give the chaps your blessing?

Archbishop: Yes, most gladly. I think they must know we're always thinking of them and wishing them well. Good-night to all of you. God bless you and keep you safe, and your homes and the good folks in them.

Padre: Well, that was my interview, and as I told the Archbishop, I'm quite sure it helps to clear the ground a lot. But in the time I've got left, may I just outline some of the points that the Archbishop brings out in the book he mentioned, and has also brought out in much of his speaking and active work today. (May I remind you also of some words of his, spoken some time ago.

'When people say', he said, 'that the church should rise up and *do* something, what is too often meant is that the bishops should get up and *say* something.') Here then are some of his points, some of the things he wants to see, some of the things the church under his leadership is going to see:

> There should be decent homes for the people of this country.
> Every child should have adequate and right nutrition.
> There should be genuinely available for everybody the kind of education that will develop their faculties to the full.
> There should be adequate leisure for personal and family life.
> There should be universal recognition of holidays with wages.
> There should be recognition by employers and employees that service comes first and opportunity to make profits comes afterwards:
> And the opportunity for all people to achieve the dignity and decency of his own personality.

These are some of the points the Archbishop briefly referred to tonight; but do remember that he also said, and said very emphatically, that the first duty of the church is to preach the gospel. Do you wonder, perhaps, why he said that? Well, may I suggest that you look up St Luke's Gospel, chapter twelve, at the thirty-first verse, to get the answer. Good-night to you all and God bless you.

Ronald Selby Wright
1942

Report on the Public for Broadcast Religious Services
LR 411: November 1941

The Inquiry was carried out during one single week (Sept. 21–27), among a random sample of 5,000 adult listeners, who were questioned as to their *general* attitude to broadcast religious services, and as to what they had listened to in particular during that week.

The General Attitude of the Public   The general attitude reported can be summarized as follows:

Very enthusiastic about religious broadcasts	16·6% of the people
Favourably disposed	24·5%
Neutral	29·5%
Unfavourably disposed	18·2%
Hostile	11·2%
	100·0%

How they listened that week   The returns show this as follows:

	Enthusiastic	Favourable	Neutral	Unfavourable	Hostile
Sunday	%	%	%	%	%
Morning Service (*Home*)	48	20	7	1	–
Morning Service (*Forces*)	18	7	4	1	–
Sunday Half Hour (*Forces*)	29	22	13	3	5
Evening Service (*Home*)	32	15	3	2	1
Epilogue (*Home*)	18	8	5	2	1
Epilogue (*Forces*)	8	9	5	4	1

It will be seen from this table that the differences in percentages of actual listeners in the top categories are sharper for Home Service listeners than for Forces listeners. In other words, the Forces Programme draws relatively *more* of its listeners (than does the Home Programme) from the *less*-religiously minded people.

	Enthusiastic	Favourable	Neutral	Unfavourable	Hostile
	%	%	%	%	%
Lift Up Your Hearts	30	10	7	3	2
Daily Service	32	10	2	2	–
Evening Prayers	14	9	2	–	1
Sunday Forces Talk (2.50 p.m.)	8	4	3	1	2
Wednesday (Home) Talk (7.45 p.m.)	17	12	3	3	–

Appendix 5

Religious Minorities and Sects

(i) Compiled by J. W. Welch, 1946

BBC policy from the beginning of broadcasting was dominated by a concept of 'mainstream' Christianity. Special consideration was given to certain Christian sects and other movements which claimed a religious basis.[1] The post-war analysis is as follows:

Religious Sect	Application	Broadcasts
Baha'i Movement	–	–
Bible Pattern Church Fellowship	–	–
Bible Testimony Fellowship	anti-Evolution	–
British Israelites	Continuous Pressure 1931–46	–
Brotherhood Movement	Continuous Pressure 1926–44	Talks and Services to 1932
Christadelphians	1930–39	–
Christian Contemplatives Charity (White Sisters)	–	–
Christian Scientists	Continuous Pressure 1930–46	–
Confraternity of Christ the King	–	–
Countess of Huntingdon's Connexion	–	–
Elim Four Square	1934, anti-Evolution 1946	–
Jehovah's Witnesses	Letter of protest only 1944	–
Moravian Churches	1932–40	–
Mormons (Church of Jesus Christ of Latter Day Saints)	Request from New York, 1936	–
Oxford Group (Moral Re-armament)	Continuous Pressure 1933–41	Talks 1938, 1939, 1936 Wartime Ban
Peculiar People	–	–
Plymouth Brethren	1937–43	–
Seekers (Spiritual Healing)	–	–
Seventh Day Adventists	–	–
Society of Friends	–	Talks from time to time

Spiritual Healing (Guild of St Raphael) (Under the discipline of the Church of England)	1935–45	3 talks in 1936 but by individuals
Spiritualism	Continuous Pressure 1925–46	Talks in 1941
Swedenborg Society	Intermittent 1927–38	Talk, 250th Anniversary, 1938
Theosophists	Intermittent 1925–43	Talk 1934
Unitarianism	Continuous Pressure 1933–46	Pre-war broadcasts and in 1944
White Knights Crusade	–	–
Faith Healers	Intermittent	–

Of these, in the opinion of [the Director of Religious Broadcasting] only the following need to be taken into consideration:

British Israelites
Christadelphians
Christian Scientists
Jehovah's Witnesses
The Oxford Group
Plymouth Brethren
Seventh Day Adventists
Spiritualists
Unitarians

J. W. Welch
October 1946

(ii) The Situation in 1954

By 1954 the RBD distinguished two fundamental types of minority:

(*a*) *Gnostic minorities*   These are the groups which have something to say to serious people and from which we can hope for occasional broadcasts of some distinction, appealing to the more intellectual and spiritually sensitive among listeners. In England at the moment[2] the two chief groups of this type are the Society of Friends and the Unitarians: of the same type are the Churches of Christ, the Moravians, Lutherans and Strict Baptists. If there are good broadcasters among them, they can provide broadcasts well suited to the Home Service.

(*b*) *Montanist minorities*   The distinctive character of this type is the enthusiasm with which their message is delivered and their use of un-orthodox means of gaining converts. We should expect from those groups fervent broadcasts, generating heat rather than light; and the object of putting one on would be to communicate to the listener a special kind of experience. The chief group here is, of course, the Salvation Army, but with them we can number the Pentecostal Churches and the Elim Four Square

Gospel Alliance and all other groups which tend to favour a 'corybantic Christianity'.[3]

The policy was set for 1955–60 on the following basis:

(*a*) Gnostics

Society of Friends	4 broadcasts per annum
Unitarians	2 broadcasts per annum

By the end of 1954 House believed it was not possible to find Unitarian preachers or churches which could provide services 'of the standards we expect' (24.11.54).

All other groups	2 or 3 broadcasts per annum

(*b*) Montanists

Salvation Army	2 or 3 broadcasts per annum

The Salvation Army had enjoyed consistently good relations with the Corporation and exercised no pressure on the RBD.

Pentecostalist Churches
Elim and Four Square ⎫ one broadcast per year
Assemblies of God ⎭ in each region

They had been granted access in 1952; House said: 'We should be on our guard lest pressure from these peripheral groups might lead to an aggregate disproportionate representation' (25.1.52).

(*c*) The Moral Re-armament Movement maintained a strenuous pressure on the Corporation and despite pressure from a number of parliamentary and other influential persons, broadcasts were not granted to Frank Buchman on the basis of the RBD policy which regarded the Christian claims of MRA to be unfounded. MRA representatives were consistently invited to take part in forum discussions but refused on the grounds of their right to evangelize at the microphone.

(*d*) Christian Science maintained a strenuous pressure particularly with the support of Lady Astor. The Corporation resisted with equal vigour. The Christian Science Campaign began to dwindle after the failure of a 1952–3 effort which widely publicized the claim for parity with mainstream churches. Similar to the MRA, the reaction of the Christian Science movement to the Board of Governors' policy, that such bodies outside the mainstream should be non-propagandist, was negative.[4]

NOTES

1. See also *Broadcasting Policy* 8, Minorities, BBC 1943.

2. This classification into types is based on the present practice of those groups; but, e.g., the Society of Friends might well become Montanist in expression of worship, and one or other of the more enthusiastic groups might well change its ways and methods of worship.

3. J. A. Fisher, Discussion document for Staff Meeting, 22.2.54.

4. Board of Governors Minutes, 8.1.53.

Appendix 6

Sunday Listening
LR3732 (extract), August 1945

Sunday, 19th August, 1945

Sunday Listening
On Sundays, for example, daytime listening is naturally much greater than on weekdays. In Week 34 the average daytime audiences were:

	Home Service %	Light Prog. %	Combined %	Ratios H:L
Sunday	9·4	7·3	16·7	56:44
Weekdays	8·0	4·0	12·0	66:34

It will be seen that though the general level of listening is considerably higher on Sundays, the major part of this increase is captured by the Light Programme. The average evening audiences for Sunday and weekdays in Week 34 were:

	%	%	%	H:L
Sunday	9·1	11·0	20·1	45:55
Weekdays	14·8	9·7	24·5	60:40

Sunday evening listening was on a substantially *lower* level than on other evenings, and in this Week 34 followed the same pattern as the previous three weeks. Even so, the whole of the decline is in the Home Service, for the level of listening to the Light Programme is actually higher on Sunday evening than on the other nights of the week.

Audiences for Religious Broadcasts in 1948

Extract by House from his policy document: 'The Aims and achievements of Religious Broadcasting 1922–1948'.

1. During the six months beginning March 1948 a number of special investigations were made into the size and composition of the audiences for religious services and other religious broadcasts of the BBC. These investigations consisted of

(a) detailed analysis of the regular returns of Listener Research on a number of Sundays, and

(b) a variety of special supplementary enquiries.

2. The average *adult* audiences for the more popular religious broadcasts on the occasions which were investigated were estimated as follows:

	Millions
Sunday Half Hour (Community hymn-singing)	7
The People's Service (Light Programme 11.30 am)	4
Think on These Things (Light Programme 10.45 pm)	3·5
Lift Up Your Hearts (Home Service 7.50 am daily)	2
Morning and Evening Sunday Services in the Home Service	1·5
Daily Service (Home Service 10.15 am)	1·2

3. When overlapping of audiences for the different religious broadcasts had been accounted for the figures show that on a typical Sunday 37 per cent of the adult population of Great Britain hears at least one of the broadcasts – i.e. a *total of 13 million individual listeners per Sunday*. Of these 13 million, 7 million hear at least one service, and many of these also hear *Sunday Half Hour* and/or *Think on These Things*. 6 million hear one or both of these hymn programmes but do not listen to a service.

4. Other facts of interest are:

(a) The ratio of *working-class to middle-class* listeners varies from 4:1 for the broadcasts in the Light Programme to 2·5:1 for the Evening Service in the Home Service.

(b) The ratio of *men to women* varies from 1:1·7 for the *People's Service* to 1:1·1 for the Evening Service in the Home Service.

(c) The proportion of listeners in the *higher age groups* is greater than in the lower; but the evidence does not support the suggestion that the average age of listeners to religious broadcasts is much above the average age of listeners to programmes in general, and for some religious broadcasts the figures for the audiences in the 16–19, 20–29 and 30–49 age groups are encouraging.

5. Reliable evidence regarding the relation between church-attendance and listening to religious broadcasts is extraordinarily difficult to obtain, but the best evidence available indicates that regular churchgoers are always in a minority and that for many religious broadcasts they are a very small minority (e.g. for the *People's Service* the ratio is probably as small as 1:10).

6. A number of parochial clergy and ministers were asked to answer questions regarding the effect of religious broadcasting on church attendance.

18 per cent replied that they did know of individuals who had been brought to active church-membership partly at least through listening.

20 per cent knew of individuals who could be described as making listening a 'substitute' for taking part in public worship.

40 per cent thought that listening was not made a 'substitute' though it was often made an 'excuse'.

Signed F. H. House
27 October 1948

Appendix 8

Silver Lining
Listener Research Analysis, 1949

The four June broadcasts of *Silver Lining* analysed for their 'penetration' into different sections of the listening population. Here are the results.

	%
Average 'listening figure'	4·1
Average 'listening figure' among men	1·0
Average 'listening figure' among women	7·1
Upper Middle Class	2·4
Lower Middle Class	3·7
Working Class	4·3
16–19 age group	1·1
20–29 age group	3·1
30–49 age group	4·1
50+ age group	5·6

The series is clearly listened to most by older working class women. (Its placing is, of course, calculated to exclude most men from the audience.)

Signed R. J. Silvey
12 July 1949

Appendix 9

Services and Talks: Denominational Allocations
1937–1945

	ANGLICAN			FREE CHURCH			ROMAN CATHOLIC			CHURCH OF SCOTLAND		
April–March	*Services* %	*Talks* %	*Lift Ups** %	*Services* %	*Talks* %	*Lift Ups** %	*Services* %	*Talks* %	*Lift Ups** %	*Services* %	*Talks* %	*Lift Ups** %
1937–1939 (Services 1938–1939 only)	81.25	72.75	–	11.25	15.5	–	4.0	9.5	–	3.5	2.0	–
1939–1940	63.25	55.25	–	20.5	38.75	–	7.25	8.25	–	9.0	–	–
1940–1941	62.0	42.25	68.5	15.0	28.5	11.5	9.0	7.25	3.0	14.0	22.0	17.0
1941–1942	62.0	72.0	56.75	17.0	17.75	24.25	9.5	7.75	8.0	11.0	2.5	10.75
1942–1943	58.25	45.0	50.0	21.75	41.0	30.75	10.5	11.0	3.75	9.5	3.0	15.5
1943–1944	56.25	58.25	59.25	19.5	32.75	22.25	10.0	3.75	7.25	14.5	5.25	11.25
1944–1945	61.5	48.5	56.0	15.75	44.0	28.0	13.5	3.0	–	9.25	4.5	16.0

* *Lift Up Your Hearts*, early morning religious talk (7.55 am)

Appendix 10

Jewish Broadcasts and Policy on Anti-Semitism

The outset of the war brought the Corporation's commitment to Jewish interests into sharp focus. It had two facets, one distinctly concerned with religion and the other with the much wider phenomenon of anti-Semitism both in Britain and elsewhere. Once the war had begun the Corporation was under pressure to take note of both areas and there were consequent policy changes.

Requests for Jewish religious programmes and services had been consistently made to the Corporation since the beginning of broadcasting. At the second meeting of the Sunday Committee, A. R. Burrows felt the company should make provision and the policy was defined: Jewish matters were for the Company and not for the churches to decide.[1] Burrows, however, believed that being religious talks they belonged to the Committee. But a year later the point was made plain: this was a Christian Committee offering advice on the Christian Sunday and to introduce non-Christian programmes on this particular day would 'open the door to possible abuse'. The Committee was anxious to keep the Unitarians and Christian Scientists out of this area. Sunday belonged to the 'established' churches and for this reason the Committee were happy to have Reith issue an invitation to the Chief Rabbi for a talk at Passover time but emphatically not on a Sunday.[2]

This policy broadly obtained well into the thirties. However, as the BBC variety output increased there were requests for programmes about Jewish culture and especially programmes in Yiddish. Eric Maschwitz expressed the Corporation's caution at broadcasting exclusively Jewish material for fear of causing offence to the Puritan element in the orthodox Jewish community. He thought much Yiddish material was dreary and whilst it might give a big kick to some Jews it all had a depressing effect upon the general audience.[3] Cecil Graves ruled in late 1935 that Yiddish programmes should be 'rare events'.[4] When the news got out, the *Jewish Daily Post* was not a little disappointed and the Corporation was at pains to see that at least orthodox Jewish opinion was not provoked. Maschwitz was in touch with Jewish affairs through Oscar Pulvermacher, a Jewish journalist on the staff of the *Daily Telegraph*. Pressure continued and the Corporation was obliged to look again: two Yiddish programmes per year were eventually allowed.[5] The Board of Deputies of British Jews, however, thought that much of the Yiddish material was of poor quality and did not approve the apparent lack of respect for 'Jewish sacralities'. John Watt, the Director of Variety, thought the material of these more or less regular programmes were in bad taste and he fully endorsed the embarrassment of the Board of Deputies that the comedy was low and not representative. The Secretary of the Board, however, was not angry with the BBC. Indeed, the

Jewish community, he said, was 'deeply indebted to the BBC for its impartiality and fairness'.[6] It was clear to Watt and Gielgud that there was almost a case for a Jewish Advisory Committee, particularly as there seemed to be a great variety of Jewish opinion focused in organizations both religious and secular.

In July 1938, Archbishop Lang circularized the Anglican Dioceses asking for intercessions for persecuted Jewry to be offered in all Church of England congregations and Iremonger dutifully sent a 'suggestion rather than an injunction' around the regions. CRAC had already considered a variety of Jewish requests for Jewish services. The organist of the Central Jewish Synagogue was one among many who wanted not merely talks but actual services on the air. CRAC would only give approval if the Chief Rabbi agreed. The Committee insisted that it could only advise on Sunday questions and in effect counselled the Corporation to make up its own mind. Reith wanted Iremonger to make the contacts necessary.[7] Later in the year Garbett hoped Iremonger would extend talks on the Jewish faith to embrace the vexed plight of European Jewry under Hitler. Iremonger shared a popular belief at that time that the Christians had expressed enough regret for Hitler's policies. Moreover, the Jewish 'record' had not been 'blameless enough to make most Christians to feel a sense of vicarious shame for Hitler's misdoings'.[8] Garbett, however, was concerned about anti-Semitism in Britain and although Iremonger agreed that Hitler's treatment of the Jews was 'abominable' he wondered if everyone had forgotten 'the treatment of Gentiles by Jews in the East End'. In his view, 'we have treated the Jews remarkably well'.[9] Iremonger temporized and nothing was done.

In spring 1939, there was increasing pressure on the Corporation from the Jewish community that services and other programmes should be broadcast not only to Jews in Britain but to those in central Europe. Iremonger was obliged to inform CRAC yet again that policy decisions had been made which disallowed such an approach. Nor would Nicolls allow Lawrence Gilliam of the BBC Features Department to embark upon a project in the North Region on the 'Jewish question' (as it became increasingly called).[10] In the meantime, the Chief Rabbi, J. H. Hertz, had a number of consultations with his own clergy and met with Welch and Iremonger in April. CRAC decided to encourage Hertz to respond to a BBC (rather than CRAC) inviation to conduct a Jewish religious service.[11] It would be the Chanukah celebration of the Feast of the Maccabees in December, 'a most appropriate day', thought Welch, 'to emphasize in this conflict with Hitler'. Hertz fell ill and the service was not broadcast. He would give instead a fifteen-minute talk at Passover time in April 1940.[12] In terms of the broadcasting of specifically religious programmes the pattern was set: the occasional service and two annual talks at, New Year and Passover.

Welch, however, was rather more anxious and much troubled by the British anti-Semitic expression and encouraged W. W. Simpson, an Anglican priest with the Christian Council for Refugees from Germany, to prepare a talk on the Christian debt to Judaism. Welch, much to his annoyance, had to settle for a sermon in the context of a broadcast church service, whereas he had originally requested two straight talks on some such title as 'The Christian Looks at the Jewish Question'. Nicolls supported the idea and was sorry that Welch was refused by the Home Board. Maconachie had carried the day: in his view such talks would have shirked the real issue which was not religious but entirely political, and could not be separated from propaganda. (Maconachie and Iremonger had agreed over Garbett's suggestion in 1938.) In his June sermon, Simpson reminded the audience that Jesus was a Jew and from this point of departure assured the sceptic that the Jews were putting their own house in order. If Christians were to be true to Jesus then love must be shown to his descendents.[13] It was all very mild, but nevertheless Welch had to play a careful part in the context of growing resistance to religious broadcasts becoming the platform for political comment. Maconachie was firmly against such ambiguity.[14]

The Board of Deputies of British Jews continued to pressurize the Corporation: more programmes should provide positive information about Jews and strengthen their efforts to resist the general anti-Semitic feelings, particularly in the North of England; such sentiments rumoured that Jews were unsavoury people and against the war effort. The Ministry of Information Jewish Secretary (H. A. Goodman) requested such programmes, as indeed did Hugh Martin. The Board of Deputies eventually arranged a modest delegation to meet the BBC in April 1942, the result being an informal agreement to have A. G. Brottman and Sydney Saloman as mediators between the Board and the BBC.[15] Elsewhere in the Corporation other attempts were being made to examine the issue. Louis MacNeice wanted a programme in the light of Anthony Eden's statement in the Commons[16] that those responsible for 'these crimes' would not escape judgment. MacNeice wanted to answer Rosenberg's charges against Jews with positive references to Jews in the arts, etc. and include the figure of Christ. He was refused. In October Welch wanted CRAC to take a bolder approach: perhaps a Jew could have a share in the *Lift Up Your Hearts* series. It was, however, consonant with the religious policy that a clear distinction was to be made between 'talks' and 'liturgical spaces' in the schedules: *Lift Up Your Hearts* belonged to the latter. Moreover, the Christian Scientists were pressing for a share of these programmes. CRAC could only say 'No' to the Jews, for fear of encouraging requests from Hindus, Muslims and Unitarians. Since special provision had been made to admit Unitarians into these 'liturgically sacrosanct' spaces it seems surprising that the Committee – notwithstanding its belief that 'the Jews merited special sympathy at this present time' – could not find its way to an innovation in their favour.[17] It was a surprising decision in the light of the increasingly widespread knowledge of Jewish persecution which the Interallied Information Committee in London disseminated that year.[18]

This publication prompted a question in the House as to what was being done by Jews in British radio for Jewry.[19] Bracken was in touch with Sir Allen Powell and with Foot and together they decided that the present time was not 'opportune' for dealing with the Jewish problem in programmes.[20] Barnes, then Director of Talks, believed it was right not to touch the subject 'except by implication in talks on other subjects'. With the agreement of the Chief Rabbi it was decided that there should be no attempt by the Corporation to counter what Fenn called 'latent anti-Semitism in this country today'[21] with progammes of a rational or discursive kind. Such an attempt would be sure to provoke a demand that the other side of the picture should have equal representation. It would do more harm than good.[22] Maconachie assured Violet Bonham Carter that the

BBC was only carrying out the wishes of the Board of Jewish Deputies backed by the Chief Rabbi. The policy thereafter was

> that we should not promote ourselves or accept any propaganda in the way of talks, discussion, features with the object of trying to correct the undoubted anti-Semitic feeling which is held very largely throughout the country; but that we should confine ourselves to reporting in the news bulletins the facts, as they are reported from time to time, of Jewish persecutions, as well as any notable achievements by Jews particularly in connection with the war effort.[23]

This remained Corporation policy throughout the war in spite of various overtures by the Board of Deputies and the oldest Jewish religious society, the Mizrachi Federation. It was, as Nicolls admitted to an irritated Maconachie, an inconsistency but one which seemed to work: CRAC was not able to make official recommendations, but quite informally supported what were in effect 'mainstream' Jewish broadcasts, especially by the Chief Rabbi or those approved by him. There would be occasional Jewish services and several talks but the Governors insisted that the arrangements should be informal and that there should be no allotment of programmes as Welch had asked.[24] After the war the situation eased somewhat but the policy remained firmly grounded in news and reporting; any specific pro-Semitic policy was to be rigorously avoided.

The situation had been complicated by Welch's attempt to use the radio for teaching the New Testament. It raised grave theological and political issues in this context. The Jewish press consistently made gentle appeals to the Corporation for more services not only to serve the Jewish community but to assist their public relations, consonant with the Corporation's policy to present the best profile.[25] As we have seen, Welch and Williams (in the Schools output) were convinced that any educative initiative over the figure of Jesus of Nazareth would best deploy the dramatic medium to convey not only a realistic recital of the New Testament gospels but considerable historical background to clarify the character of Jesus in his time. In the Jewish context, *The Man Born to be King* was supremely problematic, not the least because substantial rabbinic opinion objected to the inevitable inference to be drawn that the Jews were the villains of the story. The churches' concern for the plight of wartime Jewry was most notably expressed by William Temple, whose efforts resulted in the formation of the Council of Christians and Jews, whose first General Secretary was W. W. Simpson. Simpson was much concerned with the inbuilt anti-Semitic potential in both the Sayers cycle and a good deal of the Schools dramatic interludes for which Williams was then finally responsible. Like Sayers, the schools dramatists used by the Corporation put considerable weight upon the 'historical' veracity of the Gospel of John, which expressed so much feeling against the Jews. Simpson's office had regularly received complaints from Jews as well as Christians around the country. The feeling among many respected Jews was that both the Sayers cycle and the attempts at the life of Christ in the schools interludes contributed to the fostering of prejudice and lacked sufficient emphasis upon the part the Romans played in the story. Most Christian response was predictable and even the scholarly Fenn had to agree that anti-

Semitism was 'inherent in any attempt to understand the historical background – after all the Jews did reject the Messiah!'[26] There were times when Welch was obliged to provide scripts in order to prove how easily wrong impressions could be gained. Welch began to think that there should be a Jewish adviser to his Department as well as a Roman Catholic.

He was introduced to a prominent Jewish theologian, Ephraim Levine, through Israel Sieff and from 1946 had the benefit of informal liaison with one he understood to be among the most learned and tolerant of all ministers in Jewry.[27] Welch managed to increase the number of Jewish broadcasts but there was still a strong belief that at any rate in terms of numbers, there were insufficient Jews to justify more than four talks each year. Levine was helpful in practical programme questions and responsible for the good public relations between the controller of the Home Service and the Jewish community. The other positive influence was Simpson, and the Council of Christians and Jews; they were constantly vigilant to ensure that notwithstanding the Christian monopoly in the output and the preoccupation with Jesus in history, Jewish programmes should have the widest possible appeal. It was a characteristic emphasis of the Department that the broadest possible and simplest amalgam of Christian belief could and should be broadcast to a fundamentally Christian culture. The Department similarly emphasized that Jewish Festival programmes should be educational and simple.

By the early fifties the post-war pattern was broadly maintained and the new Chief Rabbi, Israel Broadie, was co-operative and unassuming. The Board of Deputies monitored the BBC's general output and particularly the parodies and joking which so badly misrepresented Jewish life. Their campaign was unceasing. The Chief Rabbi, however, was fully in accord with the evolving policy of educative talks with two or three programmes in which he himself addressed his own community. As the regional policy developed it was agreed that in the North, where there were considerably more liberal Jews, more deference to their representation was possible. The Jewish issue did not appear on the CRAC agenda for more than five years. Jewish broadcasts had slipped into a singularly special category of minorities to which the Corporation remained committed, and would do so until the situation radically changed with the appointment of non-Christians to CRAC in the late 1970s.

NOTES

1. Sunday Committee Minutes, 5.6.23.
2. Ibid., 1.8.24.
3. Eric Maschwitz to Val Gielgud, 11.2.35.
4. Cecil Graves to Maschwitz, 17.10.35.
5. Programme Board Minutes, March 1936, no. 121.
6. A. G. Brottman to Sir Stephen Tallents, 22.7.37.
7. CRAC Minutes, 1.10.36 (8.ii).
8. Iremonger to Garbett, 11.8.38.

9. Ibid.
10. Charles Siepmann to Laurence Gilliam, 16.3.39.
11. CRAC Minutes, 2.3.39.
12. Control Board, 9.5.39.
13. *The Listener*, 26.6.41, vol. 25, pp. 913f.
14. See above, ch. 17.A.
15. Report of delegation from Jewish Board of Deputies, submitted to Maconachie, 1.5.42.
16. Hansard, 17.12.42, vol. 285, col. 2083.
17. CRAC Minute, 1.10.42.
18. Interallied Information Committee, Report no. 6, *Persecution of the Jews*, HMSO, December 1942.
19. Hansard, 7.4.43, vol. 388, col. 610.
20. Maconachie to Barnes, 27.4.43.
21. Eric Fenn to W. W. Simpson, 1.10.43.
22. Maconachie to Refugee Aliens' Protection Committee, 9.10.43.
23. Board of Governors Minutes, 18.11.43.
24. Ibid., 2.11.44.
25. See especially *Jewish Chronicle*, 26.5.44.
26. Fenn to Simpson, 21.7.44.
27. Welch to Rendall (Controller of Talks), 26.3.46.

SOUND BROADCASTING 1951–1955

Combined Output – London Sound Broadcasting / Analysis of 1954-55 by Services

	1951-52		1952-53		1953-54		1954-55		London Home Service		Light Programme		Third Programme		Total	
	Hours	%	Hours	%	Hours	%	Hours	%	Hours	%	Hours	%	Hours	%	Hours	%
Serious Music	2,767	20	2,694	20	2,592	19	2,637	19	1,117	18·3	396	7·0	1,124	52·6	2,637	19
Light Music	2,732	20	2,754	20	2,767	20	2,781	20	987	16·1	1,782	31·4	12	0·6	2,781	20
Features and Drama	1,690	12	1,755	13	1,748	13	1,786	13	611	10·0	637	11·2	538	25·2	1,786	13
Variety	1,180	9	1,097	8	1,102	8	1,006	7	500	8·2	506	8·9	—	—	1,006	7
Dance Music	978	7	1,104	7	1,201	9	1,273	9	339	5·5	934	16·5	—	—	1,273	9
Talks and Discussions	1,344	10	1,367	10	1,357	10	1,475	11	618	10·1	464	8·2	393	18·4	1,475	11
News	1,029	8	1,023	8	1,019	7	1,075	7	618	10·1	457	8·0	—	—	1,075	8
Schools	461	3	418	3	418	3	405	3	405	6·6	—	—	—	—	405	3
Children's Hour	441	3	469	3	406	3	416	3	337	5·5	79	1·4	—	—	416	3
Religion	410	3	386	3	412	3	406	3	274	4·5	114	2·0	18	0·8	406	3
Outside Broadcasts	404	3	372	3	427	3	373	3	128	2·1	244	4·3	1	0·1	373	2
Miscellaneous	241	2	242	2	256	2	296	2	183	3·0	64	1·1	49	2·3	296	2
	13,677	100	13,681	100	13,705	100	13,929	100	6,117	100	5,677	100	2,135	100	13,929	100

LONDON TELEVISION SERVICE 1951–1955

	1951-52		1952-53		1953-54		1954-55	
	Hours	%	Hours	%	Hours	%	Hours	%
Opera, Music Productions, and Ballet	58	3·4	58	3·2	66	3·4	61	2·8
Drama	256	15·0	251	13·7	251	12·8	244	11·2
Light Entertainment, including Musical Comedy	160	9·4	194	10·6	249	12·7	248	11·4
Talks, Demonstrations, and Documentary Programmes	232	13·6	254	13·9	255	13·0	335	15·4
Children's Programmes	326	19·1	366	20·0	347	17·7	373	17·1
Religion	9	0·5	18	1·0	31	1·6	26	1·2
Newsreel and Documentary Films	194	11·4	238	13·0	249	12·7	220	10·1
Outside Broadcasts of Sporting Events	240	14·1	247	13·5	298	15·2	340	15·6
Outside Broadcasts other than Sport, including National Occasions	123	7·2	110	6·0	116	5·9	181	8·3
Entertainment Films	80	4·7	81	4·4	60	3·0	94	4·3
Other Broadcasts	27	1·6	13	0·7	39	2·0	57	2·6
	1,705	100	1,830	100	1,961	100	2,179	100
News (on Sound only)	104		100		97		98	
	1,809		1,930		2,058		2,277	

BBC Handbook, pp. 214f.

BIBLIOGRAPHY AND SOURCES

1. Broadcasters and Broadcasting

Allighan, G., *Sir John Reith*, Stanley Paul and Co., 1938

Boyle, Andrew, *Only the Wind Will Listen: Reith of the BBC*, Hutchinson 1972

Bridson, D. G., *Prospero and Ariel: the Rise and Fall of Radio*, Gollancz 1971

Briggs, Asa, *The History of Broadcasting in the United Kingdom*: I, *The Birth of Broadcasting*, OUP 1961; II, *The Golden Age of Wireless*, 1965; III, *The War of Words*, 1970; IV, *Sound and Vision*, 1979

Broadcasting House, BBC 1932

Burrows, A. R., *The Story of Broadcasting*, Cassell 1924

Clow, W. M., *Dr George Reith: A Scottish Ministry*, Hodder and Stoughton 1928

Cooper, B. G., Religious Broadcasting 1922–39, unpublished B. Litt. thesis, 1961

Dakers, Andrew, *The Big Ben Minute*, Dakers 1943

Dinwiddie, Melville, *Religion by Radio: its Place in British Broadcasting*, Allen and Unwin 1968

Eckersley, P. P., *The Power Behind the Microphone*, Cape 1941

Eckersley, Roger, *BBC and All That*, Sampson Low 1946

Falconer, Ronald, *Success and Failure of a Radio Mission*, SCM Press 1951

Fraser, Ian, *Whereas I Was Blind*, Hodder and Stoughton 1942

Gielgud, Val, *One Year of Grace*, Longmans 1950

— *British Radio Drama 1922–1956*, Harrap 1957

— *Years in a Mirror*, Bodley Head 1965

Gorham, Maurice, *Sound and Fury: Twenty-one Years in the BBC*, Percival Marshall 1948

— *Broadcasting and Television since 1900*, Dakers 1952

Grisewood, Harman, *Broadcasting and Society: Comments from a Christian Standpoint*, SCM Press 1949

— *One Thing at a Time: an Autobiography*, Hutchinson 1968

Hibberd, Stuart, *This is London*, Macdonald and Evans 1950

Kirkpatrick, Ivone, *The Inner Circle*, Macmillan 1959

Knox, Ronald, *Broadcast Minds*, Sheed and Ward 1932

Lambert, Richard S., *Ariel and All His Quality*, Gollancz 1940

Lewis, C. A., *Broadcasting from Within*, Newnes 1924

Lysacht, R., *Brendan Bracken*, Penguin/Allen Lane 1979

Madge, Charles, and others, *To Start You Talking*, Pilot Press 1945

Maine, Basil, *The BBC and its Audience*, Nelson 1939

Mansell, G., *Let Truth Be Told: Fifty Years of BBC External Broadcasting*, Weidenfeld and Nicolson 1982

Matheson, Hilda, *Broadcasting* (Home University Library), Thornton Butterworth 1933

McKay, Roy, *Take Care of the Sense: Reflections on Religious Broadcasting*, SCM Press 1964

Moseley, S. A., *Broadcasting in My Time*, Rich and Cowan 1935

New Ventures in Broadcasting, Report of a Committee to the BBC [under Sir Henry Hadow], BBC 1928

Palmer, Richard, *School Broadcasting in Britain*, BBC 1947

Reith, J. C. W., *Broadcast over Britain*, Hodder and Stoughton 1924

— *Personality and Career*, Newnes 1925

— *Into the Wind*, Hodder and Stoughton, 1949

— *Wearing Spurs*, Hutchinson 1966

Religion on the Air: three talks given to the St Paul's Lecture Society by R. J. E. Silvey, Roy McKay and George Reindorp, BBC 1955

Sendall, Bernard, *History of Independent Television in Britain*: I, *Origin and Foundation, 1946–62*, Macmillan 1982; II, *Expansion and Change, 1958–68*, 1983

Silvey, Robert, *Who's Listening?*, Allen and Unwin 1974

Simon of Wythenshawe, Lord, *The BBC from Within*, Gollancz 1953

Smith, Anthony, *British Broadcasting*, David and Charles 1974 (documents from 1863–1972)

Smithers, S. W., *Broadcasting from Within: Behind the Scenes at the BBC*, Pitman 1938

Stuart, Charles, *The Reith Diaries*, Collins 1975 (see note on p. 569)

Thomas, Howard, *Britain's Brains Trust*, Chapman and Hall 1944

Thompson, D. Cleghorn, *Radio is Changing Us*, Watts 1937

Wilson, H. H., *Pressure Group: the Campaign for Commercial Television*, Secker and Warburg 1961

Young, Filson, *Shall I Listen*, Constable 1933

2. General

Almedingen, M. E., *Dom Bernard Clements*, Bodley Head 1945

Bell, G. K. A., *Randall Davidson, Archbishop of Canterbury*, OUP, 3rd ed., 1952

Brabazon, James, *Dorothy L. Sayers*, Gollancz 1981

Busch, Eberhard, *Karl Barth*, Eng. trs. SCM Press 1976

Caraman, Philip, *C. C. Martindale*, Longmans 1967

Coles, H. C., *Walford Davies*, OUP 1942

Currie, R., Gilbert, A., and Horsley, L., *Churches and Churchgoers*, OUP 1977

Deane, A. C., *Time Remembered*, Faber and Faber 1945

Dillistone, F. W., *Charles Raven, Naturalist, Historian, Theologian*, Hodder and Stoughton 1975

— *C. H. Dodd*, Hodder and Stoughton 1977

Eliot, T. S., *The Idea of a Christian Society*, Faber and Faber 1939

Elliott, W. H., *Undiscovered Ends*, Peter Davies 1951

Falconer, Ronald, *The Kilt Beneath My Cassock*, Handsel Press 1978

Fox, Adam, *Dean Inge*, John Murray 1960

Heenan, John, *Cardinal Hinsley*, Burns Oates 1944

— *Not the Whole Truth*, Hodder and Stoughton 1971

— *Crown of Thorns*, Hodder and Stoughton 1974

Hitchman, Janet, *Such a Strange Lady: an Introduction to Dorothy L. Sayers, 1893–1957*, New English Library 1975

Iremonger, F. E., *William Temple, Archbishop of Canterbury: His Life and Letters*, OUP 1948

— (ed.), *Men and Movements in the Church*, Longmans 1928

Jackson, Eleanor M., *Red Tape and the Gospel*: a study of the significance of the ecumenical missionary struggle of William Paton (1886–1943), Phlogiston Press 1980

Jasper, R. C., *George Bell, Bishop of Chichester*, OUP 1967

Lea, F. A., *The Life of John Middleton Murry*, Methuen 1959

Lloyd, Roger, *The Church of England 1900–1965*, SCM Press 1966

Lockhart, J. G., *Cosmo Gordon Lang*, Hodder and Stoughton 1949

Matthews, W. R., *Memories and Meanings*, Hodder and Stoughton 1969

Martin, David, *Pacifism; an Historical and Sociological Study*, Routledge and Kegan Paul 1965

McCulloch, Joseph, *My Affair with the Church*, Hodder and Stoughton 1976

Nicolson, Harold, *Diaries and Letters 1939–45*, Atheneum Press 1967

Northcott, R. J., *Dick Sheppard and St Martin's*, Longmans 1937

Purcell, William, *Fisher of Lambeth*, Hodder and Stoughton 1969

Roberts, R. Ellis, *H. R. L. Sheppard: Life and Letters*, John Murray 1942

Rouse, Ruth, and Neill, Stephen, *A History of the Ecumenical Movement, 1517–1948*, SPCK 1956

Rowntree, B. S., and Lavers, G. R., *English Life and Leisure*, Longmans 1951

Scott, Carolyn, *Dick Sheppard*, Hodder and Stoughton 1977

Sheppard, H. R. L., *The Impatience of a Parson*, Hodder and Stoughton 1927

Smyth, Charles, *Cyril Forster Garbett, Archbishop of York*, Hodder and Stoughton 1964

Spinks, Stephen, *Religion in Britain since 1900*, Dakers 1952

Stockwood, Mervyn, *Chanctonbury Ring*, Hodder and Stoughton 1983

Sykes, Christopher, *Nancy Astor*, Collins 1972

Temple, William, *Christianity and Social Order*, Penguin Books 1942

Waugh, Evelyn, *Ronald Knox*, Chapman and Hall 1959

Weatherhead, Kingsley, *Leslie Weatherhead*, Hodder and Stoughton 1975

Wilkinson, Alan, *The Church of England and the First World War*, SPCK 1978

Wright, Ronald Selby, *Another Home*, Blackwood 1980

3. Journals and Serials

Radio Times
The Listener
BBC Quarterly
Aerial (BBC Staff Magazine)
BBC Handbooks, Year Books and *Annuals*
Annual Reports and Accounts of the BBC
St Martin's Review

4. Articles and Pamphlets

Barnes, George, *Television Broadcasting* (address to the BCC), BBC 1952

Chorley, G. F., 'The Work of Basil Yeaxlee', *British Journal of Religious Education* 6.2, Spring 1984

Demant, V. A., 'Unintentional Influences of Wireless', *BBC Quarterly*, October 1948

Empire Broadcasting Service, The, BBC 1933

Falconer, Ronald, 'Barclay the Broadcaster' in *Biblical Studies: Essays in Honour of William Barclay*, ed. J. R. McKay and J. F. Miller, Collins 1976, pp. 15ff.

Grayston, K. G., 'Religious Broadcasting in Britain', *World Dominion*, January 1951

Haley, Sir William, *Moral Values in Broadcasting* (an address to the British Council of Churches), BBC 1948

— *The Responsibilities of Broadcasting*, the Lewis Fry Memorial Lecture at the University of Bristol, BBC 1948

— *The Central Problem of Broadcasting*, BBC 1950

Homan, Roger, 'Sunday Observance and Social Class', *Sociological Yearbook of Religion*, 3, SCM Press 1970, pp. 78–92.

House, Francis, *The Church on the Air*, BBC 1949

— 'Some Aspects of Christian Broadcasting', *BBC Quarterly*, Summer 1950

Jennings, Hilda, and Gill, Winifred, *Broadcasting in Everyday Life*, BBC 1939

Observations by the Governors on [the] Ullswater [Report], BBC 1936

Welch, J. W., *Religious Broadcasting*, BBC 1942

— 'Religion and the Radio', *BBC Quarterly*, October, 1946

5. Prayer Books for Broadcast Services

Hugh Johnston, *This Day*, St Martin's Press 1928

— *When Two or Three*, St Martin's Press 1932

Services for Broadcasting [compiled by F. W. Dwelly], BBC 1930

New Every Morning: The prayer book of the daily broadcast service [compiled by F. W. Dwelly], BBC 1936

Each Returning Day: Prayers for use in time of war, BBC 1940

The Broadcast Psalter, BBC/SPCK 1948

The BBC Hymn Book, OUP 1951

6. Government and Other Reports and Surveys

Broadcasting Committee Report (Sykes), Cmd. 1951, 1923
      (Crawford), Cmd. 2599, 1925
      (Ullswater), Cmd. 5091, 1935

Broadcasting Policy, Cmd. 6852, 1946

Broadcasting Committee Report (Beveridge), Cmd. 8116, 1949

Appendix H: Memoranda Submitted to the Beveridge Committee, Cmd. 8117, 1949

Broadcasting. Memorandum of the Report of the Broadcasting Committee, Cmd. 8550, 1952

Memorandum on Television Policy, Cmd. 9005, 1953

Proceedings of Convocation of Canterbury, Report No. 578 (the Ely Report), SPCK 1931

The Conversion of England: Report of a Commission on Evangelism appointed by the Archbishops of Canterbury and York, SPCK 1945

Puzzled People, a survey by Mass Observation for the Ethical Union, Gollancz 1947

Relations with the BBC, Church Assembly Proceedings Vol. XXVII (CA. 872), 1948

British Council of Churches, *Christianity and Broadcasting*, SCM Press 1950

Religious Broadcasting and the Public, BBC 1955

7. Published Broadcast Religious Talks, Plays and Sermons, in Chronological Order
Several of the following were originally printed (either in whole or in part) in *The Listener*.

1930 McCormick, Pat, *Be of Good Cheer*, Longmans
       Temple, William, and others, *Points of View* and *More Points of View*, Allen and Unwin
1931 Barnes, E. W., and others, *Science and Religion*, Gerald Howe
1932 Jacks, L. P., and others, *St Martin's-in-the-Fields Caling*, Athenaeum Press
       Martindale, C. C., *What are Saints?*, Sheed and Ward
1933 Elliott, W. H., *Thursday Evening Talks*, Mowbray
       Modern Sermons (also entitled *Sermons of the Year 1932*), ed. W. F. Stead, Faber and Faber
       Temple, William, and others, *God and the World Through Christian Eyes*, Series I, SCM Press
1934 Elliott, W. H., *More Thursday Evening Talks*, Mowbray
       God and the World Through Christian Eyes, Series II, SCM Press
       MacLeod, George, *Govan Calling*, Methuen
       Whale, J. S., *Man and his Need of God*, Lutterworth
1935 Matthews, W. R., and others, *The Way to God*, Series I and II, SCM Press
       Soper, Donald, *Will Christianity Work?*, Lutterworth
1936 D'Arcy, Martin, *Christian Morals*, Longmans Green
       Deane, A. C., *Sixth Form Religion*, Hodder and Stoughton
       Elliott, W. H., *Midweek Talks*, Mowbray
       – *New Thursday Evening Talks*, Mowbray
       Matthews, W. R., *The Hope of Immortality*, SCM Press
       McCormick, Pat, *St Martin's on the Air*, Athenaeum Press
       Whale, J. S., *The Christian Answer to the Problem of Evil*, SCM Press
1937 Sayers, Dorothy L., *Four Sacred Plays*, Gollancz
1938 Elliott, W. H., *Thursday at Ten*, Mowbray
       Whale, J. S., *This Christian Faith*, SCM Press
1939 Matthews W. R., *What is Man?*, James Clarke
       Sayers, Dorothy L., *He That Should Come*, Gollancz
       Wright, Ronald Selby, *Asking Why*, OUP
1940 *A Thought for the Day (Lift Up Your Hearts)*, Frederick Muller
       Clements, Dom Bernard, *The Weapons of a Christian*, SCM Press
       Murry, John Middleton, *Europe in Travail*, Sheldon Press
       Temple, William, *The Hope of a New World*, SCM Press

1941 Bell, G. K. A., *The Church and Humanity*, Longmans Green
Carey, Walter, *As Man to Man*, Mowbray
Cockin, F. A., and others, *Three Men and a Parson*, Longmans Green
Heenan, John C., *Untruisms*, Burns Oates
Hinsley, A., *The Bond of Peace*, Burns Oates
Knox, Ronald, and others, *The World We are Fighting for*, SCM Press
Oldham, J. H., and others, *The Church Looks Ahead*, Faber and Faber
Sister Penelope, CSMV, *If Any Man Serve Me*, Pax House
Temple, William, *Palm Sunday to Easter*, SCM Press
Woods, E. S., *A Life Worth Living*, SCM Press

1942 Fenn, Eric, ed., *How Christians Worship*, SCM Press
Lewis, C. S., *Broadcast Talks*, Geoffrey Bles
Sayers, Dorothy L., *The Man Born to be King*, Gollancz
Wright, Ronald Selby, *Let's Ask the Padre*, Oliver and Boyd
– *The Average Man*, Oliver and Boyd
– 'Jimmie', in *Our Club*, Oliver and Boyd

1943 Clements, Dom Bernard, *Speaking in Parables*, SCM Press
Lewis, C. S., *Christian Behaviour*, Geoffrey Bles
Temple, William, *The Church Looks Forward*, Macmillan
Wright, Ronald Selby, *The Greater Victory*, Longmans Green

1944 Lewis, C. S., *Beyond Personality*, Geoffrey Bles
Temple, William, and others, *The Crisis of the Western World*, Allen and Unwin
Welch, J. W. and others, *Man's Dilemma and God's Answer*, SCM Press
Wright, Ronald Selby, *The Padre Presents*, McLagan and Cumming

1945 Cockin, F. A., and others, *People Matter*, SCM Press
Williamson, Hugh Ross, *Paul a Bondslave*, SCM Press
Wright, Ronald Selby, *Small Talks*, Longmans Green

1946 Bell, G. K. A., and others, *My Brother's Keeper*, SCM Press
Davies, D. R., *The World We have Forgotten*, Paternoster Press

1947 Grantham, Wilfrid, *Men of God* (six plays), Gollancz
Scott, W. M., *The Creed of a Christian*, Epworth Press
Williamson, Hugh Ross, *The Story without an End*, Mowbray
Wright, Ronald Selby, *Whatever the Years*, Epworth Press

1948 *The Existence of God* (the debate between F. C. Copleston, SJ, and Bertrand Russell), Allen and Unwin
Dearmer, Geoffrey, ed., *Told on the Air* (Children's Hour), Latimer House
Vann, Gerald, *The Two Trees*, Collins
Williams, John G., *Children's Hour Prayers*, SCM Press

1949 Hodges, H. A., and others, *Man and his Nature* (Schools), Macmillan
Williams, Austen, *Touching the Fringe*, St Martin's Press
Williams, John G., *Listen on Wednesday*, SCM Press

1950 Wright, Ronald Selby, *What Worries Me*, Epworth Press

1951 Williams, John G., *Switch on for the News* (Children's Hour), SCM Press
Guntrip, H. J. S., *You and Your Nerves (Silver Lining)*, Allen and Unwin

1952 *The Faith of a District Nurse*, Nursing Mirror
Lord Horder and others, *Men Without God*, Vox Mundi

1954 Phillips, J. B., *Plain Christianity*, Epworth Press
      Tatlock, Richard, *The Silver Lining*, Bodley Head
1955 Harington, Joy, *Jesus of Nazareth*, Brockhampton Press
      Knight, Margaret, *Morals without Religion*, Dennis Dobson
      Tatlock, Richard, *The New Silver Lining*, Bodley Head
1956 Walton, Robert, Manson, T. W., and Robinson, J. A. T., *Jesus Christ: History, Interpretation and Faith*, SPCK

8. Archives

Archbishop of Westminster
BBC Archive Press Cuttings Library
British Council of Churches, Selly Oak, Birmingham
Lambeth Palace Library
Public Record Office, Kew
York Minster Library
Church House, London

Reith Diaries

The diaries of John Reith have been in part published by Charles Stuart (Collins 1975). They have been extensively used by Professor Briggs throughout his four volumes. The complete diaries and his private scrapbooks have, however, now been given to the BBC Archive including hitherto unexamined and unpublished sections which have been used in this study.

Garbett Diaries

These are in the possession of the Rt. Rev. Gerald Ellison, former Bishop of London, who has kindly produced selected transcripts from Cyril Garbett's wartime entries.

NOTES

1. Beginnings

1. *Daily Telegraph*, 31.7.22; see also *The Times* of the same date.
2. Peter Eckersley, *The Power behind the Microphone*, 1941, Ch. 3.
3. Asa Briggs, *The History of Broadcasting in the United Kingdom*: I, *The Birth of Broadcasting*, 1961 (cited henceforth as Briggs, I), pp. 123ff.
4. Reith, Diary, March 1920.
5. Ibid. See also Andrew Boyle, *Only the Wind Will Listen*, 1972, chs. 1-5.
6. Ibid., March 1922.
7. *The Army and Religion: an enquiry and its bearing upon the religious life of the nation*, with a preface by the Bishop of Winchester (E. S. Talbot), Macmillan 1919.
8. Ibid., pp. 425ff.
9. Reith, Diary, June 1922.
10. J. C. W. Reith, *Personality and Career*, 1925, p. 28.
11. The Sunday evening addresses were first given during the interval of the Sunday Symphony concert.
12. *The Reith Diaries*, ed. C. Stewart, 1975, p. 131; Reith, *Into the Wind*, 1949, p. 100. Reith believed that the BBC monopoly gave protection to Christianity and to Sunday observance: 'The Christian religion, not just as a sectional activity among many others but as a fundamental.' See also R. C. D. Jasper, *George Bell, Bishop of Chichester*, 1967, p. 40.
13. G. K. A. Bell, *Randall Davidson*, 3rd ed., 1952, p. 1211.
14. Sunday Committee Minutes, 18.5.23.
15. Gainford to Bishop E. S. Woods, 2.9.40: 'It was left to my discretion to avoid controversy.'
16. See Alan Wilkinson, *The Church of England and the First World War*, 1978, ch. 6.
17. Sunday Committee Minutes, 27.7.23; Reith, *Into the Wind*, p. 94.
18. *The Star*, 31.7.22.
19. *St Martin's Review*, December 1937, p. 533.
20. Roger Homan, 'Sunday Observance and Social Class', *Sociological Yearbook of Religion* 3, 1970, ch. 6; R. Currie, A. Gilbert and L. Horsley, *Churches and Churchgoers*, 1977.
21. See R. Ellis Roberts, *H. R. L. Sheppard: Life and Letters*, 1942; Carolyn Scott, *Dick Sheppard*, 1977.
22. *Men and Movements in the Church*, ed. F. A. Iremonger, 1928, p. 59.
23. Reith, Diary, March 1951; see also his *Wearing Spurs*, 1966.
24. Ellis Roberts, op. cit., pp. 111ff.; Sunday Committee Minutes, 10.10.23.
25. Sheppard, *St Martin's Calling*, Atheneum Press, 1932, p. 14.
26. Scott, op. cit., p. 130; Ellis Roberts, op. cit., p. 113.
27. For an example of the Postmaster-General's involvement see Reith, *Into the Wind*, p. 160.
28. Sunday Committee Minutes, 10.10.23 and 1.8.24.
29. Ibid., 1.8.24, p. 10.

30. Briggs, I, p. 170; cf. Reith's oral evidence to the Sykes Committee, 8.5.23.
31. Sunday Committee Minutes, 4.6.25.
32. Ibid., 22.2.27.
33. Reith, *Broadcast over Britain*, 1924, p. 193.
34. *Church of England Newspaper*, 16.1.25.
35. Reith, op. cit., p. 200.
36. Bell to Reith, 29.9.25.
37. Reith, op. cit., p. 200. He confessed to Bell (7.10.26), 'How difficult it is to attend the ordinary church service with any satisfaction and benefit; and the fault is so often with the clergyman. In our broadcasting work we try so hard not to prejudice church attendance.'
38. *BBC Handbook*, 1929, p. 208.
39. For the genesis of the Daily Service see p. 46 below and Briggs, II: *The Golden Age of Wireless*, 1965, 229–32.
40. Bishops' Meeting, Minutes, 27.10.27.
41. *BBC Handbook*, 1928, p. 35.
42. Roger Eckersley, *BBC and All That*, 1946, p. 100.
43. Reith, Diary, 15.4.24.
44. Reith, *Broadcast over Britain*, p. 149. See also Maurice Gorham, *Broadcasting and Television since 1900*, 1952, ch. 2.
45. Reith to Nicolls, 2.9.26.
46. Hadow Report on Adult Education, 1928, p. 89.
47. Sunday Committee Minutes, 1.8.24.
48. The Teaching Church Group comprised a number of head teachers, clergy and college principals.
49. Published in 1930 as *Points of View* by G. Lowes Dickinson and others, *More Points of View* by William Temple and others.
50. *The Listener*, 16.1.29, vol. 1, p. 13.
51. *The Listener*, 8 January and 26 March 1930, vol. 3, pp. 75 and 263.
52. F. T. Woods, *What is God Like?*, Hodder and Stoughton 1930.

2. Anglican Approval: the Ely Committee of 1931

1. See also W. M. Clow, *Dr George Reith*, 1928, pp. 196ff.
2. See below p. 95. F. A. Iremonger, then Editor of the church paper *The Guardian*, praised it warmly (5.9.30), as did the Methodists. The *Evening Standard* thought the BBC was trespassing: 'We do not want revivalism by microphone' (23.9.30).
3. Reith, Diary, 16.9.29.
4. Verbatim report of Reith's address, approved by him, in the *Birmingham Post*, 6.7.29.
5. Reith, 'Religion, the Church and, Incidentally, Broadcasting', *St Martin's Review*, January 1930.
6. Reith, Diary, June 1926.
7. Ibid., 29.10.29.
8. *Proceedings of Convocation of Canterbury* (Lower House), 13.2.30, SPCK 1931, p. 110.
9. H. Hensley Henson, *The Times*, 14.2.30; cf. his words in the *Daily Express*, 3.10.28: 'The broadcasting of sermons may assist Christian people to forget the gravity of abandoning their religious habits.'

10. Reith, Diary, 18.6.29.

11. Policy Document submitted to the Ely Committee, 1930.

12. E.g. the Farewell Service for Archbishop Davidson, cf. the *Eastern Daily Press*, 5.11.28.

13. *Proceedings of the Lambeth Conference*, SPCK 1930, p. 80.

14. Garbett Papers Coll., 1973/1.

15. *Proceedings of Convocation*, 21.1.31, SPCK 1931, Lower House pp. 16–31; Upper House pp. 52–62.

16. *The Times* thought that the greatest gain from religious broadcasting was to the sick and housebound (24.1.31.)

17. Report of the Ely Committee to Convocation (No. 578), p. 6.

18. See below, chs. 10.B, 24.B.

19. Ely Committee report, loc. cit.

20. *Science and Religion*, by E. W. Barnes and others, delivered 1930, published 1931; reviewed in the *Daily Telegraph*, 21.1.31.

21. See below, ch. 23.C.

3. Religious Controversy

1. See Briggs, I, pp. 170ff.; II, *The Golden Age of Wireless, 1965*, pp. 128–31.

2. Reith to the Postmaster-General, 27.5.26.

3. Ibid., 6.7.26.

4. Crawford Committee, Paper No. 67, 21.1.26.

5. *The Times*, 2.2.27.

6. The Postmaster-General to Reith, 27.3.27.

7. Reith, Diary, 19.7.27.

8. CRAC Minutes, 13.3.28, 4(iii).

9. See below ch. 14, pp. 130ff.

10. See above, pp. 24f.

11. Reith, Diary, May 1930.

12. Basil Yeaxlee to Reith, 6.6.30.

13. Reith to Temple, 23.6.30. See also Briggs, II, p. 227.

14. Reith, ibid.

15. Sunday Committee Minutes, 1.8.24.

16. Board of Governors Minutes, 9.3.27, 35(d).

4. The Roman Catholics

1. *BBC Handbook*, 1928, p. 131.

2. See Currie, Gilbert and Horsley, *Churches and Churchgoers*, ch. IV, and the table on p. 31. After 1933 totals for the 'major Protestant' churches began to decline. 'Two world wars had a most adverse effect on church growth; . . . post-war revivals of church membership have been precursors of new setbacks for organized religion.'

3. Reith, Evidence to the Crawford Committee, p. 7 (in answer to questions on policy).

4. Sheppard in *BBC Handbook*, 1929, p. 20.

5. See Currie, Gilbert and Horsley, op. cit., p. 31.

6. See Ronald Knox, *Broadcast Minds*, 1932, and *A Forgotten Interlude* (broadcast in 1926), Sheed and Ward 1928; also Evelyn Waugh, *Ronald Knox*, 1959.

7. Reith to all Station Directors, 8.11.25.

8. The British Broadcasting Company became the British Broadcasting Corporation on 1 January 1927.

9. Fr. Parker, memorandum to Cardinal Hinsley, May 1936.

10. H. Ward to Cardinal Bourne, March 1927.

11. *The Universe*, 15.2.29.

12. Bourne papers, Westminster Cathedral Archives.

13. See *The Universe*, 3.5.27.

14. Bourne to Ward, 23.4.1927.

15. J. C. Stobart to Bourne, 16.4.1928.

16. See Reith, *Broadcast over Britain*, p. 194.

17. Roman Catholic Archives: 'BBC Papers'.

18. See above, p. 26, and CRAC Minutes, 13.2.28.

19. CRAC Minutes, 3.4.28 (3).

20. Reith, *Broadcast over Britain*, p. 192.

21. Martindale to Bourne, April 1928.

22. Ibid.

23. Newcastle Station Director to Stobart, 18.3.29.

5. Expansion and Resistance

1. Reith, Supplementary memorandum to the Crawford Committee, p. 7.

2. Reith, *Broadcast over Britain*, p. 196.

3. The *Daily Mirror*, 19.3.28, complained that the Sunday policy begrudged the nation its right to a little pleasure.

4. See Val Gielgud, *Years in a Mirror*, 1965.

5. CRAC Minutes, 13.3.28, (5).

6. CRAC Minutes, 17.10.30, (7).

7. Siepmann to Reith, 21.10.29.

8. The Free Churches felt the strong domination of what they understandably regarded as the 'Anglican' St Martin's – even though Sheppard and McCormick had enthusiastically maintained the tradition of regularly inviting Free Churchmen to broadcast from its pulpit.

9. Barkby to Reith, 15.10.30.

10. See Reith, *Broadcast over Britain*, p. 200.

11. CRAC Minutes, 30.10.31 (7).

12. See Briggs, II, pp. 229–34.

13. Hugh Johnson, *When Two or Three*, St Martin's Press, 1932.

14. Eckersley to Station Directors, 16.11.27.

15. See ch. 10.G below.

16. See the discussion in the *Radio Times*, 23.10.31, p. 255.

6. Popular Theology: God and the World through Christian Eyes

1. Reith to Stobart, 17.5.32.

2. Ronald Knox, *Broadcast Minds*, p. 10.

3. CRAC Minutes, 29.9.32.

4. Stobart to Reith, 17.10.31.

5. C. H. Dodd, *The Bible and its Background*, Allen and Unwin 1931. See also F. W. Dillistone, *C. H. Dodd*, 1977, pp. 183ff.

6. Reith had once 'censored' Dodd's scripts; he had not cared for 'legends' and Dodd obediently agreed to 'traditions'.

7. See Bishops' Committee Minutes, October 1932.

8. Temple in *The Times* (5.12.32) called for the clergy to organize listening groups. *The Universe*, 16.12.32, hoped Catholics would view the series with sympathetic interest.

9. L. Hodgson, BBC Pamphlet No. 626, *God and the World through Christian Eyes*, p. 42.

10. See Appendix 1.

11. *Proceedings of Convocation of Canterbury*, Upper House, 18.1.33 (SPCK, 1933, pp. 7ff).

12. Alan Don, Diaries (Lambeth Palace Library MS. 2861, p. 5). See *God and the World through Christian Eyes*, Series I, SCM Press 1933, p. 33.

13. See the *Church of England Newspaper*, 15.6.34; *Morning Post*, 28.10.32; CRAC Minutes, 11.5.33 (6); *British Weekly*, 21.9.33.

14. G. M. Bland, the Leicester Borough Librarian, to Stobart, January 1934.

7. The Search for a Director

1. Briggs, II, *The Golden Age of Wireless*, 1965, p. 242.
2. Lang to Wilfrid Parker, 27.8.26.
3. Press Release, 31.3.27.
4. See Ellis Roberts, *H. R. L. Sheppard: Life and Letters*, p. 171.
5. Don, Diaries.
6. H. R. L. Sheppard, *The Impatience of a Parson*, 1927, p. 28.
7. Reith accepted this in a document for the Governors, 12.10.27.
8. Reith, Diary, 22.5.33.
9. Ibid.
10. Reith in an interview with Francis House, January 1953.
11. Iremonger to Reith, 17.2.38.

8. Frederick A. Iremonger

1. In *Broadcasting Policy* 6, 1943, a policy review prepared by the BBC Secretariat.
2. W. H. Elliott, *Undiscovered Ends*, 1951, pp. 153–75.
3. Ibid., p. 171.
4. See Appendix 2.
5. See above, pp. oof.
6. Don, Diaries, Lambeth Palace Library MS. 2861, p. 109.
7. See Briggs, II, pp. 351–69.
8. CRAC Minutes, 11.5.33. (4).
9. See F. A. Iremonger, *William Temple*, 1948, pp. 220ff.
10. Ronald Knox, *Broadcast Minds*, 1932, pp. 9ff.
11. LR 79: 20.7.39, *The Audience for Religious Broadcasts*; see below, ch. 13.
12. Reith, Lecture to the Royal Institute of Great Britain, delivered 13 May 1932, p. 17.

9. Sunday Policy

1. On the wider question of programme timing see Briggs, II, pp. 48ff.

2. Lang to Iremonger, 31.1.34.

3. Temple to Iremonger, 30.1.34.

4. This was to be the demand of the Catholic Radio Guild, founded by Martindale and Ferdinand Valentine, Hinsley's chaplain; see the *Catholic Times*, 25.5.34.

5. Iremonger to Lang, 20.4.34.

6. Aubrey to Iremonger, 5.2.34.

7. In the 20s the Sunday services were followed by an opportunity to respond to *This Week's Appeal*, later *The Week's Good Cause*. Religion was not only hearing but doing; it was an appeal to listeners in general whatever their religious motivation.

8. See below chs. 10.B and 24.B.

9. *Ripon Diocesan Gazette*, April 1934; see also *Yorkshire Post*, 21.5.34.

10. See Briggs,II, pp. 229ff.

11. Iremonger to Dawnay, 9.7.34.

12. Iremonger to Dawnay, 4.3.35.

13. Decision of the Control Board, May 1936.

14. Dawnay to Reith, 27.3.35.

15. *Church Times*, 9.8.35. In 1933 the *Birmingham Post* had begun a campaign under the heading 'Save Sunday from the Saxophone!' Letters continued for weeks.

16. See pp. 88f. below.

17. CRAC, 7.3.35.

18. Briggs, II, p. 364.

19. Ibid.

20. See below, ch. 10.A.

21. Iremonger to Martindale, 16.9.36.

22. Iremonger to Siepmann, 5.3.38.

23. CRAC, 3.3.38, Min. 8.

24. Ibid.

25. Briggs, II, p. 248.

26. Scottish RAC Minutes, 11.3.38.

27. On Dinwiddie see p. 138 below.

28. Briggs, II, ch. IV.

29. Graves' report to Reith, 4.5.38.

30. Programmes Board, 5.5.38, Min. 1098.

31. Nicolls to Reith, 16.11.38.

32. The Ullswater Report, Cmd. 5091, 1936, para. 100.

33. See below ch. 12.C.

34. See also Briggs, II, pp. 242ff.

10. Initiatives and Innovations

1. CRAC Minutes, 4.10.34 (4).

2. Iremonger to all Station Directors, 4.1.35.

3. Dinwiddie to Iremonger, 2.2.35; CRAC Minutes, 7.3.35 (6).

4. Sung Eucharist was the increasingly popular morning service before Matins.

5. Hence the pressure from the Catholic press for the Roman Catholics to have their own wavelength and station to broadcast what they pleased.

6. Sunday Committee Minutes, 27.7.23.

7. Reith to Garbett, 16.7.26.

8. Iremonger to Gooch, 5.2.35.

9. Don, Diaries, October 1932 (Lambeth Palace MS. 2862).

10. Iremonger to Lang, 17.11.34.

11. See Reith, *Into the Wind*, p. 94.

12. Garbett to Lang, 31.5.35.

13. See Lang Papers, MS (Lambeth) no. 3.

14. Ellis Roberts to Iremonger, 11.6.34. See also J. G. Lockhart, *Cosmo Gordon Lang*, 1949, p. 414.

15. Temple to Iremonger, 13.6.35.

16. Ibid.

17. CRAC Minutes, 4.3.37 (4).

18. Iremonger's report to Graves, 7.5.36, p. 2.

19. At St Mary Redcliffe, Bristol, where a radio receiver had been installed, there had been so few present that a collection taken about the middle of the series realized only 1s. 2½d!

20. The Belfast Programme Director to Iremonger, 5.4.33.

21. Leonard Hodgson to Iremonger, 9.1.34.

22. See e.g. W. R. Matthews against G. B. Shaw, *Gabriel in his Search for Mr Shaw*, Hamish Hamilton 1933. (See also *Daily Telegraph*, 1.9.33.)

23. See Briggs, II, pp. 121ff.

24. Temple, Foreword to *The Way to God*, First Series, 1935, p. 9.

25. Iremonger, ibid., p. 17.

26. Whale, ibid., pp. 31ff.

27. Not without considerable complaint from the Spiritualist National Union, who had been campaigning for access to the microphone for some years. See *Light*, 16.7.36, and *Psychic News*, 25.1.36; also *Hansard*, 1.7.36. At its meeting in March 1936 CRAC had issued a firm refusal; the SNU failed to comply with the Christian criteria. Martindale told Iremonger that any positive response to them would cause the Roman Catholics to withdraw from CRAC.

28. See H. C. Coles, *Walford Davies*, 1942, pp. 139ff.

29. Ibid., p. 140.

30. See Reith, Diary, Christmas 1923.

31. See N. Goodall, *The Ecumenical Movement*, OUP 1961, ch. III.

32. *Church, Community and State*, Vol. 8: *The Churches Survey their Task*, the Report of the Conference at Oxford, 1937, introd. by J. H. Oldham, G. Allen and Unwin 1937.

33. The first conferences on 'Faith and Order' and 'Life and Work' had been held in Lausanne and Stockholm respectively in 1927.

34. According to Iremonger's secretary (the only woman present).

35. Iremonger to Reith.

36. John Maud in *The Listener*, 4.8.37, vol. 18, p. 237.

37. See Briggs, II, pp. 256–80.

38. See *Radio Times*, 7.5.37, p. 12.

39. The whole question would be raised again in 1952.

40. *The Listener*, 14.7.37, vol. 18, p. 66.

41. Iremonger once told him that 'the BBC was accustomed to working with gentlemen'. Martindale for his part described Iremonger to Hinsley as 'unbelievably muddle-headed with a violent temper' (11.10.36). They had quite

distinct and irreconcilable views on broadcast religious policy, each with a justifiable logic of its own: Iremonger wanted the Catholics to contribute to the popular programme of Christian witness and Martindale represented the urge to retain the peculiar identity of denominations and serve those who benefited most from broadcast religion. The *Listener* leader only served to publicize this dispute.

42. Eventually the BBC would produce its own hymn book, and raise a good deal of confessional and theological dust in the process.

43. The *Church Times* gave qualified support, rather hinting that it was an example of 'BBC religion' (25.9.36); the rest of the church press were delighted; the Baptists 'commended it without reserve' (*Baptist Times*, 1.10.36).

44. *The Times*, 29.9.36.

45. *Daily Mirror*, 29.9.36.

46. See Briggs, II, pp. 286ff.

47. Iremonger to Reith, 25.5.37.

48. Ibid.

49. Control Board, 12.4.27.

50. J. R. Fleming, Chairman of the Hymn Society, to Iremonger, 2.7.37.

51. The Oxford University Press had already published the *English Hymnal* in 1906 and *Songs of Praise* in 1925.

52. Temple to Ogilvie, 17.3.39.

53. R. Vaughan Williams to H. A. L. Fisher, 10.3.39. Fisher told Ogilvie that Vaughan Williams' complaint was 'worthy'.

54. The view of V. H. Goldsmith, Director of BBC Business Relations, to Iremonger, 31.5.39.

55. Minutes of Hymn Book Committee, 30.8.39.

56. Iremonger to Walford Davies, 23.8.39.

57. Iremonger to BBC Publications Manager, 24.2.39.

58. Iremonger to Walford Davies, 23.8.39.

59. For his earlier work on the *English Hymnal* see Roger Lloyd, *The Church of England 1900–1965*, 1966, pp. 154–9.

60. Iremonger to Welch, 24.9.39.

11. For Children and Schools

1. See Briggs, I, pp. 253ff.

2. Sunday Committee Minutes, 1.8.24.

3. Report by J. C. Stobart, December 1930.

4. See p. 213 below. *Joan and Betty's Bible Stories* were published as *The Greatest Adventure*, 2 vols., BBC Publications, 1932.

5. See Nan Dearmer, *Percy Dearmer*, Jonathan Cape 1940, pp. 313f.

6. The Corporation paid Dearmer's teenage daughter a box of paints for collecting suitable children for the programme!

7. Briggs, II, pp. 58–61.

8. Ibid., pp. 185ff.

9. Ibid., pp. 190ff.

10. CCSB Executive Minutes, 18.2.35.

11. Ibid., 28.5.35.

12. A. C. Deane, *Time Remembered*, 1945, ch. 10.

13. Deane, *Sixth Form Religion*, 1936, p. viii.

14. Deane to Iremonger, 17.5.36.
15. *Time Remembered*, p. 185.
16. BBC Secretariat to CCSB, 5.5.37.
17. These talks went out on the National Programme each Monday morning.
18. Yeaxlee to Iremonger, 3.5.37.

12. The BBC and Christian Orthodoxy

1. General Advisory Committee, Minutes, Spring 1937.
2. Hinsley papers (Westminster Cathedral).
3. Not until the National Viewers' and Listeners' Association did such Protestant vigour organize itself around a single forceful leader; see Michael Tracey and David Morrison, *Whitehouse*, Macmillan 1979. Iremonger for his part had thought birth control was a contribution 'to a sex obsession quite without parallel in our history' (to Graves, 25.10.35).
4. CRAC Minutes, 22.2.27.
5. Iremonger to Reith, 18.8.33.
6. H. A. L. Fisher, *Our New Religion* (Thinkers' Library 31), Watts 1933.
7. Iremonger to Reith, 12.7.34.
8. Fisher, op. cit., pp. 319ff. He told Reith (16.5.35) that the BBC ought to concede an 'occasional talk' without the medical reply.
9. Lothian to Reith, 2.5.35.
10. CRAC Minutes, 4.10.34.
11. Even though Dean Inge had made an abusive reference to Christian Science in a broadcast on 16.6.34; he spoke of the 'sovereign efficacy of make-believe' (Northern Ireland Script).
12. Iremonger to Reith, 13.5.35.
13. Garbett to Stobart, 25.3.31. See also Basil Maine, *The BBC and its Audience*, 1939, pp. 95ff.
14. Reith to Iremonger, 30.11.33.
15. L. P. Jacks had given the Hibbert Lectures, *Religious Perplexities*, Hodder and Stoughton 1922.
16. North Region RAC Minutes, 17.4.31.
17. See Briggs, II, pp. 48ff.
18. Iremonger to Siepmann (now Director of Regional Relations), 18.2.36.
19. See also Maurice Gorham, *Broadcasting and Television since 1900*, p. 46.
20. Tirly Garth, MRA Archives: Lawson Wood (Secretary to Buchman, 1936–39) Files.
21. *What is the Oxford Group?*, foreword by L. W. Grensted, OUP 1933.
22. Grensted, *The Person of Christ*, Nisbet 1933.
23. W. R. Matthews, *Memories and Meanings*, 1969, p. 126.
24. Don, Diaries, Lambeth Palace Library MS. 2862.
25. J. W. C. Wand, 'Buchmanism', *Theology* XXI, August 1930, pp. 79–84.
26. Only half the Committee voted to invite Grensted, though Garbett later denied that he could remember any such divided vote. See Charles Smyth, *Cyril Forster Garbett, Archbishop of York*, 1959, p. 201.
27. Charles Raven and Evelyn Underhill in *The Meaning of the Groups*, ed. F. A. M. Spencer, Methuen 1934, p. 12.
28. Buchman's speech is printed in his *Remaking the World*, Blandford Press, new and rev. ed., 1958, p. 35.

29. Scripts Library: 2nd News Bulletin, 8.7.37.
30. Lang, address to Canterbury Clergy, August 1934.
31. CRAC Minutes, October 1937.
32. Buchman's talk, *Chaos against God*, appeared in *The Listener*, 1.12.38, vol. 20, p. 1190.
33. See below, chs. 23.B; 25.B.

13. Broadcasting Statistics: Defining the Audience

1. See Briggs, II, pp. 256ff., and Robert Silvey, *Who's Listening?*, 1974.
2. LR 79: 20.7.39: *The Audience for Religious Broadcasts*.
3. Ibid.,p. 2.

14. The Central Religious Advisory Committee: the Constitution

1. CRAC Minutes, 2.3.39, no. 7.
2. Iremonger to all Regional Directors, 8.3.39.
3. Smyth, *C. F. Garbett*, p. 202.
4. The *Daily Herald* and some provincial papers made enormous efforts to articulate the popular feeling against the Reithian Sunday.
5. CRAC Minutes, 2.3.39, no. 6.

15. The End of an Era: Reith and Iremonger Retire

1. See Briggs, II, pp. 632ff.
2. Reith had complained to Bell of being 'underworked' (7.7.28) and 'disgruntled' (16.4.32).
3. Reith, Diary, October 1928.
4. Lang wrote to Reith (18.6.38): 'I can never be sufficiently thankful for the tone and spirit and ideal which you have brought to the service of this wonderful wireless.'
5. Reith later told the biographer of Robert Barrington-Ward (whom he had once wanted to be Director-General after him) that his successor should be 'just left of centre, a Christian believer [who] should give the Christian religion a privileged place in the BBC's output'. See Donald MacLachlan, *In the Chair: Barrington-Ward of 'The Times', 1927–1948*, Weidenfeld and Nicolson 1971, p. 181.
6. Iremonger was to fall out with Graves during the war over pacifism. See below, ch. 16.D.
7. See Smyth, *C. F. Garbett*, ch. 8.
8. See Currie, Gilbert and Horsley, *Churches and Churchgoers*, pp. 153ff.
9. Board of Control, Minutes, 29.7.38.
10. Briggs has documented the period region by region; see II, esp. pp. 292–339.
11. Siepmann, *Report on Regions*, 1936, quoted by Briggs, II, p. 331.
12. Ibid., quoted p. 333.
13. Reith to Dinwiddie, 25.3.37.
14. Dinwiddie to J. G. Drummond, 3.1.39.
15. Dinwiddie to Professor Archibald Main, Chairman of SRAC, 30.6.36.
16. Ibid.; Proceedings of Presbytery of Ayr, 24.6.36.
17. See George MacLeod, *We Shall Rebuild*, Iona Community 1942.

18. Iremonger to Tallents, 4.4.38.
19. Lloyd George had attended the first meeting of the Welsh Regional RAC. 'His sole interest was the monthly services in Welsh' (Reith, Diary, March 1932).
20. See below, pp. 147ff.
21. Nicolls to H. B. Moore, 19.8.38.
22. Lang to Welch, 2.9.38.
23. 'Much against my will' Welch told Dorothy L. Sayers in 1941.

16. New Approaches: James Welch

1. Welch's report, 19.6.39.
2. MacLeod to Fenn, 17.7.40.
3. See pp. 123ff below, *Three Men and a Parson*.
4. See above, p. 196.
5. Welch to Lang, 17.6.39.
6. Briggs, III, *The War of Words*, 1970, pp. 92ff.
7. Welch to J. S Whale, 15.12.39.
8. John Middleton Murry, *Europe in Travail*, 1940. See also Mary Middleton Murry, *To Keep Faith*, Constable 1959, and F. Lea, *The Life of John Middleton Murry*, Methuen 1959.
9. See Briggs, III, p. 94.
10. In a letter to Hinsley, 15.12.39 (Hinsley papers).
11. Iremonger had told E. K. Talbot of Mirfield (July 1935) that in Milan in the previous year he had met a man who reported that he and his friends 'now attend Mass on the radio'. See also the *Catholic Herald*, 3.5.40, with recollections of unqualified approval.
12. Welch to Fr John Murray, 6.12.39.
13. Welch to Nicolls, 21.5.40.
14. Welch to Cardinal Griffin, 5.10.45.
15. After the Bristol blitz the Department moved to Bedford in July 1941.
16. Welch to D'Arcy, 21.7.44.
17. See below, pp. 197ff.
18. *Catholic Herald*, 8.10.43.
19. *The Month*, 22.4.42.
20. See the *Church Gazette*, March 1942: 'Graves must go!'
21. Graves to Nicolls, 15.10.42.
22. Foot to Vice-Admiral E. A. Taylor, MP, 20.2.42.
23. Welch to D'Arcy, 30.3.45.
24. *Clergy Review*, April 1942.
25. Reaffirmed in a broadcasting context by the (Roman Catholic) Bishops' Committee, Easter 1951 (Minute 27).
26. CRAC Minutes, 5.10.39 (6).
27. Lord Chatsfield to Reith, 31.1.40.
28. During the days of his League of Prayer for Peace, Elliott had believed almost fanatically that there could be no war. He was not however in sympathy with the pacifists. See his *Undiscovered Ends*, p. 197.
29. Reith to Graves, 7.2.40.
30. Nicolls to Welch, 22.1.40.
31. See below, pp. 196f.

32. Welch later told Francis House that although Iremonger had removed Appleton and the *Silent Fellowship* 'he had left me the job of removing Elliott' (6.9.52).
33. See below, pp. 297ff.
34. Hansard, 19.12.34, vol. 296, cols. 1149f.
35. Welch to Temple, 4.6.40.
36. Home Board Minutes, 28.6.40.
37. Ogilvie to Lindsay Wellington (now at the Ministry of Information), 1.7.40.
38. Silvey to Nicolls, 18.7.40.
39. Ogilvie's minutes of meeting with Tudor-Pole, 21.8.40.
40. Ogilvie to Nicolls, 30.8.40.
41. Lang to Ogilvie, via his Chaplain, Alan Don, 5.9.40.
42. Temple to Ogilvie, 20.9.40.
43. Ogilvie to Lord Halifax, 4.9.40.
44. Welch to Nicolls, 3.10.40.
45. Welch to Temple, 16.10.40.
46. Minutes of meeting of 'Angelus' Committee, 28.10.40.
47. Home Board Minutes, 1.11.40, no. 443.
48. *The Listener*, 14.11.40, vol. 24, p. 690.
49. The Bishop of Lincoln to Welch, 12.3.41.
50. Sir Waldron Smithers was Conservative MP for Chislehurst.
51. Cooper to Ogilvie, 14.5.41.
52. Board of Governors Minutes, 22.5.41.
53. New Zealand High Commission Papers, 29.10.41.
54. Ministry of Information File B/6.34: 1940–42.
55. The Chief Rabbi, Dr J. H. Hertz, recommended special pieces to be read from the Bible and from the Rabbis.
56. Temple Papers, vol. 57, pp. 1–50 (Lambeth Palace Library).
57. Graves, note of meeting with Major-General Hoare, 11.11.42.
58. Hoare to Brendan Bracken, 13.4.43.
59. Briggs, III, p. 593.
60. William Haley to Hoare, 25.2.44.
61. Air Chief Marshal Dowding to Haley, 25.2.44.
62. Temple to Powell, 7.3.44.
63. Welch, report to Haley, 28.4.44.
64. Tudor-Pole had been long in the Middle East before starting up his movement in 1940.
65. *Round the World at Nine o'Clock*, Big Ben Council Publications, December 1950, p. 5.
66. Ogilvie, Minute of meeting with Tudor-Pole, 19.8.40.
67. Welch to Archbishop Geoffrey Fisher, 30.4.45.
68. See p. 145 above.
69. See leader in *The Listener*, 4.9.35, p. 382.
70. See David Martin, *Pacifism: an Historical and Sociological Study*, 1967.
71. Temple, 'The Christian and the World Situation', *The Listener*, 4.9.35, vol. 14, pp. 375f.
72. Ibid., p. 382.
73. CRAC Minutes, 3.10.35 (12).
74. Iremonger to Weatherhead, 17.10.35.
75. Temple, op. cit., p. 412.

76. Canon Charles Raven had given a talk on pacifism in January 1935. See his exchanges with Temple in *The Times*, June 1935.

77. *The Way of Peace*, in *The Listener*, 2.3.38, vol. 19, pp. 445f., 477–9.

78. Leslie Weatherhead was simply cut off when he once departed from his script.

79. Welch to Middleton Murry, 1.11.39. See also Middleton Murry in *Peace News*, 19.4.40: he claimed that the war was 'immoral'. There was no pacifism in *Europe in Travail*, however. See further F. Lea, *The Life of John Middleton Murry*, pp. 274f. and 279.

80. Welch to the Director of Public Relations, War Office, 12.12.39.

81. Henry Strauss, MP, took this line in *The Times*, 8.6.40.

82. Fenn Papers, 1979.

83. Maconachie to Nicolls, 22.11.39.

84. Welch to Aubrey, 10.10.41.

85. See George MacLeod, *Govan Calling*, 1934. He had become the 'Dick Sheppard' of Scotland, as Iremonger had hoped. (One listener to MacLeod, thinking he heard St Martin's, sent his offertory gift to McCormick!)

86. See P. Hartill (Archdeacon of Stoke), ed., *Into the Way of Peace*, SCM Press 1941, and C. E. Raven, *The Cross and the Crisis*, Fellowship of Reconciliation 1940.

87. MacLeod to Welch, 2.2.40. (MacLeod had served with distinction in The Argyll and Sutherland Highlanders in the First World War.)

88. Welch to MacLeod, 2.2.40.

89. F. A. Cockin, in *The Listener*, 28.12.39, vol. 22, p. 1287.

90. E. S. Woods, ibid., 12.10.39, p. 723.

91. Temple in a talk on 'The Spirit and Aim of Britain' given on 2.10.39 (*The Listener*, 5.10.39, vol. 22, p. 670). See below, p. 285.

92. See above, p. 172 and n. 86.

93. C. E. Raven, *The Listener*, 21.12.39, vol. 22, p. 1247.

94. See F. W. Dillistone, *Charles Raven: Naturalist, Historian, Theologian*, 1975.

95. L. P. Richards had broadcast a sermon on 'The Christian Substitute for Armaments' on 7.2.32 (published in *Modern Sermons = Sermons of the Year 1932*, ed. W. F. Stead, Faber and Faber 1933, pp. 179–90). He upheld 'the irreconcilable contradiction between war and Christianity' (p. 182). See also his book *The Christian's Alternative to War*, SCM Press 1929.

96. Richards, *The Crisis and World Peace*, SCM Press 1939.

97. Ogilvie to Mrs Lyon, 15.2.40.

98. See for instance Hansard, 3.9.39, vol. 351, cols. 295f.

99. Ogilvie to Reith, 29.3.40 and 4.4.40.

100. Ogilvie to Welch, 5.8.40.

101. Welch, statement to CRAC, 7.3.40.

102. C. V. Taylor, transcript, 1981.

103. Welch's report of the meeting on 7.3.40.

104. Welch to Raven, 16.2.40.

105. Board of Governors Minutes, 24.4.40, no. 118, later amended: 'For *Corporation* read *Dr Welch*.'

106. CRAC, however, would not remove Welch's statement from the Minutes.

107. Powell to Garbett, 3.6.40.

108. By H. Strauss, Hansard, 28.5.40, vol. 361, cols. 463–6.

109. Garbett to Powell, 5.6.40.

110. Board Minutes, 6.6.40, no. 152.

111 Garbett, Diary, 10.3.41.

112. It would also make the BBC's relationship with the Roman Catholics more difficult; they objected to a state institution making ecclesial and theological judgments.

113. Ogilvie to Powell, 15.8.40.

114. See below, ch. 19.C.

115. Fenn Papers, 1981.

116. Ibid.

117. Transcript of interview with Fenn, 1981. See also E. M. Jackson, *Red Tape and the Gospel* (biography of William Paton), 1980, pp. 8off.

118. Nathaniel Micklem to Powell, 13.11.40.

119. William Paton to Powell, 19.11.40.

120. Fenn had deeply regretted the ban on A. C. Craig, and told him (14.11.40) that he had little faith that CRAC would resist it.

121. CRAC meeting on 21.11.40, verbatim report and Minutes, no. 5.

122. Ibid.

123. Secretariat Directive to all Regions, 3.12.40.

124. Hansard, 11.12.40, vol. 367, col. 900.

125. *News Chronicle*, 4.1.41.

126. See further Dillistone, *Raven*, pp. 211ff.

127. Temple, letter to *The Times*, 31.1.41.

128. Harold Nicolson, *Diaries and Letters, 1939–45*, 1967, p. 247.

129. Garbett, Diaries, 5.2.41.

130. Powell, report, 5.2.41.

131. The Peace Pledge Union Form of Association included the words: 'I renounce war and will never sanction or support another.'

132. Temple, *A Conditional Justification of War*, Hazell, Watson and Viney 1940, p. 27.

133. Hansard, 6.2.40, vol. 368, cols. 1185f.

134. Temple to Powell, 22.2.41.

135. Powell to Temple, 4.3.41.

136. Hansard, 12.3.41, vol. 369, col. 1271.

137. Hansard, 20.3.41, vol. 370, cols. 282f.

138. See Jackson, *Red Tape and the Gospel*, pp. 317 and 396.

139. Joseph McCulloch, *My Affair with the Church*, 1978, pp. 171ff.

140. Programme Planning Meeting, 20.11.45.

141. Iremonger had complained to Welch at his use of Middleton Murry; he thought him an 'ignorant and dishonest man'.

142. *Broadcasting Policy* 7, January 1943, p. 7.

143. Hansard, 11.3.41, vol. 369, col. 1149.

144. Ogilvie to Mrs Lyon, 15.2.40.

145. *Malvern, 1941. The Life of the Church and the Order of Society*: being the Proceedings of the Archbishop of York's Conference, Longmans 1941.

146. T. S. Eliot, *The Idea of a Christian Society*, 1939, pp. 59ff.

147. V. A. Demant was the founder, with Maurice Reckitt, of the Christian Sociology Group; both were involved with the Malvern Conference. See Roger Lloyd, *The Church of England 1900–1965*, pp. 308ff.

148. Minutes of meeting between Welch and the 'hierarchy', 7.2.41.

149. 'Foundations of Peace', in *The Times*, 21.12.40.

150. See also *The Churches Survey their Task* (see ch. 10 n. 32 above), p. 115.

151. A. P. Ryan to Duff Cooper, 24.2.41.

152. *The Listener*, when reprinting these talks, also omitted these references (March 1941, vol. 25, pp. 333, 371, 415, 457).

153. Hansard, 26.3.41, vol. 370, cols. 569f.

154. Ibid.

155. Nicolson to Maconachie, 28.3.41.

156. Nicolson to Ogilvie, 3.4.41. Ogilvie told Nicolson (4.4.41) that 'All of us here are trying to help the cause of religion and not hinder it.'

157. The 'Concordat' as approved by the Chairman of Governors, 23.8.41.

158. CRAC Minutes, 2.10.41 (9).

159. When *Three Men and a Parson* was published, Hugh Redwood in the *News Chronicle*, 22.2.41, complained of the BBC's policy of anonymity. The names of the speakers were eventually revealed. See also *The Times*, 10.2.41.

160. Temple, *Christianity and Social Order*, 1942, p. 18. See also Appendix 3 below.

161. Nicolson to Ogilvie, 3.4.41.

162. Garbett to Welch, 2.5.41.

163. See *The Listener*, 23.7.42, vol. 28, p. 114.

164. Guy Burgess told Fenn that when the revolution came the RBD would be the first to be strung up! (Fenn papers, 1980).

165. Welch to C. S. Lewis, 7.2.41.

166. The background to C. S. Lewis's talks is well set out by Walter Hooper, Lewis's private secretary, in the introduction to the fortieth anniversary edition of *Mere Christianity*, Macmillan, New York, 1981.

167. Interview with Fenn, 1978.

168. Barbara Ward, Dorothy L. Sayers, William Temple, *Commentary on the Ten Peace Points*, SCM Press 1941.

169. *Cambridge Review*, 14.11.42.

170. Welch's University sermon had been approved by Nicolls and Powell.

171. Maconachie to the Director-General, 4.1.43.

172. Fenn Papers.

173. C. S. Lewis, *Broadcast Talks*, Geoffrey Bles 1942.

174. Welch had innocently hoped that Watts, a Director of the Rationalist Press Association, might have taken part in *The World Looks at the Christian*.

175. Nicolson to Ogilvie, 3.4.41.

176. Board Minutes, 5.1.43.

177. Foot to Graves, 30.10.42.

17. Restoring Old Images: Christianity in the Culture

1. LR 230, 3.3.41.

2. Fenn to Woodward, 18.1.40.

3. Howard Thomas to C. E. M. Joad, 13.12.40.

4. See Briggs, III, 318ff., 560ff. and elsewhere on the Brains Trust; also Howard Thomas, *Britain's Brains Trust*, 1944.

5. In a *Brains Trust* broadcast on 18.5.41.

6. Board of Governors Minutes, 4.6.42.

7. Thomas, op. cit., p. 100.

8. Temple to Graves, 14.10.42.

9. LR 1543, 19.2.42.

10. *Catholic Herald*, 15.1.43; see also the *Church Times*, 18.12.42, and *The Observer*, 17.1.43.

11. *Church Times*, 15.1.43.

12. Temple to Graves, 15.1.43.

13. Graves to Temple, 15.1.43.

14. J. B. Clark, C. E. M. Joad, Julian Huxley, Victor Murray and Leslie Howard to Powell, 19.1.43.

15. Board of Governors Minutes, 21.1.43.

16. Temple to Foot, 2.2.43.

17. Lord Hailsham, transcript, 1981.

18. CRAC Minutes, 13.3.28.

19. Ronald Knox proved an excellent example.

20. LR 2847, 6.9.44.

21. Haley, Paper for the British Association, 18.1.44.

22. Paul Rowntree Clifford, Iremonger, J. S. Stewart, John Maud, C. H. Dodd and others.

23. *People Matter* (on justice), by F. A. Cockin, N. H. Snaith, Ronald Lunt, A. S. Duncan Jones and others, 1945; *My Brother's Keeper*, by G. K. A. Bell, Daniel Jenkins, Mervyn Stockwood and others, 1946.

24. After the war there were increased efforts to involve the churches in the concept of 'mission' in a more practical way. Reconstruction bulked large in the churches' deliberations and activities. With the return to normality it was possible to encourage greater church co-operation.

25. Courses of sermons included *Man's Dilemma and God's Asnwer* by Welch and others, 1944; *Beyond Personality* by C. S. Lewis, 1944; *The Crisis of the Western World* by Temple and others, 1944; also *How Christians Worship*, ed. Fenn, 1942.

26. Minutes, 16.9.43.

27. Notably the series on *Man's Dilemma and God's Answer*.

28. CRAC Minutes, 4.6.25.

29. See p. 102 above.

30. CRAC Minutes, 5.10.33.

31. Martin Browne was in touch with G. K. A. Bell, in 1934 still Dean of Canterbury, who himself had gained such strong support from Reith for his Canterbury Festivals. Dorothy L. Sayers' play *The Zeal of Thy House* (Gollancz 1937) was performed at the Festival of 1937. See J. Brabazon, *Dorothy L. Sayers*, 1981, pp. 160ff.

32. See Briggs, II, 164ff.

33. Geoffrey Dearmer, son of Canon Percy Dearmer, had first been invited by Iremonger to help with the selection of sermons, as H. W. Fox had helped Stobart (see pp. 18f. above). He had been assistant censor of plays for the Lord Chamberlain's Office and on the council of the Stage Society, and had worked with Lance Sieveking of the Drama Research section.

34. Laurence Housman to Iremonger, 2.8.34.

35. Sayers in the *Radio Times*, 23.12.38, p. 13.

36. Sayers, *He That Should Come*, Gollancz 1939, p. 10.

37. She had published a tract, *The Greatest Drama Ever Staged* (Hodder and Stoughton 1938), in which she complained that by neglecting Christian dogma the churches had neglected the central drama: 'The drama is in the Creed' (pp. 5ff.).

38. See Janet Hitchman, *Such a Strange Lady*, 1975, p. 143.

39. Sayers, *Radio Times*, December 1938.
40. R. Palmer, *School Broadcasting in Britain*, 1947, pp. 9ff.
41. Welch in the *Radio Times*, 20.10.39.
42. Welch to Nicolls, 12.1.40.
43. See particularly *Education*, 1.3.40, p. 175.
44. See James Murphy, *Church, State and Schools in Britain*, Routledge and Kegan Paul 1971, chs. 4 and 5; also the *Cambridge Syllabus*, 1924, revised, with Introduction by J. S. Whale, 1939.
45. CCSB Meeting, Minutes, 6.6.40.
46. John G. Williams had been recommended to Welch by Parsons of the National Society.
47. The Worship Service for Schools was in the hands of the RBD until 1944 when it was taken over by the Schools Department for the later SBC.
48. Welch and Cameron had set up an advisory committee of teachers and inspectors under Sir Henry Richards.
49. CCSB Minutes, 25.7.40.
50. L. du Garde Peach, a D.Litt., produced more radio plays than any other dramatist. See his *Radio Plays*, Newnes 1932.
51. Welch to McCulloch, 12.3.40.
52. Sayers to Welch, 18.2.40.
53. Ibid., 11.1.41.
54. Sayers, 'Divine Comedy', in *The Guardian*, 15.8.40.
55. Sayers to Welch, 4.3.40.
56. Sayers, *Creed or Chaos?*, broadcast 11.8.40, publ. Hodder and Stoughton 1940, reprinted in *Creed or Chaos and other essays in popular theology*, Methuen 1947. See also W. E. Williams in *The Listener*, 15.8.40, vol. 24, p. 248.
57. May Jenkin to Sayers, 19.11.40.
58. Sayers to McCulloch, 28.11.40.
59. Cf. Val Gielgud, *Years in a Mirror*, 1965, p. 93.
60. So-called by Nicolls.
61. As Brabazon suggests, this was hardly fair; she must have expected some editing of her work. Brabazon traces her venom here to hatred for her former governess, 'forever looking over her shoulder as she worked' (op. cit., p. 198).
62. Jenkin to Sayers, 19.12.40.
63. Sayers to Welch, 11.1.41.
64. See above, p. 196.
65. Welch had earlier approached T. S. Eliot without result.
66. Gielgud to Sayers, 28.2.41.
67. Sayers to Welch, 1.8.41.
68. Lord Clarendon to Ogilvie, 28.8.40.
69. William Temple, *Readings in St John's Gospel*, 2 vols., Macmillan 1939–40.
70. Welch to Sayers, 15.9.41.
71. Sayers to Welch, 17.9.41.
72. Sayers to Welch, 20.11.41.
73. Ibid.
74. Ibid., 24.9.41.
75. Welch told Sayers that Harman Grisewood was 'far and away the best radio actor we have had' (13.2.41).
76. Sayers' prepared speech to the press, 10.12.41. See Brabazon, op. cit., p. 202.

77. H. H. Martin, General Secretary of the Lord's Day Observance Society, to Ogilvie, 12.12.41.

78. Welch to Sayers, 13.12.41.

79. Ibid., 24.12.41.

80. See e.g. the *Daily Telegraph*, 31.12.41, and the *Sunday Dispatch*, 28.12.41.

81. See Hansard, 19.12.41, vol. 376, cols. 2233f.

82. Report by Farquharson, 17.12.42.

83. Lord Clarendon to Ogilvie, 17.12.41.

84. Hansard, loc. cit.

85. Garbett to Welch, 22.12.41.

86. Welch to Garbett, 19.12.41.

87. Welch in the *Radio Times*, 19.12.41, p. 5.

88. Sayers would not have approved of her biographer's remark that the gospels are a 'rag-bag' of anecdotes (Brabazon, op. cit., p. 201).

89. In the *Glasgow Herald*, 30.12.41.

90. *The Times*, 30.12.41; see also *The English Churchman*, which on 18.12.41 printed a full-page protest.

91. The Winchester Diocesan leaflet, no. 64, 1942.

92. CRAC Minutes, 7.1.42. Garbett, however, later told Welch that he thought that 'The King of Sorrows', on the crucifixion, was her 'greatest masterpiece', but that it was 'quite unsuitable for children' (27.8.42). Roger Armfelt of the Schools Department thought the plays 'just the thing the schools want'. He encouraged the CCSB to have the cycle broadcast during school hours.

93. Welch to Sayers, 8.1.42.

94. Ibid.

95. Sayers to Welch, 27.1.42.

96. Welch to Sayers, 16.2.42.

97. Sayers to Welch, 19.2.42.

98. Welch to Sayers, 27.2.42.

99. Sayers to Welch, 17.3.42.

100. Ibid.

101. Ibid., 20.3.42.

102. Welch to Sayers, 21.3.42.

103. Ibid., 5.6.42.

104. See the text of 'The King of Sorrows', in *The Man Born to be King*, 1943, esp. pp. 303–6.

105. Sayers to Gielgud, 18.8.42.

106. Cf. Rudolf Otto, *The Idea of the Holy*, Eng. trans. 1923.

107. Sayers to Gielgud, 22.9.42.

108. Nicolls to Sayers, 16.10.42.

109. Welch later suggested to Temple that Sayers be awarded the Lambeth DD for her contribution to religion, but she was reluctant to accept and finally refused it (see Brabazon, op. cit., p. 214).

110. LR 631, 7.2.42.

111. Sayers, *The Man Born to be King*, p. 20.

112. Ibid., p. 37.

113. Ibid., p. 20.

114. Ibid., p. 37.

115. Ibid., p. 41.

116. In 1956 Joy Harington produced *Jesus of Nazareth* for Children's TV.

117. Out of over 7000 letters received, 94% were critical, but 80% of this criticism 'suggests that the correspondents are activated by blind prejudice. . . Nonconformists, largely Baptists and Evangelicals, predominate' (Programme Correspondence Section, January 1942).

118. So Heenan later told CRAC.

119. *The Universe*, 16.1.42.

120. Sister Penelope, *If Any Man Serve Me*, 1941.

121. Welch to Wellington, 11.1.45.

122. Welch to Mary Somerville, 7.4.43.

123. Sayers to Welch, 20.5.43.

124. Welch to Sister Penelope, 1.6.44.

125. Welch to Somerville, 14.7.44.

126. Somerville to Welch, 28.7.44.

127. Williamson's play *Gladstone* was running at the Gate Theatre, London.

128. CCSB Reports: from Cameron, 16.5.43; from Thornhill, 18.5.43. See also Board of Education Conferences, August 1943.

129. Williamson, *Paul a Bondslave*, 1945.

130. CCSB Minutes, 29.7.43. See Williamson's *Story without an End*, 1947.

131. See Palmer, *School Broadcasting in Britain*, ch. 9.

132. CCSB Minutes, 12.10.44.

133. See J. Murphy, *Church, State and Schools in Britain, 1800–1970*, Routledge and Kegan Paul 1971, and M. Cruickshank, *Church and State in English Education*, Macmillan 1963, ch. 7.

134. Welch to Wellington, 4.2.45.

135. Somerville to Wellington, 25.1.45.

136. See e.g. L. Elliott-Binns, *Jeremiah: A Prophet for the Time of War*, SCM Press 1941, ch. III.

137. CCSB Minutes, 18.12.44.

138. Somerville to Welch, 24.8.45.

139. See above, ch. 16.E, pp. 195ff.

140. CCSB Minutes, Sixth Form Committee, 29.1.43.

141. Welch to Somerville, 30.1.43.

142. Ibid.

143. See LR 1841, 23.6.43. This report made it quite clear that the listening public, while favourable to the series as a whole, resented the Christian 'last word' and dogmatic and 'undiscussed' character of the talk on Chrstianity by Nathaniel Micklem.

144. CCSB Postal Survey Report, 1946, Part II, para. 8.

145. Kenneth Grayston's Report to CCSB, December 1946, I.3.

146. Tissington Tatlow's Report to Senior Education Inspectors' Association, 12.3.47, para. 1(a): '50% of all grammar schools are giving no Religious Instruction beyond Third Form. . . . There are insufficient teachers to deal with the new style of questions being asked by senior pupils.'

147. The same point had been made strongly in an article by G. N. Whitfield in *Religion in Education*, Autumn 1946.

148. Ministry of Education Report of Broadcasting Panel, January 1948, no. 2.

149. SBC 80/48, Part III: Religious Instruction in Sixth Forms, p. 9.

150. Ibid., p. 10.

151. *Religion and Philosophy* Course Documents, BBC 1950.

152. Charles Madge, *To Start You Talking*, 1945, p. 6.

153. Somerville to Armfelt, 22.5.44.
154. Ibid.
155. Somerville to Fenn, 8.6.42.
156. Somerville to Lindsay Wellington, the Controller of the Home Service, 25.2.43.
157. Report, Schools Department, 7.5.43.
158. Cyril Taylor to Welch, 22.10.43.
159. See below, ch. 18.B(ii).
160. Somerville's proposals, 4.5.44.
161. See below, ch. 22.B.
162. See also Minutes of Programme Policy Meeting, 7.11.44.
163. See above, pp. 244ff.
164. See above, ch. 17.B(ii).
165. Hunter to Welch, 19.4.45.
166. *Youth Seeks an Answer* sought 'to present to youth in modern terms Christianity in action by dramatizing key parables as they might happen in Scotland today' (Scottish RAC Minutes, 28.10.47).
167 Saxon to Taylor, 21.2.47.
168. North Region RAC Minutes, 20.2.47. See also an article by Peter Green in the *Manchester Guardian*, 20.2.47.
169. Saxon to Taylor, 25.2.47.
170. Report of meeting of Standing Committee, 19.3.47.
171. Francis House to Wellington, 11.5.49.
172. Report from Falconer (Scottish Region Religious Broadcasting Organizer) to Schools Department, 14.6.49.
173. Falconer to House, 28.4.50.
174. Ibid.
175. LR 49/2390, 30.11.49.
176. Youth Broadcasting Committee, Minutes, 6.7.50.
177. See Briggs IV, pp. 63 and 807ff.
178. In 1928 about 2000 schools were listening to BBC broadcasts of various kinds. In 1941 there were about 1200, in 1945 about 1400. In 1949 there were about 1800 out of a possible 3500 (SBC Report to UNESCO, 1949, p. 2).
179. For a contemporary debate see John Hull, *School Worship. An Obituary*, SCM Press, 1975.
180. The Director of Talks, R. A. Rendall, told the Director of Schools Broadcasting that he was the responsible officer of the Corporation, 16.4.47.
181. Minutes of meeting between Postgate and House, 7.10.49.
182. *Reception in Schools*, BBC Chief Engineer, June 1943.
183. See the conclusions by G. Dixon in a report for SBC, *Schools Service Books*, 28.6.48.
184. SBC Conference Report by Sir G. Cater, 16.12.48, b. (a–d).
185. SBC Commission to BBC for a religious service, 1949.
186. Williams was about to retire from the Department.
187. SBC Commission, para. 8(1).
188. Robert Walton to House, 19.12.49.
189. Williams to House, 7.1.50.
190. From the outset of the service there had been persistent appeals for a separate service for younger children.
191. SBC Postal Report, 1951, pp. 7ff.

192. SBC Commission on Educational Policy, 72/54, 15.10.54.
193. See *Educational Forum*, March 1957, pp. 297ff.
194. K. V. Bailey, *The Listening Schools*, BBC 1957, pp. 52ff.
195. Report of conference, 9.5.52, p. 5.
196. Ibid., conclusions 2 (1–3).

18. The Audience across the Channel

1. Gerard Mansell, *Let Truth Be Told: Fifty Years of BBC External Broadcasting*, 1982, chs. 1 and 2; Briggs, II, pp. 369ff.
2. *The Listener*, 21.12.32, vol. 8, p. 884.
3. Reith, *Into the Wind*, p. 169.
4. Reith to Dawnay, 1.12.34.
5. See the *BBC Handbook*, 1934, pp. 249ff.
6. B. W. Kirke of the Australian Broadcasting Commission, 30.1.33.
7. R. Ellis Roberts, *H. R. L. Sheppard*, pp. 253ff.; W. R. Matthews, *Memories and Meanings*, pp. 183ff.
8. See Ruth Rouse and Stephen Neill, *A History of the Ecumenical Movement, 1517–1948*, SPCK 1954, and Barry Till, *The Churches Search for Unity*, Penguin Books 1972.
9. For fuller treatment see Briggs, II, pp. 363ff.
10. Briggs, III, p. 125.
11. Board of Governors Minutes, 6.12.39.
12. Briggs, III, p. 133.
13. Welch to Nicolls, 21.9.39.
14. See also Alan Wilkinson, *The Church of England and the First World War*, 1978.
15. Board of Governors Minutes, 22.12.39, no. 275: 'Variety should be broadcast with discretion on Sundays in the Services programme.'
16. Welch to Nicolls for the Home Board, 2.1.40.
17. Briggs, III, p. 125.
18. A. P. Ryan, report to Deputy Director-General, 24.1.40.
19. Welch to Nicolls, 15.1.40.
20. Ryan, op. cit.
21. Dom Bernard Clements was the Anglo-Catholic Vicar of All Saints, Margaret Street, London. Few knew that his broadcasts included short weekly talks to the island of Malta which covered the period when the attack on it was at its fiercest. See M. E. Almedingen, *Dom Bernard Clements*, 1945, p. 118. See also the Introduction by Eric Fenn to Clements' *Speaking in Parables*, 1943.
22. Roger Wilson's report to Welch, 28.3.40.
23. See Briggs, III, p. 134.
24. Welch, Report to Home Board, April 1940 (HB 1/40, p. 2).
25. LR 42/1157, 7.9.42.
26. See Wilkinson, op. cit., p. 339.
27. Ibid., pp. 156ff. See also *National, Patriotic and Devotional Hymns for Use during the War*, Novello 1915.
28. See *Three Men and a Parson*, above pp. 196ff.
29. Welch to Nicolls, 20.11.40.
30. Andrew Stewart of the Ministry of Information to Adams, 16.12.40.
31. Welch to Nicolls, 9.4.41.
32. Taylor to the RBD, 31.3.42.

33. Welch to Fenn, 4.4.42. The letter from Stanton-Jeans (see p. 272 above) had left an indelible mark on Welch's thinking. (Fenn transcript, 1981).

34. Ronald Selby Wright, *Asking Them Questions*, 1936, 1938. (See also his autobiography, *Another Home*, 1980, ch. 6.) He produced a remarkable collection of 'Christian answers' to questions framed by his boys and answered by the cream of British theological scholarship. They were and remain a unique attempt to reply intelligibly to the young, at least those within the orbit of a Christian congregation.

35. Garbett assured Welch he could see 'no kind of objection' to the project being undertaken by a Church of Scotland minister.

36. War Office Chaplains Department paper 75153, C.I.

37. LR 42/1114, 27.8.42.

38. Selby Wright, *Let's Ask the Padre*, 1942, p. 33.

39. W. E. Williams in *The Listener*, 11.12.41, vol. 26, p. 800.

40. See Appendix 3: *The Padre Asks the Archbishop*.

41. The popularity of *Sunday Half Hour* was confirmed by Silvey, LR 43/2058, 24.9.43.

42. Selby Wright, *Another Home*, p. 116.

43. M. R. D. Foot and J. M. Langley have outlined the coded use of these talks to convey messages to prisoners-of-war; see *MI9. Escape and Evasion*, Bodley Head 1979, p. 115.

44. See Selby Wright, *The Average Man*, Longmans 1942, and *The Greater Victory*, Longmans 1943.

45. Briggs, III, pp. 589ff.

46. Ibid., p. 649.

47. See Charles Siepmann, *Radio, Television and Society*, OUP 1950, pp. 243ff.

48. Welch to Gorham, 18.4.44.

49. *BBC Handbook*, 1941, p. 96.

50. Franklin Report, October, 1945.

51. See ch. 23.C below.

52. Briggs, II, p. 649. See also Mansell, op cit., ch. 4.

53. Nathaniel Micklem had published *National Socialism and the Roman Catholic Church*, OUP 1939, and *National Socialism and Christianity* (Oxford Pamphlets on World Affairs, no. 18), OUP 1939.

54. This conclusion was soon to be confirmed by the Overseas Intelligence Department of the BBC in an extensive report, *National Socialism and Religious Broadcasting*, March 1940. Welch told Bell that he had been trying to get these broadcasts for six months, 'largely at the instigation of Karl Barth' (27.11.39).

55. Ogilvie to Graves, 31.7.39.

56. See *National Socialism and Religious Broadcasting*, paras. 7–19. See also Ansgar Diller in *Rundfunk in Deutschland*, ed. H. von Bauches, vol. 2, *Die Rundfunkpolitik des Dritten Reiches*, Munich 1979, p. 313. He notes that Goebbels' proposal to reintroduce religious broadcasts after the outbreak of war was vetoed by Hitler. However by the end of the first year of the war Goebbels had developed a series of Sunday evening quasi-religious programmes involving classical music and 'prayers' of thanksgiving for the Führer. On 12 January 1941 Munich Radio broadcast a 'service' celebrating the mystical conception of the Reich, and Breslau Radio broadcast *The Creed of Our Times* which declared that the scriptures were dead and that the divinity was in the sunrise in which light was their leader. (See also Review of European Programmes by the European

Programme Director, J. Tudor Jones, 6.3.41.)

57. Fenn had met Gerstenmaier in July 1939.

58. Visser 't Hooft to Fenn, 14.9.39.

59. William Temple in *The Listener*, 5.10.39, vol. 22, p. 672.

60. R. A. Butler to Ogilvie, 1.10.39.

61. CRAC Minutes, 5.10.39.

62. See Briggs, III, pp. 169ff. See also Mansell, op cit., ch. 4.

63. E. M. Jackson, *Red Tape and the Gospel*, pp. 247ff.

64. J. B. Clark to Hugh Martin, Ministry of Information, 18.11.39.

65. Welch to Clark, 27.11.39.

66. Overseas Service Board Minutes, 28.12.39.

67. Welch to Clark, 8.1.40.

68. Board of Governors Minutes, 10.1.40.

69. This extraordinary attitude was singularly unreasonable; the Ecumenical Movement was not 'universally accepted' by any church body in any country.

70. R. J. Shaw, Report of Planning Committee, to Ogilvie, 16.1.40.

71. Ogilvie to Shaw, 18.1.40.

72. Hugh Martin to R. L. Carton (Foreign Publicity at Electra House), 31.1.40.

73. Report of Ministry of Information (Religion) Church Advisory Group, January 1940.

74. Op. cit., para. 5.

75. An article by a German priest in *The Tablet*, October 1939, called for a religious service in German.

76. Burns, Ministry of Information Report, 1.2.40, para. 5.

77. Ogilvie to Shaw, 7.2.40.

78. Jackson, op. cit., p. 248.

79. See Ivone Kirkpatrick, *The Inner Circle*, 1959, ch. VII.

80. Temple to Welch, 28.6.41.

81. German Religious Advisory Committee (Electra House), Minutes, 20.8.41. On Crossman see Mansell, op cit., p. 88.

82. The BBC's representatives were Lindley Fraser and Tangye Lean, both accomplished foreign broadcasters. See Briggs, III, p. 182.

83. See p. 289 above.

84. Welch to Nicolls, 29.8.41.

85. See Briggs, III, passim.

86. See pp. 195ff. above.

87. Tudor Jones to Welch, 6.3.41.

88. Welch to Tudor Jones, 24.3.41.

89. See above, ch. 16.C.

90. Welch to Nicolls, 31.8.41.

91. Welch to Salt, 9.10.41.

92. Newsome to Welch, 21.10.41.

93. Welch to Nicolls, 6.10.41.

94. Control Board for Overseas, Minutes, 6.11.41.

95. Welch to Micklem, 19.11.41.

96. Clark to Graves, 21.2.42.

19. Ecumenical Initiatives

1. William Temple, *The Church Looks Forward*, Macmillan 1944, p. 3.

2. Silvey explained his methodology in LR 41/392, July 1941.

3. LR 41/411, 'The Public for Religious Broadcasts', November 1941, reproduced in Appendix 4.

4. Ibid., para. 9.

5. Iremonger had impressed on Reith that unity should be expressed more within the churches' utterances on a 'common social and ethical philosophy than [by] endless, futile discussions on the validity of Anglican orders' (14.12.35).

6. See BBC Overseas Intelligence Report (see p. 284 above and ch. 18 n.54).

7. Fenn (ed.), *How Christians Worship*, 1942, p. 17.

8. *The Listener*, 26.2.42, vol. 27, p. 264.

9. Garbett to Fenn, 14.10.41.

10. Reith, *Into the Wind*, p. 95.

11. Fenn papers, 1981.

12. Maconachie to Welch, 19.8.40.

13. Nicolls to Welch, 11.9.40.

14. A. Hinsley, *The Bond of Peace*, 1941, p. 110.

15. Lang to Welch, 9.7.41.

16. Danson to Welch, 5.6.41. He gave essentially the same reply to Temple, 10.6.41.

17. Dinwiddie to Main, 27.6.41.

18. Welch to Dinwiddie, 11.7.41.

19. Welch, Minute of meeting with Lang, 23.7.41.

20. See F. A. Iremonger, *William Temple*, 1948, p. 595.

21. 'God the All-terrible', *Hymns Ancient and Modern Revised*, no. 491.

22. In 1943 the National Days of Prayer reverted to Sunday and there were complaints, this time from the Free Churches, that they were playing 'second fiddle' and not getting their fair share of broadcasts. The General Secretary of the Free Church Federal Council told Sir Alexander Maxwell at the Home Office that 'there were no more loyal subjects of His Majesty' than Free Churchmen (14.8.44). See also CRAC Minutes, 6.3.45. Welch thought the Council was simply bickering and jockeying and exploiting this national broadcast out of jealousy of the national churches. This meeting infuriated him; he considered resignation.

23. Welch in *Man's Dilemma and Gods' Answer*, 1944, p. 9.

24. LR 44/2765, 24.7.44.

25. *Church Times*, 17.1.44.

26. BBC Publicity Leaflet, Summer 1946.

27. The Livingstone Report, *The Church and Adult Education*, National Society for Religious Education, 1945.

28. See above, ch. 17.B (vi).

29. Op. cit., pp. 25f.

30. Eric Saxon to Programme Director, 16.12.46; Minutes of Senior Engineers' meeting, 26.11.46.

31. Saxon to House, 24.5.48.

32. Report, 1951, Saxon to Elsie Chamberlain, p. 3.

33. Ibid., p. 4.

34. See p. 200 above.

35. Oldham had begun, in the first number of the *Christian Newsletter* in October 1939, 'to bridge the gap between organized religion and the general life of the community . . . Our main concern is big news rather than hot news.'

36. Minutes of meeting by Fenn, 21.7.42.

37. Since pre-war days the BBC had always encouraged both kinds of review. Ogilvie thought that Iremonger's reviews were the very best; Nicolls thought him 'irreplaceable'.

38. See below ch. 22.B, 'Controversy'.

39. See below, ch. 22.C, 'Talks Policy'.

40. Grayston to Welch, 1.2.46.

41. Foster's talks were published in the church weekly, *The Guardian*.

42. Welch risked a CRAC rebuttal when he decided to drop the midweek service in favour of *What are The Churches Doing?* See CRAC Minutes, 10.10.46 and 4.3.47.

43. See E. Busch, *Karl Barth. Life and Letters*, Eng. trans. 1976, p. 314.

20. The Concept of Mission

1. Welch's sermon was printed in the *Cambridge Review*, 14.11.42. The BBC had approved the text before it was delivered.

2. Harman Grisewood, transcript, 1981.

3. Fisher to Welch, 3.4.44. (The Free Churches, surprisingly, had all agreed to this piece of Anglican/BBC empire-building!)

4. See above, ch. 17.B (iii).

5. See D. L. Sayers, *The Man Born to be King*, pp. 20ff.: 'It is the business of the dramatist . . . to trust the theology to emerge undistorted from the story; he has to eschew the didactic approach.'

6. See Wilfrid Grantham's *Men of God* (six plays on the Hebrew prophets), 1947. Joseph McCulloch was another successful radio dramatist; see his autobiography, *My Affair with the Church*, 1976, pp. 132f.

7. Secretariat to Williams, 27.12.46.

8. Dinwiddie to Welch, 16.1.40.

9. See *Towards the Conversion of England*, 1945, pp. 105ff. Welch had written the section on radio.

10. Welch to House, 17.9.45.

21. Post-war Reorganization

1. *BBC Handbook*, 1945, p. 41.

2. Briggs, III, p. 541.

3. Briggs, II, pp. 309ff.

4. Welch to Dinwiddie, 25.9.39.

5. See above, pp. 147, 151, 217.

6. Dinwiddie had asked Fenn to let it 'emphasize something of the Scottish character' (24.10.39).

7. Welch to Nicolls, 17.2.40.

8. Nicolls to Dinwiddie, 22.1.40.

9. Welch quoted Whitaker's *Almanack*.

10. Welch to Dinwiddie, 20.2.40.

11. Minute of meeting with Regional Directors, 1.8.40; Welch to all Directors, 14.8.40.

12. General Assembly of the Church of Scotland, 23.5.41.

13. Welch to Dinwiddie, 24.6.41.

14. Eric Saxon subsequently evolved an enormously successful programme, *The Parson Calls*, which featured Wilfrid Garlick, who became a nationwide personality comparable to W. H. Elliott. Haley however did not approve of such BBC personalities, least of all in religion. See CRAC Minutes, October 1945.

15. Welch to G. C. Beadle, Director of West Region, 15.6.45.

16. Scottish RAC Minutes, 25.10.44.

17. See R. H. W. Falconer, *The Kilt Beneath my Cassock*, 1978, pp. 57ff.

18. Macleod to Dinwiddie, 9.4.52.

19. Francis House to all Religious Broadcasting Organizers, 28.3.49.

20. See e.g. Saxon's article in the *BBC Handbook*, 1950, p. 60.

21. J. O. Greenwood to Mary Somerville, 20.11.51.

22. Greenwood to T. S. Eliot, 28.2.52.

23. Haley to Somerville, 22.11.50.

24. Falconer, Report to Dinwiddie, 14.11.50.A.

25. R. H. W. Falconer, *Success and Failure of a Radio Mission*, 1951, pp. 31f.

26. See LR 50/1885, 2097, 2199, 2247 and 2276.

27. Falconer, Report to Dinwiddie, 22.2.51.

28. Falconer, *Success and Failure*, p. 62.

29. Woodward had hoped that Welch would succeed him as Bishop of Bristol. (I am grateful to Bishop Mervyn Stockwood for this information.)

30. D'Arcy to Welch, 19.7.44.

31. Agnellus Andrew to Cardinal Griffin, 26.9.45.

32. Ibid.

33. See pp. 319ff. above.

34. Report of Manchester Conference, 9.10.46, p. 2, no. 2.

35. Andrew, Report to Low Week Meeting, 1947, p. 8.

36. Griffin to Andrew, 27.11.46.

37. See below, ch. 24.B.

38. Andrew to House, 4.10.49. See also *Catholic Herald*, 23.9.49.

39. The CCSB had asked Charles Raven to examine and approve both scheme and scripts before broadcasting was considered.

40. Andrew to House, 27.9.49.

41. Andrew, Report to Low Week Meeting, 1950, p. 5.

42. M. E. Aubrey, General Secretary of the Baptist Union, to House, 26.9.49.

43. Fisher to House, 22.4.50.

44. Ibid., 21.2.51.

45. See below, ch. 25.A(ii), on their evidence to the Beveridge Enquiry.

46. See below, ch. 23.C.

47. House, statement to Roman Catholic Conference, 24.5.50, no. 3.

48. See Andrew, Report to the Roman Catholic Hierarchy, 1951, p. 3.

49. Briggs, IV, *Sound and Vision*, 1979, pp. 50ff.

50. Welch to Gorham, 21.6.45.

51. LR 41/482, 17.12.41; 51/2506, 27.11.51; both gave an enormous 'hearing' figure.

52. George Barnes to Welch, 15.1.46.

53. Welch, Report to Secretariat, 31.3.46.

22. *Pressure on the Christian Cartel*

1. Welch to Temple, 16.3.44.

2. Welch to Nicolls, 7.4.44.

3. CRAC Minutes, 3.10.44.

4. Ibid.

5. Ibid., 7.3.44.

6. Haley to Nicolls, 28.11.44.

7. See Briggs, IV, p. 624.

8. Silvey to Haley, 26.4.46.

9. CRAC Minutes 1.10.46 (9).

10. The Home Board, 1941 (HB6/41); Welch to Foot, 24.2.43.

11. *The Freethinker*, 16.8.42. Welch had been approached by Hewlett Johnson, the so-called 'Red Dean' of Canterbury, with a document by the newly formed Radio Freedom League, *Radio Freedom League Calling* by Elizabeth Milford (April 1943). It enjoyed high-powered suport including that of J. B. Priestley, J. B. S. Haldane, Sybil Thorndike and H. G. Wells.

12. Kenneth Adam to F. C. C. Watts, 9.2.42.

13. C. E. M. Joad in the *New Statesman*, 31.1.42.

14. Hansard, 29.6.44, vol. 401, col. 925.

15. Maconachie to Julian Huxley, 29.9.43.

16. Welch to Nicolls, 3.9.43.

17. They appeared in *The Listener* in December 1943 (vol. 30, pp. 655f., 696f., 711f.)

18. Geoffrey Dearmer had once been hauled over the coals for replying rather curtly, 'We try to be Christian rather than orthodox' (15.3.40).

19. Welch to Foot, 24.2.44.

20. Haley, 26.2.44. He had said in 1943, 'The BBC must provide for all classes of listener equally.' See Briggs, IV, p. 28.

21. The following is taken from a 58-page verbatim report of the meeting by A. J. Lee of the BBC Secretariat, 16.6.46. Haley realized that this would be a crucial meeting and wanted every word recorded.

22. Haley had agreed to receive a deputation from the RPA, including Bertram Russell. Russell said to Haley, 'For so long I have listened to clergymen telling people that only the spread of Christianity can avert the decay of morale that I feel entitled to put the opposite proposition.' See Haley's paper for the Board of Governors, G73/46, April 1946.

23. CRAC, report by Secretariat, p. 26.

24. Ibid., p. 52.

25. See Appendix 5: 'Religious Minorities and Sects'.

26. Haley, G73/46, p. 7.

27. Report of RPA deputation, 15.10.46. Appendix to G73/46, 28.11.46.

28. Board of Governors, 28.11.46.

29. Board of Governors, G3/47; CRAC Minutes, 4.3.47.

30. *The Listener*, 13.3.47, vol. 37, p. 375.

31. J. B. S. Haldane, 'I Believe in Reason and Man', *The Listener*, 26.6.47; Bertram Russell, 'The Faith of a Rationalist', ibid., 29.5.47 (vol. 37, pp. 1004f., 826).

32. See the debate between Russell and Fr F. Copleston in *Why I am not a Christian*, Allen and Unwin 1957. The RPA warmly approved the debate.

33. LR 41/253, 8.5.41: 'By far the most generally held view is that broadcast sermons should not fail to deal with the application of Christianity to public affairs'.

34. See LR 45/3732, September 1945, 'Sunday Listening', reproduced in Appendix 7.

35. Haley to Wellington, 1.10.45.

36. LR 44/2765, 24.7.44: 'Within the churches, many confessed to considerable obscurity on the fundamentals. Outside the churches, the ignorance of some listeners would be difficult to overestimate' (para. 3).

37. Welch to Wellington, 25.4.46.

38. Fenn to Grayston, 13.3.46.

39. Welch to Wellington, 2.10.46.

40. Wellington to Rendall, 9.10.46.

41. Grayston to the RBD, 6.3.47.

42. See also Briggs, IV, ch. VI.1.

43. Grayston to A. C. F. Beales, 23.9.47.

23. Francis House and William Haley: New Policies

1. Briggs, IV, p. 764.

2. See below, ch. 25.

3. Midland Region RAC Minutes, 30.10.47.

4. See Grayston, Digest of Conference on Religious Broadcasting, Oxford, June 1947.

5. CRAC Minutes, 7.10.47.

6. LR 45/3732, August 1945.

7. Herbert Thurston, SJ, *The Church and Spiritualism*, Bruce Publication Co., Chicago 1933; cf. also G. W. Butterworth, *Spiritualism and Religion*, SPCK and Macmillan, New York, 1944.

8. Home Service Committee, 9.3.48.

9. See F. Buchman, *Remaking the World*, Blandford Press 1947, p. 156.

10. Barnes to Haley, 21.6.49. See also Tom Driberg, *The Mystery of MRA*, Secker and Warburg 1964.

11. Cf. above ch. 12.A, pp. 113ff.

12. Board of Governors, G113/41; Minutes 15.12.41. See e.g. *The Listener*, 22.5.47, vol. 37, p. 789.

13. Board of Governors, G114/48; Minutes 6.1.49.

14. See Appendix 5: 'Religious Minorities and Sects'.

15. Francis House, *The Church on the Air*, BBC 1949 (8 pages) is an abridgement of 'The Aims and Achievements of Religious Broadcasting: 1922–1948' (14 pages unpublished). The latter included 'Audiences for Religious Broadcasts, 1948', reproduced as Appendix 8 below.

16. See above, ch. 2.

17. House, 'Aims and Achievements', p. 6(c).

18. Ibid.

19. Haley, *The Responsibilities of Broadcasting*, 1948, p. 10.

20. House, op. cit., para. 12(d). See also his article in the *Church of England Newspaper*, 6.5.55, headlined: 'The Aim of Religious Broadcasting – to give the very best of the great Christian traditions.'

21. See Agnellus Andrew, transcript, 1980, p. 3.

22. House, transcript, 1982, p. 5.

23. These figures did not, of course, distinguish degrees of commitment.

24. See Briggs' comments on this section of House's document (IV, pp. 769ff.).

House also contributed to *English Life and Leisure* by Seebohm Rowntree, and G. R. Lavers, Longmans 1951. Their conclusion was that religious broadcasting was 'wholesome' but too clerical! (p. 362).

25. Aubrey complained to House in 1947 that religious broadcasting under Welch was 'too SCM – it was remote from the people'. House replied, as Welch might have done, 'Find us the prophets who can speak the language of the *People's Service*' (17.12.47).

26. CRAC Minutes, 5.10.48.

27. See Lord Simon of Wythenshawe, *The BBC from Within*, 1953, p. 311.

28. See above on the Concordat, ch. 16.E: 'Talkers and Radicals'.

29. Falconer to House, 30.9.48.

30. Oldham's friend Archie Craig had been the first General Secretary of the British Council of Churches, and both C. S. Woodward, the Chairman of CRAC, and F. A. Cockin were enthusiastic supporters.

31. E.g. House to Rendall, 26.7.50.

32. House, *The Church on the Air* [p. 8], called it 'probably the most valuable "supplement" to church teaching'.

33. See Haley's letter to Reith, 14.3.50, in C. Stuart, *The Reith Diaries*, 1975, p. 469.

34. See Val Gielgud, *Years in a Mirror*, 1965.

35. House to Barnes, 29.9.48.

36. House's report, 'Aims and Achievements', provided the basis for the BBC's deliberations. See Appendix 8.

37. BCC Minutes, 28.2.49, no. 4.

38. Harman Grisewood, *Broadcasting and Society*, 1949, p. 71.

39. BCC Minutes, 16.11.49.

40. Grisewood, op. cit., p. 64.

41. See below, ch. 26.C.

42. Minutes of Cockin's Committee, 12.1.50, no. 6.

43. Ibid., p. 5.

44. BCC, *Christianity and Broadcasting*, 1950, p. 13.

45. Minutes, 12.1.50, no. 5 (iii).

46. *Christianity and Broadcasting*, pp. 25f.

47. Cockin to Haley, 27.10.50.

24. Post-war Innovations

1. *BBC Year Book*, 1946, p. 15.

2. See LR 41/496, 24.12.41, and LR 50/2279, 16.11.50.

3. House to the RBD, 20.9.46.

4. Welch, 'Religion and the Radio', *BBC Quarterly*, October 1946.

5. For this reason Welch had urged the BBC to purchase All Souls, Langham Place; the RBD would then be directly involved in parish work.

6. J. S. Whale, digest of listeners' letters, 1941.

7. Tom Chalmers to House, 11.8.48.

8. LR 50/1121, 8.6.50; see also Appendix 8.

9. House to Norman Collins, 27.9.48.

10. See above, ch. 21.C.

11. House to Haley, 31.10.51.

12. Tatlock to Somerville, 21.10.51.

13. Mai Jones to Chalmers, 13.5.48.
14. See above, pp. 276f.
15. Haley to Somerville, 15.5.51.
16. House to Chalmers, 12.9.49.
17. House, Press release (BBC Press Service No. 27011), 14.10.48.
18. Board of Governors Minutes, 8.7.48; Haley to Somerville, 8.8.48.
19. Sunday Committee Minutes, 27.7.23.
20. See above, ch. 16.A, pp. 148f.
21. North Region RAC Minutes, 3.12.45. In a speech to a Diocesan Conference in 1944 Welch had said: 'It is impossible to broadcast a sacrament; we don't propose to invade the sacramental activities of the church.'
22. Welch to Fenn, 14.10.41: 'Anglicans . . . deeply resent Matins and Evensong being taken as representative.'
23. Lyonnaise Society for the Broadcast Mass, Lyon 1946.
24. CRAC Minutes, 24.2.48.
25. Agnellus Andrew, transcript, 1979.
26. Private note to House from the Clerk to the Board of Governors, 12.7.48.
27. Board of Governors Minutes, 8.7.48.
28. The decision was approved by the Lambeth Bishops' Committee in January 1949, as Woodward informed House, 12.1.49. (Minutes of this Committee are under a 50-year restriction.) See also Woodward to Fisher, 12.11.48 (Fisher Papers, vol. 46).
29. Welsh RAC Minutes, 25.11.48.
30. *Radio Times*, 17.12.48.
31. Written Archive Centre Script, 17.4.49.
32. Convocation of Canterbury, Proceedings, 18.5.49.
33. *Daily Telegraph*, 19.5.49.
34. General Assembly of the Presbyterian Church of England, Proceedings, 1949.
35. Report of BBC-Methodist Consultations, 27.9.49. Benson-Perkins was in the chair; Grayston was the BBC representative.
36. I Corinthians 11.26.
37. R. L. Child to E. H. Robertson, 19.9.49.
38. Baptist Union of Scotland, September 1949.
39. See W. H. Pike, 'Holy Communion by Radio', in the *Observer* (of the Presbyterian Church of Canada), 15.2.49.
40. House to Cardinal Heenan, 5.10.49.
41. *The Christian World*, 27.10.49.
42. Manson to House, 6.2.50.
43. Proceedings of the Public Worship Committee of the Church of Scotland, Edinburgh, 23.5.50.
44. Listener Research Returns, 26.12.48; 2.1.49 (Home Service) and 25.12.48 (Light Programme).
45. Board of Governors, G75/50, 3.5.50.
46. Board of Governors Minutes, 25.5.50.
47. E. R. Appleton, Welsh Regional Director, to Reith, 1.5.33.
48. See ch. 2 above.
49. Welch to Nicolls, 21.5.41.
50. See above ch. 10.E.
51. Welch to Stanton, 16.12.40.

52. Welch to Nicolls, 21.5.41.
53. Welch to Stanton, 26.2.41.
54. See ch. 10.G.
55. Welch to Iremonger, 3.9.40.
56. Iremonger complained to Walford Davies (23.8.40) that Stanton's only experience of congregational singing was a school chapel where, with the right direction, boys could be made to sing anything!
57. Welch to Iremonger, 17.5.41.
58. Hymn Book Committee, Minutes, 15.7.41, no. 2.
59. Nicolls, document for the Home Board, 18.8.41.
60. Ibid.
61. Cyril Taylor, transcript, 1981.
62. Stanton to Welch, 11.3.42..
63. In the *English Hymnal*, no. 646.
64. Millar Patrick to Welch, 3.5.45.
65. Taylor to the Hymn Book Committee, 1.8.44.
66. Welch to the Music Committee, 31.8.44.
67. Ibid.
68. See *Congregational Praise*, Independent Press 1951, p. iii.
69. E. Milner-White had collaborated with G. W. Briggs in *Daily Prayer*, OUP 1941.
70. Milner-White, report to Welch, summer 1945.
71. Ibid.
72. Welch to Dinwiddie, 18.3.46.
73. See above, ch. 22.B.
74. Minutes, 10.1.47, no. 4.
75. Nicolls to Haley, 14.2.47.
76. CRAC Minutes, 4.3.47; 7.10.47.
77. Scottish RAC Minutes, 25.3.47.
78. Stanton to Taylor, 20.3.47: 'The poor old man was sitting in an overcoat and no fire; carpet slippers, the picture of utter forlornness. . . . There he was laboriously copying out some orchestral parts . . . hardly a job for England's most distinguished composer.'
79. Iremonger to Taylor, 14.5.47.
80. Iremonger to Nicolls, 28.7.47.
81. Welch to Taylor, 22.5.47.
82. Stanton to Taylor, May 1947.
83. Ibid., 31.5.47.
84. Ibid., 16.6.47.
85. Hymn Book Committee Minutes, 30.9.47, no. 5.
86. Iremonger to Nicolls, 28.2.48.
87. Sir Hugh Allen had died, and the BBC subcommittee had no chairman.
88. Music Committee, Minutes, 30.12.48, no. 5.
89. House to Nicolls, 1.2.49.
90. Cumberlege to Nicolls, 15.3.49.
91. G. Strode, General Manager of Publications, to Nicolls, 25.7.49.
92. Minutes, 3.8.50, no. 2.
93. House to Grisewood, 4.7.51.
94. Haley to Reith, 26.9.51.
95. *The Christian World*, 11.10.51.

96. Dean Inge in the *Evening Standard*, 5.10.51.
97. *The Friend*, 22.10.51.
98. *English Church Music*, vol. 22, January 1952.
99. *Journal of Education*, March 1952.
100. There are no statistics which tell how far this was achieved, but Edwin Cox, until 1983 Reader in Religious Education in the Institute of Education, University of London, remembers how his public school, Cheltenham, was attracted to the book for chapel use, as were some universities and teacher training colleges. The University Church in Oxford took the book, largely because the Vicar, R. S. Lee, had been Overseas Religious Broadcasting Organizer.
101. C. V. Taylor, transcript, March 1978.
102. House to Regional Directors, 15.10.51.
103. In 1947 there were very few television sets (approximately 35,000), and reception was limited to the London area.
104. CRAC Minutes, 28.2.46.
105. Welch to Garbett, 23.3.43.
106. Haley to Nicolls, 10.2.48.
107. CRAC Minutes, 24.2.48.
108. Christmas Day Planning Document, 17.8.48.
109. CRAC Minutes, 24.2.48, Appendix B.
110. Barnes to House, 28.7.49.
111. See the TV Programme Review in *Presbyterian Life*, Philadelphia, 28.5.49.
112. See *Broadcasting House*, 1932, p. 22.
113. See Briggs, IV, pp. 226ff.
114. House to the RBD, 3.11.49.
115. Garbett to House, 13.1.50.
116. Don to House, 20.3.50; see also Briggs, IV, p. 784.
117. C. McGivern to Gorham, 31.3.50.
118. Board of Governors, G115/50, 20.7.50.
119. S. J. de Lotbinière to producers of Outside Broadcasts, 15.8.51.
120. See also Briggs, IV, pp. 785ff.
121. BCC, *Christianity and Broadcasting*, 1950, p. 39.

25. The Beveridge Enquiry: Clamour and Reprieve, 1949–1951

1. See Briggs, IV, p. 298.
2. *Tribune*, 30.12.49.
3. Briggs, IV, pp. 296 and 787.
4. Joseph Reeves to Haley, 20.2.48.
5. Haley to Reeves, 9.3.48.
6. LR 46/4322. 12.2.46, had made it clear that at that time straight talks were more acceptable.
7. Grayston, Policy Document, 12.1.46.
8. Board of Governors Minutes, 6.1.49.
9. Board of Governors Paper G70/50.
10. CRAC Minutes, 3.10.50.
11. Board of Governors Paper G 61/50, 5.4.50.
12. The evidence given to the Beveridge Committee is published (separately from the Report) as *Appendix H: Memoranda Submitted to the Committee*, Cmd. 8117, 1951.

13. Part I (pp. 7–27) of the BCC report, *Christianity and Broadcasting*, 1950, is reprinted in Cmd. 8117, pp. 410–18.

14. Para. 7, *Christianity and Broadcasting*, p. 14 = Cmd. 8117, p. 412.

15. Para. 30, p. 25 = p. 417.

16. Para. 19, p. 20 = p. 415.

17. Para. 21, p. 21 = p. 415.

18. Recommendation (c), p. 26 = p. 418.

19. Verbatim report by Treasury Official Reporter, 4.5.50.

20. Ibid., p. 7.

21. Ibid.

22. Ibid., p. 13.

23. See above, ch. 22.B, 'Controversy: Policy Change, 1947'.

24. See above, ch. 23.B, 'Clamouring Sects'.

25. For the Roman Catholic submission see Cmd. 8117, pp. 419–22.

26. Ibid., p. 421, para. 4(c).

27. Agnellus Andrew believed that the preoccupation with numbers was a reaction to Welch's pressure on the Roman Catholics to bury their identity in the predominantly Protestant BBC. Andrew, transcript, 1979.

28. See Briggs, IV, ch. IV. 2, pp. 311–43, 'The BBC Evidence'.

29. General Survey of the Broadcasting Service, paras. 65–7, Cmd. 8117, pp. 22f. It had essentially been prepared by Woodward, Masterson, and J. T. Christie, the Principal of Jesus College, Oxford, who had prepared the first draft.

30. Cmd. 8117, pp. 289–91.

31. Ibid., p. 290, para. 4(i).

32. J. W. C. Wand, Bishop of London, had campaigned alongside the Roman Catholics for an allocation based on numbers.

33. Cmd. 8117, p. 290, Para. 4 (iib).

34. Ibid.

35. Ibid., para. 4 (iia).

36. Unitarian evidence, ibid., pp. 453–6.

37. Briggs, IV, p. 355.

38. Christian Scientists' evidence, Cmd. 8117, p. 446.

39. The Spiritualist National Union, ibid., p. 447.

40. The Ethical Union, ibid., p. 448.

41. Evidence of the Rationalist Press Association, ibid., pp. 450–52.

42. Ibid., p. 451.

43. Currie, Gilbert and Horsley, *Churches and Churchgoers*, pp. 194f.

44. BCC, *Christianity and Broadcasting*, p. 11.

45. See p. 408 above.

46. CRAC Minutes, 6.3.51. Archbishop Fisher complained to House that he was 'besieged' by correspondents claiming that the Roman Catholics were in league with the Free Churches 'exploiting their position in the BBC to deplete the Church of England services' (22.4.50). House produced figures to refute these claims.

47. House, 'Aims and Achievements', p. 3.

48. CRAC 'Mainstream' document, 9.3.51.

49. As the BCC Commission had upheld.

50. CRAC Minutes, 6.3.51.

51. The 'two named exceptions' were the Unitarians and the Jews. House to Haley, 9.3.51.

52. The Jehovah's Witnesses had always been regarded by CRAC as 'subversive'.

53. The Jews had always understood and accepted this ruling. Whilst CRAC had put the Jews alongside the 'clamouring sects' and would not advise in their favour, the Corporation had allowed them four 'festival' talks, including the Passover talk by the Chief Rabbi, each year. CRAC Minutes, 1.10.42. Relations between the Department and the Chief Rabbi were always cordial.

54. CRAC Minutes, 6.3.51.

55. Wand to House, 26.1.51.

56. House to Wand, 29.1.51.

57. The Beveridge Report, Cmd. 8116, p. 65, para. 252.

58. *Christianity and Broadcasting*, p. 14.

59. Board of Governors Paper G112/51.I(IVB), 19.6.51.

60. Woodward to W. G. Moore of St John's College, Oxford, 2.3.51.

61. Minutes of Roman Catholic discussion on Beveridge, June 1951.

62. Woodward to Haley, 19.7.51. See also Hansard, 19.7.51, vol. 490, cols. 142–3ff.

63. Memorandum on the Report of the Broadcasting Committee, 1949, Cmd. 8291, 1951.

64. See Briggs, IV, pp. 410ff. Hansard, 25.7.51, vol. 172 (Lords), cols. 1213ff.

65. Briggs, IV, p. 420.

66. Lord Simon, the Chairman, thought the Governors' decision 'inevitable, in view of public opinion' (*The BBC from Within*, 1953, p. 310). See also Board of Governors' Minutes, 25.10.51, 22.11.51 and 17.1.52.

67. For the complex political background to the reception of the Report, see Briggs, IV, ch. IV.5, pp. 393–420.

68. See above, ch. 2.

26. Moral Values: Corporation Initiatives

1. G. M. Trevelyan, *English Literature and its Readers*, OUP 1952.

2. See above, ch. 22.

3. Sunday Committee Minutes, 5.6.23.

4. House, 'Basis of the BBC's Policy' (to Haley, 18.4.50.), p. 3, 5(c).

5. Mary Somerville to Harman Grisewood, 23.5.52.

6. *The Listener*, 4.1.51, vol. 45, p. 18.

7. Report of Deputation and Memorandum from the Parliamentary Committee for Freedom of Religious Controversy, 18.10.51.

8. Board of Governors Minutes, 17.1.52, no. 3a.

9. Minutes of RBD meeting with Chalmers, 31.10.50; Haley to Reith, 2.10.51 (in Stuart, *The Reith Diaries*, 1975, p. 477).

10. See above, ch. 22.B.

11. In October 1950 E. H. Robertson and House had organized in Chichester a European conference on religious broadcasting. The statement of aims published later made it quite clear that 'the function of religious broadcasting is not considered to be that of raising doubts' (Chichester Informal Conference, October 1950, BBC No 4).

12. Robertson to the Department, 12.9.51.

13. See above, ch. 19.C.

14. Somerville to Bliss, 12.2.51.

15. Programme Contracts, 28.2.51.
16. G. Barnes to Bliss, 25.6.51.
17. Bliss to Somerville, 15.9.51.
18. Cockin to Lord Simon, 24.9.51.
19. Board of Governors Minutes, 19.1.52, 3(f).
20. CRAC Minutes, 31.1.52, no. 5.
21. See Barbara Wootton, *Testament of Social Science*, Allen and Unwin 1950, p. 158.
22. Somerville to Haley, 15.2.52.
23. Board of Governors Paper, G18/52, 13.2.52, and Minutes, 28.2.52.
24. Minutes, ibid., no. 3.
25. Grisewood to Ian Jacob, 8.12.52.
26. Michael Stephens to Somerville, 20.2.52.
27. Somerville to Kenneth Adam (Controller, Light Programme), 20.6.52.
28. CRAC Minutes, 31.1.52 (5).
29. Report to Governors, G 40/53, 19.3.53, no. 6.
30. Ronald Lewin to Somerville, 6.1.53.
31. Home Service Board Minutes, 24.8.51.
32. House to E. H. Robertson, 23.1.53.
33. Wellington to Somerville, 26.5.52.
34. K. Bliss, reports to Governors, September 1951, paras. 10, 20, 19; 21.5.53, p. 1.
35. Ibid., p. 6, para. 18.
36. BCC evidence to Beveridge Committee, verbatim report, 4.5.50, p. 9.
37. Bliss, report to Somerville, 17.11.52.
38. Cockin to Bliss, 19.8.52.
39. CRAC Minutes, 24.10.52, no. 4.
40. Bliss, statement to CRAC, 24.10.52.
41. The English translations of Karl Heim, *Christian Faith and Natural Science* and *The Transformation of the Scientific World View*, were both published by SCM Press in 1953.
42. Oldham told Baillie (13.6.52) that if he (Baillie) could not attend he had Emil Brunner in reserve.
43. A. MacIntyre to Bliss, 23.7.52.
44. Bliss, report, 21.5.53, p. 2.
45. Ibid., p. 4.
46. Sir Herbert Read to Bliss, 16.10.52.
47. V. A. Demant to Bliss, 21.12.52.
48. Bliss, op. cit., p. 7.
49. Lorna Moore to Somerville, 13.3.53.
50. Bliss, op. cit., p. 8.
51. Home Service Meeting, 23.12.52, no. 1668.
52. Michael Polanyi, *Personal Knowledge* (Gifford Lectures for 1951), Routledge and Kegan Paul 1958.
53. See Briggs, IV, pp. 444ff. The BBC also had a new Chairman of Governors, Sir Alexander Cadogan; he replaced Lord Simon, who like Haley had always shown a particular interest in religious policy.
54. Haley to House, 11.11.52.
55. See the *Sunday Times* and *The Observer*, 8.2.53, and *New Statesman*, 14.2.53.
56. Roy Pascal to Bliss, 22.1.53.

57. Ibid., 4.2.53.
58. Bliss, report, 21.5.53, p. 8.
59. Oldham to Somerville, 9.2.53.
60. Ibid.
61. Edward Crankshaw to Bliss, 31.1.53.
62. Bliss to Hugh Trevor-Roper, 9.2.53.
63. Bliss, report, 21.5.53, p. 8.
64. Oldham to Bliss, 25.2.53, p. 3, quoting A. MacIntyre.
65. Bliss to Somerville, 5.5.53.
66. Oldham to Bliss, 25.2.53.
67. Haley to General Advisory Committee, 5.2.51 (GAC Paper no. 163).
68. GAC 11.3.53, p. 37.
69. *The Universe*, 27.3.53.
70. LR 53/554, 9.4.53.
71. Board of Governors Paper G112/51, para. 22.
72. Oldham to Bliss, 18.9.52.
73. Bliss to J. A. Scupham, Head of Schools Broadcasting, 28.10.53.
74. Lorna Moore to Somerville, 27.5.53.
75. Philip Unwin to Bliss, 14.5.53.
76. The *Manchester Guardian* had commended Bliss's scripts as 'polished and logical', 9.2.53.
77. See Briggs, IV, p. 582; see also E. L. E. Pawley, *BBC Engineering 1922–1972*, BBC 1972, pp. 389ff., on the development of the tape recorder.
78. Bliss, report, October 1953, p. 4; see also above, ch. 17.C.
79. Grisewood to Somerville, note on 'Evolution', 12.1.53, p. 2.
80. See *The Listener*, 9.3.50, vol. 43, pp. 419ff.
81. Haley to Reith, 4.6.51.
82. Michael Polanyi, *Science, Faith and Society*, OUP 1946.
83. Bliss, report, 5.1.54.
84. Home Service Board Minutes, 20.8.54, nos. 669 and 821.
85. Board of Governors Paper G 42/53, 8.4.53.
86. James Thornton to Grisewood, 12.4.54.
87. Robertson to Thornton, 28.7.54.
88. Thornton, report of meeting, 9.11.54.
89. Somerville to Thornton, 11.11.54.
90. Weltman to Somerville, 9.9.54.
91. House to Somerville, 11.10.54.
92. Margaret Knight, *Morals without Religion*, 1955, p. 33.
93. Ibid., p. 35.
94. Lord Horder and others, *Man without God*, 1952.
95. Bliss to Mrs Jenny Morton, 10.11.54.
96. Duty Officer's report to Grisewood, 13.1.55.
97. Knight, op. cit., p. 39.
98. *Sunday Graphic*, 9.1.55.
99. *Daily Telegraph*, 20. 1.55.
100. *The Times*, 22.1.55.
101. Board of Governors Minutes, 20.1.55, no. 26; verbatim report, 24.1.55.
102. Roche to Thornton, 12.1.55. House also supported the contention that there could be a contravention of the 1947 policy in Mrs Knight's talks.
103. See Briggs, IV, pp. 801ff.

104. Quoted by Knight, op. cit., pp. 56f.
105. Cockin in *The Observer*, 27.2.55.
106. Sayers in the *Daily Telegraph*, 12.1.55.
107. 'For two talks on a serious subject broadcast fairly late in the evening, nearly 1600 letters is phenomenal . . . it is the largest number of letters ever received about a broadcast talk' (Report by Kathleen Haacke, Secretary of the Programme Correspondence Section, 18.1.55).
108. CRAC Minutes, 1.3.55, no. 4.
109. See above, ch. 22.B.
110. House to Somerville, 18.1.55.
111. Winston Churchill, letter to the Bishop of Coventry, a copy of which he sent to Jacob.
112. *Illustrated London News*, 29.1.55.
113. Talks Editorial Board Minutes, 20.1.55.
114. Grisewood to Wellington (Director of Sound Broadcasting), 19.9.55.
115. Knight, op. cit., pp. 51ff., 'The Reaction'.
116. Weltman to Knight, 2.12.55.
117. Four programmes were broadcast, two in February and two in November 1956.
118. Grisewood to Somerville, 23.3.55.
119. Ibid.
120. Agnellus Andrew to Grisewood, 17.1.55.
121. Somerville to Jacob, 18.1.55.
122. Bliss to Thornton, 3.11.56.
123. *Foundations of Western Values*, see *The Listener*, 21.4 to 26.5.55, vol. 53, pp. 704f., 752f., 786f., 874 and 923.
124. Somerville to Welch, 8.7.55.
125. Kathleen Bliss's contract ended in November 1956. Though Thornton told her that the Fundamental Debate was not threatened 'in any root and branch sort of way' (9.11.56), the initiative as she had known it was effectively over. Just over a year later, following some work with the YWCA, she became Secretary of the Church of England's Board of Education.
126. House to R. S. Lee, 21.12.54.
127. On Roy McKay's appointment see below, ch. 31.C.
128. Welch, now in Africa, was much impressed with Robertson's work; he wrote to House (6.9.52): 'His Third Programme stuff is so good; you may well have in him a better than Grayston or Fenn.'
129. House to R. S. Lee, 21.12.54.
130. McKay to Grisewood, 18.6.56.
131. See Roy McKay, *Take Care of the Sense: Reflections on Religious Broadcasting*, 1964.

27. Missions: Departmental Experiments

1. Welch, an essay to J. H. Oldham, 16.1.45.
2. See Proceedings of RBD Conference, June 1950, section IV (10).
3. J. O. Greenwood to Martin Browne, 15.6.51.
4. Greenwood to Somerville, 20.11.51.
5. J. L. Forsyth in the *Radio Times*, 26.11.50.
6. Delderfield's friend, the poet John Pudney, passed on this comment from

Iremonger, 1.6.38.

7. Conference report by Greenwood, 20.5.52, section 4.

8. Conference statement, 10.5.52.

9. House later lamented to Wellington that Shaw's *Adventures of a Black Girl in her Search for God* had not instead been written by a biblical scholar!

10. S. Pritchard, Notes to Contributors [to *Sunday Half Hour*], July 1950.

11. Richard Tatlock to House, 24.10.51.

12. Minutes of meeting with Adam, 21.11.51.

13. Falconer to all RBD staff, 30.11.51.

14. This was, however, allowed in the broadcasting of the five-minute daily service in the Overseas Programme.

15. R. Dougall to House, 22.1.52.

16. Most notable was Tom Rees of Hildenborough Hall, Kent, a prominent evangelist whose Albert Hall rallies were drawing great numbers, especially from the churches.

17. *In This Sign Conquer* (Lent pamphlet, BBC 1952).

18. See Falconer, *The Kilt Beneath my Cassock*, ch. 8.

19. Report to Scottish RAC (SRAC/5/52 B), 14.10.52.

20. Ibid.

21. House in *The Listener*, 10.1.52, vol. 47, p. 62.

22. House to David Say, 10.7.52.

23. See *Towards the Conversion of England*, para. 138, and House in *Modern Churchman*, September 1952.

24. CRAC Minutes, 24.10.52, no. 11.

25. Richard Tatlock, Report to Conference on 'Parochial Mission and Religious Broadcasting', Mirfield, April 1953.

26. House to Hugh Gough, 23.4.53.

27. Falconer to Head of Scottish Programmes, 6.8.53; BBC/Church of Scotland Statement, 26.1.53.

28. Conference on 'pre-evangelism', verbatim report, 2.6.54.

29. Jacob to Grisewood, 13.5.52.

30. MacLeod called himself 'a Soperman, socialist, pacifist, and altogether terrible!' (to Malcolm Muggeridge, 4.6.54).

31. See below, p. 476.

32. Report by House to CRAC, 28.10.54.

33. See *Baptist Times*, 14.10.54.

34. H. Grisewood, 'Christian Communication – Word and Image', paper delivered to an Audio-Visual Consultation, World Council of Churches, Bossey, May 1956 (*Proceedings*, pp. 28ff.).

35. See above, ch. 25.

36. See also *BBC Handbook* for 1956, pp. 72ff.

37. Grisewood to J. H. Lloyd, Secretary of the Humanist Council, 17.11.54 and 6.12.54.

38. Lloyd to Somerville, 20.4.55. See also above, ch. 26.D.

39. Weltman to Thornton (Controller of Talks), 4.5.55.

40. Memorandum from the Humanist Association to the BBC, 18.3.58, Appendix I.

41. Conference on 'pre-evangelism', Report, 16.7.54, no. 3.

42. Board of Governors Minutes, 17.1.52, no. 3.

43. *Religious Broadcasting and the Public*, BBC 1955. See also Robert Silvey, *Who's*

Listening?, 1974, p. 150.

44. Briggs, IV, p. 779.

45. Robert Silvey, 'The Audiences for Religious Broadcasts', in *Religion on the Air*, 1955, pp. 5–14.

46. Ibid., p. 14.

47. *Religious Broadcasting and the Public*, Part II 5(e).

48. Ibid., Part III 18(c).

49. See above, ch. 17.C.

50. *Religious Broadcasting and the Public*, Part III 12.

51. Ibid., Part III 28.

52. See above, ch. 17.C.

53. *Religious Broadcasting and the Public*, Part V 15.

54. CRAC Minutes, 1.3.55.

55. Conference on 'pre-evangelism': Appendix to Report; CRAC Minutes, 1.3.55.

56. Ibid.

57. House to Thornton, 18.1.55.

58. Falconer, *The Kilt Beneath my Cassock*, p. 78.

59. CRAC Minutes, 28.10.54.

60. Conference on Religious Broadcasting and Mission, 14–18.6.54, Report, no. 5.

61. See Marshall Frady, *Billy Graham*, Hodder and Stoughton 1979; John Pollock, *Billy Graham*, Hodder and Stoughton 1966.

62. Eric Fenn to House, 20.7.54.

63. BBC Secretariat Document, 1955, from figures supplied by the Billy Graham Organization.

64. C. F. Beale to Cecil McGivern, Controller of TV, 29.6.55. Cf. Scottish RAC (SRAC/4/55), 1.11.55.

65. Luke 11.34 (New English Bible).

66. Falconer to House, 16.5.55.

28. The New Medium

1. George Barnes, *Television Broadcasting* (address to the BCC, 24.9.52), BBC 1952, p. 3; BCC, *Christianity and Broadcasting*, 1950, p. 39.

2. Silvey to Nicolls, 18.6.47, quoted by Briggs, IV, p. 217.

29. BBC Expansion

1. T. S. Eliot in *The Times*, 20.12.50.

2. Norman Collins, ibid., 23.12.50.

3. F. A. Cockin, to a discussion group in Swindon, 10.10.50.

4. Conference on, 'TV: Help or Hindrance', 12.10.51, reported in *The Schoolmaster*, 18.10.51.

5. An open letter to Francis House, *Daily Graphic*, 31.1.51.

6. *The London Churchman* (the magazine of the Diocese of London), November 1950.

7. Board of Governors Minutes, 20.7.50.

8. See p. 401 above.

9. *Methodist Recorder*, 6.12.51.

10. *Methodist Recorder*, 29.6.50.
11. Scottish RAC Minutes, 29.5.51; Dinwiddie to Barnes, 4.12.51.
12. House to Barnes, 3.1.52.
13. Report in the *Methodist Recorder*, 28.2.52.
14. See Briggs, IV, ch. V.3, esp. pp. 491–5.
15. Colin Beale, report of visit to Paris, 25–28.1.52.
16. 'Spoken Word' Meeting, Minutes, 19.10.51.
17. Beale, report to CRAC, 'Scope and Character of Religious TV', 31.1.52, p. 4.
18. See above, ch. 24.B.
19. Beale, op. cit., Appendix 2.
20. CRAC Minutes, 31.1.52.
21. House, paper for CRAC, 31.1.52, no. 2.
22. Board of Governors Paper G58/52.
23. Board of Governors Minutes, 17.7.52, no. 125.
24. Agnellus Andrew, report, Low Week, 1953, p. 3.
25. Archbishop Fisher, address to SPCK, 6.3.52.
26. Garbett to House, 26.9.52.
27. Ibid., 28.5.52.
28. *The Scotsman*, 17.3.52; Falconer, *The Kilt Beneath my Cassock*, pp. 84ff.
29. Andrew, op. cit., p. 2.

30. Protecting the Sacred

1. For detailed technical and other observations see Briggs, IV, ch. V.2, pp. 457ff.
2. Barnes, *Television Broadcasting*, p. 15.
3. See *The Scotsman*, 21.7.52.
4. House to the RBD, 11.7.52.
5. Cyril Taylor to House, 15.7.52.
6. Barnes to McGivern, 27.2.53.
7. Agnellus Andrew to House, 8.8.52.
8. CRAC Minutes, 24.10.52.
9. Report of Haley's meeting with the Archbishops, 22.7.52.
10. House, transcript, January 1982.
11. Hansard, 28.10.52, vol. 505, col. 1742.
12. Lord Woolton (Churchill's Private Secretary) to Barnes, 14.10.52.
13. Barnes to Lotbinière, 9.12.52.
14. House, report of meeting with Fisher, 18.12.52.
15. Peter Dimmock, report to Barnes, 2.3.53.
16. William Purcell, *Fisher of Lambeth*, 1969, pp. 238ff.
17. House to Cardinal Griffin, 10.2.53. Griffin refused to participate in the Memorial Service for George VI in the Concert Hall.
18. A. Andrew, Report to the Roman Catholic hierarchy, Low Week 1953–54, p. 4.
19. Presbyterian Church of Wales, reported in the *Western Mail*, 29.4.54.
20. *Manchester Guardian*, 11.1.54.
21. See John Heenan, *Crown of Thorns*, 1974, pp. 79–91.
22. See above, ch. 27.
23. Thomas Goodall (Methodist Press Officer), 17.1.52; and in the *Daily Telegraph*, 17.3.52.

24. Falconer to House, 5.1.53.
25. House, statistics for CRAC, 2.3.53.
26. CRAC Minutes, 3.3.53, no. 5.
27. The seeds for later programmes such as *Songs of Praise* and *Stars on Sunday* were sown by CRAC early in 1953.
28. House to Barnes, 28.4.53.
29. Barnes to McGivern, 28.12.53.
30. CRAC Minutes, October 1953.
31. Beale, Preliminary Report, November 1953.
32. See Briggs, IV, p. 283.
33. Beale to the RBD, 9.7.54.
34. F. H. Littman, Assistant Head of Listener Research, to McGivern, 8.12.53; E. H. Robertson to House, 15.3.54. See also Currie, Gilbert and Horsley, *Churches and Churchgoers*, p. 89, on the decline of Sunday school attendance.
35. Bishop Wynn to House, 1.3.54.
36. Board of Management, Minutes, 16.8.54 (405).
37. Freda Lingstrom to McGivern, 21.5.54.
38. Joy Harington to McGivern, 1.9.54.
39. Harington to House, 11.10.54.
40. Scupham to McGivern, 9.11.54.
41. Harington to Lingstrom, 20.12.54.
42. E. V. Rieu's modern translation of the Gospels had been published by Penguin Books in 1952.
43. Report of consultation on *Jesus of Nazareth*, 6.7.55.
44. Joy Harington, *Jesus of Nazareth*, Introduction to the American edition, Doubleday, New York 1957, pp. 5ff.
45. House to Harington, 8.10.54.
46. Donald Soper in *Illustrated*, 3.3.56.
47. S. Pritchard to Colin Beale, 21.2.56.
48. Viewer Research had as yet no means for assessing how many children were watching.
49. For Episode 1, see VR/56/93; for Episode 8, VR/56/172.
50. Programme Organization Report, 16.3.56.
51. Jacob to Harington, 1.4.56.
52. Lingstrom, Report, 22.8.56; see also *Times Educational Supplement*, 21.12.56.
53. McKay to Lingstrom, 19.6.56.
54. Don Cupitt and Peter Armstrong, *Who was Jesus?*, BBC 1977.
55. Lingstrom, op. cit., p. 14.

31. Competitive Television: the End of Radio Supremacy

1. BCC, *Christianity and Broadcasting*, p. 26, para. 30(g).
2. Ibid., p. 15, para. 10. See also Appendix 5: Religious Minorities and Sects.
3. T. S. Eliot in *The Times*, 20.12.50.
4. Fisher in the *Manchester Guardian*, 20.9.52.
5. Barnes, *Television Broadcasting*, 1952, p. 10.
6. See *The Schoolmaster*, 18.10.51.
7. Barnes, op. cit., p. 9.
8. *Broadcasting. Memorandum of the Report of the Broadcasting Committee* (Cmd. 8550), 1952.

9. Garbett reported in *The Times*, 7.11.52.

10. For a detailed analysis of the progress of the debates in Parliament, Press and nation, see Briggs, IV, chs. V.1. and VII; see also Bernard Sendall, *History of Independent Television in Britain*: I *Origin and Foundation, 1946–62*, 1982.

11. Cockin in *The Times*, 2.4.52.

12. Hansard, House of Lords, 2.7.53, vol. 183, cols. 115f.

13. BCC press release, 2.7.53.

14. Fisher to Canterbury Diocesan Conference, 30.11.53.

15. Free Church leaders in *The Times*, 18.7.53.

16. See Briggs, IV, pp. 911ff.

17. *The Tablet*, 4.7.53.

18. *Catholic Herald*, 17.7.53.

19. *Memorandum on Television Policy* (Cmd. 9005), 13.11.53.

20. Ibid., para. 10(a).

21. *Lutheran Hour News* (British edition), July 1953.

22. Hansard, House of Lords, 25.11.53, vol. 184, col. 559.

23. BCC Executive Minutes, 2.12.53.

24. Assistant Postmaster-General to David Say, 11.1.54.

25. Church Assembly, Proceedings, 18.2.54, vol. 34, p. 101.

26. BCC Delegation, 17.2.54; Say's report to Executive, 4.3.54.

27. See Briggs, IV, pp. 927f.

28. National Television Council press release, 12.3.54.

29. Wand to the Postmaster-General, 9.3.54.

30. CRAC Minutes, 2.3.54.

31. Postmaster-General to Wand, 19.3.54.

32. Fisher to Say, 26.2.54.

33. Ibid., 22.1.54.

34. Randall Phillips, Procurator of the Church of Scotland, to Fisher and James Stewart, Secretary of State for Scotland, 7.4.54.

35. General Administrative Committee of the Church of Scotland, Minutes, 20.4.54.

36. Proceedings of Parliamentary Committee, 20.5.54, vol. 184, no. 10, col. 2375.

37. Postmaster-General to Cockin, 10.6.54.

38. Hansard, House of Lords, 30.6.54, vol. 188, col. 262.

39. Ibid., cols. 353f.

40. Fisher to Say, 2.7.54.

41. House to Cockin, 9.7.54.

42. Television Act, 1954, Section 3 (4a).

43. CRAC Minutes, 28.10.54.

44. Sir Kenneth Clark to Cockin, 9.3.55.

45. Board of Governors Minutes, 17.3.55, 71(c).

46. Cockin to House, 7.6.55.

47. House to Deane, 31.1.55.

48. House to Barnes, 6.5.55.

49. Report of meeting with Sir Kenneth Clark, 17.6.55.

50. Ben Barnett to Jacob, 15.7.55.

51. Jacob to Barnett, 19.7.55.

52. Say to Cockin, 9.5.55.

53. Cockin to Kenneth Slack, the newly-appointed General Secretary of BCC, 6.9.55.

54. *Church Times*, 3.6.55.
55. See Briggs, IV, ch. VII, and Sendall, *History of Independent Television* I.
56. ITA Minutes, 4.10.55.
57. Fraser to Cockin, 12.10.55.
58. CRAC Minutes, 13.10.55.
59. CRAC, Minutes of meeting with Clark, 21.10.55; Cockin to Grisewood, 22.10.55.
60. Board of Governors Minutes, 27.10.55, 220(c).
61. Grisewood to Sendall, 1.11.55.
62. Sendall to Grisewood, 28.11.55.
63. Sendall, op. cit., p. 103.
64. Ibid., p. 279.
65. ITA/BBC Joint Statement, 2.1.56.
66. See R. McKay, *Take Care of the Sense*, 1964, ch. 2.
67. Jacob to Cockin, 4.2.55.
68. Mervyn Stockwood, *Chanctonbury Ring*, 1983, pp. 82ff.
69. See above, ch. 26.C.
70. Andrew's diplomacy was particularly necessary over a television play, *Family Portrait*, which went out at Easter 1955 and portrayed the Holy Family, with Mary as the mother of a large family. (Derek Warlock and Gilbert Harding quarrelled publicly over the programme.) Andrew was obliged to draft both a strong rebuke from Cardinal Griffin to the BBC and an equally confident reply from Jacob to the Cardinal!
71. See above, pp. 470ff.
72. Barnes to House, 9.6.55.
73. See above, ch. 27.D. ch. 27.E., pp. 470ff.
74. McKay to Cockin, 13.7.55.
75. House, 'Religious Broadcasting, 1944–55: Personal Reflections' (a paper for a Departmental Conference), June 1955.
76. Beale to McKay, 22.12.55.
77. Falconer, 'Barclay the Broadcaster', in *Biblical Studies: Essays in Honour of William Barclay*, ed. J. R. McKay and J. F. Miller, 1976, pp. 15ff.
78. R. McKay, 'The Aims of Religious Broadcasting', *Religion on the Air*, 1955, p. 22.
79. *Church Times*, 2.12.55.
80. Board of Management Minutes, 30.1.56.
81. CRAC Minutes, 13.10.55.
82. McGivern to McKay, 10.1.56.
83. See Sendall, op. cit., p. 280.
84. Religious Advisory Panel, Report to the ITA, 18.2.56.
85. Barnes to McKay, 12.1.56.
86. Board of Management Minutes, 5.3.56 (134).
87. McKay to McGivern, 21.7.56.

INDEX